MATCHBOX® TOYS 1947 to 2003
FOURTH EDITION

IDENTIFICATION & VALUE GUIDE

DANA JOHNSON

cb

COLLECTOR BOOKS
A Division of Schroeder Publishing Co., Inc.

The following are registered trademarks of Mattel, Inc.: MATCHBOX, SUPERFAST, LASER WHEELS, LASERTRONICS, LIGHTNING, WORLD CLASS, SUPER GT, TWO PACK, TWIN PACK, TRAILERS, CONVOY, HIGHWAY EXPRESS, TEAM CONVOY, TEAM MATCHBOX, SKY BUSTERS, MAJOR PACK, KING SIZE, SPEED KINGS, SUPER KINGS, MATCHBOX MILITARY, BATTLE KINGS, SEA KINGS, ADVENTURE 2000, SKYBUSTERS, MODELS OF YESTERYEAR, DINKY, ROLAMATICS, and others.

DAYS OF THUNDER is a copyrighted trademark licensed by Paramount Pictures. INDY 500 and INDIANAPOLIS 500 are licensed from IMS Corp. PETERBILT, KENWORTH, KW, and AERODYNE are licensed trademarks of Paccar, Inc., Bellevue, Washington. GOODYEAR is a trademark of Goodyear Tire and Rubber Company. JEEP is a trademark of the Chrysler Corporation. ROLLS ROYCE is a trademark of Rolls Royce, Ltd. CATERPILLAR and CAT are licensed trademarks of Caterpillar Tractor Company. Other trademarks have been used with permission. MATCHBOX and MATCHBOX COLLECTIBLES are registered trademarks of Mattel, Inc.

On The Cover

Front cover:
Top left: Rescue Crane, 2003 Hero City 5-pack #9
Top right: Volvo Container Truck, 1998 5-pack
Center left: Alfa Carabo #75, 1971
Center right: 1956 Ford Fairlane Sunliner, Matchbox Collectibles #560, 2003
Bottom left: Austin A50, #36, 1957
Bottom right: Jaguar E-Type/Jaguar XKE, #32, 1962

Back cover:
Clockwise from top:
Aston Martin DB-7, 1994 Premier Collection Series #10;
Ford Model A #73 1979/#55 1991;
1997 Chevy Tahoe, 2003 Coca-Cola 5-pack;
Chevy Highway Maintenance Truck, 1999 Airport 5-pack;
Lotus Racing Car #19, 1966;
1957 Chevy BelAir #4, 1997 American Street Machines 5-pack;
1956 Ford Pickup Truck #7

Cover design: Beth Summers
Book design: Holly C. Long

Collector Books
P.O. Box 3009
Paducah, KY 42002-3009

www.collectorbooks.com

Copyright © 2004 by Dana Johnson

Searching For A Publisher?

We are always looking for people knowledgeable within their fields. If you feel there is a real need for a book on your collectible subject and have a large comprehensive collection, contact Collector Books.

Contents

Preface

Since 1953, Matchbox toys have captured the hearts, minds, and imagination of children all around the world. As those early children grew up, they remembered the fun and fascination they had for those little toys. As adults, they were transformed into Matchbox collectors.

From their humble beginnings in 1947 in a burned-out London pub, partners Leslie and Rodney Smith built an everlasting legacy to their ingenuity and entrepreneurial spirit through their company Lesney and their Matchbox brand of diecast toys. Fifty years and several owners later, Matchbox toys remain one of the world's most popular toys and collectibles.

This book is the result of author Dana Johnson's fifty-year fascination with these wonderful toys. His first book on Matchbox toys was published in 1994, to fill a void in the collector's reference library. He has since produced three more books on the subject, the latest of which is this one. The key difference between this latest effort and the rest is that this book is arranged alphabetically, for reasons which will later be made clear. Suffice it to say that it's about time such a book was published; it promises to be the most useful and user-friendly book ever produced about Matchbox toys. . . . But I'll let you decide.

Dedication
Edgar M. Strauss

The Matchbox Volvo Container Truck pictured at left was sent to me by the late Ed Strauss around 1995. It was a simple process to remove the existing label on the container and replace it with his own custom label, thereby creating a customized Matchbox variation. This particular model lent itself well to such adaptations, since it was originally produced with no additional markings. His customized version is now valued at around $12 – 16.

Through his various letters, e-mails, and phone conversations from Closter, New Jersey, Ed Strauss demonstrated a tremendous enthusiasm and appreciation for toy cars. In support of his hobby, Ed had been a member of my own Toy Car Collectors Association (TCCA), and its predecessor, the Diecast Toy Collectors Association, as well as Charlie Mack's Matchbox USA club and likely several other collectors clubs, for many years. Even with his busy schedule, he at one time was able to represent the TCCA at the Atlantique City antiques and collectibles show in Atlantic City, New Jersey. His passing on November 15, 2002, was a great loss to the hobby and to all the friends he made along the way. His fellow collectors and I will miss him dearly. Ed Strauss is survived by his wife Bernice and by his children.

About the Author

Dana Johnson has enjoyed collecting and studying Matchbox toys since he was seven years old, in 1962. Originally from Skandia, Michigan, he lived in several other places in Michigan before moving to Bend, Oregon, in 1985. He has lived there ever since.

His interest in diecast toys has since expanded to many other brands besides Matchbox, including Majorette, Tomica, Siku, Hot Wheels, Bburago, Maisto, Yatming, and hundreds of other brands. He has discovered so many brands of automotive toys and models (over 800) that he has written a book on them entitled *Toy Car Collector's Guide*, available from Collector Books, your favorite bookstore, or from the author for $19.95 retail plus shipping and handling.

While holding down a full-time job, Dana also finds time to produce *Toy Car Collector Magazine* for his club, the Toy Car Collectors Association. He also maintains a worldwide website, at www.toynutz.com, through his home-based business, Dana Johnson Enterprises.

In addition, he has written several self-published books, including *Tomica — Japan's Most Popular Diecast Toys, Siku Toys of Germany, Majorette Toys of France*, and others. For a catalog of book titles and membership rates, send two first class stamps to:

Dana Johnson Enterprises
PO Box 1824
Bend OR 97709-1824

Other contact information:
phone: (541) 318-7176
e-mail:toynutz@earthlink.net
website: www.toynutz.com

INTRODUCTION

How to Use This Book

This book is arranged in two sections: The Introduction, and An Alphabetical Guide to Values.

The Introduction provides information on how to most effectively use this book and how to identify, date, and evaluate your collection, and offers a short history of Matchbox toys. An Alphabetical Guide to Values is an illustrated guide to values and variations by model name and/or description.

Model Number Designations

There is a good reason for making this book an alphabetical, rather than numerical, collector's guide. Since 1953, each Matchbox toy has been issued with a corresponding model number assigned to each model, but the model number was originally only on the box, not on the model itself. The eventual assortment of 75 models in the primary Matchbox Series, also known as Matchbox Miniatures or the 1-75 Series, established the size of the series at 75 models for any given year. In addition, model numbers 76, 77, 78, and 79 were applied to variations of Japanese cars offered to the Japanese market.

In 1996, an error in the planning department resulted in four models issued for the US being misnumbered as 76, 77, 78, and 79. Also, a series of inexpensive versions with no interiors and less detail were at one time assigned Roman numerals from I to X (1 to 10). To further complicate matters, Super GT's and Neon Racers were assigned two consecutive numbers per model, for a total of 24 numbers for 12 models.

The latest change to this system was in 1999, when the series was expanded to 100 models. The 100-model series continued through another year before being returned to 75 models in 2001.

The problem with listing models by model number is that they have to be in their original package to identify them by that method, since neither the earliest Matchbox models nor the ones issued after 1982 had numbers imprinted on their bases.

In the case of a model with many variations, the variations are arranged in order of color, starting with red and proceeding through the color spectrum to orange, yellow, green, blue, and purple, with black, gray, white, silver, and gold following.

Guide to Determining Values

Values indicated in this book generally represent the average value for a given model. Although collectors are often willing to pay top dollar (occasionally even higher than book value), for a model in new, or mint, condition, especially when the model is in its original box or package, it is often possible to purchase models for considerably less. In the same spirit, you will often need to sell models at a much lower price than indicated by this or any book; this is particularly likely when you need to sell an entire collection, since buyers of entire collections usually wish to quickly sell individual models at a reasonable profit. It is also important to know that most dealers will not buy toys in less than near-mint condition.

For standardization, all values mentioned in this book are for models in new condition. Two values are provided. The first value is for the model in new condition but without its original container; the second value is for the model in its original container. Among collectors, a numerical value from 0 to 10 is most commonly used to define an item's condition. The chart below is intended to assist in determining value on less-than-mint-condition toys. Note that "mint condition" denotes a model with no wear, no chips, and no flaws. Models in a sealed blisterpack, for instance, may sometimes suffer wear from rubbing on the insides of the plastic blister and are therefore considered less-than-mint condition. So not everything still in the package should automatically be considered mint.

Rating	Percent of Book Value	Evaluation
10	100%	Mint condition with original container
9	90 – 95%	Mint condition without container
8	80 – 85%	Near mint condition, close inspection reveals minor wear
7	70 – 75%	Excellent condition, visible minor wear
6	25 – 35%	Very good condition, visible wear, all parts intact
5	7 – 10%	Good condition, excessive wear, paint chipped or heavily worn
4	4 – 5%	Fair condition, parts broken or missing
1 – 3	2 – 3%	Poor condition, paint worn off, parts broken or missing
0	0.5 – 1%	Salvage, for parts only

History of Matchbox Toys

BEGINNINGS

It was 1947, and two school chums, Leslie and Rodney Smith, unrelated but sharing the same dream and last name, decided to start a diecasting firm in a vacant pub previously known as the Rifleman, which had been burned out during the German invasion of London in 1940. Leslie and Rodney Smith got together enough funds to purchase the building and start manufacturing diecast zinc alloy components for industry and the military.

It wasn't long before the Smiths started tinkering with the idea of producing a toy or two. Early toys included a walking Jumbo the Elephant tin windup and a marionette puppet named Muffin the Mule.

One of the earliest diecast toys ever produced by Lesney was a horse-drawn "rag and bone" cart, a rag and bone cart being the English equivalent of a junk wagon. This unusual toy featured a driver and assorted junk: a bicycle frame, a washtub, part of a bed frame, a bucket, a crate, and what appears to be a kitchen sink.

Other models included a soap-box racer, a road roller, a Caterpillar tractor and bulldozer, a Massey Harris Tractor, a Hand Cement Mixer, and a Prime Mover truck with a low-loader trailer, and a bulldozer.

THE CORONATION COACH

The introduction of the Coronation Coach in 1953 secured Lesney's honored place in British industry. A large and small version were produced to commemorate Queen Elizabeth II's coronation. But producing the coach to commemorate her coronation was not the original intent.

In 1949, Lesney originally planned to produce a 15¾" long toy coach to commemorate the silver wedding celebrations of King George VI and Queen Elizabeth I (now referred to as the Queen Mother), which had revived interest in British royalty. At the same time, England was planning a celebration in 1951 known as the Festival of Britain. The miniature coach would have been perfect for both occasions. But by the time the toy was ready to market, a ban on the use of zinc was declared, as it was needed for the Korean War effort.

The molds remained unused for two years. Meanwhile, King George VI died, and the throne passed to the oldest daughter, Elizabeth. It was only then that the ban on zinc use was lifted, and the coach went into production.

Approximately 200 large Coronation Coaches were produced with the king and queen inside, now intended to represent Queen Elizabeth II and her husband Prince Philip. But as her June 2nd coronation neared, it was discovered that the queen would be riding alone in the coach.

So Lesney removed the male figure from the mold, and added "Made In England" to the casting to conform to new government regulations requiring the name of the country of origin on all products. Roughly 32,800 models were made with these modifications.

Most models issued were painted gold. But a few versions were released with the queen in either a gold-plated or silver-plated coach.

The smaller 4½" version of the coach was also produced in 1953, either chrome-plated or painted gold and embossed with "A Moko Toy by Lesney, British Made."

Benbros of England made a similar version, but with "Made in England" on the upper side of the center bar and the abbreviation "E II R" (for *Elizabeth the Second Regina*) on the doors of the coach.

MATCHBOX IS BORN

Leslie and Rodney realized they had a good thing going, and in 1953 introduced the Matchbox series of toys, starting with three models, the Number 1 Diesel Road Roller, Number 2 Dumper, and Number 3 Cement Mixer, each based on early Lesney toys, but smaller.

By 1960, the Matchbox Miniatures series had settled at 75 models each year, but in 1981 numbers 76 through 79, miniatures of popular Japanese cars, were issued for the Japanese market. Another exception to the 1-75 series was a set of vehicles issued with Roman numerals I through X.

MATCHBOX MARKETING

The first Matchbox toys were marketed through the Moko firm, a century-old firm founded by Moses Kohnstam in 1875 and carried on by his sons until 1959.

Later, the Fred Bronner Corporation took over marketing. The relationship continued through the mid-1960s, when Lesney took over its own marketing.

JACK ODELL PROVIDES DIECASTING EXPERTISE

Almost from the beginning, John W. (Jack) Odell provided the diecasting expertise. After leaving Lesney, returning, and leaving again in 1982, Jack Odell started his own toy company, Lledo, which is Odell spelled backwards. His toys remain as popular today as when he first started the company. Lledo is now a subsidiary of Zindart, which also now owns the Corgi brand of diecast toys.

COMPETITION CUTS INTO MATCHBOX MARKET

Until 1968, Matchbox toys had a solid corner on the market of diecast toys. But then Mattel introduced Hot Wheels. The popularity of these new toys forced Lesney to introduce Superfast. These revamped Matchbox toys sported thinner axles and new-style wheels, and were designed to be able to compete with Hot Wheels cars on their own track.

One year later, Johnny Lightnings were introduced by Topper Toys, representing yet another threat to the market for Matchbox toys. By their third year, Johnny Lightnings were making a notable dent in both Matchbox and Hot Wheels markets. If it weren't for indictments for business fraud, which forced the company out of business, Topper would have surely dominated the diecast toy market through the 1970s.

Only now are Johnny Lightnings making a comeback, through a new company, Playing Mantis, founded by Tom Lowe. He himself is an aficionado of the original Topper versions.

MATCHBOX SELLS OUT — THREE TIMES

First Time — 1982 was the year that Lesney finally called it quits in the toy business and sold the Matchbox line to Universal Holding Company of Hong Kong, headed by David Yeh, himself a toy enthusiast. While in possession of the brand, Universal also purchased the venerable Dinky brand of England in 1987 and incorporated it into the Matchbox product line. "Matchbox Toys Intl." and "Matchbox Toys Inc." replaced the Lesney name on the bases of all models. Model numbers no longer appeared on the bases of new models released after 1983, making identification more difficult. The reason for this change was that it enabled the company to assign different model numbers for different markets. At the same time, Universal purchased Kidco and inherited Burnin' Key Cars, which was briefly incorporated into the Matchbox lineup.

Second Time — The Matchbox name was sold again in October 1992, to Tyco Toys. With the purchase of Matchbox by Tyco, several of the lines — Dinky, Models of Yesteryear, King Size — were discontinued or absorbed into the newly formed Matchbox Collectibles division.

Third Time — Once again, the Matchbox name was purchased, along with Tyco Toys and The Dinky Collection, this time by Mattel. The purchase began in the fall of 1996 and was completed in May of 1997. New Mattel Matchbox toys started appearing on the market after the New York Toy Fair in February 1998.

MATCHBOX COLLECTIBLES, INC.

In 1994, Matchbox Collectibles were introduced as a new outlet for marketing the Models of Yesteryear and the Dinky Collection from Matchbox. Previously sold only through direct marketing, an effort started in September 1998 to sell them through retail stores. They were first offered through high-end gift and specialty stores, including a few Hallmark shops, starting at twenty dollars each. Within two years, the marketing strategy changed, and Matchbox Collectibles started showing up in retail chain stores such as Target, Wal-Mart, ShopKo, Fred Meyer, and many others, for about half the original price.

WHITE ROSE AND NUTMEG COLLECTIBLES

As the collector market expanded, Universal (and later Tyco) established a symbiotic relationship, which it has maintained, with two independent companies that take stock Matchbox models and modify them especially for the collectibles market.

White Rose Collectibles has marketed limited edition variations of Matchbox models under contract to Tyco, mostly racing transporters and customized race cars, but also produced a line of 24 versions of production models for 1994 with particularly nice color and detail. White Rose agreed to purchase and market a quantity of models produced by Matchbox to White Rose's specifications. In turn, Matchbox packaged them as White Rose Collectibles. The practice is not unlike, say, Sears contracting Whirlpool to produce appliances under the Kenmore brand.

Nutmeg Collectibles, meanwhile, focused on Sprint Racers and Modified Racers and produced a distinctive line of modified Matchbox models that has since been mimicked by Racing Champions, Road Champs, and others.

ASAP and COLOR COMP

ASAP and Color Comp are the two primary companies responsible for producing custom promotional models from Matchbox blank castings. Primarily, they take a plain model and apply a simple message, logo, or design, usually a corporate name or an event designation.

MATCHBOX LIVES

While having sometimes experienced great challenges in its almost fifty years, Matchbox continues to offer a diversity of diecast toys, producing new models and updated versions of older models to replace existing models in the 1-75 series. Mattel has made a commitment to maintain the integrity of the Matchbox series by continuing to produce realistic models of cars and trucks under the Matchbox brand while maintaining the Hot Wheels series as a more sporty, hot, wild, and imaginative line of models. Meanwhile, Models of Yesteryear and Dinky Toys survive thanks to Matchbox Collectibles, Inc., the direct marketing subsidiary maintained by Mattel, Inc.

Alphabetical Guide to Values and Variations

EARLY LESNEY TOYS

Lesney Products Company started manufacturing toys in 1948, a year after the company was begun. As industrial orders declined, Leslie and Rodney Smith, with the help of their friend Jack Odell, started experimenting with the manufacture of diecast toys. Many of the early models created were later reproduced in smaller versions as the first of the Matchbox series.

Aveling Barford Diesel Road Roller, 4³/₈", 1948
1. green with driver, yellow flywheel, red wheels......................$1,250 – 1,500
2. green with no driver, no flywheel, unpainted wheels ....$600 – 750
3. green with driver, no flywheel, unpainted wheels...........................$600 – 750
4. green with no driver, no flywheel, red wheels............................$600 – 750
5. gray-brown with no driver, no flywheel, green wheels................$800 – 1,100

Bread Bait Press, 2", 1954
1. red with green wing nut, green inner mechanism, "Lesney Milbro" ....$100 – 150
2. red with unpainted wing nut, green inner mechanism, "Lesney"..$75 – 125
3. red with unpainted wing nut and inner mechanism, "Lesney".........$75 – 125

Caterpillar Bulldozer, with blade, 4¹/₂", 1948
1. green...........................$900 – 1,200
2. yellow.............................$600 – 800
3. orange ....$600 – 800

Caterpillar Tractor, no blade, 3¹/₈", 1948
1. green...........................$750 – 1,000
2. yellow...............................$650 – 900
3. orange ....$650 – 900

Cement Mixer, 3⁹/₁₆", 1948
1. light green with red barrel and handle, red wheels ....$300 – 500

2. dark green with red barrel and handle, red wheels......................$300 – 500
3. dark green with red barrel and handle, yellow wheels...................$300 – 500
4. dark green with green barrel and handle, green wheels.............$300 – 500
5. dark green with green barrel and handle, red wheels ....$300 – 500
6. red with dark green barrel & handle, green wheels...................$300 – 500
7. red with dark green barrel and handle, yellow wheels...................$300 – 500

Conestoga Wagon, 4⁷/₈", 1955
1. no barrels on sides ....$175 – 225
2. red barrels on sides ....$175 – 225

Coronation Coach, large, 15³/₄", 1952
1. gold-painted coach with king and queen inside ....$1,250 – 1,500
2. gold-painted coach with queen only...................................$500 – 650
3. gold plated, queen only .....$600 – 750
4. silver plated, queen only .$700 – 1,000

Coronation Coach, small, 4¹/₂", 1953
1. silver plated....................$150 – 200
2. gold painted ....$225 – 350

Horse-Drawn Milk Float, 5³/₈", 1949
1. orange ....$1,250 – 1,750
2. blue ....$2,500 – 3,750

Jumbo The Elephant, lithographed tin windup with key, 4", 1950........$900 – 1,200

Massey Harris Tractor, red with beige wheels, black rubber tires, 7¹³/₁₆", 1954.........................$900 – 1,200

Muffin The Mule, cast metal marionette, 5¹/₂", 1951....$500 – 650

Prime Mover with Trailer & Bulldozer, 18", 1950
1. orange with orange trailer, green bulldozer ....$2,000 – 2,500
2. orange with blue trailer, orange bulldozer ....$1,250 – 1,750
3. orange with blue trailer, yellow bulldozer with red blade ....$900 – 1,200

Rag and Bone Cart, 5¹/₄", 1949
1. yellow.....................$2,500 – 3,750
2. green.....................$3,500 – 4,750

Ruston Bucyrus 10RB Power Shovel Excavator, 4", 1949.....$900 – 1,200

Soap Box Racer, gold painted, 3¹/₈", 1949 ....$2,250 – 2,750

MATCHBOX MINIATURES BASIC SERIES

From 1953 to the present, the mainstay of the Matchbox product line has been the 1-75 series, or basic series, also referred to as Matchbox Miniatures. (In 1999 and 2000, the series was expanded to 100 models.) Below is an alphabetical listing of Matchbox Miniatures and variations, with current values.

Abrams M1 A1 Tank, #54, 1995 – 1998; #84, 1999; #61, 1995, international

1. green with black and brown camouflage, multipack .... $2 – 3

2. **army green with white star and "T-7521-6," 1996** .... **$2 – 3**
3. army green with brown and black camouflage, 1996, 5-pack .... $2 – 4
4. army green with black and tan camouflage, Premiere Collection.......... $5 – 7
5. army green with gray and brown camouflage, play set...................... $2 – 3

6. **light army green with yellow "476 BD98675," 1999 Military Patrol series** .... **$2 – 3**
7. dark army green with yellow "476 BD98675"................................. $2 – 3
8. black with rose and white design, Australia issue .... $4 – 6

9. **black with green and brown camouflage, 5-pack** .... **$2 – 3**

10. **white with gray and army green camouflage, 1997 Tundra Defense Force 5-pack** .... **$2 – 3**
11. light brown with white star and "T-7521-6," multipack.................................. $3 – 4
12. khaki with brown and white camouflage, 1995 .... $2 – 3

13. **khaki with brown camouflage, 1997, Desert Assault Force 5-pack** ..**$2 – 3**
14. dark khaki with detailed graphics, 2003, Matchbox Heroes series .$3 – 4

Abrams M1A1 Tank, 2001, Feature Cars, with opening features, designed to replace Premiere Collection

1. beige with painted black treads .... $9 – 12

Abrams Main Battle Tank (see Abrams M1 A1 Tank)

AEC Ergomatic Eight-Wheel Tipper, yellow with metallic silver dumper, 3", #51, 1969

1. orange cab, metallic silver dumper, white grille, "Douglas," black plastic wheels, 1969.................. $160 – 240

2. **orange cab, metallic silver dumper, silver grille, "Douglas," black plastic wheels, 1969** .... **$40 – 60**
3. yellow cab, metallic silver dumper, silver grille, "Douglas," black plastic wheels, 1969................................. $30 – 50

4. **yellow cab, metallic silver dumper, silver grille, "Pointer," black plastic wheels, 1969** .... **$15 – 20**
5. yellow cab, metallic silver dumper, "Pointer," Superfast wheels, 1970.........$30 – 50
6. yellow cab, metallic silver dumper, no labels, Superfast wheels, 1970..........$30 – 50

AEC Ergomatic Horse Box, with two horses, 2¾", #17, 1969

1. red cab, green box, gray door, black plastic wheels, 1969................$6 – 9
2. red cab, green box, gray door, Superfast wheels, 1970 ....$30 – 40
3. mustard yellow, green box, gray door, Superfast wheels, 1970 ....$25 – 35

4. **orange cab, light gray box, light brown door, Superfast wheels, 1970.............................$25 – 35**

Aero Junior, #95, 1999; #70, 2000; #75, 1999, international; #50, 2000, international

1. **red and yellow with blue pilot, 1999 Mountain Cruisers series.......$2 – 3**
2. metallic blue with red pilot, "NP – 20035," 2000 Air Travel series..$2 – 3
3. metallic blue with red pilot, "NP – 20035, "Matchbox 2000," 2000 Air Travel series ....$3 – 4

Air-Lift Helicopter, #68, 2000; #73, 2001; #34, 2002; #47, 2003; #48, 2000, international

1. dark red with yellow and black design, gray base, 2000 Air Travel series ....$2 – 3
2. dark red with yellow and black design "Matchbox 2000," gray base, 2000 Air Travel series ....$3 – 4

3. lime green with black, red and white illustration, black base, 2002 Ultimate Rescue series .... $2 – 3

4. black with green, yellow and red graphics, blue base, 2003 Hero City 5-pack #3 .... $2 – 3

5. gold with green base, 2003 Forest Rescue series .... $2 – 3

6. gold with green base, 2003 Hero City 10-pack #2 .... $2 – 3

Airboat, #63, 2001

1. white hull with red accents, light blue "Rescue 2," bordered in black, red deck, metallic gray fan cage, 2001 Scuba Dudes series ...... $4 – 5

Airplane Transporter, 3", #72, 1985; #65, 1986; #10, 1999; #69, 2000; #49, 2000, international (similar casting: NASA Rocket Transporter)

1. yellow, "Rescue," checkerboard pattern, China cast .... $7 – 9

2. yellow, "Rescue," checkerboard pattern, Macau cast .... $7 – 9

3. army green with black and tan camouflage, China cast, Commando series .... $45 – 55

4. black with red, blue and yellow design, 2003 Hero City 5-pack #3 ...... $2 – 3

5. black with yellow dashes and plane silhouette graphics, "Matchbox 2000," China cast, 2000 Air Travel series .... $3 – 4

6. black with yellow dashes and plane silhouette graphics, China cast, 2000 Air Travel series .... $2 – 3

7. metallic gray with red dashes and plane silhouette graphics, China cast, 1999 Air Traffic series .. $2 – 3

8. white, "NASA," Macau cast .... $4 – 5

9. white, "Rescue," checkerboard pattern, Thailand cast .... $3 – 4

10. white with gray and olive green camouflage, Thailand cast, 1997 Tundra Defense Force 5-pack .... $4 – 5

Airport Coach, 3," #65, 1977

1. "Alitalia," white with white roof, amber windows, England cast .... $8 – 10

2. "Alitalia," white with white roof, amber windows, Macau cast .... $4 – 5

3. "Alitalia," white with green roof, amber windows, Thailand cast .... $6 – 8

4. "American Airlines," metallic blue with white roof, amber windows, England cast .... $5 – 6

5. "American Airlines," metallic blue with white roof, amber windows, no-origin cast, Brazil issue .... $40 – 50

6. "American Airlines," metallic blue with white roof, clear windows, England cast .... $5 – 6

7. "Australian," metallic blue with white roof, amber windows, Macau cast, Australia issue .... $8 – 10

8. "British," metallic blue with white roof, amber windows, England cast.. $8 – 10

9. "British Airways," metallic blue with white roof, amber windows, England cast .... $5 – 6

10. "British Airways," metallic blue with white roof, no-origin cast, Brazil issue .... $40 – 50

11. "British Airways," metallic blue with white roof, clear windows, England cast .... $5 – 6

12. "Girobank," metallic blue with white roof, blue windows, Macau cast, UK issue .... $8 – 10

13. "KLM," white with blue roof, amber windows, Thailand cast .... $6 – 8

14. "Lufthansa," metallic blue with white roof, amber windows, England cast ..... $5 – 6

15. "Lufthansa," metallic blue with white roof, amber windows, no origin cast, Brazil issue .... $40 – 50

16. "Lufthansa," metallic blue with white roof, clear windows, England cast .... $5 – 6

17. "Lufthansa," orange with white roof, amber windows, Macau cast ..... $4 – 5

18. "Lufthansa," white with white roof, amber windows, England cast........... $30 – 40

19. "Lufthansa," white with white roof, amber windows, Thailand cast ... $6 – 8

20. "Pan Am," white with white roof, amber windows, Macau cast .... $4 – 5

21. "Qantas," red with white roof, amber windows, England cast............ $9 – 12

22. "SAS," white with blue roof, amber windows, Thailand cast.................. $6 – 8

23. "Schulbus," orange with white roof, amber windows, England cast, Germany issue................................ $40 – 50

24. "Stork SB," white, amber windows, Macau cast, on-package premium, Australia issue .... $9 – 12

25. "TWA," red with white roof, amber windows, England cast .... $8 – 10

26. "TWA," green with white roof, amber windows, Manaus cast, Brazil issue. $50 – 60

27. "TWA," red with white roof, amber windows, Manaus cast, Brazil issue................................. $40 – 50

28. "Virgin Atlantic," red with white roof, amber windows, Macau cast ..... $4 – 5

29. "Virgin Atlantic," red with white roof, amber windows, Thailand cast ... $4 – 5

Airport Fire Pumper/Runway Hero, with extending snorkel and translucent tank, 3"; #26, 2001; #71, 2002; #41, 2003

1. red with white, yellow and blue design, translucent blue tank, 2003 Airport series .... $2 – 3

2. red with white, yellow and blue design, translucent blue tank, 2003 Hero City 10-pack #2 .... $2 – 3

3. yellow, "Birthday Party" .... $30 – 40

4. metallic silver with blue tank, red snorkel, 2002 Kids' Cars Of The Year series.................................. $2 – 3

5. fluorescent yellow with orange and black, blue tank, 2001 Flame Eaters series ....**$2 – 3**

Airport Fire Tender (see Airport Fire Truck, Airport Fire Pumper)

Airport Fire Truck, with short nozzle and ladder, 3", #8, 1992 – 1999; #24, 1992, international; #29, 2000; #41, 2002
1. red with white ladder, "5 Alarm," yellow stripes ....$2 – 3

2. **red with white ladder, "Matchbox Fire Dept.," white stripe, 1997 Fire 5-pack**..................**$2 – 3**
3. red with white ladder, "Feuerwehr" .$4 – 5

4. **light orange with red, white and black, "Alarm," 2002 Airport Alarm series** ....**$2 – 3**
5. orange with red, white and black, "Alarm," 2003 Hero City 5-pack..$2 – 3

6. **fluorescent orange with white ladder, blue and white accents, "Airport Fire Service"**..................**$2 – 3**
7. fluorescent orange with white ladder, blue and white accents, "Airport Fire Service," "IC," Intercom City ...$40 – 50

8. yellow with metallic gray ladder, "Metro Alarm," red stripes ....$2 – 3

9. **yellow with silver ladder, "Matchbox Fire Dept.," red stripe, 2000 Fire 5-pack** ....**$2 – 3**

10. **yellow with red ladder, "Airways Fire & Rescue," 1999 Airport 5-pack** ....**$2 – 3**
11. yellow with white ladder, "Newfield Airport Fire Rescue," rubber tires on chrome rims, Premiere Collection ....$4 – 5

12. **fluorescent yellow with metallic gray ladder, "34" and dashed line, 1998 Emergency Rescue 5-pack**......**$2 – 3**
13. fluorescent yellow with metallic gray ladder, "Westford Airport Fire Rescue," rubber tires on chrome rims, Premiere Collection ....$4 – 5

14. **fluorescent lime green with metallic gray ladder, "DIA 2," rubber tires on chrome rims, Premiere Fire Collection #3** ....**$12 – 16**
15. fluorescent lime green with metallic gray ladder, "Metro 24," blue stripe, Germany issue..................$4 – 6
16. bright blue with metallic gray ladder, "Runway Rescue," yellow stripe, 2000 Fire Fighters series ....$2 – 3

17. white and red with metallic gray ladder, "Fire Dept.," gold crest and star, pack ....$2 –
18. white with black ladder, "34," hash mark 2000 Fire Fighters series ....$2 –
19. white with black ladder, "34," has marks, "Matchbox 2000," 2000 Fi Fighters series ....$3 –

20. **yellow with red windows, "Matchb FDMB" with flame graphics on shie "14," 2001 Action Launcher Fi Truck set** ....**$3 –**

Airport Foam Pumper, 3¼", #54, 198 nozzle, sirens, and lights on forward pa of roof (similar castings: Command Vel cle, Mobile Home, NASA Tracking Vehicl
1. red with "3" and Japanese letterin Japan issue..................$9 – 1
2. red with red roof, "Fire Rescue," go crest, white band, black and go stripes ....$2 –
3. red with red roof, "Foam Unit 3 "Metro Airport," metal base.......$3 –

4. **red with red roof, "Foam Unit 3, "Metro Airport," plastic base Macau cast**..................**$3 –**
5. red with red roof, "Foam Unit 3, "Metro Airport," plastic base, Thailan cast..................$2 – 3
6. red with white roof, "Foam Unit, black and white checkerboar pattern ....$40 – 50

7. **yellow with yellow roof, "Foam Uni 3," "Metro Airport," metal base Macau cast**..................**$3 – 4**

8. yellow with yellow roof, "Foam Unit 3," "Metro Airport," plastic base, Thailand cast ....$2 – 3
9. fluorescent orange, "Foam Unit," "City Airport," "Emergency Rescue," Emergency multipack ....$2 – 3
10. blue, "Police Command Center," white diagonal stripes, 1997 Police 5-pack ....$2 – 3
11. black with tan and green camouflage, tan nozzle and roof light, 5-pack ..$2 – 3

Airport Foamite Crash Tender, 2¼", #63, 1964
1. silver nozzle...........................$5 – 10
2. gold nozzle ....$20 – 25

Airport Pumper (see Airport Fire Pumper, Airport Fire Truck)

Airport Tender (see Airport Fire Truck)

Albion Chieftain Flatbed Transporter, "Portland Cement," 2½", #51, 1958
1. metal wheels......................$30 – 40

2. **gray plastic wheels ....$30 – 40**
3. silver plastic wheels..............$60 – 80
4. black plastic wheels............$80 – 100

Alfa 155 (see Alfa Romeo 155)

Alfa Carabo, 3", #75, 1971; BR 21 – 22, 1985
1. red with yellow base, accents ..$9 – 12
2. pink with yellow base, no accents...........................$80 – 120
3. pink with yellow base, accents ....$20 – 30

4. **metallic pink with no accents.$12 – 18**
5. yellow, England cast, Super GT's, BR 21 – 22, 1985 ....$30 – 40
6. orange with blue and white, England cast, Super GT's, BR 21 – 22, 1985 ....$4 – 6
7. orange, no markings, England cast, Super GT's, BR 21 – 22, 1985 ....$12 – 15
8. orange with light and dark blue accents, England cast, Super GT's, BR 21 – 22, 1985 ....$12 – 15
9. orange with green and light blue accents, England cast, Super GT's, BR 21 – 22, 1985 ....$12 – 15

10. green, China cast, Super GT's, BR 21 – 22, 1985............................$3 – 5
11. green, England cast, Super GT's, BR 21 – 22, 1985 ....$12 – 15
12. pale blue, China cast, Super GT's, BR 21 – 22, 1985 ....$3 – 5
13. light purple with unpainted base .$16 – 24
14. light purple with yellow base...$16 – 24
15. silver, China cast, Super GT's, BR 21 – 22, 1985.............................$8 – 10
16. silver, England cast, Super GT's, BR 21 – 22, 1985 ....$12 – 15
17. silver with accents, England cast, Super GT's, BR 21 – 22, 1985.........$5 – 10
18. beige, England cast, Super GT's, BR 21 – 22, 1985 ....$30 – 40

Alfa Romeo 155, # 3, 1997; #62, 1998
1. red, "7," cross and snake, chrome hubs, rubber tires.....................$5 – 7
2. unpainted, chrome hubs, rubber tires ....$5 – 7

3. **red, "8," cross and snake, 5-spoke concave star wheels.............$2 – 3**
4. red, "7," cross and snake, 5-spoke concave star wheels, China issue ..$35 – 40
5. white, "8," cross and snake, 5-spoke concave star wheels ....$2 – 3
6. metallic gold, 1997 75 Challenge series...................................$6 – 12
7. red, "Coca-Cola" and polar bears, Coca-Cola 5-pack ....$2 – 3

Alfa Romeo SZ, 2⅞", #15, 1991, US; #6, 1991, international

1. **red with black roof, no markings ....$2 – 4**
2. red with red roof, no markings, Germany gift set ....$9 – 12
3. red with black roof, "Alfa Romeo"..$2 – 4
4. red with red roof, "Alfa Romeo"..$2 – 4
5. lime with lime roof, "Alfa Romeo"..$9 – 12
6. blue, "Go Eagles! 1997," Australia issue......................................$4 – 6

All-Terrain Fire Tanker, #64, 2002; #67, 2003
1. **metallic red with metallic gray interior and tank, 2002 Rescue Rookies series ....$2 – 3**

2. black with metallic gray interior and tank, 2003 Pumper Squad series........$2 – 3

Alvis Stalwart "BP Exploration," 2⅝", #61, 1966
1. yellow wheels......................$30 – 40

2. **green wheels ....$9 – 12**

Ambulance (see Chevrolet Ambulance, Bedford Lomas Ambulance, Mercedes-Benz Ambulance, etc.)

Ambulance, #41, 2001; #26, 2002: #12, 2003
1. white with blue windows; green plastic grille, fenders, and base; "Medis M3," 2001 Rescue Squad series ....$2 – 3

2. **metallic gold with orange, brown, and white; "Ultra Med Alert," blue windows; metallic gray plastic grille, fenders, and base; 2002 Red Hot Rescue series ....$2 – 3**

3. **blue with orange and yellow, amber windows; metallic gray plastic grille, fenders, and base; 2003 Hospital series ....$2 – 3**

4. **white with red windows; blue plastic grille, fenders, and base; labels, 2003 McDonald's Happy Meal premium**...............**$3 – 4**

AMC Javelin AMX, 3", #9, 1972
1. lime with chrome hood scoop, bright yellow interior, doors open.....$12 – 16

2. **lime with black hood scoop, bright yellow interior, doors open.....$6 – 9**
3. lime with black hood scoop, orange interior, doors open..................$12 – 16
4. lime with black hood scoop, white interior, doors open.........................$60 – 80
5. lime with black hood scoop, blue interior, doors open......................$120 – 160
6. lime with black hood scoop, yellow-orange interior, doors open.......$6 – 9
7. metallic blue with black hood scoop, doors open ....$6 – 9
8. metallic blue with black hood scoop, doors don't open.....................$6 – 9
9. metallic green with black hood scoop, doors open ....$6 – 9
10. red with black hood scoop, doors don't open ....$40 – 50

AMC Javelin AMX Pro Stocker, 2⅝", #17, 1983

1. **metallic gray with red and black stripes, "AMX," Macau cast ..$2 – 4**
2. metallic gray with red and black stripes, "AMX," China cast.................$9 – 12
3. maroon with "Dr. Pepper" ....$6 – 9

AMG Mercedes-Benz 500 SEC (see Mercedes-Benz AMG 500 SEC)

Amphibious Personnel Carrier, #55, 2000
1. olive green with mud spatter, "Bravo Co. 17," 2000 Military series ....$2 – 3

2. olive green with mud spatter, "Bravo Co. 17," "Matchbox 2000," 2000 Military series ....$3 – 4
3. dark khaki with dark brown and yellow detailed graphics, 2003 Matchbox Heroes series.........................$3 – 4

AMX Javelin (see AMC Javelin AMX)

AMX Pro Stocker (see AMC Javelin AMX Pro Stocker)

Arctic Track Truck (see Snow Doctor)

Armored Police Truck (see Armored Response Vehicle)

Armored Response Vehicle, #47, 2001; #39, 2002

1. **red with black base, black canopy, 2003 Hero City 5-pack #3.....$2 – 3**

2. **metallic burgundy with red base, phosphorescent canopy, 2002 Nite Glow series ....$2 – 3**

3. **blue sides, red-brown front, metallic gray canopy, "Stratos," graphics, 2003 Matchbox Collectibles Masters of the Universe series.....$4 – 6**

4. dark gray with black base, gray canc "ARV 05," 2001 Pull Over series..$2 –
5. gray with pale green base, "Sec Force," detailed graphics, 2003 Mat box Heroes series....................$3 –

Armored Truck, 2¹³⁄₁₆", #69, 1978
1. red, "Wells Fargo," "732 – 203 clear windows, England cast ..$35 –

2. **red, "Wells Fargo," "732-2031 blue windows, England cast ...$5 –**
3. red, "Wells Fargo," "QZ – 2031," b windows, England cast..............$5 –
4. red, no markings, blue windows, Er land cast ....$30 –
5. green, "Dresdner Bank," blue window England cast, Germany issue .$40 – 5
6. dark army green, "Dresdner Bank blue windows, England cast, Germa issue..................................$60 – 8

Army Halftrack (see Army M3 Halftra Personnel Carrier)

Army Jeep (see Jeep, #38)

Army M3 Halftrack Personnel Carrie 2½", #49, 1958
1. metal front wheels and rollers .$40 – 5
2. gray plastic front wheels, metal rollers ....$45 – 6
3. gray plastic front wheels and rollers ....$90 – 10
4. gray plastic front wheels, silver plast rollers ....$70 – 8
5. black plastic front wheels and rollers ....$30 – 4

Army M3 A2 Halftrack, 2001, Featu Cars, with opening features, designe to replace Premiere Collection
1. olive green with star and black treads ....$9 – 1

Army Saracen Personnel Carrier (se Saracen Personnel Carrier)

Artic Track Truck (see Snow Doctor)

Articulated Trailer, 3", #50, 1980 (goe with #50 Articulated Truck)
1. blue container, yellow trailer base, pack.....................................$5 – (
2. metallic gray container, red trailer base 2-pack ....$7 – 8

Articulated Truck with removable traile 3¹⁄₁₆", #50, 1973

1. red cab with purple windows, blue trailer, red trailer base....................$40 – 50
2. red cab with purple windows, metallic gray trailer, red trailer base with tow hook, 2-pack ....$9 – 12
3. red cab with red windows, metallic gray trailer, red trailer base with tow hook, 2-pack..........................$9 – 12
4. red cab with red windows, blue trailer, red trailer base....................$40 – 50
5. orange-yellow cab with red windows, light blue trailer, orange yellow trailer base ....$4 – 5
6. orange-yellow cab with purple windows, light blue trailer, orange yellow trailer base, labels...........................$7 – 8
7. orange-yellow cab with purple windows, light blue trailer, orange trailer base, no labels ....$4 – 5
8. orange-yellow cab with purple windows, light blue trailer, yellow trailer base with tow hook, no labels, 2-pack ....$5 – 6
9. yellow cab with red windows, light blue trailer, orange trailer base, no labels...................................$4 – 5
10. yellow cab with red windows, light blue trailer, yellow trailer base, no labels...................................$4 – 5
11. yellow cab with red windows, dark blue trailer, yellow trailer base with tow hook, no labels, UK issue ....$90 – 120
12. yellow cab with purple windows, light blue trailer, yellow trailer base, no labels ....$4 – 5

13. yellow cab with purple windows, light blue trailer, yellow trailer base, with labels ....$7 – 8
14. yellow cab with purple windows, light blue trailer, yellow trailer base with tow hook, no labels, 2-pack ....$5 – 6

Aston Martin DB-2 Saloon, 2¹⁵/₁₆", #53, 1958
1. metallic light green with metal wheels ....$35 – 45
2. metallic light green with gray plastic wheels................................$30 – 40
3. metallic red with gray plastic wheels................................$130 – 150
4. metallic red with black plastic wheels...............................$80 – 100

Aston Martin DB-7, #59, 1994; #63, 1994, international
1. metallic red, detailed trim, rubber tires on chrome rims, JC Penney Premiere Collection...............................$4 – 5

2. metallic green, "DB-7," and stripe on sides ....$2 – 3
3. metallic green, no markings.......$2 – 3
4. blue, no markings, 6-spoke spiral wheels...................................$4 – 5
5. blue, no markings, 5-spoke concave wheels...................................$3 – 4

6. silver-blue, detailed trim, rubber tires on chrome rims, Ultra Class ..$9 – 12
7. dark gray, detailed trim, rubber tires on chrome rims, World Class ....$3 – 4
8. metallic gray, detailed trim, rubber tires on chrome rims, international Premiere Collection 1 ....$8 – 10

9. pearl white, detailed trim, rubber tires on chrome rims, Premiere Collection 10 ....$4 – 5

Aston Martin Racing Car, metallic green, 2½", #19, 1961
1. gray driver, "52," decal ....$40 – 50
2. gray driver, "41," decal ....$40 – 50
3. gray driver, "5," decal ....$40 – 50
4. gray driver, "19," decal ....$25 – 35
5. white driver, "19," decal........$25 – 35
6. white driver, "3," decal ....$40 – 50
7. white driver, "53," decal........$40 – 50

Atkinson Grit Spreader (see Ford Atkinson Grit Spreader)

Atlantic Trailer, 3⅛", #16, 1956
1. tan with metal wheels.......$175 – 200

Atlantic Trailer, 3¼", #16, 1957
1. tan with tan tow bar, gray plastic wheels..............................$35 – 45
2. orange with black tow bar, gray plastic wheels..........................$100 – 125
3. orange with black tow bar, black plastic wheels...........................$30 – 40
4. orange with unpainted tow bar, black plastic wheels.....................$30 – 40
5. orange with orange tow bar, black plastic wheels ....$40 – 50

Atlas Dump Truck, 3", #23, 1975
1. blue with orange dumper.......$10 – 15

2. blue with yellow dumper ......$9 – 12
3. red with metallic silver dumper..$9 – 12

Atlas Excavator, #32, 1981; #6, 1990 – 1998; #30, 1999; #10, 1999, Germany; #92, 2000; #72, 2000, international
1. red with black deck, red boom, red scoop, black and white stripes, Thailand cast.....................................$2 – 3

2. red with black deck, red boom, red scoop, white stripes, Thailand cast ....$2 – 3
3. orange with black deck, black boom, black scoop, England cast ....$7 – 9
4. orange with black deck, orange boom, orange scoop, black and white stripes, Thailand cast.........................$2 – 3

5. orange with black deck, orange boom, orange scoop, China cast, Germany issue.....................$4 – 5

6. orange with gray deck, gray boom, gray scoop, England cast ....$7 – 9
7. orange with orange deck, black boom, orange scoop, white stripes, 1997 ....$2 – 3
8. fluorescent orange with black deck, black boom, black scoop ....$2 – 3
9. pumpkin orange with black deck, black boom, black scoop, "Blue Ridge Construction," ASAP promotional ....$80 – 120
10. pumpkin orange with black deck, black boom, black scoop, "CAT Service Co.," ASAP promotional ....$80 – 120
11. pumpkin orange with black deck, black boom, black scoop, "Hemler Bros.," ASAP promotional ....$80 – 120
12. pumpkin orange with black deck, black boom, black scoop, "Redi-Way, Inc.," ASAP promotional ....$80 – 120
13. yellow with black deck, metallic gray boom, metallic gray scoop, "X-4970" and dust, 2000 Build It! series...$2 – 3
14. yellow with black deck, metallic gray boom, metallic gray scoop, "X-4970" and dust, "Matchbox 2000," 2000 Build It! series ....$3 – 4
15. yellow with black deck, black boom, black scoop, England cast ....$3 – 4
16. yellow with black deck, black boom, black scoop, Macau cast..........$2 – 3
17. yellow with black deck, black boom, black scoop, Thailand cast.........$2 – 3

18. yellow with black deck, black boom, red scoop, red stripes, Thailand cast.$2 – 3
19. yellow with black deck, yellow boom, yellow scoop, "JCB," label ....$9 – 10
20. yellow with yellow deck, black boom, black scoop, Macau cast.........$8 – 10
21. yellow with yellow deck, black boom, black scoop, China cast, 5-pack .$2 – 3

22. bright green with black deck, black boom, bright green scoop, black and white stripes, 1998 Stars & Stripes series ....$2 – 3
23. metallic gray with gray deck, orange boom, gray scoop, "MC21," "Matchbox," China cast, 5-pack ....$2 – 3

24. metallic gold with black deck, black boom, black scoop, 1997 75 Challenge series...................$6 – 12

25. blue with blue deck, bright yellow boom, bright yellow scoop, "MC21," "Matchbox," 2003 Hero City 5-pack #4.......................................$2 – 3

26. white with gray deck, metallic gray boom, black scoop, "X4970" and dust, 1999 Road Work series..$2 – 3

Atlas Skip Truck, 2¹¹⁄₁₆", #37, 1976
1. red with yellow skip, chrome interior, black base, amber windows ....$6 – 7
2. red with yellow skip, gray interior, black base, amber windows ....$5 – 6

3. red with yellow skip, gray interior, black base, clear windows......$5 – 6
4. red with yellow skip, gray interior, black base, tinted windows ....$5 – 6
5. red with yellow skip, gray interior, black base, blue windows ....$5 – 6
6. red with yellow skip, gray interior, brown base, clear windows......$9 – 12
7. red with yellow skip, gray interior, brown base, tinted windows.....$9 – 12
8. red with yellow skip, gray interior, dark gray base, clear windows ....$5 – 6
9. red with yellow skip, gray interior, unpainted base, clear windows...$5 – 6
10. red with yellow skip, orange interior, black base, clear windows ....$5 – 6
11. red with yellow skip, orange interior, dark gray base, clear windows ...$5 – 6
12. red with blue skip, gray interior, black base, clear windows ....$100 – 150

13. orange with red skip, gray interior, black base, clear windows, Germany issue..............................$90 – 120
14. orange with yellow skip, gray interior, black base, clear windows, Germany issue..............................$90 – 120
15. blue with yellow skip, black interior, black base, clear windows ....$7 – 8
16. blue with yellow skip, gray interior, black base, clear windows ....$4 – 5
17. blue with yellow skip, gray interior, dark gray base, clear windows ....$4 – 5
18. blue with yellow skip, gray interior, metallic gray base, clear windows ....$4 – 5
19. dark blue with yellow skip, gray interior, dark gray base, clear windows, UK issue.............................$200 – 300

Audi Avus Quattro, #12, 1995; #31, 1995, international; #19, 1999; #18, 1999, international

1. chrome burgundy with black interior, tinted windows, "0000 Avus"..$2 – 3

2. chrome gold with black interior, tinted windows, "0000 Avus," 5-pack .$2 – 3
3. chrome green with black interior, tinted windows, "0000 Avus," 1999 international issue............................$2 – 3

4. chrome silver with red interior, clear windows, no markings ....$2 – 3

5. chrome silver with red and black interior, clear windows, rubber tires on chrome rims, Premiere Collection ....$4 – 5

6. chrome orange with red and black interior, clear windows, rubber tires on chrome rims, international Premiere Collection.................................$4 – 5
7. chrome red with black interior, tinted windows, "0000 Avus" ....$2 – 3
8. iridescent white with red interior, tinted windows, "Avus Quattro," 5-pack ..$2 – 3

9. **iridescent white with red and black interior, clear windows, "Avus Quattro," rubber tires on chrome rims, Premiere Collection ....$4 – 5**
10. metallic gold with black interior, clear windows, 1997 75 Challenge ..$6 – 12
11. metallic green with black interior, tinted windows, "0000 Avus" ....$2 – 3
12. metallic gray with black interior, clear windows, no markings, ASAP promotional blank..........................$30 – 40
13. metallic gray with black interior, clear windows, "Iscar," ASAP promotional ....$75 – 125

14. **red with red and black interior, clear windows, rubber tires on chrome rims, Select Class ....$4 – 5**
15. white with gray interior, green windows, "Quattro"...............................$2 – 3

Audi Quattro, 3", #23, 1982; #25, 1982, international
1. white with "Audi 20," England cast ..$3 – 4
2. white with "Audi 20," Macau cast ..$3 – 4
3. white with "Audi 20," Manaus cast, Brazil issue...........................$40 – 60
4. white with Duckhams, "Pirelli".....$4 – 5
5. purple with "Quattro 0000" ....$4 – 6
6. blue with "Quattro 0000" ....$8 – 10
7. metallic dark gray with pictogram and "Audi 2584584," China issue ..$40 – 60

. metallic gray with Audi logo, "Quattro" ....$2 – 4

Audi TT, #44, 2000, US; #37, 1999, Germany; #74, 2000, Germany; #67, 2000, international
1. red, US issue..........................$3 – 4
2. metallic light green, 1999 Germany issue ....$4 – 5

3. **metallic dark green, 2001 Eurosports 5-pack................$2 – 3**
4. metallic blue, 2000 International issue ....$3 – 4

5. **metallic blue, "TT Coupe," 2001 Show Cars, US issue ....$2 – 3**
6. metallic blue, Target Eggmobiles 3-pack....................................$9 – 12
7. black, Launcher 5-pack ....$2 – 3
8. metallic gray, 2000 Germany issue....................................$4 – 5

Austin 200-Gallon Water Truck, 2³/₈", #71, 1959
1. olive green with black plastic wheels..............................$30 – 40

Austin A50, blue-green, 2⁵/₈", #36, 1957

1. metal wheels ....$35 – 45
2. **gray plastic wheels...........$35 – 45**

Austin A55 Cambridge, two-tone green, 2³/₄", #29, 1961
1. gray wheels.........................$35 – 45
2. silver wheels........................$20 – 30
3. black wheels........................$20 – 30

Austin FX4R London Taxi, 2⁵/₈", #4, 1987
1. black, "Great Taxi Ride London To Sidney"......................................$6 – 8
2. yellow, "ABC Taxi," Preschool/Live 'N Learn series ....$5 – 7
3. black, "London Taxi" and British flag on left side only ....$3 – 5

4. black, "Old Eight" and British flag ....$80 – 100

5. **black, no markings ....$3 – 5**
6. black, "Taxi"...........................$2 – 3

Austin London Taxi, 2¹/₄", #17, 1960
1. maroon with gray plastic wheels.$40 – 50
2. maroon with silver plastic wheels.$65 – 75

Austin Mk 2 Radio Truck, 2³/₈", #68, 1959

1. **olive green with black plastic wheels..........................$40 – 50**

Auxiliary Power Truck (see Mack Floodlight Heavy Rescue Auxiliary Power Truck)

Aveling Barford Diesel Road Roller, 1⁷/₈", #1, 1953
1. dark green with red metal wheels ....$100 – 150
2. light green with red metal wheels ....$150 – 200
3. commemorative replica, green, 1988, made in China, 40th Anniversary Gift Set.............................$8 – 12
4. dark blue, 1991 Matchbox Originals, made in China.......................$4 – 6
5. orange, 1992 Matchbox Originals, made in China.......................$4 – 6

Aveling Barford Tractor Shovel, 2⁵/₈", #43, 1962
1. yellow with yellow shovel, base and driver.....................................$40 – 50
2. yellow with yellow shovel, red base and driver ....$25 – 35

3. **yellow with red shovel, yellow base and driver........................$25 – 35**

4. yellow with red shovel, base and driver ....$40 – 50

B

Badger Cement Truck, Rolamatic, 3", #19, 1976

1. **red with orange-yellow barrel, green windows.................................$6 – 9**
2. red with orange-yellow barrel, no windows ....$6 – 9
3. red with orange barrel, purple windows ....$6 – 9
4. red with orange barrel, green windows ....$6 – 9
5. red with gray barrel, no windows ..$6 – 9
6. red with gray barrel, green windows ....$6 – 9
7. red with gray barrel, purple windows ....$6 – 9
8. red with light yellow barrel, green windows...................................$6 – 9
9. red with light yellow barrel, purple windows...................................$6 – 9

Badger Exploration Truck, with Rolamatic radar antenna, 2⅞", #16, 1974

1. **metallic orange-red with metallic gray base, green windows, ivory radar**...................................$9 – 12
2. metallic orange-red with light gray base, green windows, ivory radar ....$5 – 7

3. metallic orange-red with dark gray base, green windows, ivory radar ....$5 – 7
4. metallic orange-red with dark gray base, green windows, black radar ....$5 – 7
5. metallic orange-red with dark gray base, blue-green windows, ivory radar ..$5 – 7
6. metallic orange-red with dark gray base, blue-green windows, black radar ..$5 – 7
7. metallic orange-red with black base, green windows, ivory radar ....$5 – 7
8. metallic orange-red with black base, green windows, black radar ....$5 – 7
9. metallic orange-red with black base, purple windows, ivory radar ....$5 – 7
10. metallic orange-red with black base, blue-green windows, ivory radar ..$5 – 7
11. army green with light gray base, green windows, ivory radar, Two Pack .....$65 – 85

12. **olive green with light gray base, green windows, ivory radar, Two Pack ....$6 – 8**

Baja Buggy, 2⅝", #13, 1971
1. metallic light green with orange interior, red flower label, black exhausts ....$12 – 16
2. metallic light green with orange interior, red flower label, red exhausts ..$12 – 16
3. metallic light green with orange interior, orange flower label, black exhausts ....$12 – 16
4. metallic light green with orange interior, orange flower label, red exhausts ..$12 – 16
5. metallic light green with orange interior, police shield label, red exhausts .$30 – 45
6. metallic light green with red interior, police shield label, red exhausts........$30 – 45
7. metallic light green with red interior, orange flower label, red exhausts ....$12 – 16
8. metallic light green with orange interior from #47 Beach Hopper, orange flower label, red exhausts ....$30 – 45
9. metallic light green with orange interior, no label, red exhausts ....$12 – 16
10. metallic dark green with orange interior, orange flower label, red exhausts ....$12 – 16
11. metallic green with orange interior, sunburst label, red exhausts ....$24 – 36
12. bright lime green with orange interior, orange flower label, red exhausts, Brazil issue ....$400 – 600

Baja Dune Buggy (see Baja Buggy)

Battering Ram, #90, 2000
1. blue, "Police," white and silver stripes, 2000 Police Patrol series..........$2 – 3

2. **blue, "Police," white and silver stripes, "Matchbox 2000," 2000 Police Patrol series ....$3 – 4**

3. **white, "Metro Patrol," "Police 3," blue, yellow and red design, 2001 On Patrol 5-pack.......................$2 – 3**

BEA (British European Airways) Coach, 2½", #58, 1958

1. **"British European Airways" decals, gray plastic wheels............$30 – 40**
2. "BEA" decals, gray plastic wheels................................$40 – 50
3. "BEA" decals, silver plastic wheels................................$80 – 100
4. "BEA" decals, black plastic wheels................................$80 – 100

Beach 4x4, #46, 2003

1. **metallic green with yellow interior, black plastic base, 2003 Forest Rescue series............................$2 – 3**

Beach Buggy, 2⅝", #30, 1971

1. metallic pink with white interior ..$20 – 25
2. metallic pink with yellow interior ..$12 – 16
3. metallic lavender with yellow interior ....$16 – 24

Beach Hopper (Rolamatic), 2⁵/₈", #47, 1974
1. dark blue, orange interior, metallic gray base.................................$25 – 30
2. dark blue, orange interior, pink base.................................$12 – 16
3. dark blue, yellow interior, pink base.................................$16 – 24
4. dark blue, orange interior, lavender base.................................$12 – 16
5. dark blue, orange interior, unpainted base.................................$12 – 16

Beach Rescue, Real Talkin' (see Real Talkin' Beach Rescue)

Bedford Car Transporter, 3", #11, 1976; cars are listed in order: top front, top rear, bottom.
1. orange with beige carrier, blue windows; red, yellow, blue cars ....$5 – 7
2. orange with beige carrier, blue windows; red, yellow, dark blue cars ....$5 – 7
3. orange with beige carrier, blue windows; yellow, red, blue cars ....$5 – 7

4. **orange with beige carrier, blue windows; red, yellow, blue cars ...$5 – 7**
5. orange with beige carrier, blue windows; red, blue, blue cars ....$8 – 10
6. orange with beige carrier, blue windows; blue, blue, blue cars ....$12 – 16
7. orange with beige carrier, blue windows; yellow, yellow, yellow cars.......$12 – 16
8. orange with beige carrier, blue windows; red, red, red cars.................$12 – 16
9. orange with beige carrier, green windows; red, yellow, blue cars.................$5 – 7
10. orange with beige carrier, purple windows; red, yellow, blue cars ....$5 – 7
11. orange with off-white carrier, blue windows; red, blue, blue cars..................$8 – 10
12. orange with off-white carrier, blue windows; red, yellow, blue cars...............$5 – 7
13. orange with off-white carrier, blue windows; yellow, yellow, blue cars..........$8 – 10
14. orange with off-white carrier, blue windows; yellow, yellow, blue cars ....$8 – 10
15. orange with gray carrier, blue windows; blue, red, yellow cars.............$8 – 10
16. red with beige carrier, blue windows; red, yellow, blue cars ....$5 – 7

17. red with beige carrier, blue windows; red, orange, blue cars ....$5 – 7
18. red with beige carrier, blue windows; red, orange, red cars ....$8 – 10
19. red with beige carrier, purple windows; red, yellow, blue cars ....$5 – 7
20. red with beige carrier, purple windows; red, orange, blue cars ....$5 – 7
21. red with gray carrier, blue windows; yellow, red, blue cars ....$5 – 7
22. red with gray carrier, blue windows; red, red, red cars ....$12 – 16

Bedford Compressor Truck, 2¼", #28, 1956

1. **orange-yellow, metal wheels.........................$35 – 55**

Bedford "Dunlop" 12 CWT Van, 2⅛", #25, 1956
1. blue...................................$40 – 55

Bedford Duplé Long Distance Coach, 2¼", #21, 1956
1. green ....$45 – 55

Bedford Duplé Long Distance Coach, 2⁵/₈", #21, 1958
1. light green.........................$45 – 60
2. dark green ....$80 – 100

Bedford "Evening News" Van, yellow-orange, 2¼", #42, 1957
1. metal wheels ....$40 – 50
2. gray plastic wheels ....$40 – 50
3. black plastic wheels ....$40 – 50

Bedford Horse Box, with two horses, 23/16", #40, 1977; #87, 1999, US; #49, 2000; #2, 1999, international; #29, 2000, international
1. red with beige box, light brown door, green windows, black base, England cast ....$50 – 60
2. red with dark tan box, brown door, green windows, black base, Manaus cast, Brazil issue..................$40 – 50
3. red with light brown box, white door, green windows, black base, England cast ....$12 – 16
4. red with light brown box, white door, green windows, metallic gray base, England cast...........................$12 – 16
5. orange with beige box, dark brown door, clear windows, black base, England cast..............................$9 – 12

6. orange with beige box, dark brown door, clear windows, dark gray base, England cast.........................$9 – 12
7. orange with beige box, dark brown door, green windows, dark gray base, England cast.........................$5 – 6
8. orange with beige box, dark brown door, green windows, metallic gray base, England cast ....$5 – 6
9. orange with beige box, dark brown door, green windows, unpainted base, England cast.........................$5 – 6

10. **orange with beige box, light brown door, green windows, black base, England cast ....$5 – 6**
11. orange with beige box, light brown door, green windows, black base, England cast ....$5 – 6
12. orange with beige box, dark brown door, purple windows, dark gray base, England cast..........................$6 – 8
13. orange with ivory box, light brown door, green windows, black base, England cast ....$5 – 6
14. orange with ivory box, lime green door, green windows, black base, England cast ....$12 – 16
15. orange with light brown box, lime green door, green windows, black base, England cast....................................$6 – 8
16. orange with light brown box, white door, green windows, black base, England cast ....$6 – 8
17. orange with light brown box, white door, green windows, black base, Macau cast ....$5 – 6
18. orange with light brown box, white door, green windows, metallic gray base, England cast................................$6 – 8
19. orange with light brown box, white door, green windows, unpainted base, England cast................................$6 – 8
20. orange with clear windows.......$8 – 10
21. orange with purple windows.......$5 – 8
22. dark orange with beige box, brown door, green windows, dark gray base, England cast..........................$6 – 8
23. dark orange with light brown box, lime green door, green windows, black base, England cast..........................$5 – 6
24. dark orange with light brown box, lime green door, green windows, black base, England cast, black wheel hubs ....$6 – 8
25. dark orange with light brown box, lime green door, green windows, unpainted base, England cast ....$5 – 6

26. dark orange with light brown box, lime green door, green windows, unpainted base, England cast, black wheel hubs .... $6 – 8
27. dark orange with light brown box, white door, green windows, black base, England cast .... $5 – 6
28. yellow with light brown box, lime green door, green windows, black base, England cast .... $6 – 8
29. yellow with light brown box, white door, amber windows, black base, Thailand cast, Farming series gift set ...... $4 – 5
30. yellow with light brown box, white door, green windows, black base, England cast .... $6 – 8
31. dark green with beige box, dark brown door, green windows, dark gray base, England cast .... $6 – 8
32. dark green with beige box, dark brown door, green windows, metallic gray base, England cast .... $6 – 8
33. dark green with beige box, dark brown door, green windows, unpainted base, England cast .... $6 – 8
34. dark green with beige box, lime green door, green windows, black base, England cast .... $8 – 10
35. dark green with beige box, lime green door, green windows, metallic gray base, England cast .... $8 – 10
36. dark green with light brown box, white door, green windows, unpainted base, England cast .... $12 – 16
37. dark green with translucent ivory box, dark brown door, green windows, unpainted base, England cast ... $8 – 10
38. light green with beige box, dark brown door, green windows, black base, England cast .... $6 – 8
39. light green with beige box, dark brown door, green windows, unpainted base, England cast .... $6 – 8
40. light green with beige box, white door, green windows, unpainted base, England cast .... $6 – 8
41. blue with yellow box, lime green door, green windows, red base, lime green wheels with blue hubs, Live 'N Learn/Matchbox Preschool series, Thailand cast .... $16 – 24
42. blue with yellow box, lime green door, green windows, red base, lime green wheels with lime green hubs, Live 'N Learn/Matchbox Preschool series, Thailand cast .... $16 – 24
43. blue with yellow box, lime green door, green windows, red base, lime green wheels with red hubs, Live 'N Learn/ Matchbox Preschool series, Macau cast .... $6 – 8

44. **metallic turquoise with translucent pale gray box, black door, tinted windows, "Express," 1999 On The Farm series, China cast, US issue ... $2 – 3**
45. metallic turquoise with translucent pale gray box, black door, tinted windows, "Kentucky Stables," 1999 Farming series, international window box .... $3 – 4
46. white with white box, white door, blue windows, red base, "Circus Circus," Thailand cast, Motor City .... $5 – 6
47. dark gray with mustard yellow box, light brown door, tinted windows, "Express," 2000 Farming series .... $2 – 3
48. dark gray with mustard yellow box, light brown door, tinted windows, "Express," "Matchbox 2000," 2000 Farming series .... $3 – 4

Bedford Lomas Ambulance, 2⅝", #14, 1962

1. gray plastic wheels .... $100 – 125
2. silver plastic wheels .... $50 – 60

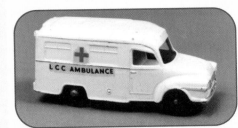

3. **black plastic wheels .... $15 – 20**

Bedford Low Loader, 1⅜", #27, 1956
1. light blue cab, dark blue trailer .... $625 – 800
2. dark green cab, tan trailer ..... $35 – 60

Bedford Low Loader, 3¾", #27, 1959
1. light green cab with metal wheels .... $40 – 50

2. **light green cab with gray plastic wheels .... $65 – 75**
3. dark green cab with gray plastic wheels .... $75 – 95

Bedford "Matchbox Removal" Van, 2⅛", #17, 1956
1. maroon or blue body .... $150 – 180
2. green .... $30 – 50
3. light green .... $60 – 75

Bedford Milk Delivery Van, 2¼", #29, 1956
1. tan, metal wheels .... $60 – 80
2. tan, gray plastic wheels .... $65 – 85

Bedford Petrol Tanker, with tilt cab, 3", #25, 1964
1. yellow cab, "BP," gray plastic wheels .... $140 – 160

2. **yellow cab, "BP," black plastic wheels .... $25 – 40**
3. dark blue cab, "ARAL," black plastic wheels .... $80 – 100

Bedford Tipper Truck, red with tan dumper, 2⅛", #40, 1957
1. metal wheels .... $30 – 45
2. gray plastic wheels .... $30 – 45
3. black plastic wheels .... $25 – 30
1. metal wheels .... $40 – 50
2. gray plastic wheels .... $50 – 60

Bedford Ton Tipper, gray cab, 2½", #3, 1961
1. maroon dumper, gray wheels .. $90 – 100
2. red dumper, gray wheels .... $30 – 40
3. maroon dumper, black wheels .. $15 – 20

4. **red dumper, black wheels .. $15 – 20**

Bedford Wreck Truck, no number cast in base, 2", #13, 1955
1. tan, metal wheels .... $60 – 80

Bedford Wreck Truck, number 13 cast in base, 2⅛", #13, 1958
1. tan, metal wheels .... $60 – 80
2. tan, gray plastic wheels .... $80 – 100

Bedford Wreck Truck, 2", 1993, Matchbox Originals replica of #13
1. red with yellow boom, Made in China .... $4 – 5

Beef Hauler (see Dodge Stake Truck)

Beetle 4x4 (see Volkswagen Beetle 4x4)

eetle Streaker (see Hot Chocolate)

erkeley Cavalier Travel Trailer, 2½",
#23, 1956
- pale blue, metal wheels, no number on base, faint door outline.........$60 – 80
- pale blue, metal wheels, number 23 on base, prominent door outline ..$60 – 80
- lime green, metal wheels, number 23 on base, prominent door outline ..$100 – 120
- lime green, gray plastic wheels, number 23 on base, prominent door outline ....$100 – 120
- metallic green, gray plastic wheels, number 23 on base, prominent door outline ....$750 – 1000

ig Banger, 3", #26, 1972 (similar castings: Cosmic Blues, Flame Out, Pi-Eyed Piper, Red Rider)
- red, "Big Banger" labels, unpainted metal base, blue windows......$15 – 20
- red, "Big Banger" labels, unpainted metal base, amber windows...$15 – 20
- red, "Big Banger" labels, chrome plastic base, blue windows, Premiere Collection #13 ....$4 – 5
- red, "Big Banger" labels, chrome plastic base, blue windows, "Pi-Eyed Piper" on base.................................$90 – 120

ig Blue (see Hot Chocolate)

ig Bull Bulldozer, 2⅜", #12, 1975
- orange with green blade, orange rollers ....$5 – 7
- orange with green blade, yellow rollers ....$15 – 20
- orange with green blade, black rollers ....$55 – 65

illboard Truck, #56, 2003
- blue, 2003 Kids' Shoppes series ....$2 – 3

lack Widow, Roman numeral VIII, 1978 (variation of #41 Siva Spider, 1972)
- powder blue with clear windows, Roman Numeral Limited Edition.........$12 – 15
- powder blue with black windows, Roman Numeral Limited Edition...........$9 – 12

laze Buster Fire Engine, "Fire" labels, 3", #22, 1975
- red with white ladder, chrome interior, unpainted base, "Fire" labels ..$275 – 425
- red with black ladder, chrome interior, unpainted base, "Fire" labels ..$25 – 40
- red with yellow ladder, chrome interior, unpainted base, "Fire" labels ....$6 – 10
- red with yellow ladder, chrome interior, unpainted base; Manaus, Brazil cast ....$40 – 55
- red with yellow ladder, chrome interior, gray base; Manaus, Brazil cast ....$70 – 90
- red with yellow ladder, chrome interior, black base..............................$6 – 10

7. red with yellow ladder, white interior, black base.............................$6 – 10
8. red with yellow ladder, white interior, charcoal base........................$6 – 10
9. dark red with yellow ladder, white interior, black base ....$6 – 10
10. dark red with yellow ladder, white interior, charcoal base........................$6 – 10
11. dark red with yellow ladder, white interior, gray-brown base ....$6 – 10
12. dull red with orange-yellow ladder, white interior, gray-brown base........$6 – 10
13. dull red with orange-yellow ladder, white interior, gray-brown base, "No.32" labels ....$9 – 12

Blimp, #455, 1999
1. red, "Coca-Cola," Premiere Collection ....$7 – 9
2. red, "Coca-Cola," "www.cocacolastore.com," Color Comp promotional.........$80 – 120

Bloodmobile, #15, 2003 (see Police Mobile Command Center)

Bluebird Dauphine Travel Trailer, 2½", #23, 1960
1. metallic green with gray plastic wheels..............................$300 – 350
2. metallic tan with gray plastic wheels...............................$50 – 60
3. metallic tan with silver wheels..$50 – 60
4. metallic tan with black plastic wheels..............................$80 – 100

Blue Shark, 3", #61, 1971
1. dark blue, "69" label, amber windshield ....$16 – 24
2. dark blue, "69" label, clear windshield ....$16 – 24
3. dark blue, "86" label, amber windshield ....$16 – 24
4. dark blue, "86" label, clear windshield ....$16 – 24
5. dark blue, "scorpion label, amber windshield ....$30 – 40
6. dark blue, "scorpion label, clear windshield ....$30 – 40

BMC 1800 Pininfarina, 2¾", #56, 1970

1. metallic gold ....$16 – 24

2. pink ....$20 – 25

3. orange ....$16 – 24

BMW 3.0 CSL, 2⅞", #45, 1976
1. red..............................$70 – 80
2. orange with clear windows.......$8 – 10
3. orange with dark green windows ..$8 – 10

4. orange with green windows ....$7 – 9
5. white, "BMW," "Manhalter" labels, Action System.....................$60 – 70
6. white "Polizei" label, amber dome light, Germany/Japan issue...............$40 – 50
7. white, "Polizei" label, blue dome light, Germany/Japan issue...............$40 – 50
8. white, "Polizei" label, green hood and trunk, Germany/Japan issue ....$60 – 70
9. white, no "Polizei" label, green hood and trunk, Germany issue..........$90 – 120

BMW 323i Cabriolet, 2¾", #39, 1985
1. red, "323i," no tow hook ....$2 – 3
2. red, "323i," tow hook...............$2 – 3
3. red, "Gliding Club," tow hook, Two Pack (with glider trailer) ....$4 – 5
4. metallic light blue, "323i," no tow hook....................................$3 – 4
5. metallic light blue, "323i," tow hook..$2 – 3
6. metallic light blue, dark blue stripe, tow hook, Two – Pack ....$3 – 4
7. dark blue, "323i," "BP," the Netherlands issue ....$10 – 12
8. white, "323i," "BMW," no tow hook....................................$10 – 12
9. white, "323i," "BMW," tow hook..$10 – 12
10. white, "323i," blue and red design, tow hook, Two Pack........................$3 – 4
11. white, "Alpina," Laser wheels, tow hook....................................$5 – 6
12. white, "Alpina," new Superfast wheels, no tow hook.............................$5 – 6
13. white, "Alpina," new Superfast wheels, tow hook................................$5 – 6
14. white with purple, orange and blue design, tow hook, Two Pack.......$2 – 3

BMW 328i, #69, 1999, Germany
1. metallic dark green, light tan interior, clear windows, 1999...............$4 – 5
2. metallic blue, light gray interior, tinted windows, 5-pack.....................$2 – 3
3. dark metallic blue, black interior, tinted windows, Launcher 5-pack.........$2 – 3

BMW 328i

4. **metallic silver-blue, rubber tires on chrome rims, Sharon Osbourne, Matchbox Collectibles "The Osbournes" ....$5 – 6**
5. dark gray, "BMW328i," light gray interior, clear windows ....$3 – 4

BMW 328i Police Car, #11, 2000; #31, 2001; #29, 2003
1. white and green, "Polizei," blue and green light bar, 2000 ....$3 – 5
2. white with red band, blue stripes, crest, "35-1," 2000 ....$3 – 5
3. metallic silver, "Police" with orange band and checks, blue light bar, 2001 ..$2 – 3

4. **blue with red and white design, tinted windows, black interior, red light bar, 2001 On Patrol 5-pack ...$2 – 3**

5. **metallic blue with red and yellow design, amber windows, white interior, red light bar, 2003 Police Squad series ....$2 – 3**

BMW 3 – Series Coupe, #83, 2000; #63, 2000, international
1. metallic blue, "3 Series," gradient black to gray stripe, 5-pack...............$2 – 3

2. **metallic gray with white and yellow headlights, 2000 Worldwide Wheels ....$2 – 3**

3. metallic gray with white and yellow headlights, "Matchbox 2000," 2000 Worldwide Wheels...........................$3 – 4
4. white with silver headlights, black Matchbox logo, 2003 Auto Carrier Launcher 5-pack ....$2 – 3

BMW 5-Series 535i, 3", #26, 1989; #31, 1990, international
1. red, no markings, Show Stoppers, Thailand cast................................$4 – 5
2. metallic dark gray, no markings, Macau cast ....$3 – 4
3. metallic dark gray, no markings, Thailand cast................................$3 – 4
4. white, "BMW Team," Thailand cast.....................................$3 – 4

BMW 850i, 3", #49, 1993; #2, 2001; #2, 1993, international; #73, 1998, international; #54, 1998, Germany

1. **red, "Ripper" on sides, skull and crossbones on hood, 1995.....$2 – 3**
2. red, "Ripper" on sides, no markings on hood, 1996 ....$2 – 3
3. red, detailed trim, black and red interior, rubber tires on chrome rims, Premiere Collection #15 ....$4 – 5
4. red, detailed trim, black and tan interior, rubber tires on chrome rims, JC Penney Premiere Collection....................$4 – 5
5. red, no markings, Kentucky Fried Chicken Kids Meal premium ....$40 – 60
6. metallic red, no markings, 1998 Street Cruisers series, international issue .$2 – 3
7. metallic red, no markings, Germany issue ....$4 – 5

8. **metallic red, "BMW 850I" on doors, 10-spoke wheels, 2000 Daddy's Dreams series ....$2 – 3**
9. metallic red, "BMW 850I" on doors, 5-spoke wheels, 2000 Daddy's Dreams series ....$4 – 5

10. yellow, "Coca-Cola" and polar bears, pack ....$2 –
11. dark blue, no markings..............$2 –
12. maroon with pink and yellow streak, 1994 ....$2 –

13. **maroon, detailed trim, rubbe tires on chrome rims, Premier Collection ....$4 –**
14. purple, detailed trim, rubber tires o chrome rims, Ultra Class ....$9 – 1
15. black, "850i," yellow flash, gold whe hubs....................................$2 –
16. black, "850i," yellow flash, silver whe hubs....................................$3 –
17. black, "Go Tigers! 1997," Australa issue ....$5 –
18. white, Show Stoppers ....$4 –

19. **metallic silver, clear windows, brigh blue interior, 1994................$3 –**
20. metallic gray, detailed trim, chrome wi dows, rubber tires on chrome rim World Class ....$4 –

BMW Cabriolet (see 323i Cabriolet)

BMW M1, 3", #52, 1981

1. **red, "1," stripes, hood doesn't open ....$2 –**

2. **yellow, "11" and stripes, hood does n't open................................$2 –**
3. dark yellow, detailed trim, chrome wi dows, rubber tires on chrome rims hood doesn't open, World Class ..$6 –

metallic blue, detailed trim, rubber tires on chrome rims, hood doesn't open, Gold Coin Collection ....$16 – 24

black, "Pirelli 59," hood doesn't open, Macau cast ....$4 – 5
. black, "Pirelli 59," hood doesn't open, Manaus cast, Brazil issue......$40 – 50
. metallic gray, "52," hood opens, clear windows...................................$3 – 4
. metallic gray, "52," hood opens, tinted windows...................................$3 – 4
. metallic gray, "52," hood opens, amber windows...................................$12 – 16
O. metallic gray, "52," hood opens, green windows...................................$70 – 80

1. white, "BMW M1," hood doesn't open ....$3 – 4
2. chrome, hood doesn't open, custom ....$16 – 24

MW Z-3, #25, 1997; #61, 1997, international; #5, 1998; #72, 1998, international; #50, 1999; #45, 1999, international; #3, 2000, international; #74, 2002
. unpainted with tan and black interior, rubber tires on chrome rims, detailed trim, 1997 Inaugural Edition ......$5 – 6
. black with dark red interior ....$2 – 3
. black with dark red interior, plastic base, Target Eggmobile.............$3 – 4
. black with dark red interior, metal base, Target Eggmobile ....$10 – 12
. black with dark red interior, "Millions of Reasons To Celebrate! Compaq," ASAP promotional.........................$60 – 90

. **blue with gray interior, "Z3," white splash design bordered in red, 1998 Stars & Stripes series...........$2 – 3**
7. **metallic blue with tan and black interior, rubber tires on chrome rims, detailed trim, 1997 Inaugural Edition.......$5 – 6**

8. metallic red with black interior, silver "Z3," 1999 Drop Tops series.....$2 – 3

9. metallic red with black interior, 2002 Kids' Cars of the Year ..$2 – 3
10. metallic red with black interior, silver "Z3" and "007," ASAP promotional ....$80 – 120
11. metallic gold with black interior, 1997 75 Challenge series...............$6 – 12

12. metallic green with black interior, 5-pack ....$2 – 3
13. metallic green with tan interior ...$3 – 4
14. metallic gray with gray interior....$4 – 5

15. metallic gray with maroon and black interior, rubber tires on chrome rims, Premiere Collection #12.........$4 – 5
16. red with black interior, "3Com," ASAP promotional ....$80 – 120
17. red with black interior, "Compaq," ASAP promotional ....$60 – 90
18. red with black interior, "Macola Software," ASAP promotional ....$80 – 120
19. red with black interior, "Millions of Reasons To Celebrate! Compaq," ASAP promotional..............................$60 – 90
20. red with black interior, "Retek Broadvision," ASAP promotional......$80 – 120
21. red with black interior, "Rigid Keenserts,"ASAP promotional...$80 – 120

22. red with black interior, "Z3," white splash design bordered in blue, 1998 Stars & Stripes series ..$2 – 3
23. red with black interior, "Z3," white splash design bordered in blue, "Espe," ASAP promotional ....$120 – 160
24. red with black interior, "Z3," white splash design bordered in blue, "Fiery Driven," ASAP promotional.............$120 – 160

25. red with gray and black interior, rubber tires on chrome rims, Premiere Collection #16 ....$4 – 5
26. white with dark red interior, rubber tires on chrome rims, "Coca-Cola," Premiere Collection ....$7 – 8

BMW Z-8, #9, 2002; #10, 2003
1. metallic blue with tan interior, 2002 Style Champs series.........................$
2. metallic blue with cream interior, 2003 Family Wheels series ....$2 – 3
3. metallic gold with silver-gray interior, 2003 Auto Carrier Launcher 5-pack ....$2 – 3

Boat and Trailer, plastic boat, 3¼", #9, 1966

1. **white hull, dull blue deck, blue trailer, black plastic wheels .....$12 – 16**
2. white hull, bright blue deck, blue trailer, black plastic wheels ....$5 – 8
3. white hull, blue deck, no label, blue trailer, Superfast wheels, 1969...$20 – 25
4. white hull, blue deck, no label, blue trailer, Two Pack ....$4 – 5
5. white hull, blue deck, "8" label, blue trailer, Two Pack...................$12 – 16
6. white hull, blue deck, no label, orange trailer, Two Pack......................$6 – 8

7. white hull, black deck, no label, blue trailer, Two Pack..................$65 – 85
8. white hull, white deck, "8" label, orange trailer, Two Pack..................$8 – 10

9. **white hull, white deck, "Seaspray," black trailer, Two Pack ....$4 – 5**
10. white hull, white deck, "yellow dash, Two Pack....................$4 – 5
11. blue hull, white deck, "8" label, blue trailer, Two Pack..................$12 – 16
12. blue hull, white deck, "8" label, orange trailer, Two Pack....................$6 – 8

13. **blue hull, blue deck, orange spatter, black trailer, Two Pack ....$4 – 5**

Bomag Road Roller, #72, 1979; #40, 1991; #68, 1992; #29, 1999; #68, 1991, international; #9, 1998, Germany
1. orange with blue stripes, gray interior, Thailand cast, 1991 ....$2 – 3
2. orange with red stripes and design, gray interior, Thailand cast ....$2 – 3
3. orange with black stripes and design, gray interior, Thailand cast ....$2 – 3
4. orange with white roof, black dashes, "R75," China cast, Germany issue...$4 – 5

5. **yellow with red interior, yellow hubs, England cast, 1979 ....$5 – 6**
6. yellow with red interior, chrome hubs, England cast, 1979..................$4 – 5

7. yellow with red stripes, bridge and road graphics, 1992 ....$2 – 3
8. **blue with white stripes and "PR-510" and dots, China cast, 1999 Road Work series..................$2 – 3**

Boss Mustang (see Ford Mustang 1970 Boss Mustang)

Boulevard Blaster (see Mazda RX7 Savannah)

Bradley M2 Fighting Vehicle, #47, 1998; #83, 1999

1. **army green, "Mountain Tiger," "J020764," "476," black base and barrel, 1999 Military Patrol series ..$4 – 5**
2. army green, black and tan camouflage, army green base, black barrel, Premiere Collection ....$4 – 5

3. **khaki, "T-0927," black star on front and sides, black base and barrel, 1998 Rough 'N Tough series ..$2 – 3**

4. **black with green turret, green tanks, white and red globe graphics, yellow Matchbox logo, gray base and barrel, 2003 Hero City 5-pack #3......$2 – 3**

Bradley M2 Fighting Vehicle, 2001 Feature Cars, with opening features, designed to replace Premiere Collection
1. dark tan with green, black and white camouflage ....$9 – 12

Breakdown Van (see Chevrolet Breakdown Van)

BRM Racing Car, black tires on plastic hubs, 2⁵/₈", #52, 1965

1. blue with "5" decal or label.......$8 – 12
2. blue with "3" decal ....$40 – 50
3. red with "5" decal or label......$20 – 25

Brown Sugar, Roman numeral VII, 1978 (similar castings: #26 Big Banger, 1972; #26 Cosmic Blues, 1980)

1. **brown, Roman Numeral Limited Edition ....$9 – 12**

Bucket Fire Truck, #2, 2003

1. **metallic red with metallic gray interior and bumpers, black boom, 2003 Sky Fire series ....$2 – 3**

Buick LeSabre Stock Car, 3", #10, 1987
1. black with white base, "4," "355 CID" ....$2 – 4
2. pale purple and white, "Ken Wells," "Quicksilver," Laser wheels.........$6 – 8
3. light green with white base, "4," "355 CID" ....$3 – 5
4. light brown with white base, "4," "355 CID" ....$3 – 5
5. orange with white base, "4," "355 CID" ....$6 – 8
6. red with white base, "4," "355 CID" ..6 – 8
7. yellow with red base, "10," "Shell," "Marshall" ....$2 – 4
8. white with red base, "10," "Shell," "Marshall"..$2 – 4

9. **red with white base, "07," "Total Racing"...............................$2 – 4**

Bulldozer (see Caterpillar Bulldozer, Caterpillar Crawler Bulldozer, Caterpillar D8, Caterpillar Tractor, Case Bulldozer)

Bulldozer Dirt Machine, #37, 2001 Earth Crunchers (see Super Dozer)

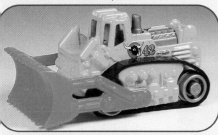

Bulldozer Dirt Machine, 2003 Hero city 5-pack, #9 (see Super Dozer)

Bulldozer Super Dozer, #67, 2003 (see Super Dozer)

Buster (see The Buster)

C

Cadillac Allante, 3", #65, 1988; #72, 1988
1. metallic red, "Official Pace Car 76th Indy," gray interior, clear windshield, Thailand cast ....$8 – 10
2. metallic red with dark gray interior, chrome windshield, rubber tires on gray rims, Thailand cast, World Class ..$4 – 5
3. pink with gray interior, "Cadillac," clear windshield, China cast...............$2 – 3
4. pink with gray interior, "Cadillac," clear windshield, Macau cast.............$2 – 3
5. pink with gray interior, "Cadillac," clear windshield, Thailand cast ....$2 – 3

6. pink with white interior, green zigzag and blue stripe design, "Cadillac," clear windshield, Thailand cast ....$2 – 3
7. pink with white interior, green zigzag and blue stripe design, clear windshield, China cast...............................$2 – 3

8. black with red interior, red and silver stripes, clear windshield, Macau cast, Laser wheels ....$4 – 5
9. metallic dark gray with red interior, chrome windshield, rubber tires on gray rims, Macau cast, World Class ..$6 – 8

10. metallic gray with red interior, clear windshield, China cast ....$2 – 3
11. metallic gray with red interior, clear windshield, Macau cast.............$2 – 3
12. cream with black and tan interior, clear windshield, rubber tires on gray rims, Thailand cast, JC Penney Premiere Collection 8-car display set.............$4 – 5

13. white with red and black interior, clear windshield, rubber tires on chrome rims, Thailand cast, Ultra Class ....$9 – 12
14. white with red interior, clear windshield, rubber tires on gray rims, China cast, US issue ....$120 – 160

Cadillac Ambulance (see Cadillac S&S Ambulance)

Cadillac Eldorado 1956, #501, 2001, Matchbox Collectibles Elvis Presley Collection with Graceland diorama
1. metallic purple, detailed trim, rubber white wall tires on chrome rims ....$12 – 16

Cadillac Escalade, #21, 2003

1. black with yellow and white on sides, "Matchbox Hero City," "Escalade," "21," 2003 Bridge Crew series .$2 – 3

Cadillac Fleetwood 1955, #500, 2001, Matchbox Collectibles Elvis Presley Collection with Graceland diorama

1. pink with white roof, detailed trim, rubber white wall tires on chrome rims..................................$12 – 16

Cadillac S&S Ambulance, white, 2⁵/₈", #54, 1965

1. white with black base, black plastic wheels, 1965 ....$9 – 12
2. white with black base, Superfast wheels, 1970.....................$40 – 50

Cadillac Sixty Special, 2³/₄", #27, 1960
1. metallic light green with white roof...............................$500 – 600
2. metallic gray with white roof...$35 – 45

3. lavender with pink roof ....$75 – 100

Camaro (see Chevrolet Camaro)

Car Carrier, #16, 2003
1. orange with dark gray ramp, blue windows, 2003 Public Works series.....................................$2 – 3

Car Transporter (see Bedford Car Transporter)

Caravan Travel Trailer (see Eccles Caravan Travel Trailer)

Caravan Travel Trailer, 2¹¹/₁₆", #31, 1977; #52, 1999; #47, 1999, international
1. beige, "Mobile 500," Two Pack...$3 – 4
2. gray with blue and red stripes, black base, gray door, amber windows..........$3 – 4
3. white with unpainted base, door and interior various colors, England casting..$5 – 6
4. white with black base, "Mobile 500," Two Pack ....$4 – 5
5. white with red door; yellow, orange, and red stripes ....$3 – 4
6. white with "Caravan 2000," 5-pack....................................$2 – 3
7. white with turquoise and blue design, 1999 Beach series ....$3 – 4

Carmichael Commando (European model), 3", #57, 1982
1. red, "Fire" ....$16 – 24
2. white, "Police Rescue"..........$20 – 30

Case Bulldozer, 2½", #16, 1969

1. **green treads.......................$9 – 12**
2. black treads ....$12 – 15

Caterpillar Articulated Dump Truck, #403, 1999, Caterpillar series
1. orange-yellow, "CAT" ....$4 – 5

Caterpillar Backhoe/Loader, #353, 1998 Dirt Machines 2-pack with accessories, retooled Hot Wheels casting

1. **orange-yellow, "CAT" ....$4 – 5**

Caterpillar Bulldozer (see Caterpillar Crawler, Caterpillar D8, Caterpillar Tractor)

Caterpillar Bulldozer, yellow, no blade braces, 2", #18, 1958

1. **yellow with yellow blade .....$55 – 70**

Caterpillar Bulldozer, yellow with blade braces, 2¼", #18, 1961
1. metal rollers........................$30 – 40

2. silver plastic rollers..............$85 – 95
3. black plastic rollers..............$20 – 30

Caterpillar Bulldozer, with plastic roof, 2⅝", #64, 1979; #9, 1983, #14, 1998
1. red with lime green blade, blue canopy, gravel design, Thailand cast, Live 'N Learn/Matchbox Preschool ....$7 – 9

2. **red with metallic gray blade, black canopy, no markings, China cast, 1996 ....$2 – 3**
3. red with yellow blade, blue canopy, yellow stripes, Macau cast, Live 'N Learn/Matchbox Preschool ....$7 – 9
4. orange with metallic gray blade, black canopy, detailed trim, Thailand cast, Collector's Choice, White Rose Collectibles.................................$3 – 4
5. orange with orange blade, black canopy, "Losinger," Macau cast, Switzerland issue ....$9 – 12
6. orange with orange blade, black canopy, "Metro DPW" on blade, China cast, 1998 Big Movers series ....$2 – 3
7. orange with orange blade, black canopy, black stripes on blade, Thailand cast, 5-pack......................................$2 – 3
8. pumpkin orange with gray blade, black canopy, no markings, China cast, 5-pack......................................$2 – 3
9. pumpkin orange with metallic gray blade, black canopy, "Amavia," China cast, ASAP promotional ......$80 – 120
10. pumpkin orange with metallic gray blade, black canopy, "Blue Ridge Construction Co.," China cast, ASAP promotional ....$80 – 120
11. pumpkin orange with metallic gray blade, black canopy, "Cat Service Co.," China cast, ASAP promotional.......$80 – 120
12. pumpkin orange with metallic gray blade, black canopy, "CT Tank Removal," China cast, ASAP promotional ....$80 – 120
13. pumpkin orange with metallic gray blade, black canopy, "General Fill," China cast, ASAP promotional ......$80 – 120
14. pumpkin orange with metallic gray blade, black canopy, "Hemler Bros.," China cast, ASAP promotional.......$80 – 120
15. pumpkin orange with metallic gray blade, black canopy, "LCT," China cast, ASAP promotional ....$80 – 120
16. fluorescent orange with black blade, black canopy, no markings, Thailand cast, 5-pack ....$2 – 3

17. fluorescent orange with gray blade, black canopy, no markings, China cast, 5-pack....................................$2 – 3
18. orange-yellow with black blade, yellow canopy, "Matchbox," detailed trim, China cast, Premiere Collection/Convoy ..$3 – 4
19. orange-yellow with orange-yellow blade, orange-yellow canopy, detailed trim, China cast, Premiere Collection ..$4 – 5
20. orange-yellow with yellow blade, black canopy, no markings, Thailand cast..............$2 – 3
21. orange-yellow with yellow blade, red canopy, red stripes on blade, Thailand cast ....$2 – 3
22. orange-yellow with yellow blade, red canopy, no markings on blade, Thailand cast ....$2 – 3
23. yellow with black blade, black canopy, Caterpillar "C" logo, England cast...$5 – 6
24. yellow with black blade, tan canopy, Caterpillar "C" logo, England cast..........$5 – 6
25. yellow with black blade, yellow canopy, small Caterpillar "C" logo, detailed trim, China cast, Premiere Collection/Convoy ...$3 – 4
26. yellow with gray blade, black canopy, no markings, Macau cast, 5-pack ...$3 – 4
27. yellow with gray blade, black canopy, no markings, Thailand cast..............$2 – 3
28. yellow with yellow blade, black canopy, Caterpillar "C" logo, England cast...$5 – 6

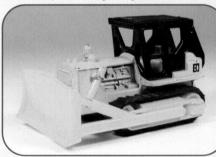

29. **yellow with yellow blade, black canopy, backwards Caterpillar "C" logo ....$6 – 8**
30. yellow with yellow blade, black canopy, Caterpillar "C" logo and "Cat," China cast...$2 – 3
31. yellow with yellow blade, black canopy, Caterpillar "C" logo and "Cat," Macau cast ....$2 – 3
32. yellow with yellow blade, black canopy, no markings, Macau cast ....$2 – 3
33. yellow with yellow blade, black canopy, no markings, Thailand cast ....$2 – 3

34. **yellow with yellow blade, red canopy, red stripes on blade ....$2 – 3**

35. yellow with yellow blade, tan canopy, Caterpillar "C" logo, England cast ..$5 – 6
36. yellow with yellow blade, tan canopy, no markings, England cast ....$5 – 6
37. yellow with no blade, black canopy, Caterpillar "C" logo and "Cat," England cast...................................$12 – 16
38. fluorescent yellow with gray blade, black canopy, no markings, China cast ..$2 – 3

39. fluorescent green with yellow blade, black canopy, "Unit #3", China cast, 1999 Highway Crew 5-pack ...$2 – 3
40. fluorescent green with black blade, black canopy, 1998 Big Movers series .$2 – 3
41. metallic gold with black blade, black canopy, no markings, China cast, 1997 75 Challenge series ....$6 – 12

Caterpillar Bulldozer, #345, 1998 Dirt Machines 2-pack with accessories, retooled Hot Wheels casting

1. orange-yellow, "CAT" ....$4 – 5

Caterpillar Challenger AG Tractor, #351, 1998 Dirt Machines 2-pack with accessories, retooled Hot Wheels casting
1. orange-yellow with tinted windows, 1998 Dirt Machines.................$4 – 5
2. orange-yellow with clear windows, Premiere Collection ....$6 – 9

Caterpillar Crawler Bulldozer, 2³⁄₈", #18, 1964
1. silver plastic rollers.............$90 – 100
2. black plastic rollers...............$15 – 20

Caterpillar D8 Bulldozer with blade, 1⁷⁄₈", #18, 1956
1. yellow with red blade.............$40 – 60

Caterpillar Dump Truck, #344, 1998 Dirt Machines 2-pack with accessories, retooled Hot Wheels casting

1. orange-yellow, "Caterpillar".........$4 – 5

Caterpillar Excavator, #343, 1998 Dirt Machines 2-pack with accessories, retooled Hot Wheels casting
1. orange-yellow, "CAT" ....$4 – 5

Caterpillar Material Handler, #381, 1999
1. orange-yellow with tinted windows, "CAT," Caterpillar series ....$4 – 5
2. orange-yellow with clear windows, "CAT," Premiere Collection.......$9 – 12

Caterpillar Motor Grader, #350, 1998 Dirt Machines 2-pack with accessories, retooled Hot Wheels casting

1. orange-yellow, "Caterpillar"....$4 – 5
2. olive green, "Caterpillar" ....$4 – 5

Caterpillar Quarry Dump Truck, #462, 2000
1. orange-yellow with black cab, "CAT," "Caterpillar" ....$6 – 8

Caterpillar Road Roller, #347, 1998 Dirt Machines 2-pack with accessories, retooled Hot Wheels casting
1. orange-yellow, "Caterpillar".........$4 – 5
2. chrome plated, "Caterpillar" ....$4 – 5

Caterpillar Scraper, #348, 1998 Dirt Machines 2-pack with accessories, retooled Hot Wheels casting
1. orange-yellow, "CAT" ....$4 – 5
2. chrome plated with black cab and back section, "CAT".........................$4 – 3

Caterpillar Skidder, #404, 1999
1. orange-yellow, "CAT" ....$4 – 5

Caterpillar Soil Compactor, #354, 1998 Dirt Machines 2-pack with accessories, retooled Hot Wheels casting

1. orange-yellow, tinted windows, 1998 Dirt Machines ....$4 – 5

2. orange-yellow, clear windows, Premiere Collection ....$6 – 9

Caterpillar Tool Carrier, #382, 1999 Caterpillar series
1. orange-yellow, black forks ....$4 – 5

Caterpillar Tractor, driver, no blade, 1½", #8, 1955
1. orange with orange driver....$80 – 100
2. light yellow with red driver....$80 – 100
3. dark yellow with dark yellow driver ....$30 – 40

Caterpillar Tractor, driver, no blade, 1⁵⁄₈", #8, 1959
1. yellow with metal rollers ....$50 – 60

Caterpillar Tractor, driver, no blade, 1⁷⁄₈", #8, 1961
1. metal rollers ....$45 – 60
2. silver plastic rollers.............$65 – 80
3. black plastic rollers..............$40 – 60

Caterpillar Tractor, no driver, no blade, 2", #8, 1964
1. yellow with black plastic rollers ..$15 – 20

Caterpillar Tractor Shovel, #383, 1999
1. orange-yellow with tinted windows, Caterpillar series.....................$4 – 5
2. orange-yellow with clear windows, Premiere series ....$16 – 24

Caterpillar Trailer, #352, 1998 Dirt Machines 2-pack with accessories, retooled Hot Wheels casting
1. orange-yellow with black treads...$4 – 5

Caterpillar Trailer, #443, 1999
1. orange-yellow, "CAT," Caterpillar series.....................................$3 – 4

Caterpillar Wheel Loader, #346, 1998 Dirt Machines 2-pack with accessories, retooled Hot Wheels casting

1. orange-yellow, "CAT" ....$4 – 5

Cattle Trailer, #792, 1979, Two Pack
1. red with beige stakes, black cattle, England cast...............................$3 – 4
2. red with beige stakes, brown cattle, England cast...........................$3 – 4
3. red with orange-yellow stakes, black cattle, England cast ....$3 – 4

4. red with yellow stakes, no cattle, blue wheels with yellow hubs, no-origin cast, Live 'N Learn/Matchbox Preschool ....$7 – 9
5. yellow with light brown stakes, brown cattle, England cast ....$3 – 4
6. yellow with light brown stakes, brown cattle, Macau cast...................$3 – 4
7. yellow with light brown stakes, brown cattle, no origin cast.................$3 – 4
8. green with yellow stakes, black cattle, no origin cast ....$3 – 4
9. pale blue with light brown stakes, black cattle, no origin cast.................$3 – 4

Cattle Truck (see Dodge Cattle Truck, Dodge Stake Truck)

Cavalier (see Opel Vectra/Chevrolet Cavalier)

Cement Mixer, 1⅝", #3, 1953
1. blue with orange metal wheels ..$30 – 40
2. blue with gray plastic wheels ..$40 – 50

Cement Mixer Truck, 3", #40, 2001; #22, 2003

1. **white with red drum, 2001 Earth Crunchers series...................$2 – 3**

2. **metallic blue with white drum, 2003 5-pack #9...........................$2 – 3**

3. **white with yellow drum, 2003 Bridge Crew series ....$2 – 3**

Cement Truck, Peterbilt (see Peterbilt Cement Truck)

Cement Truck, Badger (see Badger Cement Truck)

Center-Console Boat, #44, 2003 (see Sea Speeder)

Chevrolet 1939 Sedan Delivery, #58, 1997, Australia; #245, 1992, White Rose Collectibles (larger than #215, no rear bumper)
1. "1995 Temecula Rod Run," red with white chassis, White Rose Collectibles....................$12 – 16
2. "49ers 1992," gold with red chassis, White Rose Collectibles.............$4 – 5
3. "Angels 1993," white with dark blue chassis, White Rose Collectibles ..$6 – 8
4. "Astros 1993," dark blue with orange chassis, White Rose Collectibles ..$6 – 8
5. "Bears 1992," orange with dark blue chassis, White Rose Collectibles ..$4 – 5
6. "Bengals 1992," orange with black chassis, White Rose Collectibles........$4 – 5
7. "Bills 1992", white with dark blue chassis, White Rose Collectibles ....$4 – 5
8. "Blue Ridge Brewing Co.," "Hawksbill Lager," silver-blue and black with cream chassis, rubber tires on chrome rims, Matchbox Collectibles Microbreweries Collection ....$9 – 12
9. "Boston Celtics 1995," green with white chassis, Australia issue...........$9 – 12
10. "Braves 1993," white with metallic blue chassis, White Rose Collectibles ..$6 – 8
11. "Brewers 1993," blue with yellow chassis, White Rose Collectibles ....$6 – 8
12. "Broncos 1992," orange with blue chassis, White Rose Collectibles ....$4 – 5
13. "Browns 1992," white with brown chassis, White Rose Collectibles ....$4 – 5
14. "Buccaneers 1992," white with orange chassis, White Rose Collectibles ..$4 – 5
15. "Cardinals 1992," yellow with rust chassis, White Rose Collectibles ....$4 – 5
16. "Cardinals 1993," red with dark blue chassis, White Rose Collectibles ..$6 – 8
17. "Chargers 1992," yellow with dark blue chassis, White Rose Collectibles ..$4 – 5
18. "Charlotte Hornets 1995," turquoise with blue chassis, Australia issue ......$9 – 12
19. "Chicago Bulls 1995," dark blue w... red chassis, Australia issue .....$9 – 1
20. "Chicago Cubs 1993," gray with r... chassis, White Rose Collectibles ..$6 –
21. "Chiefs 1992," yellow with red chass... White Rose Collectibles.............$4 –
22. "Colts 1992," white with dark blue cha... sis, White Rose Collectibles........$4 –
23. "Cowboys 1992," metallic gray wi... dark blue chassis, White Rose C... lectibles ....$4 –
24. "Dallas Mavericks 1995," green wi... blue chassis, Australia issue ....$9 – 1
25. "Dallas Stars 1993," black with go... chassis, White Rose Collectibles ..$6 –
26. "Denver Nuggets 1995," dark re... with dark blue chassis, Austral... issue ....$9 – 1
27. "Detroit Pistons 1995," red with bl... chassis, Australia issue...........$9 – 1
28. "Dodgers 1993," blue with white cha... sis, White Rose Collectibles ....$6 –
29. "Dolphins 1992," white with turquois... chassis, White Rose Collectibles ..$4 –
30. "Dubuque Red," red and black wi... black chassis, rubber tires on chrom... rims, Matchbox Collectibles Microbre... eries Collection ....$9 – 1
31. "Eagles 1992," white with green cha... sis, White Rose Collectibles ....$4 –
32. "Expos 1993," blue with red chassi... White Rose Collectibles.............$6 –
33. "Falcons 1992," white with red chassi... White Rose Collectibles.............$4 –
34. "Florida Panthers 1993," white wi... dark blue chassis, White Rose C... lectibles ....$6 –
35. "Gator Lager Beer," yellow and bla... with green chassis, rubber tires ... chrome rims, Matchbox Collectible... Microbreweries Collection........$9 – 1
36. "Giants 1992," red with dark blue cha... sis, White Rose Collectibles ....$4 –
37. "Giants 1993," gray with black chassi... White Rose Collectibles.............$6 –
38. "Golden State Warriors 1995," da... blue with orange-yellow chassis, Au... tralia issue ....$9 – 1
39. "Houston Rockets 1995," dark blue wi... red chassis, Australia issue......$9 – 1
40. "Indians 1993," gray with dark blu... chassis, White Rose Collectibles .$6 –
41. "Jets 1992," white with green chassi... White Rose Collectibles.............$4 –
42. "Knicks 1995," blue-green with orang... chassis, Australia issue...........$9 – 1
43. "LA Rams 1992," yellow with blue cha... sis, White Rose Collectibles ....$4 –
44. "Lions 1992," metallic gray with blu... chassis, White Rose Collectibles ..$4 –
45. "Los Angeles Lakers 1995," lavende... with orange-yellow chassis, Austral... issue ....$9 – 1
46. "Mariners 1993," metallic gray wit... blue-green chassis, White Rose C... lectibles ....$6 –
47. "Marlins 1993," white with light blu... chassis, White Rose Collectibles ..$6 –

8. "Matchbox Get In The Fast Lane — Hershey 1995," fluorescent orange, US issue ....$9 – 12
9. "Mighty Ducks 1993," white with purple chassis, White Rose Collectibles ..$6 – 8
0. "NY Mets 1993," blue with orange chassis, White Rose Collectibles........$6 – 8
1. "Oakland A's 1993," orange-yellow with green chassis, White Rose Collectibles ....$6 – 8
2. "Oilers 1992," white with dark blue chassis, White Rose Collectibles ....$4 – 5
3. "Orioles 1993," orange with black chassis, White Rose Collectibles ....$6 – 8
4. "Orlando Magic 1995," blue with white chassis, Australia issue...........$9 – 12
5. "Pacers 1995," orange-yellow with dark blue chassis, Australia issue ....$9 – 12
6. "Packers 1992," yellow with green chassis, White Rose Collectibles........$4 – 5
7. "Padres 1993," white with orange chassis, White Rose Collectibles ....$6 – 8
8. "Patroits 1992," white with bright blue chassis, White Rose Collectibles ....$4 – 5
9. "Penn State 1993," white and blue with blue chassis, White Rose Collectibles ....$6 – 8
0. "Phillies 1993", red with white chassis, White Rose Collectibles.............$6 – 8
1. "Phoenix Suns 1995," orange with purple chassis, Australia issue......$9 – 12
2. "Pioneer Distributors — Gowings," yellow with black chassis, Australia issue ....$12 – 16
3. "Pirates 1993," black with yellow chassis, White Rose Collectibles ....$6 – 8
4. "Raiders 1992," metallic gray with black chassis, White Rose Collectibles ....$4 – 5
5. "Rangers 1993," white with red chassis, White Rose Collectibles ....$6 – 8
6. "Raptors 1995," red with purple chassis, Australia issue ....$9 – 12
7. "Red Ale," yellow and black with red chassis, rubber tires on chrome rims, Matchbox Collectibles Microbreweries Collection ....$9 – 12
8. "Red Sox 1993," dark blue with red chassis, White Rose Collectibles ..$6 – 8
9. "Reds 1993," red with black chassis, White Rose Collectibles.............$6 – 8
0. "Redskins 1992," white with rust chassis, White Rose Collectibles ....$4 – 5
1. "Redskins 1993," rust with yellow chassis, White Rose Collectibles ......$6 – 8
2. "Reithoffer's — Tickets For All Attractions," white with orange chassis, White Rose Collectibles gift set............$5 – 6
3. "Rockies 1993," black with purple chassis, White Rose Collectibles ....$6 – 8
4. "Royals 1993," pale blue with dark blue chassis, White Rose Collectibles ..$6 – 8
5. "Saints 1992," green-gold with black chassis, White Rose Collectibles..................................$4 – 5
6. "Sam Adams," white and black with lavender chassis, rubber tires on

chrome rims, Matchbox Collectibles Microbreweries Collection........$9 – 12
77. "San Andreas Brewing Co.," dark purple and black with blue-green chassis, rubber tires on chrome rims, Matchbox Collectibles Microbreweries Collection ....$9 – 12
78. "San Antonio Spurs 1995," dark blue with orange chassis, Australia issue . $9 – 12
79. "Seahawks 1992," metallic gray with blue chassis, White Rose Collectibles ....$4 – 5
80. "Seattle Sonics 1995," dark green with orange-yellow chassis, Australia issue ....$9 – 12
81. "Steelers 1992," yellow with black chassis, White Rose Collectibles ....$4 – 5
82. "Tigers 1993," white with blue chassis, White Rose Collectibles.............$6 – 8
83. "Toronto Blue Jays 1993," blue with bright blue chassis, White Rose Collectibles ....$6 – 8
84. "Twins 1993," dark blue with red chassis, White Rose Collectibles ....$6 – 8
85. "Utah Jazz 1995," green with orange-yellow chassis, Australia issue ..$9 – 12
86. "Vancouver Grizzlies 1995," black with turquoise chassis, Australia issue ....$9 – 12
87. "Vikings 1992," yellow with purple chassis, White Rose Collectibles ....$4 – 5
88. "Washington Capitals 20th Anniversary 1974 – 1994," white with blue chassis, White Rose Collectibles.............$6 – 8
89. "White Sox 1993," metallic gray with black chassis, White Rose Collectibles....$6 – 8
90. "Yankees 1993," white with blue chassis, White Rose Collectibles ....$6 – 8
91. "York Fair 1992," fluorescent orange with lavender chassis, White Rose Collectibles ....$7 – 9
92. "York Fair 1994," light blue with lavender chassis, White Rose Collectibles ..$6 – 8
93. black with money bags and bullet marks, Australia issue ....$5 – 6

Chevrolet 1939 Sedan Delivery, #215 (smaller than #58/#245)

Chevrolet 4x4 Van (see Chevrolet Van 4x4)

Chevrolet Ambulance, 2¹⁵/₁₆", #41, 1978; #25, 1983; #34, 1999
1. red, "Notarzt," Germany issue, England cast ....$30 – 40
2. red, "Fire Rescue," gold and white trim, 1996 5-pack, China cast..........$2 – 3
3. red with white, gold and black accents, blue windows, 1996 5-pack.......$2 – 4
4. fluorescent orange, "Ambulance 7," "Intercom City," bar code on base, China cast..........................$12 – 16
5. fluorescent orange, "Ambulance 7," "Intercom City," no bar code on base, China cast..........................$10 – 12
6. yellow, "Paramedics E11," orange band, China cast..........................$10 – 12

7. fluorescent yellow, "Emergency Unit 3," "3 EMT," Collectors Choice, White Rose Collectibles, China cast.............$3 – 4
8. black, "SWAT," "MB County Sheriff," 1999 Law & Order series, China cast....................................$2 – 3
9. metallic gray, "Paris Dakar 81," England cast ....$25 – 35
10. white, "Action System," on-package premium, China cast...................$9 – 10

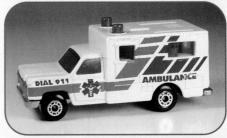

11. white, "Ambulance," "Dial 911," red and blue design, China cast....$2 – 3

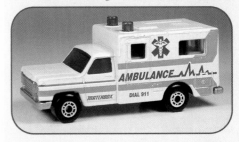

12. white, "Ambulance," "Dial 911," orange and blue design, 1996 ....$2 – 3
13. white, "Ambulance," "EMS" labels, England cast...............................$7 – 9
14. white, "Ambulance," cross labels, gray interior, England cast................$7 – 9
15. white, "Ambulance," cross labels, gray interior, England cast, towing tab on front of base, UK issue ....$40 – 60
16. white, "Ambulance," cross labels, light yellow interior, England cast......$7 – 9
17. white, "Ambulance," cross labels, orange interior, England cast ..$9 – 12
18. white, "Emergency Medical Services," dark tan interior, England cast ...$7 – 9
19. white, "Emergency Medical Services," gray interior, England cast.........$7 – 9
20. white, "Emergency Medical Services," light yellow interior, England cast..................................$7 – 9
21. white, "Emergency Medical Services," orange interior, England cast ...$9 – 12
22. white, "EMT Ambulance," Action Pack, China cast...............................$4 – 5
23. white, "LeBonheur Children's Medical Center," orange band on sides, ASAP promotional, China cast.........$30 – 45
24. white, "Manhattan National Life," orange band on sides, ASAP promotional, China cast ....$120 – 160
25. white, "Matchbox Ambulance Dial 911," orange and blue design, 1997 City Streets 5-pack, China cast........$2 – 3

26. white, "Methodist Healthcare," orange band on sides, ASAP promotional, China cast..................$30 – 45
27. white, "Methodist LeBonheur Healthcare," orange band on sides, ASAP promotional, China cast.............$30 – 45
28. white, "Pacific Ambulance," England cast, Code Red series...............$7 – 9
29. white, "Pacific Ambulance," China cast ....$6 – 7
30. white, "Pacific Ambulance," Macau cast ....$6 – 7
31. white, "Paramedics E11," orange band, China cast.............................$2 – 3
32. white, "Paramedics E11," orange band, Macau cast............................$2 – 3

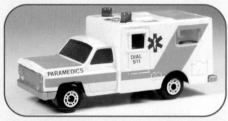

33. white, "Paramedics," "Dial 911," orange band, China cast ....$3 – 4
34. white, no markings, Graffic Traffic, China cast...........................$12 – 16
35. white, orange band on sides, ASAP promotional blank, China cast .....$30 – 45

Chevrolet Avalanche, #58, 2002; #49, 2003

1. metallic green with dark gray base, 2002 Rescue Rookies series .....$2 – 3
2. bright green with dark gray base, 2003 Forest Rescue series ....$2 – 3
3. bright green with dark gray base, 2003 Hero City 10-pack #1 ....$2 – 3

Chevrolet Bel Air 1955 Convertible, #46, 1999

1. red and ivory two-tone, detailed trim, rubber tires on chrome rims, Premiere Collection ....$9 – 12

2. pale blue, "1999 Matchbox Official Parade Car," gray interior, 1999 Classic Decades ....$2 – 3
3. black, "The Brady Bunch," white stripe, white and black interior, Avon Star Cars ....$12 – 16

4. white, "Coca-Cola," red interior, 5-pack ....$2 – 3

5. bright purple, "Patrick," light blue interior, bright coral pink base, 2003 Nickelodeon Spongebob Squarepants 5-pack ....$2 – 3

Chevrolet Bel Air 1955 Hardtop, #73, 1999
1. red, "Midwest Collector's Dinner Model," white roof, white interior, ASAP promotional ....$25 – 35
2. red, "RCA," white roof, white interior, ASAP promotional ....$25 – 35
3. red with white roof, white interior, ASAP promotional blank ....$30 – 40
4. yellow, "Coca-Cola," white roof, black interior, rubber tires on chrome wire rims, Premiere Collection ....$5 – 6
5. yellow, "Coca-Cola," white roof, red interior, Avon Two Pack.................$4 – 5
6. dark green and cream with silver stripes, cream roof, rubber tires on chrome rims, 1999 First Editions ....$6 – 8

7. blue, "Bel Air," white stripes, white roof, 1999 Classics series .....$2 – 3
8. blue, "Cruisin' New England Magazine," white roof, black interior, Color Comp promotional ....$45 – 55
9. blue, "D.A.R.E.," white roof, red light bar on roof, 2001 DARE 5-pack ....$2 – 3
10. blue, "Matchbox USA Road Race Participant," white roof, white interior, Color Comp promotional ....$80 – 120
11. blue, "Westfield NJ Reunion 2000," "W.H.S.," Color Comp promotional.........................$16 – 24
13. unpainted, rubber tires on chrome rims, 1999 First Editions ....$6 – 8

Chevrolet Bel Air 1955 Police, #507, 2001

1. "D.A.R.E.," metallic blue with white sides, red roof light, 5-pack....$2 – 3

Chevrolet Bel Air 1957, hood open, 2¹⁵/₁₆", #4, 1979; #43, 1990

1. metallic magenta......................$6 – 8

2. red, "Cherry Bomb," unpainted or metallic gray base, chrome interior ....$3 – 4
3. red, "Cherry Bomb," black base, chrome interior....................$60 – 80
4. black with red hood, flames, chrome interior ....$2 – 3
5. pink with red hood, flames, chrome interior, chrome hubs, rubber tires, Select Class ....$4 – 5
6. pale green with red hood, flames, chrome interior, chrome hubs, rubber tires, Select Class ....$4 – 5
7. peach with red hood, flames, chrome interior, chrome hubs, rubber tires, Select Class ....$5 – 8
8. metallic rose red with red hood, flames, chrome interior, chrome hubs, rubber tires, Select Class ....$4 – 5
9. metallic purple with red hood, flames, chrome interior, chrome hubs, rubber tires, Select Class ....$4 – 5
10. red with red hood, chrome interior, "Heinz 57 Chevy"................$16 – 24
11. metallic purple with "Milky Way," chrome interior, Mail-Away Premium...$16 – 24
12. black with dark red hood, flames, chrome interior.......................$2 – 3
13. metallic red with red hood, chrome windows, silver stripes, chrome interior, chrome hubs, rubber tires, World Class................................$4 – 6
14. yellow with blue and red stripes, "57," black windows, Triple Heat........$4 – 5

15. red with yellow flame outlines, silver trim, chrome interior............$2 – 3
16. white with pink and blue accents, chrome interior.......................$2 – 3

. black with black hood, yellow accents, chrome interior, 5-pack............$2 – 3

. metallic blue, chrome interior, Collectors Choice ....$3 – 4

. red, "Chubby's Diner," chrome interior ....$8 – 12

. **black with yellow hood, yellow flames, chrome interior, 5-pack ....$2 – 3**

. pearl white, chrome interior.......$2 – 3

. metallic gray with red and white interior, white roof, chrome hubs, rubber tires, Premiere Collection ....$4 – 5

. black with red and white interior, chrome hubs, rubber tires, Premiere Collection ....$4 – 5

. red with red hood, red and white interior, white roof............................$12 – 16

. **bright blue with yellow hood, chrome interior, yellow flames, 5-pack ..$2 – 3**

. **maroon with maroon hood, red and white interior, white roof, Select Class....................................$4 – 5**

. red with yellow hood, black and chrome interior, orange flames, Premiere Collection, chrome hubs, rubber tires ....$4 – 5

. black with chrome interior, "Night Stalker," flames ....$3 – 4

. black with red hood, yellow flames, chrome interior, chrome hubs, rubber tires, Premiere Collection ....$4 – 5

. red with yellow flames, black and chrome interior, chrome hubs, rubber tires, U.S. Hot August Nights .$12 – 16

. metallic gold with black and chrome interior, chrome hubs, rubber tires, 75 Challenge Winner's Car.....$175 – 250

. orange with orange hood, chrome interior, "Enjoy Fanta"............$150 – 200

Chevrolet Bel Air 1957, 1999, Taco Bell; Matchbox mold retooled by Strottman International Inc. through a licensing

agreement with Mattel. Strottman manufactures toy premiums for Taco Bell. Base is marked "Made in China by S.I.I."

1. white with green and blue bands, black windows, Taco Bell premium ......$3 – 4

Chevrolet Bel Air 1957 Convertible, #36, 1998; #47, 1999

1. black, "Toy Fair 98 — Matchbox," rubber tires on chrome rims, white interior ....$90 – 120

2. red, silver flash, detailed trim, rubber tires on chrome rims, red and white interior, 1998 First Editions.......$5 – 6

3. unpainted, rubber tires on chrome rims, red and white interior, 1998 First Editions............................$5 – 6

4. turquoise, silver flash with purple and white accents, white interior, rubber tires on chrome rims, 1998 First Editions (likely a manufacturer packaging error) ....$120 – 160

5. turquoise, silver flash with purple and white accents, white interior, 1998 Classic Decades series ....$2 – 3

6. **turquoise, silver flash with purple and white accents, white and turquoise interior, rubber tires on chrome rims, Premiere Collection................$5 – 6**

7. turquoise, "Matchbox 2000 Convention — Hershey, PA — Color Comp Inc. Demo Model," white interior, Color Comp promotional ....$20 – 25

8. turquoise, "Cruisin New England Magazine Elite Dream Machines," "Mohegan Sun," white interior, Color Comp promotional ....$40 – 50

9. silver blue, "Coke Brightens Every Bite," red interior, Avon 2-pack ....$6 – 7

10. **pale yellow, red and black accents, red interior, 1999 Drop Tops series ....$2 – 3**

11. pale yellow, "American Wheels Show," red and black accents, red interior, Color Comp promotional ....$20 – 30

12. pale yellow, "Parsippany Demo Model," "Matchbox USA Toy Show & Convention," Color Comp promotional ....$20 – 25

Chevrolet Bel Air 1957 Convertible, 2000 Feature Cars, with opening features, designed to replace Premiere Collection

1. light yellow with cream and black interior ....$9 – 12

Chevrolet Bel Air 1957 Hardtop, #31, 1998

1. **blue with blue and white interior, rubber tires on chrome rims, 1998 First Editions........................$5 – 6**

2. **unpainted metal with gray plastic roof, white interior, rubber tires on chrome rims, 1998 First Editions.........$5 – 6**

3. **black with white interior, green and white design on sides, 1998 Classic Decades..............................$2 – 3**

4. black with white interior, green and white design on sides, larger tires, 1998 Classic Decades..........$12 – 16

5. purple with beige roof, "Matchbox Premiere Collectors Club," rubber tires on chrome rims......................$12 – 16

6. **red with white interior, 5-pack ..$2 – 3**

Chevrolet Bel Air 1957 Hardtop, 2000 Feature Cars, with opening features, designed to replace Premiere Collection

1. red with white roof, red and white interior ....$9 – 12

2. baby blue with white roof, blue and white interior ....$12 – 16

Chevrolet Blazer 4x4 (see Chevrolet Blazer 4x4 Police)

Chevrolet Blazer 4x4 Police, 3", #50, 1984 – 1997; #22, 1998; #32, 1999; #71, 2000; #6, 2002

1. metallic red, black base, no markings, Thailand cast, 5-pack ....$2 – 3

2. **olive green, "Chief," yellow and brown, 2003 Hero City 5-pack #7 ......$2 – 3**
3. blue, "682," green stripes, chrome base, China cast, 5-pack ....$4 – 5
4. blue, "Police 50," "Police Dial 911," star, chrome base, blue windows, Thailand cast................................$2 – 3
5. blue, "Police 50," "Police Dial 911," star, chrome base, red windows, Thailand cast ....$2 – 3
6. blue, "Rocky Mountain Rescue MB County 682", China cast, 5-pack........$2 – 3
7. blue and white, "Police 50," "Police Dial 911," China cast, 5-pack...........$2 – 3

8. **blue and white, "Police Dial 911," China cast, 1996..................$2 – 3**

9. **blue and white, "Police Unit 14," chrome base, Thailand cast, 5-pack........$2 – 3**
10. blue with black and white accents, orange "50" on roof, blue windows..........$2 – 3
11. blue with black and white accents, orange "50" on roof, red windows...........$2 – 3
12. purple with orange, red and black accents, armaments, Roadblasters...........$6 – 8
13. black, "Action Radar," "Xtreme Mission," 5-pack...........................$2 – 3

14. **black, "Off Road Patrol Matchbox Police," white canopy, white accents, 1997 ....$2 – 3**
15. black, "Police Unit 3," gold star, Thailand cast, 5-pack......................$2 – 3
16. black with pink and yellow design, chrome base and windows, Super Trucks ..$3 – 4
17. brown, "Action Tours," 2000 On Tour series....................................$2 – 3
18. brown, "Action Tours," "Matchbox 2000," 2000 On Tour series .....$3 – 4
19. beige and green, "Park Police," China cast, 5-pack ....$2 – 3
20. white, "7 Eleven," black base, Thailand cast ....$5 – 6

21. **white, "MB Metro Police," yellow and blue accents, red star, black base, 2001 On Patrol 5-pack .$2 – 3**

22. **white, "Emergency Unit 50," "Off Road Patrol," black canopy, chrome base, 1998 To The Rescue series ......$2 – 3**
23. **white, "Metro EMS," black base, Thailand cast ....$2 – 3**
24. white, "Police MB To Protect and Serve," chrome base, China cast, 1999 Law & Order series ....$2 – 3

25. **white, "Police Unit 3," blue hood a doors, chrome base, Thailand cas 5-pack..................................$2 –**
26. white, "Sheriff 7," chrome base, Mad cast ....$2 –
27. white, "Sheriff 7," black base, Mad cast ....$2 –
28. white, "Sheriff 7," black base, Mana cast, Brazil issue ....$50 – (
29. white, "Sheriff 7," black base, Thaila cast ....$2 –
30. white and black, "Emergency Unit 50," " Road Patrol," chrome base, China ca 1998 To The Rescue series.........$2 –
31. white and black, "Emergency Unit 50," " Road Patrol," chrome base, Thailand ca 1998 To The Rescue series.........$2 –
32. white with blue, peach and magen design, chrome base and window Super Trucks ....$3 –

33. **white. "Smokey Says... Prevent F est Fires," green canopy, teal bas red windows, Smokey The Bea 2002 Safety Stars...............$2 –**
34. metallic gold, chrome base, 1997 Challenge series....................$6 –

Chevrolet Breakdown Van, #21, 198 #53, 1990

1. army green with metallic gray boom, "Gen IV," "The Lost World," Jurassic Park series ....$7 – 9
2. black with gray boom, yellow stripes, black hubs, multipack, China issue..................................$20 –.25
3. black with gray boom, yellow stripes, silver hubs, Commando series ......$5 – 7
4. black with red boom, "24," hand and car logo, multipack...................$2 – 3

5. **blue with gray boom, "MB" logo and dirt, 5-pack ....$2 – 3**
6. fluorescent orange with black boom, "Intercom City Auto Services," Intercom City.......................................$12 – 16
7. lemon yellow with black boom, "Rob's Towing 24 Hours," Action System ......$2 – 3
8. metallic gray with black boom, "Rob's Towing 24 Hours," Action Pack..$2 – 3
9. orange with black boom, "Auto Relay 24 Hr. Tow"...............................$2 – 3
10. orange with orange boom, "Auto Relay 24 Hr. Tow," Action Pack..........$4 – 5
11. red with green boom, blue wheels, Live 'N Learn/Matchbox Preschool series ....$6 – 8
12. red with white boom, "24 Hour Service"...................................$2 – 3
13. white and purple with purple boom, "Metro Alarm MA-BU1," 5-pack...$2 – 3
14. white with black boom, "Auto Rescue," Emergency Pack ....$3 – 4
15. white with white boom, no markings, Graffic Traffic ....$12 – 16
16. yellow with black boom, "Auto Relay 24 Hr. Tow"...............................$2 – 3

Chevrolet Camaro 1969 SS 396, #40, 1997; #33, 1998
1. red with white racing stripes, black interior, Action Pack.....................$2 – 3
2. orange with black stripes, black interior, 5-pack..................................$2 – 3
3. orange with white and black stripes, black and white interior, Premiere Collection #20 ....$4 – 5
4. dark green with white side stripes, black and white interior, rubber tires on chrome rims, Premiere Collection #17 ....$4 – 5

5. **metallic blue with white racing stripes, black interior, 1998 Classic Decades series ....$2 – 3**
6. metallic blue with white racing stripes, black interior, "Great Camaro Gathering 1997," promotional.............$40 – 50

7. **white with black racing stripes, red interior, 1998 Classic Decades series ....$2 – 3**
8. white with "Coca-Cola" and red bands, red and black interior, rubber tires on chrome rims, Premiere Collection ....$5 – 6
9. white with "Coca-Cola" and red bands, red and black interior, rubber tires on chrome rims, "www.cocacolastore.com," Color Comp promotional ....$60 – 80
10. white with "East Coast Camaro Gathering IV," red interior, Color Comp promotional ....$24 – 36
11. metallic gold with black interior, 1997 75 Challenge series ....$6 – 12

Chevrolet Camaro 1971 Z-28, #39, 1998; #18, 2000
1. red, "Coca-Cola Play Refreshed," tire marks, Premiere Collection........$4 – 5

2. **metallic green with white stripes, 1998 Classic Decades series .$2 – 3**
3. dark green with white stripes, "Great Camaro Gathering 1999, Color Comp promotional........................$40 – 50
4. metallic light blue with black stripes, rubber tires on black rims, Premiere Collection............................$30 – 40

5. **metallic gold with black stripes, 2000 Great Drivers series.....$2 – 3**
6. metallic gold with black stripes, "Matchbox 2000," 2000 Great Drivers series ....$3 – 4

Chevrolet Camaro 1994 Z-28, #43, 1994 – 1997; #75, 1998
1. red, black roof, detailed trim, rubber tires on chrome rims, Premiere Collection #5 ....$5 – 6

2. metallic red, black roof, detailed trim, rubber tires on chrome rims, Gold Coin Collection............................$16 – 24
3. orange with white stripes, rubber tires on chrome rims, Premiere Collection #14.......................................$5 – 6
4. fluorescent orange, "Matchbox Get In The Fast Lane — 95 Premium Show".................................$40 – 50
5. fluorescent orange, "Matchbox Get In The Fast Lane — Melbourne Motor Show 96" ....$40 – 50
6. fluorescent orange, "Matchbox Get In The Fast Lane — Sydney Motor Show" ....$20 – 30
7. yellow, black roof, rubber tires on chrome rims, Special Class #4 ..$5 – 6
8. dark green, black roof, detailed trim, rubber tires on chrome rims, Premiere Collection #2 ....$5 – 6
9. metallic turquoise, black roof, rubber tires on chrome rims, Special Class #5..$5 – 6
10. blue with orange flame and checkered flag design on sides, 1998 Street Cruisers series ....$2 – 3

11. **blue with black roof, detailed trim, rubber tires on chrome rims, Premiere Collection 8-car display set......$5 – 6**

12. **metallic purple with orange flame and checkered flag design on sides, 1998 Street Cruisers series..$2 – 3**

13. **purple chrome with orange and yellow design on sides, 1997 Sleek Riders 5-pack............................$2 – 3**
14. dark purple with black roof, detailed trim, rubber tires on chrome rims, Special Class #2 ....$5 – 6
15. metallic gray with white, magenta and cyan stripes on sides and hood, 1996...............................$2 – 3
16. metallic gray with white, magenta and cyan stripes on sides only, 1996 .$2 – 3
17. dark gray with stripes on sides, 1997 ....$2 – 3

18. black, "DDCM DuPage Diecast Collectors Meet," ASAP promotional ......$20 – 30
19. black, "Novell 6," ASAP promotional ....$20 – 30
20. black, "RCA," ASAP promotional .$20 – 30
21. black, "Real Cars Wear Bow Ties," ASAP promotiOonal ....$80 – 120
22. black, "Speed Equipment World," ASAP promotional.......................$80 – 120
23. black, no markings, ASAP promotional blank.................................$30 – 40

24. **black with white, magenta and cyan stripes on sides and hood, gold chrome wheel hubs, 1994 .....$2 – 3**

25. **black with white, magenta and cyan stripes on sides only, silver chrome wheel hubs, 1995.................$2 – 3**
26. white with black roof, chrome windows, rubber tires on chrome rims, World Class......................................$4 – 5
27. silver with lavender, purple and blue stripes on hood and sides, 1997 Matchcaps.............................$5 – 6
28. gold chrome, blue and yellow design, yellow windows, 1996 5-pack ....$2 – 3
29. metallic gold, "Great Camaro Gathering II 1998," rubber tires on chrome rims, promotional model ....$40 – 50
30. metallic gold, "Matchbox Collectors Club," rubber tires on chrome rims...$12 – 16
31. metallic gold, 1997 75 Challenge series....................................$6 – 12

Chevrolet Camaro 1994 Z-28 Police, #59, 1995 – 1997; #27, 1998; #98, 1999; #89, 2000; #7, 2002; #30, 2003; #457, 2000; #458, 2000
1. "5," red with crest and white band, 5-pack......................................$2 – 3
2. "5," blue with crest and white band, lace wheels, Launcher 5-pack ....$2 – 3
3. "5," blue with crest and white band, 5-spoke concave wheels, Launcher 5-pack....................................$9 – 12
4. "City of Miami 7630," white, rubber tires on chrome rims, Premiere Collection #22.........................$150 – 200
5. "D.A.R.E.," black with yellow and red stripes, 2000 D.A.R.E. series...$4 – 5

6. **"D.A.R.E.," orange with dark blue, white and gray accents, 2001 D.A.R.E. series ....$2 – 3**

7. **"D.A.R.E.," white with lion and US flag graphics, 2000 Police Patrol series ....$2 – 3**
8. "D.A.R.E.," white with lion and US flag graphics, "Matchbox 2000," 2000 Police Patrol series ....$3 – 4
9. "D.A.R.E.," "Crimestopper," black with stripes and stars, D.A.R.E. series..$4 – 5
10. "D.A.R.E. America," "Matchbox," white and black, rubber tires on chrome rims, D.A.R.E. series.......................$9 – 12
11. "Dial 1-888-Road Rescue," white with dashed road, "Dial" slants left, 1999 At Your Service series ....$2 – 3
12. "Dial 1-888-Road Rescue," white with dashed road, "Dial" slants right, 1999 At Your Service series ....$40 – 50

13. **"Emergency Dial 911," white with black, blue and silver accents, silver "Police" shield, 2003 Police Squad Series ....$2 – 3**
14. "Highway Patrol," "DWI Enforcement," white, 5-pack...........................$2 – 3
15. "Highway Patrol," black and white, rubber tires on chrome rims, Premiere Collection #8 ....$4 – 5

16. **"Kansas State Trooper," black with shield on doors, rubber tires on chrome rims, World Class #18 State Police II ....$4 – 5**

17. "Matchbox Police," blue, 5-pack..$2 –

18. **"Matchbox Police," white with bl[u]e doors and hood, silver star on do[or] 1996 Police 5-pack ....$2 –**
19. "Matchbox Police," white ....$2 –
20. "Matchbox Police 911," black, 1998 The Rescue series ....$2 –

21. **"Matchbox Police Unit 04," blue wi[th] white shield and accents, 199[?] Police 5-pack ....$2 –**
22. "Medford Police," "D.A.R.E. — No Drug[s] stripes, white, D.A.R.E. series .....$4 –

23. **"Nevada Highway Patrol," metal[lic] blue and silver, rubber tires [on] chrome rims, World Class #18 Sta[te] Police II...............................$4 –**
24. "NY State Police," bright blue, rubb[er] tires on chrome rims, Premiere Colle[c]tion #8.................................$4 –
25. "Police," gold on white star on doors ....$2 –
26. "Police," black on white star on doors ....$2 –
27. "Police Unit 4", blue, 5-pack.......$2 –
28. "Police," "Unit 6," white with star [on] blue doors, blue hood, 1996 Police 5-pack..................................$2 –

29. **"Police," "Unit 21," black with shie[ld] design on hood, white accents, 199[?] To The Rescue series............$3 –**
30. **"Police," "Unit 21," white with bl[ue] shield design on hood, blue accent[s] 1997..................................$2 –**

1. "Police," "Matchbox Police," black with star on white doors, white hood, 1996 $2 – 3
2. "Police D.A.R.E.," "New Rochelle," white and pale blue, D.A.R.E. series....$4 – 5
3. "State Patrol Nebraska," white, rubber tires on chrome rims, Premiere Collection ....$5 – 6

4. "Take A Bite Out Of Crime," metallic gray with crime dog graphics, 2002 Safety Stars series...............$2 – 3
5. "Texas Dept. Public Safety Trooper," white and black, rubber tires on chrome rims, Premiere Collection #8 .....$4 – 5

6. "Utah Highway Patrol," white, rubber tires on chrome rims, World Class #18 State Police II.......$4 – 5
7. "Wyoming Highway Patrol," black and white, rubber tires on chrome rims, Premiere Collection ....$5 – 6

8. metallic gold, 1997 75 Challenge series ....$6 – 12

---

39. red with silver and blue stripes and crest, 5-pack..........................$2 – 3

Chevrolet Camaro 1998 Convertible, #2, 2000
1. dark red, "Matchbox 2000" logo, black interior, 2000 Open Road series 1 ....$3 – 5

2. **dark red, without "Matchbox 2000" logo, black interior, 2000 Open Road series 1 ....$2 – 3**
3. salmon, "Sydney 2000," orange-yellow interior, 5-pack.......................$2 – 3
4. red, Coca-Cola, white interior, Avon 2-pack.....................................$5 – 6
5. black, Coca-Cola with polar bear, chrome wheels, rubber tires, Premiere Collection.................................$5 – 6
6. black, trim detailing, chrome wheels, rubber tires, First Editions ....$5 – 6
7. unpainted, chrome wheels, rubber tires, First Editions ....$5 – 6
8. dark red, with "Matchbox 2000" logo, "South Jersey Camaro Group Productions," "East Coast Camaro Gathering IV," Color Comp promotional ..$30 – 40

Chevrolet Camaro IROC Z, 3", #51, 1985; #68, 1987
1. red, "Carter," "Goodyear" ....$4 – 5
2. red with white stripes, Show Stoppers..................................$3 – 4
3. metallic red, "Carter," "Goodyear"..$4 – 5
4. metallic orange, "Carter," "Goodyear" ....$5 – 6
5. yellow, "IROC Z" ....$2 – 3
6. green, "BP Stunt Team" stripes, the Netherlands issue ....$10 – 12
7. green, "IROC Z" ....$5 – 6
8. blue, "IROC Z" on sides only ....$3 – 4
9. blue, "IROC Z" on sides and hood ..$3 – 4
10. metallic blue, "350Z"; pink, purple, and lime green stripes; Triple Heat...$4 – 5
11. dark purple, "Z28" and silver stripe, Collectors Choice, White Rose Collectibles.............................$3 – 4
12. black, "Z28," red accents.........$2 – 4

13. **black, "Z28," orange and white accents..............................$2 – 3**

Chevrolet Camaro IROC Z-28 Police (see Chevrolet Camaro 1994 Z-28 Police)

Chevrolet Camaro Police (see Chevrolet Camaro 1994 Z-28 Police)

Chevrolet Camaro Z-28 (see Chevrolet Camaro 1994 Z-28)

Chevrolet Camaro Z-28 Police (see Chevrolet Camaro 1994 Z-28 Police)

Chevrolet Cavalier (see Opel Vectra/Chevrolet Cavalier GS)

Chevrolet Corvette 1957 Convertible, #362, 1999
1. red, "Coca-Cola," Santa illustration, white flash, rubber tires on chrome wire rims, Premiere Collection ...$7 – 9
2. red, "Coca-Cola," Santa illustration, white flash, rubber tires on chrome mag rims, Premiere Collection ...$7 – 9
3. red with "FTD" license plate, sold with 1950s diner ceramic planter, sold exclusively through FTD florists ......$20 – 30
4. red with detailed trim, rubber tires on chrome rims, 1999 First Editions..$6 – 8
5. yellow, "Coke," white flash, 5-pack .$4 – 5
6. unpainted, rubber tires on chrome rims, 1999 First Editions ....$6 – 8

Chevrolet Corvette 1957 Hardtop, 2⅞", #75, 1999
1. red with white roof, "Cruisin' New England Magazine All Wheels Festival 2001," white interior and side flash, Color Comp promotional........$60 – 80
2. red with white roof, "Vettes in Glasstown XXI," "Corvettes Unlimited," white interior and side flash, Color Comp promotional................$16 – 24

3. **red with white roof, white interior and side flash, chrome base, 1999 Classics series.....................$2 – 3**
4. black with black roof, white interior and side flash, black base, rubber tires on chrome rims, Premiere Collection..$6 – 8

Chevrolet Corvette 1961 (see Chevrolet Corvette 1962)

Chevrolet Corvette 1962, 2¹⁵⁄₁₆", #71, 1982; #32, 1993 reissue; #72, 1994 international reissue (also see Chevrolet Corvette 1962, #374)
1. red, "454 Rat," gold wheels, Macau cast ....$3 – 4
2. red, "454 Rat," silver wheels, China cast ....$2 – 3
3. red, "454 Rat," silver wheels, Macau cast ....$3 – 4

4. red, "62" and white stripes on roof, China cast, Australia issue ....$5 – 6
5. red, "Animal House," white roof and side flash, China cast, Star Cars ......$5 – 6
6. red, "Chubby's," "Pepsi-Cola," China cast, US issue ....$6 – 12
7. red, "Heinz 57," Macau cast, US issue ....$30 – 40
8. red with white roof and side flash, rubber tires on chrome rims, China cast, 1997 Corvette Premiere Collection ....$5 – 6
9. red with white roof and side flash, Thailand cast, gift set ....$3 – 4
10. red with white stripes, China cast, Australia issue ....$5 – 6
11. pale red, "62 and white stripes on roof, gold 6-spoke spiral wheels, China cast, China issue ....$80 – 120

12. metallic red, "Corvette 62," China cast, 1996 Racing 5-pack......$2 – 3
13. metallic red with white roof, "Matchbox," "DMB & B," rubber tires on chrome rims, Thailand cast, US issue ......$300 – 400
14. metallic red with white roof, rubber tires on chrome rims, Premiere Collection #3 ....$5 – 6
15. orange, "11" and white stripe, Macau cast, New Superfast Wheels .....$4 – 5
16. metallic orange, "4," black roof, rubber tires on black rims, China cast, Whales Project ....$6 – 8
17. metallic orange, "11," white stripes, Macau cast, Laser Wheels........$4 – 5

18. yellow with white roof, silver detailed trim, rubber tires on chrome rims, Premiere Collection Select Class #3 ....$5 – 6
19. yellow with white roof and side flash, gold 6-spoke spiral wheels, China cast, 1997 75 Challenge series ..$80 – 120

20. metallic blue with white and magenta accents on sides and hood, 1994...$2 – 3

21. metallic blue with blue and red design, Thailand cast..........................$2 – 3
22. metallic blue with white and red design, China cast ....$2 – 3
23. metallic blue with white and red design, Thailand cast..........................$2 – 3
24. metallic blue with white roof and side flash, silver 5-spoke spiral wheels, China cast, China issue ....$80 – 120
25. metallic blue with white roof and side flash, rubber tires on chrome rims, 1997 Corvette Premiere Collection........$5 – 6
26. blue with white and magenta accents on sides only, 1996......................$2 – 3
27. blue with white and red design on sides only, China cast ....$2 – 3
28. blue with white accents, blue interior, England cast ....$4 – 5
29. blue with white accents, chrome interior, England cast............................$4 – 5
30. blue with white roof and side flash, gold 6-spoke spiral wheels, China cast, China issue ....$80 – 120

31. blue with white roof and side flash, silver detailed trim, rubber tires on chrome rims, 1961 Corvette, 1997 Corvette Premiere Collection..$5 – 6
32. bright blue, "Firestone," Macau cast, Japan issue..........................$8 – 10
33. blue with magenta and white accents, chrome interior, 1994 ....$2 – 3
34. metallic green, "11" and white stripes, Macau cast, Laser Wheels........$4 – 5
35. turquoise with white roof, chrome windows, rubber tires on gray rims, China cast, World Class ....$4 – 5

36. purple with fluorescent green-yellow and white tiger stripes, 1997 American Street Machines 5-pack...$2 – 3
37. purple with orange and yellow flames, 5-spoke concave wheels, engine cast on hood, China cast, China issue ....$80 – 120
38. purple with orange and yellow flames, rubber tires on chrome rims, Premiere Collection #11 ....$4 – 5
39. black, "Bloomberg Fair Association," "Millennium 2000," ASAP promotional.$60 – 80
40. black, "BS Auto Seaside Oregon," ASAP promotional.........................$16 – 24

41. black, "DDCM DuPage Diecast Collecto[rs] Meet," ASAP promotional.......$16 – 2[ ]
42. black, "Matchbox," "Hot August Nigh[t] 1998," pink roof, rubber tires [on] chrome rims, US issue ....$16 – 2[ ]
43. black, "Matchbox USA 18th Conventio[n] Toy Show," ASAP promotional..$16 – 2[ ]
44. black, "X Xedia," ASAP promotional ....$80 – 1[ ]
45. black, no markings, ASAP promotio[nal] blank.................................$35 – 4[ ]
46. black with silver, blue and purp[le] accents, engine cast on hood, rubb[er] tires on chrome rims, Premiere Colle[c]tion #9...........................$4 [–]
47. black with white roof and side flash, C[ol]lectors Choice, White Rose Collectible[s,] China cast ....$3 – [ ]
48. black with white roof and side flash, r[ub]ber tires on chrome rims, 199[ ] Corvette Premiere Collection......$5 – [ ]
49. white with blue base, red accents, silv[er] interior ....$8 – [ ]

50. white with fluorescent oran[ge] flames, 5-spoke concave wheel[s,] China cast.........................$2 – [ ]
51. white with fluorescent orange flames, spoke spiral wheels, China cast..$3 – [ ]
52. white with fluorescent orange flame[s,] Hong Kong cast......................$3 – [ ]
53. white with fluorescent orange flame[s,] Macau cast.........................$3 – [ ]
54. white with no markings, China cas[t,] Graffic Traffic ....$7 – [ ]
55. white with red accents, blue interio[r,] England cast ....$8 – [ ]
56. white with red accents, chrome interio[r,] England cast ....$8 – [ ]
57. white with red flames, Hong Kong cast.................................$3 – [ ]
58. white with red flames, Macau cast.................................$3 – [ ]
59. white with white roof and side flas[h,] rubber tires on chrome rims, 199[ ] Corvette Premiere Collection......$5 – [ ]

60. metallic silver with white roof and si[de] flash, detailed trim, rubber tires [on] chrome rims, 1961 Corvette, 19[ ] Corvette Premiere Collection ...$5 – [ ]

36

metallic silver with white roof and side flash, gold 6-spoke spiral wheels, China cast, China issue ....$80 – 120

2. metallic gold with white roof, silver detailed trim, rubber tires on chrome rims, Premiere Collection World Class #6 ....$5 – 6

3. metallic gold, 5-spoke concave wheels, China cast, 1997 75 Challenge series...................................$6 – 12

Chevrolet Corvette 1962, #374, 1998, Taco Bell; Matchbox mold retooled by Strottman International Inc. through a licensing agreement with Mattel. Strottman manufactures toy premiums for Taco Bell. Base is marked "Made in China by S.I.I."

black with Taco Bell logo and red bands on sides ....$4 – 5

Chevrolet Corvette 1983/1984 Convertible, 3", #14, 1983; #69, 1983; #28, 1990

red upper, light gray lower, black interior, "Vette," silver and black stripes ...$3 – 5
red upper, metallic silver lower, black interior, blue and silver, Dinky, 1983.....................................$9 – 12
red and white upper and lower, black interior, "350 CID" ....$4 – 6
red and white upper, red lower, black interior, "Chef Boyardee," on package promotional........................$15 – 20
red and white upper, red lower, black interior, "Chef Boyardee," Laser Wheels, on package promotional ......$80 – 100
red and white upper, red lower, "350 CID" ....$3 – 5
gray upper, lavender lower, interior replaced by gold chrome armament, Roadblasters...........................$6 – 9
gray upper, bluish purple lower, interior replaced by gold chrome armament, Roadblasters...........................$6 – 9
metallic silver with red interior, "83 Vette".....................................$4 – 6

Chevrolet Corvette 1987/1988 Convertible, 3", #14, 1987; #28, 1990, international

1. **red upper and lower, "Corvette" and logo, black interior, clear windshield$2 – 3**

2. red upper and lower, flame, black interior, clear windshield ....$9 – 12

3. red upper and lower, "Corvette" and "Matchbox Line Preview 1994," black interior, clear windshield ...$300 – 400

4. **red upper and lower, detailed trim, black and red interior, clear windshield, rubber tires on chrome rims, Ultra Class ....$9 – 12**

5. red to orange upper, metallic gray lower, "Corvette" and logo, black interior, clear windshield, Super Color Changers.$3 – 5

6. metallic red upper and lower, rubber tires on chrome rims, detailed trim, gray and black interior, clear windshield, Corvette Premiere Collection......$4 – 6

7. orange-yellow upper and lower, "Corvette" and logo, black interior, clear windshield..............................$2 – 3

8. **yellow upper and lower, detailed trim, black and gray interior, clear windshield, rubber tires on chrome rims, Corvette Premiere Collection........................$4 – 6**

9. lemon yellow upper and lower, black interior, clear windshield, "Corvette" and logo ....$2 – 3

10. **yellow upper and lower with black interior, clear windshield, "Corvette" and logo...............................$2 – 4**

11. lime green upper and lower, "Rally Official," "Joe Bulgin," black interior, clear windshield, rubber tires on gray rims, Whales Project........................$7 – 9

12. metallic yellow-green upper and lower, detailed trim, gray and black interior, clear windshield, rubber tires on chrome rims, Corvette Premiere Collection.........$4 – 6

13. **bright green upper and lower, pink side molding, "White's Guide Car of the Month — December 1998", white interior, clear windshield, Color Comp promotional ....$12 – 16**

14. bright green upper and lower, "70th Shenandoah Apple Blossom Festival 1997," white interior, clear windshield.................................$12 – 16

15. dark green upper and lower, detailed trim, black and gray interior, clear windshield, rubber tires on chrome rims, Corvette Premiere Collection......$4 – 6

16. blue-green upper and lower, Corvette," black interior, clear windshield, Show Stoppers..................................$3 – 4

17. bright blue upper and lower, white stripes, black and red interior, clear windshield, rubber tires on chrome rims, Premiere Collection ....$4 – 6

18. metallic blue upper and lower, black and gray interior, chrome windshield, rubber tires on chrome rims, World Class..$6 – 8

19. **purple upper and lower, white, orange interior, clear windshield, 1987..................................$2 – 3**

20. **burgundy, "Corvette," black interior, clear windshield, 1987 ....$3 – 5**

21. purple upper and lower, detailed trim, gray and black interior, clear windshield, rubber tires on chrome rims, Corvette Premiere Collection ....$4 – 6

22. black upper, green-gold lower, gray and black interior, clear windshield, gold hubs, China issue.............$100 – 150

23. black upper and lower, "Corvette Cologne," red and black interior, clear windshield, rubber tires on chrome rims....$12 – 16

24. black upper and lower, detailed trim, red and black interior, clear windshield, rubber tires on chrome rims, Corvette Premiere Collection...........................$4 – 6

24. black upper and lower, pink and yellow, fluorescent yellow interior, clear windshield ....$2 – 3
25. black upper and lower, detailed trim, red interior, clear windshield, White Rose Collectors Choice ....$3 – 5

26. **black, detailed trim, rubber wheels on chrome rims, Corvette Premiere Series.................$4 – 6**
27. white and red upper, red lower, black interior, clear windshield, "350 CID," Laser wheels.................$4 – 6
28. white and red upper, red lower, "350 CID," black interior, clear windshield, new Superfast wheels.............$4 – 6

29. **white upper and lower, stripes and zigzag, pink interior, clear windshield, Dream Machines 3-pack........$2 – 4**
30. white upper and lower, maroon interior, chrome windshield, rubber tires on gray rims, World Class...................$3 – 5
31. white upper and lower, orange and blue, blue interior, clear windshield .....$2 – 3
32. metallic gold upper and lower, black interior, clear windshield, 1997 75 Challenge series ....$6 – 12
33. metallic light bronze upper and lower, detailed trim, gray and black interior, clear windshield, rubber tires on chrome rims, Corvette Premiere Collection......................................$4 – 6
34. metallic light bronze upper and lower, fluorescent yellow interior, clear windshield, gold hubs, China issue ....$100 – 150

Chevrolet Corvette 1997, #4, 1997; #58, 1998
1. red, "Corvette" on windshield, black interior ....$2 – 3
2. red, "8th Toy Show Demo Model — Hershey," Color Comp promotional.$25 – 35
3. red, "Corvette Cologne," chrome hubs, rubber tires, black interior.....$30 – 45

4. red, "Corvette Expo.," ASAP promotional............................$50 – 100
5. red, "Fiery Driven," black interior, ASAP promotional.....................$100 – 125
6. red, "Launch Commemorative Jan. 6th, 1997," black interior ....$175 – 225
7. red, "Matchbox USA Hershey 2001," Color Comp promotional........$25 – 35
8. red, "Mid Town Bank," ASAP promotional ....$100 – 150

9. **red, chrome hubs, rubber tires, gray and black interior, Corvette Premiere Edition ....$4 – 6**
10. maroon, "Frohe Weihnachten"..$20 – 30
11. metallic red, chrome hubs, rubber tires, gray and black interior, Corvette Premiere Edition ....$4 – 6
12. yellow, "Corvette," white and black checked, play set ....$6 – 8
13. green, chrome hubs, rubber tires, gray and black interior, Corvette Premiere Edition ....$4 – 6

14. **blue, "Corvette" on windshield, #58, 1998..................$2 – 3**
15. metallic blue, chrome hubs, rubber tires, 1997 Inaugural Edition .....$5 – 7
16. lavender, lime interior, "Scooby Do," "Like Who," "Daphne," Warner Bros....$6 – 8
17. black, "Coca-Cola," Premiere Collection ....$5 – 7
18. black, chrome hubs, rubber tires, red and black interior, Corvette Premiere Edition ....$4 – 6
19. dark gray, chrome hubs, rubber tires, Toys "R" Us gift set ....$4 – 6
20. metallic gray, chrome hubs, rubber tires, gray and black interior, Corvette Premiere Edition ....$4 – 6

21. **white, chrome hubs, rubber tires, red and black interior, Corvette Premiere Edition ....$4 – 6**
22. white, no markings, ASAP blank ..$25 – 50
23. white, "Lucent Technologies," red "Gigaspeed," ASAP promotional ....$100 – 150

24. white, "Lucent Technologies," bla "Gigaspeed/Optispeed," ASAP promotional.............................$25 – 5
25. white, "Route 66 Promotions," ASA promotional........................$25 – 5
26. white, "Progress Pit Crew," ASAP pr motional ....$100 – 15
27. white, "Sandvik Coromant," ASAP pr motional ....$100 – 15
28. white, "Cisco Systems," ASAP promotional...............................$100 – 15
29. white, "Colorado Auto Auctions," ASA promotional........................$25 – 5

30. **white, "White's Guide Car the Month #7," ASAP prom tional ....$9 – 1**
31. white, "Datamax," ASAP prom tional ....$75 – 12
32. white, "RCA," ASAP promotional.$25 – 5
33. white, "Progressive AE," ASAP prom tional...............................$75 – 12
34. white, "Kitchen Aid," ASAP prom tional...............................$100 – 15
35. white, "IBM" on left side, ASAP prom tional...............................$100 – 15
36. white, "Pras, ASAP promotional.$15 – 2
37. white, "ND Go Irish," ASAP prom tional...............................$15 – 2
38. white, Consumer Finance Services ASAP promotional............$100 – 15
39. white, "Serena," ASAP prom tional...........................$100 – 15
40. white, "Alabama Crimson Tide," ASA promotional........................$75 – 12
41. white, "Huskers," ASAP promotional.............................$12 – 1
42. white, "Novell," ASAP promotional .$20 – 2
43. white, "Eds," "eds.com," ASAP prom tional...............................$40 – 5
44. white, "Bud's Cruise-In," ASAP prom tional...............................$50 – 10
45. white, "Phillips," "Sy's Samson," ASA promotional........................$50 – 10
46. unpainted, chrome hubs, rubber tire 1997 Inaugural Edition ....$5 –
47. metallic gold, 1997 75 Challeng series.................................$6 – 1

Chevrolet Corvette 1997, 1999, Tac Bell; Matchbox mold retooled Strottman International Inc. through licensing agreement with Matte Strottman manufactures toy premium for Taco Bell. Base is marked "Made China by S.I.I."
1. green with blue and white design, blac windows, Taco Bell..................$3 –

Chevrolet Corvette 1998, 2000 Feature Cars, with opening features, designed to replace Premiere Collection
dark blue with gray interior......$9 – 12

Chevrolet Corvette 1998 Convertible, 2000 Feature Cars, with opening features, designed to replace Premiere Collection
red with tan and black interior..$9 – 12

Chevrolet Corvette 2000, #57, 2001, #11, 2002; #8, 2003
metallic burgundy with black interior, no markings, 2001 Wheeled Envy series ....$2 – 3

metallic silver with black interior, "Corvette" in white on sides, 2002 Style Champs series..............$2 – 3

metallic green with butterscotch interior, yellow and white on sides, 2003 Family Wheels series....$2 – 3

Chevrolet Corvette Grand Sport, 3", #2, 1990; #15, 1990; #3, 1998
metallic blue with "15" on doors, black base ....$3 – 5
metallic red with "63," black base ....$15 – 20
metallic red with "63," chrome base ....$5 – 10

metallic blue with "Corvette" on doors, black base..................$3 – 5
metallic blue with "15" on doors, black base ....$4 – 5
metallic blue with "Heinz 57"..$20 – 25
white with red stripes, "Corvette," black base ....$2 – 3
bright yellow with purple and black, dark gray base ....$2 – 3
metallic blue with "2" on doors, 40th Anniversary Corvette Collection, 1993........$5 – 7

10. chrome plated, white base ....$3 – 5
11. dark orange, black tire tread .....$2 – 3
12. metallic red, chrome windows, black base, World Class series ......$12 – 16
13. metallic red, chrome windows, chrome base, World Class....................$4 – 6
14. white and blue with "9" and red stripes, Goodyear tires ....$6 – 8
15. white with red accent stripe, "Corvette," 1993 ....$2 – 4
16. orange with black tire tread pattern, 1994 ....$2 – 3

17. white with black widow, 1995 .$2 – 3

18. black with black widow, 1996 .$3 – 5

19. dark purple with orange flames..$2 – 3
20. 1998 Stars & Stripes series 1 ..$3 – 5
21. metallic gray with "50" and white stripes, chrome wheels, rubber tires, Premiere Collection ....$4 – 6
22. metallic gold, Challenge series .$5 – 10

23. white with "4" and black stripes, chrome wheels, rubber tires, Select Class series ....$4 – 6

24. light metallic blue, chrome wheels, rubber tires, Premiere Collection...........................$4 – 6

25. metallic blue with yellow flames on hood and doors, 1995 Hot Rods 5-pack ....$3 – 5
26. dark gray, chrome wheels, rubber tires, Corvette Premiere series ....$4 – 6
27. blue, chrome wheels, rubber tires, Corvette Premiere series ....$4 – 6
28. white with orange flames, chrome wheels, rubber tires, Premiere Collection...........................$4 – 6
29. lemon yellow, chrome wheels, rubber tires, Corvette Premiere series ..$4 – 6
30. metallic gold, chrome wheels, rubber tires, Corvette Premiere series ..$4 – 6
31. metallic green, chrome wheels, rubber tires, Corvette Premiere series ..$4 – 6

32. black, chrome wheels, rubber tires, Corvette Premiere series.......$4 – 6
33. red with white stripe.................$3 – 5
34. black, gold 6-spoke pinwheel wheels, Challenge series prize...........$60 – 80
35. gold, gold 6-spoke pinwheel wheels, Challenge series prize...........$60 – 80
36. blue with white stripe................$2 – 3

Chevrolet Corvette Hardtop, 3¹/₁₆", #62, 1979; #21, 1983
1. "Angels 1992," yellow, rubber tires on gray rims, White Rose Collectibles ....$4 – 5
2. "Astros 1992," white, rubber tires on gray rims, White Rose Collectibles ....$4 – 5
3. "Athletics 1992," green, rubber tires on gray rims, White Rose Collectibles...$4 – 5
4. "Brut," "Faberge," green, gray interior, clear windows, Macau cast, Team Matchbox ....$3 – 4
5. "Blue Jays 1992," blue, rubber tires on gray rims, White Rose Collectibles ....$4 – 5
6. "Braves 1992," metallic blue, rubber tires on gray rims, White Rose Collectibles ....$4 – 5
7. "Brewers 1992," blue, rubber tires on gray rims, White Rose Collectibles ....$4 – 5
8. "Cardinals 1992," red, rubber tires on gray rims, White Rose Collectibles ....$4 – 5
9. "Coca-Cola Play Refreshed," red band, black interior, tinted windows, Premiere Collection................................$4 – 5

10. "Cooperstown 1993," white, rubber tires on gray rims, White Rose Collectibles ....$4 – 5

11. "Cubs 1992," red, rubber tires on gray rims, White Rose Collectibles ....$4 – 5

12. "Dodgers 1992," blue, rubber tires on gray rims, White Rose Collectibles .$4 – 5

13. "Expos 1992," blue, rubber tires on gray rims, White Rose Collectibles .....$4 – 5

14. "Giants 1992," gray, rubber tires on gray rims, White Rose Collectibles.......$4 – 5

15. "Indians 1992," blue, rubber tires on gray rims, White Rose Collectibles.......$4 – 5

16. "Mariners 1992," blue, rubber tires on gray rims, White Rose Collectibles ..$4 – 5

17. "Marlins 1992," white, rubber tires on gray rims, White Rose Collectibles .....$4 – 5

18. "Mets 1992," blue, rubber tires on gray rims, White Rose Collectibles .....$4 – 5

19. "Orioles 1992," black, rubber tires on gray rims, White Rose Collectibles ....$4 – 5

20. **"Pace Car" on sides and trunk, metallic gray with blue accents........$6 – 8**

21. "Pace Car" on sides only, metallic gray with blue accents ....$6 – 8

22. "Padres 1992," white, rubber tires on gray rims, White Rose Collectibles ....$4 – 5

23. "Phillies 1992," red, rubber tires on gray rims, White Rose Collectibles.......$4 – 5

24. "Pirates 1992," black, rubber tires on gray rims, White Rose Collectibles ....$4 – 5

25. "Rangers 1992," red, rubber tires on gray rims, White Rose Collectibles ....$4 – 5

26. "Reds 1992," red, rubber tires on gray rims, White Rose Collectibles ....$4 – 5

27. "Red Sox 1992," blue, rubber tires on gray rims, White Rose Collectibles ......$4 – 5

28. "Rockies 1992," blue, rubber tires on gray rims, White Rose Collectibles.......$4 – 5

29. "Royals 1992," blue, rubber tires on gray rims, White Rose Collectibles......$4 – 5

30. "The Force," black, gray interior, clear windows, Macau cast ....$3 – 4

31. "The Force," black, gray interior, opaque windows, Macau cast ....$9 – 12

32. "The Force," black, red plastic base, gray interior, clear windows, Manaus cast, Brazil issue ....$40 – 50

33. "Tigers 1992," orange, rubber tires on gray rims, White Rose Collectibles...................................$4 – 5

34. "Turbo Vette," black, red interior, clear windows, Macau cast, New Superfast Wheels ....$4 – 5

35. "Turbo Vette," black, red interior, clear windows, Macau cast, Laser Wheels ....$4 – 5

36. "Turbo Vette," metallic red, red interior, clear windows, Macau cast, Laser Wheels ....$12 – 16

37. "Twins 1992," blue, rubber tires on gray rims, White Rose Collectibles.....$4 – 5

38. "White Sox 1992," black, rubber tires on gray rims, White Rose Collectibles ....$4 – 5

39. "Yankees 1992," white, rubber tires on gray rims, White Rose Collectibles...................................$4 – 5

40. red with white hood and sides, black interior, clear windows, England cast..$5 – 6

41. red with white hood and sides, gray interior, clear windows, no "Corvette" cast at rear or front, England cast....................................$40 – 50

42. red with white hood and sides, gray interior, clear windows, England cast..$5 – 6

43. red with white hood and sides, black interior, clear windows, England cast..$5 – 6

44. red with white hood only, black interior, clear windows, England cast......$5 – 6

45. black with green and orange stripes on hood, gray interior, clear windows, England cast ....$4 – 5

46. black with green and orange stripes on hood, gray interior, opaque windows, England cast ....$12 – 16

47. black with yellow and orange stripes on hood, gray interior, clear windows, Macau cast............................$3 – 4

48. metallic gray with white and purple design, purple interior, clear windows, China cast ....$9 – 12

49. white with red stripes, maroon interior, Thailand cast...........................$3 – 4

Chevrolet Corvette Pace Car, #21, 1983 (see Chevrolet Corvette Hardtop)

Chevrolet Corvette Police, #464, 2000

1. "D.A.R.E. America," "Moorehead Police," white, triangular roof lights, D.A.R.E. series.......................$4 – 5

2. "D.A.R.E. Suffern Police," yellow with purple flames, D.A.R.E. series ...$4 – 5

Chevrolet Corvette Stingray III Convertible, #38, 1994; #2, 1998

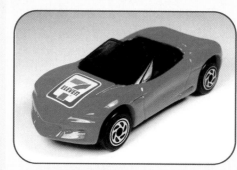

1. **red, "7-Eleven" ....$5 – 6**

2. red, "Matchbox USA 97," black interior, chrome windshield, rubber tires on chrome rims, promotional ....$120 – 160

3. **red with white and blue accent light gray interior, tinted windshiel 1998 Stars & Stripes series..$2 –**

4. red with detailed trim, black interic chrome windshield, rubber tires on chrom rims, US on-package premium ..$30 – 4

5. red, detailed trim, brown and black interic clear windshield, rubber tires on chrom rims, Premiere Collection #12 .....$4 –

6. **metallic dark red, detailed trim, tw tone gray interior, clear windshiel rubber tires on chrome rims, Pr miere Collection #16.............$4 –**

7. fluorescent orange, "Ice Breaker," gr interior ....$8 – 1

8. fluorescent orange and yellow, "Matc box Get In The Fast Lane," "Toy Fa 1995," US issue.................$20 – 2

9. fluorescent orange and yellov "Matchbox Get In The Fast Lane "Toy Fair 1995," England/Germar issue ....$20 – 2

10. lemon yellow with detailed trim, two tone gray interior, rubber tires o chrome rims, clear windshield, Pr miere Collection #5.................$4 –

11. fluorescent yellow, "Ice Breaker," gr interior ....$8 – 1

12. blue with orange and white accent "Corvette," 1998 Stars & Stripe Series ....$2 –

13. **blue chrome with pink and orang design, light gray interior, clea windshield, 1997 Sleek Riders pack ....$2 –**

14. metallic blue with detailed trim, tw tone gray interior, rubber tires o chrome rims, clear windshield, Pr miere Collection #2.................$4 –

15. purple, white interior, tinted windshiel 5-pack...................................$2 –

. purple with pink and white accents, dark gray interior, clear windshield, 1994 .... $2 – 3

7. purple with pink and white accents, gray interior, tinted windshield .... $2 – 3

3. purple with pink and white accents, light gray interior, tinted windshield ... $2 – 3

9. purple, detailed trim, dark gray interior, chrome windshield, rubber tires on chrome rims, World Class .... $4 – 5

0. black, detailed trim, red and gray interior, clear windshield, rubber tires on chrome rims, Gold Coin Collection .... $16 – 24

1. black and fluorescent orange, white interior, tinted windshield, 5-pack ..... $3 – 4

2. white with red and yellow design, red interior, tinted windshield, 1996 .... $3 – 4

3. white with blue and black spray design, blue interior, tinted windshield, 5-pack .... $2 – 3

4. white, detailed trim, brown and black interior, clear windshield, rubber tires on chrome rims, Select Class #4 .... $4 – 5

5. metallic silver with white and peach accents, white interior, amber windshield .... $4 – 5

6. metallic silver, detailed trim, dark gray interior, clear windshield, rubber tires on chrome rims, Select Class #2 .... $4 – 5

7. metallic gold with black interior, clear windshield, 1997 75 Challenge series .... $12 – 16

Chevrolet Corvette T-Roof, 3¹/₁₆", #40, 1982; #58; 1992 – 1997; #74, 1998; #62, 1982, international

. red, "Vette," "Chevy" logo, white interior, China cast .... $2 – 3

. red, "Vette," white stripe, white interior, 1993, Thailand cast................. $2 – 3

. red with white accents, no "Corvette" cast on front or rear .... $35 – 45

. red with white accents, "Corvette" cast on front and rear .... $4 – 6

. red with white and purple design, black interior, 1998 Street Cruisers series .... $2 – 3

---

6. red with detailed trim, black and red interior, rubber tires on chrome rims, Corvette Premiere Collection...... $4 – 5

7. candy apple red with black and white design, black and white interior, rubber tires on chrome rims, Premiere Collection #9 .... $4 – 5

8. candy apple red with black and white design, purple interior, Canada issue. $60 – 80

9. metallic red, "Turbo Vette," Laser Wheels .... $8 – 10

10. salmon pink, detailed trim, white and black interior, rubber tires on chrome rims, Gold Coin Collection ..... $16 – 24

11. orange with chrome windshield, rubber tires on gray rims, World Class.. $6 – 8

12. yellow, "Corvette," metallic gray interior, Macau cast............................ $2 – 3

13. yellow, "Corvette," metallic gray interior, China cast .... $2 – 3

14. yellow with purple and blue accents. $2 – 4

15. yellow with detailed trim, black and white interior, rubber tires on chrome rims, Corvette Premiere Collection.......................... $4 – 5

16. green, "Brut," "Faberge".......... $8 – 10

17. green with white and purple design, black interior, China cast........... $2 – 3

18. dark green, detailed trim, orange interior, Thailand cast, Collectors Choice, White Rose Collectibles........................ $3 – 4

19. dark green, detailed trim, white and black interior, rubber tires on chrome rims, Corvette Premiere Collection .... $4 – 5

20. metallic green, white accents with lavender border .... $2 – 3

21. blue with flames, red interior, silver wheel hubs, Macau cast .... $3 – 4

22. blue with flames, red interior, gold wheel hubs, Macau cast .... $5 – 6

23. blue with flames, red interior, New Superfast wheels, Macau cast....... $80 – 100

24. blue with yellow and red stripes, red interior, Manaus cast, Brazil issue ... $40 – 50

25. teal blue with pink interior, white and pink grid design, Thailand cast ... $2 – 3

26. metallic blue with chrome windshield, dark gray interior, World Class .. $6 – 8

27. metallic blue with white and red accents, 1994 .... $2 – 4

28. bright blue, detailed trim, white and black interior, rubber tires on chrome rims, Corvette Premiere Collection....... $4 – 5

29. black with chrome windshield, World Class..................................... $6 – 8

30. black "22," green and orange stripes, clear windows, rubber tires on black rims, Whales Project............... $6 – 8

---

31. black, detailed trim, red and black interior, rubber tires on chrome rims, Corvette Premiere Collection.................... $4 – 5

32. black with opaque windows, green and orange stripes .... $8 – 10

33. black with clear windows, yellow and orange stripes .... $2 – 4

34. black with gray interior, "The Force" .... $2 – 4

35. black with red interior, "The Force," Manaus cast, Brazil issue ..... $20 – 30

36. metallic gray with white and purple design, purple interior, China cast .... $2 – 3

37. metallic dark gray, "Corvette," white stripes, white interior, Corvette 40th Anniversary set........................ $3 – 4

38. dark cream with red and gray stripes, red interior, Manaus cast, Brazil issue .... $40 – 50

39. white front, black rear, pink blotch design, pink interior, China cast .... $2 – 3

40. white front, black rear, pink blotch design, pink interior, Thailand cast........... $2 – 3

41. white with pink design, black interior, China cast .... $2 – 3

42. white with stripes, gray interior, England cast................................. $5 – 6

43. white with stripes, red interior, Macau cast................................. $3 – 4

44. white, detailed trim, red and black interior, rubber tires on chrome rims, Corvette Premiere Collection...... $4 – 5

45. black with "Turbo Vette" .... $4 – 6

46. metallic silver, purple interior, gray base .... $2 – 3

47. metallic gold, black interior, 1997 75 Challenge series .... $6 – 12

48. various baseball team logos (29 variations) .... $4 – 6

Chevrolet Corvette T-Top (see Chevrolet Corvette T-Roof)

Chevrolet El Camino 1970, #32, 1998; #74, 1999; #60, 2000

1. red, "Coca-Cola It's The Real Thing," metallic gray metal base, Avon... $4 – 5

2. red and white, "Coca-Cola," rubber tires on chrome rims, Premiere Collection..$5 – 6
3. red with white stripes on hood, rubber tires on chrome rims, 1998 First Editions ....$5 – 6
4. maroon, chrome plastic base, "Canyon Base," 5-pack..........................$2 – 3
5. maroon, metallic gray metal base, "Canyon Base," Target Eggmobiles 5-pack.............................$9 – 12
6. metallic blue, "Freestyle," skateboarder, 2000 Speedy Delivery series .....$2 – 3
7. metallic blue, "Freestyle," skateboarder, "Matchbox 2000," 2000 Speedy Delivery series ....$3 – 4

8. **metallic gold with black stripes on hood, chrome base, 1998 Classic Decades series ....$2 – 3**
9. metallic gold with black stripes on hood, translucent white base, 1998 Classic Decades series....................$60 – 80
10. unpainted with no markings, rubber tires on chrome rims, 1998 First Editions ....$5 – 6

11. **yellow with dark brown and blue design, 1999 Classics series .$2 – 3**

Chevrolet Highway Maintenance Truck, 3¹/₁₆", #45, 1990 – 1997; #11, 1998; #79, 2000; #20, 2003; #69, 1990, international

1. **"Airport Plowing," white, blue dumper and plow, 1999 Airport 5-pack ....$2 – 3**
2. "Aspen Snow Removal," red, gray dumper and plow, Action Pack...$4 – 5
3. "Blue Ridge Construction," pumpkin orange, gray dumper and plow, ASAP promotional.......................$80 – 120
4. "CAT Service Co.," pumpkin, gray dumper and plow, ASAP promotional...$80 – 120

5. "DOT 13", fluorescent yellow, gray dumper and plow, "2000 Snow Explorer series......................................$2 – 3
6. "DOT 13," "Matchbox 2000," fluorescent yellow, gray dumper and plow, 2000 Snow Explorer series ......$3 – 4
7. "DOT 103," orange, black dumper and plow, 1999 Highway Haulers series ....$2 – 3
8. "Hemler Bros.," pumpkin orange, gray dumper and plow, ASAP promotional..............................$80 – 120

9. **"Highway Crew," fluorescent green, black dumper, yellow plow, 1999 Highway Crew 5-pack ....$2 – 3**

10. **"Highway Dept.," white, blue dumper and plow, 1995 ....$2 – 3**
11. "Highway Maintenance 45," orange, gray dumper and plow, Collectors Choice, White Rose Collectibles ..$4 – 5
12. "Intercom City," green, yellow dumper and plow................................$8 – 10
13. "International Airport Authority 45," dark orange, red dumper and plow...$9 – 12
14. "International Airport Authority 45," yellow, red dumper and plow ....$2 – 3
15. "International Airport Authority 45," yellow, yellow dumper and plow......$2 – 3
16. "Matchbox," pumpkin orange, gray dumper and plow, 5-pack ....$2 – 3

17. **"Matchbox Road Crew," red, black dumper and plow, 1998 Big Movers series ....$2 – 3**
18. "Minnesota Guidestar," pumpkin orange, gray dumper and plow, ASAP promotional.......................$80 – 120

19. "Redi-Way Inc.," pumpkin orang gray dumper and plow, ASAP prom tional ....$80 – 12

20. **"Road Crew," orange, black dumpe and plow, 1997 ....$2 –**
21. "Test Centre," orange, gray dumper an plow, polar bear design, Launcher pack....................................$2 –

22. **metallic green, orange dumper an plow, charging ram design, 200 Public Works series ....$2 – 3**
23. metallic gold, black dumper and plow 1997 75 Challenge series ......$6 – 1
24. 2002 Matchbox Across America 50t Birthday Series #39 North Dakota - Central Collection, black with orang dumper and plow ....$4 –

Chevrolet Impala, metallic blue with ligh blue roof, 2³/₄", #57, 1961
1. gray plastic wheels, black base.............................$150 – 17
2. silver plastic wheels, black base ....$70 – 90
3. silver plastic wheels, dark blu base ....$70 – 90
4. silver plastic wheels, light blu base ....$70 – 90
5. silver plastic wheels, pale light blu base ....$80 – 100
5. black plastic wheels, black base.........................$70 – 90

Chevrolet Impala Police, #34, 2000; #53 2001; #5, 2002; #53, 2003

1. **black, "Test Mission," yellow and re with white space shuttle design 2000 Space Mission 5-pack...$2 – 3**

blue with white and yellow accents, "53 Crossing Guard," 2003 School Time series.....................$2 – 3

blue with light blue, white and yellow design, 2003 Hero City 5-pack #2.....................$2 – 3
white, "D.A.R.E.," 2002 Safety Stars series.....................$2 – 3

white with blue design, "Cleveland, Ohio, Police," 2000 Matchbox USA series.....................$2 – 3
white with blue design, "Cleveland, Ohio, Police," "Matchbox 2000," 2000 Matchbox USA series.....................$3 – 4
white and blue, "Metro Alarm," "Police," 5-pack.....................$2 – 3
yellow-orange and blue, "Sydney 2000," 5-pack.....................$2 – 3
2001 Police series.....................$2 – 3
⊃. 2002 Matchbox Across America 50th Birthday Series #9 New Hampshire — Northeastern Collection.....................$4 – 6
1. 2002 Matchbox Across America 50th Birthday Series #10 Virginia — Southern Collection.....................$4 – 6

hevrolet Impala Police, 2000 Feature Cars, with opening features, designed to replace Premiere Collection "Chevrolet Police Vehicle," white.$9 – 12
. "FDMB R32," white, K B Toys exclusive $9 – 12
. "NYPD 2419," white.....................$9 – 12
. "State Highway Patrol Ohio," dark gray.....................$9 – 12
. "Twp. of Franklin," "43-5," white with red band.....................$9 – 12

hevrolet Impala Taxi Cab, 3", #20, 1965
. orange with gray wheels, ivory interior.....................$250 – 350
. orange with black wheels, ivory or red interior.....................$20 – 25
. yellow with black wheels, ivory or red interior.....................$12 – 16

hevrolet K-1500 4x4 Pick-Up, #72, 1996; #54, 1998; #100, 1999

1. white, "World Cup Field Maintenance," "France 98," 1998 World Cup 5-pack.....................$2 – 3

2. red with yellow lightning bolt, black and white specks on sides, 1998 Rugged Riders 5-pack.....................$2 – 3

3. fluorescent orange with blue snowcapped mountain design, 1996 Off-Road 5-pack.....................$2 – 3

4. yellow with red and white design on sides, 1998 Rough 'N Tough series.....................$2 – 3

5. fluorescent green with orange lightning bolt, black and white specks on sides, 1997 Rugged Riders 5-pack.....................$2 – 3

6. blue, "Evergreen Landscaping," "Keeping Lawns Beautiful," 1999 At Your Service series.....................$2 – 3

7. metallic blue with green and white design on sides, 1998 Rough & Tough series.....................$2 – 3
8. metallic blue with red and white accents.....................$2 – 3
9. black, "Farm Credit Services," yellow and pink accents, ASAP promotional...$120 – 160

10. black with yellow and pink accents.....................$2 – 3
11. metallic gold, no markings, 1997 75 Challenge series.....................$12 – 16

Chevrolet K-1500 Pickup 1980, 1999, Taco Bell; Matchbox mold retooled by Strottman International Inc. through a licensing agreement with Mattel. Strottman manufactures toy premiums for Taco Bell. Base is marked "Made in China by S.I.I."
1. blue with white wave design, black windows, Taco Bell premium.....................$3 – 4

Chevrolet Lumina Stock Car, 3", #54, 1990; #267, 1994, White Rose Collectibles
1. "3," "GM Parts," black, Goodyear rubber tires on gray rims, Winross promotional, White Rose Collectibles.....................$20 – 30
2. "7 Time Champion 3," gold plated, Goodyear rubber tires on black rims, White Rose Collectibles.....................$4 – 5
3. "98 Cutler-Hammer," white, ASAP promotional.....................$60 – 80
4. "AC Delco 52," Goodyear rubber tires on black rims, White Rose Collectibles .$4 – 5
5. "Active 32," red, Goodyear slicks, White Rose Collectibles.....................$4 – 5
6. "American Zoom 93," white and blue, white, Goodyear slicks, White Rose Collectibles.....................$12 – 16
7. "Avis," white, Goodyear slicks, ASAP promotional.....................$60 – 80
8. "Baltimore Colts 29," white, Hoosier rubber tires on black rims, White Rose Collectibles.....................$20 – 30

9. "Caterpillar," black and orange-yellow, Goodyear rubber tires on black rims, White Rose Collectibles.............$4 – 5

10. "Champion 4," black, Hot Stocks...$3 – 4

11. "Cintas 87," white, Goodyear slicks, White Rose Collectibles..........$8 – 10

12. "City Chevrolet 46," green and lime, China cast ....$4 – 5

13. "City Chevrolet 46," green and lime, Macau cast, Days of Thunder ....$7 – 9

14. "Dentyne 87," red and white, Goodyear slicks, White Rose Collectibles ...$4 – 5

15. "Detroit Gasket," "MGM Brake 70," red, Goodyear rubber tires on black rims, White Rose Collectibles.............$4 – 5

16. "Dewalt 08," yellow, Goodyear slicks, White Rose Collectibles.............$4 – 5

17. "Dewalt 08," yellow, Goodyear rubber tires on black rims, White Rose Collectibles ....$5 – 6

18. "Drive," "A-Pix Entertainment," white, Goodyear slicks, ASAP promotional ....$120 – 160

19. "Dupont 24," metallic blue and fluorescent orange, Goodyear slicks, White Rose Collectibles......................$4 – 5

20. "Dupont 24," metallic blue and fluorescent orange, Goodyear rubber tires on black rims, Team Convoy, White Rose Collectibles........................$5 – 6

21. "Dupont 24," "1993 Rookie of the Year," metallic blue and fluorescent orange, Goodyear rubber tires on black rims, Team Convoy, White Rose Collectibles ....$4 – 5

22. "Dupont 99," metallic blue, Goodyear slicks, White Rose Collectibles ...$4 – 5

23. "Dupont Automotive Finishes 2," metallic blue, Goodyear rubber tires on black rims, White Rose Collectibles ....$4 – 5

24. "Enck's Custom Catering 71," blue, Goodyear slicks, White Rose Collectibles ....$4 – 5

25. "Exxon 51" with signature, black, China cast, Days of Thunder...............$4 – 5

26. "Exxon 51" with signature, black, Macau cast, Days of Thunder...............$7 – 9

27. "Exxon 51," no signature, black, Macau cast, Days of Thunder...........$30 – 40

28. "FDP Brakes 9," metallic turquoise and pink, Goodyear slicks, White Rose Collectibles ....$4 – 5

29. "Fiddle Faddle 34," red, Goodyear rubber tires on black rims, White Rose Collectibles ....$4 – 5

30. "Ferree Chevrolet 49," white and orange, White Rose Collectibles..$4 – 5

31. "Freedom Village," "Jasper 55," white, Goodyear slicks, White Rose Collectibles ....$4 – 5

32. "Goodwrench," "GM," "Mom N Pops," "Western Steer," black, Goodyear slicks, on-package premium, White Rose Collectibles......................$7 – 9

33. "GM," "Goodwrench," black, Goodyear slicks, Team Convoy, White Rose Collectibles ....$5 – 7

34. "Goodwrench 3," "GM," "Western Steer," black, 9-spoke Goodyear slicks, White Rose Collectibles.............$4 – 5

35. "Goodwrench 3," "GM," "Western Steer," black, Goodyear slicks, White Rose Collectibles......................$6 – 8

36. "Goodwrench 3," "GM," "Western Steer," black, Goodyear rubber tires on black rims, Team Convoy, White Rose Collectibles...............................$6 – 8

37. "Goodwrench 3," "GM," "Western Steer," black, Goodyear rubber tires on gray rims, Team Convoy, White Rose Collectibles...............................$7 – 9

38. "Goodwrench 3," "GM," black, Goodyear rubber tires on gray rims, White Rose Collectibles Winross promotional...$20 – 30

39. "Goodwrench 3," "GM," large "Goodwrench" on sides, revised small logos, black, Goodyear rubber tires on gray rims, Team Convoy, White Rose Collectibles...............................$5 – 6

40. "Goodwrench 3," "Melbourne Motor Show," black, Goodyear rubber tires on black rims, promotional.........$20 – 30

41. "Goodwrench 3," "Sydney Motorshow 1997," black, Goodyear rubber tires on black rims, promotional.........$20 – 30

42. "Hardees 18," bright orange and blue, Macau cast, Days of Thunder ....$7 – 9

43. "Hardees 18," bright orange and blue, China cast, Days of Thunder ....$4 – 5

44. "Hendricks 25," white and green, Goodyear rubber tires on gold rims, Team Convoy, White Rose Collectibles ....$7 – 9

45. "Ica Citrix," "CDN," Goodyear slicks, ASAP promotional..............$80 – 120

46. "Ideal," white, Goodyear slicks, ASAP promotional......................$80 – 120

47. "Interstate Batteries 18," lime green and black, White Rose Collectibles.....$4 – 5

48. "Ireland 31," black, Goodyear slicks, White Rose Collectibles.............$4 – 5

49. "Ithaca Finish First," "607-257-8901," white, Goodyear slicks, ASAP promotional...................................$60 – 80

50. "Kandi & Steve," "October 1, 1994," purple, Goodyear rubber tires on black rims, White Rose Collectibles .....$400 – 500

51. "Kellogg's 5," gray, Goodyear rubber tires on black rims, White Rose Collectibles ....$5 – 6

52. "Kellogg's Corn Flakes," red and yellow, Goodyear rubber tires on black rims, White Rose Collectibles.............$4 – 5

53. "Kellogg's Corn Flakes," red and yellow, yellow disc wheels, Team Convoy, White Rose Collectibles......................$5 – 6

54. "Kodak 4," orange-yellow, Goodyear rubber tires on black rims, White Rose Collectibles ....$4 – 5

55. "Kodak Film 4 Racing," orange-yellow, Goodyear rubber tires on black rims, Team Convoy, White Rose Collectibles ....$6 – 8

56. "Kodak Film 4 Racing," orange-yellow, Goodyear slicks, White Rose Collectibles ....$4 – 5

57. "Kodak Funsaver 4," orange and whit[e] Goodyear rubber tires on black rim[s] White Rose Collectibles.............$4 –

58. "Lifetime Achievement Award — Har[ry] Gant," gold plated, Team Convoy, Wh[ite] Rose Collectibles...................$20 – 3[0]

59. "Lipton Tea 74," pink-red and yello[w] Goodyear rubber tires on black rim[s] White Rose Collectibles.............$4 –

60. "Luxaire 99," white, Goodyear rubb[er] tires on black rims, White Rose C[ol]lectibles................................$4 –

61. "Mac Tool Distributors 10," yellow White Rose Collectibles........$16 – 2[0]

62. "Mac Tool Distributors 10," "Cham[pi]on 3," yellow, Goodyear slicks, H[ot] Stocks..................................$3 –

63. "Mac Tools 7," yellow, White Rose C[ol]lectibles................................$8 – 1[0]

64. "Mac Tools 10," yellow, White Rose C[ol]lectibles................................$8 – 1[0]

65. "Manheim 41," fluorescent yellow a[nd] lime green, Goodyear slicks, Whi[te] Rose Collectibles....................$4 –

66. "Manheim Auctions 7" in black letter[s] fluorescent lime green, Hoosier ru[b]ber tires on black rims, White Ros[e] Collectibles........................$4 –

67. "Manheim Auctions 7" in white letter[s] fluorescent lime green, Goodyear ru[b]ber tires on lime green rims, Whi[te] Rose Collectibles....................$4 –

68. "Matchbox," "White Rose 29," whit[e] Goodyear slicks, White Rose Co[l]lectibles................................$4 –

69. "Matchbox," "White Rose 29," "Brad[s] Toys," white, Goodyear slicks, Whit[e] Rose Collectibles....................$7 –

70. "Matchbox," "White Rose 29," "Car[s] Plus," white, Goodyear slicks, Whit[e] Rose Collectibles....................$7 –

71. "Matchbox," "White Rose 29," "Cra[ig] Hill," white, Goodyear slicks, Whit[e] Rose Collectibles....................$7 –

72. "Matchbox," "White Rose 29," "Diecas[t] Toy Exchange," white, Goodyear slicks White Rose Collectibles.............$7 –

73. "Matchbox," "White Rose 29," "Kidd[ie] Kar Kollectibles," white, Goodyea[r] slicks, White Rose Collectibles ...$7 –

74. "Matchbox," "White Rose 29," "Matc[h]box Road Museum," white, Goodyea[r] slicks, White Rose Collectibles ...$7 –

75. "Matchbox — White Rose Collectible[s] 29," dark blue and yellow, Hoosier ru[b]ber tires on black rims, White Rose Co[l]lectibles................................$4 – 5

76. "Matchbox Motorsports 35," fluores[cent] cent green, black grille, Goodyea[r] slicks ....$3 – 4

77. "Matchbox Motorsports 35," fluorescent gree[n] without black grille, Goodyear slicks .....$2 – 3

78. "Matchbox Motorsports 35," dar[k] blue ....$3 – 4

79. "Matchbox Racing 1," white and metalli[c] blue, Hot Stocks ....$3 – 4

80. "Matchbox Racing 7," red and yello[w] Goodyear slicks, Hot Stocks.......$3 – 4

"Matchbox USA 12," yellow and red, Goodyear slicks.........................$7 – 9

"Matchbox USA 13," yellow and red, Goodyear slicks.........................$7 – 9

"Matchbox USA 14," metallic gray, Goodyear slicks, Parlor City Collectibles ....$8 – 10

"Meineke 41," black and yellow, Goodyear rubber tires on black rims, White Rose Collectibles............$5 – 6

"Mello Yello 51," black, Macau cast...................................$6 – 8

"Mello Yello 51," black, China cast, Days of Thunder.....................$4 – 5

"Molly Black Gold 98," black, Goodyear slicks, White Rose Collectibles ...$4 – 5

"MW Windows," "Freedom 14," white, Goodyear slicks, White Rose Collectibles ....$4 – 5

"Nationwide Auto Parts," yellow, Goodyear slicks.....................$30 – 40

"Penrose 44," "Firecracker Sausage," "Big Mama," maroon, White Rose Collectibles................................$7 – 9

"Performance Parts 12," red, white-lettered Goodyear slicks............$2 – 3

"Performance Parts 12," red, yellow-lettered Goodyear slicks, Aquafresh on-package premium....................$5 – 6

3. **"Performance Parts 12," baby blue, Goodyear slicks, Collectors Choice, White Rose Collectibles ....$4 – 5**

4. **"Performance Parts 12," purple with yellow lettering, Goodyear slicks, Collectors Choice, White Rose Collectibles ....$4 – 5**

5. "PG Tags," white, UK on-package premium..................................$90 – 120

6. "Phil Parsons Racing 29," "Matchbox," dark purple and white, White Rose Collectibles................................$16 – 24

7. "Pic N Pay," "Shoe World 32," yellow, Goodyear rubber tires on black rims, White Rose Collectibles...........$9 – 12

8. "Pic N Pay Shoes," "Shoe City 32," yellow, Goodyear slicks, White Rose Collectibles................................$4 – 5

9. "Polaroid 46," orange, Goodyear rubber tires on black rims, White Rose Collectibles................................$20 – 30

100. "Purolator 10," fluorescent orange and white, Goodyear slicks, White Rose Collectibles.............................$4 – 5

101. "Purolator 10," fluorescent orange and white, Goodyear rubber tires on gray rims, Team Convoy, White Rose Collectibles................................$5 – 6

102. "Raybestos 12," without "Tic Tac," metallic blue and white, White Rose Collectibles.........................$80 – 100

103. "Raybestos 12," "Tic Tac," metallic blue and white, White Rose Collectibles................................$4 – 5

104. "Rookie of the Year 1993," gold plated, Goodyear rubber tires on black rims, Team Convoy, White Rose Collectibles..................$8 – 10

105. "Six Time Champion 3 Dale Earnhardt," gold plated, White Rose Collectibles...........................$20 – 30

106. "Slim Jim 44," maroon, White Rose Collectibles..........................$7 – 9

107. "Stanley 92," black, Goodyear rubber tires on black rims, White Rose Collectibles................................$5 – 6

108. "Stanley Tools 92," black, Goodyear slicks, White Rose Collectibles ...$4 – 5

109. "Steph & Mike," "The Desenbergs," "December 10, 1994," Goodyear rubber tires on black rims, White Rose Collectibles.........................$400 – 500

110. "Sunoco Ultra 94," dark blue, Goodyear slicks, White Rose Collectibles................................$4 – 5

111. "Superflo 46," pink and white, Macau cast, Days of Thunder..............$7 – 9

112. "Superflo 46," pink and white, China cast, Days of Thunder..............$4 – 5

113. "Team Goodyear 11," white, Hot Stocks...............................$3 – 4

114. "Team Goodyear 22," orange, Hot Stocks...............................$3 – 4

115. "Texas Pete," "Lozito's 87," yellow and white, White Rose Collectibles ...$5 – 6

116. "Tracey Lawrence," "Yamaha 1," orange-red and white, Goodyear rubber tires on black rims, White Rose Collectibles..............................$9 – 12

117. "US Transplant Olympics — Tyler Elliott," white, Goodyear slicks, Color Comp promotional...............$30 – 40

118. "Vermont Teddy Bear," blue-green and purple, Goodyear rubber tires on black rims, White Rose Collectibles ....$4 – 5

119. "Virginia Is For Lovers 25," black, white, Goodyear slicks, White Rose Collectibles................................$4 – 5

120. "Western Auto 17," white, gray and black, Goodyear rubber tires on black rims, White Rose Collectibles ....$4 – 5

121. "WFE 69," black, Goodyear slicks, White Rose Collectibles.........$16 – 24

122. "White Rose Collectibles 29," "Matchbox," dark purple and white, White Rose Collectibles.....................$4 – 5

123. "White Rose Collectibles 94," white, light blue and dark blue, White Rose Collectibles..........................$30 – 40

124. "White Rose Series II in '94," white and dark blue, White Rose Collectibles ....$5 – 6

125. Lightning Wheels, yellow and orange with purple spatter and lightning bolts, chrome and black windows........$3 – 5

126. Lightning Wheels, yellow and orange, red spatter and lightning bolts, chrome and black windows ....$4 – 5

127. Lightning Wheels, green and white wtih purple spatter and lightning bolts, chrome and black windows.......$4 – 5

128. Lightning Wheels, white and yellow with pink spatter and lightning bolts, blue chrome and black windows ......$8 – 10

129. Lightning Wheels, white and black..................................$8 – 10

130. yellow, Goodyear slicks, White Rose Collectibles..........................$16 – 24

131. white with no markings, Thailand cast, Graffic Traffic ....$6 – 8

132. white with no markings, China cast, ASAP promotional blank........$20 – 30

133. chrome plated, no markings, Goodyear slicks, customized model.......$15 – 20

Chevrolet Monte Carlo, #283, 1995, White Rose Collectibles

1. "1995 Champion — Lipton Tea 74," gold plated, Goodyear rubber tires on black rims, White Rose Collectibles..$20 – 30

2. "1995 Rookie of the Year — Ricky Craven 41," gold plated, Goodyear rubber tires on black rims, White Rose Collectibles................................$20 – 30

3. "Bell South Mobility 87," blue and white, Goodyear rubber tires on black rims, White Rose Collectibles.........$12 – 16

4. "Budweiser 25," red, Goodyear rubber tires on black rims, White Rose Collectibles, sealed in plexiglas box ....$20 – 25

5. "Budweiser 25," red, Goodyear rubber tires on black rims, White Rose Collectibles, sealed in glass bottle ....$30 – 40

6. "Burger King 87," black and orange-yellow, Goodyear rubber tires on black rims, White Rose Collectibles ..$8 – 10

7. "Burger King 87," purple and yellow, Goodyear rubber tires on black rims, White Rose Collectibles.............$4 – 5

8. "Caterpillar," "Cat 95," black, Goodyear rubber tires on black rims, Team Convoy, White Rose Collectibles ......$7 – 9

9. "Caterpillar," "Cat 96," orange-yellow, Goodyear rubber tires on black rims, White Rose Collectibles............$4 – 5

10. "Caterpillar 96," black and orange-yellow, Goodyear rubber tires on black rims, White Rose Collectibles............$4 – 5

11. "Channellock 10," blue, Goodyear rubber tires on black rims, White Rose Collectibles................................$4 – 5

12. "Coor's Light 40," dark blue, metallic gray and pale yellow, Goodyear rubber tires on black rims, White Rose Collectibles, sealed in glass bottle ....$30 – 40

13. "Dewalt 1," orange-yellow, Goodyear rubber tires on black rims, White Rose Collectibles..............................$4 – 5
14. "Dupont 24," metallic blue and fluorescent orange, Goodyear rubber tires on black rims, White Rose Collectibles ....$4 – 5
15. "Dupont 95 Points Champion," gold plated, Goodyear rubber tires on black rims, White Rose Collectibles...........$20 – 30
16. "Fina 74," blue, Goodyear rubber tires on black rims, White Rose Collectibles .$4 – 5
17. "Fina 74 — 1996 Champion," gold plated, Goodyear rubber tires on black rims, White Rose Collectibles.........$20 – 30
18. "Goodwrench 3," black, Goodyear rubber tires on black rims, White Rose Collectibles..............................$4 – 5
19. "Hyde Tools 08," blue and white, Goodyear rubber tires on black rims, White Rose Collectibles.............$4 – 5
20. "Hype 88," black, Goodyear rubber tires on black rims, White Rose Collectibles................................$4 – 5
21. "Interstate Batteries," green and black, Goodyear rubber tires on black rims, White Rose Collectibles.............$4 – 5
22. "Kellogg's 5," yellow and red, Goodyear rubber tires on black rims, White Rose Collectibles..............................$4 – 5
23. "Kellogg's Corn Flakes 5," "1996 Champion," gold plated, Goodyear rubber tires on black rims, White Rose Collectibles...............................$20 – 30
24. "Kellogg's Corn Flakes 5," lemon and red, Goodyear rubber tires on black rims, White Rose Collectibles ....$4 – 5
25. "Kodak Film 4," orange-yellow, Goodyear rubber tires on black rims, White Rose Collectibles..............................$4 – 5
26. "Kodiac 41," white and green, Goodyear rubber tires on black rims, White Rose Collectibles, sealed in plexiglas box..............................$20 – 30
27. "Lance Snacks 43," blue, Goodyear rubber tires on black rims, White Rose Collectibles..............................$4 – 5
28. "Lance Snacks 43"; blue, white, and red; Goodyear rubber tires on black rims, White Rose Collectibles ....$4 – 5
29. "Lipton Tea 74," red, Goodyear rubber tires on black rims, White Rose Collectibles...............................$4 – 5
30. "Matchbox 1995," "1," fluorescent pink, Goodyear rubber tires on black rims, White Rose Collectibles; 1995 Hershey, PA, convention raffle prize ..$100 – 150
31. "Matchbox 1995," "1," fluorescent yellow, Goodyear rubber tires on black rims, White Rose Collectibles; 1995 Hershey, PA, convention raffle prize ..$100 – 150
32. "Rookie of the Year — Ricky Craven 41," gold plated ....$20 – 25
33. "Royal Oak Charcoal," red and yellow, Goodyear rubber tires on black rims, White Rose Collectibles.............$4 – 5
34. "Skoal 33," green and white, Goodyear rubber tires on black rims, White Rose Collectibles, sealed in plexiglas box ..$30 – 40

35. "The Budget Gourmet," white, Goodyear rubber tires on black rims, White Rose Collectibles..............................$4 – 5
36. "White Rose Collectibles 96," blue, white and dark rose, Goodyear rubber tires on black rims, White Rose Collectibles................................$9 – 12

Chevrolet Panel Van, #215, 1995
1. red, "Texaco," rubber tires on chrome rims, Premiere Collection ....$4 – 5
2. metallic red, "American Iron Cruise 95".....................................$15 – 20
3. fluorescent orange, "Matchbox — Get In The Fast Lane — Hershey Convention 1996"................................$10 – 12
4. metallic green, "25th Anniversary S.J.S.R.A. South Jersey Shore Rod Run," Color Comp promotional.........$16 – 24
5. metallic green, "American Iron Cruise 1998," custom promotional ..$16 – 24
6. metallic green, "Season's Greetings — Matchbox Collectors Club 1995" ....$10 – 12
7. purple, "Continental Aero" .....$12 – 16
8. metallic gray, "Andale — www.andale.com," ASAP promotional...................$60 – 80
9. metallic gray, "Hot August Nights," Color Comp promotional........$16 – 24
10. metallic gray, "Penn State," ASAP promotional ....$16 – 24
11. metallic gray, no markings, ASAP promotional blank ....$35 – 45
12. white, "1st Annual Salmon River Festival," rubber tires on chrome rims, Color Comp promotional................$15 – 20
13. white, "Alpenglow," "Appie House," rubber tires on chrome rims, Color Comp promotional..........................$20 – 30
14. white, "FAO Schwarz World of Wheels," rubber tires on chrome rims, Color Comp promotional................$60 – 80
15. white, "Mac's Roller Rink, Inc.," rubber tires on chrome rims, Color Comp promotional ....$20 – 30
16. white, "Omps Funeral Home," rubber tires on chrome rims, Color Comp promotional ....$15 – 20
17. white, no markings, rubber tires on chrome rims, Color Comp promotional blank.................................$35 – 45

Chevrolet Pro Stocker, 3", #34, 1981
1. white with no markings ....$16 – 24
2. white, "Lightning," "34," metallic gray base ....$6 – 8
3. white, "Lightning," "34," red base.$16 – 24

4. white, "Lightning," "34," unpainted base ....$6 – 8

5. light orange, "4" and stripe........$3 –
6. white, "Pepsi Challenger," "14," r interior ....$3 –

7. white, "Pepsi Challenger," "14," bla interior, Team Matchbox .....$70 – 9
8. white, "Superstar 217," Team Mato box ....$4 –
9. black, "Halley's Comet"...........$9 – 1

10. white and orange, "21," "355 CID" ....$5 –
11. white, "7-Up," red interior..........$4 –
12. white, "7-Up," black interior....$80 – 12
13. blue and white, "70 Bailey Excavating White Rose Collectibles.............$5 –

Chevrolet Sedan Delivery (see Chevro 1939 Sedan Delivery)

Chevrolet Silverado 1999, #86, 199 #49, 2002
1. red, "Classic Home Builders," chrom plastic grille and base, 5-pack ....$2 –
2. red with tool designs, chrome plast grille and base, 5-pack.............$2 –

3. yellow, "Aqua Centre" on sides, multicolo on hood, chrome plastic grille and bas 2000 Ocean Dock 5-pack..........$2 – 3

4. yellow, "Hammer & Nails Qualit Carpentry," black plastic grille an base, 2002 Hammer and Nail series ....$2 – 3
5. white, "5 Alarm," "Hangar 34," "67 chrome plastic grille and base, Launche 5-pack..................................$2 – 3

6. white, "Action Radar," "Xtreme Mission," red plastic grille and base, 5-pack ..$2 – 3

7. white, "Fresh Eggs," "Farm Fresh Dairy," brown mud, chrome plastic grille and base, 1999 On The Farm series ....$2 – 3

8. white, "HQ Chief," aqua, green and black design, green plastic grille and base, 2003 Hero City 5-pack #7 ....$2 – 3

Chevrolet Silverado 1999 4x4, #70, 1999; #11, 2000; #7, 2001; #22, 2002; #65, 1999, international
1. yellow, "Zero," mountain design, 5-pack ....$2 – 3

2. purple, "Surfshop — The Hottest Boards on the Beach!" 2000 To The Beach series...........................$2 – 3
3. purple, "Surfshop — The Hottest Boards on the Beach!" "Matchbox 2000," 2000 To The Beach series ....$3 – 4
4. purple, 2002 Great Outdoors series ....$2 – 3
5. black, "Canyon Mission," 1999 Ranger Patrol international series ....$3 – 4
6. black, "Game Warden," "Protect Wild Life," 1999 Ranger Patrol US series.....................................$2 – 3
7. white, "Fast Ride Snowboards 22," 2001 Team Tundra series ....$2 – 3

Chevrolet SSR, #70, 2002; #57, 2003
1. metallic blue, 2002 Kids' Cars of the Year ....$2 – 3
2. yellow, "Tony's Pizza," 2003 Kids' Shoppes ....$2 – 3

Chevrolet Suburban, 2000 Feature Cars, with opening features, designed to replace Premiere Collection

1. "Chevrolet Police Vehicle," white ..$9 – 12
2. "DC1," "City of Miami," "Fire Rescue," red ....9 – 12
3. "FDMB," "TR3," white, K B Toys exclusive......................................$9 – 12
4. "Fire MBFD 45," red and white .$9 – 12
5. "NYPD," white ....$9 – 12

Chevrolet Suburban 2000, #80, 2000; #477, 2000; #60, 2000, international

1. white, "zero test base," "Matchbox 2000," red and black design, 2000 Snow Explorer series ....$3 – 4
2. white, "zero test base," red and black design, 2000 Snow Explorer series.............$2 – 3
3. white with blue logo, ASAP promotional ....$60 – 80

4. blue with red roof lights, white and yellow, 2003 Hero City 5-pack #2 ....$2 – 3
5. black, "D.A.R.E. America," "Pima County Sheriff," D.A.R.E. series ....$4 – 5

Chevrolet Super Truck, 1995, #284, White Rose Collectibles
1. "3 — 1995 Super Truck Champion," gold plated, Goodyear rubber tires on black rims ....$20 – 25
2. "Dupont 24," metallic blue and orange, Goodyear rubber tires on black rims ....$4 – 5
3. "Goodwrench 3," black, Goodyear rubber tires on black rims.............$4 – 5
4. "Lance Snacks 43"; blue, white, and red; Goodyear rubber tires on black rims.....................................$4 – 5
5. "Manheim Auctions 33," purple, Goodyear rubber tires on black rims ....$4 – 5
6. "Quaker State 24," white and green, Goodyear rubber tires on black rims ....$4 – 5
7. "Sears Diehard 1," black, Goodyear rubber tires on black rims.............$4 – 5
8. "The Magic Mile 96," black, Goodyear rubber tires on black rims ....$8 – 10
9. "Total 6"; white, blue, and red; Goodyear rubber tires on black rims ....$4 – 5
10. "Westview Capital 33," purple, Goodyear rubber tires on black rims ....$4 – 5

Chevrolet Tahoe 1997, #46, 1998; #99, 1999; #28, 2000; #33, 2001; #51, 2002

1. bright yellow with "Coca-Cola" and logo on side.....................$12 – 16
2. yellow with red windows, 2003 Coca-Cola 5-pack............................$4 – 5
3. red with black flare and mud spatter, gray interior, play set...........$12 – 16

4. metallic red, "454," white and yellow design, tan interior, 1998 To The Rescue series ....$2 – 3
5. metallic red, "454," "Matchbox Madness," white and yellow design, tan interior, Color Comp promotional................$80 – 120
6. dark green, silver band, detailed trim, rubber tires on chrome rims, tan and black interior, 1998 First Editions 2-car set..$5 – 6
7. bright blue, "Sydney 2000," red interior, 5-pack..................................$2 – 3
8. black, "Hammer Demolition," 2002 Hammer and Nails series..........$2 – 3
9. black, "Chicago Bulls 23," "Michael Jordan," white interior, NBA 2-pack ....$6 – 8
10. metallic gray, "Clogs," blue interior, 1999 At Your Service series, Canada/Mexico issue, not released in US...$12 – 16
11. metallic gray, "Coca-Cola" and logo, red interior, 5-pack.........................$2 – 3
12. white, "Chicago Bulls 23," "Michael Jordan," black interior, NBA 2-pack ....$6 – 8
13. white, "Rough Riders," red interior, ASAP promotional ....$80 – 120
14. white, "Ford Tough Mud Run," red interior, ASAP promotional ....$80 – 120
15. unpainted, rubber tires on chrome rims, tan interior, 1998 First Editions 2-car set ....$5 – 6

Chevrolet Tahoe 1997 Police/Fire Chief, #30, 1998; #78, 1999; #33, 2000; #28, 2001
1. red, "City of Seattle," rubber tires on chrome rims, Premiere Collection ..$6 – 8

2. red, "Fire 3 Dept.," "Dial 911," "Fire Chief," 2000 Fire Fighters series .... $2 – 3

3. red, "Fire 3 Dept.," "Dial 911," "Fire Chief," "Matchbox 2000," 2000 Fire Fighters series .... $10 – 12
4. red, "5 Alarm," "67," "Hangar 34," Action Launcher Airplane set ..... $2 – 3
5. metallic red, "Fire Chief," 2000 Fire Fighters series .... $2 – 3
6. blue, "City of Cleveland Ohio," red interior, 2000 Matchbox USA series .... $2 – 3
7. blue, "City of Cleveland Ohio," "Matchbox 2000," red interior, 2000 Matchbox USA series................................ $3 – 4
8. green and yellow, "York Fair Police 1998," US issue .... $8 – 10
9. army green, "Military Police," rubber tires on green rims, Premiere Collection .... $12 – 16
10. blue, "Wisconsin State Police," rubber tires on chrome rims, Premiere Collection .... $12 – 16
11. black, "Matchbox Official Collectors Club" .... $7 – 9

12. black, "NJ Diecast Collectors Club," 1998, ASAP promotional ... $20 – 25

13. black, "Official Matchbox Collectors Club," "Matchbox USA Membership Drive 2001," Color Comp promotional .... $20 – 25
14. black, "Official Matchbox Collectors Club," "Penn Matchbox Collectors Club 2001," Color Comp promotional .... $20 – 25

15. metallic gray with red interior, "Matchbox FDMB" on shield with flame graphics, "14," 2001 Action Launcher Fire Truck set .... $3 – 4

16. white, "Fire Chief," red and black design, 1999 Fire Rescue series .... $2 – 3
17. white, "H2O Force," red, orange and black design, 2001 Flame Eaters series .... $2 – 3
18. white, "Nassau County Police," stripes, Color Comp promotional .... $20 – 25
19. white, "Open Space Officer," ASAP promotional .... $80 – 120

20. white, "Police," "Dial 911," blue accents, red trim, 1998 To The Rescue series .... $2 – 3

21. white, "Police," "Matchbox," two-tone blue stripes, Pleasant Books ...... $4 – 5
22. white, "Salt Lake City Police," rubber tires on chrome rims, Premiere Collection #23 .... $20 – 25
23. white, "Thomas Hines Retired Finally," ASAP promotional .... $80 – 120
24. white, no markings, ASAP promotional blank .... $30 – 40

Chevrolet Tahoe 1997, 1999, Taco Bell; Matchbox mold retooled by Strottman International Inc. through a licensing agreement with Mattel. Strottman manufactures toy premiums for Taco Bell. Base is marked "Made in China by S.I.I."

1. white with green, blue and black design, black windows, Taco Bell premium .... $3 – 4

Chevrolet Transport Bus, #24, 1999; #73, 2000

1. blue with red and yellow, 2000 Wilderness Road Trip 5-pack .. $2 – 3

2. red, "Coca-Cola" and polar bears, Premiere Collection .... $5 – 6
3. white, black interior, clear windows, ASAP promotional blank .... $30 – 45

4. white, "Serving Meridian Since 1927," ASAP promotional .... $80 – 120
5. white, "Happy Birthday Michelle," ASAP promotional .... $80 – 120

6. ivory, "Metro Motel Shuttle" and globe design, 2000 On Tour series .... $2 – 3

7. ivory, "Metro Motel Shuttle" and globe design, "Matchbox 2000," 2000 On Tour series .... $3 – 4

8. green, "National," 1999 Speedy Delivery series .... $2 – 3

9. dark green, "National," 1999 Canada issue .... $15 – 20

Chevrolet Van, 2$^{15}/_{16}$", #68, 1979; #44, 1982; #26, 1991 (similar casting: Chevrolet Van 4x4)

1. red-orange, "Claws," black and white accents, 1997 .... $2 – 3
2. orange, "Matchbox Collectors Club," blue windows, England cast .... $20 – 30
3. orange with blue and red stripes, blue windows, Macau cast, Premiere Collection #13 .... $4 – 5
4. orange with no markings, blue windows, England cast .... $9 – 12
5. orange with wide blue and narrow red stripes, clear windows, England cast .... $35 – 45
6. orange with wide blue and narrow red stripes, blue windows, England cast .... $4 – 5
7. orange with wide blue and narrow white stripes, blue windows, England cast .... $5 – 6
8. orange with wide red and narrow black stripes, blue windows, England cast .... $5 – 6
9. orange with wide red and narrow black stripes, green windows, England cast .... $7 – 9
10. orange with wide red and narrow black stripes, orange windows, England cast .... $5 – 6

1. orange with wide red and narrow black stripes, red windows, England cast.................................$5 – 6
2. dark orange with wide blue and narrow red stripes, blue windows, England cast.................................$16 – 24
3. fluorescent orange and white, "Purolator 10," blue windows, Thailand cast, Team Convoy, White Rose Collectibles..$5 – 6
4. orange-yellow, "DeWalt 08," clear windows, Thailand cast, Team Convoy, White Rose Collectibles............$5 – 6
5. orange-yellow, "Kodak Film 4 Racing," blue windows, Thailand cast, Team Convoy, White Rose Collectibles ......$5 – 6
6. yellow, "Matchbox Collecting," kangaroo illustration, blue windows, Australia issue.................................$12 – 16
7. yellow, "Pennzoil 30," blue windows, Thailand cast, Team Convoy, White Rose Collectibles......................$5 – 6
8. yellow, "Pepsi Challenge," blue windows, Macau cast, Team Matchbox.....$5 – 6
9. yellow, "STP Son Of A Gun," blue windows, Macau cast, Team Matchbox...$60 – 80
10. green, "Chevy," brown stripes, blue windows, England cast ....$9 – 12
11. green, "Chevy," yellow stripes, blue windows, England cast ....$9 – 12
22. pale blue, "Boston Gas," blue windows, Thailand cast, US issue.......$80 – 120
23. blue and fluorescent orange, "43 STP Oil Treatment," blue windows, Thailand cast, Team Convoy, White Rose Collectibles.................................$5 – 6
24. blue and dark orange, "21st National Truckin' VAM," Thailand cast, US issue.................................$9 – 12
25. black, "Automodels 98912244," "Melbourne Motorshow," blue windows, Thailand cast, Australia custom promotional issue.........................$16 – 24
26. black, "Automodels 98912244," "Sydney Motorshow," blue windows, Thailand cast, Australia custom promotional issue.................................$16 – 24
27. black, "Goodwrench 5 Time National Champion Dale Earnhardt," blue windows, Thailand cast, Team Convoy, White Rose Collectibles.............$5 – 6
28. black, "Goodwrench Racing Team Pit Crew," blue windows, Macau cast, Team Convoy, White Rose Collectibles ....$5 – 6
29. black, "Goodwrench Racing Team Pit Crew," blue windows, Thailand cast, Team Convoy, White Rose Collectibles ....$5 – 6
30. black, "Pontiac Excitement 2," blue windows, Thailand cast, Team Convoy, White Rose Collectibles.............$5 – 6
31. black and green, "Mello Yello 42," blue windows, Thailand cast, Team Convoy, White Rose Collectibles.............$5 – 6
32. metallic gray, "Vanpire," blue windows, England cast ....$4 – 5
33. pearl silver, "Vanpire," blue windows, Macau cast..................................$4 – 5

34. white, "25" and green accents, blue windows, Thailand cast, Team Convoy, White Rose Collectibles............$5 – 6
35. white, "Adidas," blue windows, England cast, Germany issue.............$40 – 50
36. white, "American International Recovery" in black lettering, blue windows, Thailand cast, ASAP promotional issue.....................$120 – 160
37. white, "American International Recovery" in blue lettering, blue windows, Thailand cast, ASAP promotional issue.....................$120 – 160
38. white, "Bulldog Castor Co.," blue windows, China cast, ASAP promotional issue.................................$20 – 30
39. white, "Consolidated Engineering," blue windows, Thailand cast, ASAP promotional issue.....................$120 – 160
40. white, "MCI Scholar Award," blue windows, Thailand cast, ASAP promotional issue.............................$120 – 160
41. white, "Huffman," blue windows, China cast, ASAP promotional issue..$30 – 40
42. white, "RCA," blue windows, China cast, ASAP promotional issue........$25 – 35
43. white, "Sears Home Central," blue windows, Thailand cast, ASAP promotional issue.................................$30 – 40
44. white, "Sears May I Reward," blue windows, Thailand cast, ASAP promotional issue.................................$30 – 40
45. white, "USA 1," blue windows, England cast.................................$9 – 12
46. white, no markings, blue windows, Thailand cast, ASAP promotional blank...$30 – 40
47. white and maroon, "Dr. Pepper," blue windows, Macau cast, Team Matchbox.................................$8 – 10
48. white and yellow, "Renault Canon Williams," Thailand cast, Nigel Mansell.........$5 – 6
49. white with purple and lime green graphics, 1996 ....$2 – 3

Chevrolet Van 4x4, 2⁷/₈", #68, 1979; #44, 1982; #26, 1991; #96, 1998; #10, 1993, international (similar casting: Chevrolet Van)

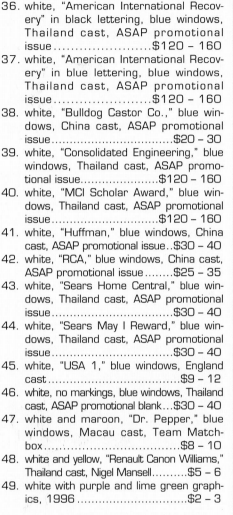

1. **red, "Claws," black and white rip graphics, 1997....................$2 – 3**
2. red, "Coca-Cola," polar bears at pool table, 5-pack ....$2 – 3
3. green and purple, "23rd National Truck-In"..............................$9 – 12
4. metallic green, "Ridin' High," no graphics on hood ....$4 – 5

5. **fluorescent yellow with blue and pink graphics, 1994....................$2 – 3**
6. metallic green, "Ridin' High," black horseshoes, white "4x4" on hood........$4 – 5
7. metallic green, "Ridin' High," white horseshoes, black "4x4" on hood ......$8 – 10
8. metallic emerald green, black horseshoes, white "4x4" on hood ...$16 – 24

9. **metallic blue with white snowflake and cross on sides, 2003 Hero City 5-pack #8 ....$2 – 4**
10. black, "S.W.A.T. Unit 5," gold star, 5-pack.....................................$2 – 3
11. black, "Stegosaurus," skeleton graphics, 5-pack ....$

12. **black with pink and light green graphics, 1993 Off Road 5-pack......$2 – 3**

13. **white, "100 Amazing Flavors," "Ice Cream," purple, orange and lime green graphics, 1999 At Your Service series ....$2 – 3**

14. white, "Castrol Racing Team," Australia issue..................$8 – 10
15. white, "Matchbox Collectors Club 20th Anniversary," ASAP promotional .$12 – 16

16. white, "Matchbox Motorsports," yellow orange and red design, 1993....$2 – 3
17. white, "Matchbox Racing".........$3 – 4
18. white, "Surf's Up," wave design, 5-pack ....$2 – 3
19. white, "Tokyo Giants," "Egawa 30," Japan issue.........................$10 – 12
20. white, "Tokyo Giants," "Hara 8," Japan issue.........................$10 – 12
21. white, "Tokyo Giants," "Matsumoto 2," Japan issue.........................$10 – 12
22. white, "Tokyo Giants," "Nakahata 24," Japan issue.........................$10 – 12
23. white, "Tokyo Giants," "Nishimoto 26," Japan issue.........................$10 – 12
24. white, "Tokyo Giants," "Shinozuka 6," Japan issue.........................$10 – 12
25. white, "Tokyo Giants," "Yamakura 15," Japan issue.........................$10 – 12
26. white, no markings, Graffic Traffic, labels included with set ....$12 – 16

27. white with purple and green graphics, 1996..........................$2 – 3
28. metallic gold, 1997 75 Challenge series...................................$6 – 12

Chevy (see Chevrolet)

Chevy Pro Stocker (see Chevrolet Pro Stocker)

Chevy Van (see Chevrolet Van)

Chevy Van 4x4 (see Chevrolet Van 4x4)

Chop Suey Motorcycle, 2¾", #49, 1973
1. magenta with chrome handlebars ....$400 – 450
2. magenta with orange handlebars ....$16 – 24

3. magenta with red handlebars..$12 – 16
4. magenta with black handlebars.........................$20 – 25
5. magenta with dark red handlebars.........................$12 – 16

Chrysler Atlantic, #11, 1997; #19, 1998, #39, 1999; #34, 2000
1. metallic tan with tan interior, 1997 ..$3 – 4
2. metallic gold with black interior, chrome wheel hubs, 1997 75 Challenge ....$6 – 12
3. metallic gold with black interior, black wheel hubs, 1997 75 Challenge........$30 – 40
4. metallic tan with brown interior, 1998 Cool Concepts series ....$2 – 3
5. metallic tan with light tan interior, 1999 Car Shows series ....$2 – 3
6. metallic tan with brown interior, rubber tires on chrome rims, "Matchbox," "www.Matchboxtoys.com" ....$9 – 12
7. metallic tan with brown and tan interior, rubber tires on chrome rims, Chrysler gift set ....$4 – 6
8. metallic tan with tan interior, "Merry Christmas 1997 Seasons Greetings from Color Comp," Color Comp promotional...........................$100 – 150

Chrysler Panel Cruiser, #30, 2002

1. metallic gold with wood panel, 2002 Cool Rides series ....$2 – 3
2. white, "Richie's Burgerama," 2003 Mom and Pop Shops series.......$2 – 3
3. white, "Richie's Burgerama," 2003 Hero City 10-pack #2 ....$2 – 3

Chrysler PT Cruiser Convertible, #72, 2003

1. red, 2003 Car Shop series ....$2 – 3

Chrysler Voyager, #262, 1994, Belgium, modified casting of #64/#68 Dodge Caravan
1. blue with detailed trim..........$16 – 24
2. blue with detailed trim, "Kipling" label on roof ....$16 – 20

Citroen 15CV (European model), 3", #44, 1983
1. dark green with chrome base, China cast, 1983 Dinky Collection from Matchbox ....$9 – 12

2. dark blue with chrome base, Macau cast ....$3 – 4
3. black with chrome base, England cast..............................$3 – 4
4. black with chrome base, Macau cast.................................$3 – 4
5. black with gray base, China cast .$5 – 7

Citroen CX Ambulance (European model), 3", #12, 1980 (similar casting: Citroen CX Station Wagon)
1. white with red interior, metallic gray base, blue windows, "Ambulance," England cast ....$3 – 5
2. white with red interior, black base, blue windows, "Ambulance," England cast.....................................$3 – 5
3. white with red interior, unpainted base, blue windows, "Ambulance," England cast.....................................$3 – 5
4. white with red interior, metallic gray base, blue windows, "Marine Division Police," Two Pack, England cast..$3 – 5
5. white with red interior, unpainted base, blue windows, "Marine Division Police," Two Pack, England cast ....$3 – 5
6. white with red interior, pearly silver base, blue windows, "Marine Division Police," Two Pack, Macau cast...$5 – 7

Citroen CX Station Wagon, 3", #12, 1979 (similar casting: Citroen CX Ambulance)
1. metallic light blue with ivory interior, metallic gray base, blue windows ......$12 – 16
2. metallic light blue with ivory interior, metallic gray base, clear windows.........$6 – 9
3. metallic light blue with yellow interior, metallic gray base, clear windows ..$6 – 9
4. metallic light blue with tan interior, unpainted base, clear windows...$6 – 9
5. metallic light blue with tan interior, black base, clear windows ....$6 – 9
6. metallic light blue with tan interior, dark gray base, clear windows ....$6 – 9
7. metallic light blue with tan interior, metallic gray base, clear windows ....$6 – 9
8. metallic dark blue with ivory interior, metallic gray base, clear windows.........$6 – 9
9. metallic dark blue with yellow interior, metallic gray base, clear windows ..$6 – 9
10. metallic dark blue with yellow interior, metallic gray base, blue windows...$6 – 9

11. metallic dark blue with red interior, metallic gray base, clear windows.....$200 – 275
12. yellow with red interior, black base, clear windows........................$6 – 9
13. yellow with red interior, dark gray base, clear windows........................$6 – 9
14. yellow with red interior, black base, clear windows, "Team" in blue, Two Pack ....$5 – 7
15. yellow with red interior, black base, clear windows, "Team" in black, Two Pack ....$5 – 7
16. yellow with red interior, dark gray base, clear windows, "Team" in blue ....$5 – 7
17. yellow with red interior, black base, blue windows, "Team" in black, Two Pack ....$5 – 7
18. yellow with red interior, black base, blue windows, no markings, Two Pack ..$6 – 9
19. yellow with red interior, metallic gray base, clear windows, no markings, Two Pack ....$6 – 9

Citroen DS19, yellow, 2½", #66, 1959
1. gray plastic wheels...............$50 – 60
2. silver plastic wheels.........$120 – 130

Citroen SM, 3", #51, 1972
1. metallic orange with orange interior ....$25 – 35
2. metallic orange with ivory interior ....$10 – 12
3. metallic orange with yellow interior ....$10 – 12
4. metallic orange with tan interior ....$10 – 12
5. metallic blue, no markings.....$16 – 24
6. metallic blue, "8"..................$10 – 12
7. metallic blue with roof rack....$60 – 80

Claas Combine Harvester, 3", #65, 1967

1. **red with black plastic wheels .$6 – 9**

Clipper, fantasy car with opening cockpit, 3", #39, 1973
1. hot pink, yellow interior, amber windows, unpainted base, chrome tailpipes ....$200 – 300
2. metallic magenta, yellow interior, amber windows, green base, chrome tailpipes..........................$12 – 16
3. metallic magenta, yellow interior, amber windows, green base, white tailpipes..........................$12 – 16
4. metallic magenta, yellow interior, amber windows, unpainted base, chrome tailpipes..........................$12 – 16

5. metallic magenta, yellow interior, amber windows, unpainted base, white tailpipes..........................$12 – 16
6. metallic magenta, yellow interior, clear windows, green base, chrome tailpipes..........................$12 – 16
7. metallic magenta, yellow interior, clear windows, green base, white tailpipes..........................$12 – 16

Combine Harvester (see Claas Combine Harvester)

Combine Harvester, 2¾", #51, 1978; #89, 1999; #47, 2000; #3, 2000, Germany
1. red with yellow rotor and chute ..$5 – 6
2. orange with yellow rotor and chute, no-origin cast, Brazil issue.....$400 – 600
3. orange-yellow with red rotor and chute, "2" and stripes, Motor City........$2 – 3
4. orange-yellow with maroon rotor and chute, "2" and stripes, Motor City..$2 – 3

5. **yellow with red rotor and chute, "2" with stripes, Motor City........$2 – 3**
6. lime green and blue with yellow rotor, lime green chute, Matchbox Preschool/ Live 'N Learn series..................$7 – 9
7. green with yellow rotor and chute, Germany issue.............................$4 – 5

8. **dark green with yellow rotor and chute, no-origin cast, Brazil issue .$400 – 600**
9. dark green with yellow rotor and chute, China cast, 2000 Farming series ..$2 – 3
10. dark green with yellow rotor and chute, "Matchbox 2000," China cast, 2000 Farming series ....$3 – 4

11. **dark blue with yellow rotor and chute, 1999 On The Farm series ....$2 – 3**

Command Vehicle, 3¼", #54, 1984, radar, beacons and lights on forward part of roof (similar castings: Airport Foam Pumper, Mobile Home, NASA Tracking Vehicle)

1. **army green, "9," red and white diagonal stripes, black wheels, Commando Strike Team ....$4 – 5**
2. army green, "9," red and white diagonal stripes, chrome wheels, Commando Strike Team ....$20 – 25

3. **black, "LS150," yellow design, black wheels, Commando Dagger Force .$4 – 5**

4. **black, khaki and green camoflage, Commando Dagger Force.................$4 – 5**

5. **blue, white lettering, "Police," "Command Center," white stripes ......$4 – 5**
6. white, "NASA Space Shuttle Command Center," Thailand cast ....$2 – 3

Commer 30 CWT "Nestle's" Van, gray plastic wheels, 2⅜", #69, 1959

1. maroon ....$30 – 40
2. dark red ....$30 – 40
3. red ....$60 – 70

Commer Ice Cream Canteen, 2⁷/₁₆", #47, 1963
1. blue with gray plastic wheels .$150 – 175

2. blue with black plastic wheels .$30 – 35
3. metallic blue with black plastic wheels............................$100 – 120
4. ivory with square roof decal, striped side decals, black wheels ......$60 – 70
5. ivory with oval roof decal, plain side decals, black plastic wheels ...$40 – 50

Commer Milk Delivery Truck, 2¼", #21, 1961

1. silver wheels ....$25 – 35
2. gray wheels.........................$65 – 75
3. black wheels.....................$15 – 25

Commer Pickup, 2½", #50, 1958
1. dark tan with metal wheels ....$40 – 50
2. light tan with metal wheels ....$40 – 50
3. light tan with gray plastic wheels ....$40 – 50
4. dark tan with gray plastic wheels ....$40 – 50
5. dark tan with silver plastic wheels ....$80 – 100
6. red and white with silver plastic wheels ....$275 – 300
7. red and gray with silver plastic wheels ....$80 – 100
8. red and gray with gray plastic wheels ....$60 – 80

9. red and gray with black plastic wheels...............................$60 – 80

Compressor Truck (see Bedford Compressor Truck, Thames Trader Compressor Truck)

Corvette (see Chevrolet Corvette)

Cosmic Blues, 3", #26, 1980; #41, 1993 (similar castings: Big Banger, Flame Out, Pi-Eyed Piper, Red Rider)
1. white with blue "Cosmic Blues," clear windows, Hong Kong cast .....$40 – 50
2. white with chrome exhausts, blue "Cosmic Blues," blue windows, Hong Kong cast......................................$4 – 5
3. white with chrome exhausts, blue "Cosmic Blues," blue windows, Macau cast......................................$2 – 3
4. white with chrome exhausts, blue "Cosmic Blues," blue windows, China cast......................................$2 – 3
5. blue with chrome exhausts, white "Cosmic Blues," blue windows, China cast......................................$2 – 3
6. blue with black exhausts, white "Cosmic Blues," blue windows, China cast ....$2 – 3

7. bright orange-yellow with black exhausts, "Hemi," magenta and black design, 1993..............$2 – 3

8. black with gray exhausts, fluorescent orange and white flames, 1996 .$2 – 3

9. metallic green with orange and white flames, 1997 ....$2 – 3
10. orange-red with gray exhausts, "Dandelion," "Dyslexicon" ....$9 – 12

11. metallic gold with black exhausts, 199 75 Challenge series ....$6 – 1₂

Cosmobile, 2⁷/₈", #68, 1975
1. metallic red upper, beige lower, chrom interior, amber windows........$16 – 2₄
2. metallic red upper, beige lower, whit interior, amber windows........$16 – 2₄
3. metallic avocado upper, black lower chrome interior, purple windows, Adver ture 2000 ....$30 – 4₀
4. metallic avocado upper, black lower white interior, purple windows, Adver ture 2000 ....$30 – 4₀
5. metallic avocado upper, black lower chrome interior, amber windows Adventure 2000 ....$30 – 4₀
6. metallic blue upper, black lower chrome interior, purple windows, Adver ture 2000 ....$50 – 6₀
7. metallic blue upper, yellow lower, chrom interior, amber windows........$12 – 1₆
8. metallic blue upper, yellow lower, whit interior, amber windows.......$12 – 1₆

Crane, #72, 2001; #24, 2003 (see Res cue Crane)

Crane Truck, 2¹⁵/₁₆", #49, 1976
1. red with yellow boom, green windows Germany issue.....................$70 – 8₀
2. yellow with yellow boom, green win dows ....$5 – 6
3. yellow with black boom, blu windows ....$9 – 1₂
4. yellow with black boom, green win dows ....$5 – 6
5. yellow with black boom, purple win dows ....$5 – 6
6. yellow with black boom, red win dows ....$5 – 6

Crown Victoria (see Ford Crown Victoria)

D

D.I.R.T. Modified Racer, #217, 1992 White Rose Collectibles
1. "35," blue ....$7 – 9
2. "Alfair Studio 21"; red, white, and black..................................$7 – 9
3. "Auto Palace 72," red..............$6 – 8
4. "BR Dewitt 12," orange and yellow.$7 – 9
5. "Doherty Bros. 115," white and black ....$7 – 9
6. "Freightliner 6," white ....$6 – 8
7. "Kinney 9," orange and white .....$6 – 8
8. "Phil's Chevrolet 1," brown.........$6 – 8
9. "Pontiac — Kneisel Race Cars 44," white and orange ....$7 – 9
10. "R.P. LeFrois 14," white............$7 – 9
11. "Smith Brothers 74," dark blue and white..................................$7 – 9
12. "Steak Out Restaurants 1," white .$7 – 9
13. "Turbo Blue 7X," light orange.....$6 – 8
14. "Wheels 91," light orange ....$6 – 8
15. "White Rose Collectibles 1," light blue ....$70 – 90

-Type Jaguar (see Jaguar D-Type)

AF 3300 Space Cab, #15, 1999
orange, "DAF 3300 SC56"........$3 – 4

AF Girder Truck, 2⅝", #58, 1968

• **cream with 8 red girders in back,
black plastic wheels, 1968..$12 – 16**
cream with 8 red girders in back,
Superfast wheels, 1970 ....$70 – 90
metallic gold with 8 red girders in back,
Superfast wheels, 1970 ....$24 – 32

AF Tipper Container Truck, 3", #47,
1968
blue with yellow container, gray
container cover, black plastic
wheels ....$25 – 30
metallic silver with yellow container,
gray container cover, black plastic
wheels................................$6 – 9
metallic silver with yellow container,
gray container cover, Superfast wheels,
1970.................................$30 – 40

Daimler Ambulance, 1⅞", #14
1956 ....$50 – 65

Daimler Ambulance, 2⅛", #14, 1958
metal wheels.......................$35 – 45
gray plastic wheels ....$30 – 40
silver plastic wheels.........$100 – 125

Daimler London Bus, 3", #74, 1966
"Baron of Beef," red, Superfast
wheels ....$200 – 250
"Beefeater Gin," red, Superfast
wheels ....$400 – 500
"Esso Extra Petrol," red, black plastic
wheels..............................$15 – 20
"Esso Extra Petrol," red, Superfast
wheels, ...$20 – 30
"Esso Extra Petrol," green, black plastic
wheels..............................$15 – 20

• **"Esso Extra Petrol" decals, cream,
black plastic wheels ....$20 – 30**
• **"Esso Extra Petrol" labels, cream,
black plastic wheels ....$16 – 24**

8. "Fly Cyprus Airways," "London Frank-
furt Athens Nicosia," red, Superfast
wheels ....$350 – 450
9. "Inn On The Park," red, Superfast
wheels...........................$250 – 300
10. "The Miniature Vehicle," "N.A.M.C.,"
red, Superfast wheels.......$250 – 300

Datsun 126X, 3", #33, 1973; BR5-6, 1985
1. yellow with orange base, no
markings.....................$12 – 16
2. yellow with unpainted base, no
markings..........................$30 – 45
3. yellow with orange base, orange and
red flames ....$16 – 24
4. yellow with orange base, black and red
flames...............................$16 – 24
5. dark blue with black windows, England
cast, Super GT BR5-6, 1985 ....$4 – 6
6. silver with black windows, England cast,
Super GT BR5-6, 1985 ....$4 – 6
7. silver with black windows, China cast,
Super GT BR5-6, 1985 ....$8 – 10
8. powder blue with black windows, China
cast, Super GT BR5-6, 1985 ....$3 – 5
9. beige with black windows, China cast,
Super GT BR5-6, 1985 ....$3 – 5

Datsun 260Z 2+2, #67, 1978
1. metallic burgundy, doors open, Lesney
England cast ....$4 – 5
2. metallic purple, doors open, Lesney
England cast ....$9 – 12
3. metallic magenta, doors open, Lesney
England cast ....$6 – 8
4. metallic blue, doors open, Lesney England cast ....$7 – 9
5. black, doors cast shut, black interior,
clear windows, Matchbox International
England cast ....$5 – 6
6. black, doors cast shut, black interior,
opaque windows, Matchbox International
England cast.........................$9 – 12
7. black, doors cast shut, white interior,
clear windows, Matchbox International
England cast ....$3 – 4
8. black, doors cast shut, white interior,
opaque windows, Matchbox International
England cast.........................$9 – 12
9. metallic gray, doors open, red interior,
Lesney England cast ....$3 – 4
10. metallic gray, doors open, light yellow
interior, Lesney England cast .....$7 – 9
11. metallic gray, doors cast shut, red interior, black base, clear windows, China
cast ....$9 – 12
12. metallic gray, doors cast shut, black
interior, black base, clear windows,
China cast ....$12 – 16

13. metallic gray, doors cast shut, black interior, black base, clear windows, Matchbox International England cast .....$6 – 8
14. metallic gray, doors cast shut, black
interior, metallic gray base, clear windows, Matchbox International England
cast ....$4 – 5
15. metallic gray, doors cast shut, black
interior, opaque windows, Matchbox
International England cast ....$9 – 12
16. metallic gray with green and blue
accents, doors cast shut, black interior,
China cast, Chinese issue..$150 – 200
17. metallic gray with red and black
accents, doors open, white interior,
Lesney England cast.................$3 – 4
18. metallic gray with two-tone blue
accents, doors cast shut, black interior,
black base, Matchbox International England cast ....$3 – 4
19. metallic gray with two-tone blue
accents, doors cast shut, black interior,
metallic gray base, Matchbox International England cast ....$5 – 6

Datsun 280ZX, hood doesn't open, 3",
#24, 1981
1. black with white interior ....$3 – 4
2. black with red interior ....$4 – 5

Datsun 280ZX 2+2, hood opens, 3", #24,
1983

1. **black with gold pin stripes .....$3 – 4**

2. **black, "Turbo ZX," silver wheels .$3 – 4**
3. black, "Turbo ZX," gold wheels .$9 – 12
4. white, "Turbo 33," Japan issue .$9 – 12

5. **black with orange, yellow and
white "Turbo," new Superfast
wheels ....$4 – 5**

DATSUN 280ZX 2+2

6. gray with orange, yellow and white accents, Laser Wheels ....$7 – 8
7. red with black and orange, armaments, Roadblasters ....$7 – 9
8. metallic red, China issue ....$60 – 80

Datsun 280ZX Police Car, #44, 1987, Japan
1. white and black, Japanese pictograms, red dome lights, tan interior, Macau cast..................................$9 – 12

Datsun Fairlady Z, #78, 1981; #5, 1981, Japan
1. red, Japan cast, Japan issue ..$16 – 24
2. black, "Z," Hong Kong cast, issued in US as Phantom Z ....$6 – 8
3. black, no markings, Australia issue and US Speedsticks issue................$3 – 4
4. pearl white, no markings, Australia issue.................................$16 – 24
5. pearl silver, Japan cast, Japan issue ....$16 – 24

Deep Diver (see Submersible)

Delivery Truck, #48, 2000; #28, 2000, international (similar casting: Flatbed Truck)
1. red with white container, barn and rooster labels ....$2 – 3
2. red with white container, barn and rooster, "Matchbox 2000" ....$3 – 4

3. **metallic orange with gray container, "Test Mission," 2000 Space Mission 5-pack ....$2 – 3**
4. dark orange with bright blue container, "MC 09" and rhinoceros head, Matchbox City 5-pack ..$2 – 3

5. **fluorescent yellow, black box, orange rhino, 2003 Hero City 5-pack ..$2 – 3**

Demolition Machine, #38, 2001; #25, 2003
1. **white with blue claw, The Wall Eater, 2001 Earth Crunchers series ....$2 – 3**

2. **metallic blue with orange claw, 2003 Bridge Crew series...............$2 – 3**

3. **orange with blue claw, 2003 Hero City 5-pack #9.....................$2 – 3**

Dennis Fire Escape, 2¼", #9, 1955
1. no front bumper, no-number cast...................................$45 – 60

Dennis Fire Escape, with front bumper, number 9 cast, 2³⁄₈", #9, 1957
1. metal wheels.......................$50 – 60
2. gray plastic wheels...........$125 – 150

Dennis Fire Escape, 1988, commemorative replica of #9, 2¼"
1. made in China, red reels, 40th Anniversary Gift Set, 1988 ....$8 – 10
2. yellow reels, 1991 Matchbox Originals................................$2 – 4

Dennis Refuse Truck, dark blue with gray container, 2½", #15, 1963
1. no porthole in rear hatch ......$45 – 50
2. porthole in rear hatch..........$15 – 20

Dennis Sabre Fire Truck, #30, 2001; #44, 2002; #61, 2003; #68, 1999, international
1. red, "35 – 3," white dashes.......$3 – 4

2. red, "44," white and silver accents 2002 Airport Alarm series ......$2 –

3. **red, "4589," "54," "Matchbox" i circle, white stripes and panels 2000 5 Alarm 5-pack...........$2 –**

4. **red, "911 Emergency," yellow an white stripes, silver panels shield.................................$4 – **
5. red, "London Fire Brigade," silve panels ....$3 –
6. red, "Matchbox"; white, blue, an yellow graphics; 2003 Pumpe Squad series.........................$2 –
7. red, "Metro Alarm," "WR – 1168," ye low bands, 5-pack ....$2 –
8. red with yellow and silver panels, 199 Fire Rescue international series...$3 –

9. **yellow with red, maroon, silver, an white; red windows, metallic gra plastic base, 2003 Hero City 5-pac #1.....................................$2 – **

10. **black, "Oregon 33," "Mount Hoo Fire Rescue," volcano and mountai graphics, Matchbox Across Americ 50th Birthday Series #33 — West ern Collection ....$4 – **

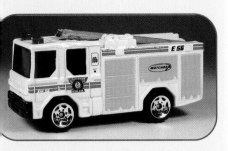

1. white, "Universe Action Base," red stripes, yellow panels, shield, 2001 Flame Eaters series ....$2 – 3

Desert Dawg 4x4 Jeep, 2⁵⁄₈", #20, 1982; #14, 1987
1. white with red roof, "Desert Dawg," England cast ....$2 – 4

DeTomaso Pantera, 3", #8, 1975; BR 39 – 40, 1986 (similar castings: Greased Lightning)
1. white with blue base, "8" label on hood ....$8 – 12
2. white with unpainted base, "8" label on hood ....$8 – 12
3. white with blue base, "9" label on hood ....$15 – 20
4. white with blue base, sunburst label on hood ....$20 – 25
5. white with lavender base, "8" label on hood, Brazil issue................$60 – 80
6. blue with black base ....$4 – 6
7. maroon, China cast, Super GTs BR 39 – 40, 1986 ....$3 – 5
8. orange, China cast, Super GTs BR 39 – 40, 1986 ....$3 – 5
9. fluorescent yellow, China cast, Neon Racers BR 39 – 40, 1986........$4 – 6

DeTomaso Pantera Greased Lightning, 3", #8, 1983
1. red with white base, black interior, Macau cast...........................$6 – 9
2. red with white base, black interior, Hong Kong cast......................$6 – 9

Diesel Road Roller (see Aveling Barford Diesel Road Roller)

Diesel Shunter Locomotive, 3", #24, 1978
1. dark green with red metal undercarriage, red base, "Rail Freight" ....$9 – 12
2. dark green with red metal undercarriage, red base, "D1496-RF"..............$9 – 12
3. yellow with red metal undercarriage, red base, "D1496-RF," England cast..$5 – 6
4. yellow with red metal undercarriage, red base, "D1496-RF," no-origin cast................................$80 – 120
5. yellow with yellow plastic undercarriage, black base, "D1496-RF," England cast................$80 – 120
6. yellow with red plastic undercarriage, black base, "D1496-RF," Macau cast, Motor City..........................$3 – 4

Dirt Bike, #93, 1999; #13, 2000; #33, 2001; #73, 1999, international
1. red with black seat, blue – gray rider with brown jacket, 1999 Mountain Cruisers series ....$2 – 3

2. red with black seat, yellow rider with red jacket, 2000 To The Beach series.......................$2 – 3
3. red with black seat, red rider with black jacket, "Matchbox 2000," 2000 To The Beach series ....$3 – 4
4. red with black seat, red rider with black jacket, 2000 To The Beach series ....$2 – 3
5. orange with purple seat, white rider with red jacket, 2001 Sand Blasters series....................................$2 – 3

6. yellow with blue seat, red rider with black jacket, Wilderness Tour 5-pack..................................$2 – 3
7. yellow, blue rider with orange jacket, 5-pack.....................................$2 – 3

Dirt Machine, #37, 2001; #19, 2002; #67 2003 (see Super Dozer)

Dirt Modified Racer (see D.I.R.T. Modified Racer)

Dodge Airflow Van 1938, #338, 1998, Matchbox Collectibles
1. "Catamount Porter," mustard yellow with black roof......................$9 – 12
2. "Continental Aero," "Purple Plastic Inserts...," purple..................$9 – 12
3. "Penn Brewery St. Nikolaus Bock Bier," red ....$9 – 12
4. "Zephyr Golden Ale," yellow......$9 – 12

Dodge Caravan, 2⁷⁄₈", #68, 1984; #64, 1985, international
1. red, "Red Arrows," "Royal Air Force," red door, Thailand cast, Motor City....$4 – 5

2. burgundy, "Expressly for Dodge Las Vegas," England cast..........$90 – 120
3. burgundy with black stripe, England cast, US issue....................$18 – 24
4. black, "Adidas" on hood, silver stripe, black door, England cast, US issue..........................$275 – 325
5. black with green and yellow stripes, black door, Macau cast, the Netherlands issue..........................$9 – 12
6. black with no stripe, England cast ..$4 – 6
7. black with silver side stripe, black door, England cast ....$4 – 5
8. black with silver side stripe, black door, Macau cast..........................$3 – 4
9. black with silver and gold stripes, black door, Macau cast ....$3 – 4
10. black with silver and gold stripes, black door, China cast ....$4 – 5
11. black with silver and gold stripes, black door, Manaus cast, Brazil issue..........................$40 – 50
12. gray and blue, "British Airways," gray door, barcode base, Thailand cast, Intercom City......................$40 – 50
13. gray and blue, "British Airways," gray door, Thailand cast, Motor City................................$4 – 5
14. metallic gray with black stripe, gray door, England cast ....$7 – 9
15. metallic gray with no stripe, black door, England cast ....$6 – 8
16. white, "Caravan" and stripe, white door, Macau cast..........................$3 – 4
17. white, "Fly Virgin Atlantic," white door, Macau cast, gift set ....$4 – 5
18. white, "NASA Shuttle Personnel," white door, Macau cast..........................$4 – 5
19. white, "Pan Am," white door, Macau cast, gift set..........................$4 – 5

Dodge Cattle Truck (also see Dodge Stake Truck)

Dodge Cattle Truck, with cattle and ramp tailgate, 2¹⁄₂", #37, 1966
1. yellow with gray cattle compartment, metal base, black plastic wheels..............................$12 – 16
2. yellow with gray cattle compartment, plastic base, black plastic wheels ....$20 – 25
3. yellow with brown cattle compartment, metal base.....................$120 – 160
4. yellow with gray cattle compartment, Superfast wheels, 1970.....$30 – 40
5. yellow with metallic gray cattle compartment, Superfast wheels, 1970 ....$30 – 40

Dodge Challenger, with hood grilles, no scoop, 2¹⁵⁄₁₆", #1, 1976 (similar casting: Revin' Rebel, Dodge Challenger Hot Rod)
1. red with chrome interior, dot-dash wheels................................$8 – 10
2. red with white interior, 5-arc wheels ....$4 – 6

3. red with red interior ....$9 – 12

4. **blue with red interior............$5 – 8**

Dodge Challenger, Revin' Rebel, cast hood scoop, 2⁷/₈", #1, US, 1982; #34, international, 1991

1. **orange with blue roof, "Revin' Rebel".......................$5 – 8**
2. orange with blue roof, no markings ....$10 – 15

3. **orange with white roof, "Revin' Rebel"..................$8 – 12**

Dodge Challenger Hot Rod, plastic hood scoop 2⁷/₈", #1, 1983

1. **yellow with black roof, "Toyman," England cast ....$3 – 5**
2. yellow with black roof, "Toyman," Macao cast....................................$2 – 4

---

3. yellow with black roof, "Toyman," China cast....................$2 – 4
4. yellow with black roof, no markings, China cast ....$3 – 5

5. **white with white roof, no markings, (Graffic Traffic)....................$5 – 7**

6. **light blue with black roof, "Challenger," (Action Pack with accessories)................................$4 – 6**
7. white with black roof, "Toyman," China cast....................................$4 – 6

8. **metallic blue with white roof, "Hemi," "Challenger," 1993 ...$2 – 4**

9. **fluorescent yellow with black spatter accents, black roof, hot pink interior, 1994.............................$2 – 3**

10. **white with purple spatter accents, black roof, fuchsia interior, 1996.........................$2 – 3**

11. **dark purple with black roof, gra plastic base, Thailand cast.....$2 – 4**
12. dark purple with black roof, chrom plastic base, China cast ....$4 – 6
13. dark purple with black roof, gray plasti base, China cast..................$45 – 60
14. red with black roof, chrome wheels rubber tires (Premiere Collection #11) ....$5 – 8

15. **green, black roof, 1996 Hot Rods pack ....$2 – 3**

Dodge Challenger/Mitsubishi Galan Eterna, 2⁷/₈", #63, 1980; #79, 1981 #J-22, 1979, Japan

1. two-tone green with white "2," whit interior, Japan cast.............$16 – 24
2. green with black "2," green interior Japan cast.........................$16 – 24
3. light green, "Hot Points," Hong Kong cast iUS issue as Hot Points Challenger .$6 – 8
4. light green, Hong Kong cast, Australi issue and US Speedsticks issue..$3 – 4
5. dark green, Hong Kong cast, Australi issue and US Speedsticks issue..$3 – 4

Dodge Charger (see Orange Peel Dodg Charger)

Dodge Charger Mk III concept car, 2⁷/₈ #52, 1970

1. metallic red with metallic green base.................................$12 – 16
2. metallic magenta with metallic gree base ....$12 – 16
3. metallic light green with red base, "5 on roof, side labels...............$16 – 24
4. metallic light green with red base, "Cas trol" label ....$600 – 800
5. metallic light green with red base, n label..............................$12 – 16
6. metallic light green with unpainted base no label ....$12 – 16
7. purple with green base ....$16 – 24

Dodge "Copperhead" Concept, #40, 1999

metallic copper, rubber tires on chrome rims, 1999 First Editions.........$5 – 6

metallic copper, 1999 Car Shows series.....................$2 – 3

unpainted, rubber tires on chrome rims, 1999 First Editions ....$5 – 6

Dodge Crane Truck, 2³/₄", #63, 1968

yellow with green windows, red hook, black plastic wheels, 1968....$12 – 16

yellow with green windows, yellow hook, black plastic wheels, 1968 ...$12 – 16

yellow with green windows, Superfast wheels, 1970......................$30 – 40

Dodge Dakota Pickup, 3", #50, 1989; #17, 1990

bright red with black and white stripes, chrome roll bar.........$4 – 6

bright red, "Dakota ST," black and white stripes, chrome roll bar ....$2 – 3

dark red, "Dakota ST," black and white stripes, black roll bar................$2 – 3

metallic green with "MB Construction," black roll bar, Action Pack.........$4 – 6

white with no markings, white roll bar, Graffic Traffic ....$12 – 16

blue with "Dakota ST" and stripes, black roll bar, gift set......................$9 – 12

fluorescent orange, "Fire Chief 1," "Intercom City," white roll bar.........$12 – 16

purple with yellow and pink on sides, chrome roll bar, 1997 Rugged Riders 5-pack.............................$2 – 3

olive with white bands, black roll bar, China multipack ....$24 – 36

10. **yellow, "Highway Crew," "Crew Chief," black roll bar, 1999 Highway Crew 5-pack ....$2 – 3**

11. black and gray with logo on door and gray and beige spots, Salvage Yard 5-pack.....................................$2 – 3

12. **black and gray, "Hershey 99" in silver print, black roll bar, 1999 Color Comp promotional..............$9 – 12**

13. black and gray, "Hershey 99" in gold print, black roll bar, 1999 Color Comp promotional..........................$9 – 12

14. **metallic blue with gray plastic base, red interior and roll bar, monkey and wrench, 2003 Hero City 5-pack #11...$2 – 3**

15. **Spongebob Squarepants 5-pack, 2003....................................$2 – 3**

Dodge Daytona 1984 Turbo Z, 2⁷/₈", #28, 1984

1. red with yellow and blue "Turbo Z," silver wheels ....$2 – 3

2. **red with yellow and blue "Turbo Z," Superfast wheels..................$6 – 7**

3. metallic burgundy with metallic gray lower body, "Expressly For Dodge Las Vegas," England cast..........$90 – 120

4. **metallic burgundy with metallic gray lower body, England cast.......$4 – 5**

5. metallic burgundy with metallic gray lower body, Macau cast........$60 – 80

6. metallic burgundy with gold lower body, plastic armament, Roadblasters.$7 – 8

7. dark blue with black lower body, "5 Goat Racing Team," Hong Kong issue ....$10 – 12

8. white with blue lower body, red and blue stripes, new Superfast wheels ...$4 – 5

9. white with blue lower body, red and blue stripes, Laser Wheels ....$4 – 5

10. **metallic silver with black lower body, red and black stripes, Macau cast ....$3 – 4**

Dodge Delivery Truck, 2³/₄", #72, 1982

1. "Big Top Circus," red with white container, Thailand cast........$4 – 5

2. "British Airways Cargo," light gray and dark blue, Thailand cast, Motor City ....$4 – 5

3. "C Plus Orange," dark green with orange container, Macau cast, Canada issue..................................$12 – 16

4. "H & B," "Harris & Bailey Ltd.," red with red container, Thailand cast, UK issue..................................$12 – 16

5. "Hertz," orange-yellow with orange-yellow container, Macau cast ....$3 – 4

6. "Hertz," yellow with yellow container, Macau cast............................$3 – 4

7. "Jetspress Road Express," white with white container, Macau cast, Australia issue......................................$7 – 9

8. "Kellogg's" labels, red with white container, gold wheels, England cast ....$5 – 6

9. "Kellogg's" labels, red with white container, silver wheels, England cast..........$5 – 6

10. "Kellogg's" labels, red with white container, silver wheels, Macau cast............$5 – 6

11. "Kellogg's," "Milch-Laite-Latte," red with white container, Macau cast, Germany/Switzerland issue ....$40 – 50

12. "Kit Kat," red with red container, Macau cast, UK on-package premium .$8 – 10

13. "Matchbox USA Sheraton Inn 1989," red with white container, Macau cast, US issue..............................$9 – 12

14. "MD," white with white container, Thailand cast, UK issue ....$12 – 16

15. "Minties," green with white container, Macau cast, Australia issue.......$7 – 9
16. "Mitre 10," blue with blue container, Macau cast, Australia issue.......$7 – 9
17. "Nestles Chokito," red with red container, Macau cast, Australia issue........$7 – 9
18. "Pepsi" labels, red with white container, gold wheels, England cast ....$5 – 6
19. "Pepsi" labels, red with white container, silver wheels, England cast........$5 – 6
20. "Pirelli Gripping Stuff," white with white container, Macau cast, Team Convoy ....$4 – 5
21. "Risi," orange-yellow with yellow container, Macau cast, Spain issue ....$20 – 30
22. "Royal Mail Parcels," red with red container, Macau cast, UK issue.....$6 – 8
23. "Smith's" labels, red with white container, gold wheels, England cast, UK on-package premium ....$5 – 6
24. "Smith's" labels, red with white container, silver wheels, England cast, UK on-package premium ....$5 – 6
25. "St. Ivel Gold," blue with blue container, Thailand cast, UK on-package premium ....$12 – 16
26. "Stena Line Freight," blue with blue container, Thailand cast, UK issue .$12 – 16
27. "Street's Ice Cream," white with white container, Macau cast, Australia issue ....$7 – 9
28. "Wigwam," white with white container, Thailand cast, Convoy series, the Netherlands issue ....$8 – 10
29. "XP Express Parcels Systems," white with white container, Macau cast, Team Convoy ....$4 – 5
30. "XP Express Parcels Systems," white with white container, Thailand cast, Team Convoy..........................$4 – 5
31. "Yorkie," blue with blue container, Macau cast, UK on-package premium ..$8 – 10

Dodge Dragster, 3", #70, 1971 (similar casting: Orange Peel Dodge Charger)
1. pink, "Castrol" label, black base ....$800 – 1,000
2. pink, "Rat Rod" label, black base ....$30 – 40
3. pink, "Wildcat" label, black base ....$30 – 40
4. pink, snake label, black base ..$16 – 24
5. pink, snake label, unpainted base ....$16 – 24
6. pink, snake label, dark gray base ....$16 – 24
7. pink, snake label, green base..$16 – 24
8. pink, snake label, lavender base ....$16 – 24
9. pink, snake label, tan base ....$16 – 24
10. pink, snake label, yellow base ..$16 – 24
11. pink, star flame label, black base ....$250 – 300

Dodge Dump Truck, 3," #48, 1966
1. red, black plastic wheels, 1966 ..$7 – 9
2. blue cab, yellow dumper, Superfast wheels, 1970......................$30 – 40

3. metallic blue cab, yellow dumper, Superfast wheels, 1970 ....$30 – 40

Dodge Ram SRT-10, #66, 2003
1. black with red windows, red "Dodge" and Dodge Ram logo, 2003 Heavy Movers series ....$2 – 3

Dodge Stake Truck, 2⁷/₈", #4, 1967; reissued as Cattle Truck #71, 1976 – 1991; #12, 1992 – 1997; reissued as Beef Hauler #88, 1999 and #50, 2000; #30, 2000, international, England cast except where noted
1. red with cream stake bed, two black steers, blue windows, #71 Cattle Truck...................................$4 – 5
2. red with cream stake bed, two brown steers, blue windows, #71 Cattle Truck...................................$4 – 5
3. red with beige stake bed, two black steers, purple windows, #71 Cattle Truck...................................$4 – 5
4. red with beige stake bed, two black steers, red windows, #71 Cattle Truck...................................$4 – 5
5. red with yellow stake bed, no steers, red windows, blue wheels with yellow hubs, Matchbox Preschool/Live 'N Learn....................................$7 – 9
6. metallic orange with orange-yellow stake bed, two black steers, blue windows, #71 Cattle Truck ....$4 – 5
7. metallic orange with orange-yellow stake bed, two black steers, light green windows, #71 Cattle Truck ....$4 – 5
8. metallic orange with orange-yellow stake bed, two black steers, orange windows, #71 Cattle Truck ....$4 – 5
9. metallic orange with orange-yellow stake bed, two black steers, purple windows, #71 Cattle Truck ....$4 – 5
10. orange-yellow with green stake bed, Superfast wheels, no livestock, #4, 1970.................................$20 – 30
11. yellow with blue-green stake bed, regular wheels, no livestock, #4, 1967 ....$160 – 240

12. yellow with green stake bed, regular wheels, no livestock, #4, 1967 ....$12 – 16
13. yellow with green stake bed, Superfast wheels, no livestock, #4, 1970 ....$90 – 120
14. yellow with brown stake bed, amber windows, black tow hook, #71.......$4 – 5

15. yellow with brown stake bed, amber windows, no tow hook, #71 ....$8 – 10
16. yellow with brown stake bed, clear windows, #71.............................$4 – 5
17. yellow with brown stake bed, red windows, black tow hook, #71.......$4 – 5
18. yellow with brown stake bed, red windows, black tow hook, #71, Macau cast.....................................$2 – 3
19. yellow with brown stake bed, red windows, no tow hook, #71 ....$8 – 10

20. yellow with red stake bed, two black steers, #1, 1999 Beef Hauler, China cast ....$2 – 3
21. yellow with red stake bed, "Target Beef," two black steers, #1, 1999 Beef Hauler, China cast ....$2 – 3
22. yellow with tan stake bed, amber windows, no tow hook, #71 ....$5 – 6
23. yellow with tan stake bed, red windows, no tow hook, #71 ....$5 – 6

24. green with yellow stake bed, two black steers, #12, 1992 Cattle Truck...................................$4 – 5
25. green with yellow stake bed, two black steers, #71, Macau cast, Two Pack.....................................$2 – 3
26. green with yellow stake bed, two black steers, #71, Thailand cast, Two Pack ....$2 – 3
27. dark green with beige stake bed, two steers, orange windows, #71......$7 – 9
28. dark green with light brown stake bed, two steers, amber windows, #71.......$7 – 9
29. dark green with light brown stake bed, two steers, clear windows, #71 ..$7 – 9
30. dark green with light brown stake bed, two steers, orange windows, #71........$7 – 9
31. dark green with light brown stake bed, two steers, red windows, #71.....$7 – 9
32. dark green with orange-yellow stake bed, two steers, orange windows, #71 ..$4 – 5
33. dark green with orange-yellow stake bed, two steers, red windows, #71.....$4 – 5
34. metallic green with brown stake bed, two steers, amber windows, #71 ....$7 – 9

5. metallic green with brown stake bed, two steers, clear windows, #71 ....$7 – 9
6. metallic green with brown stake bed, two steers, red windows, #71 ...$7 – 9
7. light green with beige stake bed, two steers, orange windows, #71 ....$7 – 9
8. light green with orange-yellow stake bed, two steers, orange windows, #71 ..$4 – 5
9. light green with orange-yellow stake bed, two steers, red windows, #71 ....$4 – 5
0. blue with brown stake bed, amber windows, two dark brown steers, #50/30, 2000 Farm series ....$2 – 3
1. blue with brown stake bed, amber windows, two dark brown steers, "Matchbox 2000," #50/30, 2000 Farm series..........................$3 – 4
2. pale blue with brown stake bed, two black steers, red windows, #71, Macau cast..............................$3 – 4

Dodge Viper GTS Coupe, #1, US, 1997; #35, international, 1997; #1, 1998; #19, 1999

. metallic blue with white stripes, chrome wheels, rubber tires, 1997 Inaugural Edition ....$6 – 8
. unpainted, chrome wheels, rubber tires, 1997 Inaugural Edition .....$6 – 8

. **metallic blue with white stripes, 5-spoke wheels........................$2 – 4**
. black with orange interior, chrome wheels, rubber tires, Matchbox Convention...................................$12 – 16
. red with black interior, chrome wheels, rubber tires, Premiere Collection #14 ....$6 – 8
. red with black interior, 5-spoke wheels, Premiere Collection #14 ....$45 – 60

. **white with blue stripes, 1998 Stars & Stripes series 1.................$2 – 4**
. metallic gold with black interior, 75 Challenge series, 1997 ....$8 – 12
. bright blue with white stripes, Chrysler Gift Set....................................$4 – 6
0. blue with black interior, New York Knicks, NBA............................$5 – 7
1. light blue with white interior, Utah Jazz, NBA.......................................$5 – 7

12. teal blue with black interior, Detroit Pistons, NBA..............................$5 – 7
13. lavender and white with white interior, Los Angeles Lakers, NBA..........$5 – 7
14. black with gray interior, Orlando Magic, NBA.......................................$5 – 7
15. black and white with red interior, Chicago Bulls, NBA...............................$5 – 7
16. orange and black with red-orange interior, Atlanta Hawks, NBA..................$5 – 7
17. red with white interior, Houston Rockets, NBA ....$5 – 7
18. dark purple and black with orange interior, Phoenix Suns, NBA....................$5 – 7
19. orange-yellow with green interior, Seattle Supersonics, NBA................$5 – 7
20. white with purple interior, Charlotte Hornets, NBA..........................$5 – 7
21. yellow and red with black interior, Miami Heat, NBA ....$5 – 7
22. green and white with black interior, Boston Celtics, NBA ....$5 – 7
23. red and black with white interior, Portland Trailblazers, NBA ....$5 – 7
24. white with dark blue interior, Warriors, NBA.......................................$5 – 7
25. yellow and white with dark blue interior, Indiana Pacers, NBA ....$5 – 7
26. lavender and blue with orange interior, Cleveland Cavaliers, NBA...........$5 – 7
27. black and green with blue interior, Timberwolves, NBA ....$5 – 7
28. metallic gray with red interior, New York Nets, NBA.......................$5 – 7
29. metallic brown with red interior, Denver Nuggets, NBA ....$5 – 7
30. bright yellow with black interior, 5-pack....................................$2 – 4
31. metallic gray with black interior, chrome wheels, rubber tires, Premiere Collection....................................$5 – 7
32. 1998 Stars & Stripes series 1 ..$3 – 5

33. **metallic gray with tan interior, Mattel Wheels #19, 1999 ....$2 – 4**
34. metallic gray with tan interior, "Matchbox 2000" on window...............$3 – 5
35. white with black interior, blue "Midwest Regional Matchbox Convention" on hood, Color Comp ....$30 – 35
36. white with black interior, red "Midwest Regional Matchbox Convention" on hood, Color Comp ....$30 – 35
37. white with black interior, no, concave star wheels, Color Comp blank.......$30 – 40
38. metallic dark gray with metallic gray interior, 5-pack........................$2 – 3
39. metallic gray with tan interior, "Celebrating Dr. Roy R. Gal Ph.D. Astrophysics," "California Institute of Technology," Color Comp................................$45 – 55

40. **bright blue with metallic gray interior, yellow stripes and "Viper".$2 – 3**
41. metallic dark gray with metallic gray interior, 5-pack........................$2 – 3
42. white with black interior, "Hope Spring 2000," Color Comp..............$12 – 16
43. white with black interior, "Hope Spring 2001," Color Comp..............$12 – 16
44. white with black interior, "Savannah 2001," Color Comp..............$25 – 30

Dodge Viper GTSR, #56, 2001; #10, 2002
1. 2001 Wheeled Envy series........$2 – 4

2. **metallic blue with white "Viper GTSR" on sides, black plastic base, 2002 Style Champs series.....$2 – 4**

3. **black with gold "Dodge," Dodge Ram logo, snake's head, gold wheel hubs, 2003 Hero City 5-pack #12...$4 – 6**

Dodge Viper RT/10, #10, 1994; #12, 1994, international; #56, 1998; #67, 1998, international; #37, 1999; #32, 1999, international; #43, 2000; #66, 2000, international

1. **red with black interior, clear windshield, gold wheel hubs.........$2 – 3**
2. red with black interior, clear windshield, silver wheel hubs ....$2 – 3
3. red with black interior, tinted windshield, silver wheel hubs...........$2 – 3

4. red with black interior, chrome windshield, rubber tires on gray rims, World Class......................................$3 – 5

5. red with black and brown interior, clear windshield, rubber tires on chrome rims, Premiere Collection..........$4 – 6

6. red with twin yellow stripes, black and gray interior, clear windshield, rubber tires on chrome rims, Gold Collection...........................$35 – 55

7. **red with black interior, tinted windshield, yellow wheel hubs, 5-pack ....$2 – 3**

8. **red with gray interior, clear windshield ....$5 – 7**

9. red with black interior, tinted windshield, #43, 2000.....................$2 – 3

10. red with black interior, tinted windshield, "Matchbox 2000," #43, 2000...$3 – 5

111. red with black interior, clear windshield, #66, 2000.....................$2 – 3

12. red with black interior, clear windshield, "16th Annual Matchbox USA Convention 1997" decals, silver wheel hubs....................................$12 – 16

13. red with black interior, clear windshield, "Compaq," ASAP promotional .$50 – 75

14. red with black interior, clear windshield, "NCR," ASAP promotional......$50 – 75

15. red with black interior, clear windshield, small "R," ASAP promotional..$30 – 40

16. red with black interior, clear windshield, "G" in circle, ASAP promotional......$16 – 24

17. red with black interior, clear windshield, "Mahle," ASAP promotional ...$30 – 40

18. red with black interior, clear windshield, "Rensselaer Polytechnic," ASAP promotional..................................$16 – 24

19. red with black interior, clear windshield, "Microsoft," ASAP promotional.....................$75 – 125

20. red with black interior, clear windshield, "Citrix Silver," ASAP promotional...$75 – 125

21. red with black interior, clear windshield, "Intel Pill Pushing The Limits," ASAP promotional........................$75 – 125

22. red with black interior, clear windshield, "Skip Barber Driving School," ASAP promotional.........................$50 – 75

23. red with black interior, clear windshield, "Huskers" on left side, ASAP promotional ....$12 – 16

24. red with black interior, clear windshield, "Novell 6," ASAP promotional ..$20 – 25

25. red with black interior, clear windshield, "A-Pix Entertainment," "Drive," ASAP promotional.....................$120 – 160

26. red with black interior, clear windshield, "Lucent Technologies," ASAP promotional ....$25 – 45

27. red with black interior, tinted windshield, "Fiery Driven," ASAP promotional ....$100 – 150

28. red with black interior, clear windshield, "Fiery Driven," ASAP promotional ....$100 – 150

29. red with black interior, clear windshield, "1998 Sales Meeting," ASAP promotional.............................$100 – 150

30. red with black interior, clear windshield, "Concept 4," "Interact," ASAP promotional.............................$16 – 24

31. red with black interior, clear windshield, "Yasnac PCNC," "Yaskawa Can Fly!" ASAP promotional...............$50 – 75

32. red with black interior, clear windshield, "Moore," ASAP promotional ..$100 – 150

33. red with black interior, clear windshield, "Nebraska," ASAP promotional..$12 – 16

34. red with black interior, clear windshield, "Huffhines Dodge," ASAP promotional.........................$100 – 150

35. red with black interior, clear windshield, "Oberon Software," ASAP promotional...........................$75 – 125

36. red with black interior, clear windshield, "X," ASAP promotional........$75 – 125

37. red with black interior, clear windshield, "RCA," ASAP promotional......$20 – 25

38. red with black interior, clear windshield, "Season's Greetings Color Comp Inc.," "Christmas 1998," Color Comp promotional.............................$250 – 300

39. red with black interior, clear windshield, "Marathon Ashland," ASAP promotional.........................$75 – 125

40. red with black interior, clear windshield, "Faith," "Sunday School Evangelism Strategy," ASAP promotional.....$100 – 150

41. red with black interior, tinted windshield, "Matchbox Collectors," "Color Comp Inc. Conference," Color Comp promotional.........................$30 – 45

42. red with black interior, clear windshield, "Project Vertigo," "Citrix Developer Network," ASAP promotional ....$75 – 125

43. red with black interior, clear windshield, "Citrix Vertigo," ASAP promotional ....$75 – 125

44. red with black interior, clear windshield, "Me, Mom & Matchbox," Color Comp promotional.........................$16 – 24

45. green with tan interior, tinted windshield, "Hope Spring Cancer Support Center 1997".....................$90 – 120

46. green with tan interior, tinted windshield, no markings ....$3 – 4

47. yellow with black interior, clear windshield, "Me, Mom & Matchbox," Color Comp promotional................$16 – 2

48. **green with tan interior, clear windshield, "Me, Mom & Matchbox" Color Comp promotional ..$80 – 10**

49. **white with black interior, clear windshield, "March 1999," "White Guide," ASAP promotional .$30 – 3**

50. **red with black interior, clear windshield, yellow-lettered "White's Guide Car of the Month #8 July 1999 ASAP promotional...............$9 – 1**

51. **red with black interior, clear windshield, white-lettered "White's Guide Car of the Month #8 July 1999 ASAP promotional...............$9 – 1**

52. red with black interior, tinted windshield, "Hope Spring Cancer Support Center 1997".....................$16 – 2

53. green with twin white stripes, gray and black interior, clear windshield, rubber tires on chrome rims, Premiere Collection......................................$4 –

54. metallic green with black and gray interior, clear windshield, rubber tires on chrome rims, Select Class....................$12 – 1

5. dark gray with black and gray interior, clear windshield, rubber tires on chrome rims, Australia issue Premiere Collection.............................$9 – 12

6. **yellow with black interior, clear windshield, #56, 1998 ....$2 – 3**
7. yellow, black interior, tinted windshield, #56, 1998.............................$2 – 3
8. yellow with black and gray interior, clear windshield, rubber tires on chrome rims, Premiere Collection........$8 – 10
9. yellow with black interior, chrome windshield, "California Viper's Club," rubber tires on gray rims ....$15 – 20
0. yellow with black interior, tinted windshield, "Matchbox Forum 1998," "First Shot"..................................$20 – 25
1. yellow with black interior, tinted windshield, "Matchbox Convoys Collectors Club," "M3CG," Color Comp promotional ....$30 – 45
2. yellow with black interior, clear windshield, "Pratiker" ....$45 – 65
3. yellow with black interior, tinted windshield, "PMCC Happy Holidays," Color Comp promotional...............$30 – 45
4. yellow with black interior, tinted windshield, "Color Comp Demo Model 2000," Color Comp promotional.........$20 – 25
5. yellow with black interior, tinted windshield, "NJ Die-cast Collectors Club"....$30 – 45
6. yellow with black interior, tinted windshield, "Matchbox Forum International Matchbox Collectors Club Deutschland"....$30 – 45
7. yellow with black interior, tinted windshield, "Keystone Kollectible Kars," Color Comp promotional........$16 – 24
8. blue with metallic gray interior, clear windshield, "Keystone Kollectible Kars," Color Comp promotional........$16 – 24
9. blue with twin yellow stripes, gray interior, clear windshield, "Praktiker".....$16 – 24
0. red with black interior, clear windshield, "Keystone Kollectible Kars," Color Comp promotional...........................$16 – 24
1. black with gray interior, chrome windshield, rubber tires on gray rims, "Matchbox 1995 Line Preview" .....$275 – 350

2. **black with tan interior, clear windshield, 5-pack ....$2 – 3**

73. **black with twin silver stripes, gray and black interior, clear windshield, rubber tires on chrome rims, Select Class ....$4 – 6**
74. white with black interior, clear windshield, "69th Shenandoah Apple Blossom Festival 1996".............$12 – 15
75. white with black interior, clear windshield, "Merry Christmas Ad-Ventures"..$20 – 25
76. white with twin red stripes, black and gray interior, clear windshield, rubber tires on chrome rims, Select Class..........$4 – 6
77. white with brown interior, clear windshield, "Viper," 5-pack...............$2 – 3
78. white with black interior, clear windshield, "1st Annual Golf Outing — Mattel," Color Comp ....$300 – 375
79. white with twin white stripes, black, blue and gray interior, clear windshield, rubber tires on chrome rims, Premiere Collection ....$5 – 7
80. white with blue stripes, tan interior, clear windshield, "District 16B Lion's Club New Jersey," Color Comp promotional..................................$25 – 40

81. **metallic blue with twin white stripes, gray and black interior, clear windshield, rubber tires on chrome rims, Premiere Collection ....$4 – 6**
82. gold with black interior, clear windshield, no markings, 1997 75 Challenge..................................$12 – 16

Dodge Wreck Truck, "BP", 3", #13, 1965
1. green cab, yellow body, black plastic wheels, prototype...........$900 – 1000

2. **yellow cab, green body, black plastic wheels ....$10 – 15**
3. yellow cab, green body, Superfast wheels, 1970.....................$60 – 80

Dodge Zoo Truck, #72, 1992, international
1. white with red, orange and yellow stripes, blue windows, metallic gray cage, brown lions, Thailand cast, Motor City.....$4 – 5

Dragon Wheels (see Hot Chocolate)

Draguar (see Hot Rod Draguar)

Drott Excavator, 2⅝", #58, 1962
1. red with silver motor and base, metal rollers ....$25 – 35
2. red with silver motor and base, silver rollers ....$80 – 100
3. red with silver motor & base, black rollers ....$25 – 35
4. orange with silver motor and base, black rollers ....$35 – 45
5. orange with orange motor and base, black rollers ....$35 – 45

DUKW Army Amphibian, 2¾", #55, 1958
1. metal wheels......................$30 – 45
2. gray plastic wheels..............$30 – 45
3. black plastic wheels.............$30 – 45

Dumper, 1⅝", #2, 1953
1. green metal wheels..........$120 – 150
2. unpainted metal wheels.........$45 – 60

Dumper, 1⅞", #2, 1957
1. with driver ....$45 – 60

Dumper, Muir Hill, red with green dumper, black plastic wheels, 2³⁄₁₆", #2, 1961

1. **"Laing" decals..................$20 – 25**
2. "Muir Hill" decals.................$65 – 80

Dump Truck (see Articulated Dump Truck, Atlas Earth Mover Dump Truck, Caterpillar Dump Truck, DAF Tipper Truck, Dodge Dump Truck, 8-Wheel Tipper, Euclid Quarry Truck, GMC Highway Maintenance Truck, GMC Tipper Truck, Leyland Articulated Truck, Mack Dump Truck, Peterbilt Quarry Truck, Quarry Truck)

Dump Truck, #55, 2002; #69, 2003
1. metallic red with metallic gray plastic dumper with "Matchbox Demolition Force" and wrecking ball on sides, 2002 Rescue Rookies series ....$2 – 3

2. **metallic red with metallic gray plastic dumper with "Matchbox Demolition Force" and wrecking ball on sides, Christmas 2002 3-pack with gift box.............................$4 – 5**
3. red with black dumper, 2003 Heavy Movers series ....$2 – 3

Dune Buggy/Sand Speeder, #92, 1999; #15, 2000; #35, 2001; #46, 2002; #72, 1999, international

1. **red, "Beach Patrol," black interior, black roll cage, "Matchbox 2000," 2000 To The Beach series .....$3 – 4**
2. red, "Beach Patrol," black interior, black roll cage, 2000 To The Beach series....................................$2 – 3

3. **red, "Beach Patrol," blue interior, yellow base, red roll cage, 2002 Sand Castle Rescue Team 5-pack ....$4 – 5**

4. **orange with phosphorescent yellow roll cage, blue interior, 2003 Camp Fun 3-pack with flashlight......$4 – 5**

---

5. yellow with red interior, blue roll cage, yellow base, 2002 Weekend Cruisers series......................................$2 – 3
6. light blue with white band, metallic gray interior, black roll cage ....$2 – 3
7. pale blue with dark blue band, mountain scene, light blue base, metallic gray interior, 1999 Mountain Cruisers series ....

8. **turquoise, "Rt450," mountain scene, black interior, metallic gray roll cage, yellow base, 1999 Mountain Cruisers international series ..$3 – 4**
9. purple, "Sand Blaster," black interior, black roll cage, yellow base, 2001 Sand Blasters series ....$2 – 3
10. black, "Rugged Adventures," "88," orange interior, yellow roll cage, orange base ....$3 – 4
11. black with purple and blue sting rays design, black roll cage, metallic red base, 5-pack ....$2 – 3

Dune Man Volkswagen Beetle, 2¹³⁄₁₆", #49, 1984 (similar castings: Hi Ho Silver, Hot Chocolate, Sand Digger, Volks Dragon, Big Blue)
1. red ....$3 – 4

Dunes Racer 4x4 Pickup, 3", #13, 1982; #63, 1984, #76 error package (similar castings: Mini Pickup 4x4, Mountain Man)
1. white, #63 on package ....$4 – 6

2. **white, #76 on package ....$3 – 5**

3. **white, #13 on package ....$2 – 4**

E

Earth Mover (see Faun Earth Mover Dump Truck)

Eccles Caravan Travel Trailer, 3", #57, 1970
1. light yellow with orange roof, brown stripe and flower label, green interior, black axle cover ....$12 – 16

2. **dark yellow with dark orange roof, black stripe and flower label, white interior, black axle cover ......$6 – 8**
3. dark yellow with dark orange roof, dots label, white interior, black axle cover ....$9 – 12
4. beige with orange roof, stripe label, green interior, black axle cover........$12 – 16

5. **beige with orange roof, brown stripe and flower label, green interior, black axle cover ....$12 – 16**
6. beige with orange roof, brown stripe and flower label, green interior, red axle cover ....$12 – 16
7. beige with dark orange roof, black stripe and flower label, white interior, black axle cover ....$6 – 8
8. beige with dark orange roof, stripe and seagull label, white interior, black axle cover ....$9 – 12
9. white with dark orange roof, "Sun Set" design, white interior, black axle cover ....$10 – 14

Eight-Wheel Crane Truck, 3", #30, 1965

1. **mint green, black plastic wheels, pre-production ....$900 – 1,000**
2. green, black plastic wheels, 1965...$5 – 10
3. red with orange boom, Superfast wheels, 1970.................$400 – 500
4. red with gold boom, Superfast wheels, 1970...............................$40 – 50

ight-Wheel Tipper (see AEC Ergomatic Eight-Wheel Tipper)

mergency Power Truck, #60, 2002; #68, 2003

red with white light tower, 2002 Rescue Rookies series ....**$2 – 3**
orange with white light tower, 2003 Heavy Movers series ....$2 – 3

mergency Response 4x4, #11, 2003

metallic silver with red gear and base, 2003 Hospital series ....**$2 – 3**

RF 686 Truck "Eveready For Life," blue, 2⅝", #20, 1959
gray plastic wheels ....$40 – 50
silver plastic wheels..............$85 – 95
black plastic wheels..............$45 – 55

uclid Quarry Truck, 2⅝", #6, 1964
yellow with black plastic wheels..$10 – 15

xcavator (see Atlas Excavator, Caterpillar Excavator)

xtending Ladder Fire Engine, 3", #18, 1984; #23, 1998; #79, 1999; #32, 2000; #29, 2001; #4, 2003

1. **fluorescent orange with "4" and checkered bar accents, 1994 $2 – 3**
2. fluorescent orange, "5," "Intercom City," black base with bar code.......$12 – 16

3. **fluorescent orange, "5," "Intercom City," chrome base............$9 – 12**
4. fluorescent orange with white accents...................................$2 – 3
5. metallic gold with white ladder, 1997 75 Challenge series ....$6 – 12
6. metallic maroon with gray ladder, gold design, "14" and "Matchbox," Pleasant Books....................................$5 – 7

7. **red with gray ladder, gold stripe, 5-pack** ....**$2 – 3**
8. red with gray ladder, "54" and "Matchbox" in circle, 5-pack...........$2 – 3
9. red with gray ladder, "FDMB-E64" and "Ladder 3 Fire Rescue," rubber tires on chrome rims, K B Toys Feature Car ....$6 – 9
10. red with white ladder, no markings...$2 – 3
11. red with white ladder, "Fire Dept," "7," shield ....$2 – 3
12. red with white ladder, Japan lettering....................................$10 – 15
13. red with white ladder, "3" and crest..$3 – 5
14. red with white ladder, "Fire Dept," no-origin cast ....$10 – 15
15. red with white ladder, "4" and checkered bar accents...........................$8 – 10
16. red with white ladder, "FD No. 1," 5-pack....................................$2 – 3
17. red with white "12th," gold "Rescue Squad," gold trim, 1995 ....$2 – 3
18. red with white upper, gold and black accents, "FD No.1" on gold shield, 1996 5-pack..........................$2 – 4
19. red with white "12th Rescue Squad," white trim, 1996 ....$2 – 3

20. **red with white stripes on sides, "Matchbox Fire Dept." in black** .**$2 – 3**

21. red with white ladder, "Metro Fire Department," Collectors Choice, White Rose Collectibles.....................$3 – 5
22. red with white ladder, white accents, "Laurel Springs Fire Rescue," rubber tires on chrome rims, Premiere Collection 21 ....$4 – 6
23. red with white ladder, white accents, "City of Miami," rubber tires on chrome rims, Premiere Collection ....$4 – 6
24. red with white ladder, white accents, "Cleveland Fire Div.," 2000 Matchbox USA series............................$2 – 3
25. red with white ladder, white accents, "Cleveland Fire Div.," "Matchbox 2000," 2000 Matchbox USA series ......$3 – 5
26. red with white ladder, white accents, "Westworth Fire Dept. 8," 2001 Flame Eaters series...........................$2 – 3
27. red with yellow ladder, blue tires, Live 'N Learn/Matchbox Preschool.......$7 – 9

28. **red with yellow ladder, black plastic base; gold, white, and yellow accents; 2003 Sky Fire series$2 – 3**
29. white with gray ladder, "Metro Alarm," orange and red stripes, 5-pack ..$2 – 3

30. **white with metallic gray ladder, blue, metallic gray metal base, 2001 Flame Eaters series** ....**$3 – 4**
31. white with orange ladder, 1996 ..$2 – 3
32. white with red ladder, red bands and yellow hash marks on ladder, 5-pack.$2 – 3

33. **white with translucent red ladder, red band, 1998 To The Rescue series** ....**$2 – 3**
34. white with white ladder, Graffic Traffic ....$12 – 16

35. white with white ladder, red accents, "Springfield Fire Dept.," rubber tires on chrome rims, Premiere Collection 7 ....$4 – 6

36. yellow with white ladder, no markings ....$4 – 6

37. **yellow with gray ladder, "Matchbox Fire Dept." and red stripe, 5-pack....$2 – 3**

38. yellow with gray ladder, "Ladder 3 Bay District," rubber tires on chrome rims, Premiere Collection 7 ....$4 – 6

39. yellow with gray ladder, "Park Ridge Fire Dept.," rubber tires on chrome rims, Premiere Collection 21 ....$4 – 6

40. yellow with gray ladder, "21" and crest, 1999 Fire Rescue series ....$2 – 3

41. yellow with gray ladder, "21 Laurel Ladder" and crest, 1999 Fire Rescue series.....................................$2 – 3

42. 2002 Matchbox Across America 50th Birthday series #20 Mississippi — Southern Collection ....$4 – 6

F

F1 Racer, 2⁷/₈", #16, 1984, USA; #6, 1985, Europe; Indy Racer, #65, 1985

1. "123456" and flames, white with red airfoil, blue wheels, red driver, Matchbox Preschool/Live 'N Learn series, Macau cast...............................$7 – 9

2. "123456" and flames, white with red airfoil, blue wheels, red driver, Matchbox Preschool/Live 'N Learn series, Thailand cast...........................$7 – 9

3. "Agfa Film 29," white and dark orange with orange driver, "Agfa" on orange airfoil, Thailand cast, US issue .....$8 – 10

4. "Agfa Film 29," white and red with red driver, "Agfa" on red airfoil, Thailand cast, US issue.......................$8 – 10

5. "Amway," "Speedway 22," white with pink driver, bright pink and blue accents, "Rain-X" on pink airfoil, China cast, Indy 500...........................$4 – 5

6. "Amway," "Speedway 22"; white, bright pink, and blue; pink driver, bright pink and blue accents, "Rain-X" on pink airfoil, Thailand cast, Indy 500......$4 – 5

7. "Bosch STP 20," dark blue with red driver, "Goodyear" on red airfoil, chrome lettering on wheels, Macau cast .....$5 – 6

8. "Bosch STP 20," dark blue with red driver, "Goodyear" on red airfoil, unchromed lettering on wheels, Macau cast..$5 – 6

9. "Fiat 3," red with black driver, "Pirelli" on black airfoil ....$3 – 5

10. "Havoline 86," black with black driver, "Havoline" on black airfoil, China cast, Indy 500...............................$4 – 5

11. **"Hyflo Exhausts 5," white with purple driver, "Hyflo Exhausts" on fuchsia airfoil, Thailand cast........$2 – 3**

12. "Indy 11," lemon yellow and black with lemon yellow driver, "Goodyear" on lemon yellow airfoil, China cast, Indy 500.....................................$4 – 5

13. "Indy 11," lemon yellow and black with lemon yellow driver, "Indy" on lemon yellow airfoil, China cast, Indy 500 ....$5 – 6

14. "Kraco 18," orange-yellow and blue with orange-yellow driver, "Kraco" on orange-yellow airfoil, Thailand cast, Indy 500 ....$4 – 5

15. "Kraco," "Otter Pops 18," orange-yellow and blue with yellow driver, "Kraco" on yellow airfoil, China cast, Indy 500 ...$4 – 5

16. "Matchbox," "Goodyear," white with blue driver, "Shell" on blue airfoil ....$3 – 5

17. "Matchbox Racing Team," red with red driver, "Goodyear" on red airfoil, Macau cast, Super Color Changers.......$4 – 5

18. "Matchbox Racing Team," pink with red driver, "Goodyear" on red airfoil, Macau cast, Super Color Changers.......$4 – 5

19. "Matchbox Racing Team," light peach with with red driver, "Goodyear" on red airfoil, Macau cast, Super Color Changers ....$4 – 5

20. "Matchbox Racing Team," orange with with red driver, "Goodyear" on red airfoil, Macau cast, Super Color Changers..........$4 – 5

21. "Matchbox Racing Team," yellow with dark red driver, "Goodyear" on dark red airfoil, Macau cast ....$3 – 4

22. "Matchbox Racing Team," yellow with red driver, "Goodyear" on red airfoil, black exhausts, China cast ....$2 – 3

23. "Matchbox Racing Team," yellow with red driver, "Goodyear" on red airfoil, black exhausts, Macau cast.......$2 – 3

24. "Matchbox Racing Team," yellow with red driver, "Goodyear" on red airfoil, black exhausts, Thailand cast.....$2 – 3

25. "Matchbox Racing Team," yellow with red driver, "Goodyear" on red airfoil, chrome exhausts, Macau cast...$3 – 4

26. "Matchbox Racing Team," yellow with maroon driver, "Goodyear" on red airfoil, black exhausts, Thailand cast .....$2 – 3

27. "Matchbox Racing Team," light green with with red driver, "Goodyear" on red airfoil, Macau cast, Super Color Changers ....$4 – 5

28. "Mitre 10," "M10," blue with blue driver, "Mitre 10" on blue airfoil, Thailand cast, Convoy Australia issue ......$6 – 8

29. "Mitre 10," "Larkham," "Taubmans 3 blue and white with blue driver, "Mitr 10" on blue airfoil, Thailand cast, Tea Convoy Australia issue ....$7 –

30. "Mr. Juicy," "Sunkist"; white, orange ar green; yellow driver, "Watson's" on yello airfoil, Hong Kong issue ....$24 – 3

31. "Rad 5," black with green and whit stripes, black driver, "Rad" on black a foil, Thailand cast....................$2 –

32. "Rad 5," black with white stripes, black d ver, "Rad" on black airfoil, Thailand cas Aquafresh on-package premium....$5 –

33. "Tech Racing 3," red with black drive black airfoil, Thailand cast ....$2 –

34. "Valvoline 5," blue and white with da blue driver, "Valvoline" on blue airfoi China cast, Indy 500 ....$4 –

35. chrome with red driver, "Goodyear" red airfoil, Thailand cast, custom pr motional ....$16 – 2

Fairlady Z [see Datsun Fairlady Z]

Fandango, 3", #35, 1975; BR 31 – 3 1985

1. red, "35" label, red base, red interic silver propeller.....................$60 – 8

2. red, "35" label, red base, ivory interio silver propeller.....................$12 – 8

3. red, "35" label, unpainted base, ivo interior, silver propeller...........$9 – 1

4. red, "35" label, unpainted base, ivo interior, blue propeller ....$9 – 1

5. red, "35" label, unpainted base, whi interior, blue propeller ....$9 – 1

6. red, "35" label, white base, ivory interic silver propeller.....................$9 – 1

7. red, "35" label, white base, ivory interic red propeller......................$9 – 1

8. red, "35" label, white base, ivory interic blue propeller ....$9 – 1

9. red, "35" label, black base, white interic blue propeller, UK issue...........$75 – 9

10. red, sunburst label, unpainted bas white interior, blue propeller ..$16 – 2

11. yellow, England cast, Super GTs BR 3 – 32, 1985 ....$4 –

12. yellow, China cast, Super GTs BR 31 – 3 1985..................................$3 – 4

13. lemon yellow, China cast, Super GTs E 31 – 32, 1985 ....$8 – 1

14. maroon, England cast, Super GTs E 31 – 32, 1985 ....$4 –

15. maroon, China cast, Super GTs E 31 – 32, 1985....................$8 – 1

16. purple, "35" label, gray base, white interic light blue propeller, UK issue..$600 – 80

17. white, "6" label, red base, red interic silver propeller.....................$16 – 2

18. white, "35" label, red base, red interic red propeller ....$9 – 1

19. white, "35" label, red base, red interic silver propeller.....................$9 – 1

20. white, "35" label, unpainted base, re interior, silver propeller...........$9 – 1

21. gray, China cast, Super GTs BR 31 32, 1985............................$3 – 4

rm Trailer, #711, 1993 Farming series
yellow, black tires on gray rims ..$3 – 4

un Crane Truck (see Faun Mobile Crane)

un Dump Truck (see Faun Earth Mover
Dump Truck)

un Earth Mover Dump Truck, 2³/₄",
#58, 1976; #9, 1989; #53, 1989;
#9, 1997; #27, 1999; #95, 2000;
#18, 2002
red with metallic gray dumper, no markings, 1997 ....$2 – 3
red with black dumper, no
markings.................................$2 – 3

**primer pale red with light gray
dumper, black and brown rust and
primer colors, no markings, 5-
pack.....................................$2 – 3**

**bright orange with metallic gray
dumper, 2003 5-pack............$2 – 3**
bright orange with bright orange
dumper ....$2 – 3

**bright orange with black dumper, no
markings, 1996.....................$2 – 3**
fluorescent light orange, black dumper,
no markings ....$3 – 4
light orange with red dumper, no markings, Action Systems Pack.........$2 – 3
orange-yellow with red dumper, no
markings, China cast.................$2 – 3
0. orange-yellow with orange-yellow
dumper, orange stripes, China cast,
Action Pack..............................$3 – 4
1. orange-yellow with orange-yellow dumper,
no markings, England cast.........$4 – 6
2. yellow with yellow dumper, no markings,
England cast ....$4 – 6

13. **yellow with red dumper, no markings, England cast ....$30 – 40**
14. yellow with yellow dumper, "CAT" logo,
England cast ....$5 – 7
15. yellow with metallic silver dumper,
orange stripes, Macau cast.......$3 – 4
16. yellow, metallic silver dumper, orange
stripes, China cast..................$3 – 4

17. **metallic green with yellow Matchbox logo, yellow dumper with black
vertical stripes, 2002 Build It
Right series ....$2 – 3**
18. blue, yellow dumper, orange stripes and
tools, China cast, Live 'N Learn/
Preschool series ....$4 – 5

19. **dusty blue with pale gray dumper,
2000 Build It! series ....$2 – 3**
20. dusty blue with pale gray dumper,
"Matchbox 2000," 2000 Build It!
series ....$3 – 4
21. dusty white with green dumper, 1999
Road Work series...................$2 – 3
22. white with yellow dumper, "MC18,"
"Matchbox," rhinoceros head, 5-
pack ....$2 – 3
23. metallic gold with metallic gold dumper,
no markings, 1997 75 Challenge
series................................$12 – 16

Faun Mobile Crane, 3", #42, 1985 –
1997; #15, 1998
1. red, black crane cab, metallic gray
crane, 1998 Big Movers series ..$2 – 3
2. yellow, "Reynolds Crane Hire," England
cast......................................$3 – 4
3. yellow, "Reynolds Crane Hire," Macau
cast......................................$2 – 3

4. yellow, "Reynolds Crane Hire," China
cast......................................$2 – 3
5. yellow, "Reynolds Crane Hire," Thailand
cast......................................$2 – 3

6. **yellow, black crane cab, metallic
gray crane ....$3 – 5**
7. yellow, no markings, yellow plastic crane
cab, black crane, Motor City.........$3 – 4

8. **yellow, road and bridge graphic, red
plastic crane cab ....$2 – 3**
9. yellow, fluorescent orange crane cab,
"IC" and checkerboard pattern, Intercom City.............................$12 – 16
10. orange, road and bridge graphic, gray
crane cab, black crane, light gray
boom, 1996 ....$2 – 3
11. orange, black crane cab, metallic gray
crane, 1997 ....$2 – 3
12. orange, gray crane cab, black
crane.....................................$2 – 3

13. **blue-green, black crane cab, metallic
gray crane, dolphin and waves
design, Action Pack..............$4 – 5**

14. blue, purple crane cab, gray and brown crane, dirt pattern, 5-pack.......$2 – 3
15. blue, purple crane cab, gray and brown crane, dirt pattern, "Hershey 99," Color Comp promotional................$12 – 16
16. pale blue, black crane cab, metallic gray crane......................................$2 – 3
17. metallic gold, black crane cab, black crane, 1997 75 Challenge series.........$6 – 12

FedEx Delivery Truck (see Ford Box Van)

Ferrari 308 GTB, 2¹⁵⁄₁₆", #70, 1981
1. red, "Data East," "Secret Service," red base, Macau cast, Canada issue................................$70 – 90
2. red, "Ferrari" logo on hood, red base, Macau cast..............................$3 – 4
3. red, "Ferrari" logo on hood, red base, Thailand cast, Motor City ....$3 – 4
4. red, "Ferrari" on sides, gray plastic base, Manaus cast, Brazil issue ......$20 – 30
5. red, "Magnum P. I.," red plastic base, black roof, China cast, Star Cars..$5 – 6
6. red, "Pioneer 39," blue base, Macau cast...................................$3 – 4
7. red with chrome windows, red base, rubber tires on chrome rims, World Class, Macau cast ....$6 – 8
8. red with no markings, red base, clear windows, England cast..............$3 – 4
9. red with no markings, orange-red base, clear windows, England cast ......$3 – 4
10. dark red, "Ferrari" and logo, pearl silver base, clear windows, Macau cast.$3 – 4
11. orange-red, "Ferrari" and logo, pearl silver base, clear windows, Macau cast..$3 – 4
12. orange-red, "Ferrari" logo, orange-red base, amber windows, England cast ......$3 – 4
13. orange-red, "Ferrari" logo, orange-red base, clear windows, England cast.......$3 – 4
14. orange-red, "Ferrari" logo, metallic gray base, clear windows, England cast........$9 – 12
15. orange-red, no markings, orange-red base, clear windows, England cast........$3 – 4
16. orange, "12 Rat Racing Team," blue base, Macau cast, Hong Kong issue....$9 – 12
17. yellow, "Ferrari 308 GTB," red base, Macau cast, Laser Wheels........$4 – 5
18. yellow, "Ferrari 308 GTB," red base, Macau cast, New Superfast Wheels.........$4 – 5
19. yellow with geometric design, yellow base, 1993 Dream Machines 3-pack, Thailand cast............................$3 – 4
20. white with no markings, white base, green windows, Graffic Traffic, Macau cast ..$12 – 16

Ferrari 360 Spider, #7, 2003

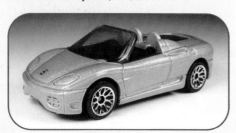

1. metallic gray with black interior, 2003 Family Wheels series....$2 – 3

Ferrari 456 GT, #17, 1994, US; #41, 1994, international; #29, 1997; #82, 2000
1. black, rubber tires on chrome rims, Premiere Collection 15 ....$4 – 5
2. metallic blue, "456 GT" in yellow on sides, gold 6-spoke spiral wheels, 1994......................................$2 – 3
3. metallic gold, 75 Challenge series, 1997.................................$12 – 16

4. metallic pale gold, #82, 2000 Worldwide Wheels series ....$2 – 3
5. metallic pale gold, #82, "Matchbox 2000," 2000 Worldwide Wheels series ....$3 – 4

6. metallic purple with white abstract design on sides, no markings on hood or roof, fluorescent yellow interior, 1996.................................$2 – 3

7. metallic purple with white design on sides, roof, and hood; "Matchbox Rush Racing," pale gray interior, 1997.............................$2 – 3

8. metallic red with no markings, butterscotch interior, 5-spoke wheels, 1996 ....$2 – 3

9. metallic red with no markings, butterscotch interior, 6-spoke pinwheel wheels, 1997 ....$2 – 3
10. metallic red, Ferrari logo, rubber tires on chrome rims, J C Penney's Premiere Collection..............................$4 – 5

11. metallic blue with white design on sides, roof, and hood; "Matchbox Rush Racing," pale gray interior, 1997 ....$2 – 3
12. metallic red, small logo on hood, 1998 ....
13. metallic dark red, Ferrari logo, 5-spoke wheels ....$2 –
14. pale yellow, small Matchbox logo, 1997..................................$3 –

Ferrari Berlinetta, 3", #75, 1965
1. red, black tires on chrome wheels, prototype...................$1200 – 160
2. red, plain grille, Superfast wheels, 1970.................................$30 – 4
3. red, silver grille, Superfast wheels, 1970.................................$30 – 4
4. metallic green, unpainted base, black tires on spoked wheels, 1965 ....$16 – 2
5. metallic green, metallic gray base, black tires on spoked wheels, 1965 ....$65 – 8
6. metallic green, unpainted base, black tires on chrome wheels, 1966.........................$16 – 2
7. metallic green, plain grille, Superfast wheels, 1970...................$80 – 10

8. metallic light blue-green, black tires, spoked wheels, 1965.....$160 – 24

Ferrari F1 Racing Car, red, 2⅝", #73, 196
1. white driver.........................$20 – 3
2. gray driver ....$20 – 3

Ferrari F40, 3", #24, 1989; #70, 198 #57, 1998; #19, 1999; #23, 2000
1. black with black and chrome windows, Lightning series ....$4 –
2. black with clear windows, "It's Matchbox," '93 Tyco".........................$40 – 5
3. black with clear windows, tan and black interior, rubber wheels on chrome rims, International Premiere Collection #2 ....$4 –

red chrome with clear windows, white interior, light blue and yellow design, 5-pack..............................$2 – 3
silver chrome with clear windows, custom model ....$15 – 20
silver chrome with pink windows ..$3 – 4

light blue chrome with red windows, 1997 Sleek Riders 5-pack......$2 – 3
metallic burgundy with clear windows, white interior, light blue and yellow design, 5-pack..........................$2 – 3
metallic gold with clear windows, black interior, 6-spoke wheels, 1997 75 Challenge series ....$6 – 12
). metallic gold with clear windows, black interior, 5-spoke concave wheels, 1997 75 Challenge series ....$30 – 50
. metallic gray with clear windows, red and black interior, rubber tires on chrome rims, Premiere Collection #19 ....$4 – 5
². gradient metallic purple to metallic pink, 1996.......................................$2 – 3
³. gradient metallic red to black, clear windows, black interior, 5-pack.......$2 – 3
⁴. gradient metallic red to purple, clear windows, black interior..............$2 – 3

⁵. **gradient white to orange, clear windows, black interior, 1996 Super Cars 5-pack..........................$2 – 3**

⁶. **orange with opaque yellow windows, black spots ....$2 – 3**

17. **purple with orange windows, orange and white design, 1997 Super Cars 5-pack ....$2 – 3**
18. red with opaque yellow windows, black spots, 1994 ....$3 – 4
19. red with black windows, Triple Heat series.....................................$4 – 5
20. red with clear windows, black interior, Ferrari logo ....$2 – 3
21. red with clear windows, black interior, Ferrari logo, painted tail lights, Show Stoppers................................$3 – 4
22. red with clear windows, black interior, Ferrari logo, Intercom City base ....$40 – 60
23. red with clear windows, black interior, "Ferrari," "Pininfarina" on doors, 1999 Top Class series ....$2 – 3
24. red with clear windows, black interior, "Ferrari," no "Pininfarina" on doors, 1999 Top Class series ....$2 – 3
25. red with clear windows, black interior, "Old Eight," UK issue..........$80 – 120
26. red with clear windows, black and red interior, detailed trim, Gold Coin Collection...................................$16 – 24
27. red with chrome windows, rubber tires on chrome rims, Ferrari logo, World Class.....................................$6 – 8
28. red with chrome and black windows, Lightning series ....$3 – 4
29. red with tinted windows, brown interior, 2000 Italian Stars series ....$2 – 3
30. red with tinted windows, brown interior, "Matchbox 2000," 2000 Italian Stars series.....................................$3 – 4
31. silver with pink windows, yellow and pink stripes ....$4 – 5
32. white with blue chrome and black windows, Lightning series ....$4 – 5
33. white with clear windows, Collectors Choice, White Rose Collectibles .$3 – 4

34. **white with clear windows, black horse, red stripe, 1998 Super Car series ....$2 – 3**
35. yellow and white with chrome windows, rubber tires on gray rims, World Class.......................$6 – 8
36. yellow with clear windows, black and red interior, rubber tires on gray rims, Premiere Collection #10................$4 – 5
37. yellow with clear windows, black interior, red stripe, black horse on hood ..$2 – 3
38. yellow with blue chrome and black windows, Lightning series ....$3 – 4
39. yellow with red racing stripe, black horse on hood, 1997 ....$2 – 3

Ferrari F50 Coupe, #75, 1996 – 1997; #59, 1998; #21, 2000; #35,

1999, international; #16, 2000, international
1. red, "Citrix," "SD2000," black interior, ASAP promotional.............$80 – 120

2. **red, "Ferrari," "50," gradient white to yellow stripes, black interior, 1997 Racing 5-pack.............$2 – 3**
3. red, "Go Swans! 1997," gray interior, 5-spoke concave wheels, Australia issue.....................................$4 – 5
4. red, "Novell 6," black interior, clear windows, ASAP promotional.......$20 – 30
5. red, "Novell 6," black interior, tinted windows, ASAP promotional ..$20 – 30
6. red with Ferrari logo, black interior, 5-spoke concave wheels...............$2 – 3

7. **red with Ferrari logo, black interior, 6-spoke spiral wheels ....$2 – 3**
8. red with detailed trim, black interior, rubber tires on chrome rims, Ultra Class.....................................$9 – 12
9. red with no markings, black interior, ASAP promotional blank........$30 – 40
10. yellow, "Ferrari" and logo, black interior, 5-spoke concave wheels, 5-pack ....$2 – 3
11. yellow, "Ferrari" and logo, black interior, 5-spoke wheels, 5-pack.............$2 – 3
12. yellow, "Ferrari" and logo, black interior, 10-spoke wheels, 5-pack...........$7 – 9
13. yellow with detailed trim, black and red interior, rubber tires on chrome rims, Toys "R" Us gift set ....$4 – 5
14. yellow with Ferrari logo, black interior, 5-spoke concave wheels...........$2 – 3
15. black with Ferrari logo, brown interior ....$2 – 3

16. **black with Ferrari logo, red interior, 1998 Super Cars series ....$2 – 3**
17. metallic gray, "Ferrari" and logo, red interior, 5-pack......................$2 – 3

18. metallic gray with detailed trim, black and red interior, rubber tires on chrome rims, Premiere Collection #15....$4 – 5
19. metallic gray with Ferrari logo, "Matchbox 2000," black interior, 5-spoke concave wheels, 2000 Italian Stars ....$7 – 9
20. metallic gray with Ferrari logo, "Matchbox 2000," black interior, 5-spoke wheels, 2000 Italian Stars ....$3 – 4
21. metallic gray with Ferrari logo, black interior, 5-spoke wheels, 2000 Italian Stars ....$2 – 3
22. metallic gray with Ferrari logo, black interior, 5-spoke concave wheels, 2000 Italian Stars........................$2 – 3
23. metallic gold, black interior, 1997 75 Challenge series ....$12 – 16

Ferrari F-50 Spyder, #75, 1996 (planned but never issued)

Ferrari Testarossa, 3", #75, 1987; #78 error package, 1996; #25, 2000; #20, 2000, international
1. red, "1," face and checkered flag, yellow wheels with blue hubs, Macau cast, Live 'N Learn/Matchbox Preschool series ....$7 – 9
2. red, "Lloyds," "Ferrari," China cast, UK issue...................................$8 – 10
3. red, "Redoxon," Macau cast, Hong Kong issue..........................$30 – 40
4. red with clear windows, detailed trim, rubber tires on chrome rims, Thailand cast, Premiere Collection #19 ...$4 – 5
5. red with chrome windows, detailed trim, rubber tires on gray rims, Macau cast, World Class ....$6 – 8
6. red with chrome windows, detailed trim, rubber tires on gray rims, Thailand cast, World Class ....$6 – 8
7. red with Ferrari logo, China cast..$2 – 3
8. red with Ferrari logo, 8-dot wheels, Thailand cast....................$2 – 3
9. red with Ferrari logo, 6-spoke spiral wheels, Thailand cast ....$4 – 5
10. red with small Ferrari logo, painted tail lights, Thailand cast, Show Stoppers ....$3 – 4
11. red with silver accents and logos, Macau cast, New Superfast Wheels.....$9 – 12
12. metallic red with silver accents, Macau cast, Laser Wheels.................$4 – 5
13. metallic red 6-spoke spiral wheels, Thailand cast ....$2 – 3
14. dark red to orange with Ferrari logos, Macau cast, Super Color Changers......................................$4 – 5
15. yellow with detailed trim, rubber tires on chrome rims, Thailand cast, international Premiere Collection #2 ....$4 – 5
16. yellow with small logo, 5-spoke concave wheels, China cast, Germany issue..$5 – 6
17. yellow with red, blue and yellow accents, armaments, Roadblasters ....$4 – 5
18. yellow, "9 Rabbit Racing Team," Macau cast, Hong Kong issue.........$10 – 12

FERRARI TESTAROSSA

19. fluorescent yellow with black accent stripes, pink flash, Thailand cast (top shows error package)....$2 – 3
20. metallic blue with small Ferrari logo, Collectors Choice, White Rose Collectibles...................................$3 – 4
21. black with detailed trim, rubber tires on chrome rims, Thailand cast, Premiere Collection #10.........................$4 – 5
22. black with Ferrari logo, silver accents, New Superfast Wheels ....$4 – 5
23. black with small logo, 5-spoke concave wheels, China cast, 2000 Italian Stars series....................................$2 – 3

24. black with small logo, "Matchbox 2000," 5-spoke concave wheels, China cast, 2000 Italian Stars series ....$3 – 4
25. metallic gray with detailed trim, rubber tires on chrome rims, Thailand cast, Gold Coin Collection.............$20 – 30
26. metallic pearl gray with gold accents, Laser Wheels..........................$4 – 5
27. white, "Miami Vice," China cast, Star Cars ....$5 – 6
28. white with chrome windows, detai trim, rubber tires on gray rims, Th land cast, World Class.............$6 –
29. white with no markings, China ca Graffic Traffic ....$12 –

Ferret Scout Car, 2¼", #61, 1959
1. olive green with black plastic wheels...............................$15 –

Fiat 1500, with luggage on roof, 2¹ #56, 1965
1. turquoise ....$8 –
2. red ....$80 – 9

Fiat Abarth, 2¹⁵/₁₆", #9, 1982; #7 1984
1. white, "Matchbox," red interior...$3 –
2. white, "Matchbox," black interior ....$160 – 20
3. white, "Alitalia".......................$4 –
4. white with red, orange, yellow strip Macau cast........................$9 –
5. white, "Matchbox 11," Manaus ca Brazil issue ....$45 – 5

Field Car, 2⁵/₈", #18, 1969
1. yellow with black plastic tires on gre plastic wheel hubs...........$250 – 30
2. yellow with black plastic tires on r wheel hubs, unpainted base.......$6 –
3. black plastic tires on red wheel hub black painted base ....$9 –
4. yellow with Superfast wheels, unpaint base ....$24 – 3
5. yellow with Superfast wheels, meta gray base ....$32 – 3
6. light olive green with Superfast wheels................................$6 –
7. dark olive green with Superfast wheels...............................$70 – 9
8. white with checked design label, Sup fast wheels ....$400 – 50
9. orange with Superfast wheels, bla interior ....$5 –
10. orange with Superfast wheels, "179 black interior ....$6 –
11. orange with Superfast wheels, wh interior ....$6 –
12. orange with Superfast wheels, "179 white interior.......................$9 – 1
13. metallic red with Superfast wheels................................$5 –
14. dark yellow with checked design lab Superfast wheels ....$5 –

Field Gun, 3", #32, 1978
1. army green, army green guard, no base ....$6 –
2. army green, army green guard, t plastic base, black wheel hubs ...$6 –
3. army green, army green guard, tan pla tic base, chrome wheel hubs..$30 – 4
4. army green, black guard, tan plastic bas black wheel hubs, UK issue......$80 – 9
5. green, green guard, tan plastic bas black wheel hubs, UK issue ..$80 – 12

Fire Chief Car (resembles a Ford Torino), 3", #64, 1976; BR 17-18, 1985
red, 1976 .... $10 – 12
red, "Rescue," England cast, Super GT's BR 17-18, 1985 .... $4 – 6
red, "Rescue," China cast, Super GT's BR 17-18, 1985 .... $8 – 10
orange, "Rescue," China cast, Super GT's BR 17-18, 1985 .... $3 – 5
blue, "Police," China cast, Super GT's BR 17-18, 1985 .... $3 – 5
white, "Police," England cast, Super GT's BR 17-18, 1985 .... $4 – 6
white, "Police," China cast, Super GT's BR 17-18, 1985 .... $8 – 10

Fire Crusher/Ladder Truck, #27, 2001; #25, 2002; #3, 2003
metallic red with white ladder, "5 Alarm Force," "Base 525," 2001 Flame Eaters series .... $2 – 3
metallic orange, 2002 Red Hot Heroes series .... $2 – 3

white with red ladder, 2003 Sky Fire series .... **$2 – 3**

Fire Engine (see Snorkel Fire Engine, Extending Ladder Fire Engine)

Fire Hovercraft, 2⅞", #62, 2001; #35, 2002; #64, 2003
2001 Scuba Dudes .... $2 – 3

2. **red plastic hull, white deck, sky blue water gun and engines, 2002 Ultimate Rescue series** .... **$2 – 3**
3. red plastic hull, white deck, sky blue water gun and engines, in Christmas box, 2002 .... $3 – 4
4. dark red plastic hull, white deck, yellow water gun and engines, 2003 Pumper Squad series .... $2 – 3

Fire Truck (see Bucket Fire Truck)

Fire Pumper (see Highway Fire Pumper)

Fire Pumper, 3", #29, 1966
1. red, "Denver" decals, regular wheels .... $9 – 12
2. red, shield labels, regular wheels .. $9 – 12

3. **red, no labels, regular wheels .. $8 – 10**
4. red, no water gun cast, Superfast wheels, 1970 .... $60 – 80
5. red, water gun cast, Superfast wheels, Code Red series .... $9 – 12

Fire Water Pumper, #75, 2002; #62, 2003

1. **dark red with metallic gray base, "Eng. 922," 2002 Rescue Rookies series** .... **$2 – 3**
2. red, "Matchbox Hero City," burning cityscape and fireman graphics, 2003 Pumper Squad series .... $2 – 3

3. **red, "Rescue Heroes" and fireman illustration, 2003 Rescue Heroes 5-pack** .... **$2 – 3**

FJ Holden Van (see Holden FJ Van)

Flame Out, 3", #67, 1983 (similar castings: Big Banger, Cosmic Blues, Pi-Eyed Piper, Red Rider)
1. white with red and orange flames, red windows, Macau cast .... $5 – 6

Flamin' Manta, Roman numeral IX, 1978 (variation of #7 Hairy Hustler, 1971)
1. yellow, Roman Numeral Limited Edition .... $9 – 12

Flareside Pickup (see Ford Flareside Pickup)

Flat Car with container, 3", #25, 1978
1. beige container, "NYK".......... $12 – 16
2. beige container, "Sea/Land".... $8 – 12
3. blue container, "United States Line" .... $45 – 60
4. blue container, "Sea/Land" labels .... $45 – 60
5. dark brown container, "NYK" ..... $7 – 9
6. light brown container, "NYK".. $16 – 24
7. orange container, "NYK" .... $45 – 60
8. orange container, "OCL"........ $45 – 60
9. red container, "NYK" .... $45 – 60
10. tan container, "NYK" .... $7 – 9
11. tan container, "United States Line"................................... $10 – 12
12. tan container, "Sea/Land"......... $7 – 9
13. tan container, "OCL" .... $12 – 16
14. white container, no labels (labels included with play set) .... $12 – 16
15. yellow container, no labels (labels included with play set)...................... $12 – 16

Flatbed Truck, #41, 2000 (similar casting: Delivery Truck)
1. lemon yellow with gray flat bed, metallic gray base, "HB Show Cars" .... $2 – 3
2. lemon yellow with gray flat bed, metallic gray base, "HB Show Cars," "Matchbox 2000".................................... $3 – 4
3. orange with black flatbed, metallic gray base, "Auto Club" .... $3 – 5

4. **metallic blue with black flatbed, metallic gray base, monkey and wrench design, 2003 Hero City 5-pack #11** .... **$2 – 3**

Floodlight Heavy Rescue Auxiliary Power Truck (see Mack Floodlight Heavy Rescue Auxiliary Power Truck)

Flying Beetle, Roman numeral IV, 1978 (variation of #11 Flying Bug, 1972)
1. orange, Roman Numeral Limited Edition .... $9 – 12

Flying Bug Volkswagen Beetle, 2⁷⁄₈", #11, 1972

1. **orange, Roman numeral IV.....$6 – 8**
2. metallic red, yellow jets, driver with chrome helmet...................$15 – 20

Foden Cement Truck (see Foden Concrete Truck, Foden "Ready-Mix" Concrete Truck)

Foden Concrete Truck, 3", #21, 1968
1. yellow with red base, black plastic wheels.................$6 – 9
1. yellow with green base, Superfast wheels.................$24 – 36

Foden "Ready-Mix" Concrete Truck, 1³⁄₄", #26, 1956
1. orange with orange mixer, metal wheels, gold grille................$65 – 85
2. orange with orange mixer, metal wheels, silver grille...............$35 – 50
3. orange with orange mixer, silver plastic wheels............................$135 – 160
5. orange with orange mixer, silver metal wheels, China casting, 1993 Matchbox Originals..............................$3 – 5

Foden "Ready-Mix" Concrete Truck, 2¹⁄₂", #26, 1961
1. orange with gray mixer, gray metal wheels.................$400 – 450
2. orange with orange mixer, gray plastic wheels.................$35 – 45
3. orange with orange mixer, silver plastic wheels.................$130 – 150
4. orange with orange mixer, black plastic wheels.................$15 – 20

Ford '33 Street Rod, #34, 1998; #13, 1999, Australia; #20, 2000
1. black, "IMCC Est. 1998," "Join Today," custom..............................$30 – 40
2. black with red stripes, rubber tires on chrome rims, First Editions.......$5 – 6

3. **gray with purple door, dirt and "MB" door logo, 5-pack ....$2 – 3**
4. gray with purple door, dirt and "American Iron Cruise Night," Color Comp promotional.............................$12 – 16
5. metallic hot pink with accents ....$2 – 3
6. maroon, "IMCC Est. 1998," "Join Today," Goodyear slicks, custom........$20 – 30

7. **maroon with black and yellow design, Goodyear slicks, 1998 Classic Decades series ....$2 – 3**

8. **metallic purple, no markings, Goodyear slicks, 2000 Great Drivers series ....$2 – 3**
9. metallic purple, "Matchbox 2000," Goodyear slicks, 2000 Great Drivers series.....................................$3 – 4
10. metallic purple, "Midwest Regional Convention," "MRMC 2000," custom...$20 – 25
11. metallic purple, "Midwest Regional Convention," "MRMC 2000 Vendor," custom ....$30 – 40
12. purple, "Hot August Nights 2000"................................$16 – 24

13. **purple with amber roof lights, "D.A.R.E." and graphics, 2001 D.A.R.E. 5-pack ....$2 – 3**
14. red and white, "Coca-Cola," rubber tires, Premiere Collection..........$5 – 6
15. unpainted, "IMCC Est. 1998," "Join Today," custom ....$30 – 40
16. unpainted with no markings, rubber tires on chrome rims, First Editions ....$5 – 6
17. yellow, "American Graffiti," rubber tires on gray rims, Star Cars ....$12 – 16

18. yellow, "2001 Ballarat 12th Super Southern Swapmeet, custom.........$12 – 1
19. yellow, "Cruise Down Memory Lane "Corvettes Unlimited," Color Comp pmotional ....$16 – 2
20. yellow, "Cruisin New England Magazi All Wheels Festival 2001, Color Co promotional.........................$50 – 6
21. yellow with black roof, "Glenside Mot Vehicle Show 2000," Color Comp pmotional ....$20 – 2
22. yellow with black roof, "Matchbox 200 Demo Model — Color Comp Inc.," Co Comp promotional................$24 – 3
23. yellow with black roof, "Midwest Region Convention," custom ....$20 – 2
24. yellow with black roof, Goodyear slic Australia issue.......................$3 –

Ford 3-Ton 4x4 Army Ambulance, 2¹⁄ #63, 1959
1. olive green with black plastic wheels ....$40 – 5

Ford Ambulance, #51, 1997; #25, 199 #5, 1999; #87, 2000; #17, 199 international
1. "27 Matchbox Ambulance," "48 – 9 "Newfield Ambulance Corps," whi with chrome base, Color Comp prom tional ....$20 – 3

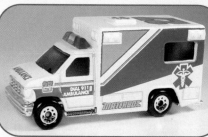

2. **"27 Matchbox Ambulance," "Di 911 Ambulance," white with chrom base, blue and silver design ...$2 – **

3. **"27 Matchbox Ambulance," yellow wi chrome base, red and white desig 1998 To The Rescue series ....$2 – **
4. "27 Matchbox Ambulance," yello with translucent white base, red a white design, 1998 To The Rescu series ....$60 – 8
5. "5 Alarm Ambulance," white wi chrome base, 5-pack................$2 –
6. "Alice 106 FM," white with chrome bas ASAP promotional issue.....$120 – 16

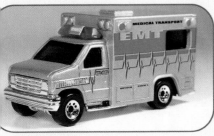

"Ambulance," "EMS" logo, metallic silver with chrome base, dark blue bands, 5-pack.....................$4 – 5
"Ambulance — Ridge, New York," bright blue with chrome base, 1999 Matchbox USA series.........................$2 – 3
"Ambulance 3-1926," white with chrome base, olive and blue stripes, 5-pack..$2 – 3
Ɔ. "Ambulance Dial 911," white with chrome base, rubber tires on chrome rims, 1997 Inaugural issue.......$5 – 6
1. "American International Recovery," white with chrome base, ASAP promotional issue......................$120 – 160
2. "Bill Cairns Realtor," white with chrome base, ASAP promotional issue...................................$12 – 16
3. "County EMS," burgundy cab, white box, burgundy accents, 1998 Around Town 5-pack...$2 – 3
4. "EMT," "Matchbox Medical Transport," metallic silver with chrome base, red band, yellow design, 2000 Police Patrol series...................................$2 – 3
5. "EMT," "Matchbox Medical Transport," "Matchbox 2000," metallic silver with chrome base, red band, yellow design, 2000 Police Patrol series.........$3 – 4
6. "Fire Rescue," red with chrome base, white band, rubber tires on chrome rims, Premiere Collection #21.......................................$4 – 5
7. "FSU," white with chrome base, ASAP promotional issue.................$12 – 16
8. "Flight Crew Transport," dark blue with chrome base, rubber tires on chrome rims, Premiere Collection......$30 – 40
9. "Kimball Day Hospital," white with chrome base, ASAP promotional issue..$12 – 16
Ɔ. "Las Vegas Fire Department," white with chrome base, rubber tires on chrome rims, Premiere Collection.......$12 – 16
1. "Matchbox Dial 911 Ambulance," white with blue and silver accents.......$2 – 3
2. "Metro Alarm," "Ambulance, orange and white with chrome base, 5-pack..$2 – 3
3. "Midwest Regional Matchbox Convention" in gold lettering, white with chrome base, ASAP promotional issue.........$12 – 16
4. "Midwest Regional Matchbox Convention" in green lettering, white with chrome base, ASAP promotional issue ....$60 – 70
5. "Midwest Regional Matchbox Convention" in red lettering, white with chrome base, ASAP promotional issue..........$30 – 40

26. "NAEMT/MAEMT 25 Years of Service," white with chrome base, ASAP promotional issue...........................$12 – 16
27. "Police," "Metropolitan Police," white with chrome base; red, yellow, and blue stripes; 2000 Police Patrol series............$3 – 4
28. "Squantz Engine Co.," white with chrome base, ASAP promotional issue .$12 – 16
29. "Sugar Grove Fire Department 2000," white with chrome base, ASAP promotional issue...........................$16 – 24
30. "Windham Hospital EMS" (left side only), white with chrome base, ASAP promotional issue...........................$12 – 16
31. "Windham Hospital EMS," "2000," white with chrome base, ASAP promotional issue...........................$12 – 16
32. "York Fair Emergency 1997," yellow with chrome base, White Rose Collectibles...................................$7 – 9
33. metallic gold with chrome base, 1997 75 Challenge series ....$6 – 12
34. red with chrome base, yellow and red snake and rod design, 5-pack ....$2 – 3
35. unpainted with chrome base, rubber tires on chrome rims, 1997 Inaugural issue.......................................$5 – 6
36. white with chrome base, no markings, ASAP promotional blank........$30 – 40

Ford Anglia, light blue, 2⅝", #7, 1961
1. gray plastic wheels...............$20 – 25
2. silver plastic wheels..............$20 – 25
3. black plastic wheels..............$15 – 20

Ford Atkinson Grit Spreader, 2⅝", #70, 1966

1. red cab, light yellow hopper, black plastic wheels, 1966.........$12 – 16
2. red cab, dark yellow hopper, black plastic wheels, 1966 ....$30 – 40
3. red cab, yellow hopper, Superfast wheels, 1970.....................$35 – 45

Ford Boss Mustang, 2⅞", #44, 1972, #11, 1982
1. orange, "Boss" outlined on sides, 1982 ....$7 – 9
2. orange, "Boss" in black on sides, 1982 ....$7 – 9
3. orange, "Boss" in white on sides, 1982 ....$7 – 9
4. orange with no markings, 1982 ..$7 – 9
5. yellow with black hood, no markings, 1972......................................$7 – 9
6. dark green, "Cobra Mustang," limited edition, 1972.....................$9 – 12

Ford Boss Mustang 1970, #37, 1998
1. lemon yellow with black stripe, lemon yellow plastic base, white and black interior, rubber tires on chrome rims, 1998 First Editions ....$5 – 6
2. lemon yellow, "Coca-Cola," black interior, metallic gray metal base, Avon....$6 – 7
3. pale blue, no markings, white and black interior, rubber tires on chrome rims, pale blue plastic base ....$5 – 6

4. metallic purple, "Boss" and stripes, yellow interior, chrome plastic base, 1998 Classic Decades series .$2 – 3
5. metallic purple, "Boss," "South Jersey Mustang" and stripes, yellow interior, chrome plastic base, Color Comp promotional ....$30 – 40
6. metallic purple, "Boss" and stripes, yellow interior, translucent white base, 1998 Classic Decades series...........$60 – 80
7. unpainted, no markings, white interior, chrome plastic base, rubber tires on chrome rims, 1998 First Editions .$5 – 6
8. black with silver design, light gray interior, chrome plastic base, Real Talkin' series ....$4 – 5
9. black with silver design, light gray interior, translucent white plastic base ..$60 – 80

Ford Box Van, #23, 1999, #59, 2000
1. blue-green with white interior, blue windows, fish logo, 5-pack ....$2 – 3

2. green with yellow interior, "Hey Arnold" and cartoon head, 2003 Nickelodeon 5-pack ....$3 – 4

3. **red with red interior, "Coca-Cola," black and white design ....$3 – 4**
4. white with white interior, clear windows, "FedEx," 1999 Speedy Delivery series ....$2 – 3
5. white with white interior, clear windows, no markings, ASAP promotional blank..................................$30 – 45
6. white with white interior, clear windows, "County Line," ASAP promotional ....$80 – 120
7. white with white interior, clear windows, "Flowers Make It Special," "Roques," ASAP promotional ....$80 – 120

8. **white with white interior, blue windows, "FedEx," 2000 Speedy Delivery series ....$2 – 3**
9. white with white interior, blue windows, "FedEx," "Matchbox 2000," 2000 Speedy Delivery series ....$3 – 4
10. white with black interior, clear windows, "FedEx," 2000 Speedy Delivery series ....$2 – 3

11. **white with black interior, amber windows, red and black design, "Matchbox," "8945," "54," circle logo, 2000 5 Alarm 5-pack............$2 – 3**
12. white with black interior, "Merry Christmas 1999," "Last Delivery — Matchbox Forum," custom model..........$24 – 32
13. white with black interior, clear windows, no markings, ASAP promotional blank..................................$30 – 45
14. yellow with red interior, clear windows, "Coca-Cola," rubber tires on chrome rims, Premiere Collection ....$5 – 6

Ford Bronco II 4x4, 3", #35, 1989; #39, 1990; #51, 1998; #25, 1999
1. red, "Vinnie's Pizza," 1999 Speedy Delivery series ....$2 – 3
2. red, map and compass design, yellow tires, Live 'N Learn/Matchbox Preschool series ....$7 – 9

3. **red with yellow "4x4 Bronco," white splash design, 1993 Off Road 5-pack ....$2 – 3**

4. **red, "Luigi's Pizza," 1998 Rough 'N Tough series..........................$2 – 3**
5. orange to dark brown, "Bronco" and stripes, Super Color Changer.....$4 – 5
6. fluorescent orange with black zebra stripes, 5-pack ....$2 – 3
7. yellow, "4x4," red flames, red interior, on-package premium, US issue ..$7 – 9
8. yellow, "World 4 Kids," blue interior, Australia issue.....................$20 – 25
9. metallic green with beige trim, Collectors Choice, White Rose Collectibles ....$4 – 5
10. purple with white stripes, modified base and interior, play set.................$4 – 5
11. metallic blue, "4x4 Bronco," white splash design ....$2 – 3

12. **metallic purple with white zebra stripes, 1998 Rugged Riders 5-pack ....$2 – 3**
13. black, "Kidz 1.75 FM," pink and yellow stripes, Australia issue ....$5 – 6
14. black, "Piranha" on hood, orange piranha design, orange interior ....$2 – 3
15. black, "Piranha" on hood, orange piranha design, red interior ....$2 – 3
16. black, without "Piranha" on hood, orange piranha design, red interior ....$2 – 3

17. **white, "Rescue Unit," "Police," shiel on door, black hood, black sid design, Emergency EM – 71...$2 – :**
18. white, "Police PD-22," 1995 Emergenc 5-pack.....................................$2 – 4

19. **white with black zebra stripes black interior, 1996 Off-Road 5 pack...................................$2 – :**
20. white, "Bronco" and stripes, red inte rior...$2 – 4
21. white, "Coast Guard Beach Patrol," re interior ....$2 – :
22. white, "Luigi's Pizza," red interior 1997...$2 – :
23. dark brown to orange, "Bronco" an stripes, red interior, Super Colo Changer ....$4 – :
24. metallic silver with orange piranh design, blue interior...................$3 – 4
25. metallic gold, black interior, 1997 7 Challenge series ....$6 – 12
26. 2002 Matchbox Across America 50t Birthday series #41 Montana — West ern Collection ....$4 – :

Ford Camper Pickup Truck (see Ford Pick up Camper)

Ford Capri, 3", #54, 1971; BR 37-38 1986 (similar casting: Hot Rocker Maxi Taxi)

- metallic bright pink ....$12 – 16
- orange..............................$9 – 12
- purple ....$12 – 15
- cream, China cast, Super GT's BR 37-38, 1986................................$3 – 5
- blue, China cast, Super GT's BR 37-38, 1986................................$3 – 5

Ford Cargo Skip Truck, 2¹³/₁₆", #70, 1988; #45, 1987, international; #317, 1999, Action Packs

- red with metallic gray cage, metallic gray arms with lever, "Big Top Circus," Action Pack............................$4 – 5
- orange-yellow with no stripe, red plastic skip, China cast ....$2 – 3
- yellow with orange stripe, gray metal skip, Macau cast ....$2 – 3
- yellow with orange stripe, gray metal skip, Thailand cast ....$2 – 3
- yellow with orange stripe, gray plastic skip, Macau cast ....$2 – 3
- yellow with orange stripe, gray plastic skip, Thailand cast ....$2 – 3
- yellow with orange stripe, red plastic skip, Thailand cast ....$2 – 3
- bright green with orange cage, black arms with lever, dark green camouflage, "The Lost World," Jurassic Park ....$4 – 5
- blue with red metal skip, yellow wheels with orange hubs, Macau cast, Matchbox Preschool/Live 'N Learn series ....$7 – 9
- 10. khaki with black cage, black arms with lever, green stripes, Action Pack......................................$3 – 4

Ford Corsair with boat and rack on roof, 2⅝", #45, 1965
1. gray wheels........................$30 – 40
2. black wheels.......................$12 – 16

Ford Cortina 1600 GL, 3¹/₁₆", #55, 1979
1. red, clear windows, doors cast shut.......................................$4 – 5
2. red, clear windows, white and orange flames, Chinese issue ....$160 – 240
3. metallic red, clear windows, doors open ....$5 – 6
4. metallic red, opaque white windows, doors cast shut ....$12 – 16
5. orange-red, "Nigel Cooper for Matchbox Toys," "Christmas 96," clear windows, Bulgarian cast, UK issue ....$9 – 12
6. green, clear windows, doors open ....$5 – 6

7. **metallic green, clear windows, doors open.............................$5 – 6**

8. **metallic tan, black stripe, clear windows, doors open.................$4 – 5**

Ford Cortina GT, 2⅞", #25, 1968

1. **metallic light brown, no roof rack, regular wheels.....................$6 – 9**
2. metallic light brown with roof rack, regular wheels ....$9 – 12
3. metallic light brown, Superfast wheels, 1970................................$60 – 80
4. metallic blue, Superfast wheels, 1970................................$20 – 25

Ford Coupe (see Ford Street Rod 1933)

Ford Coupe 1933 Police, #508, 2001
1. metallic purple, "D.A.R.E.," black and orange design, amber roof light, 5-pack ....$2 – 3

Ford Courier Delivery Van, 3," #38, 1992, European model
1. red, "Australia Matchbox News," no side cast windows, Australia issue .$16 – 24
2. red, "Australia Matchbox News," "Club Member" on roof, no side cast windows, Australia issue..........$80 – 120
3. red, "Axa Insurance?," no side cast windows, UK issue.................$80 – 120
4. red, "Ford County Emergency Services," no side cast windows, US issue.....$16 – 24
5. red, no markings, side cast windows..............................$12 – 16
6. dark blue, "Australia Matchbox News," no side cast windows, Australia issue ....$80 – 120
7. dark blue, "Axa," no side cast windows, UK issue...........................$20 – 25
8. dark blue, "Benedick's Coffee Service," no side cast windows, US issue ....$16 – 24
9. dark blue, "Matchbox — The Ideal Premium," no side cast windows, Germany issue................................$20 – 25
10. dark purple, "Milka," no side cast windows.....................................$2 – 3
11. light purple, "Milka," no side cast windows.....................................$3 – 4
12. white, "Courier," no side cast windows, UK issue...........................$12 – 16

13. white, "Dent Magician," no side cast windows, UK issue ....$50 – 60

Ford Crown Victoria Police Car, #54, 1997; #28, 1998; #33, 1999; #86, 2000; #49, 2001
1. "Aegis NT New World Systems," white with red roof lights, ASAP promotional...........................$60 – 80
2. "Atlanta Police," white with blue roof lights, rubber tires on chrome rims, Premiere Collection #22 ...$200 – 250
3. "C.E.R.T.," "Toy Show Police," "Color Comp Emergency Response Team," "Emergency Demo Model," white with red triangular roof lights, Color Comp promotional ..$30 – 40
4. "D.A.R.E.," white with blue flames, red triangular roof lights, D.A.R.E. series ....$4 – 5
5. "Dallas Police," white with red and blue roof lights, rubber tires on chrome rims, Premiere Collection #22....$300 – 350
6. "Drive," "A-Pix Entertainment," white, red roof lights, ASAP promotional ......$120 – 160
7. "Freeport Police," white with red roof lights, ASAP promotional.......$30 – 40
8. "IACP," white with red dome light, ASAP promotional.........................$60 – 80
9. "If You Don't Collect Matchbox... Get Out Of The Way," white with red triangular roof lights, Color Comp promotional .$30 – 40
10. "Justice for Police Officer Daniel Faulkner," "4699," "Philadelphia Police," white with red triangular roof lights, Color Comp promotional.................................$30 – 50

11. **"Matchbox FDMB" on shield with flame graphics, "14," white with red roof lights, 2001 Action Launcher Fire Truck ....$3 – 4**

12. **"MBI Special Agents" on hood, black with blue roof lights; blue, white, and red accents; 2001 Pull Over series.......................................$2 – 3**

13. "Minnesota State Patrol," metallic burgundy wtih red roof lights, rubber tires on chrome rims, World Class series 18 State Patrol II ....$4 – 5

14. "Missouri State Police," white with red and blue roof lights, rubber tires on chrome rims, World Class State Patrol .....$4 – 5

15. "Montana Highway Patrol," black with blue roof lights, white roof, rubber tires on chrome rims, World Class series 18 State Patrol II.........$4 – 5

16. "Nassau County Police," white with red roof lights, ASAP promotional..$30 – 40

17. "National Law Enforcement Officers Memorial 2001," white with red bar roof lights, ASAP promotional........$60 – 80

18. "North Dakota State Patrol," white with red roof lights, rubber tires on chrome rims, World Class State Patrol...$4 – 5

19. "Ocean City New Jersey Police" on shield, white with red roof lights, blue and orange stripes, 2000 Police Patrol series ....$2 – 3

20. "Ocean City New Jersey Police" on shield, white with red roof lights, blue and orange stripes, 2000 Police Patrol series.....................................$2 – 3

21. "Ocean City New Jersey Police" on shield, white with red triangular roof lights, blue and orange stripes, 2000 Police Patrol series ....$3 – 4

22. "Police," "D.A.R.E.," white with red and blue roof lights, D.A.R.E. series..$4 – 5

23. "Police," "To Serve and Protect, Scotchguard," white with red triangular roof lights, Color Comp promotional...........$30 – 50

24. "Police D-19," black and white with red roof lights ....$5 – 6

25. "Police K-9 Canine Unit," blue with red roof lights ....$2 – 3

26. "Police Landover Hills," "D.A.R.E.," white with red and blue roof lights, D.A.R.E. series....................................$4 – 5

27. "Police Unit 22," "D22" on roof, blue with red roof lights, white and pale orange design, 1997 ....$3 – 4

28. "Police Unit 22," "D22" on roof, black with red roof lights, 1998 To The Rescue series................................$2 – 3

29. "Police" with red and white design, blue with red roof lights, 1999 Law & Order series....................................$2 – 3

30. "Police" with red and blue stripes, white with red triangular roof lights, 1999 Law & Order series ....$2 – 3

31. "Police" with blue checkerboard pattern, white with red and blue roof lights, Australia issue ....$16 – 24

32. "Rhode Island State Police," gray with red roof lights, rubber tires on chrome rims, Premiere Collection ....$6 – 8

33. "Route 66 Promotions," white with red roof lights, ASAP promotional ..$20 – 30

34. "South Dakota Highway Patrol," white with red and blue roof lights, rubber tires on chrome rims, World Class series 18 State Patrol II ....$4 – 5

35. "Station 02," red with red roof lights; white, silver, and yellow graphics; 2003 Hero City 5-pack #1......$2 – 3

36. "Verona Police," white with red triangular roof lights, black interior, Color Comp promotional................$20 – 30

37. "Verona Police," white with red triangular roof lights, gray interior, Color Comp promotional..........................$60 – 80

38. "Verona Police," "Verona PBA," white with red triangular roof lights, black interior, Color Comp promotional ..$20 – 30

39. "Wanaque Police," "D.A.R.E.," black with red triangular roof lights, D.A.R.E. series....................................$4 – 5

40. blue with red and yellow stripes and crest, red roof lights, 5-pack ....$2 – 3

41. blue with red and yellow stripes and crest, red roof lights, Target Eggmobile 3-pack..............................$12 – 16

42. white with yellow roof lights, 200 McDonald's Happy Meal premiu with set of labels to apply......$3 –

43. white with red roof lights, ASAP promotional blank........................$30 – 4

44. white with red triangular roof lights, Cold Comp promotional blank.........$30 – 4

45. metallic gold with red roof lights, 199 75 Challenge series ....$6 – 1

Ford Customline Station Wagon, 2³/₄ #31, 1957

1. yellow with metal wheels ....$35 – 4

2. yellow with gray plastic wheels..$40 – 5

Ford Dump/Utility Truck, #91, 2000 #71, 2000, international (see Ford 150 Pickup)

Ford Escort, BR 25-26, 1985

1. red, England cast, Super GTs BR 25-6 1985......................................$4 –

2. blue, England cast, Super GTs BR 25 26, 1985...........................$6 –

3. beige, England cast, Super GTs BR 25 26, 1985..........................$4 –

4. yellow, England cast, Super GTs BR 25 26, 1985.........................$12 – 15

5. purple, China cast, Super GTs BR 25 26, 1985...........................$3 –

Ford Escort Cosworth (see Ford Escort R Cosworth)

Ford Escort RS200 (see Ford RS200)

Ford Escort RS Cosworth, #52, 1994 1997; #15, 2001, UK

1. red, "5," yellow splash design, blac spoiler, 5-spoke wheels.............$2 –

2. red, "5," yellow splash design, blac spoiler, 6-spoke wheels.............$4 –

3. metallic red with lime and whit design, red spoiler ....$2 – 3

4. metallic red with lime and white design black spoiler...........................$3 – 4

black, "1," yellow and white accents, yellow spoiler, 1997 ....**$2 – 3**

black, "1," yellow and white accents, black spoiler ....$2 – 3

white, "MOL," orange and two-tone green stripes, white spoiler, Hungarian issue ....$30 – 40

white with British flag, red spoiler, 2001 Union Jack series, UK issue ......$4 – 5

white, "Ford" logo on hood, "23," "Goodyear," black and orange graphics, white spoiler, 1996 Racing 5-pack ....**$2 – 3**

0. **white, "Matchbox 3," yellow and dark blue design, dark blue spoiler, 1997 Racing 5-pack** ....**$2 – 3**

1. **white, "Mobil 1," "5," "Michelin," blue design, white spoiler, white base** ....**$2 – 3**

2. white, "Mobil 1," "5," "Michelin, blue design, white spoiler, blue base .. $4 – 5

3. metallic gold, black spoiler, 1997 75 Challenge series ....$6 – 12

ord Escort RS2000, 3", #9, 1978

white with tan interior, "Dunlop" labels ....**$4 – 5**

---

2. white with red interior, "Dunlop" labels ....$150 – 180

3. white with tan interior, "Phantom" labels ....$4 – 6

4. blue with tan interior, "Phantom" labels ....$4 – 6

5. green with tan interior, "Dunlop" labels ....$4 – 6

6. green with tan interior, seagull labels ....$4 – 6

7. green with white interior, seagull labels ....$4 – 6

8. green with red interior, seagull labels ....$150 – 180

Ford Escort XR3/XR3i Cabriolet, 2¾", #17, 1985, US; #37, 1985, international

1. **white with "Ocean Explorer," 1999 Beach Fun 5-pack** ....**$3 – 5**

2. **white with "XR3i," silver wheel hubs, Macau cast** ....**$2 – 4**

3. white with "XR3i," gold wheel hubs, Macau cast.............................$4 – 6

4. white with "XR3i," Thailand cast .. $2 – 4

5. **white with "3" and stripes, new Superfast wheels** ....**$4 – 6**

6. red with "XR3i" and "FORD" .....$9 – 12

7. metallic blue with "3" and stripes, Laser wheels.................................$4 – 6

8. **metallic blue with white and orange spatter** ....**$2 – 4**

---

9. dark blue with "XR3i," Macau cast....................................$2 – 4

10. dark blue with "XR3i," Thailand cast....................................$2 – 4

Ford Expedition, #67, 1999; #54, 2000; #28, 2002; #62, 1999, international

1. yellow, "Base 2000," "3456/54," red bands, Launcher 5-pack............$2 – 3

2. yellow, "Coca-Cola," red band and polar bears, rubber tires on chrome rims, Premiere Collection ....$6 – 8

3. yellow, "Rescue," "Mountain Patrol," red stripes, 1999 Ranger Patrol US issue....................................$2 – 3

4. yellow with red stripes and medical cross, 1999 Ranger Patrol international issue....................................$3 – 4

5. dusty army green, "Military Police," "Matchbox 2000," 2000 Military series ...$3 – 4

6. **dusty army green, "Military Police," 2000 Military series** ....**$2 – 3**

7. bright blue, detailed trim, rubber tires on chrome rims, 1999 First Editions .. $5 – 6

8. unpainted, rubber tires on chrome rims, 1999 First Editions ....$5 – 6

9. black, "09-99," red and black design, 5-pack....................................$2 – 3

10. black, "09-99," red and white design, Target Eggmobile 3-pack ....$3 – 4

11. black, "Scooby-Doo," "Iriuih-Irioih," "Scooby Dooby Doo!" Warner Brothers .....$6 – 8

12. white, "100 Ford Motor Company 100 Years," 2003 Avon 2-pack ....$5 – 6

13. **metal flake silver, "RR Road Rescue Fire Patrol," purple base, 2002 Red Hot Heroes series** ....**$2 – 3**

Ford Expedition Police, #50, 2001; #5, 2003

1. **blue, "State Patrol," yellow roof light, chrome base, 2001 Pull Over series** ....$2 – 3
2. metallic blue, "042076," storm graphics, amber roof light, Launcher 5-pack .$2 – 3

3. **white, round "Matchbox" fire logo, red stripes, "54," "3456," red roof light, 2000 5 Alarm 5-pack ...$2 – 3**
4. white and metallic red, "Fire Chief PTF01," "Matchbox PTF 2001," red roof light, rubber tires on chrome rims ....$50 – 60
5. white with orange accents, amber roof light, 2002 Matchbox Across America 50th Birthday series #47 New Mexico — Western Collection...............$5 – 6

6. **white with black; red, yellow, and bronze design; blue roof light, "Metro Alarm," 2003 Sky Fire series** ....$2 – 3

Ford Explorer Sport Trac, #23, 2001; #24, 2002; #40, 2003

1. **red with gray base, 2001 Sun Chasers series** ....$2 – 3
2. orange-red with chrome base, "2001 Matchbox Toy Show," "Hershey Matchbox Pennsylvania," rubber tires on chrome rims ....$9 – 12

3. **white with gray base, red and black "Huskies Dog Sled Team," 2002 Great Outdoors series** ....$2 – 3
4. black with purple base, "Tune-Up Auto Parts" and graphics, 2003 Mom and Pop Shops ....$2 – 3
5. 2002 Matchbox Across America 50th Birthday series #45 Utah — Western Collection...............................$4 – 6

6. **metallic blue with black base, 2003 Hero City 5-pack #12** ....$2 – 3

7. **yellow with lime green base, 2003 Rescue Heroes 5-pack** ....$2 – 3

Ford F-150 1997 Pickup, #65, 1997; #50, 1998; #69, 1999; #21, 2002

1. **red, "4X4 Off Road," black interior, chrome base, 1998 Rough 'N Tough series** ....$2 – 3

2. **blue with orange and white "State Park Fish Farm," "Catch & Release," "Patrol Vehicle," 1999 Ranger Patrol series** ....$2 – 3
3. black with black and tan interior, Goodyear rubber tires, 1997 First Editions ....$5 – 6
4. black with black and tan interior, Goodyear rubber tires, "Matchbox," "MDM," "630-681-2101" .....$40 – 50
5. white, "Action Radar," "Xtreme Mission," 5-pack ....$2 – 3

6. white, "Texaco — A World of Energy," bla bed liner, Premiere Collection ....$5 –
7. metallic olive gold, blue accents, 20 Great Outdoors series ....$2 –
8. unpainted, tan interior, Goodyear ru ber tires, 1997 First Editions.....$5 –
9. unpainted, tan interior, Goodyear ru ber tires, "Matchbox," "MDM," "63 681-2101" ....$40 – 5

Ford F-150 4x4 Pickup, #65, 1995; #5 1998; #14, 2000

1. red, "Beach Patrol Unit 44," black r bar, China cast, 2000 To The Bea series ....$2 –
2. red, "Beach Patrol Unit 44," "Matchb 2000," black roll bar, China cast, 20 To The Beach series.................$3 –

3. **red, "Ford," white and blu accents, chrome roll bar, Chi cast, 5-pack** ....$2 –
4. red with white accents on sides, bla roll bar, China cast, 1995.........$2 –
5. red with white accents on sides, bla roll bar, Thailand cast, 1995 .....$2 –

6. **red with white accents on sides chrome roll bar, Thailand cas 1995** ....$2 –
7. red with white and blue splash, blu Ford logo on doors, chrome roll ba 1997 Rugged Riders 5-pack......$2 –

8. **fluorescent yellow with orange an blue rhinoceros head on doors, 200 Hero City 5-pack #4** ....$2 –

metallic blue, "Whirlpool," black roll bar, China cast, ASAP promotional ....$120 – 160

0. metallic blue with silver accents on sides, black roll bar, China cast, 1996.................$2 – 3

1. purple with light green accents on sides, chrome roll bar, China cast, 1998 5-pack.........................$2 – 3

2. purple with light green accents on sides, metallic gray roll bar, 1996 Off Road 5-pack...................$2 – 3

3. black, "Black Star Ranch," mud spatter, green roll bar, China cast, 5-pack.$2 – 3

4. black, "Don't Mess With Texas," mud spatter, green roll bar, China cast, 5-pack....................................$2 – 3

5. black, "MC15" and rhinoceros head, dark green roll bar, China cast, 5-pack.$2 – 3

6. black with red accents on sides, chrome roll bar, China cast, 1997 ....$2 – 3

17. white with orange and blue accents, blue Ford logo, blue roll bar, China cast, 1998 Rough 'N Tough series........................$2 – 3

18. metallic gold with white and blue splash design, blue Ford logo on sides, chrome roll bar, China cast, 1998 Rugged Riders 5-pack...$2 – 3

19. metallic gold with chrome roll bar, 1997 75 Challenge series ......$6 – 12

Ford F-150 Dump Truck, #91, 2000; #13, 2001; #71, 2000, international (similar casting: Ford F-150 Rescue Pickup)

1. red, "Matchbox Bilt," "CM-3527," white stripes, 8-spoke wheels, 2000 Build It! series.................................$3 – 4

2. red, "Matchbox Bilt," "CM-3527," white stripes, 8-spoke wheels, 2000 Build It! series, "Matchbox 2000" ....$4 – 5

3. red, "Matchbox Bilt," "CM-3527," white stripes, 7-spoke sawblade wheels, 2000 5-pack.......................$12 – 16

4. orange-red, "Rescue Heroes," graphics, yellow dumper, 7-spoke sawblade wheels, 2003 Rescue Heroes 5-pack ....$2 – 3

5. black with checkerboard design and winged logo, 7-spoke sawblade wheels, 2001 Highway Heroes series ....$3 – 4

6. black with checkerboard design and winged logo, 8-spoke wheels, 2001 Highway Heroes series ....$5 – 6

Ford F-150 Rescue Pickup, with boat ramp and inflatable raft, #43, 2001; #42, 2003 (similar casting: Ford F-150 Dump Truck)

1. red, "Matchbox FDMB" on shield, flame graphics, metallic gray ramp, yellow raft, 2001 Action Launcher Fire Truck set........................$3 – 4

2. red, "MBFD," white ramp, yellow raft, 2001 Rescue Squad series .....$2 – 3

3. yellow, 2002 Matchbox Across America 50th Birthday series #32 Minnesota – Central Collection....................$4 – 6

4. white, "MHC Beach Patrol," yellow ramp, yellow raft, 2003 Beach Patrol series...................................$2 – 3

Ford F-150 Utility Truck, 3", #74, 1987, international; #33, 1989 – 1997; #9, 1998; #15, 1999

1. red with white boom, "Matchbox Fire Dept.," 2000 Fire 5-pack.......$2 – 3

2. red with yellow boom, "53," yellow wheels, Matchbox Preschool/Live 'N Learn series...........................$6 – 8

3. orange with white boom, "P & L Response Unit 20," 1998 Big Movers series....................................$2 – 3

4. yellow with red front end, "Energy Inc," Action Pack ....$4 – 5

5. yellow, "Telephone Co.," "Unit 4" ..$2 – 3

6. green, "Intercom City," "Service".$8 – 10

7. **metallic green with metallic gray base, white boom, "Tree Care" and tree, 1996**.....................**$2 – 3**
8. blue with yellow boom, white lettering, yellow accents, White Rose Collectibles ....$6 – 8

9. **blue with yellow boom, "P & L Co," "Response Unit," "20," 1997**.**$2 – 3**
10. metallic gold with black boom, 1997 75 Challenge series ....$12 – 16

11. **metallic silver with red boom, "Global Electric, 1997 City Streets 5-pack** ....**$2 – 3**

12. **metallic silver with yellow boom, "Ideal Power," "Clean Safe Power," 1999 Highway Haulers series** ....**$2 – 3**

13. **black with green boom, "Highway Crew," "Caution High Voltage," "Unit 45," 1999 Highway Crew 5-pack**.....................................**$2 – 3**
14. **gray with orange front end, "Energy Inc."** ....**$2 – 3**

15. **beige with bright green base and boom, green "Tree Care" and tree design, 1995**.......................**$2 – 3**
16. white with white boom, ASAP promotional blank..........................$30 – 40
17. white with white boom, "American International Recovery," ASAP promotional ....$60 – 80
18. white with white boom, "Bell Atlantic," ASAP promotional ....$60 – 80
19. white with white boom, "Georgia Power Co.," ASAP promotional ......$80 – 120
20. white with white boom, "GI," ASAP promotional ....$120 – 160
21. white with white boom, "Gulf Power," ASAP promotional ....$60 – 80
22. white with white boom, "LCEC," ASAP promotional.........................$40 – 60
23. white with white boom, "MTI" on left side, ASAP promotional ....$60 – 80
24. white with white boom, "Pac Tel," ASAP promotional......................$80 – 120
25. white with white boom, "RMLD," ASAP promotional.........................$30 – 40
26. white with white boom, "Verizon," ASAP promotional......................$80 – 120
27. white with white boom, "Western States Co-Op," ASAP promotional .....$80 – 120
28. white with white boom, "Xcel Energy," ASAP promotional..............$80 – 120
29. white with white boom, yellow sun and green line logo, ASAP promotional ......$60 – 80

Ford F-350 (see Ford F-150 Dump Truck, Ford F-150 Rescue Pickup)

Ford F-350 KME Pumper, 2000 Feature Cars, with opening features, designed to replace Premiere Collection
1. fluorescent yellow, "Base 24"...$9 – 12
2. white and red, "Elizaville" ....$12 – 16
3. white and red, "Trucksville" ....$12 – 16

Ford F-350 Pickup, 2000 Feature Cars, with opening features, designed to replace Premiere Collection

1. metallic gray..........................$9 – 1
2. metallic pale brown ....$9 – 1

Ford F-800 Delivery Truck, FS001 WR002, container doesn't extend ov cab, White Rose Collectibles
1. "ABC Sports," white with white container ....$12 – 1
2. "All Star Game 1996," red with whit container ....$9 – 1
3. "All Star Game 1997 — Indians," whit with white container ....$7 – 9
4. "American Lung Association," white wit white container.....................$8 – 10
5. "Atlanta Braves 1996," red with blu container ....$7 – 9
6. "Baltimore Orioles 1996," orange wit black container ....$7 – 9
7. "Bill Elliot," "M," "10," red with whit container, Team Convoy..........$7 – 9
8. "Boston Red Sox 1996," dark blue wit red container ....$7 – 9
9. "California Angels 1996," metallic gra with dark blue container...........$7 – 9
10. "Cat Racing," white with white containe Team Convoy............................$7 – 9
11. "Chicago Cubs 1996," blue with whit container ....$7 – 9
12. "Chicago White Sox 1996," black wit white container......................$7 – 9
13. "Cincinnati Reds 1996," white with re container ....$7 – 9
14. "Cleveland Indians 1996," red with dar blue container ....$7 – 9
15. "Colorado Rockies 1996," purple wit metallic gray container............$7 – 9
16. "Detroit Tigers 1996," dark blue wit orange container ....$7 – 9
17. "Dutch Valley," blue with white cor tainer.................................$7 – 9
18. "Florida Marlins 1996," black wit turquoise container ....$7 – 9
19. "Houston Astros 1996," gold with dar blue container ....$7 – 9
20. "Hulkster," "Hogan 43," red with orange yellow container, Team Convoy..$8 – 10
21. "KC Royals 1996," blue with white cor tainer.................................$7 – 9
22. "Los Angeles Dodgers 1996," whit with blue container.................$7 – 9
23. "Milwaukee Brewers 1996," dark blu with gold container.................$7 – 9
24. "Minnesota Twins 1996," red with dar blue container ....$7 – 9
25. "Montreal Expos 1996," red with blu container ....$7 – 9
26. "New York Mets 1996," orange wit blue container ....$7 – 9
27. "New York Yankees 1996," white wit blue container ....$7 – 9
28. "NY Yankees World Series 1996, white with white container ....$8 – 10
29. "Oakland Athletics 1996," yellow wit green container ....$7 – 9
30. "Philadelphia Phillies 1996," blue wit red container ....$7 – 9
31. "Pittsburgh Pirates 1996," yellow wit black container ....$7 – 9

2. "Preston — The 151 Line," orange with white container...................$16 – 24
3. "Quality You Can See — Maple Donuts," white with white container.......$8 – 10
4. "Rutters Dairy Celebrates 75 Years," green with white container ....$16 – 24
5. "San Diego Padres 1996," dark blue with orange container..............$7 – 9
6. "San Francisco Giants 1996," black with orange container..............$7 – 9
7. "Seattle Mariners 1996," blue-green with dark blue container...........$7 – 9
8. "St. Louis Cardinals 1996," dark blue with red container...................$7 – 9
9. "Texas Rangers 1996," light gray with red container ....$7 – 9
10. "Toronto Blue Jays 1996," blue with dark blue container ....$7 – 9
11. "UGI Gas Service," white with white container...................................$9 – 12
12. "We Are Penn State 95," dark blue, white container with blue roof ..$8 – 10
13. "World Series 1995 — Atlanta Braves Champs," blue with white container.................................$9 – 12
14. "World Series 1995 — Atlanta Braves Champs," red with white container ....$9 – 12
15. "York Daily Record," white with white container ....$7 – 9
16. "York Fair 1995," green with orange-yellow container ....$8 – 10

ord F-800 Delivery Van, FS002, 1995, container extends over cab, White Rose Collectibles
1. "All Star Game 1997, blue with white container ....$7 – 9
2. "Nittany Lions — PSU 1996," metallic silver with metallic silver container ..$8 – 10
3. "Penn State 1996," white with white container ....$8 – 10
4. "York Fair 1996," beige with beige container ....$8 – 10

ord F-Series (see Ford F-150 Dump Truck, Ford F-150 Rescue Pickup)

ord Fairlane Fire Chief Car, 2⁷⁄₈", #59, 1963
1. red with gray plastic wheels ..$80 – 100
2. red with silver plastic wheels ..$125 – 150
3. red with black plastic wheels ..$20 – 25

ord Fairlane Police Car, 2⅝", #55, 1963
1. dark blue with black plastic wheels.............................$180 – 200

2. **light blue with black plastic wheels ....$65 – 90**

---

3. light blue with gray plastic wheels...............................$80 – 100
4. light blue with silver plastic wheels...............................$80 – 100

Ford Fairlane Station Wagon, 2³⁄₄", #31, 1960
1. yellow, silver plastic wheels ..$100 – 120
2. green with pink roof, silver plastic wheels ....$40 – 50
3. green with pink roof, gray plastic wheels ....$40 – 50
4. green with pink roof, black plastic wheels ....$100 – 120

Ford Falcon, #61, 2001, international
1. metallic blue...........................$2 – 3

2. **green, "Coca-Cola," US issue..$4 – 5**

Ford Falcon Forte, #63, 1997, Australia; #68, 1998, international; #12, 2000, international; #4, 2002, US
1. "Australia's First," gold, rubber tires on chrome rims, Australia inaugural issue $12 – 16
2. "Australia's First," unpainted, rubber tires on chrome rims, Australia inaugural issue..............................$12 – 16
3. "Australia Open 1997," white, rubber tires on chrome rims, Australia issue ..$8 – 10
4. "Blues 1998," white and dark blue, Australia issue..............................$4 – 5
5. "Brisbane 1998," yellow and purple, Australia issue.........................$4 – 5
6. "Castrol 25," white, rubber tires on chrome rims, Australia issue ...$16 – 24
7. "Cats 1998," white and black, Australia issue....................................$4 – 5

8. **"Coca-Cola," white, US issue ..$4 – 5**
9. "Crows 1998," red and dark blue, Australia issue..............................$4 – 5
10. "Eagles 1998," yellow and dark blue, Australia issue.........................$4 – 5
11. "Ford," maroon with white stripes, 2000 Australia Adventure international series.......................................$3 – 4
12. "Ford 75," white and dark blue, Australia issue..............................$3 – 4

---

13. "Ford Falcon 4," metallic purple, 1998 Street Cruisers international series ....$2 – 3
14. "Go Cats! 1997," white, Australia issue......................................$4 – 5
15. "Great Strides," "Cystic Fibrosis Foundation," "Ford," maroon with white stripes, Color Comp promotional........$20 – 30
16. "Kangaroos 1998," white and blue, Australia issue.........................$4 – 5
17. "Midwest Regional Matchbox Convention 2000," "Toy Show Demo Model," "Ford," maroon with white stripes, Color Comp promotional...............$12 – 16
18. "Mitre 10 Accent Paint Racing," blue, rubber tires on yellow rims, Australia issue......................................$8 – 10
19. "Official Matchbox Collectors Club," "Australia Matchbox News," white, rubber tires on chrome rims ......$16 – 24
20. "Official Matchbox Collectors Club," "Australia Matchbox News," gold, rubber tires on chrome rims ......$16 – 24
21. "Official Matchbox Collectors Club," "Australia Matchbox News," unpainted, rubber tires on chrome rims..$16 – 24

22. **"Roy Roo's Taxi," picture of Sydney Opera House on doors, yellow with black plastic base, 2002 Hometown Heroes series ....$2 – 3**
23. "Special Edition Puerto Rico," Puerto Rican flag, maroon, "Ford" and white stripes, Color Comp promotional ....$9 – 12
24. "Swans 1998," white and red, Australia issue......................................$4 – 5
25. "Tigers 1998," yellow and black, Australia issue ....$4 – 5

Ford Falcon Taxi (see Ford Falcon Forte)

Ford Flareside Pickup, 2⁷⁄₈", #53, 1982; #55, 1994 – 1998 (compare to Ford Flareside Pickup with Load)
1. red, "326 Baja Bouncer," 8-spoke wheels, Macau cast ....$25 – 30
2. red, "326 Baja Bouncer," 8-spoke wheels, Manaus cast, Brazil issue .....$80 – 120

3. **red with orange and yellow flames, racing slicks, chrome windows, 1994 ....$2 – 3**

4 red, "Bill Elliott 11," racing slicks, Team Convoy, White Rose Collectibles..$6 – 8

5. **orange, "326 Baja Bouncer," clear windows..............................$3 – 4**

6. **fluorescent orange with black front end ....$2 – 4**

7 yellow, "Ford 460," black interior, racing slicks with chromed lettering, Macau casting...........................$3 – 4

8. **yellow, "Ford 460," black interior, racing slicks with unchromed lettering, Macau casting................$2 – 3**

9 yellow, "Ford 460," black interior, racing slicks with unchromed lettering, Thailand casting........................$3 – 4

10. yellow, "Ford 460," black interior, 8-spoke wheels, Macau casting..$40 – 50

11. yellow, "Ford 460," white interior, 8-spoke wheels, Macau casting.......$200 – 250

12. yellow with black interior, 8-spoke wheels.............................$35 – 40

13. yellow with black interior, racing slicks ....$2 – 4

14. fluorescent yellow with no interior, chrome windows, Super Trucks..$3 – 4

15. orange, "326 Baja Bouncer," white interior, black base.......................$2 – 3

16. fluorescent orange with black design on front, chrome base, white interior..$2 – 3

17. lime green, yellow base, red interior, red racing slicks, Matchbox Preschool/Live 'N Learn series ....$7 – 8

18. khaki green with purple and blue design, racing slicks, plastic armament, Road-blasters.................................$7 – 8

19. blue, "326 Baja Bouncer," blue windows ....$50 – 60

20. blue, "326 Baja Bouncer," clear windows...................................$3 – 4

21. **light blue, "F-150" with white accents, yellow interior, chrome base.....$2 – 3**

22. metallic blue, "326 Baja Bouncer," white interior...........................$3 – 4

23. dark blue, "QC Quality Care 15," chrome interior, racing slicks with unchromed lettering, Team Convoy, White Rose Collectibles.............$4 – 5

24. metallic blue with no interior, chrome windows, Super Trucks ....$3 – 4

25. **dark purple with white accents, gray interior, chrome base, 1998 Rough 'N Tough series....................$2 – 3**

26. **black with flames on front; yellow tailpipes, roll bar, grille, and interior; chrome base, 1998 Rugged Riders 5-pack ....$2 – 3**

27. **gray with purple and magenta flames on front; purple tailpipes, roll bar, grille, and interior; 1996 Off Road 5-pack.....$2 – 3**

28. metallic gray, "Jay's Flight Team," racing slicks, Avon Light & Sound ...$2 –

29. metallic gray, "Jay's Flight Team," racing slicks, includes black launcher and white glider, Action System........$3 –

30. white, "Deb," racing slicks, UK on-package premium ....$40 – 5

31. **white with silver band, red stripe chrome interior, clear windows Collector's Choice, White Rose Collectibles ....$3 –**

32. metallic gold, chrome base, black interior, 1997 75 Challenge series .$6 – 1

Ford Flareside Pickup with Load, 1994 White Rose Collectibles

1. "Angels 94," dark blue ....$4 –
2. "Astros 94," gold ....$4 –
3. "Athletics 94," dark green ....$4 –
4. "Baltimore Football 94," white ....$4 –
5. "Blue Jays 94," light blue..........$4 –
6. "Braves 94," metallic blue ....$4 –
7. "Brewers 94 — 25th Anniversary," dark green.................................$4 –
8. "Cubs 94," red ....$4 –
9. "Dodgers 94," blue..................$4 –
10. "Expos 94," blue ....$4 –
11. "Giants 94," orange.................$4 –
12. "Indians 94," red ....$4 –
13. "Mariners 94," dark blue-green ..$4 –
14. "Marlins 94," blue-green ....$4 –
15. "Mets 94," blue ....$4 –
16. "Orioles 94," black...................$4 –
17. "Padres 94," orange ....$4 –
18. "Penn State Nittany Lions 94," dark blue ....$4 –
19. "Phillies 94," red.....................$4 –
20. "Pirates 94," black ....$4 –
21. "Rangers 94," khaki gray..........$4 –
22. "Red Sox 94," dark gray...........$4 –
23. "Reds 94," black ....$4 –
24. "Rockies 94," purple................$4 –
25. "Royals 94," gold ....$4 –
26. "St. Louis Cardinals 94," blue.....$4 –
27. "Tigers 94," orange.................$4 –
28. "Twins 94," blue ....$4 –
29. "White Sox 94," metallic gray ....$4 –
30. "Yankees 94," red...................$4 –

Ford Focus, #84, 2000; #55, 2003; #64 2000, international

1. metallic orange, "Matchbox 2000," 2000 Worldwide Wheels series ....$3 – 4

2. **metallic orange, 2000 Worldwide Wheels series.......................$2 – 3**

8. yellow, 2003 Hero City 5-pack #12..**$2 – 3**

4. **metallic blue, 2001 Eurosports 5-pack.................$2 – 3**
5. purple, "Focus," 5-pack ....$2 – 3
6. white with bears graphics, 2003 School Time series ....$2 – 3

Ford Galaxie Fire Chief Car, 2⅞", #59, 1966

1. **red, black plastic wheels, 1966 ....$15 – 20**
2. red, Superfast wheels, 1970..$30 – 40

Ford Galaxie Police Car, 2⅞", #55, 1966
1. white, blue dome light...........$50 – 60
2. white, red dome light...........$16 – 24

Ford Grit Spreader (see Ford Atkinson Grit Spreader)

Ford Group 6, 3", 45-C, 1970; BR 19-20, 1985

1. **red, England cast, Super GTs BR 19-20, 1985.............................$4 – 6**

2. red, China cast, Super GTs BR 19-20, 1985.................$8 – 10
3. dark red, China cast, Super GTs BR 19-20, 1985.............................$3 – 5
4. yellow, England cast, Super GTs BR 19-20, 1985.........................$8 – 10
5. dark enamel green, unpainted base, clear windows, round "7" label .$1,200 – 1,600
6. metallic green, black base, amber windows, "45" label.................$12 – 16
7. metallic green, black base, clear windows, "45" label.................$12 – 16
8. metallic green, black base, clear windows, round "7" label...........$12 – 16
9. metallic green, black base, square "7" label.........$12 – 16
10. metallic green, gray base, amber windows, "45" label.................$12 – 16
11. metallic green, gray base, clear windows, "45" label.................$12 – 16
12. metallic green, black base, clear windows, "45" label.................$12 – 16
13. metallic green, pink base, amber windows, "45" label.................$12 – 16
14. metallic green, pink base, clear windows, "45" label.................$12 – 16
15. metallic green, unpainted base, clear windows, round "7" label ....$12 – 16
16. metallic green, unpainted base, clear windows, square "7" label......$12 – 16
17. metallic green, yellow base, amber windows, "45" label.................$12 – 16
18. metallic green, yellow base, clear windows, "45" label.................$12 – 16
19. fluorescent lime green, China cast, Neon Racers BR 19-20, 1985............$4 – 6
20. purple, amber windows, "45" label ....$12 – 16
21. purple, amber windows, eyes label.................................$12 – 16
22. gray, China cast, Super GTs BR 19-20, 1985.................................$3 – 5
23. white, England cast, Super GTs BR 19-20, 1985 ....$4 – 6
24. white, China cast, Super GTs BR 19-20, 1985 ....$8 – 10

Ford GT, 2⅝", #41, 1965
1. metallic orange with Superfast wheels ....$12 – 16
2. yellow with black plastic tires, yellow wheel hubs, "6" decals..........$60 – 80
3. yellow with Superfast wheels, Italian issue..............................$700 – 900
4. white with black plastic tires, red wheel hubs, "6" decal ....$100 – 120

5. **white with black plastic tires, yellow wheel hubs, "6" decal.........$8 – 12**
6. white with black plastic tires, yellow wheel hubs, "9" decals..........$12 – 16

7. white with black plastic tires, yellow wheel hubs, "6" label ....$7 – 12
8. white with black plastic tires, yellow wheel hubs, "9" label ....$7 – 12
9. white with Superfast wheels, "6" label.................................$12 – 16
10. white with Superfast wheels, cat head label.................................$16 – 24

Ford Heavy Wreck Truck, "Esso," 3", #71, 1968
1. red cab, "Esso," white bed, amber windows, black plastic wheels, prototype ....$300 – 400

2. **red cab, "Esso," white bed, green windows, black plastic wheels, 1968...................................$25 – 35**
3. red cab, "Esso," white bed, Superfast wheels, 1970.....................$35 – 45
4. olive green, "3LGS64," Superfast wheels, Two Pack ....$12 – 15
5. blue, Superfast wheels, multipack ....$200 – 250

Ford IMSA Mustang (see IMSA Mustang)

Ford Kennel Truck, with four dogs, 2¾", #50, 1969
1. metallic green, tinted canopy, white grille, black plastic wheels, 1969 ......$16 – 24
2. metallic green, tinted canopy, chrome grille, black plastic wheels, 1969.......$20 – 25
3. metallic green, clear canopy, white grille, black plastic wheels, 1969.....$16 – 24
4. metallic green, clear canopy, chrome grille, black plastic wheels, 1969 ......$20 – 25
5. metallic green, chrome grille, Superfast wheels, 1970.....................$30 – 40
6. apple green, chrome grille, Superfast wheels, 1970.....................$30 – 40

Ford Lotus Europa (see Lotus Europa)

Ford LTD Police, 3", #51, 1988; #16, 1990; #24, 1998; #2, 1999 (similar casting: Ford LTD Taxi)
1. black, "Police Unit 3," gold star, 5-pack ....$2 – 3
2. black and tan, "Florida State Trooper," Premiere Collection #8 ....$4 – 6
3. black and white, "42" in shield....$6 – 9
4. blue with white trim, "Matchbox Police" shield ....$2 – 3
5. bright blue with yellow accent stripe on sides, "State Police," 1996 ....$2 – 3
6. dark blue, "Police," "R-25," Triple Heat series....................................$3 – 5

7. dark blue and gray, "Virginia State Police," Premiere Collection #8 ..$4 – 6

8. **blue with white trim, black shield, "Police," "16," White Rose Collectibles, Collectors Choice ....$4 – 5**

9. **blue with white band, "Unit 22 Police," 5-pack....................$2 – 3**

10. **metallic blue with yellow accent stripe on sides, "State Police," 1996..$2 – 3**

11. **metallic copper, "Sheriff" and "S-27," 1997 ....$2 – 3**

12. metallic gold, no markings, 1997 75 Challenge...........................$12 – 16

13. metallic gray, "Police," shield and red design, 5-pack........................$2 – 3

14. purple to red, "Police," with "PD-21" on roof, Color Changers ....$3 – 5

15. **red, "Dan's Pocket Cruisers," "Police," "1994," customized ....$5 – 10**

16. red, "Fire Chief," "FD No. 1" in gold crest, multipack......................$2 – 3

17. red, "Fire Dept. Fire Chief," Motor City series....................................$2 – 4

18. red, "Police," with "PD-21" on roof.$3 – 5

19. white, "17 Police," multipack......$2 – 3

20. white, "Corvette Unlimited Salutes Vineland Police NJ," Color Comp promo..$80 – 120

21. white, "New Jersey Police," Premiere Collection #8...........................$4 – 6

22. white, Policeman caricature, Live 'N Learn/Preschool series ....$6 – 9

23. white, "Police," with "PD-21" on roof, "Intercom City"....................$12 – 16

24. **white, "Ridge, New York, Police," 1999 Matchbox USA series...$2 – 3**

25. **white, "Sheriff," "S-27," 1998.$2 – 3**

26. **white with black accents, shield on door, "Police," with "PD-21" on roof, 1995..................................$2 – 3**

27. **white with blue accents, shield on door, "Police," with "PD-21" on roof, 1995..................................$5 – 7**

28. **white with bright orange and yellow accents, "Dial 911," "Metro," 1993 Emergency 5-pack................$3 – 5**

29. **white, blue doors, no number o roof, 1996, Police 5-pack .....$3 – 5**

30. white with no markings, Graffic Traffic ....$12 – 16

Ford LTD US Taxi, 3", #53, 1992; #56 1992; #9, 1999 (similar casting: For LTD Police)

1. **yellow, "Radio XYZ Cab" an checkerboard pattern............$4 – 5**

2. **yellow, "Taxi," black checks, Star Cars....................................$5 – 8**

3. yellow with black checks and airplane si houette on doors, 1999 Air Traffi series....................................$2 – 3

4. pumpkin orange, "Taxi," 5-pack...$2 – 3

5. pumpkin orange, "Cabbies For Life, ASAP promotional issue......$80 – 120

6. pumpkin orange, "Ronnie & Ren August 19, 2000," ASAP promotiona issue...............................$80 – 120

Ford Model A, 2¹³/₁₆", #73, 1979; #55 1991

1. **red with blue and yellow design, re fenders, clear windows, racing slicks on back axle, Thailand cast, 199 Hot Rods 5-pack ....$2 – 3**

2. red with black fenders, clear windows Macau cast.............................$3 – 4

3. red with dark green fenders, clear wir dows, China cast, UK on-package pre mium ....$16 – 24

4. red with dark green fenders, clear wir dows, Macau cast, UK on-package pre mium ....$16 – 24

5. red with dark green fenders, clear wir dows, Thailand cast, UK on-package premium...........................$16 – 24

metallic red with detailed trim, racing slicks on back axle, Thailand cast, Collectors Choice, White Rose Collectibles.....$4 – 5

orange-yellow, "GT" and yellow jacket, white fenders, Thailand cast, White Rose Collectibles......................$7 – 9

yellow, "PAVA," red fenders, clear windows, racing slicks on back axle, Macau cast, the Netherlands issue.....$9 – 12

metallic green with dark green fenders, green windows, England cast.....$5 – 6

0. metallic green with dark green fenders, no windows, England cast..$5 – 6

1. light blue with clown illustration, clear windows, racing slicks on back axle, Thailand cast, Motor City ....$8 – 10
2. dark blue with green and pink grid design, clear windows, racing slicks on back axle, Thailand cast, multipack ....$2 – 3
3. purple with stripes, yellow fenders, clear windows, racing slicks on back axle, Macau cast ....$4 – 5
4. purple with stripes, yellow fenders, clear windows, racing slicks on back axle, Thailand cast....................$3 – 4

5. black with flames, black fenders, clear windows, racing slicks on back axle, Macau cast ....$3 – 4

6. dark gray, "The Untouchables," bullet holes, clear windows, China cast, Star Cars ....$5 – 6

7. cream with dark green fenders, green windows, spare tire cast into fender, England cast ....$7 – 9

18. cream, "Hershey 2000," "Matchbox USA," England cast, Color Comp promotional................................$80 – 120
19. cream with dark green fenders, green windows, England cast..............$5 – 6
20. cream with dark green fenders, no windows, England cast ....$5 – 6
21. beige with brown fenders, amber windows, England cast ....$5 – 6
22. beige with brown fenders, clear windows, England cast ....$5 – 6
23. beige with brown fenders, clear windows, Macau cast....................$3 – 4
24. white, "Temecula Rod Run 1996," clear windows, racing slicks on back axle, Thailand cast, White Rose Collectibles................................$9 – 12
25. white with zigzag design, clear windows, racing slick on back axle, Thailand cast ....$3 – 4
26. metallic gold, "Matchbox Collectors Club," clear windows, Thailand cast...$12 – 16
27. metallic gold, "American Iron Cruise 96," "Memory Lane," Thailand cast, custom promotional ....$20 – 30

Ford Model A Van, 3", #38, 1982 – 1997
1. "Acco Chain & Lifting Products," white with black fenders and roof, ASAP promotional ....$40 – 60
2. "Adelaide Crows," dark blue with red fenders, yellow roof, Australia issue ..$8 – 10
3. "Adelaide Super Sixers," dark blue with red fenders and roof, Australia issue...$8 – 10
4. "Aldershot — 4th M.I.C.A. Convention," green, rust roof, UK issue.......$9 – 12
5. "Alex Munro Master Butcher," red, black roof, UK issue ....$9 – 12
6. "Alka-Seltzer," dark blue ....$5 – 6
7. "Arnott's Biscuits," red with black fenders and roof, Australia issue....$8 – 10
8. "Asda Baked Beans," red, red roof, on-package premium, UK issue ....$8 – 10
9. "Atlanta Braves 1990," white with blue fenders, white roof, White Rose Collectibles................................$4 – 5
10. "Atlanta Braves 1991," blue with red fenders, white roof, White Rose Collectibles................................$4 – 5
11. "Atlanta Falcons 1990," red with black fenders, light gray roof, White Rose Collectibles................................$4 – 5
12. "Atlanta Falcons 1991," red with black fenders and roof, White Rose Collectibles................................$4 – 5
13. "Aukland Warriors," green with blue fenders and roof, Australia issue......$8 – 10
14. "Australia Post," orange-red with black fenders and roof ....$6 – 8
15. "Auto 1," white with blue fenders, red roof, Australia issue ....$6 – 8
16. "Automodel Exchange," maroon with beige fenders and roof, Australia issue ..$8 – 10
17. "Avant Garde Drum & Bugle Corps," white with black fenders and roof, ASAP promotional.........................$12 – 16
18. "Bakker Bros. Seeds," white with black fenders and roof, ASAP promotional.$40 – 50

19. "Balmain Tigers," orange with white fenders, black roof, Australia issue...$8 – 10
20. "Baltimore Colts 1990," white with blue fenders and roof, White Rose Collectibles................................$4 – 5
21. "Baltimore Colts 1991," dark blue with white fenders and roof, White Rose Collectibles................................$4 – 5
22. "Baltimore Orioles 1989," black with orange fenders and roof, White Rose Collectibles................................$7 – 9
23. "Baltimore Orioles 1990," black with orange fenders, black roof, White Rose Collectibles................................$4 – 5
24. "Baltimore Orioles 1991," orange with black fenders, white roof, White Rose Collectibles................................$4 – 5
25. "Barratt's Sherbet," yellow, black chassis, red roof, on-package premium, UK issue................................$12 – 16
26. "Barratt's Sherbet," yellow, black chassis and roof, UK issue.............$9 – 12
27. "Barratt's Sherbet," yellow, red chassis and roof, UK issue ....$9 – 12
28. "Bass Museum," blue with black fenders, red roof ....$6 – 8
29. "Bayer Aspirin," tan with brown fenders, tan roof.................................$5 – 6
30. "BBC 1925," green, black roof, UK issue......................................$7 – 9
31. "Beechworth Bakery," brown with black fenders, brown roof, Australia issue...$6 – 8
32. "Beechworth Bakery," brown with black fenders, yellow roof, Australia issue...$20 – 25
33. "Beechworth Bakery," red with black fenders and roof, Australia issue ....$4 – 5
34. "Ben Franklin," white with blue fenders, red roof..........................$600 – 800
35. "Bendigo National Swapmeet," white with blue fenders, red roof, Australia promotional issue ....
36. "Big Apple Circus," blue with blue fenders and roof............................$6 – 8
37. "Big Apple Circus," red with blue fenders, white roof, US issue.......$60 – 80
38. "Big Ben," white with black fenders, red roof, Australia issue ....$7 – 9
39. "Big Sister," red, black roof, on-package premium, Australia issue...........$7 – 9
40. "Boston Bruins 1917," tan with brown fenders, white roof; "Boston Bruins 1992," black with yellow fenders, white roof, White Rose Collectibles 2-pack, for set of two ....$12 – 16
41. "Boston Red Sox 1990," white with red fenders, white roof, White Rose Collectibles................................$4 – 5
42. "Boston Red Sox 1991," dark blue with red fenders, white roof, White Rose Collectibles............................$4 – 5
43. "Brew Works," white with black fenders and roof, ASAP promotional..................$120 – 160
44. "Brisbane Bears," red with yellow fenders, red roof, Australia issue ...$8 – 10
45. "Brisbane Broncos," light purple with white fenders, yellow roof, Australia issue..................................$8 – 10

46. "Brisbane Bullets," yellow with blue fenders, yellow roof, Australia issue ..$8 – 10
47. "Buffalo Bills 1990," blue with red fenders, white roof, White Rose Collectibles ....$4 – 5
48. "Buffalo Bills 1991," white with dark blue fenders, red roof, White Rose Collectibles ....$4 – 5
49. "C-B Bulldogs," white with blue fenders, white roof, Australia issue.........$8 – 10
50. "Cadbury's Chocolate," purple with gold fenders, purple roof, Australia issue..................................$16 – 24
51. "California Angels 1990," white with red fenders, yellow roof, White Rose Collectibles ....$4 – 5
52. "California Angels 1991," yellow with red fenders, dark blue roof, White Rose Collectibles..................................$4 – 5
53. "Camperdown Cumberland," white with blue fenders, blue roof, Australia issue..................................$12 – 16
54. "Canada Dry," metallic green, Canada issue..................................$9 – 12
55. "Canada Tire," red with black fenders and roof, rubber tires, Canada issue ....$5 – 6
56. "Canada Tire Associate Store," red with black fenders and roof, rubber tires, Canada issue..........................$5 – 6
57. "Canada Tire Corp'n," red with black fenders and roof, rubber tires, Canada issue..................................$5 – 6
58. "Canberra Cannons," red with blue fenders, red roof, Australia issue ...$8 – 10
59. "Canberra Raiders," bright lime green with white fenders, blue roof, Australia issue..................................$8 – 10
60. "Carlton Blues, dark blue, Australia issue..................................$8 – 10
61. "Carmelle," green, green roof, Saudi Arabia issue..........................$16 – 24
62. "Carroll County Fair," white with black fenders and roof, ASAP promotional......................$60 – 80
63. "Cave Creek Chili Beer," fluorescent orange with black fenders and roof, Matchbox Collectibles ....$9 – 12
64. "Champion," blue with black fenders, white roof, England cast............$6 – 8
65. "Champion," blue with black fenders, white roof, Macau cast.............$5 – 6
66. "Celebrate Michigan's Greatness," "Governor John Engler 1999 Inauguration," white with black fenders and roof, ASAP promotional......................$80 – 120
67. "Celebrating a Decade of Matchbox Conventions 1991," yellow with black fenders and roof..........................$9 – 12
68. "Cheeses of England & Wales," blue, black roof, on-package premium, UK issue..................................$12 – 16
69. "Chester Heraldry Centre," pale blue, dark gray roof, UK issue ....$7 – 9
70. "Chester Toy Museum," pale blue, dark gray roof, UK issue ....$7 – 9
71. "Chesty Bonds," white, black roof, Australia issue..................................$6 – 8

72. "Chicago Bears 1990," white with dark blue fenders, orange roof, White Rose Collectibles..................................$4 – 5

73. **"Chicago Bears 1991," white with orange fenders, dark blue roof, White Rose Collectibles........$4 – 5**
74. "Chicago Black Hawks 1917," black with red fenders, white roof; "Chicago Black Hawks 1992," white with black fenders, white roof, White Rose Collectibles 2-pack, for set of two....................................$12 – 16
75. "Chicago Cubs 1990," white with blue fenders, red roof, White Rose Collectibles ....$4 – 5
76. "Chicago Cubs 1991," red with white fenders and roof, White Rose Collectibles ....$4 – 5
77. "Chicago White Sox 1990," white with blue fenders, white roof, White Rose Collectibles..................................$4 – 5
78. "Chicago White Sox 1991," white with black fenders, dark gray roof, White Rose Collectibles......................$4 – 5
79. "Cincinnati Bengals 1990," black with orange fenders, white roof, White Rose Collectibles..................................$4 – 5
80. "Cincinnati Bengals 1991," orange with black fenders and roof, White Rose Collectibles..................................$4 – 5
81. "Cincinnati Reds 1990," white with red fenders, white roof, White Rose Collectibles..................................$4 – 5
82. "Cincinnati Reds 1991," red with white fenders and roof, White Rose Collectibles..................................$4 – 5
83. "City Ford," black, Australia issue ....$8 – 10
84. "Clemson University 1992," orange with blue fenders, white roof, White Rose Collectibles..................................$5 – 7
85. "Cleveland Browns 1990," orange with brown fenders, white roof, White Rose Collectibles..................................$4 – 5
86. "Cleveland Browns 1991," brown with brown fenders, orange roof, White Rose Collectibles......................$4 – 5
87. "Cleveland Indians 1990," white with blue fenders, white roof, White Rose Collectibles..................................$4 – 5
88. "Cobb of Knightsbridge," brown with black fenders and roof, UK issue, Macau cast..........................$8 – 10
89. "Cobb of Knightsbridge," brown with black fenders and roof, UK issue, Thailand cast ....$9 – 12

90. "Coca-Cola," cream with red roof, Australia issue.........................$16 – 2⸱
91. "Coca-Cola Quality Assurance," red wit⸱ black fenders and roof, Premiere Collec⸱ tion......................................$5 – 6⸱
92. "Collingwood Magpies," black wit⸱ white fenders, black roof, Australi⸱ issue.................................$8 – 1⸱
93. "Continental Aero," purple wit⸱ black fenders and roof, US issue.................................$9 – 1⸱
94. "Cooter's Garage," "Christma⸱ 2000," white with black fenders an⸱ roof, Color Comp promotional......................$30 – 4⸱
95. "Corning Building Co.," white wit⸱ black fenders and roof, ASAP prome⸱ tional ....$80 – 12⸱
96. "Cronulla Sharks," light blue with blac⸱ fenders, bright blue roof, Australi⸱ issue.................................$8 – 1⸱
97. "Dairylea," light yellow, light blue an⸱ light blue roof, on-package premium, U⸱ issues ....$16 – 2⸱
98. "Dale Farms," dark blue with whit⸱ fenders, red roof, UK issue .....$7 – 9⸱
99. "Dallas Cowboys 1990," silver with dar⸱ blue fenders, dark blue roof, Whit⸱ Rose Collectibles......................$4 – 5⸱
100. "Dallas Cowboys 1991," dark blu⸱ with silver fenders, dark blue roof⸱ White Rose Collectibles..........$4 – 5⸱
101. "De Post," red with black fenders⸱ black roof ....$6 – 8⸱
102. "Delacre World's Finest Belgia⸱ Chocolate Biscuits," white with blac⸱ fenders and roof, Color Comp promo⸱ tional ....$160 – 24⸱
103. "Denver Broncos 1990," orange wit⸱ blue fenders, orange roof, White Ros⸱ Collectibles..................................$4 – 5⸱
104. "Denver Broncos 1991," orange wit⸱ dark blue fenders, dark blue roof⸱ White Rose Collectibles ....$4 – 5⸱
105. "Detroit Lions 1990," silver with ligh⸱ fenders, white roof, White Rose Co⸱ lectibles..................................$4 – 5⸱
106. "Detroit Lions 1991," blue with silve⸱ fenders, white roof, White Rose Co⸱ lectibles..................................$4 – 5⸱
107. "Detroit Redwings 1917," re⸱ with white fenders, white roof⸱ "Detroit Redwings 1992," whit⸱ with red fenders, white roof, Whit⸱ Rose Collectibles 2-pack, for set o⸱ two ....$12 – 16⸱
108. "Detroit Tigers 1990," white wit⸱ blue fenders, orange roof, White Ros⸱ Collectibles..................................$4 – 5⸱
109. "Detroit Tigers 1991," silver with dar⸱ blue fenders, orange roof, White Ros⸱ Collectibles..................................$4 – 5⸱
110. "Dewhurst Master Butcher," red, blac⸱ roof, UK issue ....$9 – 12⸱
111. **"Dixie Lexington Brewery," "Ken⸱ tucky Pride," cream with green fend⸱ ers, dark green roof, rubber tires⸱ Matchbox Collectibles ....$9 – 12⸱**

186. "Lion's Club Fund Raising Activity," white with black fenders and roof, Color Comp promotional...............$30 – 40

187. "Los Angeles Dodgers 1991," silver with blue fenders, orange roof, White Rose Collectibles....................$4 – 5

188. "Los Angeles Dodgers 1990," white with blue fenders, white roof, White Rose Collectibles....................$4 – 5

189. "Los Angeles Kings 1993," black with silver fenders, silver roof, White Rose Collectibles.............................$7 – 9

190. "Los Angeles Rams 1990," yellow with blue fenders, yellow roof, White Rose Collectibles............................$4 – 5

191. "Los Angeles Rams 1991," yellow with dark blue fenders, dark blue roof, White Rose Collectibles....................$4 – 5

192. "Lyceum Theatre," blue, black roof, UK issue ....$7 – 9

193. "Lyon's Tea," dark blue with black fenders, white roof, UK issue...........$7 – 9

194. "Magic," black with red fenders, blue roof, Australia issue ....$8 – 10

195. "Manx Cattery," red, black roof, UK issue...................................$12 – 16

196. "Matchbox," white with black fenders, red roof, Australia issue........$24 – 32

197. "Matchbox Collectors Club 1989," silver with silver fenders, black roof, promotional ....$120 – 160

198. "Matchbox Collectors Club 1990," fluorescent green with fluorescent orange fenders, black roof, promotional ....$90 – 120

199. "Matchbox Collectors Club 1991," white with dark pink fenders, black roof, promotional......................$60 – 80

200. "Matchbox Collectors Club 1992," brass plated with black fenders, black roof, promotional ....$50 – 70

201. "Matchbox Collectors Club 1993," black with green fenders, green roof, promotional.........................$20 – 25

202. "Matchbox Collectors Club Christmas 1994"....................................$6 – 8

203. "Matchbox Convention 2000 — Hershey Demo Model," brown with brown fenders, white roof, Color Comp promotional...............$40 – 50

204. "Matchbox Convention 2001 — Hershey Demo Model," white with black fenders and roof, Color Comp promotional..................................$16 – 24

205. "Matchbox Dinky Toy Convention 1991," yellow with black fenders, black roof, UK issue ....$9 – 12

206. "Matchbox For Serious Collectors," yellow with black roof, Germany issue ...$9 – 12

207. "Matchbox On The Move In '84," blue with black fenders, white roof....................................$30 – 50

208. "Matchbox On The Move In '84," "Toy Fair 84," blue with black fenders, white roof ....$30 – 50

209. "Matchbox Series Model A Ford Van," yellow, black roof ....$3 – 4

210. "Matchbox Speedshop," blue, orange pinstripes, non-chrome–lettered wheels.$2 – 3

211. "Matchbox Speedshop," blue, yellow pinstripes, non-chrome–lettered wheels ....$2 – 3

212. "Matchbox Speedshop," blue, yellow pinstripes, chrome-lettered wheels ....$80 – 120

213. "Matchbox USA," white with blue fenders, red roof ....$24 – 36

214. "Matchbox USA 9th Annual Convention 1990," white with maroon fenders, white roof ....$8 – 10

215. "Matchbox & Lesney Toy Museum," brown with white roof ....$6 – 12

216. "Matchbox — Get In The Fast Lane," fluorescent orange with yellow fenders, orange roof..........................$8 – 10

217. "Matchbox — This Van Delivers" with phone number on doors, blue, red roof, UK issue............................$16 – 24

218. "Matchbox — This Van Delivers" without phone number on doors, blue, red roof, Hong Kong issue ....$60 – 80

219. "Matchbox 1991," blue with red fenders, white roof, China issue ...$60 – 80

220. "Matchbox 1991," green with yellow fenders, white roof, China issue......$60 – 80

221. "Matchbox 1991," maroon with maroon fenders, white roof, China issue.$60 – 80

222. "Matchbox 1991," orange with black fenders, white roof, China issue ......$60 – 80

223. "Matchbox 1991," silver with black fenders, orange roof, China issue ...$60 – 80

224. "Matchbox 1991," white with red fenders, blue roof, China issue.....$60 – 80

225. "Matchbox 33000," white with black fenders and roof, ASAP promotional ....$80 – 120

226. "Matchbox 40th Anniversary 1990," blue, blue roof ....$8 – 10

227. "Matthew Walker," white with white fenders, white roof, UK issue...$9 – 12

228. "McVities Digestive," red with black fenders, black roof, on-package premium, UK issue ....$12 – 16

229. "Melbourne Demons," dark blue with red fenders, blue roof, Australia issue.$8 – 10

230. "Melbourne Tigers," red with yellow fenders, red roof, Australia issue .....$8 – 10

231. "Melcer Tile 30 Years," white with black fenders and roof, ASAP promotional ....$120 – 160

232. "Memories 1993," gold with black fenders, black roof, promotional.$400 – 600

233. "Merry Christmas 1993," green with red fenders, red roof, promotional..$30 – 50

234. "Mervyn Wynne," red with black fenders, black roof, UK issue.......$12 – 16

235. "Mervyn Wynne," black island design on doors, red with black fenders, black roof, UK issue ....$20 – 25

236. "Miami Dolphins 1990," blue-green with orange fenders, white roof, White Rose Collectibles....................$4 – 5

237. "Miami Dolphins 1991," orange with blue-green fenders, blue-green roof, White Rose Collectibles............$4 – 5

238. "MICA" and kangaroo, tan with blue fenders, blue roof, Australia issue ....$8 – 10

239. "MICA" and kangaroo, beige with blue fenders, blue roof, base secured by screws, Australia issue....$100 – 150

240. "Milk of Magnesia," blue with dark blue fenders, blue roof ....$5 – 6

241. "Milwaukee Brewers 1991," white with yellow fenders, white roof, White Rose Collectibles.................................$4 – 5

242. "Milwaukee Brewers 1990," white with blue fenders, white roof, White Rose Collectibles.................................$4 – 5

243. "Minnesota Twins 1990," white with blue fenders, white roof, White Rose Collectibles.................................$4 – 5

244. "Minnesota Twins 1991," dark blue with red fenders, white roof, White Rose Collectibles.................................$4 – 5

245. "Minnesota Vikings 1990," purple with purple fenders, yellow roof, White Rose Collectibles.................................$4 – 5

246. "Minnesota Vikings 1991," yellow with purple fenders, purple roof, White Rose Collectibles.................................$4 – 5

247. "Mitre 10," blue with black fenders, blue roof, Australia issue.........$8 – 10

248. "Moorland Centre," light gray, dark gray roof, UK issue ....$7 – 9

249. "Montreal Expos 1990," white with red fenders, white roof, White Rose Collectibles ....$4 – 5

250. "Montreal Canadiennes 1917," red with blue fenders, white roof; "Montreal Canadiennes 1992," white with red fenders, white roof, White Rose Collectibles, Two Pack, for set of two ....$12 – 16

251. "Montreal Expos 1991," baby blue with red fenders, white roof, White Rose Collectibles.................................$4 – 5

252. "Moto Master," black with red fenders and roof, rubber tires, Canada issue......................................$5 – 6

253. "Nat West Action Bank," blue, gray roof, UK issue ....$7 – 9

254. "New England Ice Cream 508-80-6100," white with black fenders and roof, ASAP promotional.............$120 – 160

255. "New England Patriots 1990," red with white fenders, blue roof, White Rose Collectibles.................................$4 – 5

256. "New England Patriots 1991," dark blue with red fenders, red roof, White Rose Collectibles.........................$4 – 5

257. "New Orleans Saints 1990," gold with black fenders, white roof, White Rose Collectibles.................................$4 – 5

258. "New Orleans Saints 1991," white with gold fenders, black roof, White Rose Collectibles.................................$4 – 5

259. "New York Jets 1990," white with green fenders, green roof, White Rose Collectibles.................................$4 – 5

260. "New York Jets 1991," white with green fenders, green roof, White Rose Collectibles.................................$4 – 5

261. "New York Mets 1990," white with blue fenders, white roof, White Rose Collectibles ....$4 – 5

282. "New York Mets 1991," orange with blue fenders, white roof, White Rose Collectibles.............................$4 – 5

283. "New York Rangers 1917," red with red fenders, white roof; "New York Rangers 1992," white with blue fenders, white roof, White Rose Collectibles 2-pack, for set of two ....$12 – 16

284. "New York Rangers 1990," white with blue fenders, white roof, White Rose Collectibles.............................$4 – 5

285. "New York Rangers 1991," red with blue fenders, white roof, White Rose Collectibles.............................$4 – 5

286. "New York Yankees 1991," white with red fenders, dark blue roof, White Rose Collectibles.............................$4 – 5

287. "New York Yankees 1990," white with blue fenders, white roof, White Rose Collectibles.............................$4 – 5

288. "Newcastle Falcons," dark blue with red fenders, red roof, Australia issue ....$8 – 10

289. "Newcastle Knights," blue with red fenders, red roof, Australia issue ....$8 – 10

270. "No. Melbourne Kangaroos," white with blue fenders, white roof, Australia issue....................................$8 – 10

271. "No. Melbourne Giants," turquoise with purple fenders, white roof, Australia issue....................................$8 – 10

272. "No. Queensland Cowboys," dark blue with gray fenders, gray roof, Australia issue....................................$8 – 10

273. "No. Sydney Bears," black with white fenders, black roof, Australia issue ....$8 – 10

274. "North America M.I.C.A. Convention 1988," orange, black roof........$7 – 9

275. "North Carolina 1992," pale blue with pale blue fenders, white roof, White Rose Collectibles......................$5 – 7

276. "Notre Dame 1991," yellow with green fenders, white roof, White Rose Collectibles.................................$4 – 5

277. "Oakland Athletics 1990," yellow with green fenders, white roof, White Rose Collectibles.............................$4 – 5

278. "Oakland Athletics 1991," green with yellow fenders, white roof, White Rose Collectibles.............................$4 – 5

279. "Oakland Raiders 1990," silver with black fenders, white roof, White Rose Collectibles.............................$4 – 5

280. "Oakland Raiders 1991," black with silver fenders, white roof, White Rose Collectibles.................................$4 – 5

281. "Old Tymers Model A Club Rod Run," white with black fenders and roof, ASAP promotional.......................$80 – 120

282. "Open Every Day," pale blue with dark gray fenders, dark gray roof ..$12 – 16

283. "P.M.G.," orange with black fenders, black roof, Australia issue ....$9 – 12

284. "Parramatta Eels," blue with yellow fenders, blue roof, Australia issue ...$8 – 10

285. "Pava," yellow, red roof, Denmark issue....................................$9 – 12

286. "Penn State 1990," blue with white fenders, white roof, White Rose Collectibles.................................$7 – 9

287. "Penn State 1990," white with blue fenders, white roof, White Rose Collectibles.................................$7 – 9

288. "Penn State 1991," white with dark blue fenders, dark blue roof, White Rose Collectibles......................$7 – 9

289. "Penrith Panthers," black with red fenders, black roof, Australia issue...$8 – 10

290. "Pepsi," white with blue fenders, red roof ....$5 – 6

291. "Pepsi-Cola," white with black fenders and roof, ASAP promotional ..$60 – 80

292. "Pepsi," "Come Alive," white with blue fenders, red roof ....$8 – 10

293. "Perth Wildcats," white with yellow fenders, white roof, Australia issue...$8 – 10

294. "PG Tips," cream with green fenders, red roof, on-package premium, UK issue.................................$12 – 16

295. "Philadelphia Eagles 1990," silver with green fenders, white roof, White Rose Collectibles.............................$4 – 5

296. "Philadelphia Eagles 1991," silver with green fenders, green roof, White Rose Collectibles.............................$4 – 5

297. "Philadelphia Flyers 1993," orange with black fenders, black roof, White Rose Collectibles......................$7 – 9

298. "Philadelphia Phillies 1990," white with maroon fenders, white roof, White Rose Collectibles......................$4 – 5

299. "Philadelphia Phillies 1991," maroon with maroon fenders, white roof, White Rose Collectibles......................$4 – 5

300. "Pittsburgh Pirates 1991," black with yellow fenders, white roof, White Rose Collectibles.............................$4 – 5

301. "Pittsburgh Pirates 1990," white with black fenders, black roof, White Rose Collectibles.............................$4 – 5

302. "Pittsburgh Steelers 1990," yellow with black fenders, yellow roof, White Rose Collectibles......................$4 – 5

303. "Pittsburgh Steelers 1991," yellow with black fenders, black roof, White Rose Collectibles......................$4 – 5

304. "Postes Canada Post," red with black fenders, black roof ....$6 – 8

305. "Pritt Stick," red with black fenders, black roof, on-package premium, UK issue.....................................$8 – 10

306. "Pure Cod Liver Oil," dark cream with blue fenders, cream roof...........$5 – 6

307. "RACQ," yellow with bright blue fenders, blue roof, Australia issue ....$12 – 16

308. "Rayner's Crusha," red, on-package premium, UK issue................$9 – 12

309. "RCA," white with black fenders and roof, ASAP promotional ....$30 – 40

310. "Reichspost," yellow with black fenders, white roof ....$6 – 8

311. "Ribena," blue, black roof, UK issue ....$9 – 12

312. "Richmond Tigers," black with yellow fenders, black roof, Australia issue ...$8 – 10

313. "Ritz Carlton Hotel & Casino," white with black fenders and roof, ASAP promotional ....$320 – 480

314. "Ritz Carlton Hotel, Spa & Casino," white with black fenders and roof, ASAP promotional....................$240 – 320

315. "River Horse Lager," green with yellow fenders and roof, Matchbox Collectibles...........................$9 – 12

316. "Roosevelt For President 1932 White's Guide Car #1 Presidential Campaign Series," white with black fenders and roof, Color Comp promotional ....$16 – 24

317. "Route 11 Potato Chips," white with black fenders and roof, Color Comp promotional ....$16 – 24

318. "Rowntree's Table Jelly," green, yellow roof, on-package premium, UK issue....$9 – 12

319. "Royal Mail," red, black roof, gold grille, UK issue....................$7 – 9

320. "Rugby Child Development Centre," white with blue fenders, blue roof, UK issue......................................$8 – 10

321. "Rutter Bros. Dairy," white with black fenders, black roof, White Rose Collectibles.................................$7 – 9

322. "Sammler Treffen 1988," dark blue with black fenders, yellow roof, 1997 Germany promotional ....$180 – 240

323. "San Diego Chargers 1990," dark blue with yellow fenders, white roof, White Rose Collectibles......................$4 – 5

324. "San Diego Chargers 1991," yellow with dark blue fenders, dark blue roof, White Rose Collectibles.............$4 – 5

325. "San Diego Padres 1990," white with brown fenders, orange roof, White Rose Collectibles......................$4 – 5

326. "San Diego Padres 1991," silver with dark blue fenders, orange roof, White Rose Collectibles......................$4 – 5

327. "San Francisco 49ers 1990," gold with red fenders, white roof, White Rose Collectibles......................$4 – 5

328. "San Francisco 49ers 1991," red with gold fenders, gold roof, White Rose Collectibles ....$4 – 5

329. "San Francisco Giants 1990," blue with white fenders, white roof, White Rose Collectibles......................$4 – 5

330. "San Francisco Giants 1990," white with black fenders, white roof, White Rose Collectibles......................$4 – 5

331. "San Francisco Giants 1991," lavender gray with black fenders, orange roof, White Rose Collectibles.............$4 – 5

332. "San Francisco Giants 1991," white with dark blue fenders, dark blue roof, White Rose Collectibles.............$4 – 5

333. "San Jose Sharks 1993," white with metallic turquoise fenders, black roof, White Rose Collectibles............$7 – 9

334. "Sea Eagles," dark red with white fenders, dark red roof, Australia issue ......$8 – 10

335. "Season's Greetings From Color Comp Inc.," white with red fenders, green roof, Color Comp promotional ....$120 – 160

336. "Seattle Mariners 1990," white with blue fenders, yellow roof, White Rose Collectibles..............................$4 – 5

337. "Seattle Mariners 1991," yellow with blue fenders, blue roof, White Rose Collectibles..................................$4 – 5

338. "Seattle Seahawks 1990," silver with blue fenders, white roof, White Rose Collectibles..................................$4 – 5

339. "Seattle Seahawks 1991," dark blue with green fenders, white roof, White Rose Collectibles.......................$4 – 5

340. "Selfridge & Co.," dark green with black roof, UK issue ....$6 – 8

341. "Shell Motor Oil," yellow with red fenders, yellow roof, Australia issue.......$16 – 24

342. "Ship McQuaid," white with black fenders and roof, ASAP promotional ....$30 – 40

343. "Shipyard Brewing," white with blue fenders and roof, rubber tires, Matchbox Collectibles ....$9 – 12

344. "Silvo," blue with black fenders, black roof, UK issue ....$8 – 10

345. "Smith Kline Beecham," white with black fenders and roof, ASAP promotional..............................$120 – 160

346. "Smith's Potato Crisps," blue, white roof, on-package premium, Australia issue.................................$8 – 10

347. "So. Queensland Crushers," dark blue with red fenders and roof, Australia issue.................................$8 – 10

348. "So. Sydney Rabbitohs," bright green with red fenders, bright green roof, Australia issue.......................$8 – 10

349. "South Jersey Ghost Research," white with black fenders and roof, Color Comp promotional........................$20 – 25

350. "St. George," white with red fenders, white roof, Australia issue ......$8 – 10

351. "St. Kilda Saints," white with red roof, Australia issue.......................$8 – 10

352. "St. Louis Cardinals 1990," white with rust fenders, maroon roof, White Rose Collectibles..............................$4 – 5

353. "St. Louis Cardinals 1990," white with red fenders, white roof, White Rose Collectibles..............................$4 – 5

354. "St. Louis Cardinals 1991," white with red fenders, white roof, White Rose Collectibles..............................$4 – 5

355. "St. Louis Cardinals 1991," maroon with white fenders, white roof, White Rose Collectibles.....................$4 – 5

356. "Smith's Crisps," dark blue with red fenders, yellow roof, Australia issue.................................$16 – 24

357. "Special Edition 76," white with blue fenders and roof ....$2 – 3

358. "Street's Ice Cream," light brown with red fenders and roof, Australia issue ....$16 – 24

359. "Swarfega," blue, black roof, on-package premium, UK issue.........$20 – 25

360. "Sydney Kings," purple with yellow fenders, white roof, Australia issue................................$8 – 10

361. "Sydney Swans," white with red fenders, red roof, Australia issue ...$8 – 10

362. "Syracuse University 1992," orange with blue fenders, white roof, White Rose Collectibles.....................$5 – 7

363. "Tampa Bay Buccaneers 1990," orange with black fenders, black roof, White Rose Collectibles............$4 – 5

364. "Tampa Bay Buccaneers 1991," orange with red fenders, white roof, White Rose Collectibles............$4 – 5

365. "Tandy Electronics," red, blue roof, Australia issue....................$12 – 16

366. "Tassie Devils," yellow with red fenders, red roof, Australia issue ....$8 – 10

367. "Ten Years Lion," white, blue roof, UK issue ....$8 – 10

368. "Tennessee Vol. 1992," white with orange fenders, white roof, White Rose Collectibles..............................$5 – 7

369. "Texaco Petroleum Products," black with green fenders and roof, Premiere Collection..................................$5 – 6

370. "The Australia," white with black fenders, black roof, Australia issue...$7 – 9

371. "The New Crawford," white with black fenders and roof, ASAP promotional ....$80 – 120

372. "Tiger Balm," red with dark blue fenders, red roof ....$5 – 6

373. "Tittensor First School," gray with red fenders, red roof, UK issue ....$6 – 8

374. "TMLP," white with black fenders and roof, ASAP promotional ....$30 – 40

375. "Tom's Antiques Art & Collectibles," white with black fenders and roof, ASAP promotional........................$40 – 50

376. "Toronto Blue Jays 1990," white with blue fenders, white roof, White Rose Collectibles..............................$4 – 5

377. "Toronto Blue Jays 1991," blue with blue fenders, white roof, White Rose Collectibles..............................$4 – 5

378. "Toronto Maple Leafs 1917," dark blue with white fenders, white roof; "Toronto Maple Leafs 1992," white with blue fenders, white roof, White Rose Collectibles 2-pack, for set of two..................................$12 – 16

379. "Townsville Suns," yellow with salmon pink fenders, red roof, Australia issue $8 – 10

380. "Toy Collectors Pocket Guide," yellow with green fenders, green roof, UK issue.................................$7 – 9

381. "Transply," white with black fenders and roof ....$60 – 80

382. "True Value Hardware," lime green with orange fenders, orange roof, Australia issue...........................$8 – 1[ ]

383. "Two Men And A Truck," white with black fenders and roof, ASAP promotional.............................$12 – 1[ ]

384. "Tyco-Portland, Oregon," white with black fenders and roof, ASAP promotional.............................$120 – 16[ ]

385. "Tyne Brand," dark blue with black fenders and roof, on-package premium UK issue...........................$12 – 1[ ]

386. "Tyne Brand," orange-red with black fenders and roof, on-package premium UK issue...........................$12 – 1[ ]

387. "U.S. Mail," white ....$6 – [ ]

388. "Unionville Community Fair 2000," white with black fenders and roof, ASAP promotional.........................$30 – 4[ ]

389. "Uniroyal Royal Care," black, Canada issue.................................$20 – 2[ ]

390. "University of Colorado 1992," yellow with black fenders, white roof, White Rose Collectibles.....................$5 – [ ]

391. "University of Michigan 1992," yellow with dark blue fenders, yellow roof, White Rose Collectibles............$5 – [ ]

392. "University of Washington 1992," yellow with purple fenders, white roof, White Rose Collectibles............$5 – [ ]

393. "UNLV 1991," silver with red fenders white roof, White Rose Collectibles .$4 – [ ]

394. "Vegemite," yellow with red fenders, yellow roof, Australia issue ......$8 – 1[ ]

395. "Vick's," green with blue fenders, green roof ....$5 – [ ]

396. "Vileda," red with white fenders, white roof, on-package premium, UK issue....$9 – 1[ ]

397. "W.H. Smith & Sons," red, black roof, on-package premium, UK issue ....$20 – 2[ ]

398. "W.H. Smith & Sons," yellow, black roof, UK issue ....$12 – 1[ ]

399. "Washington Capitals 1993," white with red fenders, blue roof, White Rose Collectibles..............................$7 – [ ]

400. "Washington Redskins 1990," rust with yellow fenders, white roof, White Rose Collectibles.....................$4 – [ ]

401. "Washington Redskins 1991," yellow with maroon fenders, maroon roof, White Rose Collectibles............$4 – [ ]

402. "Weetabix," "Sanitarium Food," green, on-package premium, Australia issue...................................$8 – 1[ ]

403. "Welcome Ye To Chester," yellow, blue roof, promotional UK issue ....$16 – 2[ ]

404. "West Coast Eagles," blue and yellow fenders, blue roof, Australia issue..................................$8 – 1[ ]

405. "Western Reds," red with white fenders and roof, Australia issue ....$8 – 1[ ]

406. "Western Suburbs," black with white fenders, black roof, Australia issue ....$8 – 1[ ]

407. "White's Guide Car of the Month #6 May, 1999," white with black fenders and roof, Color Comp promotional ....$16 – 2[ ]

08. "William Lusty," cream with green fenders, green roof, UK issue ....$7 – 9

09. "William Lusty," green with green fenders, green roof, UK issue..........$7 – 9

10. "XIth MICA Convention," rust with cream fenders, cream roof, UK issue..............................$12 – 16

11. "Yardley," light gray with brown fenders, brown roof, UK issue ....$9 – 12

12. "York Fair 1989," yellow, green roof, White Rose Collectibles.............$7 – 9

13. "York Fair 1990 — 225 Years," cream with red fenders, red roof, White Rose Collectibles.............$6 – 8

14. "York Fair 1991," silver with turquoise fenders, turquoise roof, White Rose Collectibles..............................$6 – 8

15. "York Fair 1993," cream with blue fenders, green roof, White Rose Collectibles..................................$5 – 6

16. "Young's Sheep Dips," green, Australia issue.....................................$8 – 10

17. "1st M.I.C.A. Australia Convention," yellow with green fenders, green roof, Australia issue.........................$9 – 12

18. "1st M.I.C.A. European Convention," red with yellow fenders, black roof, Germany issue............................$15 – 20

19. "2nd M.I.C.A. Convention," black, black roof ....$400 – 500

20. "2nd M.I.C.A. NA Convention 1989," black, orange roof.....................$7 – 9

21. "3rd M.I.C.A. Australia Convention," yellow-orange with green fenders and roof, Australia issue ....$9 – 12

22. "3rd M.I.C.A. Australia Convention," fluorescent orange with blue fenders and roof, screw mounted base, promotional...........................$90 – 120

23. "3rd M.I.C.A. Convention," yellow, red roof, UK issue ....$9 – 12

24. "8th M.I.C.A. Event," red with yellow fenders, dark blue roof, UK issue....$12 – 16

25. "10th M.I.C.A. Convention," silver black fenders, black roof, UK issue ....$9 – 12

26. "15th Anniversary Matchbox USA 1991," chrome plated with red fenders, red roof, promotional...........$40 – 50

27. "72nd Shenandoah Apple Blossom Festival," white with black fenders and roof, US issue ....$9 – 12

28. "75th Anniversary Borough of Newfield," blue with black fenders and roof, Color Comp promotional........$12 – 16

29. "2000 Southern California Rod Run Sept. 4th 2000," white with black fenders and roof, ASAP promotional ....$80 – 120

430. Australian six-piece set: "Aeroplane Jelly," "Billy Tea," "IXL," "Milo," "Uncle Toby's," "Violet Crumble," Australia issue, for set of six in original box ....$12 – 16

431. Australian six-piece set: "Hardy's Black Bottle," "Houghton White Burgundy," "McWilliams Cream Sherry," "Penfold's," "Tyrell's Dry Red," "Yalumba Port," for set of six in original box ....$40 – 50

432. Australian six-piece set: "Big Apple Circus," "Chipperfield's Circus," "Circus Barum," "Circus Krone," "Circus Oz," "Gerry Cottle's Circus," for set of six in original box ....$30 – 40

433. white, white fenders, white roof, no markings, Graffic Traffic........$12 – 16

434. white with black fenders and roof, no markings, ASAP promotional blank............................$30 – 40

Ford Model T 1921 Van, 2⁷⁄₈", #44, 1990

1. "15 Jaar Model Auto 97," yellow with black fenders, the Netherlands issue .$12 – 16

2. "1896 1996," red with black fenders, UK issue..............................$16 – 24

3. "1939 – 1945," "War & Occupation Museum," white with black fenders, the Netherlands issue ....$20 – 30

4. "3rd MICA NA Convention 1990," ivory with dark blue roof and fenders, US issue..................................$10 – 12

5. "4th MICA NA Convention," "Detroit Motor City, black, US issue....$10 – 12

6. "5th Anniversary Australian Matchbox News," white with black fenders .$16 – 24

7. "5th MICA Convention 1990," ivory with dark blue roof and fenders, UK issue..................................$10 – 12

8. "8th Super Southern Swapmeet," red with black fenders, Australia issue ....$9 – 12

9. "8th Super Southern Swapmeet," yellow with black fenders, Australia issue ....$9 – 12

10. 16th Matchbox USA Toy Show," white with black fenders, US issue ....$12 – 16

11. 16th Matchbox USA Toy Show," yellow with black fenders, US issue .$12 – 16

12. "40th Anniversary Spar," white with black fenders, UK issue ....$120 – 160

13. "50 Years Liberation," "War & Occupation Museum," white with black fenders, the Netherlands issue...........$20 – 30

14. "Adtrucks," yellow with black fenders, UK issue..............................$12 – 16

15. "Adtrucks 2001," UK issue ...$12 – 16

16. "Anderson Valley," gold with green roof and fenders, Matchbox Collectibles #5 ....$9 – 12

17. "Bala Lake Railway," yellow with black fenders, UK issue ....$12 – 16

18. "Barrettine The Independent Choice," ivory with blue fenders, UK issue ....$12 – 16

19. "BASC," "Beccles Amateur Sailing Club," dark blue with black fenders, UK issue................................$40 – 50

20. "Bendigo National Swapmeet 1996," red with black fenders, Australia issue ....$20 – 30

21. "Bendigo National Swapmeet 1996," white with black fenders, Australia issue ....$20 – 30

22. "Biddestone Village," white with black fenders, UK issue ....$12 – 16

23. **"Bird's Custard Powder," yellow with red roof, blue fenders, China cast ....$3 – 4**

24. "Bird's Custard Powder," yellow with red roof, blue fenders, Macau cast ..$2 – 3

25. "Bishop's Move," yellow with black fenders, UK issue ....$12 – 16

26. "Bostik," ivory with black fenders, UK issue...................................$12 – 16

27. "Bradford AFC," red with black fenders, UK issue...........................$20 – 30

28. "Catalogue of Matchbox Toys," ivory with black fenders, US issue........$16 – 24

29. "Catalogue of Matchbox Toys," yellow with black fenders, US issue ..$60 – 80

30. "CE Engineering Europe Ltd.," white with black fenders, UK issue ....$12 – 16

31. "Chesdale," yellow with blue roof and fenders, Australia on-package premium ....$8 – 12

32. "Chester Doll Hospital," "World's Largest Matchbox Display," white with light blue roof and fenders, UK issue .....$9 – 12

33. "Coca-Cola," red with white fenders, Premiere Collection ....$5 – 6

34. "Continental Aero," purple with black fenders, US issue..................$12 – 16

35. "Craig's," blue with red roof and fenders, Australia on-package premium....................................$8 – 12

36. "Crazy Clown," red with dark blue roof and base, Australia issue ....$9 – 12

37. "Cromer Carnival 1996," white with black fenders, UK issue ....$20 – 30

38. "Cromer Carnival 1997," red with black fenders, UK issue ....$12 – 16

39. "Dale Farm," white with red roof, dark blue fenders, UK issue............$8 – 11

40. "Daybreak at Lowestoft," "The Sunrise Coast," "The Dawn of a New Millenium," UK issue................................$12 – 16

41. "DM David Meek," dark blue with black fenders, UK issue ....$60 – 80

42. "Dunaskin," white with black fenders, UK issue.............................$12 – 16

43. "Dyspraxia Foundation," white with black fenders, UK issue ....$12 – 16

44. "Encyclopedia of Matchbox Toys," ivory with black fenders, US issue ..$40 – 50
45. "Encyclopedia of Matchbox Toys," red with black fenders, UK issue ..$12 – 16
46. "Encyclopedia of Matchbox Toys" in black lettering, yellow with black fenders, US issue ....$20 – 30
47. "Encyclopedia of Matchbox Toys" in blue lettering, yellow with black fenders, US issue............................$20 – 30
48. "Evening Gazette Car Awards 1997," yellow with black fenders, UK issue................................$12 – 16
49. "Farnham Maltings 1 – 7th January 1996," white with black fenders, UK issue......................................$20 – 30
50. "Farnham Maltings 2 – 10th March 1996," white with black fenders, UK issue......................................$20 – 30
51. "Farnham Maltings 3 – 26th May 1996," ivory with white roof, blue fenders, UK issue ....$20 – 30
52. "Farnham Maltings 3 – 26th May 1996," white with blue fenders, UK issue......................................$20 – 30
53. "Farnham Maltings 4 – 8th September 1996," white with black fenders, UK issue......................................$20 – 30
54. "Farnham 6 – 16th March 1997," white with black fenders, UK issue ..$12 – 16
55. "Farnham 7 – May 1997," white with black fenders, UK issue ....$12 – 16
56. "Farnham 8 – 11th September 1997," white with black fenders, UK issue ....$12 – 16
57. "Ferne Animal Sanctuary," white with black fenders, UK issue ....$12 – 16
58. "Financial Times," white with black roof and fenders, UK issue ....$9 – 12
59. "Finlaystone," white with black fenders, UK issue.............................$12 – 16
60. "Finlaystone," yellow with black fenders, UK issue.............................$12 – 16
61. "Firehouse Brewing Co.," black with red roof and fenders, Matchbox Collectibles #2......................$9 – 12
62. "Ford Motor Company," yellow with black fenders, UK issue ....$20 – 30
63. "Ford Motor Company 100 Years," blue with white roof, black fenders, 2003 Matchbox Collectibles ....$6 – 8
64. "Ford On Show," dark blue with black fenders, UK issue ....$80 – 120
65. "Freihofer's," white with black fenders, US issue............................$12 – 16
66. "Garde D'Or," white with black fenders, UK issue.............................$12 – 16
67. "Glenturret," white with black fenders, UK issue.............................$12 – 16
68. "Goodyear Tire & Rubber Co," light blue with black roof, dark blue fenders..$2 – 4
69. "Goodyear Tyres," powder blue with black roof, dark blue fenders......$2 – 3
70. "Great Yarmouth," "The Bloaters," yellow with black fenders, UK issue ..$12 – 16
71. "Great Yarmouth," "Wellesley Main Grandstand," yellow with black fenders,

UK issue............................$12 – 16
72. "Greetings From Philadelphia 1992," "MICA NA," ivory, dark blue roof and fenders............................$12 – 16
73. "Haig's Chocolates," beige with red fenders, spoked wheels, Australia issue............................$12 – 16
74. "Holy Cow," "Ambler Gambler," green with black roof, red fenders, Matchbox Collectibles #3......................$9 – 12
75. "Jacob's," orange with black fenders, Irish on-package premium......$20 – 30
76. "Kellogg's Apple Jacks," fluorescent green with black roof and fenders, US on-package premium ....$9 – 12
77. "Kellogg's Corn Flakes," dark blue with black roof and fenders, Australia on-package premium ....$16 – 24
78. "Kellogg's Corn Pops," yellow with red roof, blue fenders, US on-package premium ....$9 – 12
79. "Kellogg's Eggo," yellow with red roof, black fenders, US on-package premium............................$20 – 30
80. "Kla-Ora," yellow with black fenders, UK issue...................................$12 – 16
81. "Klaus Toys," red with green roof, red fenders, Holiday Express Train, Color Comp promotional................$40 – 50
82. "Kraft," blue with yellow roof and fenders, Australia on-package premium ..$9 – 12
83. "Lloyds," white with red roof, dark blue fenders, UK issue ....$12 – 16
84. "Lowestoft Town Football Club," "Blues of Crown Meadow," white with blue roof, black fenders, UK issue .$30 – 40
85. "Lowestoft Town Football Club," "Blues of Crown Meadow" with "John Grose Ford" on roof, white with black fenders, UK issue........................$200 – 250
86. "Lowestoft Town Football Club," "John Grose Ford," white with blue roof, black fenders, UK issue ....$30 – 40
87. "Mastercraft," blue with red roof and fenders, Canada issue ....$5 – 6
88. "Matchbox Collectibles," green with red roof, green fenders, Holiday Express Train, Color Comp promotional .$40 – 50
89. "Matchbox Drive Your Name Home," dark blue with black fenders, UK issue ....$20 – 30
90. "Matchbox Drive Your Name Home," red with black fenders, UK issue ..$20 – 30
91. "Matchbox Official Visitor," red with black fenders, UK issue ....$60 – 80
92. "Matchbox Drive Your Name Home," white with black fenders, UK issue.....$20 – 30

93. **"Matchbox Toy Delivery," red wit black roof, Collector's Choice, Whit Rose Collectibles...................$4 –**
94. "Matchbox USA 15th Annual T Show," dark blue with black fender US issue............................$20 – 3
95. "Matchbox USA 15th Annual T Show," red with black fenders, U issue............................$20 – 3
96. "Matchbox USA 15th Annual T Show," yellow with black fenders, U issue............................$100 – 15
97. "Matchbox USA 95," dark blue wi black fenders.....................$20 – 3
98. "Matchbox USA 96," red with bla fenders.............................$20 – 3
99. "Matchbox USA 96," white with bla fenders.............................$20 – 3
100. "Mars," black, UK issue.......$12 – 1
101. "Mars," red, UK issue ....$16 – 2
102. "MCCD 1998," ivory with black fer ers, Germany issue ....$40 – 6
103. "MCCD 1998," red with black fender Germany issue...................$16 – 2
104. "MCCD 1998," white with black fer ers, Germany issue ....$16 – 2
105. "MCCD 1998," yellow with black fer ers, Germany issue ....$60 – 8
106. "MD," white with black fenders, U issue...............................$12 – 1
107. "Merry Christmas Australia Matchbo red with black fenders ....$16 – 2
108. "Merry Christmas," "Best Wishes fro Carr Collectibles," red with black fer ers, UK issue ....$40 – 5
109. "MICA 7," "I Could Have Danced Night," white with light blue roof a fenders, UK issue ....$12 – 1
110. "MICA NA Convention," "Detroit Mot City," black ....$10 – 1
111. "Mt. Wilson Wheat Beer," pink wi dark green roof and fenders, Matchb Collectibles........................$9 – 1
112. "Mundesley Inshore Lifeboat," wh with black fenders, UK issue ..$12 – 1
113. "NGK — The Heartbeat of th Engine," white with black fenders, U issue ....$60 – 8
114. "NGK — The UK's No. 1 Profession Plug," white with black fenders, U issue..............................$70 – 9
115. "North Coast Brewing Company Scrimshaw," blue with red roof and fer ers, Matchbox Collectibles #1 ..$9 – 1
116. "North Walsham Carnival 1996," wh with black fenders, UK issue ..$20 – 3
117. "Norwich Citadel — Salvation Army," ivo with black fenders, UK issue ....$12 – 1
118. "Norwich Citadel — Salvation Army," yello with black fenders, UK issue......$12 – 1
119. "Open Business Solutions," white wi black fenders, UK issue ....$16 – 2
120. "P.M.G.," orange-red with black ro and fenders, Australia issue ....$8 – 1
121. "PARA 90," white with light blue roof and fenders, UK issue ....$10 – 1
122. "PG Tips," ivory with red roof, green fer ers, UK on-package premium ...$16 – 2

123. "Philadelphia MICA NA," black .$12 – 16
124. "Pool's Plus, Inc." dark blue with red roof and fenders, ASAP promotional .... $16 – 24
125. "QATC & EMC Projects," "QA Testing Centre," yellow with black fenders, UK issue .... $20 – 30
126. "Red Tail Ale," red with blue roof, gold fenders, Matchbox Collectibles #6 ...... $9 – 12
127. "Ritz Carlton Hotel, Spa & Casino," dark blue with red roof and fenders, ASAP promotional .... $200 – 300
128. "Royal Mail GR," red with black hood, roof and fenders, UK issue ...... $9 – 12
129. "Runnymeade Meccano Guild," red with green roof, black fenders, UK issue .... $12 – 16
130. "Runnymeade Meccano Guild," white with black fenders, UK issue ..$12 – 16
131. "SAE International," black, US issue .... $45 – 55
132. "Seadog Brewing Co.," blue with red roof and fenders, Matchbox Collectibles .... $9 – 12
133. "Springfest Extravaganza 1996," red with black fenders, Australia issue .... $20 – 30
134. "St. Marien Sandersleben," red with black fenders, Germany issue $30 – 40
135. "St. Marien Sandersleben," white with black fenders, Germany issue .... $40 – 50
136. "St. Marien Sandersleben," yellow with black fenders, Germany issue $16 – 24
137. "Starlec," white with black fenders, UK issue .... $12 – 16
138. "Stirling Old Town Jail," dark blue with black fenders, UK issue .... $60 – 80
139. "Swarfega," dark green with black roof, dark gray base, UK on-package premium .... $45 – 55
140. "The Royal Tournament," white with black fenders, UK issue .... $20 – 30
141. "The Royal Tournament" with "Earl's Court," white with black fenders, UK issue .... $150 – 200
142. "The Story of Mann," ivory with black fenders, UK issue .... $12 – 16
143. "The Sunrise Coast," UK issue .$12 – 16
144. "TTK," dark blue with black fenders, UK issue .... $40 – 50
145. "Vegemite," yellow with red roof and fenders, Australia on-package premium .... $8 – 12
146. "Weidman's Brewery," yellow with blue fenders, Matchbox Collectibles #4 .$9 – 12
147. "Welcoming the New Millennium," beige with black roof and fenders, UK issue .... $20 – 30
148. "Welcoming the New Millennium," red with black fenders, UK issue ..$20 – 30
149. "Williams Lusty," black, UK issue .$7 – 9
150. "Your Own Promotional Vehicle," "Matchbox — Put Your Logo Here," Australia Special Edition in gift box ..... $100 – 150
151. "Zonker Stout," pale orange with orange red roof and fenders, Matchbox Collectibles .... $9 – 12

152. bright blue with red roof and fenders, no markings, ASAP promotional blank .... $30 – 40

153. "Squidward," Spongebob Squarepants 5-pack .... $2 –3
Australia 2-packs with pewter medallion:
154. "St. Kilda Saints 1897;" "St. Kilda Saints 1996," pair .... $45 – 65
155. "Essendon Bombers 1897," "Essendon Bombers 1996," pair .... $45 – 65
156. "Fitzroy Lions 1897," "Fitzroy Lions 1996," pair....................... $45 – 65
157. "Carlton Blues 1897," "Carlton Blues 1996," pair....................... $45 – 65
158. "Melbourne Demons 1897," "Melbourne Demons 1996," pair ..$45 – 65
159. "Collingwood Magpies 1897," "Collingwood Magpies 1996," pair....$45 – 65
160. "South Melbourne 1897," 1996," pair .... $45 – 65
161. "Geelong Cats 1897"; "Geelong Cats 1996," pair........................ $45 – 65

Ford Mondeo, #40, 1995; #33, 1995, international
1. blue, "151CS," blue "Mondeo" on white field, tan interior, Thailand cast ..$2 – 3
2. blue, "Ford" logo, tan interior, Thailand cast .... $2 – 3

3. blue, "151CS," red "Mondeo" on white field, tan interior, Thailand cast .... $2 – 3
4. white, "Airport Security," dark blue interior, China cast.................... $12 – 16

Ford Mustang, 2⁷/₈", #8, 1966

1. white with black plastic tires and chrome hubs .... $12 – 15
2. orange with black plastic tires with chrome hubs.................. $100 – 125

3. white with red interior, Superfast wheels................................ $60 – 80
4. red with red interior, Superfast wheels................................ $300 – 360
5. red-orange with red interior, Superfast wheels.................... $300 – 360
6. red with ivory interior, Superfast wheels................................ $40 – 50
6. red-orange with ivory interior, Superfast wheels.................... $40 – 50

Ford Mustang 1965 — ½ Convertible, 2000 Feature Cars, with opening features, designed to replace Premiere Collection
1. black with red interior .... $9 – 12

Ford Mustang 1965 — ½ Soft Top, 2000 Feature Cars, with opening features, designed to replace Premiere Collection
1. dark green with white roof, tan interior .... $12 – 16

Ford Mustang 1999 Convertible, #36, 1999; #3, 2000; #12, 2002
1. black, "Toy Fair 2000 Matchbox," gray interior, rubber tires on chrome rims .... $60 – 80
2. black with tan interior, detailed trim, rubber tires on chrome rims, Premiere Collection................................ $7 – 8
3. blue with white interior, white stripes, 5-pack................................ $2 – 3
4. bronze with black interior, silver stripes and horse logo, "Mustang," 5-pack.$2 – 3
5. light red, "Subway," tan interior, "Subway Mfg. By b. little" cast into base.$4 – 5
6. red with black interior, white band and stripes, 5-pack .... $2 – 3

7. metallic red with purple interior, "Mustang" and graphics, 2002 Style Champs series..................... $2 – 3

8. white with red interior, "Coca-Cola," Coke bottles and water droplets graphics on hood, 5-pack .... $2 – 3
9. white with tan interior, black stripes, "Mustang," 1999 Car Shows series ...... $2 – 3

10. yellow, "Mustang," black interior, 2000 Open Road series ....$2 – 3

11. yellow, "Mustang," "Matchbox 2000," black stripes, black interior, 2000 Open Road series...........................$3 – 4

Ford Mustang 1999 Hardtop Coupe, #17, 2000, US; #8, 2000, Mexico; #68, 2000, international; #3, 2001; #12, 2002

1. red with rubber tires on chrome rims, 1999 First Edition....................$6 – 9
2. unpainted with rubber tires on chrome rims, 1999 First Edition...........$6 – 9
3. orange and white, "Matchbox 2," "Mattel Wheels"........................$15 – 20
4. metallic green with white headlights, ivory interior, 2000 Great Drivers series...................................$2 – 3

5. metallic green with white headlights, ivory interior, "Matchbox 2000," 2000 Great Drivers series.....$3 – 4

6. white with red stripes, "Mustang," 5-spoke wheels, 2000 international issue ..$3 – 4
7. white with red stripes, "Mustang," 10-spoke wheels, 2000 international issue...................................$9 – 12

8. white with silver and black horse, red accent and "Mustang" on sides, red and blue stripes, "Thirty Fifth Anniversary" on hood, 2001 Daddy's Dreams series ....$2 – 3

9. metallic red with purple and white design, "Mustang," 2002 Style Champs series...................................$2 – 3
10. black with dual white stripes, 5-pack...............................$2 – 3
11. red with rubber tires on chrome rims, "MDM," "Matchbox," custom ..$20 – 25

12. unpainted with rubber tires on chrome rims, "MDM," "Matchbox," custom ....$20 – 25
13. red with "Coca-Cola" and polar bears design, Avon 2-pack, chrome hubs ....$5 – 7
14. red with "Coca-Cola" and polar bears design, Avon 2-pack, black hubs.$9 – 12
15. cream, "Scooby Doo!" "Like Wow!" "Fred," Warner Bros. promotional............$6 – 8
16. red with "Coca-Cola" and polar bears design, rubber tires on chrome rims, Premiere Collection ....$7 – 9
17. black with dual white stripes, 5-pack.....................................$2 – 3

Ford Mustang 1999 Police, #460/509, 2000

1. **"D.A.R.E.," metallic red with amber roof lights, D.A.R.E. 5-pack ...$2 – 3**
2. "D.A.R.E. Police," black with blue and red roof lights, D.A.R.E. series...$4 – 5

Ford Mustang 2000 Convertible, #3, 2000; #12, 2002

1. yellow with black interior, "Mustang," black, 2000 Open Road series 1 ....$2 – 3
2. metallic red with purple interior, "Mustang"; purple, black, and white; 2002 Style Champs series 3 ....$2 – 3

Ford Mustang Boss 1970 (see Ford Boss Mustang 1970)

Ford Mustang Cobra, #44, 1972 (see Ford Boss Mustang)

Ford Mustang Cobra, #71, 1995; #73, 1998

1. **red with no markings, butterscotch interior, 1999 Beach Fun 5-pack ....$2 – 3**
2. red with no markings, tan interior, 5-pack.....................................$2 – 3
3. red with detailed trim, rubber tires on chrome rims, Premiere Collection #2 ....$5 – 6
4. metallic red with cobra on black hood, Thailand cast, 1995.................$2 – 3

5. metallic red with lime green horse head on sides, chrome wheel hubs, 1998 Street Cruisers series ..$2 – 3

6. metallic red with lime green horse head on sides, black wheel hubs, 1998 Street Cruisers series..........$16 – 24
7. pink, "71st Shenandoah Apple Blossom Festival 1998," Thailand cast, US issue ....$9 – 12

8. pink, "White's Guide Car of the Month #2," "January 1999"..........$12 – 16

9. pumpkin orange with detailed trim, white and gray interior, rubber tires on chrome rims, Gold Coin Collection ....$16 – 24
10. metallic orange with detailed trim, tan and brown interior, rubber tires on chrome rims, gift set................$5 – 6
11. green with white and gray interior, detailed trim, rubber tires on chrome rims, Select Class ....$5 – 6
12. bright blue, "District 16 Convention Lion's Club, gray interior, Color Comp promotional.........................$16 – 24
13. bright blue with no markings, gray interior, China cast, 5-pack.............$2 – 3

14. metallic blue with brown and tan interior, rubber tires on chrome rims, Premiere Collection #16........$4 – 5

15. metallic blue with lime green horse logo on sides, translucent yellow interior, Thailand cast..........................$2 – 3

5. metallic blue with white and gray interior, detailed trim, rubber tires on chrome rims, Select Class #4....$5 – 6

7. purple with white and black interior, rubber tires on chrome rims, JC Penney Premiere Collection 8-car display set.................$4 – 5

9. black with detailed trim, rubber tires on chrome rims, Select Class #2....$5 – 6

8. black with cobra on gray hood, Thailand cast, 1996.................$4 – 5

10. white, "Pace Car," Ford logo, black speckle pattern, blue interior, 1997 Convertibles 5-pack.............$2 – 3

11. white with cobra on black hood, green interior, Thailand cast, 1998 5-pack.................$2 – 3

12. white with detailed trim, rubber tires on chrome rims, Premiere Collection #5.................$5 – 6

13. metallic gold with no markings, Thailand cast, 1997 75 Challenge series.................$6 – 12

14. gold with white and gray interior, detailed trim, rubber tires on chrome rims, Premiere Collection #14 ...$4 – 5

Ford Mustang Cobra Jet 1968, #69, 1997; #40, 1998
red with white and black stripes, rubber tires on chrome rims, Premiere Collection #20.................$4 – 5
maroon with black and white stripes, rubber tires on chrome rims, Toys "R" Us gift set.................$4 – 5
yellow, "Coca-Cola," rubber tires on chrome rims, Premiere Collection..$6 – 8

yellow with white and purple accents, 1998 Classic Decades ....$2 – 3
green with gold side stripes and black hood band, rubber tires on chrome rims, Premiere Collection ....$6 – 8

---

6. dark green, "Ice Cold Coca-Cola," Avon 2-pack.................$4 – 5

7. blue with white and orange accents, chrome interior, 1998 Classic Decades.................$2 – 3

8. blue with white and orange accents, translucent white interior, 1998 Classic Decades.................$60 – 80

10. silver-blue with black band and stripes, 5-spoke wheels, 5-pack.............$2 – 3

11. silver-blue with black band and stripes, 10-spoke wheels, 5-pack...........$6 – 8

11. silver-blue with black stripes, rubber tires on chrome rims, Matchbox Collectibles.................$16 – 24

12. dark blue with black and gold stripes, rubber tires on chrome rims, Premiere Collection.......$7 – 9

13. black with red pinstripes, rubber tires on chrome rims, 1997 Inaugural Edition ....$5 – 6

14. unpainted, rubber tires on chrome rims, 1997 Inaugural Edition .....$5 – 6

15. white, "Coca-Cola Play Refreshed," Premiere Collection.................$4 – 5

16. white with black on hood and red pinstripes, rubber tires on chrome rims, Premiere Collection #17 ....$4 – 5

17. metallic gold with black stripes, 5-pack.................$2 – 3

Ford Mustang GT, #74, 1984, oversized chrome engine

1. red with black stripes, racing slicks on back axle, China cast ....$2 – 3

2. light orange with yellow and blue stripes, racing slicks on back axle, China cast ....$3 – 4

3. light orange with yellow and blue stripes, racing slicks on back axle, Macau cast.................$3 – 4

---

4. dark orange with yellow and blue stripes, racing slicks on back axle, Macau cast.................$3 – 4

5. dark orange with orange and blue stripes, racing slicks on back axle, Macau cast.................$3 – 4

6. pearl silver with purple and yellow stripes, racing slicks on back axle, China cast ....$3 – 4

7. white with red lines, racing slicks on back axle, Thailand cast.........$2 – 3

Ford Mustang GT 1965 Fastback, #72, 1999 (similar casting: Ford Mustang Fastback)

1. red, "Matchbox Toy Show," "Toy Show 98," black interior, rubber tires on chrome rims ....$9 – 12

2. red with white stripes, black and white interior, rubber tires on chrome rims, gift set ....$5 – 6

3. white, "Cruisin New England Magazine All Wheels Festival 2001," Color Comp promotional.........................$60 – 80

4. white, "Mustang," blue stripes, large 5-spoke concave wheels, 1999 Classics series...........................$2 – 3

5. white, "Mustang," blue stripes, small 5-spoke concave wheels, 1999 Classics series.................$6 – 8

Ford Mustang GT 1968, issued 2003
1. blue with white C-stripe, "Ford Motor Company 100 Years," 2003 Avon Two pack.........................$5 – 6

Ford Mustang GT 1998, issued 2003
1. red, "Ford Motor Company 100 Years," 2003 Avon Two Pack ....$5 – 6

Ford Mustang GT350, 2⅞", #23, 1979
1. white with chrome oversized engine, blue accents.......................$10 – 15

Ford Mustang IMSA, 3", #11, 1983; #67, 1983

1. black with red and white stripes, "Ford Mustang"..................................$2 – 3
2. black with yellow and green flames.$2 – 3
3. black with yellow and green stripes ....$2 – 3
4. yellow with black and red stripes, "47".......................................$4 – 5
5. red with no markings............$10 – 12
6. orange with yellow flames, 1993 .$2 – 3
7. orange with yellow and blue flames...................................$2 – 3
8. fluorescent orange with black wavy lines, black plastic base.............$2 – 3
9. fluorescent orange with black wavy lines, black metal base, Hungary issue.................................$16 – 24
10. bright red with spatter accents, 1994.....................................$2 – 3

Ford Mustang Mach III Convertible, #15, 1994, US; #28, 1994, international; #4, 1998

1. red; hood has black lines through blue field bordered in white, 1994 ....$2 – 3

2. black; hood has black lines through dark blue field bordered in white, 1994.......................................$2 – 3
3. red; hood has white stars on blue field; red stripes on trunk and sides, 1995..................................$2 – 3
4. black; hood has white stars on blue field; red stripes on trunk and sides, 1996.................................$2 – 3

5. white; hood has white stars on blue field; red stripes on trunk and sides, 1997.......................................$2 – 3

6. light blue with orange stripe down middle and on front, 1997 Cars of the Future 5-pack ....$2 – 3

7. **white; hood has white stars on red field; blue stripes on trunk and sides, 1998 Stars & Stripes series ..$2 – 3**
8. purple with neon yellow tiger stripes on doors, 1999 ....$2 – 3
9. red with rubber tires on gray rims, World Class Super Series 1994 – 1995..................................$3 – 5
10. metallic blue, "Mach III," trim detail, rubber tires on chrome rims, Premiere Collection World Class Series 12 – Convertibles ....$4 – 6
11. metallic green with rubber tires on chrome rims, Matchbox European Premiere Series 2, 1997 ....$4 – 6
12. yellow, "Nationwise Auto Parts".$16 – 24
13. pearly white, "Ice Crusher".......$9 – 12
14. metallic red, "Mach III"............$2 – 3
15. dark purple with green stripes, 5-pack..................................$2 – 3
16. metallic gold, 1997 75 Challenge series.................................$6 – 12
17. yellow with rubber tires on chrome rims, Gold Coin Collection......$16 – 24

Ford Mustang Piston Popper (Rolamatic), 2¹³⁄₁₆", #10, 1973; #60, 1982 reissue

1. orange, "Sunkist," red interior, black base, Macau cast ....$5 – 6
2. orange, "Sunkist," red interior, unpainted base, Hong Kong cast ....$5 – 6
3. yellow, "Hot Popper," flames ......$6 – 8
4. yellow, "60," red interior, England cast....................................$6 – 8
5. yellow, "60," white interior, England cast..................................$12 – 16
6. yellow, design on trunk, England cast....................................$8 – 10
7. yellow, no markings, red interior, England cast ....$8 – 10
8. metallic blue, "Superfast" cast ....$80 – 100
9. metallic blue, "Rolamatic" cast................................$9 – 12
10. white, no markings...........$250 – 350

Ford Mustang Wildcat Dragster, 2⁷⁄₈", #8, 1970

1. "Wildcat" labels....................$20 – 30
2. "Rat Rod" labels....................$30 – 45
3. no labels.............................$20 – 30
4. sailboat labels.....................$30 – 45

Ford Panel Van, #38, 2000; #474, 2000; #52, 2002; #23, 2000, international

1. "Camp Sunshine," white, Color Comp promotional.......................$20 – 30
2. "D.A.R.E. Dover Police," black, D.A.R.E. series..................................$4 – 5

3. **"H + N 24 Hour Emergency Service, "For All Your Plumbing Needs, metallic gray, 2002 Hammer and Nails series, 2003 Hero City .$2 – ?**
4. "M.J. Engineering & Land Surveying, P.C." white, Color Comp promotional..$20 – 30
5. "MICA Hershey 2000," white, Color Comp promotional...............$16 – 24

6. **"Mission 1 Base Shuttle" on doors, "Matchbox 2000," white, world map and space shuttle design, metallic gray ladders on roof, Mission Ford Van from 2000 Space Explorer series ....$3 – ?**
7. "Mission 1 Base Shuttle" on doors, white, world map and space shuttle design, metallic gray ladders on roof, Mission Ford Van from 2000 Space Explorer series ....$2 – ?
8. "Virtek," white, Color Comp promotional..............................$20 – 30
9. white, no markings, Color Comp promotional blank.........................$30 – 40

Ford Pickup 1956, #48, 1997; #35, 1998; #21, 1999; #56, 2000; #15, 2001

1. red, "2nd Annual Mattel Open," Color Comp promotional issue....$120 – 160
2. red, "Bendigo 1999 National Swap Meet, Australia issue............$16 – 24
3. red, "Coca-Cola In Bottles," rubber tires on chrome rims, Premiere Collection..$5 – 6
4. red, "Matchbox Madness," Color Comp promotional issue...............$80 – 120

red, "Matchbox USA," "www.match-box-usa.com," white roof, promotional ....$12 – 16

red, "Mr. Timmerman's," 2001 Highway Heroes series.................$2 – 3

. **red, "Texaco" logo, "Jimmy's Auto Service" on doors, 2000 Speedy Delivery series ....$2 – 3**
red, "Texaco" logo, "Jimmy's Auto Service" on doors, "Matchbox 2000," 2000 Speedy Delivery series .....$3 – 4
red, detailed trim, rubber tires on chrome rims, Premiere Collection #17 ....$4 – 5

0. red, no markings, 1998 Classic Decades series ....$2 – 3
1. metallic red, "Happy Days," Star Cars series...................................$5 – 6
2. red and white, "Coca-Cola," Avon 2-pack.................................$4 – 5
3. orange, "MBRR Service," rubber tires on chrome rims, Color Comp promotional...................................$30 – 40
4. orange with chrome trim..........$2 – 3
5. yellow with mud spray, 5-pack....$2 – 3

6. green, "Fresh Produce Delivery" 1999 Speedy Delivery series ..$2 – 3
7. turquoise, with pink and purple pinstripes, rubber tires on chrome rims, Premiere Collection #20 ....$4 – 5
8. dark blue with white flames........$2 – 3
9. metallic blue, "Matchbox Toy Show Hershey 98," rubber tires on chrome rims ....$12 – 16
1. black, "Great Connecticut Toy Show 2000," Color Comp promotional issue ....$12 – 16

20. dark purple with white and pink flames ....$3 – 4
22. black, "Great White Adventures," Australia issue ....$3 – 4
23. black with white roof, rubber tires on chrome rims, 1997 Inaugural Edition ....$5 – 6

24. white with yellow plastic base, monkey and wrench design, 2003 Hero City 5-pack #11....................$2 – 3
25. metallic gold, 1997 75 Challenge series...................................$6 – 12
26. unpainted, rubber tires on chrome rims, 1997 Inaugural Edition .....$5 – 6

Ford Pickup, red with white topper, 2³/₄", #6, 1968
1. white grille, black plastic wheels..................................$9 – 12
2. chrome grille, black plastic wheels................................$12 – 15
3. chrome grille, unpainted base, Superfast wheels ....$45 – 60
4. chrome grille, black base, Superfast wheels.................................$45 – 60
5. chrome grille, green base, Superfast wheels.................................$45 – 60
6. chrome grille, metallic green base, Superfast wheels ....$45 – 60
7. chrome grille, gray base, Superfast wheels.................................$45 – 60
8. white grille, green base, Superfast wheels.................................$45 – 60
9. white grille, gray base, Superfast wheels.................................$45 – 60
10. white grille, black base, Superfast wheels.................................$45 – 60
11. white grille, unpainted base, Superfast wheels.................................$45 – 60

Ford Pickup Camper, 3", #38, 1980
1. red, beige camper....................$5 – 6
2. orange-red, beige camper ....$5 – 6
3. orange-red, beige camper, "35" on base ....$60 – 80

Ford Prefect, 2¹/₄", #30, 1956
1. light blue.......................$100 – 125

2. gray-brown or olive brown......$35 – 50

Ford Probe GT, #44, 1994
1. metallic red, "Princeton Nassau – Conover," orange and yellow design ....$16 – 24

2. metallic red with orange and yellow design, 1994.........................$2 – 3
3. metallic blue with gray flames, oversized engine, rubber tires on chrome rims, Premiere Collection #9 ....$4 – 5
4. purple with green and white design, 1996......................................$2 – 3

5. black with blue and pink design, 1995...................................$2 – 3
6. black with peach and white design ....$2 – 3

7. metallic bronze with blue and white design...................................$2 – 3
8. metallic gold, 1997 75 Challenge series................................$12 – 16

Ford Refuse Truck, 3", #7, 1966
1. orange cab, gray container, black plastic wheels ....$12 – 16
2. orange cab, gray container, Superfast wheels, 1970.....................$30 – 40

Ford RS200, 2⁷/₈", #34, 1987

1. white, "7," blue accents ....$2 – 3

Ford RS200

2. white, "7," red accents ....$2 – 3

3. blue, "2" ....$2 – 3
4. white with no markings, Graffic Traffic series..................................$12 – 16
5. dark blue with no markings, Germany issue.................................$10 – 12
6. orange, "Enjoy Fanta," China issue.............................$160 – 200

Ford RS2000 (see Ford Escort RS2000)

Ford Scissors Truck, #7, 1999; #37, 2000, US; #22, 2000, international

1. white with white container, "World Jets," 1999 Air Traffic series $2 – 3
2. white with white container, "World Airways," 5-pack ....$2 – 3
3. white with white container, "LSG Sky Chefs" ....$2 – 3

4. light gray with white container, "VentureStar," 2000 Space Explorer series............................$2 – 3
5. light gray with white container, "VentureStar," "Matchbox 2000," 2000 Space Explorer series...$3 – 4

6. white with white container, blue and green labels, 5-pack ....$2 – 3
7. red with white container, shipping docks and ship labels, 2000 Ocean Dock 5-pack.....................................$2 – 3
8. red with gray container, jet and globe labels, Action System ....$4 – 5

Ford Sierra (see Ford Sierra XR4Ti)

Ford Sierra XR4Ti, 3", #15, 1983; #55, 1983; #40, 1990

1. black upper, dark gray lower, white and green stripes, "85" ....$3 – 5

2. black upper, black lower, "Texaco 6," "Pirelli" ....$2 – 4
3. dark blue upper, black lower, "Duckhams Race Team," Team Convoy.........$4 – 6
4. ivory upper, dark gray lower, black roof, wide stripe, "55"....................$9 – 12
5. metallic green upper, dark gray lower, black roof, Laser Wheels ....$4 – 6
6. metallic green upper, dark gray lower, black roof, Superfast wheels ....$9 – 12

7. metallic gray upper, dark gray lower body, "Ford XR4i Sport" on hood, red interior, clear windows ....$4 – 6
8. red upper, black lower, "Tizer The Appetizer," Team Convoy.................$4 – 6
9. red upper, black lower, "Fire Dept.," Siren Force ....$9 – 12

10. red upper, yellow lower, blue roof, Liv 'N Learn/Preschool series ....$12 – 18
11. white upper, red lower, black interior, "Virgin Atlantic"..................$4 – 6
12. white upper, red lower, red interior, "Virgin Atlantic"..................$12 – 18
13. white upper, gray lower, white interior, clear windows, gray metal base....................$90 – 120

14. white upper, gray lower, red interior, clear windows, gray metal base........................$4 – 6

15. white upper, gray lower, red interior, clear windows, gray metal base, metallic gray spoiler...$4 – 6
16. white upper, white lower, "Sheriff" Siren Force/Rescue 911 ....$9 – 12
17. white upper, black lower, "Police," Light & Sound ....$2 – 4
18. white upper, black lower, "Gemini," "Cooper," "1" ....$2 – 4

19. yellow upper, black lower, black roof, "XR 4x4" ....$6 – 9
20. yellow upper, black lower, black roof, "Matchbox Taxi Co. 555-7800," Light & Sound ....$4 – 6
21. yellow upper, dark gray lower, gray roof, "XR 4x4"..........................$40 – 60
22. yellow-orange upper, black lower, "Airport Security," red roof lights, Siren Force/Rescue 911 ....$9 – 12
23. yellow-orange, "Airport Security," green roof lights, Siren Force/Rescue 911 .$20 – 25

Ford Skip Truck (see Ford Cargo Skip Truck)

Ford Super Truck, FST, 1996, White Rose Collectibles

1. "Exide 7," black ....$4 – 6
2. "Larry's Heavenly," "Petron Plus 78" white..................................$6 – 8

"Ortho 21," yellow ....$4 – 5
"Quaker State 24," white and green......................................$4 – 5
"Remax 6," white and red..........$6 – 8
"Team ASE 2," blue and white ....$4 – 5

ord Supervan II, 2¹⁵/₁₆", #6, 1985, international; #72, 1987, US

white with "Ford Supervan" ....$3 – 5

white with "Starfire" ....$4 – 6
white with "Fuji Racing Team".....$4 – 6
white with roof lights, "Ambulance," Siren Force ....$12 – 16
white with roof lights, "Ambulance," "Rescue 911".......................$12 – 16
white with no markings, Graffic Traffic ....$4 – 6
red with roof lights, "Fire Observer," Siren Force ....$12 – 16
red with roof lights, "Fire Observer," "Rescue 911".......................$12 – 16
red with "Tizer Flavoured Soft Drink".$4 – 6
0. dark blue with "Duckhams QXR Engine Oils".......................................$4 – 6
1. dark blue with lights, "Police Control Unit," Siren Force.................$12 – 16
2. dark blue with lights, "Police Control Unit," "Rescue 911" ....$12 – 16
3. dark gray, "Danger High Explosive," "Heavy Load," weapons, Roadblasters .....$3 – 5
4. light gray, "Danger High Explosive," "Heavy Load," weapons ....$15 – 20
5. yellow with "Service Car BP Oil"..$12 – 15
6. yellow with "Goodyear Pit Stop"...$4 – 6

ord Thames Estate Car, yellow and turquoise, 2¹/₈", #70, 1959
. no windows, gray plastic wheels.............................$30 – 40
. clear windows, gray plastic wheels.............................$30 – 40
. green windows, gray plastic wheels.............................$30 – 40
. clear windows, silver plastic wheels.............................$30 – 40
. green windows, silver plastic wheels.............................$30 – 40
. green windows, black plastic wheels.............................$25 – 35

ord Thames "Singer" Van, 2¹/₈", #59, 1958
. light green with gray plastic wheels.............................$30 – 40
. light green with silver plastic wheels.............................$$80 – 100
. dark green with gray plastic wheels.............................$100 – 120

4. dark green with silver plastic wheels..........................$110 – 135

Ford Thames Trader Wreck Truck, 2¹/₂", #13, 1961
1. gray wheels.........................$40 – 50
2. black wheels.......................$30 – 40

Ford Thunderbird, 2⁵/₈", #75, 1960
1. ivory and pink, gray plastic wheels..............................$50 – 60
2. ivory and pink, silver plastic wheels..............................$50 – 60
3. ivory and pink, black plastic wheels..............................$80 – 100

Ford Thunderbird 1957, #42, 1982; #16, 2000

1. red, "White's Guide #3," "February 1999" ....$4 – 6
2. red, "Celebrating Patsy," white interior ....$12 – 16
3. red, detailed trim, white and red interior, rubber tires on chrome rims, Special Class ....$4 – 5

4. metallic red, detailed trim, white and red interior, rubber tires on chrome rims, Premiere Collection #6..$4 – 5
5. pink, "Pinky," "Happy Days," white and pink interior, Avon Star Cars series...................................$9 – 12
6. yellow, detailed trim, black and white interior, rubber tires on chrome rims, Premiere Collection #17 ....$4 – 5

7. pale yellow with light gray interior, 2000 Great Drivers series.....$2 – 3
8. pale yellow with light gray interior, "Matchbox 2000," 2000 Great Drivers series...................................$3 – 4
9. pale yellow, black and white interior, rubber tires on chrome rims, Matchbox Collectibles Elvis Presley series, includes Graceland diorama and plexiglass cover ....$12 – 16

10. blue with yellow and orange flames, detailed trim, white and red interior, rubber tires on chrome rims, Premiere Collection #11.....................$4 – 5
11. blue with yellow and orange flames, white interior, China issue .....$60 – 80
12. turquoise, "Chubby's," white interior...............................$9 – 12
13. turquoise, detailed trim, white and turquoise interior, rubber tires on chrome rims, Matchbox Collectibles Train Set ....$12 – 16
14. black with red interior..............$4 – 5
15. black, detailed trim, red and white interior, rubber tires on chrome rims, Premiere Collection #3 ....$4 – 5
16. ivory and red two-tone ....$4 – 5

17. white with red interior...........$2 – 3
18. white with red and pink interior, detailed trim, rubber tires on chrome rims, Gold Coin Collection.....................$16 – 24
19. metallic silver, T-Bird design, detailed trim, blue and white interior, rubber tires on chrome rims, Premiere Collection #20...............................$4 – 5
20. red with white interior.............$4 – 5

Ford Thunderbird 1996, WRP02, 1996, White Rose Collectibles, Goodyear rubber tires on chrome rims
1. "Badcock 12," orange and blue.$9 – 12
2. "Caterpillar 97," orange-yellow ...$4 – 5
3. "Circuit City 8," dark red............$4 – 5
4. "Family Channel 16," metallic blue and white.....................................$4 – 5
5. "Hayes Modems 15," purple and turquoise ....$9 – 12
6. "Jasper," "Federal Mogul 77," white......................................$4 – 5
7. "Mac Tonight," blue ....$20 – 30
8. "McDonald's," "Monopoly 94," red......................................$9 – 12
9. "McDonald's 94," red ....$4 – 5
10. "McDonald's 94," red and white..$4 – 5
11. "McDonald's 94," red and white with red wheels, Team Convoy..........$7 – 9
12. "Miller Lite," dark blue and white, sealed in plexiglas box....................$25 – 35
13. "Miller Racing 2," black, sealed in glass bottle on wooden stand........$60 – 80
14. "New Holland 94," blue ....$4 – 5
15. "QC Quality Care," "Red Carpet Lease 88," blue ....$4 – 5
16. "QVC 7," brown-gold ....$4 – 5
17. "Remington 75," metallic green, sealed in glass bottle.....................$30 – 40
18. "Remington 75," olive green, tan and black camouflage, sealed in glass bottle ....$30 – 40
19. "Remington Stren 75," purple, sealed in glass bottle ....$30 – 40

20. "Spam 9," blue ....$4 – 5
21. "Valvoline 6," white and blue ......$4 – 5

Ford Thunderbird Concept, 2000 Feature Cars, with opening features, designed to replace Premiere Collection
1. red ....$9 – 12
2. pale yellow ....$9 – 12

Ford Thunderbird Concept Convertible, 2000 Feature Cars, with opening features, designed to replace Premiere Collection
1. pale yellow with black interior ...$9 – 12

Ford Thunderbird Stock Car, 3", #7, 1993, US; #39, 1995, international; #64, 1998, US; #268, 1994, White Rose
1. "10," checkered flag, bright pink, white-lettered Goodyear slicks ....$2 – 3
2. "1994 Most Popular Driver — Bill Elliott," gold plated, Goodyear rubber tires on black rims, White Rose..........$20 – 30
3. "1994 Rookie of the Year — 8 Jeff Burton," gold plated, Goodyear rubber tires on black rims, White Rose ....$20 – 30
4. "Baby Ruth 1," white, white-lettered Goodyear slicks, White Rose......$4 – 5
5. "Baby Ruth," white, yellow-lettered Goodyear slicks, White Rose......$4 – 5
6. "Bill Elliot 11," red, white-lettered Goodyear slicks, White Rose......$4 – 5
7. "Bill Elliot 11, red, white-lettered Goodyear slicks, White Rose Team Convoy...$4 – 5
8. "Bojangles," "Easter Seals 7," white, yellow-lettered Goodyear slicks, White Rose ....$20 – 25
9. "Bojangles 98," black, Goodyear rubber tires on black rims, White Rose Team Convoy ....$5 – 6
10. "Bojangles 98," yellow, Goodyear rubber tires on black rims, White Rose Team Convoy ....$5 – 6
11. "Bojangles 98," yellow, yellow-lettered Goodyear slicks, White Rose......$4 – 5
12. "BP Car Care 25," green, Australia issue...................................$20 – 25
13. "Bud 11," flat black, Goodyear rubber tires on black rims, White Rose Ertl set ....$24 – 36
14. "Budweiser 11," red, Goodyear rubber tires on black rims, White Rose Ertl set ....$24 – 36
15. "Burn Foundation," "Motorsports 96," black, Goodyear rubber tires on black rims, White Rose.................$8 – 10
16. "Cappio 48," black, yellow-lettered Goodyear slicks, White Rose......$4 – 5
17. "Carr Auto Care 4," black.........$2 – 3
18. "Carr Auto Care 4," blue ....$4 – 5
19. "Cellular One 7," black and red, yellow-lettered Goodyear slicks, White Rose ....$6 – 9
20. "Citgo 21," white and red, yellow-lettered Goodyear slicks, White Rose ....$4 – 5

21. "Citgo 21," red and orange, Goodyear rubber tires on black rims, White Rose...$4 – 5
22. "Country Time 68," fluorescent pink, yellow-lettered Goodyear slicks, White Rose ....$4 – 5
23. "Country Time 68," fluorescent yellow, yellow-lettered Goodyear slicks, White Rose Team Convoy...................$4 – 5
24. "Evan Carr," black, racing accents, white-lettered Goodyear slicks ....$1 – 3
25. "Exide 99," black, Goodyear rubber tires on black rims, White Rose ....$4 – 5
26. "Exide Batteries," black, Goodyear rubber tires on black rims, White Rose ..$4 – 5
27. "Factory Stores of America," blue, Goodyear rubber tires on black rims, White Rose............................$4 – 5
28. "Family Channel 7," white, yellow-lettered Goodyear slicks, White Rose...$12 – 16
29. "Family Channel 16," metallic blue and white, Goodyear rubber tires on black rims, White Rose.....................$4 – 5
30. "Fingerhut 98," black, Goodyear rubber tires on black rims, White Rose .$4 – 5
31. "Fingerhut 98," black and pink, Goodyear rubber tires on black rims, White Rose.............................$4 – 5
32. "Ford 1" and checkered flag, white, Goodyear tires on chrome rims, Show Stoppers................................$3 – 4
33. "Ford Motorsports 2," black, Goodyear rubber tires on black rims, White Rose.................................$4 – 5
34. "Hanes 7," white, yellow-lettered Goodyear slicks, White Rose..$20 – 25
35. "Havoline," "Texaco 28," black, white-lettered Goodyear slicks, White Rose ....$4 – 5
36. "Havoline 28," black, Goodyear rubber tires on black rims, White Rose .$4 – 5
37. "Heilig-Meyers 90," turquoise and black, Goodyear rubber tires on black rims, White Rose............................$4 – 5
38. "Hooters 7," gray, white-lettered Goodyear slicks, White Rose....$9 – 12
39. "Hooters 7," white and orange, Goodyear slicks, White Rose Team Convoy...................................$12 – 16
40. "Hooters 7," "Classic," "Naturally Fresh," white and orange, white-lettered Goodyear slicks, White Rose......$6 – 9
41. "Hooters 7," without "Classic," "Naturally Fresh," white, white-lettered Goodyear slicks, White Rose..................$9 – 12
42. "Hooters 19," white, Hoosier rubber tires on black rims, White Rose .$4 – 5

43. "Joltage Batteries 12," black, yellow-lettered Goodyear slicks, 5-pack ....$2 – 3

44. "K-Mart," "Little Caesar's 37," purpl[e] Goodyear rubber tires on black rim[s] White Rose............................$4 –
45. "Kleenex 40," blue, Goodyear rubb[er] tires on black rims, White Rose .$4 –
46. "Kleenex 40," blue, Goodyear slick[s] White Rose..........................$12 – 1
47. "Kyle Wieder 11," blue, racing accent[s] white-lettered Goodyear slicks ....$2 –
48. "Lowe's 11," bright blue and yello[w] Goodyear rubber tires on black rim[s] White Rose............................$4 –
49. "Luxaire 1," white, black-letter[ed] Goodyear slicks, White Rose..$12 – 1
50. "Mane N Tail," "Straight Arrow 12," multicolor, Goodyear rubber tires [on] black rims, White Rose............$4 –
51. "Matchbox," "USA Bobsled 7," whit[e] yellow-lettered Goodyear slicks, Whi[te] Rose...................................$12 – 1
52. "Matchbox," "White Rose 1," whit[e] yellow-lettered Goodyear slicks, Whi[te] Rose...................................$4 –
53. "Matchbox," "White Rose 7," whit[e] yellow-lettered Goodyear slicks, Whi[te] Rose...................................$12 – 1
54. "Matchbox 92," yellow, white-letter[ed] Goodyear slicks, White Rose..$21 – 2
55. "Maui 17," white, white-letter[ed] Goodyear slicks, White Rose.....$4 –
56. "Maxwell House 22," blue, white-letter[ed] Goodyear slicks, White Rose .....$4 –
57. "Maxwell House 22," blue, yellow-lettered Goodyear slicks, Whi[te] Rose ....$4 –
58. "McDonald's," "Batman Forever 94," black, Goodyear rubber tires on bla[ck] rims, White Rose.................$12 – 1
59. "McDonald's 94," red, Goodyear rubb[er] tires on black rims, White Rose .$4 –
60. "Meineke," black, yellow-letter[ed] Goodyear slicks, White Rose......$4 –
61. "Melling 9," red, white-letter[ed] Goodyear slicks, White Rose......$4 –
62. "Mitre 10," Stanley," blue, yello[w] lettered Goodyear slicks, Austra[lia] issue...................................$6 –
63. "Motorcraft Quality Parts 15," re[d] white-lettered Goodyear slicks, Whi[te] Rose...................................$4 –
64. "Nationwise Auto Parts," yellow, yello[w] lettered Goodyear slicks ....$24 – 3
65. "Naturally Fresh," bright blue, yellow-letter[ed] Goodyear slicks, White Rose..........$6 –
66. "New Holland 94," blue, Goodyear rubb[er] tires on black rims, White Rose...$4 –

67. "Peterson Pistons 17," blue...$2 – 3

**"Peterson Pistons 17," red,
5-pack** ....$2 – 3

. "Petron," black, Goodyear rubber tires
on black rims, White Rose ....$16 – 24

. "Phillips 66," "Trop Artic," black,
white-lettered Goodyear slicks, White
Rose....................................$4 – 5

. "Phillips 66," "Trop Artic," bright red,
white-lettered Goodyear slicks, White
Rose....................................$4 – 5

. "Phillips 66," "Trop Artic," dark red,
white-lettered Goodyear slicks, White
Rose....................................$4 – 5

. "Purex 83," bright blue, yellow-lettered
Goodyear slicks, White Rose......$4 – 5

. "Purex Dial 40," blue and orange,
Goodyear rubber tires on black rims,
White Rose.............................$4 – 5

. "Quaker State 26," green, Goodyear rubber
tires on black rims, White Rose.....$4 – 5

. "Quaker State 26," green, white-lettered
Goodyear slicks, White Rose .....$4 – 5

. "Quality Care 15," metallic blue and pale
blue, Goodyear rubber tires on black
rims, White Rose....................$4 – 5

. **"Racetech," blue, white-lettered
Goodyear slicks, 1994** ....$2 – 3

. "Racetech Radios 16," blue, gold
chrome spokes, yellow-lettered
Goodyear slicks........................$2 – 3

. "Racetech Radios 16," blue, gold
chrome spokes, white-lettered Goodyear
slicks, Aquafresh promo ....$5 – 6

. "Racetech Radios," dark blue, white-lettered
Goodyear slicks, 5-pack ....$2 – 3

. **"Radical Cams 10," pink, yellow-lettered Goodyear slicks**............$2 – 3

. "Raybestos 8," blue and white,
Goodyear rubber tires on black rims,
White Rose.............................$4 – 5

84. "Raybestos 8," metallic blue, Hoosier
rubber tires on black rims, White
Rose.....................................$4 – 5

85. "Raybestos 8," metallic blue, yellow-lettered Goodyear slicks, White
Rose ....$4 – 5

86. "Smokin' Joe 23",yellow and purple,
Goodyear rubber tires on black rims,
White Rose, sealed in plexiglas box with
yellow platform base.............$20 – 30

87. "Smokin' Joe 23," yellow and purple,
Goodyear rubber tires on black rims,
White Rose, sealed in plexiglas box with
purple platform base ....$20 – 30

88. "Snickers 8," brown and red, white-lettered
Goodyear slicks, White Rose ....$4 – 5

89. "Texaco," "Havoline 28" in bright
orange, black, white-lettered Goodyear
slicks, White Rose ....$9 – 12

90. "Texaco," "Havoline 28" in bright
orange, black, Goodyear rubber tires on
black rims, White Rose...........$9 – 12

91. "Texaco 28," flat black, white-lettered
Goodyear slicks, White Rose Team Convoy......................................$9 – 12

92. "TIC Financial 0," black, yellow-lettered
Goodyear slicks, White Rose......$6 – 9

93. "USA Bobsled Project 7," white,
yellow-lettered Goodyear slicks,
White Rose,"Cummins".........$12 – 16

94. "Valvoline," "Cummins 6," white and
dark blue, Goodyear rubber tires on
black rims, White Rose.............$4 – 5

95. "Valvoline 6," white, yellow-lettered
Goodyear slicks, White Rose......$4 – 5

96. "Valvoline 6," "Reese's"; white, red, and
dark blue; Goodyear rubber tires on
black rims, White Rose.............$4 – 5

97. "White Rose Collectibles 00," orange,
Goodyear rubber tires on black rims,
White Rose........................$12 – 16

98. **"Wieder Racing 7," dark blue, yellow-lettered Goodyear slicks** ....$2 – 3

99. "Wieder Racing 7," dark blue, concave
5-spoke wheels........................$3 – 4

100. "Wynn Dixie 60," black, Goodyear rubber
tires on black rims, White Rose....$4 – 5

101. white, no markings, gold chromed spokes,
yellow-lettered Goodyear slicks ....$4 – 5

102. metallic gold, 1997 75
Challenge ....$6 – 12

Ford Thunderbird Turbo Coupe, 3", #59,
1988; #61, 1988, international; #28,
1992, international reissue
1. red, "Turbo Coupe".................$2 – 3
2. red, detailed trim, rubber tires on
chrome rims, Premiere Collection Special Class 2 ....$4 – 5

Ford Tractor, 2³/₁₆", #46, 1978

1. yellow with orange stripe, black interior, no harrow, metallic silver base, orange hubs, Macau cast, 2-pack ....$2 – 3
2. yellow with orange stripe, black interior, red harrow, metallic silver base, orange hubs, Macau cast, gift set.........$2 – 3
3. green, black interior, no harrow, metallic silver base, orange hubs, Macau cast....................................$2 – 3

4. **green, black interior, no harrow, metallic silver base, orange hubs, Thailand cast, 2-pack ....$2 – 3**
5. green, black interior, yellow harrow, metallic silver base, orange hubs, Thailand cast, Motor City................$2 – 3
6. green, white interior, red harrow, metallic silver base, orange hubs, Macau cast, Motor City ....$2 – 3
7. green, yellow interior, yellow harrow, unpainted base, yellow wheel hubs, England cast ....$6 – 8
8. lime green, yellow interior, yellow harrow, unpainted base, yellow wheel hubs, England cast ....$6 – 8
9. blue, yellow interior, no harrow, unpainted base, black wheel hubs, England cast, 2-pack ....$4 – 5
10. blue, yellow interior, orange harrow, black wheel hubs, unpainted base, England cast ....$4 – 5
11. blue, yellow interior, yellow harrow, unpainted base, black wheel hubs, England cast ....$4 – 5
12. blue, yellow interior, yellow harrow, unpainted base, yellow wheel hubs, England cast ....$4 – 5
13. blue, yellow interior, yellow harrow, unpainted base with towing tab, yellow wheel hubs, no-origin cast, Brazil issue.................................$70 – 90

14. **blue, white interior, plain wheels, no harrow ....$4 – 6**

15. blue, white interior, yellow harrow, unpainted base, black front hubs, yellow rear hubs, England cast.............$4 – 5
16. blue, white interior, yellow harrow, unpainted base, yellow front and rear hubs, England cast...................$4 – 5
17. blue, yellow interior, no harrow, metallic silver base, gold hubs, Macau cast, 2-pack.....................................$3 – 4

Ford Tractor, #236, 1993 Farming Series set

1. **blue with red scoop, Farming Series ....$4 – 5**
2. dark blue with yellow harrow, Action Pack ....$4 – 5

Ford Transit (see Ford Transit Pickup, Ford Transit Van, Ford Transit Ambulance)

Ford Transit Ambulance, with roof light, #21, 1999, Germany; #14, 2003 (similar casting: Ford Transit Van)

1. red, "112 Feuerwehr," 1999, Germany issue......................................$5 – 6
2. red with yellow stripes, "London Fire Brigade".................................$4 – 5
3. yellow with blue stripes, "Medic" ..$3 – 4

4. **white with yellow and orange stripes, blue tinted windows and roof light, 2003 Hospital series ....$2 – 3**

Ford Transit Van, 2⁷/₈", #60, 1987 – 1989; #57, 1990 – 1997; #49, 2002; #50, 2003; #5, 1998, international; #25, 1999, international; #13, 2001, UK (left hand drive unless noted; similar casting: Ford Transit Ambulance)

1. "14th Annual Toy Show — Ft. Washington, PA," red, US issue ....$20 – 30
2. "24 Hour Roofing," metallic blue, 2002 Hammer and Nails series..........$2 – 3
3. "24th Annual Truck-In 1996," red, US issue.................................$20 – 30
4. "24th Annual Truck-In 1996," white, US issue.................................$12 – 16
5. "97.5 PST," dark blue, US issue ....$20 – 30

6. "97.5 PST," white, US issue ..$16 – 2
7. "Abbey Stainless," white, UK issue..................................$12 – 1
8. "AC Auto Clenz," white, UK issue..................................$60 – 1C
9. "American International Recovery white, ASAP promotional...$100 – 15
10. "Anglian Self Drive," "Norflex," white, U issue..................................$120 – 18
11. "Auckland Warriors," green with bl roof, Australia issue ....$12 – 1
12. "Australia Post," red, Australia issue......................................$7 –
13. "Australia Post — We Deliver," orang red with white roof, left hand drive, Au tralia issue...............................$4 –
14. "Australia Post — We Deliver," re right hand drive, Australia issue .$7 –
15. "Australia Telecom," white, Austra issue......................................$7 –
16. "Balmain Tigers," black with red ro Australia issue....................$12 – 1
17. "Belfast Evening Telegraph," red, Iri issue..................................$120 – 16
18. "Bell South Americast," white, ASA promo ....$120 – 16
19. "Blick," red, Switzerland issue ..$9 – 1
20. "Brantho-Korrux," red, Germany issue.................................$30 – 4
21. "Brisbane Broncos," light yellow w purple roof, Australia issue....$12 – 1
22. "British Telecom," yellow ....$5 –
23. "Cadbury Flakes," yellow ....$2 –
24. "Canberra Raiders," lime green with y low roof, Australia issue........$12 – 1
25. "Canterbury-Bankstown Bulldogs black with dark blue roof, Austral issue..................................$12 – 1
26. "Citizens Communications," white, ASA promo ....$30 – 4
27. "Coca-Cola," yellow, rubber tires chrome rims, Premiere Collection..$5 –
28. "Coca-Cola" with hockey player bea red and white, FAO Schwarz mul pack ....$4 –

29. **"Coca-Cola" with line of bottles a couple, metallic silver, 2003 ..$4 –**
30. "Coca-Cola" with two polar bears, re and white.............................$16 – 2
31. "Coldseal," white, UK issue ....$12 – 1
32. "Council of Councils," "C of C The Old Shi metallic gray, UK issue..........$60 – 12
33. "Council of Councils," "C of C The C Ship," white, UK issue...........$16 – 1
34. "Council of Councils," "France — Win sor — London — Stonehenge," meta gray, UK issue.....................$16 – 2

129. "St. George Dragons," white with red roof, Australia issue ....$12 – 16
130. "Standish Van Hire," white, UK issue ....$12 – 16
131. "Starlec," white, UK issue ....$12 – 16
132. "Stegosaurus" and skeleton design, black ....$2 – 3
133. "Supertoys," white, Ireland issue.$20 – 30
134. "Taronga Zoomobile," metallic green, Australia issue..........................$7 – 9
135. "The Sunrise Coast," metallic gray, UK issue.................................$16 – 24
136. "The Sunrise Coast," white, UK issue..................................$12 – 16
137. "Transit" in red and black, metallic gray, UK issue ....$80 – 120
138. "Transit" in red and black, white, UK issue ....$40 – 50
139. "Transit" in red and blue, metallic gray, UK issue ....$80 – 120
140. "Transit" in red and blue, white, UK issue ....$40 – 50
141. "Transit Ford," "C of C Ford," "Transit Plant Trip 2000," metallic gray, UK issue ....$16 – 24
142. "Transit Ford," "C of C Ford," "Transit Plant Trip 2000," white, UK issue..................................$16 – 24
143. "Transit Ford," "NSVA," "Show & Shine," metallic gray, UK issue ....$16 – 24
144. "Transit Ford," "NSVA," "Show & Shine," white, UK issue ....$16 – 24
145. "Trophy Gold Pet Foods," white, UK issue ....$12 – 16
146. "Ultra Link," white, UK issue..................................$140 – 180
147. "Unichem," white, right hand drive, UK issue ....$8 – 10
148. "Upright," metallic gray, UK issue..................................$30 – 40
149. "Van Club — 25th Van Nationals — England," white, UK issue .....$12 – 16
150. "Van Club — 26 Years of Vanning," white, UK issue...................$12 – 16
151. "Viewmaster," red; US issue with wooden box, viewer, and special reel..$90 – 100
152. "Viewmaster," white, US issue .$20 – 30
153. "Vinnie's," red ....$3 – 4
154. "Waterway Recovery Group," red, UK issue..................................$12 – 16
155. "Web Force," white, UK issue .$12 – 16
156. "Welcoming the New Millennium" in red, white, UK issue ....$12 – 16
157. "Welcoming the New Millennium" in black, white, UK issue ....$12 – 16
158. "Wella," white, Germany issue ..$7 – 9
159. "Western Reds," red with yellow roof, Australia issue.....................$12 – 16
160. "Western Suburbs Magpies," white, Australia issue.....................$12 – 16
161. "Windscreen Auto," white, UK issue..................................$120 – 160
162. "Wigwam," white, the Netherlands issue..................................$8 – 10
163. "Wishing Well Appeal," white, UK issue....................................$7 – 9

164. "www rent-a-van," white, UK issue..................................$12 – 16
165. "XP Express Parcels," white, UK issue....................................$5 – 6
166. "XP Express Parcels," white, right hand drive, UK issue ....$7 – 9
167. red, no markings, left hand drive .$3 – 4
168. red, no markings, right hand drive, UK issue..................................$40 – 50
169. yellow, 2001 Union Jack series, UK issue....................................$4 – 6
170. yellow with British flag, blue and red stripes ....$3 – 4
171. lime green with no markings, the Netherlands issue ....$12 – 16
172. light blue, surfing design ....$2 – 4
173. white, no markings, Graffic Traffic ....$12 – 16
174. white, no markings, ASAP promotional blank ....$20 – 25
175. white with red cross and stripes, gray rectangle, Macau cast..............$3 – 4
176. white with red cross and stripes, gray rectangle, China cast..............$3 – 4
177. white with surfboard design, 1998..................................$2 – 3
178. white with surfing scene, 1998 Around the Town international series ....$2 – 3

Ford Transit Pickup, light to dark orange with cargo load of varying shades of brown or tan, 2³⁄₄", #66, 1977
1. amber windows, light yellow interior, unpainted base ....$7 – 9
2. amber windows, olive green interior, unpainted base ....$7 – 9
3. amber windows, tan interior, unpainted base ....$7 – 9
4. amber windows, white interior, unpainted base ....$7 – 9
5. blue-green windows, cream interior, black base ....$7 – 9
6. blue-green windows, cream interior, unpainted base ....$7 – 9
7. blue-green windows, cream interior, unpainted base with towing tab, Brazil issue..................................$40 – 60
8. blue-green windows, light yellow interior, unpainted base ....$7 – 9
9. blue-green windows, olive green interior, unpainted base ....$7 – 9
10. blue-green windows, tan interior, unpainted base ....$7 – 9
11. dark green windows, olive green interior, unpainted base ....$7 – 9
12. green windows, cream interior, dark gray base ....$7 – 9
13. green windows, light yellow interior, dark gray base ....$7 – 9

Ford Dump Truck, #91, 2000; #71, 2000, international (see Ford F-150 Dump Truck)

Ford Wildlife Truck (Rolamatic) with lion under transparent canopy, 2³⁄₄", #57,

1973 (similar casting: Ford Kenn Truck)
1. yellow with red windows, amber canopy ....$6 –
2. yellow with red windows, blue canopy ....$6 –
3. yellow with red windows, clear canopy ....$6 –
4. yellow with red windows, tinted canopy ....$6 –
5. yellow with orange windows, tinte canopy ....$6 –
6. yellow with no windows, clear canopy ....$6 –
7. white with red windows, blue canopy ....$6 –
8. white with red windows, clear canop stripes ....$6 –
9. white with red windows, tinted canop stripes ....$6 –
10. white with orange windows, blu canopy, stripes ....$6 –
11. white with orange windows, clea canopy, stripes ....$6 –
12. white with orange windows, tinte canopy, stripes ....$6 –
13. white with purple windows, blue canop stripes ....$6 –
14. white with purple windows, clea canopy, stripes ....$6 –
15. white with purple windows, tinte canopy, stripes ....$6 –

Ford Wreck Truck, 3", #61, 1978
1. red with amber windows, green boom black hooks ....$200 – 30
2. red with amber windows, red boom black hooks ....$7 –
3. red with amber windows, red boom red hooks ....$7 –
4. red with amber windows, white boom black hooks ....$5 –
5. red with amber windows, white boom red hooks ....$5 –
6. red with amber windows, white boom red hooks, "24 Hour" ....$6 –
7. red with blue windows, white boom red hooks ....$5 –
8. red with blue windows, white boom. white hooks..........................$9 – 1
9. orange-red with amber windows, whit booms, red hooks, Manaus cast, Bra issue..............................$250 – 35
10. yellow with amber windows, gree booms, black hooks................$6 –
11. yellow with amber windows, gree booms, red hooks ....$6 –
12. yellow with amber windows, red boom black hooks ....$5 –
13. yellow with amber windows, red boom red hooks ....$5 –
14. yellow with amber windows, whit booms, red hooks ....$5 –
15. white with amber windows, whit booms, red hooks, red stripe labe Manaus cast, Brazil issue .$500 – 60

Ford Zephyr 6 Mk III, 2⁵⁄₈", #33, 1963

gray plastic wheels...............$30 – 35
silver plastic wheels.............$35 – 40

black plastic wheels ....$60 – 70

rd Zodiac Convertible, pink, 2⅝", #39, 1957
tan interior and base, metal wheels..........................$100 – 125
turquoise interior and base, metal wheels................................$30 – 50
turquoise interior and base, gray plastic wheels................................$45 – 60
turquoise interior and base, silver plastic wheels ....$60 – 80

rd Zodiac Mk II, 2⅝", #33, 1957
light blue or light blue-green, no windows, metal wheels..............$30 – 40
dark green. no windows, metal wheels................................$30 – 40
dark green, no windows, gray plastic wheels................................$40 – 50
metallic gray and orange, no windows, gray plastic wheels ....$40 – 50
tan and orange to light orange, no windows, gray plastic wheels......$40 – 50
tan and orange with green windows, gray plastic wheels...............$40 – 50
tan and orange with green windows, silver plastic wheels................$40 – 50

rd Zodiac Mk IV, 2¾", #53, 1968
metallic silver blue, unpainted base, black plastic wheels..................$7 – 9
light metallic green, unpainted base, black plastic wheels..........$500 – 600
metallic light blue, unpainted base, Superfast wheels ....$400 – 450
metallic green, unpainted base, Superfast wheels ....$18 – 24
apple green, unpainted base, Superfast wheels................................$24 – 32

rdson Power Major Farm Tractor, blue, 2", #72, 1959
gray front wheels, gray rear tires on orange wheels ....$40 – 50
black front wheels, black rear tires on orange wheels ....$35 – 45
gray front and rear tires on orange wheels................................$40 – 50
gray front and rear tires on yellow wheels................................$90 – 100
black front and rear tires on yellow wheels................................$90 – 100
black front and rear tires on orange wheels................................$40 – 50

rk Lift, #63, 2002; #70, 2003

1.   **orange with black fork lift boom, yellow and blue, 2002 Rescue Rookies series ....$2 – 3**
2.   white with red fork lift boom, 2003 Heavy Movers series ....$2 – 3

Fork Lift Truck, 2½", #15, 1972

1.   **plastic steering wheel, "Lansing Bagnall" labels, gray forks ......$12 – 16**
2.   plastic steering wheel, "T6AD" labels, gray forks, Brazil issue......$250 – 400
3.   no steering wheel, "Lansing Bagnall" labels, gray forks ....$12 – 16
4.   no steering wheel, "Lansing Bagnall" labels, long red forks, part of King Size model.................................$20 – 25
5.   no steering wheel, "Lansing Bagnall" labels, black forks ....$12 – 16
6.   no steering wheel, "Lansing Bagnall" labels, yellow forks ....$12 – 16
7.   cast steering wheel, "Lansing Bagnall" labels, yellow forks ....$9 – 12
8.   cast steering wheel, "HI LIFT" labels, black roof, long black forks, part of King Size model ....$20 – 25
9.   cast steering wheel, "HI LIFT" labels, no roof, black forks...................$12 – 16

Fork Lift Truck, 3⅛". #28, 1991; #61, 1992 (see Sambron Jack Lift)

Formula 1 (see Formula One Racing Car, Formula Racer)

Formula 5000, 3", #36, 1975
1.   orange, "5000" labels ....$9 – 12
2.   red, "5000" labels ....$8 – 10
3.   red, "Texaco" on hood.............$8 – 10
4.   red, "Texaco" on hood, towing tab on base, UK issue ....$50 – 60
5.   white, "Texaco" on hood, towing tab on base, UK issue ....$350 – 450

Formula One Racing Car, 2⅞", #34, 1971

1.   metallic pink, "16" and "Wynn's" labels, UK issue.........................$100 – 150
2.   metallic pink, "16" label only...$16 – 24
3.   orange, "16" label ....$12 – 16
4.   yellow, "15" label ....$12 – 16
5.   yellow, "16" label..................$12 – 16
6.   metallic blue, "15" label.........$12 – 16
7.   blue, "15" label ....$12 – 16
8.   blue, "16" label ....$12 – 16

Formula Racer, #28, 1982; #16, 1984;#74, 1996; #61, 1998 (see Williams Renault Formula Racer)

Four-Wheeler, #91, 1999; #63, 2000; #34, 2001; #71, 1999, international; #43, 2000, international

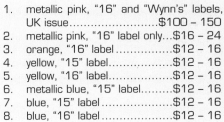

1.   **red with black chassis, white cross, yellow driver, 2002 Sand Castle Rescue Team 5-pack ....$2 – 3**
2.   red with metallic gray chassis, "5," mud spray, black driver, 2001 Sand Blasters series....................................$2 – 3
3.   red with metallic gray chassis, "400," blue stripes, yellow driver with black pants, 5-pack ....$2 – 3
4.   light red with metallic gray chassis, "Matchbox 2000," white and black design, gray driver with dark gray pants, 2000 Great Outdoors series......$2 – 3
5.   light red with metallic gray chassis, white and black design, gray driver with dark gray pants, 2000 Great Outdoors series....................................$2 – 3
6.   green with metallic gray chassis, brown mud, brown driver with black pants, 5-pack.......................................$2 – 3

7.   **olive green with metallic gray chassis, beige driver with blue pants, 1999 Mountain Cruisers series ....$2 – 3**

Freeman Inter-City Commuter Coach, 3", #22, 1970
1. metallic purple ....$16 – 24
2. metallic gold ....$16 – 24
3. metallic magenta ....$16 – 24

Freeway Gas Tanker, 3", #63, 1973 (goes with #63 Freeway Gas Tanker Trailer, 1978)
1. "95 High Octane," olive green cab, purple windows, olive green tank, Two Pack ....$8 – 10

2. **"95 High Octane," dark army green cab, purple windows, dark army green tank ....$70 – 90**
3. "Aral," blue cab, purple windows, blue and white tank ....$30 – 40
4. "BP," white cab, purple windows, white and yellow tank ....$60 – 80
5. "BP," white cab, purple windows, white and green tank ....$9 – 12
6. "Burmah," red cab, purple windows, red and white tank ....$7 – 9
7. "Burmah," red cab, purple windows, red and white tank with tow hook, Two Pack ....$7 – 9
8. "Castrol," red cab, purple windows, red and white tank ....$100 – 125
9. "Chevron," red cab, purple windows, red and white tank ....$7 – 9
10. "Chevron," red cab, purple windows, red and white tank with tow hook, Two Pack ....$7 – 9
11. "Exxon," white cab, purple windows, white tank ....$8 – 10
12. "Exxon," white cab, purple windows, white tank with tow hook, Two Pack ......$7 – 9
13. "Exxon," white cab, purple windows, yellow and white tank ....$20 – 30
14. "Exxon," red cab, purple windows, white tank with tow hook, Two Pack .$60 – 80
15. "Shell," white cab, amber windows, white and yellow tank ....$7 – 9
16. "Shell," white cab, red windows, white and yellow tank ....$7 – 9
17. "Shell," white cab, purple windows, white and yellow tank ....$7 – 9
18. "Shell," white cab, purple windows, white and yellow tank with tow hook, Two Pack ....$7 – 9
19. "Shell," yellow cab, purple windows, white and yellow tank ....$9 – 12
20. Canadian flag labels, army green cab, purple windows, army green tank, Two Pack ....$300 – 400
21. French flag labels, army green cab, purple windows, army green tank, Two Pack ....$70 – 90

Freeway Gas Tanker Trailer, 3", #63, 1978 (issued as part of Two Pack with #63 Freeway Gas Tanker, 1973)
1. "BP" labels, yellow coupling, yellow base ....$40 – 50
2. "BP" labels, white coupling, yellow base ....$7 – 9
3. "Burmah" labels, red coupling, red base ....$7 – 9
4. "Chevron" labels, red coupling, red base ....$7 – 9
5. "Exxon" labels, red coupling, white base ....$60 – 80
6. "Exxon" labels, yellow coupling, white base ....$8 – 10
7. "Shell" labels, yellow coupling, yellow base ....$7 – 9

G

Galant Eterna (see Dodge Challenger/Mitsubishi Galant Eterna)

General Service Lorry, 2⅝", #62, 1959
1. olive green with black plastic wheels..............................$40 – 50

Glider Trailer, #794, 1976, with white glider and wings
1. red with amber canopy, "Gliding Club," England cast ....$400 – 450
2. red with clear canopy, "Auto Glide," no origin cast ....$3 – 4
3. yellow with amber canopy, "Gliding Club," England cast................$3 – 4
4. lemon yellow with clear canopy, purple and pink spatters, no-origin cast.$3 – 4
5. green with clear canopy, "Seagull Gliding Club," England cast..................$3 – 4
6. green with clear canopy, England cast ....$3 – 4
7. dark green with amber canopy, "Seagull Gliding Club," England cast.........$3 – 4
8. dark blue with clear canopy, yellow stripes, no-origin cast...............$3 – 4

GMC Bucket Truck, #99, 2000
1. dark blue, "Power Inc.," white boom and bucket, 2000 On The Road Again series....................................$2 – 3

2. **dark blue, "Power Inc.," white boom and bucket, "Matchbox 2000," 2000 On The Road Again series ....$3 – 4**

GMC Dump Truck (see GMC Tipper Truck)

GMC Refrigerator Truck, 3", #44, 1967

1. **red with turquoise container, bla plastic wheels.......................$6 –**
2. red with turquoise container, Superfa wheels, 1970.....................$50 – 6
3. yellow with red container, Superfa wheels...........................$20 – 3
4. yellow with turquoise container, Sup fast wheels ....$2000 – 250

GMC Terradyne, #62, 2002; #58, 2003

1. **metallic gray, no markings, 200 Rescue Rookies series ....$2 –**
2. metallic green, "Extreme," 2003 Kid Shoppes ....$2 –

GMC Tipper Truck, 2⅝", #26 ,1968

1. **red with metallic gray dumper, reg lar wheels, 1968 ....$6 –**
1. red with metallic gray dumper, Supe fast wheels, 1970 ....$30 – 4

GMC Wrecker, 2⅞", #21, 1987; #7 1987; #72, 1989; #63, 1998; #1 1999
1. black with chrome plastic base, "Offic Wrecker Indy 500" ....$8 – 1
2. black with chrome plastic base, "Matc box," yellow and white design, 199 Motor Sports series ....$2 –
3. black with chrome plastic base, "Poli Emergency Unit 4" and gold star, pack.......................................$2 –
4. black with chrome plastic base, "Servi GMC," yellow and white design, 199 Motor Sports series ....$2 –

black with chrome plastic base, "Service GMC," "Matchbox," yellow and white design, Pleasant Books issue.....$4 – 5

metallic gold with chrome plastic base, black boom, 1997 75 Challenge series ....$6 – 12

metallic green with chrome plastic base, "Ron's," yellow and white design, 2000 Police Patrol series ....$2 – 3

metallic green with chrome plastic base, "Ron's," "Matchbox 2000," yellow and white design, 2000 Police Patrol series ....$3 – 4

metallic purple with chrome plastic base, white boom, yellow and white design...................................$2 – 3

. metallic purple with chrome plastic base, "Parkhill Towing," "24 Hour Towing" on hood, fluorescent yellow boom, 1996 ....$2 – 3

. metallic purple with chrome plastic base, "Parkhill Towing," black boom, no printing on hood, international issue ....$7 – 9

. metallic purple with chrome plastic base, "Parkhill Towing," fluorescent yellow boom, no printing on hood ...$2 – 3

. red with chrome plastic base, white accents, "Ron's Towing," Collectors Choice, White Rose Collectibles .$4 – 5

. red with chrome plastic base, "Parkhill Towing," fluorescent yellow boom, no printing on hood......................$2 – 3

. red with chrome plastic base, "Matchbox 24 Hour Towing," yellow and white accents ....$2 – 3

6. red with chrome plastic base, "Ron's," yellow and white accents, black boom, 1999 Highway Haulers series ....$2 – 3

7. white with unpainted metal base, "Accessory Wholesalers Inc.".$20 – 25

8. white with unpainted metal base, "Frank's Getty," "557-1117," Macau cast ....$3 – 4

19. white with chrome plastic base, "3 Rescue".......................................$2 – 3

20. white with chrome plastic base, "CAA Member Service," red windows, blue boom, Canada issue ....$120 – 160

21. white with chrome plastic base, "CAA Member Service," amber windows, blue boom, Canada issue ....$12 – 16

22. white with chrome plastic base, "Frank's Getty," "557-1117," China cast...$2 – 3

23. white with chrome plastic base, "Frank's Getty," "557-1117," Macau cast ....$2 – 3

24. white with chrome plastic base, "Frank's Getty," "557-1117," no origin cast ....$4 – 5

25. white with chrome plastic base, "Frank's Getty," "557-1117," Thailand cast ....$2 – 3

26. white with chrome plastic base, "Frank's Getty," no phone number, China cast..............................$2 – 3

27. white with chrome plastic base, "Frank's Getty," no phone number, Thailand cast ....$2 – 3

28. white with chrome plastic base, "Matchbox 24 Hr. Towing," 5-pack ....$3 – 4

29. white with chrome plastic base, "Police," "Metro Emergency," 1993 Emergency 5-pack.................$2 – 3

30. white with chrome plastic base, "Helmrich Towing & Recovery," Color Comp promotional......................$80 – 120

31. white with chrome plastic base, "Riehl's Towing," Color Comp promotional ....$80 – 120

32. white with chrome plastic base, white boom, "Alenco Service," ASAP promotional...............................$80 – 120

33. white with chrome plastic base, white boom, "American International Recovery," ASAP promotional.....$120 – 160

34. white with chrome plastic base, white boom, "Matchbox 33000," ASAP promotional ....$60 – 80

35. white with chrome plastic base, white boom, "Phil's Body Works," ASAP promotional ....$120 – 160

36. white with chrome plastic base, white boom, "PTROI," ASAP promotional ....$30 – 40

37. white with chrome plastic base, white boom, no markings, ASAP promotional blank.................................$25 – 30

38. white with chrome plastic base, "3 Rescue".......................................$3 – 4

Golden X, Roman Numeral X, 1978 (variation of #33 Datsun 126X, 1973)

1. yellow, Roman Numeral Limited Edition ....$15 – 20

2. gold plated, Roman Numeral Limited Edition ....$9 – 12

Golf Cart, #75, 2000; #55, 2000, international

1. gray, "Canyon Golf 232," 2000 On Tour series...................................$3 – 4

2. gray, "Canyon Golf 232," "Matchbox 2000," 2000 On Tour series.....$4 – 5

3. gray, "Canyon Golf 232," "PMCC Christmas Dinner," Color Comp promotional............................$20 – 30

4. white, "3rd Annual Mattel Open," Color Comp promotional................$20 – 30

5. white, "EMC2 Where Information Lives," "Global Financial Services," ASAP promotional ....$35 – 45

6. white, "RCA," ASAP promotional.$25 – 35

7. white, "Together For Tyler," "Memorial Golf Tournament," Color Comp promotional.................................$20 – 30

8. white, no markings, ASAP/Color Comp promotional blank.................$30 – 40

Grain Grabber (see Combine Harvester)

Gran Fury Police (see Plymouth Gran Fury Police)

Grand Prix Racer, 3", #74, 1988; #14, 1989

1. red, "Fiat 27," black metal base ..$3 – 4

2. red, "Fiat 27," black plastic base ....$16 – 24

3. red, "Kids World," "Fiat," Australia issue...................................$45 – 55

4. red, "Scotch," "Target," Indy 500 series...................................$4 – 5

5. red, "Scotch 9," Indy 500 series...................................$4 – 5

6. orange, lavender and white, "Indy 1," Indy 500 series ....$4 – 5

7. orange and white, "Indy 4," Indy 500 series...................................$4 – 5

8. fluorescent orange and yellow, "Matchbox Get In The Fast Lane 7," Collectors Choice, White Rose Collectibles ....$4 – 5

9. yellow, "Pennzoil 2," Indy 500 series...................................$4 – 5

10. yellow, "Pennzoil 4," Indy 500 series...................................$4 – 5

11. yellow, "Pennzoil 8," Indy 500 series ....$4 – 5
12. yellow, "Squirt," on-package premium ....$20 – 30
13. green and white, "4," black lines .$2 – 3
14. blue, "Mackenzie," Indy 500 series ..$4 – 5
15. blue, "Panasonic," Indy 500 series ..$4 – 5
16. blue and white, "Valvoline," "Kraco 3",Indy 500 series ....$4 – 5
17. blue and yellow, "Panasonic 11," Indy 500 series...........................$4 – 5

18. **purple, "Matchbox," "20," fluorescent yellow airfoil and base, 1997 Racing 5-pack......................$2 – 3**
19. black, "Indy 5," green and pink spatter, Indy 500 series ....$4 – 5
20. white, "7," blue dots ....$2 – 3
21. white, "Indy 500," "77," Indy 500 series....................................$4 – 5
22. white, "XP 6," the Netherlands issue $9 – 12
23. white and black, "Havoline," "K-Mart," Indy 500 series ....$4 – 5
24. white and black, "Texaco," "K-Mart," Indy 500 series ....$4 – 5
25. white and blue, "Indy 76," Indy 500 series....................................$4 – 5

26. **white and orange, "4," black lines, 1996 Racing 5-pack.............$2 – 3**
27. white and pale blue, "15," "Goodyear," "Shell" ....$4 – 5
28. metallic tan, "Peugeot," "Special 11," international issue ....$3 – 4
29. chrome plated, custom promotional.....................$16 – 24

Greased Lightning (see DeTomaso Pantera Greased Lightning)

Grayhound Bus, 3", #66, 1967
1. metallic gray, clear windows, black plastic wheels, 1967 ....$175 – 225
2. metallic gray, amber windows, black plastic wheels, 1967...........$20 – 30
3. metallic gray, black base, 1970, Superfast wheels ....$30 – 40
4. metallic gray, pink base, 1970, Superfast wheels ....$30 – 40
5. metallic gray, yellow base, 1970, Superfast wheels ....$30 – 40

Gruesome Twosome, 2⁷/₈", #4, 1971; BR 3 – 4, 1985
1. metallic gold with amber windows ....$125 – 150
2. metallic gold with purple windows..........................$12 – 16
2. metallic orange-gold with purple windows..........................$12 – 16
3. red with purple windows........$16 – 24
4. yellow, England cast, Super GT BR 3 – 4, 1985..........................$4 – 6
5. powder blue, England cast, Super GT BR 3 – 4, 1985 ....$4 – 6
6. dark blue, England cast, Super GT BR 3 – 4, 1985 ....$6 – 8
7. yellow, China cast, Super GT BR 3 – 4, 1985................................$8 – 10
8. white with black windows, China cast, Super GT BR 3 – 4, 1985........$3 – 5
9. white with translucent white windows, China cast, Super GT BR 3 – 4, 1985.................................$20 – 25
10. gray, China cast, Super GT BR 3 – 4, 1985................................$3 – 5
11. fluorescent orange, China cast, Neon Racers BR 3 – 4, 1985...........$4 – 6

H

Hairy Hustler, 2⁷/₈", #7, 1971 (similar casting: Flamin' Manta)
1. metallic orange-red with purple windows, "5" labels ....$120 – 160
2. metallic orange-red with amber windows, "5" labels ....$16 – 24
3. metallic orange-red with amber windows, scorpion label............$30 – 40
4. white with amber windows, no labels ....$60 – 80
5. white with amber windows, checkers and stripes ....$16 – 24
6. yellow, England cast, Super GTs BR 13 – 14, 1985....................$5 – 10
7. green, England cast, Super GTs BR 13 – 14, 1985....................$4 – 6
8. dark green, England cast, Super GTs BR 13 – 14, 1985 ....$8 – 10
9. gray, China cast, Super GTs BR 13 – 14, 1985 ....$3 – 5
10. yellow, China cast, Super GTs BR 13 – 14, 1985.......................$8 – 10
11. red, China cast, Super GTs BR 13 – 14, 1985 ....$3 – 5

Halftrack (see Army M3 Halftrack Personnel Carrier)

Harley Davidson Chopper, #50, 1993 Harley Davidson series
1. red, chrome handlebars...........$3 – 4
2. metallic maroon, chrome handlebars.........................$3 – 4
3. fluorescent orange, black flames, chrome handlebars ....$3 – 4
4. yellow, chrome handlebars ....$3 – 4
5. yellow chrome, chrome handlebars...........................$3 – 4
6. turquoise, chrome handlebars .$12 – 16

7. blue, chrome handlebars...........$3 –
8. metallic blue, chrome handlebars..$3 –
9. dark purple, chrome handlebars ..$9 – 1
10. black, chrome handlebars ....$3 –
11. metallic gray, chrome handlebars.$3 –

Harley Davidson Electraglide, #50, 199 Harley Davidson series
1. red, "Harley Davidson," chrome hand bars, black saddlebags ....$3 –
2. metallic red, "Harley Davidson," chrom handlebars, black saddlebags ..$9 – 1
3. orange-red, "PMG," orange hand bars, orange saddlebags, Austra issue................................$12 – 1
4. gold chrome, "Harley Davidson," chrom handlebars, black saddlebags .....$3 –
5. metallic blue, "MBPD," chrome hand bars, black saddlebags ....$3 –
6. dark blue, "Harley Davidson," chrom handlebars, black saddlebags ....$3 –
7. black, "Harley Davidson," chrom handlebars, black saddlebags..$3 –
8. black, "MBPD," chrome handlebar black saddlebags ....$3 –
9. pale gray, "MBPD," chrome handlebar black saddlebags ....$3 –
10. white, "Police," chrome handlebar blue saddlebags ....$3 –
11. white, "MBPD," chrome handlebar white saddlebags ....$3 –

Harley Davidson H-D FXSTS Springer S tail, #393, 1995
1. metallic blue..........................$4 –
2. metallic turquoise....................$4 –
3. metallic purple ....$4 –
4. metallic red ....$4 –

Harley Davidson H-D Knucklehead, #39 1995
1. pale blue...............................$4 –
2. black....................................$4 –

Harley Davidson Motorcycle, 2¹¹/₁₆", #5 1980
1. red, chrome handlebars, no driver, Chi cast, Harley Davidson series.......$3 –
2. metallic red, chrome handlebars, no d ver, Thailand cast, Harley Davidso series................................$3 –
3. orange-red, "PMG," orange-red hand bars, no driver, China cast, Austral issue....................................$5 –
4. orange-red, "PMG," orange-red hand bars, no driver, Thailand cast, Austral issue....................................$5 –
5. metallic orange, black handlebars, t driver, England cast..................$4 –
6. metallic orange, chrome handlebars, driver, Thailand cast, Harley Davidso series.....................................$3 –
7. metallic dark orange, chrome hand bars, no driver, Thailand cast, Harl Davidson gift set ....$3 –
8. metallic dark orange, chrome handl bars, no driver, China cast, Harl Davidson series ....$3 –

fluorescent orange, chrome handlebars, no driver, Thailand cast, Harley David-son series ....$3 – 4

0. metallic yellow, chrome handlebars, no driver, Thailand cast, Harley Davidson series ....$3 – 4

1. fluorescent yellow, chrome handlebars, no driver, Thailand cast, Harley David-son gift set ....$3 – 4

2. gold plated, chrome handlebars, no dri-ver, Thailand cast, Harley Davidson series ....$3 – 4

3. metallic turquoise, chrome handlebars, no driver, Thailand cast, Harley David-son gift set ....$3 – 4

4. metallic turquoise, chrome handlebars, no driver, Thailand cast, Harley David-son series ....$3 – 4

5. metallic blue, chrome handlebars, no driver, Thailand cast, Harley Davidson series ....$3 – 4

6. dark purple, chrome handlebars, no dri-ver, Thailand cast, Harley Davidson series ....$4 – 3

7. metallic brown, black handlebars, brown driver, Macau cast..................$3 – 4

8. metallic tan, black handlebars, no dri-ver, England cast ....$4 – 5

9. metallic dark gray, chrome handlebars, no driver, Thailand cast, Harley David-son series ....$3 – 4

0. metallic gray, chrome handlebars, no driver, Thailand cast, Harley Davidson series ....$3 – 4

1. white, chrome handlebars, no dri-ver, Thailand cast, Harley Davidson play set ....$3 – 4

Harley Davidson Motorcycle and Sidecar, 2⅝", #66, 1962

. **metallic bronze with black tires ....$85 – 95**

Matra Tractor Shovel, 3", #69, 1965
. yellow with red wheels, black tires ....$12 – 16

. **yellow with yellow wheels, black tires ....$10 – 15**

---

3. orange with orange wheels, gray tires..................................$20 – 30
4. orange with orange wheels, black tires..................................$12 – 16
5. orange with red wheels, black tires..................................$12 – 16
6. orange with yellow wheels, black tires..................................$12 – 16

Hay Trailer, 3¼", #40, 1967
1. blue with yellow plastic fences, yellow hubs, black plastic tires ....$6 – 9

Hay Trailer, 1993 Farming Series set

1. **yellow ....$3 – 5**

Heavy Rescue Auxiliary Power Truck (see Mack Floodlight Heavy Rescue Auxiliary Power Truck)

Helicopter, with pilot, large windows, 3", #75, 1982; #29, 1998; #6, 1999
1. red with red base, "Fire Dept.," China cast......................................$2 – 3

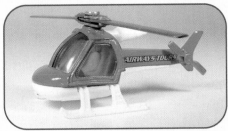

2. **red with white base, "Airways Tours," China cast ....$2 – 3**

3. **red with white base, "Fire Dept.," Macau cast ....$3 – 4**
4. red with white base, "Fire Dept.," Thai-land cast ....$2 – 3
5. red with white base, "Red Rebels," Macau cast, Motor City ....$3 – 4
6. red with white base, "Red Rebels," Thai-land cast, Motor City ....$2 – 3
7. red with white base, "Royal Air Force," Thailand cast, Motor City ....$3 – 4

---

8. orange with brown base, "Magnum P.I.," brown stripes, China cast, Avon Star Cars..........................$9 – 12
9. yellow with black base, "702," black stripes, China cast, Germany issue............$4 – 5
10. black with black base, "Air Car," Macau cast, Convoy series ....$3 – 4
11. black with black base, "Air Car," Thai-land cast, Convoy series............$3 – 4
12. metallic gray with orange base, "600," England cast, Convoy series.........$3 – 4
13. metallic gray with orange base, "600," Macau cast, Convoy series........$3 – 4
14. metallic gray with black base, "600," England cast, Convoy series......$3 – 4
15. white with red base, "35-2," medic logo and red stripes, China cast ......$3 – 4

16. **white with red base, "87," yellow design, China cast, 1999 Air Traffic series ....$2 – 3**
17. white with red base, "Aerobatic Team," Thailand cast..........................$3 – 4

18. **white with red base, "Fire Dept.," black interior, China cast, 1998 To The Rescue series ....$2 – 3**
19. white with red base, "Fire Dept.," white interior, China cast...................$2 – 3
20. white with red base, "Fire Rescue," China cast, Avon Action Pack.....$2 – 3
21. white with red base, "NASA," Macau cast ....$3 – 4
22. white with red base, "Virgin Atlantic," Macau cast, gift set ....$3 – 4
23. white with orange base, "MBTV News," England cast ....$4 – 5
24. white with orange base, "Police," China cast, Action Pack.....................$3 – 4
25. white with orange base, "Police 36," England cast ....$16 – 24
26. white with orange base, "Rescue," Macau cast..............................$3 – 4
27. white with fluorescent orange base, "Air Rescue 10," "IC" logo, Thailand cast, Intercom City......................$12 – 16
28. white with fluorescent orange base, blue checkerboard design, Thailand cast, Emergency Pack ....$2 – 3

29. white with yellow base, "123456," Macau cast, Live 'N Learn/Matchbox Preschool series ....$7 – 9
30. white with yellow base, "123456," Thailand cast, Live 'N Learn/Matchbox Preschool series ....$7 – 9
31. white with yellow base, "JCB," Macau cast, gift set...........................$5 – 6
32. white with yellow base, "Fire Dept.," Macau cast...............................$3 – 4
33. white with yellow base, "Fire Dept.," Thailand cast...........................$3 – 4
34. white with black base, "MBTV News," England cast ....$9 – 12
35. white with black base, "Newscam," "News 8," China cast, Real Talkin'..........$3 – 4
36. white with black base, "Police 36," England cast ....$5 – 6
37. white with black base, "Rescue," England cast ....$3 – 4
38. white with black base, "Rescue," Macau cast ....$3 – 4
39. white with black base, "Rescue," Thailand cast, Motor City ....$3 – 4
40. white with black base, Japanese lettering, Japanese gift set ....$10 – 12
41. metallic gold with white base, China cast, 1997 75 Challenge series ......$6 – 12

Hellraiser, 3", #55, 1975
1. white with red stripes, white stars on blue field.............................$16 – 24
2. blue with red stripes, white stars on blue field.............................$12 – 16
3. blue with no labels................$12 – 16
4. blue with "3" label ....$12 – 16

Hi Ho Silver! Volkswagen Beetle (similar castings: Hot Chocolate, Volks Dragon, Sand Digger, Dune Man, Big Blue)
1. metallic silver with red interior, "Hi Ho Silver!"....................................$9 – 12

Hi-Tailer Team Matchbox Racer, 3", #56, 1974; BR 33 – 34, 1986
1. white, unpainted base.............$8 – 10
2. white, red base......................$9 – 12
3. lemon, China cast, Super GT's BR33 – 34, 1986.............................$4 – 5
4. yellow, China cast, Super GT's BR33 – 34, 1986.............................$4 – 5
5. white, China cast, Super GT's BR33 – 34, 1986.............................$4 – 5

Highway Fire Pumper, #1, 2003

1. **metallic red with white plastic components, 2003 Sky Fire series ....$2 – 3**

Highway Maintenance Truck (see Chevrolet Highway Maintenance Truck)

Hillman Minx, 2⅝", #43, 1958
1. green with metal wheels ...$200 – 225
2. blue-gray with gray roof, metal wheels................................$40 – 50
3. blue-gray with gray roof, gray plastic wheels................................$40 – 50
4. turquoise with ivory roof, gray plastic wheels................................$30 – 40

Holden Commodore, #54, 1997, Australia; #64, 1998, international; #11, 2000, international
1. "50," unpainted, rubber tires on chrome rims, promotional.....$16 – 24
2. "50th Anniversary," metallic silver, rubber tires on chrome rims, promotional....................................$16 – 24
3. "99 Holden Commodore," pumpkin orange, 1998 Motor Sports series, international issue....................$4 – 5
4. "Australia's First," metallic silver, rubber tires on chrome rims, Australian Inaugural issue..........................$12 – 16
5. "Bombers," red and dark blue, Australia issue....................................$4 – 5
6. "Bulldogs 1998," red and black, Australia issue..............................$4 – 5
7. "Castrol 11," white, rubber tires on chrome rims, Australia issue....$16 – 24
8. "Commodore Race Team 25," white, Australia issue.........................$4 – 5
9. "Demons 1998," red and dark blue, Australia issue.........................$4 – 5
10. "Fremantle 1998," red and green, Australia issue.............................$4 – 5
11. "Hawks 1998," yellow and brown, Australia issue.............................$4 – 5
12. "Holden," white, 2000 Australian Adventure series, international issue....................................$4 – 5
13. "Magpies 1998," white and black, Australia issue.............................$4 – 5
14. "Olympic Torch Relay," metallic gray, Australia issue......................$9 – 12
15. "Power 1998," turquoise and black, Australia issue.............................$4 – 5
16. "Saints 1998," white and red, Australia issue....................................$4 – 5
17. unpainted, rubber tires on chrome rims, Australian Inaugural issue......$12 – 16

Holden Commodore Police Car, #35, 2001, international
1. blue, "Police," crest and blue designs ....$2 – 3

Holden Pickup, 2⅞", #60, 1977 (similar casting: Holden Ruff Trek)
1. red with star label, yellow motorcycles, yellow interior ....$20 – 30
2. red with sunburst label, olive motorcycles, red interior ....$12 – 16
3. maroon with "500" labels, yellow motorcycles, orange interior ....$12 – 16

4. **red with "500" label on hood, yelle** motorcycles, red interior ......$9 – 1
5. red with "500" labels, yellow motorcycles, yellow interior.................$8 – 1
6. red with "500" labels, olive green motorcycles, red interior.....$12 – 16
7.. metallic blue with "Paris Dakar" label yellow motorcycles, yellow interior French issue ....$40 – 5
8. cream with "Honda" labels, red motorcycles, red interior ....$16 – 2

9. **cream with "Superbike" label, re** motorcycles, red interior ....$7 –
10. cream with "Superbike" label, yellow motorcycles, red interior.........$9 – 1
11. cream with "Superbike" label, yellow motorcycles, tan interior ....$7 –
12. white with "Superbike" label, red motorcycles, red interior ....$12 – 1

Holden Ruff Trek Pickup, with tires back, 2⅞", #58, 1983 (similar casting Holden Pickup)
1. yellow, "Matchbox Rescue Team Support," black cargo, clear windows, re interior, Macau cast, Motor City ..$4 –
2. yellow, "Matchbox Rescue Team Support black cargo, clear windows, red interior Thailand cast, Motor City ....$4 –
3. dark blue, "STP," "Goodyear," black cargo, clear windows, red interior Macau cast, Team Matchbox .$50 – 6

4. **white, "217," black cargo, amber windows, red interior, Macau cast Team Matchbox ....$4 – **
5. white, "217," black cargo, clear windows, red interior, Macau cast, Team Matchbox ....$4 –

6. white, "7-Up," black cargo, clear windows, red interior, Macau cast, Team Matchbox ....$4 – 5
7. white, "Brut," "Faberge," black cargo, clear windows, black interior, Macau cast, Team Matchbox ....$4 – 5
8. white, "Brut," "Faberge," black cargo, clear windows, red interior, Macau cast, Team Matchbox ....$50 – 60
9. white, "Ruff Trek," black cargo, amber windows, red interior, Macau cast, Japan issue............................$8 – 10
10. white with flames, black cargo, clear windows, black interior, Macau cast, James Bond gift set ....$9 – 12

11. metallic tan, "Ruff Trek," black cargo, amber windows, Macau cast ...$3 – 4
12. brown with red, yellow, and blue accents; green cargo, armaments, Macau cast, Roadblasters.........$7 – 9
13. brown with red, yellow, and blue accents; green cargo, armaments, Thailand cast, Japan issue, Tomy box....................................$12 – 16

Holden FJ Van, #282, 1995, Australia; #40, 1998, international; #21, 1999, international; #14, 2000, international
1. "Auto One," white, Australian issue......................................$5 – 6
2. "Automodels for Model Cars 1995," black, Australia issue............$30 – 40
3. "Automodels for Model Cars 1996," black, Australia issue............$30 – 40
4. "Bears," burgundy and yellow, Australia issue......................................$4 – 5
5. "Bevic," baby blue, Australia issue......................................$20 – 30
6. "Blues," white and dark blue, Australia issue......................................$4 – 5
7. "Bombers," red and black, Australia issue......................................$4 – 5
8. "Bulldogs, red and blue, Australia issue......................................$4 – 5
9. "Cats," white and dark blue, Australia issue......................................$4 – 5
10. "Coca-Cola Good with Food," green, Avon 2-pack ....$6 – 8
11. "Crows," yellow and dark blue, Australia issue................................$4 – 5
12. "Demons," red and dark blue, Australia issue................................$4 – 5
13. "Dockers," red and green, Australia issue................................$4 – 5
14. "Hawks," brown and yellow, Australia issue................................$4 – 5
15. "Kangaroos," white and dark blue, Australia issue..........................$4 – 5

16. "Kids World," white, 1995 Australia issue......................................$5 – 6

17. "Laverne & Shirley," "Shotz," Star Cars series, US issue ....$5 – 6
18. "Lions," red and blue, Australia issue $4 – 5
19. "Magpies," white and black, Australia issue......................................$4 – 5
20. "Matchbox," red, 1998 international issue......................................$2 – 3
21. "Premiers 1995," white and dark blue, Australia issue.........................$4 – 5
22. "Royal Mail," orange-red, Australia issue $5 – 6
23. "Saints," light red and black, Australia issue......................................$4 – 5
24. "Sunday Age/View," black, Australia issue................................$30 – 40
25. "Sydney," red and white, Australia issue......................................$4 – 5
26. "Tigers," yellow and black, Australia issue......................................$4 – 5
27. "True Blue," blue, Australia issue......................................$4 – 5
28. "West Coast," yellow and blue, Australia issue................................$4 – 5
29. "Your Own Promotional Van," "Matchbox — Your Logo Here," blue, Australia issue................................$20 – 30
30. green with fruit design, 1999 Special Delivery international series ....$3 – 4
31. black, no markings, Australia issue ....$5 – 6
32. beige with surfer design, 2000 Australia issue ....$3 – 4

Honda CB750 (see Police Motorcyclist)

Honda ATC, #23, 1985
1. red ....$9 – 12
2. fluorescent green....................$5 – 8

Honda Motorcycle and Trailer, 2⁷⁄₈", #38, 1967

1. **yellow with "Honda" decals, black plastic wheels.....................$9 – 12**
2. orange trailer with no decals, black plastic wheels.....................$20 – 25
3. orange trailer with "Honda" decals, black plastic wheels.............$30 – 35
4. orange trailer with blue-green motorcycle, Superfast wheels ....$6 – 8
5. yellow trailer with blue motorcycle, Superfast wheels, 1970 ....$16 – 24
6. yellow with purple motorcycle, Superfast wheels.................................$24 – 32
7. yellow trailer with pink motorcycle, Superfast wheels ....$24 – 32
8. yellow trailer with blue-green motorcycle, Superfast wheels.....................$6 – 8

Honda Passport (see Isuzu Rodeo)

Hondarora Motorcycle, 2³⁄₈", #18, 1975
1. red with chrome handlebars, black seat, chrome engine, wire wheels, no rider, England cast..............$12 – 16

2. **red with black handlebars and seat, chrome engine, wire wheels, no rider, England cast ....$6 – 8**
3. red with black handlebars and seat, chrome engine, mag wheels, no rider, England cast ....$6 – 8
4. red with black handlebars and seat, black engine, mag wheels, no rider, England cast ....$6 – 8
5. red with black handlebars, white seat, chrome engine, wire wheels, no rider, England cast ....$100 – 150
6. orange with black handlebars and seat, chrome engine, wire wheels, no rider, England cast ....$8 – 12
7. dark olive green with black handlebars and seat, black engine, wire wheels, no rider, England cast...............$60 – 80
8. light olive green with black handlebars and seat, black engine, wire wheels, no rider, England cast...................$4 – 6
9. metallic red with black handlebars and seat, black engine, wire wheels, no rider, England cast...............$40 – 50
10. metallic red with black handlebars and seat, chrome engine, wire wheels, no rider, England cast............$80 – 120
13. yellow with black handlebars and seat, chrome engine, mag wheels, no driver, England cast ....$5 – 7
14. yellow with black handlebars and seat, chrome engine, mag wheels, tan driver, England cast ....$5 – 7

15. yellow with black handlebars and seat, chrome engine, mag wheels, brown driver, England cast ....$5 – 7
16. yellow with black handlebars and seat, chrome engine, mag wheels, green driver, England cast ....$60 – 80
17. yellow with black handlebars and seat, chrome engine, mag wheels, tan driver, Macau cast...........................$4 – 6

11. metallic green with black handlebars and seat, chrome engine, mag wheels, no rider, England cast ....$6 – 8
12. metallic green with black handlebars and seat, black engine, mag wheels, no rider, England cast..................$6 – 8
18. metallic silver with black handlebars and seat, black engine, mag wheels, red rider, Macau cast ....$9 – 12
19. metallic silver with black handlebars, dark gray seat, black engine, mag wheels, red rider, Macau cast..$9 – 12
20. orange with black handlebars and seat, chrome engine, mag wheels, tan rider, Macau cast............................$4 – 6

Horse Box (see AEC Ergomatic Horse Box, Bedford Horse Box)

Horse Drawn Milk Float, 2¼", #7, 1955
1. orange with silver bottles, metal wheels, made in England ....$100 – 125

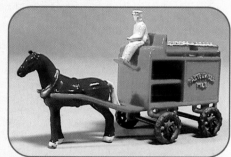

2. orange with white bottles, metal wheels, made in England .$125 – 150
3. orange with orange bottles, metal wheels, made in England ....$50 – 75
4. orange with gray plastic wheels, made in England ....$75 – 100
5. orange, 1988 40th Anniversary Gift Set, made in China ....$8 – 10
6. light blue, 1991 Matchbox Originals, made in China ....$3 – 5

Hospital Helicopter, #13, 2003 (similar casting: Rescue Helicopter, #63, 2003)

1. black metal upper, red plastic lower and tail, red and yellow design on sides, #13 Hospital Helicopter, 2003 Hospital series ....$2 – 3

2. white metal upper, blue plastic lower and tail, red and blue "Med Alarm," #63 Rescue Helicopter, 2003 ....$2 – 3

Hot Chocolate Volkswagen Beetle, 2¹³⁄₁₆", #46, 1982; Dragon Wheels, #43, 1972 (similar castings: Beetle Streaker, Big Blue, Dragon Wheels, Dune Man, Hi Ho Silver, Sand Digger, Volks Dragon)

1. black with metallic brown sides, no roof stripes, "Hot Chocolate" on base, Hong Kong cast ....$9 – 12
2. black with metallic brown sides, white roof stripes, "Hot Chocolate" on base, Hong Kong cast......................$5 – 6

3. metallic blue, "Big Blue," "Beetle Streaker" on base, Macau cast .$4 – 5

4. metallic blue, "Big Blue," "Beetle Streaker" on base, Hong Kong cast ....$4 – 5
5. blue, "Big Blue," "Beetle Streaker" on base, Hong Kong cast ....$4 – 5
6. green, "Dragon Wheels" tampo, "Beetle Streaker" on base, China cast, Premiere Collection #13 ....$5 – 6
7. green, "Dragon Wheels" label, England cast ....$16 – 24

Hot Points Challenger (see Dodge Challenger/Mitsubishi Galant Eterna)

Hot Rocker, 3", #67, 1973 (similar casting: Ford Capri, Maxi Taxi)
1. metallic lime green ....$12 – 16
2. metallic green ....$12 – 16
3. orange-red ....$12 – 16

Hot Rod Draguar, 2¹³⁄₁₆", #36, 1970
1. metallic red ....$16 – 24
2. metallic pink ....$16 – 24

Hot Smoker, Roman numeral V, 1978 (variation of #70 Dodge Dragster, 1971, and #74 Orange Peel Dodge Charger, 1981)
1. yellow, Roman Numeral Limited Edition ....$9 – 12

Hovercraft, 3⅛", #2, 1976
1. metallic light green ....$5 – 10

2. avocado green, Adventure 2000 series ....8 – 12

Hovercraft, 2⅞", #62, 2001; #35, 2002 (see Fire Hovercraft)

Hovercraft SRN6, 3", #72, 1972
1. white.....................................$6 – 8

Hoveringham Tipper, 2⅞", #17, 1963

1. red cab, orange tipper.......$15 – 20

Hummer/Humvee, with roof-mounted gun, small opening rear hatch, #3, 1994; #48, 1998; #53, 2000; #32, 2002 khaki-gray with brown and white camouflage, pink cross .... $2 – 3

2. pink-tan with green and brown camouflage, 5-pack .... $2 – 3

3. light khaki with brown camouflage, bright orange cross on rear hatch, 1994.................................... $2 – 4

4. light khaki with brown camouflage, bright orange vertical bar on rear hatch, 1995....................... $2 – 3

5. army green with white star on doors and hood, "A-4873-2," 1996.. $2 – 3

6. white with blue "Police," "Police Unit 7," 1996 Police 5-pack.......... $2 – 3

7. army green with brown and black camouflage, 1996 5-pack .... $2 – 4

8. white with gray and army green camouflage, 1997 Tundra Defense Force 5-pack .... $2 – 3

9. dark khaki with brown star, "A-4873-2," 1998..................... $2 – 3

10. light khaki with mud splash, "Alpha Co.," 2000 Military series................ $2 – 3

11. light khaki with mud splash, "Alpha Co.," "Matchbox 2000," 2000 Military series........................... $3 – 4

12. metallic green, no gun, 2002 Cool Rides series .... $2 – 4

13. flat army green, "Unit 01," "476 Convoy Follows," 1999 Military Patrol.................................... $3 – 4

14. army green, "Unit 5 Communications," Real Talkin' series .... $2 – 3

15. dark green, "Gen IV," "The Lost World," Jurassic Park play set.............. $4 – 5

16. black with green and brown camouflage, 5-pack .... $2 – 3

17. flat army green, green hubs with rubber tires, Premiere Collection .... $5 – 6

Humvee, #375, 1998, Taco Bell; Matchbox mold retooled by Strottman International Inc. through a licensing agreement with Mattel. Strottman manufactures toy premiums for Taco Bell. Base is marked "Made in China by S.I.I."

1. black with white and red swirls, metallic silver windows, Taco Bell premium ... $4 – 5

Hummer H2, #73, 2003

1. yellow, 2003 Car Shop series $2 – 3

Hummer Rescue Vehicle, with large opening compartment, ATV molded into interior, #33, 2002; #65, 2003

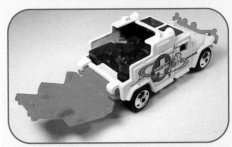

1. white with opening red hatch, black interior, red and blue "BASE 33," 2002 Ultimate Rescue series .... $2 – 3

2. yellow with opening white hatch, burning cityscape and fireman graphics, 2003 Pumper Squad.........................$2 – 3

3. **metallic red with opening metallic gray hatch, "Matchbox FDMB" on shield with flame graphics, "14," 2001 Action Launcher Fire Truck set...........$3 – 4**

Hummer School Bus, #16, 2001; #69, 2002; #52, 2003
1. yellow, "Burton Hill Elementary Buffalos," 2001 City Dudes series .....$2 – 3

2. **yellow, "Bulldogs Football," "State Champions 2002," 2002 Kids' Cars of the Year series ....$2 – 3**
3. yellow, "Hero City Elementary Bears," 2003 School Time series..........$2 – 3

Humvee (see Hummer)

Hydroplane, #44, 1999; #10, 2000; #39, 1999, international
1. red, "Coca-Cola" and polar bears design, Premiere Collection ......$5 – 6
2. red, "Coca-Cola," "www.cocacolastore.com," polar bears design, Color Comp promotional...................................$60 – 80

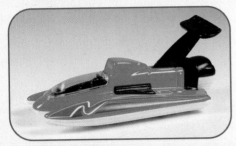

3. **red with white base, black wing, 1999 Ocean series ....$2 – 3**
4. dark blue, "492," red and white design, red base, metallic gray wing, black wheels, 5-pack ....$2 – 3
5. dark blue, "492," red and white design, red base, metallic gray wing, white wheels, 5-pack ....$4 – 5

6. **bright blue, "492," orange and white design, orange base, metallic gray wing, 2000 Ocean Explorer series ....$2 – 3**
7. bright blue, "492," "Matchbox 2000," orange and white design, orange base, metallic gray wing, 2000 Ocean Explorer series.......................$3 – 4

Ice Breaker, #61, 2002 – 2003

1. **metallic red hull, white cabin, blue deck and stacks, white cross, illustration on sides, 2002 Rescue Rookies, 2003 Hero City ....$2 – 3**

2. **blue hull, white cabin, aqua deck and stacks, "Spongebob Squarepants," 2003 Nickelodeon 5-pack ......$2 – 3**

Ice Cream Canteen (Commer Ice Cream Canteen)

Ice Cream Truck, #65, 2002; #60, 2003

1. **white with yellow plastic base, red door, "Jimmie's Ice Cream," 2002 Kids' Cars of the Year series..$2 – 3**

2. white with blue trim, ice cream cone graphics, 2003 Kids' Shoppes series .....$2 – 3

Ikarus Coach, European model, 3", #67, 1987; #2, 1998, international
1. "2384584," "FT," Chinese pictograms, white with green roof, tinted windows, China cast, China issue.........$40 – 50
2. "Airport Limousine 237," white and orange with white roof, tinted windows, China cast, Japanese gift set...$9 – 12
3. "Canary Island," white with white roof, tinted windows, China cast, UK issue.....$8 – 10

4. **"City Line Tourist," white with green roof, tinted windows, China cast ....$3 – 4**

5. **"España," white with white roof, tinted windows, China cast ....$2 – 3**
6. "Gibraltar," white with red roof, clear windows, Macau cast, Spain issue....$6 – 8
7. "Gibraltar," white with red roof, tinted windows, China cast, Spain issue.......$6 – 8
8. "Ikarus," cream with cream roof, tinted windows ....$3 – 4
9. "Marti," beige with brown roof, tinted windows, China cast, Switzerland issue...................................$9 – 12

10. **"Shuttle," purple with purple roof, tinted windows, China cast, 5-pack...................................$2 – 3**

1. "Voyager," white with orange roof, amber windows, Macau cast .....$3 – 4

2. **"Voyager," white with orange roof, clear windows, Macau cast....$3 – 4**
3. "Voyager," white with orange roof, tinted windows, China cast .....$3 – 4
4. "Voyager," white with orange roof, tinted windows, Macau cast ....$3 – 4
5. "World Cup Tour Bus," white with red roof, blue windows, China cast, 5-pack ..$2 – 3
6. yellow with white roof, sunset scene, tinted windows, China cast, 1998 Around the Town international series ....$2 – 3
7. light blue, Matchbox Across America 50th Birthday Series #3 New Jersey — Northeastern Collection ....$4 – 5
8. white with red roof, smiling face design, tinted windows, China cast, 5-pack ....$4 – 5
9. white with white roof, no markings, Graffic Traffic ....$9 – 12
0. white with white roof, tinted windows, China cast, ASAP promotional blank............................$30 – 40

ce Maker (see Zamboni)

MSA Mazda (see Mazda IMSA)

MSA Mustang (see Ford Mustang IMSA)

dy Racer, #65, 1985 (see F1 Racer, #16, 1984)

flatable Raft and Trailer, #793, 1984, Two Pack except where noted

. **red deck, white hull, black motor, blue "SR," England cast; black trailer, England cast ....$6 – 8**

2. **red deck, yellow hull, black motor, "Red Valley Camp," no-origin cast; black trailer, no-origin cast, 5-pack..........$2 – 3**
3. red deck, yellow hull, black motor, "Red Valley Camp," no-origin cast; black trailer, China cast, 5-pack ....$2 – 3

4. **orange deck, black hull, black motor, "R1," no-origin cast; white trailer, "Rescue" and stripes, no-origin cast ..$3 – 4**
5. orange deck, black hull, black motor, blue "SR," no-origin cast; black trailer, no-origin cast ....$3 – 4
6. orange deck, black hull, white motor, anchor emblem, no-origin cast; white trailer with black and orange stripes, no-origin cast ....$3 – 4
7. orange deck, black hull, white motor, no-origin cast; white trailer with dark blue and red stripes, no-origin cast ...$3 – 4
8. orange deck, metallic gray hull, white motor, "Rescue," no-origin cast; white trailer with anchor design, no-origin cast......................................$3 – 4
9. orange deck, white hull, black motor, blue "SR," England cast; black trailer, England cast ....$3 – 4
10. orange deck, white hull, black motor, blue "SR," England cast; black trailer, Macau cast...........................$3 – 4
11. orange deck, white hull, black motor, red "SR," England cast; black trailer, England cast ....$3 – 4
12. orange deck, white hull, black motor, England cast; black trailer, England cast......................................$3 – 4
13. lemon yellow deck, white hull, black motor, England cast; blue "SR," black trailer, England cast ....$6 – 8
14. dark blue deck, gray hull, white motor, no-origin cast; white trailer with blue and red stripes, no-origin cast ...$3 – 4
15. black deck, orange hull, white motor, no-origin cast; black trailer, "2," no-origin cast ....$3 – 4

International Armored Car, #58, 2000; #17, 2001; #38, 2003; #53, 2001, international
1. lime green with piggy bank illustration, "MHC Bank," 2003 Mom and Pop Shops series ....$2 – 3

2. **metallic blue-gray, "Mr. Krabs" and cartoon illustration, 2003 Nickelodeon Spongebob Squarepants 5-pack......................................$2 – 3**
3. lime green with piggy bank illustration, "MHC Bank," 2003 Hero City 10-pack #2.......................................$2 – 3

4. **light gray, "Matchbox Armored Car Service," blue windows, 2000 Speedy Delivery series..........$2 – 3**
5. light gray, "Matchbox Armored Car Service," "Matchbox 2000," blue windows, 2000 Speedy Delivery series .....$3 – 4
6. pearl gray, red and yellow crest, tinted windows, 5-pack ....$2 – 3
7. 2001 City Dudes series ....$2 – 3
8. 2002 Matchbox Across America 50th Birthday series #36 Nevada — Western Collection ....$5 – 6
9. beige and brown, "AMSA," blue windows, Color Comp promotional, repainted, rivets glued ....$40 – 50
10. white, "Selmac Savings," blue windows, ASAP promotional..............$80 – 120
11. white, no markings, blue windows, ASAP promotional blank........$30 – 40

International Fire Pumper, #76, 1999; #30, 2000; #27, 2002; #66, 1999, international
1. red, "73rd Apple Blossom Festival" ....$9 – 12
2. red, "Fort Wayne Fire Dept.," rubber tires on chrome rims, Premiere Collection...................................$16 – 24
3. red, "Hot Springs Vol. Fire Dept.," Color Comp promotional................$20 – 30

4. **red, "Matchbox" logo, "Station 5," yellow and white trim, 2003 Hero City 5-pack #1....................$2 – 3**
5. red, MB Fire Dept No. 7," stripes, door crest, 1999 Fire Rescue series...$2 – 3
6. red, "Metro Alarm," black stripe, 5-pack......................................$2 – 3
7. red with white roof and back section, stripes, door crest, 1999 Fire Rescue international series..................$3 – 4

8. red with yellow flame and hood trim, Kidde First Alert Carbon Monoxide Detector on-package premium (+ cost of various detectors/alarms if still in package) ....$4 – 5

9. metallic red, "Fire Hunter AMR 977," yellow, red and black design, 2002 Red Hot Heroes series..$2 – 3

10. orange-red with self-stick set of labels, McDonald's Happy Meal premium..........................$2 – 3

11. orange-yellow, "6532," "54," black bands, "Matchbox" in circular logo, 2000 5 Alarm 5-pack...........$2 – 3

12. white, "Engine Co. 34," 5-pack ...$3 – 4

13. white, "Engine Co. 77," pale green trim, black detail, 1998 Emergency Rescue 5-pack ....$2 – 3

14. white and red, "Radio E-75" .....$9 – 12
15. metallic gold, "MB Fire Dept. No. 7," "Matchbox 2000," 2000 Fire Fighters series......................................$3 – 4
16. metallic gold, "MB Fire Dept. No. 7," 2000 Fire Fighters series ....$2 – 3

International Fire Truck (see International Fire Pumper)

International Pumper (see International Fire Pumper)

Iron Fairy Crane, 3", #42, 1969

1. red with yellow crane, black plastic wheels ....$12 – 16
2. red with yellow crane, Superfast wheels, 1970......................$70 – 90
3. red with lime green crane, Superfast wheels...........................$300 – 400
4. orange-red with yellow boom, Superfast wheels................................$50 – 60
5. orange-red with lime green, Superfast wheels................................$50 – 60

Iso Grifo, 3", #14, 1968; BR 3 – 4, 1985
1. metallic blue with light blue interior, black plastic wheels on chrome hubs, 1968....................................$6 – 9
2. enamel dark blue with light blue interior, Superfast wheels, 1969 ....$20 – 25
3. enamel dark blue with dark blue interior, Superfast wheels, 1969 ....$20 – 25
4. enamel dark blue with white interior, Superfast wheels, 1969 ....$20 – 25
5. metallic dark blue with white interior, Superfast wheels ....$20 – 25
6. enamel light blue with white interior, Superfast wheels ....$20 – 25
7. enamel blue with white interior, Superfast wheels ....$20 – 25
8. enamel pale blue with white interior, Superfast wheels, Japan issue .$20 – 25
9. cream with black windows, England cast, Super GT BR 3 – 4, 1985 .$3 – 5
10. cream with translucent white windows, England cast, Super GT BR 3 – 4, 1985..................................$12 – 15
11. yellow with black windows, England cast, Super GT BR 3 – 4, 1985 ....$8 – 10
12. light blue with black windows, England cast, Super GT BR 3 – 4, 1985 .$4 – 6

13. metallic blue with black windows, Englan cast, Super GT BR 3 – 4, 1985 ..$3 – 8
14. metallic blue with translucent whit windows, England cast, Super GT BI 3 – 4, 1985......................$12 – 15
15. bright green with black windows, China cas Neon Racers BR 3 – 4, 1985.......$3 – 5
16. metallic blue with black windows, Chin cast, Super GT BR 3 – 4, 1985..$8 – 10
17. cream with black windows, China cast Super GT BR 3 – 4, 1985.........$6 – 8
18. yellow with black windows, China cas Super GT BR 3 – 4, 1985.........$3 – 5

Isuzu Amigo, 2⅞", #52, 1991
1. red, "Amigo," silver and orang stripes.....................................$3 – 5
2. light yellow, pink stripes and pat terns, gray interior, Dream Machine 3-pack.....................................$3 – 4
3. metallic blue, "Isuzu Amigo," gray inte rior...$6 – 8

4. dark blue with green design gray interior, 1999 Beach Fun 5 pack ....$2 – 3
5. purple, "Hadrosaur," skeleton design black interior ....$2 – 3

6. white, "Surf Shop," "Surf's Up, orange and blue design, black interio 1999 Beach series ....$2 – 3

7. white with blue design, fluorescen orange interior, 1997 Land Sea Air 5-pack ....$2 – 3

Isuzu Rodeo/Vauxhall Opel Frontera #56, 1995; #100, 2000; #59, 1995 international
1. metallic red, no markings, "Frontera" o black base ....$3 – 4

. **red, "Power Parts 21," blue and white accents, "Rodeo" on gray base .$3 – 4**

. **yellow, "555-RES-Q Roadside Rescue," "Rodeo" on black base, 2000 On The Road Again..............$2 – 3**
. yellow, "555-RES-Q Roadside Rescue," "Matchbox 2000"; "Rodeo" on black base, 2000 On The Road Again ..$3 – 4
. green, "Brontosaurus" and skeleton, no name on gray base, 5-pack ....$2 – 3
. blue, red tail lights, "Opel Frontera" on black base, 1995 Germany issue..$4 – 5

. **black with bright pink mud splash pattern on sides only, "Rodeo" on gray base..........................$2 – 3**

. **black with bright pink mud splash pattern on sides and hood, "Rodeo" on gray base ....$2 – 3**
. black with red and white design, "Rodeo" on gray base, 5-pack ....$2 – 3
0. black with red and white design, "Frontera" on gray base, 5-pack ....$2 – 3
1. metallic gray, no markings, "Frontera" on black base ....$2 – 3

12. pink-beige, "Operations Safari 1999," "Matchbox," green camouflage, "Rodeo" on black base ....$20 – 25

13. **white, "Wilderness Tours," "Rodeo" on turquoise base, Wilderness Tours 5-pack ....$2 – 3**

14. **white with bright pink mud splash pattern on sides only, "Rodeo" on gray base............................$3 – 4**
15. white with brown mud splash pattern on sides only, "Frontera" on black base....................................$4 – 5
16. white with orange and blue design, "Frontera" on black base, international issue....................................$3 – 4
17. white with no markings, "Frontera" on black base ....$12 – 16
18. white with no markings, "Frontera" on turquoise base, Wilderness Tours 5-pack......................................$2 – 3
19. metallic gold, no markings, "Rodeo" on gray base, 1997 75 Challenge series ....$6 – 12

J

Jaguar 3.4 Litre, gray plastic wheels, 2½", #65, 1959
1. metallic blue.........................$30 – 40
2. blue ....$30 – 40

Jaguar 3.8 Litre Saloon, 2⅝", #65, 1962
1. red with gray wheels............$25 – 35
2. red with silver wheels ....$35 – 45
3. metallic red with silver wheels .$35 – 45

4. **red with black wheels, Union Jack on roof...............................$25 – 35**

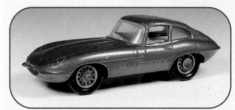

5. **red with black wheels.......$20 – 30**

Jaguar D-Type, green, 2³/₁₆", #41, 1957
1. metal wheels, "41" decal......$30 – 40
2. gray plastic wheels, "41" decal..................................$40 – 50

Jaguar D-Type, green, 2⁷/₁₆", #41, 1960
1. gray plastic wheels, "41" decal..................................$40 – 50
2. silver plastic wheels, "19" decal................................$125 – 150
3. black plastic tires on spoked hubs ....$40 – 50
4. black plastic tires on red hubs ....$175 – 200

Jaguar Mark 10, metallic tan, 2¾", #28, 1964

1. gray plastic wheels..........$140 – 160
2. **black plastic wheels ....$15 – 20**

Jaguar SS-100, 3", #47, 1982
1. red with partially painted hood, England cast....................................$9 – 12
2. red with red hood, England cast..$4 – 5
3. red with red hood, Macau cast ..$4 – 5
4. blue with gray hood, Macau cast .$5 – 6
5. dark green, Thailand cast, UK on-package premium, US gift set.......$12 – 16
6. metallic gray with dark gray hood, Thailand cast, gift set....................$4 – 5

Jaguar XJ-6, 3", #1, 1987; #41, 1987; #14, 2001, UK (similar casting: Jaguar XJ-6 Police)
1. metallic red, tan interior, doors open ....$2 – 3
2. green, "Redoxon," "Jaguar," maroon interior, doors open, Hong Kong issue ....$20 – 25
3. dark green, black and tan interior, detailed trim, doors don't open, chrome windows, rubber tires on gray rims, Ultra Class...........................$9 – 12
4. blue, tan interior, doors don't open, Show Stoppers ....$3 – 4
5. blue, gray interior, British flag, 2001 Union Jack series, UK issue .....$4 – 5

6. metallic blue, tan interior, detailed trim, doors don't open, chrome windows, rubber tires on gray rims, World Class.....................$3 – 4

7. black, "W&M" and crest, maroon interior, doors open, on-package premium, UK issue.................$30 – 40

8. metallic dark gray, black and red interior, detailed trim, doors don't open, chrome windows, rubber tires on gray rims, JC Penney Premiere Collection.........................$4 – 5

9. metallic silver with white interior ..$3 – 4

10. white, black interior, doors open, part of King Size set......................$9 – 12

11. white with no markings, Graffic Traffic.................................$6 – 8

Jaguar XJ-6 Police, 3", #1, 1991; #27, 1998, international (similar casting: Jaguar XJ6)

1. white, "Police," blue and yellow stripes..............................$4 – 5

2. white, "Police," shield and checkerboard design, blue interior, doors don't open..................................$2 – 3

Jaguar XJ-220, 3¹⁄₈", #31, 1993; #75, 1998, international; #12, 2001, international

1. blue with white interior, "Old Eight," UK issue...............................$80 – 120

2. blue with yellow and green accents, 1997....................................$2 – 3

3. **blue with ivory interior, clear windows, 1993.........................$2 – 3**

4. blue with ivory interior, clear windows, Jaguar logo...........................$4 – 5

5. blue with white interior, tinted windows, "50," "XJ220," gift set..............$4 – 5

6. chrome plated with white interior, amber windows, Graffic Traffic...$3 – 4

7. fluorescent orange with black accents, 1996....................................$2 – 3

8. fluorescent yellow and orange with blue interior, bright blue design, 1994....................................$2 – 3

9. **gradient metallic red to black with yellow interior, 2001 Union Jack series, international issue......$2 – 3**

10. green with gray and black interior, rubber tires on chrome rims, Premiere Collection #19...........................$4 – 5

11. **green with ivory interior, tinted windows, white and lime green flames........................$2 – 3**

12. green with tan interior, "Jaguar," 1998 Street Cruisers series, international issue.....................................$2 – 3

13. metallic blue with gray and black interior, rubber tires on chrome rims, international Premiere Collection #2......$4 – 5

14. metallic gold with black interior, clear windows, 1997 75 Challenge series.................................$6 – 12

15. metallic gray with blue interior, tinted windows, blue and yellow design..$2 – 3

16. metallic gray with red interior, clear windows, 1993 Show Stoppers series.................................$3 – 4

17. metallic maroon with gray and black interior, rubber tires on chrome rims, Premiere Collection #10...........$4 – 5

18. metallic purple with chrome windows, rubber tires on chrome rims, 1995 World Class...........................$3 – 5

19. metallic silver-blue with chrome interior, 1998 Street Cruisers, international issue......................................$3 – 4

20. metallic turquoise with yellow interior, tinted windows, yellow and white flames ....$2 – 3

21. **metallic teal blue with yellow and green design, #31.................$3 – 4**

22. red with silver-gray interior, British flag and white band, 1997..............$3 – 4

Jaguar XK-8 1997, #71, 1998; #48, 1999; #43, 1999, international; #2, 2000, international; #2, 2001, UK; #43, 2002, international

1. **metallic red with gray interior, silver headlights, 1999 Roadsters international series ....$4 – 5**

2. metallic red with metallic gray interior, silver headlights, 10 spoke wheels, 2002 Roadster international series ....$3 – 4

3. metallic red with tan and black interior, detailed trim, rubber tires on chrome rims, 1998 First Editions ....$5 – 6

4. green with gray interior, no markings 5-spoke wheels.....................$3 – 4

5. green with gray interior, no markings 10-spoke wheels, Target Eggmobile 3 pack.................................$9 – 12

6. green with metallic gray interior white Jaguar design, 1999 Drop Tops series ....$2 – 3

7. green with tan interior, no markings Germany issue.......................$4 – 5

8. **metallic blue, "Jaguar XK8" an silver design, 1998 Street Cruisers series ....$2 – 3**

9. metallic blue with black interior, red tail lights, white Matchbox logo, 2003 Auto Carrier Launcher 5-pack ....$2 – 3

10. **metallic light blue with silver head lights, black interior, 200 Eurosports 5-pack ....$2 – 3**

11. unpainted with pale tan interior, rubber tires on chrome rims, 1998 First Editions ....$5 – 6

Jaguar XK-120, 3", #22, 1984

1. **black with orange interior, Collectors Choice, White Rose Collectibles..$3 – 5**

black with light brown interior,
Select Class #3 ....\$4 - 5
. dark green with red interior, no markings ....\$4 - 5
. dark green with tan and brown interior,
rubber tires on chrome rims, Premiere
Collection #3 ....\$4 - 5
. dark green with tan interior, no markings, China issue ....\$80 - 120
. pale olive with maroon interior ...\$3 - 4
. ivory with red interior, "414" .....\$2 - 3
. red with white interior, Show Stoppers ....\$3 - 4
. red with white interior, "Coca-Cola," rubber tires on chrome rims, Premiere Collection ....\$4 - 5

0. red with light brown interior, rubber
tires on chrome rims, Premiere Collection #6 ....\$4 - 5
1. red with tan interior, no markings,
China issue ....\$80 - 120
2. white with chrome windshield, rubber tires
on chrome rims, World Class ......\$6 - 8

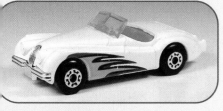

3. white with blue and fluorescent orange
flames, Dream Machines ....\$4 - 5

aguar XK-140 Coupe, 2³/₈", #32, 1957
. ivory ....\$40 - 50
. red ....\$75 - 100
. Matchbox Originals replica, 1993, black
with silver metal wheels ....\$3 - 5

aguar XKE, 2⁵/₈", #32, 1962
. metallic red, clear windows, gray plastic
wheels ....\$50 - 75
. metallic red, green windows, gray plastic wheels ....\$30 - 40
. metallic red, clear windows, black plastic wheels ....\$25 - 35
. metallic bronze, clear windows, black
wheels ....\$40 - 50

avelin AMX (see AMC Javelin AMX)

avelin AMX Pro Stocker (see AMC
Javelin AMX Pro Stocker)

eep, #38, 1976, with or without gun, no
roof (similar casting: U.S. Mail Jeep,
Sleet 'N Snow, Jeep 4x4)

1. light army green, no gun, star in circle
label on hood, black hubs ......\$20 - 25
2. light army green, no gun, "21*11"
label, black hubs ....\$9 - 12
3. light army green, with gun, star in circle
label on hood, black hubs ....\$9 - 12
4. light army green, with gun, "21*11"
label, silver hubs ....\$9 - 12
5. light army green, with gun, "21*11"
label, black hubs ....\$6 - 8
6. green, with gun, "21*11" label, silver
hubs, UK issue ....\$160 - 240
7. green, with gun, no label, silver hubs,
UK issue........................\$160 - 240
8. dark army green, no gun, "21*11"
label, black hubs ....\$70 - 90
9. red, no gun, "Gliding Club," silver hubs,
Two Pack ....\$360 - 480
10. yellow, no gun, "Gliding Club," silver
hubs, Two Pack ....\$9 - 12
11. yellow, no gun, "Gliding Club," black
hubs, Two Pack ....\$9 - 12

Jeep, Army, #38, 1976 (see Jeep, #38)

Jeep 1960, #505, 2001, Matchbox Collectibles Elvis Presley Collection with
Graceland diorama
1. pink with white roof, pink stripes,
rubber white wall tires on chrome
rims ....\$12 - 16

Jeep 4x4, with or without roof, 2⁷/₁₆", #5,
1982, US; #20, 1982, US; #14, 1984,
international; #56, 1990, international
(similar castings: US Mail Jeep, 4x4 Jeep
Eagle, 4x4 Golden Eagle Off-Road Jeep,
Jeep Laredo, Jeep Wrangler)

1. beige with beige roof, camouflage .\$2 - 3

2. beige with black roof, camouflage .\$2 - 3
3. black with red roof, "Laredo," Macau
cast ....\$14 - 21
4. black with white roof, "Laredo," Macau
cast ....\$2 - 3

5. black with white roof, "Laredo,"
Hong Kong cast ....\$21 - 28
6. black with white roof, "Laredo," Thailand
cast ....\$2 - 3
7. blue, "Mork & Mindy," Star Cars
series..................................\$6 - 9

8. metallic blue with pink, white, and
yellow accents, no roof, 1993 5-
pack ....\$3 - 4
9. brown, "Golden Eagle," no roof ...\$3 - 4
10. pale brown with pale brown roof, "V-
9873-3," 5-pack ....\$2 - 3
11. metallic copper with red roof, England
cast ....\$3 - 5
12. army green with black roof, "RB104,"
play set ....\$2 - 3
13. army green with black roof, "V-
9872-3" ....\$2 - 3

14. army green with army green roof,
white star, "V-9872-3," 1996 .\$2 - 3
15. army green with tan roof, camouflage,
Macau cast, black metal base, Commando series ....\$5 - 7
16. army green with tan roof, camouflage,
Macau cast, black plastic base, Commando series ....\$5 - 7
17. army green with plastic armaments,
Roadblasters ....\$7 - 8
18. light army green with army green roof,
red cross, "M*A*S*H," Star Cars
series..................................\$5 - 7

19. pale army green with pale olive roof, white cross, "RB104," play set ..$2 – 3

20. **metallic gray, "Bad To The Bone" on hood, black interior, no roof, 1996**.....................$3 – 4

21. **fluorescent pink with white interior, no roof, 1993 Dream Machines 3-pack**....................$3 – 4

22. metallic purple, "Bad To The Bone" on hood, teal blue interior, no roof, 1995 ....$2 – 3

23. red, "Golden Eagle," metal base, no roof ....$3 – 4

24. red, "Golden Eagle," plastic base, no roof ....$2 – 3

25. red, "Wolff Systems" ....$20 – 25

26. red with white roof, "Golden Eagle," Macau cast.....................$9 – 12

27. **tan with tan roof, brown camouflage** ....$2 – 3

28. dark tan, "Golden Eagle," red roof, England cast ....$21 – 28

29. metallic dark tan, "Golden Eagle," no roof ....$4 – 5

30. metallic light tan, "Golden Eagle," no roof ....$4 – 5

31. metallic turquoise, "Jeep," no roof, White Rose Collectors Choice ....$3 – 4

32. white, "Desert Dawg," red roof, England cast ....$4 – 6

33. white with black cow spots, 5-pack.$2 – 3

34. yellow "50th Anniversary Jeep," no roof ....$16 – 24

35. yellow with lime green roof, Macau cast, Matchbox Preschool/Live 'N Learn series.....................$7 – 9

36. **yellow with black roof, pink and blue design on hood, 5-pack** ....$2 – 3

37. metallic gold, 75 Challenge....$12 – 16

Jeep Cherokee, 2⁷⁄₈", #27, 1987; #73, 1994; #1, 1996, international; #36, 1998; #97, 1999

1. beige, "Holiday Club," Two Pack ..$3 – 4

2. black with pink-red and white flames ....$2 – 3

3. black, no markings, ASAP promotional blank.....................$30 – 40

4. black, "American International Recovery," ASAP promotional.....$120 – 160

5. black, "Linux Solutions," ASAP promotional.....................$80 – 120

6. black, "Microsoft," ASAP promotional.....................$80 – 120

7. blue, "Hellman's," "Best Foods" ..$80 – 120

8. blue with black lower, "Camp Jeep 2000," 5-pack.....................$2 – 3

9. brown, "Mr. Fixer"....................$3 – 5

10. **dark green with tan lower, no markings, 1997 Rugged Riders 5-pack, China cast**.....................$2 – 3

11. green, no markings, Thailand cast, Belgium issue ....$20 – 25

12. light green to dark brown, "Mr. Fixer," Super Color Changers...............$4 – 5

13. metallic green with light tan interior and trim, black base, 1997 Rugged Riders 5-pack.....................$2 – 3

14. **metallic silver with black lower "Sport," red stripe**................$3 – 4

15. orange-red with black lower, "Hilti expertise in every case"...............$12 – 16

16. purple with orange and ivory flames 1994.....................$2 – 3

17. red with black lower, gold trim and shield, 5-pack.....................$2 – 3

18. red with black lower, "Fire Chief," "F No. 1," 5-pack.....................$2 – 3

19. **red with black lower, "Matchbox Fir Chief," 1999 Fire 5-pack** ....$2 – 3

20. red with black lower, "Fire Chief," rubber tires on chrome rims, Premiere Collection #7 ....$4 – 5

21. **red with blue lower; blue, white, an gold winged design; 5-pack**.....$2 – 3

22. turquoise with black lower, "Animal Rescue," 2000 international Rescue series ....$2 – 3

23. white, "Giant," ASAP promotional ....$80 – 120

24. white, "Linux Solutions," ASAP promotional.....................$80 – 120

25. white, "Microsoft," ASAP promotional.....................$80 – 120

26. white, "National Ski Patrol" ......$9 – 12

27. white, "Quadtrak" ....$4 – 5

28. white, "Rescue EMT," 5-pack .....$2 – 3

29. white, "Unix User Conference San Jose ASAP promotional ....$80 – 120

30. white with black lower, no markings ASAP promotional blank........$30 – 40

31. **white with blue lower, "Water Work City Division" logo, teal wave design 1999 At Your Service series** ..$2 – 3

2. white with blue lower, black and orange design, polar bear logo, Launcher 5-pack.......................................$2 – 3

3. white with dark blue lower, "Rescue EMT," "Dial 911," orange and blue stripes, 2000 City Streets 5-pack......................................$2 – 3
4. white with orange lower, blue and red design, Launcher 5-pack ....$2 – 3

5. white with red lower, red flames, gold and black star, "Chief" on sides, 2003 Hero City 5-pack #7 .....$2 – 3
6. white, "AT&T Network Management Services," ASAP promotional .....$80 – 120
7. white, "V8 Splash," ASAP promotional ....$120 – 160
8. yellow, "Forest Ranger County Park".$8 – 10
9. yellow, "BP Chief," green and red stripes, the Netherlands issue ....$10 – 12
10. yellow, "Mr. Fixer" ....$2 – 3

Jeep CJ5, Standard, 2³⁄₈", #72, 1966

1. yellow with red interior, black plastic tires on plastic wheel hubs, 1966 ....$16 – 20
2. yellow with white interior, black plastic tires on plastic wheel hubs, prototype ....$1,200 – 1,600
3. yellow, Superfast wheels, 1970..$35 – 45

Jeep CJ6, 2¹⁵⁄₁₆", #53, 1977

1. red with tan canopy, orange-yellow interior, metallic gray base ....$5 – 6
2. red with tan canopy, orange-yellow interior, unpainted base ....$5 – 6
3. red with tan canopy, black interior, unpainted base ....$7 – 8
4. yellow with brown canopy, black interior, black base ....$6 – 7

3. red with tan canopy, orange-yellow interior, unpainted base, black hubs..................................$6 – 7
6. green with tan canopy, orange-yellow interior, unpainted base ....$7 – 8
7. green with tan canopy, orange-yellow interior, metallic gray base ....$7 – 8
8. green with tan canopy, black interior, metallic gray base ....$5 – 6

Jeep Eagle 4x4 (see Jeep 4x4)

Jeep Gladiator Pickup Truck, 2⁵⁄₈", #71, 1964
1. red with green interior ....$40 – 50

2. red with white interior.......$20 – 25

Jeep Golden Eagle Off-Road Jeep (see Jeep 4x4)

Jeep Grand Cherokee, with river raft on roof, 3", #65, 2000; #22, 2001; #48, 2002; #45, 2000, international
1. red, "Camp Jeep 2000," no roof raft, black stripes and design, 5-pack..$2 – 3
2. red, "Metro Alarm," yellow band, no roof raft, 5-pack ....$2 – 3

3. gradient red, "Hospitality," "Coca-Cola," yellow interior, rubber tires on chrome rims, Matchbox Collectibles Coca-Cola Collection ....$5 – 6

4. dark blue with yellow raft, "Action Canyon," 2001 Sun Chasers series..................................$2 – 3

5. purple with river rafting graphics, yellow raft, 2003 Hero City ...$2 – 3

6. metallic silver with red raft, "Grand Cherokee," 2000 Great Outdoors series, 5-spoke wheels..........$2 – 3
7. metallic silver with red raft, "Grand Cherokee," "Matchbox 2000," 2000 Great Outdoors series, 5-spoke wheels ....$3 – 4
8. metallic silver with red raft, "Grand Cherokee," 2000 Great Outdoors series, 10-spoke wheels........$12 – 16

Jeep Grand Cherokee, 2000 Feature Cars, with opening features, designed to replace Premiere Collection
1. red, "FDMB," "EMT," red, K B Toys exclusive ....$9 – 12
2. maroon ....$9 – 12
3. metallic gray, "FDMB," "EMT," K B Toys exclusive ....$9 – 12

Jeep Hot Rod, 2⁵⁄₁₆", #2, 1971
1. fuchsia with green base ....$20 – 25
2. red with green base ....$20 – 25
3. red with white base ....$15 – 25
4. light olive ....$10 – 15
5. dark olive ....$70 – 80

JEEP HOT ROD

6.   pink with green base.............$15 – 20

7.   pink with white base ....$15 – 20

Jeep Laredo (see Jeep 4x4)

Jeep Liberty

1.   metallic gold with black plastic base, monkey and wrench, 2003 Hero City 5-pack #11 ....$2 – 3

Jeep Off-Road 4x4, with black roll cage and winch, white antenna, 2⅞", #37, 1984 – 1997; #52, 1998; #25, 1994, international; #57, 1998, Germany

1.   metallic red, black base, Germany issue......................................$5 – 6

2.   metallic red, gray base, 1996 Off-Road 5-pack ....$2 – 3

3.   pink, "Cool Mud" ....$4 – 5

4.   fluorescent orange, "Cool Mud," 1997....................................$2 – 3

6.   yellow with blue roll cage, blue and red circle design, 5-pack.................$4 – 5

5.   yellow with red flames, 1998 Rugged Riders 5-pack...........$2 – 3

7.   yellow with blue roll cage, "Wilderness Tours," Wilderness Tours 5-pack...................................$2 – 3

8.   lime green with green roll cage, black antenna, "Jeep" and mud design, 5-pack ....$2 – 3

9.   blue with white splash design, 1998 Rough 'N Tough series...........$2 – 3

10.   pale blue, "Cool Mud"............$4 – 5

11.   black with red, orange and yellow design....................................$3 – 4

12.   metallic gray with purple and pink flames, Action System ....$2 – 3

13.   metallic blue with orange flames, 1997 Rugged Riders 5-pack...$2 – 3

14.   beige with green stripes, Action System/Action Pack ....$2 – 3

15.   white with blue, red and orange design ....$2 – 3

16.   metallic gold, 1997 75 Challenge series ....$12 – 16

Jeep, U.S. Mail (see U.S. Mail Jeep)

Jeep Willys, #71, 2003

1.   metallic light blue, 2003 Car Shop series ....$2 – 3

Jeep Wrangler 1998, #68, 1999; #9, 2000; #25, 2001; #63, 1999, international

1.   yellow, "Coca-Cola," red interior and roll cage, black base, Premiere Collection ....$5 – 6

2. yellow, "Coca-Cola," "www.cocalastores.com," red interior and roll cage, black base, Premiere Collection .... $60 – 80

3. **metallic orange, "Tours"; butter-scotch roll cage, base and roof rack with gear, green interior, 2001 Sun Chasers series ....$2 – 3**
4. metallic orange, "Matchbox New York Toy Fair 2000," "Matchbox 2000" ..$50 – 75
5. green, "Forest Ranger," black roll cage and base, 1999 Ranger Patrol international series ....$3 – 4
6. green with yellow and white accents, black roll cage and base, 1999 Ranger Patrol US series ....$2 – 3
7. green, "Jeep," "Matchbox," mud spatter, gray interior, black roll cage and base, Pleasant Books issue ....$4 – 5

8. **blue, "10-17MB," octopus graphics, metallic gray roll cage and base, no roof rack or gear, 2000 Ocean Explorers series....................$2 – 3**
9. blue, "10-17MB," "Matchbox 2000," octopus graphics, metallic gray roll cage and base, no roof rack or gear, 2000 Ocean Explorers series ....$3 – 4
10. metallic blue, metallic gray roll cage, interior and base, no roof rack or gear, 2000 Ocean Explorers series ....$2 – 3

11. **metallic blue with fishing pole graphics, bright red interior; phosphorescent roll cage, roof rack, and gear, 2003 Camp Fun 3-pack..................$2 – 3**

12. beige, "Black Star Ranch" and mud spatter, black roll cage and base, 5-pack...................................$2 – 3
13. metallic gray, "Jeep" and mud spatter, gray interior, black roll cage and base, 5-pack...................................$2 – 3
14. white, "Base 2000," red roll cage and interior, black base, Launcher 5-pack...................................$2 – 3

Jiminy Cricket's Old Timer, WD – 8, 1979
1. Hong Kong casting ....$35 – 45
2. Macau casting ....$60 – 80

John Deere Tractor, 2⅛", #50, 1964
1. gray plastic tires ....$25 – 30
2. black plastic tires ....$20 – 25

John Deere Trailer with three barrels, 2⅝", #51, 1964
1. gray plastic tires ....$25 – 30
2. black plastic tires ....$20 – 25

Jumbo Crane (see Taylor Jumbo Crane)

Jumbo Jet Motorcycle, 2¾", #71, 1973
1. dark blue, red elephant's head...................................$16 – 24

K

Karrier Bantam 2-Ton Coca-Cola Lorry, 2¼", #37, 1957
1. no base, uneven caseload ...$75 – 100
2. no base, even caseload.........$60 – 75
3. black base, even caseload, gray plastic wheels, 1960......................$50 – 60
4. black base, even caseload, silver plastic wheels............................$125 – 150
5. black base, even caseload, black plastic wheels...............................$50 – 60

Karrier Refuse Truck, 2⅜", #38, 1957
1. grayish brown with metal wheels ....$100 – 125
2. dark gray with metal wheels ..$30 – 40
3. dark gray with gray plastic wheels..................................$30 – 40
4. silver with gray plastic wheels ....$40 – 50

Kennel Truck (see Ford Kennel Truck)

Kenworth COE Aerodyne, 2¾", #45, 1982 (other variations exist as part of Convoy series)
1. white with brown and blue stripes, England cast ....$4 – 5
2. white with brown and blue stripes, Macau cast............................$3 – 4
3. metallic silver with purple and orange ....$3 – 4
4. white with "Chef Boyardee" labels, US on-package premium ....$40 – 50
5. red with yellow, orange, and white stripes ....$2 – 3

Kenworth Conventional Aerodyne, 2¾", #41, 1982 (other versions exist as part of Convoy and White Rose Race Transporter series)
1. red with black and white flared stripes, Lesney England cast ....$4 – 5
2. red with black and white straight stripes, Lesney England cast......$4 – 5
3. red with black and white straight stripes, Matchbox International England cast ....$4 – 5
4. red with black and white curved stripes, Matchbox International England cast.............................$4 – 5
5. blue, Macau cast ....$5 – 6
6. black with orange, yellow, and white stripes, Macau cast ....$5 – 6
7. metallic gray with red and blue stripes, Macau cast............................$4 – 5

Kenworth T-2000, #13, 1998 – 1999
1. metallic red, chrome interior and base, rubber tires on chrome rims, 1998 First Editions ....$6 – 9
2. unpainted, chrome interior and base, rubber tires on chrome rims, 1998 First Editions ....$6 – 9

3. **bright blue, metallic gray interior and base, "Eagle Express," stripes, 1999 Highway Haulers series $2 – 3**
4. bright blue, metallic gray interior and base, "Express," stripes, 1999 Highway Haulers series ....$2 – 3
5. dark gray, chrome interior and base, rubber tires on chrome rims, "Matchbox Toy Show 2000" ....$7 – 9

King Tow, #11, 2001; #1, 2002; #17 Tow Truck, 2003

1. **white, blue boom, "Police," 2001 On Patrol 5-pack ....$2 – 3**
2. black with gray boom, chrome plastic base, "Auto Max Crash 00-207-600," 2001 Highway Heroes series ..$2 – 3
3. black with black boom, chrome plastic base, "Matchbox Mattel Toy Fair 2001"................................$30 – 40

4. **metallic blue with red boom, chrome plastic base, "All-Star Towing," 2002 Hometown Heroes series ....$2 – 3**

5. **red with bright blue boom, yellow plastic base, monkey and wrench design, 2003 Hero City 5-pack #11 ....$2 – 3**

6. **metallic gray with red boom, red plastic base, snarling dog design, 2003 Public Works series .....$2 – 3**

Ladder Fire Truck (see Extending Ladder Fire Engine)

Lady Bug, Roman numeral VI, 1978 (variation of #31 Volks Dragon, 1971, and #15 Hi Ho Silver! 1971)
1. red, Roman Numeral Limited Edition ....$15 – 20

---

2. **black, Roman Numeral Limited Edition ....$9 – 12**

Laing Dumper (see Dumper, Muir Hill)

Lamborghini Countach, with opening rear cowl, 2⁷⁄₈", #27, 1973
1. yellow with chrome interior, purple windows, "3"............................$12 – 16
2. yellow with chrome interior, red windows, "3"............................$12 – 16

3. **yellow with chrome interior, amber windows, "3"....................$12 – 16**
4. dark green with light gray interior, blue-green windows, "Shell" labels, UK issue..............................$600 – 800
5. red with chrome interior, amber windows, "3"............................$12 – 16
6. red with chrome interior, red windows, "3".....................................$12 – 16
7. red with chrome interior, amber windows, "8," yellow and blue design ....$9 – 12
8. red with chrome interior, blue-green windows, "8," yellow and blue design.$9 – 12
9. red with chrome interior, red windows, "8," yellow and blue design ......$9 – 12
10. red with gray interior, blue-green windows, "8," yellow and blue design.........$9 – 12
11. red with gray interior, blue-green windows, "8," green and blue design.........$9 – 12
12. red with gray interior, green windows, "8," green and blue design ......$9 – 12
13. red with gray interior, green windows, "8," yellow and blue design ......$9 – 12
14. red with gray interior, tinted windows, "8," yellow and blue design ......$9 – 12
15. red with gray interior, tinted windows, no design, UK issue..........$160 – 240
16. red with tan interior, blue-green windows, "8," yellow and blue design ....$9 – 12
17. red with tan interior, clear windows, "8," yellow and blue design ......$9 – 12
18. red with tan interior, green windows, "8," yellow and blue design ......$9 – 12
19. red with tan interior, purple windows, "8," yellow and blue design ......$9 – 12
20. red with white interior, blue-green windows, "8," yellow and blue design..........$9 – 12
21. red with white interior, clear windows, "8," yellow and blue design ......$9 – 12
22. red with yellow interior, blue-green windows, "8," yellow and blue design ....$9 – 12
23. red with yellow interior, tinted windows, "8," yellow and blue design ......$9 – 12

Lamborghini Countach LP500S, no opening features, 3", #67, 1985 – 1997; #60, 1998; #16, 1999; #24, 2000; #11, 1985 – 1997, international; #19, 2000, international

---

1. red, "Countach," "Lamborghini," clear windows, gold wheels, Thailand cast...$3 – 4
2. red, "Countach," clear windows, red metal base, Thailand cast.........$2 – 3
3. red, "Countach," clear windows, red plastic base base, 5-spoke concave wheels, Thailand cast ....$2 – 3

4. **red, "Countach," clear windows, red plastic base base, 6-spoke wheels, Thailand cast........................$4 – 5**
5. red, "Countach," clear windows, bar code base, Thailand cast, Intercom City....................................$40 – 50
6. red, "Countach," clear windows, China cast ....$2 – 3
7. red, "Countach," detailed trim, chrome windows, rubber tires on gray rims, China cast, World Class............$6 – 8

8. **red with white "lamborghini" and bull logo, black interior, 1996 Super Cars 5-pack.........................$2 – 3**

9. **red, detailed trim, rubber tires on chrome rims, Premiere Collection ....$5 – 6**
10. red, detailed trim, rubber tires on chrome rims, Thailand cast, Ultra Class..................................$9 – 12
11. red, Lamborghini logo on hood, silver wheels, Macau cast ....$3 – 4
12. red, Lamborghini logo on hood, gold wheels, Macau cast ....$9 – 12
13. red with green "15" and "BP," Macau cast, the Netherlands issue.....$9 – 12

4. red chrome with purple, white and yellow design, Thailand cast, 1997 Sleek Riders 5-pack..............$2 – 3

5. metallic red with white "lamborghini" and bull logo on sides, 1995, Thailand cast ....$2 – 3
6. metallic light red, "Lamborghini," "Bloomberg," Thailand cast, ASAP promotional ....$120 – 160
7. orange, detailed trim, rubber tires on chrome rims, Thailand cast, Gold Coin Collection...........................$16 – 24
8. yellow, "10 Tiger Racing Team," Macau cast, Hong Kong issue............$9 – 12

9. yellow, "Lamborghini" in script, 2000 Italian Stars series ......$2 – 3
0. yellow, "Lamborghini" in script, "Matchbox 2000," 2000 Italian Stars series ....$3 – 4
1. yellow, "Lamborghini" and "Countach," Macau cast............................$3 – 4
2. yellow, "LP500," chrome windows, rubber tires on gray rims, Macau cast, World Class ....$6 – 8
3. fluorescent yellow and metallic blue with blue design on sides and hood, pink interior, Thailand cast, 1994.....$2 – 3
4. fluorescent yellow and metallic blue with blue design on sides only, pink interior, Thailand cast, Aquafresh on-package premium................................$5 – 6
5. fluorescent green, Thailand cast, Show Stoppers................................$3 – 4
6. dark green, "Lamborghini," Thailand cast, 1998 Super Cars series ...$2 – 3

7. metallic light blue, "Lamborghini" in script, China cast, 1999 Top Class series ....$2 – 3
8. metallic blue with pink windows, Thailand cast, 5-pack ....$5 – 6
9. metallic purple, detailed trim, rubber tires on chrome rims, Thailand cast, Premiere Collection #10...........$4 – 5

30. black, "5" and stripes, silver wheels, Macau cast............................$3 – 4
31. black, "5" and stripes, gold wheels, Macau cast............................$4 – 5
32. black, "LP500" and stripes, New Superfast Wheels, Macau cast......$12 – 16
33. black with white "Lamborghini" and bull on sides, Thailand cast, 1997 ...$2 – 3
34. pearl ivory, "Countach" and logo, Thailand cast, Triple Heat ....$4 – 5
35. pearl silver, "LP500S" and stripes, Macau cast, Laser wheels.........$4 – 5
36. metallic silver with lavender, blue and white design, Thailand cast, Matchcaps..$4 – 5
37. metallic gray, "Countach," detailed trim, Thailand cast, Collector's Choice, White Rose Collectibles......................$3 – 4

38. white, "lamborghini" and bull logo, red windows, 1997 Super Cars 5-pack ....$2 – 3
39. white, "LP500S" and stripes, New Superfast Wheels, Macau cast ..$4 – 5
40. white, detailed trim, rubber tires on chrome rims, international Premiere Collection #2...........................$4 – 5
41. white with no markings, China cast, clear windows, silver wheels, Graffic Traffic ....$12 – 16
42. white with no markings, Thailand cast, pink windows, gold wheels, Graffic Traffic.................................$3 – 4
43. chrome with no markings, Macau cast, custom promotional ....$16 – 24
44. metallic gold, Thailand cast, 1997 75 Challenge series ....$12 – 16

Lamborghini Diablo, 3",#22, 1992; #49, 1992, international; #17, 2000, international
1. black with black interior, chrome windows, rubber tires on gray rims, World Class series ....$3 – 4
2. black with red interior, clear windows, "Lamborghini," international issue ....$2 – 3

3. blue with brown interior, clear windows, white "Diablo," white and black design, 1997 ....$2 – 3
4. blue with gray and blue interior, rubber tires on chrome rims, Premiere Collection Select Class series #2........$4 – 5
5. bright blue with gray interior, 2000 Italian Stars series ....$2 – 3
6. bright blue with gray interior, "Matchbox 2000," 2000 Italian Stars series..$3 – 4
7. metallic blue with pink and white accents, 1994 ....$2 – 3
8. metallic blue with white and black accents, "Diablo," 1997............$2 – 3

9. metallic blue to black gradient with orange interior, clear windows, orange and white flash design $2 – 3
10. metallic turquoise with black and gray interior, clear windows, rubber tires on chrome rims, Japan Premiere Collection ....$4 – 5
11. gold with gray and black interior, clear windows, rubber tires on chrome rims, Premiere Collection series 19....$4 – 5
12. metallic gold with black interior, clear windows, 1997 75 Challenge series ....$6 – 12
13. metallic gray with blue and black interior, clear windows, rubber tires on chrome rims, Premiere Collection World Class series 6...............$4 – 5
14. fluorescent pink with black interior, clear windows, black spots, 5-pack .....$2 – 3
15. metallic pinkish purple with blue and black interior, clear windows, rubber tires on chrome rims, Premiere Collection World Class series 3..........$4 – 5

16. dark purple with orange interior, clear windows, white spots, 5-pack...$2 – 3
17. dark purple with gray interior, clear windows.....................................$4 – 5
18. metallic purple with black and gray interior, clear windows, rubber tires on chrome rims, Premiere Collection Select Class series 5................$4 – 5
19. red with black interior, chrome windows, rubber tires on gray rims, World Class....................................$6 – 8
20. red with black interior, clear windows, "Diablo," Thailand cast, UK issue.....$60 – 80
21. red with black and red interior, rubber tires on chrome rims, Premiere Collection Select Class series 4..........$4 – 5
22. red with fluorescent yellow interior, black spots, 1996 ....$4 – 5
23. silver with white interior, amber windows, orange and yellow flames .$4 – 5

24. white with blue and gray interior, clear windows, rubber tires on chrome rims, Gold Coin Collection ....$16 – 24

25. **yellow with black interior, clear windows, "Diablo," silver chrome hubs, 1992 ....$2 – 3**

26. yellow with black interior, clear windows, "Diablo," gold chrome hubs, 1992......................................$3 – 4

27. yellow with gray and black interior, clear windows, rubber tires on gray rims, Australia Premiere Collection series 1.$4 – 5

28. yellow chrome with black interior, clear windows; orange, white, and pink design; 5-pack.........................$2 – 3

29. **fluorescent yellow with bright pink interior, black spots, clear windows, 1995 ....$2 – 3**

30. fluorescent yellow with black interior, clear windows, Show Stoppers...$4 – 5

Lamborghini Marzal, with Superfast wheels, 2³⁄₄", #20, 1969; BR 27 – 28, 1985

1. **metallic red ....$16 – 24**
2. metallic red with labels, gift set.$20 – 25
3. salmon ....$16 – 24
4. salmon with labels, gift set ....$20 – 25
5. yellow...................................$40 – 50
6. fluorescent pink ....$12 – 16
7. fluorescent pink ....$16 – 24
8. green, "8," England cast, Super GTs BR 27 – 28, 1985 ....$4 – 6
9. green, "16," England cast, Super GTs BR 27 – 28, 1985 ....$12 – 15
10. blue, England cast, Super GTs BR 27 – 28, 1985...........................$8 – 10
11. cream, England cast, Super GTs BR 27 – 28, 1985 ....$4 – 6
12. white, England cast, Super GTs BR 27 – 28, 1985 ....$12 – 15
13. cream, China cast, Super GTs BR 27 – 28, 1985 ....$8 – 10

14. yellow, China cast, Super GT's BR 27 – 28, 1985.............................$3 – 5
15. green, China cast, Super GT's BR 27 – 28, 1985.............................$8 – 10
16. red, China cast, Super GT's BR 27 – 28, 1985.............................$3 – 5

Lamborghini Miura, 2³⁄₄", #33, 1969
1. yellow with ivory interior, black plastic wheels on chrome hubs ....$60 – 75
2. yellow with red interior, black plastic wheels on chrome hubs ....$6 – 9
3. metallic gold with ivory interior, black plastic wheels on chrome hubs .....$60 – 75
4. yellow, red interior, Superfast wheels, 1970..............................$80 – 100
5. metallic dark orange, red interior, Superfast wheels, 1970 ....$30 – 45
6. metallic light orange, red interior, Superfast wheels, 1970 ....$20 – 25
7. metallic gold, red interior, Superfast wheels, 1970.....................$20 – 25
8. metallic gold, ivory interior, Superfast wheels, 1970.....................$16 – 24

Lambretta TV175 Scooter and Sidecar, 2", #36, 1961
1. metallic green, black wheels ...$60 – 75

Land Rover, with driver, 1³⁄₄", #12, 1955
1. olive green, metal wheels ......$40 – 50

Land Rover, without driver, no roof, olive green, 2¹⁄₄", #12, 1959
1. gray plastic wheels ....$85 – 100
2. black plastic wheels..............$25 – 30

Land Rover Discovery, #67, 2001; #50, 2003
1. 2001 Storm Watch series........$2 – 3
2. green camouflage, 2002 Matchbox Across America 50th Birthday Series #14 Vermont — Northeastern Collection.........................$4 – 6
3. metallic bronze with red windows, 2003 Forest Rescue series................$2 – 3

Land Rover Freelander, #66, 1999; #64, 2000; #9, 2001; #61, 1999, international; #44, 2000, international

1. **yellow with metallic gray fenders; red, maroon, silver, and white accents; 2003 Hero City 5-pack #1......$2 – 3**
2. metallic pale green with green fenders, "Canyon Base," 5-pack..............$2 – 3
3. metallic blue with blue fenders, "Canyon Park," green band and door crest, 2000 Great Outdoors series .....$2 – 3

4. **metallic blue with blue fenders "Canyon Park," "Matchbox 2000," green band and door crest, 2000 Great Outdoors series, 5-spoke wheels ....$3 – 4**
5. metallic blue with blue fenders, "Canyon Park," "Matchbox 2000," green band and door crest, 2000 Great Outdoors series, 5-spoke concave wheels .$6 – 8

6. **bright blue with bright orange fenders, "Powder," "Turbo," unpainted metal base, 2001 Team Tundra series ....$2 – 3**
7. metallic gray with dark gray fenders, "Canyon Park," green band and door crest, 1999 Ranger Patrol international series....................................$2 – 3
8. metallic gray with dark gray fenders, "Canyon Park," "Ranger," green band and door crest, 1999 Ranger Patrol US series, larger 5-spoke concave wheels...................................$2 – 3
9. metallic gray with dark gray fenders, "Canyon Park," "Ranger," green band and door crest, 1999 Ranger Patrol US series, smaller 5-spoke concave wheels ....$6 – 8

Land Rover Fire Truck, 2⁷⁄₈", #57, 1966
1. "Kent Fire Brigade," red, gray plastic wheels, 1966..................$325 – 475
2. "Kent Fire Brigade," red, black plastic wheels, 1966.......................$9 – 12
3. "Kent Fire Brigade," red, Superfast wheels, 1970.....................$50 – 60

Land Rover Ninety, 2¹⁄₂", #35, 1990, US; #16, international, 1990; #53, 1998, international; #41, 1998, Germany

1. red with white roof, "Red Valley Camp," 1997 Land Sea & Air 5-pack .....$2 – 3
2. red with white roof, "County," blue and gray stripes....................$2 – 3
3. red with white roof, "Red Arrows," "Royal Air Force," Motor City.....$4 – 5

4. orange with black roof, "Safari Park," black tiger stripes, 1993 Off-Road 5-pack ....$2 – 3
5. yellow with black roof, "Canyon," crest and dashes design ....$3 – 4
6. yellow with white roof, "Park Ranger" ....$2 – 3
7. yellow with black roof, "Mountain Trails," 5-pack.............................$2 – 3

8. green with white roof, yellow and orange stripes, Motor City ....$2 – 3
9. dark green with black roof, "0321" and tree design, Germany issue ....$4 – 5
10. blue with white roof, yellow and orange stripes, Motor City ....$3 – 4
11. dark blue with white roof, "Royal Navy" ....$3 – 4
12. black with gray roof, gray and yellow camouflage, Commando series ..$5 – 6
13. light gray and navy blue with light gray roof, red stripes ....$4 – 5
14. white with black roof, "Land Rover," 1998 international Rough and Tough series...............................$2 – 3
15. white with black roof, "Metropolitan Police," stripes, UK issue ....$3 – 4
16. white with blue roof, "Alitalia" .....$4 – 5
17. white with blue roof, "KLM".......$4 – 5
18. white with blue roof, "SAS" ....$4 – 5
19. white with green roof, "Garden Festival Wales," Wales issue ....$7 – 8
20. white with white roof, "Bacardi Rum," on-package premium ....$30 – 40
21. white with white roof, "Circus Circus," Motor City............................$3 – 4
22. white with white roof, "County," black and red stripes ....$2 – 3

23. white with white roof, "Rescue Police," checkerboard pattern, Emergency series....................................$2 – 3
24. white with white roof, "Rijkspolitie," "55," the Netherlands issue.......$4 – 5
25. white with white roof, black and red stripes, "Country"....................$2 – 4
26. white with white roof, bright pink, bright yellow and blue splash design.....$4 – 5
27. white with white roof, no markings, Graffic Traffic ....$12 – 16

Land Rover Safari (see Safari Land Rover)

Leyland Articulated Tanker, 3", #14, 1982, international
1. red with white tank, "Elf" labels...$3 – 5
2. yellow with white tank, "Shell," Japan issue....................................$9 – 12
3. red with white tank, Shell" .....$65 – 90
4. black with black tank, "Gas," Commando series...................................$5 – 6

Leyland Articulated Truck, 3", #30, 1982

1. blue cab, metallic gray trailer, no markings..............................$3 – 4
2. blue cab, metallic gray trailer, "International"....................................$5 – 7
3. red cab, metallic gray trailer, no markings ....$8 – 10
4. red cab, yellow trailer, "International"...........................$6 – 8
5. blue cab, yellow trailer, "International" ....$6 – 8
6. bright blue cab, yellow trailer, "International"...........................$4 – 5
7. bright blue cab, bright blue trailer, "Paul's," UK issue.................$30 – 40

Leyland Petrol Tanker, 3", #32, 1968
1. green with white tank, "BP" labels, silver grille, black plastic wheels ....$6 – 9
2. green with white tank, "BP" labels, white grille, black plastic wheels ....$9 – 12
3. dark blue with white tank, "Aral" labels, silver grille, black plastic wheels ....$40 – 50
4. blue with white tank, "Aral," Superfast wheels...............................$60 – 80

5. green cab with white tank, chrome base, "BP," Superfast wheels ....$16 – 24
6. green cab with white tank, gray base, "BP," Superfast wheels ....$20 – 25
7. red cab with white tank, "N. A. M. C.," "The Miniature Vehicle," 1972 .....$500 – 750
8. purple cab with metallic gray tank, "National Association of Matchbox Collectors," 1972 ....$200 – 250
9. purple cab, metallic gray tank, chrome base, no labels, 1994 .....$150 – 200

Leyland Pipe Truck, with six pipes, 2⁷/₈", #10, 1966

1. red with chrome grille and base, gray pipes, black plastic wheels ..$40 – 50
2. red with white grille and base, gray pipes, black plastic wheels.....$20 – 30
3. red with chrome grille and base, gray pipes, Superfast wheels ....$40 – 50
4. orange with chrome grille and base, yellow pipes, Superfast wheels...$20 – 30
5. orange with gray grille and base, gray pipes, Superfast wheels ....$20 – 30
6. orange with gray grille and base, yellow pipes, Superfast wheels ....$20 – 30

Leyland Royal Tiger Coach, metallic blue, 3", #40, 1961
1. gray wheels.........................$35 – 45
2. silver wheels ....$25 – 35

3. black wheels....................$20 – 30

Leyland Site Office Truck, 2¹/₂", #60, 1966

1. blue, yellow plastic building with green roof, black plastic wheels, 1966 ....$15 – 20

2. blue, yellow plastic building with green roof, Superfast wheels, 1970..$30 – 40

Leyland Tanker, #32 (see Leyland Petrol Tanker)

Leyland Tanker, with separate tank trailer (European model), 3⅛", #14, 1982
1. red cab with "ELF" and red stripe ..$4 – 6
2. yellow cab with "Shell," white tank with yellow base ....$6 – 8
3. red cab with "Shell," white tank with red base ....$40 – 50
4. black cab tank, "GAS" ....$4 – 6

Leyland Titan London Bus (see London Bus, Leyland Titan)

Limousine, #66, 2002; #32, 2003

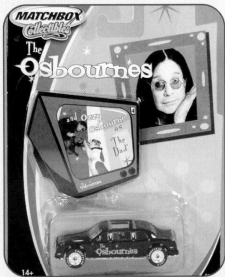

1. **black, 2002 Kids' Cars of the Year series ....$2 – 3**
2. metallic gray, "Matchbox VIP Shuttle," 2003 Airport series ....$2 – 3
3. metallic gray, "Matchbox VIP Shuttle," 2003 Hero City 10-pack #2 ......$2 – 3

4. **black, "The Osbournes," Ozzie Osbourne, 2003 Matchbox Collectibles the Osbournes series ....$4 – 6**
5. metallic red with silver Matchbox logo, 2003 Auto Carrier Launcher 5-pack ....$2 – 3

Lincoln Continental, 2¾", #31, 1964
1. metallic blue, black plastic wheels.................................$15 – 20
2. mint green, black plastic wheels .$6 – 10
3. metallic lime green, black plastic wheels............................$500 – 600
4. mint green, Superfast wheels, 1970......................$2,000 – 2,500
5. green-gold, Superfast wheels, 1970.................................$50 – 60

Lincoln Continental Mark V, 3", #28, 1979
1. red with white roof, tan interior ..$4 – 5
2. red with white roof, gray interior ..$5 – 6
3. red with white roof, brown interior ....$5 – 6

4. **red with white roof, light brown interior ....$6 – 7**

Lincoln Premiere, 1957

1. **pink with whitewall tires, Matchbox Collectibles, Barrett-Jackson collection, 2003 ....$4 – 6**

Lincoln Town Car, 3", #43, 1989; #24, 1990
1. metallic red, brown back half of roof ....$4 – 5

2. **metallic red ....$2 – 3**
3. yellow with blue wheels, Live 'N Learn/ Matchbox Preschool.............$12 – 16
4. black with chrome windows, whitewall rubber tires on gray rims, World Class....................................$7 – 9

5. **metallic dark gray, purple back half of roof, rubber tires on chrome rims, Ultra Class........................$9 – 12**

6. **white with metal base ....$2 – ?**
7. white with plastic base.............$2 – ?

8. **metallic silver with pink and yellow design, Dream Machines........$3 – ?**

Lockheed Martin X-33 Reusable Launch Vehicle (RLV), #36, 2000; #21, 2000, international

1. **white with black base, "Venture Star, "USA," "X-33 RLV" on base .....$2 – ?**
2. white with black base, "Venture Star, "USA," "X-33 RLV" on base, "Matchbox 2000".................................$3 – ?
3. white with black base, "Venture Star, "USA," "X-33 Lockheed" on base, 200? Space Mission 5-pack.............$2 – ?
4. white with black base, "Citrix MetaFrame XP, "X-33 Lockheed" on base, Colo Comp promotional ....$25 – 3?

London Bus, red, 2, #5, 1954
1. "Buy Matchbox Series," metal wheels made in England ....$60 – 7?
2. "Buy Matchbox Series," 1988 40t? Anniversary Gift Set replica, made ? China ....$8 – 1?
3. "Matchbox Originals," 1991 Matchbox Originals replica, made in China..$2 – ?

London Bus, 2¼", #5, 1957
1. metal wheels, "Buy Matchbox Series" ....$45 – 6?
2. gray plastic wheels, "Buy Matchbox Series" ....$65 – 8?

London Bus, red body, plastic wheels 2⁹⁄₁₆", #5, 1961
1. "Player's Please," gray wheels ....$100 – 12?
2. "Visco Static," gray wheels.....$35 – ?

"Drink Peardrax," gray wheels..................$150 – 175
"Drink Peardrax," black wheels..................$150 – 175
"Baron of Beef," gray wheels..................$175 – 200
"Baron of Beef," black wheels..................$175 – 200
"Visco Static," black wheels ...$30 – 40

London Bus (also see Daimler London Bus, Routemaster London Bus)

London Bus, 2³⁄₄", #5, 1965
"Longlife" decals..................$9 – 12
"Visco Static" decals or stickers .$9 – 12
"Baron of Beef"..............$180 – 200

London Bus, The Londoner, with solid door in left side center, small windows, 3", #17, 1972
red, "Swinging London" labels, black base ....$9 – 12
red, "Swinging London" labels, gray base ....$9 – 12
red, "Swinging London" labels, unpainted base with cast screw mounts .$15 – 20
gold plated, "Swinging London" labels, unpainted base with cast screw mounts..................$800 – 1200
silver plated, "Swinging London" labels, unpainted base with cast screw mounts..................$800 – 1200
red, "Preston Guild Merchant 1972"..................$175 – 225
red, "London Kensington Hilton"..................$175 – 225
red, "Typhoo Tea"............$300 – 350
red, "Impel 73"..........$60 – 80
red, "Berger Paints"..............$9 – 12
red, "ICP Interchemicals & Plastics"..................$800 – 1200
red, "Borregard Paper"...$800 – 1200
red, "Sellotape Selbstklebander"..................$800 – 1200
red, "Sellotape Packaging Systems"..................$175 – 225
red, "Sellotape Electrical Tapes"..................$800 – 1200
red, "Sellotape International Operations"..................$800 – 1200
red, "Chambourcy Yogurt"...$90 – 120
red, "Esso Extra Petrol"........$40 – 50
butterscotch and ivory, "Berger Paints"..................$175 – 225
butterscotch and ivory, "Impel 76"..................$90 – 120
red, "Selfridges"..................$65 – 75
red, "Aviemore Centre," "Santa Claus Land"..................$75 – 100
red, "Amcel"..................$180 – 240
red, 'Baron Of Beef'........$180 – 240
yellow and red, "Swinging London"..................$400 – 500
red, "AIM Building Fund 1976".$45 – 60
red with no labels..................$6 – 9
white and red, "Berger Paints"..................$400 – 500

29. white and blue, "Berger Paints"..................$200 – 250
30. yellow and blue, "Berger Paints"..................$600 – 800
31. metallic red, "Lufthansa"...$600 – 800
32. red, "Army & Navy".............$55 – 70
33. red, "Eduscho Kaffee".......$600 – 800
34. orange, "Jacob's Biscuit Makers"..................$35 – 50
35. red, "Jacob's Biscuit Makers"..$70 – 90
36. red, "Ilford Hp5 Film".......$400 – 500
37. red, "Museum Of London".....$60 – 90
38. red, "Silver Jubilee".........$200 – 250
39. metallic gray, "Silver Jubilee"..$12 – 16
40. metallic gray, "Berger Paints"..$80 – 120
41. blue, "Deutschlands Autopartner"..................$40 – 60
42. blue, "Matchbox 1953 – 1978"..................$40 – 60
43. orange, "Matchbox 1953 – 1978"..................$80 – 120
44. red, "Matchbox 1953 – 1978"..$7 – 10
45. red, "Busch Gardens"..........$50 – 70
46. red, "The Bisto Bus"............$10 – 15
47. red, "3rd A.I.M. Inc. Convention & Toy Show"..................$40 – 50
48. red, "Matchbox Collectors Club 1997," "Hershey 1997"..................$16 – 24

London Bus, Leyland Titan, with double doors on left side, large windows, 3", #17, 1982; #51, 1984; #28, 1990; #2, 2002
1. Red, "Berger Paints" labels....$12 – 15
2. red, "Laker Skytrain" labels......$9 – 12
3. white upper, light blue lower, "Matchbox No. 1," "Montepna".............$30 – 40
4. red, "Matchbox No. 1," "Montepna"..................$30 – 40
5. dark green, "Chesterfield Centenary" labels..................$12 – 16
6. red, "Matchbox London Bus," England cast..................$5 – 8
7. red, "Matchbox London Bus," Macau cast..................$2 – 4
8. red, "Nice To Meet You! Japan 1984," Japan issue..................$16 – 24
9. red, Japan writing on labels, Japan issue..................$16 – 24
10. red, "York Festival & Mystery Plays"..................$12 – 16
11. dark blue, "Nestle Milkybar"...$12 – 16
12. red, "Nestle Milkybar"..........$12 – 16
13. dark green, "Rowntree Fruit Gums"..................$12 – 16
14. red, "Rowntree Fruit Gums".....$8 – 10
15. dark blue, "Keddies No. 1 In Essex"..................$50 – 70
16. maroon, "Rapport"................$9 – 12
17. white upper, black lower, "Torvale Fisher Engineering Co."..................$9 – 12
18. white upper, orange lower, "W H Smith Travel"..................$12 – 16
19. red, "You'll [Love] New York"......$2 – 4
20. "Space For Youth 1985," "Staffordshire Police"..................$9 – 12
21. blue, "Cityrama"..................$9 – 12
22. red, no labels, England cast.......$4 – 6

23. red, no labels, China cast..........$6 – 8
24. red, "Nurenburg 1986," Macau cast..................$120 – 160
25. red, "First M.I.C.A. Convention," Macau cast..................$240 – 300
26. red, "First M.I.C.A. Convention," England cast..................$240 – 300
27. red, "First M.I.C.A. Convention," England cast..................$240 – 300
28. "M.I.C.A. Matchbox Intl Collectors Association"..................$9 – 12
29. red, "Around London Tour Bus," China cast..................$2 – 4
30. blue, "National Tramway Museum," China cast..................$9 – 12
31. white upper, red lower, "Midland Bus Transport Museum," China cast..................$9 – 12
32. red, "Band-Aid Plasters Playbus," China cast..................$9 – 12
33. blue, "National Girobank," China cast..................$9 – 12
34. red, "Matchbox — Niagara Falls," China cast..................$6 – 8
35. red, "Feria Del Juguete Valencia," "12 Febrero 1987"..................$180 – 240
36. beige upper, blue lower, "West Midlands Travel," China cast..................$9 – 12
37. white, "Denney — Happy 1000th Birthday, Dublin"..................$8 – 10
38. red, "123abc," "My First Matchbox — Nurenburg 1990"..................$12 – 16
39. red, "123abc," Matchbox Preschool/ Live 'N Learn..................$6 – 8
40. yellow, "It's The Real Thing — Coke," China cast..................$15 – 20
41. maroon, "Corning Glass Center," China cast..................$9 – 12
42. chrome, "Celebrating A Decade Of Matchbox Conventions"..................$30 – 45
43. red, "Markfield Project Support Appeal 92," China cast..................$16 – 24
44. red, "London Wide Tour Bus," China cast..................$2 – 4
45. white, no labels, China cast, Graffic Traffic..................$12 – 16

46. red, "Union Jack Tours," #2, 2002 Hometown Heroes series ....$2 – 3

47. red, "Takashimaya," Japan issue.............................$120 – 150
48. white with no markings, ASAP promotional blank.........................$20 – 25
49. white, "American International Recovery" on roof, ASAP promotional..$125 – 175
50. orange, "Fanta" labels on sides, "Enjoy Fanta" on roof, China issue..$175 – 225

51. red, scenery design, 2000 On Tour series ....$2 – 3
52. red, scenery design, "Matchbox 2000," 2000 On Tour series................$3 – 4
53. red, "Scansource & Symbol" on roof, ASAP promotional ....$75 – 125
54. red, "www.citrix.com/cdn" on sides, "Citrix Meta Frame for Unix Operating Systems" on roof, ASAP promotional.....$75 – 125
55. red, "www.mbxroad.com" on sides, "Matchbox Road Museum" on roof, Color Comp promotional........$16 – 24

London Taxi (see Austin FX4R London Taxi)

London Trolley Bus, red, 2⅝", #56, 1958
1. black rods, metal wheels...$180 – 200
2. red rods, metal wheels ....$35 – 45
3. red rods, gray plastic wheels .$25 – 40

Lotus Elise, #69, 2000, international
1. yellow with black interior, tinted windows, 2000 Power international series ....$3 – 4

2. metallic green with black metal base, 2003 Hero City 5-pack #12, US issue ....$5 – 6

Lotus Europa, Superfast wheels, 2⅞", #5, 1969; BR 9 – 10, 1985

1. metallic blue, does not say "Superfast" on base ....$80 – 100
2. metallic blue, says "Superfast" on base ....$12 – 16
3. metallic blue, "20" labels, gift set.....................................$16 – 24
4. metallic lavender, no labels....$12 – 16
5. metallic lavender, "20" labels, gift set.....................................$16 – 24
6. black, "JPS," Japan issue ......$20 – 25
7. black, no labels.....................$16 – 24
8. Bulgarian issue, various colors..$40 – 50
9. white, England cast, Super GT BR 9 – 10, 1985 ....$4 – 6
10. metallic blue, England cast, Super GT BR 9 – 10, 1985 ....$4 – 6
11. purple, China cast, Super GT BR 9 – 10, 1985 ....$3 – 5
12. white, China cast, Super GT BR 9 – 10, 1985 ....$8 – 10
13. blue, China cast, Super GT BR 9 – 10, 1985 ....$3 – 5

Lotus Racing Car, 2¾", #19, 1966
1. orange with black tires on yellow plastic hubs ....$25 – 30
2. green with black tires on yellow plastic hubs ....$15 – 20

3. purple with Superfast wheels, 1970.............................$40 – 50

Lotus Super Seven, 3", #60, 1971
1. orange with flames label........$16 – 24
2. yellow with flames label ....$60 – 80

3. yellow with checkerboard pattern and "60"..........................$20 – 30

Luna – C (see UFO)

LVTP7 Landing Craft, 2001 Feature Cars, with opening features, designed to replace Premiere Collection
1. beige with black painted treads..$9 – 12

Lyons Maid Ice Cream Truck (see Commer Ice Cream Canteen)

M

M1 A1 Abrams Tank (see Abrams M1 A1 Tank)

M1 Abrams Tank (see Abrams M1 A Tank)

M2 Bradley Tank (see Bradley M2 Fighti Vehicle)

M3 Army Halftrack Personnel Carrier (s Army M3 Halftrack Personnel Carrier)

M4 A3 Sherman Tank (see Sherman N A3 Tank)

Mack CH600 Aerodyne, 3", #8, 1990, U #39, 1990, international; other var tions in Convoy and White Rose series
1. white with black and red stripes ..$2 –
2. red and white, "Coke," chrome hub rubber tires............................$5 –

Mack Dump Truck, 2⅝", #28, 1968
1. orange with black plastic tires orange plastic hubs ....$9 – 1
1. metallic dull gold, Superfast whee 1970................................$24 – 3
2. dark olive green, Superfast wheels, Tv Pack ....$70 – 9

**3. light olive green, Superfast whee Two Pack ....$6 – **

Mack Floodlight Heavy Rescue Auxilia Power Truck, 3", #57, 1991 – 199 #21, 1998; #77, 1999; #45, 200 #42, 2002; #50, 1991, international

**1. "42 Metro," yellow with red ro black, red and white design, 20 Airport Alarm series ....$2 – **
2. "Acorn Hill Fire Dept.," red a white with white roof, rubber tir on chrome rims, Premiere Colle tion #7 ....$4 –
3. "American International Recover red with white roof, ASAP prom tional ....$120 – 18

"Action Metro Base," "33," safety green with blue roof, white and black design, "Action Metro" shield, 1999 Fire Rescue series.................$2 – 3

10. **"Emergency Power" in blue field, red with white roof, "77," white accents, blue shield on doors, 1998 Emergency Rescue 5-pack ....$2 – 3**
11. "Emergency Power 34," red with white roof, 5-pack ....$4 – 5
12. "Fire Rescue Unit 2," orange-red with white roof, "Action System," on-package premium...............................$8 – 10
13. "Fire Rescue Unit 2," fluorescent orange with white roof, black and white checkerboard design ....$2 – 3
14. "Floodlight Rescue Unit," metallic gold, 1997 75 Challenge series ....$12 – 16
15. "Floodlight Heavy Rescue," red with white roof, "Fire Rescue Unit 2," gift set ....$9 – 12
16. "Floodlight Heavy Rescue," fluorescent orange with white roof, "Fire Rescue Unit 2," blue and white checkerboard design ....$5 – 6

26. "Metro Alarm," white and green with black roof, "MA-RC1," 5-pack.....$2 – 3
27. "Reithoffer's," orange with white roof, White Rose Collectibles gift set ....$5 – 6
28. "Shrewsbury Fire Co.," red with white roof, White Rose Collectibles .$12 – 16
29. "Sugar Grove Fire Department" on left side only, red with white roof, ASAP promotional.......................$16 – 24
30. "Sugar Grove Fire Department 2000," red with white roof, ASAP promotional ....$20 – 25

"Bridge & Highway Dept," red with white roof, "57," "Give Us A Brake," black roadway design, red lettering, 1998 To The Rescue series....$2 – 3
"Bridge & Highway Dept," yellow with white roof, "57" ....$3 – 4

17. **"Floodlight Heavy Rescue," fluorescent orange with white roof, "Newfield Borough Fire Co.," "Fire Rescue Unit 2," 1995 ....$2 – 3**
18. "Floodlight Heavy Rescue," yellow with white roof, "Newfield Borough Fire Co.," shield on doors, 1995 ....$2 – 3
19. "Floodlight Rescue Unit," red with white roof, "Fire Rescue" ....$6 – 8
20. "Garage 33," red with white roof, "5 Alarm," Launcher 5-pack...........$2 – 3
21. "Garage 33," yellow with white roof, "5 Alarm," Launcher 5-pack...........$2 – 3
22. "Houston Fire Dept. 11," white and red with white roof, "Heavy Rescue," Premiere Collection ....$5 – 6
23. "Main Transit Fire Dept. Amherst NY," red with white roof, ASAP promotional ....$16 – 24

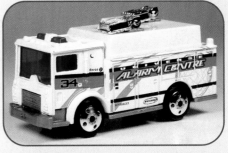

31. **"Universe Alarm Centre," white with white roof, red and black design, 2001 Rescue Squad series ....$2 – 3**
32. red with white roof, no markings, ASAP promotional blank.................$30 – 40
33. white with white roof, no markings, Graffic Traffic ....$12 – 16

Mack Junior Van 1937, #339, 1998, Matchbox Collectibles
1. "Arapahoe Amber Ale," dark green...................................$9 – 12
2. "Continental Aero," "Purple Plastic Inserts...," purple...................$9 – 12
3. "Dixie Jazz Beer," black...........$9 – 12
4. "Pony Express," yellow.............$9 – 12

Magirus-Deutz Six-Wheel Crane Truck, 2⅝", #30, 1961
1. tan with gray plastic wheels.$800 – 850
2. metallic silver with silver plastic wheels................................$40 – 50
3. metallic silver with gray plastic wheels................................$40 – 50

"Bridge & Highway Dept," white with white roof, "57," "Give Us A Brake," black roadway design, red lettering, 1996.............................$2 – 3
"Clearbrook Fire & Rescue," red with white roof ....$9 – 12
"Eagle Point Fire Rescue," metallic red and white with white roof, rubber tires on chrome rims, Premiere Collection #21...$4 – 5

24. **"Matchbox Fire Rescue," red with white roof, "Fire Dept.," white bands, 1997 Fire 5-pack ......$2 – 3**
25. **"Matchbox Fire Rescue," white with white roof, "Fire Dept.," red bands, 2000 Fire 5-pack ....$2 – 3**

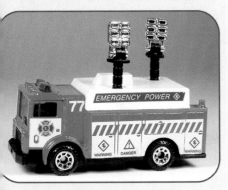

4. **metallic silver with black plastic wheels** ....**$30 – 40**

Maintenance Truck (see Chevrolet Highway Maintenance Truck)

Mark 10 Jaguar (see Jaguar Mark 10)

Marshall Horse Box Truck, red cab, brown horse box, 2", #35, 1957
1. metal wheels ....$35 – 45
2. gray plastic wheels ....$40 – 50
3. silver plastic wheels ....$80 – 100
4. black plastic wheels ....$125 – 150

Maserati 4CL T/1948 Racer, 2½", #52, 1958

1. **red with black plastic wheels.** **$50 – 70**
2. red with black plastic tires on spoked wheels ....$100 – 125

3. **yellow with black tires on spoked wheels** ....**$60 – 80**

Maserati Bora, 3", #32, 1972; BR 29 – 30, 1985 (similar casting: Sunburner)
1. metallic burgundy with unpainted metal base, "8" label ....$60 – 80

2. **metallic burgundy with green base, "8" label** ....**$9 – 12**
3. beige, China cast, Super GTs BR 29 – 30, 1985 ....$3 – 5

4. **metallic gold with metallic gray base** ....**$16 – 24**

5. fluorescent lime, China cast, Neon Racer BR 29 – 30, 1985 ....$4 – 6
6. yellow, England cast, Super GTs BR 29 – 30, 1985.....................$5 – 10
7. yellow, China cast, Super GTs BR 29 – 30, 1985....................$8 – 10
8. powder blue, China cast, Super GTs BR 29 – 30, 1985 ....$3 – 5
9. light blue, England cast, Super GTs BR 29 – 30, 1985 ....$5 – 10
10. light blue, China cast, Super GTs BR 29 – 30, 1985 ....$8 – 10
11. dark blue, England cast, Super GTs BR 29 – 30, 1985 ....$6 – 10

Massey Harris Tractor, with fenders, 1⅝", #4, 1954
1. red, made in England............$60 – 75
2. red, from 40th Anniversary Gift Set, made in China, 1988 ....$8 – 10
3. green, Matchbox Originals, made in China, 1991 ....$3 – 4

Massey Harris Tractor, no fenders, 1⅝", #4, 1957
1. red ....$50 – 70

Matra Rancho, 2⅞", #37, 1982, international
1. turquoise, no markings, blue tailgate, turquoise base......................$9 – 12
2. light blue, no markings, blue tailgate, light blue base ....$9 – 12
3. blue, "Marine Rescue," blue tailgate, yellow base ....$4 – 5

4. **dark blue, "Surf Rescue," black tailgate, white base** ....**$5 – 6**
5. dark blue, "Surf Rescue," black tailgate, yellow base ....$5 – 6
6. dark blue, "Surf Rescue," blue tailgate, white base ....$5 – 6
7. dark blue, no markings, blue tailgate, black base, silver wheel hubs ...$8 – 10
8. dark blue, no markings, blue tailgate, black base, gold wheel hubs ..$16 – 24
9. dark blue, no markings, blue tailgate, dark blue base, silver wheel hubs ....$16 – 24
10. dark blue, no markings, blue tailgate, yellow base, silver wheel hubs ....$16 – 24
11. dark blue, no markings, yellow tailgate, yellow base, gold wheel hubs .$20 – 25
12. orange, "Surf 2," orange tailgate, black base ....$3 – 4
13. yellow, no markings, yellow tailgate, yellow base ....$7 – 9

14. **yellow, red stripes, yellow tai[l] gate, yellow base, silver whee[l] hubs** ....**$8 – 1[0]**
15. yellow, red stripes, yellow tailgate, ye[l] low base, gold wheel hubs .....$16 – 2[4]

16. **fluorescent yellow, "Marine Rescue,["] fluorescent yellow tailgate, yellow base** ....**$2 – [3]**
17. black, "Surf 2," orange tailgate, blac[k] base ....$3 – [4]
18. white, no markings, white tailgate, whit[e] base, Graffic Traffic (stickers and mark ers included with set)...........$12 – 1[6]

Maxi Taxi, 3", #72, 1973 (similar castings Ford Capri, Hot Rocker)
1. yellow, "M" on roof, Hong Kong cast....................................$8 – 1[0]
2. yellow, "M" on roof, Macau cast ..$4 – [5]
3. yellow, "I" on roof, Hong Kong cast....................................$3 – [4]
4. yellow, no markings, Hong Kong cast....................................$4 – [5]

Mazda IMSA, 3", #6, 1983, US; #7[ ] 1983, Europe
1. dark blue, red interior, white an[d] orange, Macau cast ....$3 – [4]
2. dark blue, red interior, white an[d] stripes, Manaus cast...........$40 – 5[0]

Mazda RX500, 3", #66, 1971
1. red with amber windows, chrom[e] interior, unpainted base, "77," Eng land cast.............................$9 – 1[2]
2. red with amber windows, chrom[e] interior, white base, "77," England cast....................................$9 – 1[2]
3. red with amber windows, tan interior white base, "77," England cast.$9 – 1[2]
4. red with purple windows, chrom[e] interior, white base, "77," England cast....................................$12 – 1[6]
5. red with purple windows, chrome interi or, white base, "Castrol" labels, England cast....................................$700 – 90[0]

red with purple windows, chrome interior, white base, England cast ..$20 – 30
red with purple windows, tan interior, white base, England cast.......$20 – 30
orange with amber windows, chrome interior, unpainted base, England cast ....$60 – 80
orange with purple windows, chrome interior, unpainted base, England cast ....$12 – 16
). orange with purple windows, chrome interior, white base, England cast ....$12 – 16

green with amber windows, chrome interior, pearl silver base, "66," Hong Kong cast ....$12 – 16

azda RX7, with no spoiler, #31, 1982
white with wide stripe on sides, ivory interior ....$4 – 5
white with thin stripe on sides, ivory interior ....$4 – 5
white with wide stripe on sides, tan interior ....$4 – 5
white with thin stripe on sides, tan interior ....$4 – 5
black with gold stripe on sides, tan interior ....$4 – 5

azda RX7, with spoiler, #31, 1983

black with gold stripe on sides, Macau cast ....**$3 – 4**

white with "7" and stripe accents, Macau cast ....**$3 – 4**
black with "RX7" and "MAZDA," Manaus cast, Brazil issue ....$40 – 50

azda RX7, #8, 1994; #54, 1994, international; #67, 1998; #41, 1998, international; #20, 1999

1. fluorescent orange, "Matchbox Get In The Fast Lane," "Toy Fair 1994"......$40 – 50
2. black, no markings, chrome windows, gray wheel hubs, rubber tires, World Class.....................................$3 – 4

3. **black with silver stripes, "Mazda," 1999**.............................**$2 – 3**
4. blue, rubber tires on chrome rims, Gold Collection...........................$16 – 24
5. red with black and yellow on roof and hood ....$2 – 3
6. red with black and yellow on hood.$3 – 4

7. **red with trim detail, rubber tires on chrome rims, Premiere Collection** ....**$4 – 5**
8. red, "Go Bombers! 1997," Australia issue.......................................$4 – 5
9. red, rubber tires on chrome rims, Premiere Collection ....$5 – 6
10. metallic bronze to black gradient, no, 1998....................................$2 – 3
11. metallic gold, no markings, 1997 75 Challenge series ....12 – 16

12. **metallic green to black gradient, no markings** ....**$2 – 3**

13. **metallic green, rubber tires on chrome rims, JC Penney Premiere Collection** ....**$4 – 5**
14. metallic silver with red blotch .....$4 – 5
15. yellow-orange with black and pink on hood and sides ....$2 – 3

16. yellow-orange with black and pink on sides only, Aquafresh promotional........$5 – 6
17. yellow-orange with black and pink on hood and sides, "Nationwise Auto Parts" on roof.....................$25 – 35
18. yellow, rubber tires on chrome rims, Premiere Collection ....$4 – 5
19. lavender chrome with yellow and blue, 5-pack...................................$2 – 3

20. **metallic orange to black gradient, no, 1998** ....**$2 – 3**

21. **metallic yellow to red gradient, no** ....**$2 – 3**

22. **purple chrome with yellow and orange, 5-pack**.....................**$2 – 3**

Mazda RX7 Savannah, no spoiler, #76, 1981; #2, 1981, Japan
1. yellow with stripe and "RX7," Japan cast, Japan issue.................$16 – 24
2. green with stripe and "RX7," Japan cast, Japan issue.................$16 – 24
3. light green, no markings, Hong Kong cast, Australia issue.............$16 – 24
4. blue, no markings, Hong Kong cast, Speedsticks, US issue...............$4 – 5
5. blue with black stripe, "RX7," Hong Kong cast, US issue ....$25 – 35
6. blue with red and white stripes, issued in US as Boulevard Blaster, Hong Kong cast ....$6 – 8

Mazda Savanna RX7 (see Mazda RX7 Savannah)

Mechanical Horse and Trailer, #10, 1955
1. red cab, gray trailer, metal wheels 2³⁄₈".....................................$60 – 75

Mechanical Horse and Trailer, red cab, tan trailer, 2^{15}/$_{16}$", 10 – B, 1958
1. metal wheels ....$45 – 60
2. gray plastic wheels ....$50 – 60

Mercedes (see Mercedes-Benz)

Mercedes-Benz Trac 1600 Turbo Farm Tractor, 2^3/$_4$", #73, 1990; #90, 1999; #46, 2000; #27, 1991, international; #5, 1999, international; #26, international
1. mustard yellow and brown, "Power," China cast, 2000 Farming series ....$2 – 3
2. mustard yellow and brown, "Power," "Matchbox 2000," China cast, 2000 Farming series ....$3 – 4
3. green, "FA2318," black interior, China cast, Germany issue ....$5 – 6
4. green, no markings, yellow interior, Thailand cast, Team Convoy Two Pack .$3 – 4
5. dark green, no markings, green interior, Thailand cast, 1999 Farming series ....$3 – 4
6. light green, no markings, green interior, Macau cast....................$2 – 3
7. light green, no markings, green interior, Thailand cast.................$2 – 3
8. light green, "MB Trac," green interior, Thailand cast ....$2 – 3

9. **blue and orange-red, "Chiefton Power," China cast, 1999 Farming series ....$2 – 3**
10. "Iowa," Matchbox Across America 50th Birthday Series #29 — Central Collection ....$4 – 5

Mercedes-Benz 220 SE, 2^3/$_4$", #53, 1963

1. **red with black plastic wheels ....$100 – 120**
2. maroon with gray plastic wheels................................$25 – 30
3. red with gray plastic wheels...$25 – 30
4. maroon with silver plastic wheels................................$30 – 35

5. maroon with black plastic wheels.................................$25 – 30

Mercedes-Benz 230 SL Convertible, 3", #27, 1966
1. ivory, regular wheels.................$6 – 8
2. white, regular wheels..............$8 – 10
3. ivory with red interior, Superfast wheels.................................$30 – 40
4. off-white with red interior, Superfast wheels..................................$30 – 40
5. yellow with red interior, Superfast wheels..................................$20 – 25
6. yellow with black interior, Superfast wheels..................................$16 – 24

Mercedes-Benz 280 GE G-Wagon, 3", #30, 1984; #40, 2000
1. army green with tan roof, "LS 2014," Commando series ....$5 – 6
2. beige with dark green roof, green stripes, Avon Light & Sound ......$5 – 6
3. blue with blue roof, "SWAT Unit Team Support," Siren Force/Rescue 911 series.................................$10 – 12
4. fluorescent orange with white roof, "Auto Rescue 24 Hr. Towing," Thailand cast ....$2 – 3
5. fluorescent orange with white roof, "Police 8," "Intercom City"......$12 – 16
6. fluorescent orange with white roof, "Rescue" and checkerboard pattern, Emergency Pack ....$2 – 3
7. metallic gray with black roof, red stripe and fish design, 5-pack ....$3 – 4
8. metallic gray with black roof, "Marine Research," 5-pack....................$2 – 3
9. orange with white roof, "Lufthansa"..........................$4 – 5
10. red with black roof, "Mission Satellite Top Secret," 2000 Space Explorer series....................................$2 – 3
11. red with black roof, "Mission Satellite Top Secret," "Matchbox 2000," 2000 Space Explorer series ....$3 – 4
12. red with gray roof, "Matchbox Rescue Unit," Light & Sound ....$4 – 5
13. red with red roof, "Fire Metro Airport," Siren Force/Rescue 911 series.................................$10 – 12
14. red with white roof, "Matchbox Fires Rescue Dept.," Avon Light & Sound ....$5 – 6
15. red with white roof, "Matchbox Rescue Unit," "Fire Dept.," Light & Sound ....$4 – 5
16. red with white roof, "Rescue Unit" and checkerboard pattern, Motor City.....................................$2 – 3
17. white with blue roof, "Test Centre," Launcher 5-pack ....$2 – 3
18. white with fluorescent orange roof, "Marine Rescue" and checkerboard pattern, Emergency Pack.............$2 – 3
19. white with green roof, Polizei, Germany issue ....$4 – 5
20. white with green roof and doors, "Polizei" ....$6 – 7

21. white with orange roof, "Ambulance and checkerboard pattern, Motor City ....$4 –
22. white with white roof, "Auto Rescue Hr. Towing," Siren Force/Rescue 9 series.................................$10 –
23. white with white roof, "Polizei," check board pattern, Two Pack...........$3 –
24. white with white roof, "Polizei," gre doors ....$3 –
25. white with white roof, "Polizei," gre doors and hood ....$2 –
26. white with white roof, "Lufthansa Macau cast.............................$5 –
27. white with white roof, "Lufthansa," Th land cast ....$2 –
28. yellow with black roof, "Tough Constru tion — Construction Foreman," Light Sound ....$4 –

29. **yellow with blue roof, red and whi on doors with "S.C.U.B.A." a "Beach Patrol," 2002 Sand Cast Rescue Team 5-pack with plast bucket ....$3 –**
30. yellow with white roof, "Beach Pat Unit 2," Light & Sound ....$4 –

Mercedes-Benz 300 E, 3", #58, 1987
1. metallic light blue, dark blue interio Macau cast............................$2 –
2. metallic light blue, dark blue interio Thailand cast..........................$2 –
3. blue-gray, "Go Blues! 1997," gray interio China cast, Australia issue..........$4 –
4. white, "Polizei 5075," green stripe, silv star, tan interior, Thailand cast ...$2 –
5. white, "Polizei 5075," green stripe, t interior, China cast...................$3 –
6. white, "Polizei 5075," green stripe, t interior, Thailand cast ....$2 –
7. white, "Rijkspolitie," dark blue interio Thailand cast, the Netherlands Conv issue ....$5 –

Mercedes-Benz 300 SE, with 2^7/$_8$", #4 1968
1. green, black plastic wheels....$16 – 2

2. **metallic blue, black plastic whee 1968....................................$30 – 3**

metallic blue, Superfast wheels, 1970 ....$80 – 100
metallic orange, Superfast wheels ....$20 – 25
metallic gold, Superfast wheels ....$20 – 25
army green with "Staff" labels, Superfast wheels ....$9 – 12
metallic gray, Superfast wheels ....$90 – 120

Mercedes-Benz 350 SL Convertible (also Mercedes Tourer), 3", #6, 1973
orange with black roof ....$9 – 12
yellow with black roof ....$6 – 9
metallic gray with black roof, no markings ....$30 – 45
metallic gray with black roof, "Rennservice" labels, Germany issue....$40 – 50
metallic orange with black roof.$9 – 12
metallic orange with white roof...$6 – 9
maroon with white roof ....$9 – 12
red with white roof ....$6 – 9
blue with no roof ....$6 – 9
purple with no roof ....$9 – 12

. **white with no roof, translucent red interior** ....$9 – 12
. pale gray with no roof, translucent white interior, UK issue ....$40 – 50
. beige with no roof, translucent white interior, UK issue ....$40 – 50
. red with no roof, translucent white interior ....$40 – 50
. black with no roof, white interior ....$40 – 50

Mercedes-Benz 430 Wagon, #68, 1999, Germany
metallic dark blue ....$4 – 5
white, "Euro Taxi" and green band ....$4 – 5

Mercedes-Benz 450 SEL/Taxi/Polizei, 3", #56, 1979
metallic blue with tan interior .....$3 – 4
metallic blue with red interior .....$6 – 8

beige with ivory "Taxi" sign on roof, tan interior ....$3 – 4
beige with ivory "Taxi" sign on roof, brown interior...........................$4 – 5
white with blue roof light ....$8 – 10

6. white and green, "Polizei," blue roof light ....$3 – 4
7. white and green, no markings, blue roof light ....$3 – 4

Mercedes-Benz 500 AMG (see Mercedes-Benz AMG 500 SEC)

Mercedes-Benz 500 SEC (see Mercedes-Benz AMG 500 SEC)

Mercedes-Benz 500 SL Convertible, 3", #12, 1990; #33, 1990, international
1. metallic gray with dark blue interior, clear windshield ....$2 – 3

2. **white with brown interior, "500SL," clear windshield** ....$2 – 3
3. metallic gray with maroon interior, chrome windshield, rubber tires on gray rims, World Class.....................$6 – 9
4. black with dark gray interior, chrome windshield, rubber tires on gray rims, World Class ....$6 – 9
5. red with white interior, clear windshield, Show Stoppers ....$3 – 4

6. **black with gray interior, pink and white, clear windshield** ....$2 – 3
7. white with maroon and black interior, rubber tires on chrome rims, Gold Collection ....$15 – 20
8. red with gray and black interior, clear windshield, rubber tires on chrome rims, Premiere Collection ....$4 – 6
9. black with black interior, clear windshield, rubber tires on chrome rims, Premiere Collection ....$4 – 6
10. dark blue with two-tone gray interior, clear windshield, rubber tires on chrome rims, Premiere Collection ....$4 – 6
11. bright green with reddish brown interior, Mattel Wheels 5-pack ....$2 – 3
12. bright green with reddish brown interior, "Merry Christmas," "Ad-Ventures 1999," Color Comp promotional ....$20 – 25
13. metallic silver with black interior, no markings, ASAP promotional blank ..$35 – 45
14. metallic silver with black interior, "Personal Lines 25 Years, ASAP promotional ....$50 – 100
15. metallic silver with black interior, "Citrix Technology Directions 2000," ASAP promotional.......................$75 – 125

16. metallic silver with black interior, "Classic Collision," ASAP promotional ..$75 – 125
17. metallic silver with black interior, "Thunder Machines AMG Line," ASAP promotional...............................$75 – 125

Mercedes-Benz 600 SL/SEL, 3", #38, 1992; #39, 1991, international
1. metallic red, detailed trim, two-tone gray interior, clear windows, rubber tires on chrome rims, Ultra Class.........$9 – 12
2. dark green, detailed trim, two-tone gray interior, clear windows, rubber tires on chrome rims, Australia Premiere 3 Collection #1 ....$4 – 5
3. blue, detailed trim, two-tone gray interior, clear windows, rubber tires on chrome rims, Premiere Collection #2 ......$4 – 5
4. silver blue, detailed trim, two-tone gray interior, clear windows, rubber tires on chrome rims, JC Penney Premiere Collection ....$4 – 5
5. black, detailed trim, two-tone gray interior, clear windows, rubber tires on chrome rims, Premiere Collection #5........$4 – 5
6. white, detailed trim, two-tone gray interior, clear windows, rubber tires on chrome rims, Special Class #2 ..$4 – 5

7. **metallic silver, light gray interior, clear windows**......................$2 – 3
8. metallic brown, light gray interior, clear windows, Show Stoppers...........$3 – 4

Mercedes-Benz A-Class, #56, 1999; #51, 1999, international

1. **red, New Hope Auto Show 2000" with kayak and splash design, purple interior, Color Comp promotional** ....$16 – 24
2. red with kayak and splash design, purple interior, 1999 Wilderness Adventure series ....$2 – 3
3. red with no design, black interior, 1999 Forest Run international series ..$3 – 4
4. metallic gray, "New Hope Auto Show 2000," Color Comp promotional.$16 – 24
5. metallic gray, no design, black interior, 2000 Germany Classics international series....................................$3 – 4

6. **white with snowflake on sides, 2003 Hero City 5-pack #8.............$4 – 6**

Mercedes-Benz AAV, #319, 1997, Jurassic Park; #337, 1997, Jurassic Park
1. light green, "The Lost World," green camouflage, roof turret with arms......$6 – 8
2. light green, "The Lost World," green camouflage, roof luggage rack ...$6 – 8

Mercedes-Benz Actros 1857 Semi-Tractor, #64, 1999, Germany
1. yellow with black base, no markings, China cast ....$6 – 8

Mercedes-Benz AMG 500 SEC, #43, 1984
1. red, "AMG," black interior, clear windows, Macau cast...................$3 – 4
2. red, "AMG" and stripes, black interior, clear windows, new Superfast wheels.....................................$5 – 6
3. red with green and yellow stripes, brown interior, clear windows, the Netherlands issue ....$10 – 12
4. metallic red, "AMG" and stripes, black interior, clear windows, Laser wheels....................................$5 – 6
5. army green, "Matchbox Military Police MP-090196," Light & Sound .....$5 – 6
6. black, "500SEC," brown interior .$3 – 4
7. black, "500SEC" and stripes, brown interior, black base...................$3 – 4
8. black, "500SEC" and stripes, brown interior, silver base ....$5 – 6
9. black, "Redoxon," "500SEC," brown interior, Hong Kong issue..........$20 – 25

10. **black, "Pace Car Heuer," "Rescue 911," black metal base, Siren Force...............................$8 – 10**
11. black, "Pace Car Heuer," "Rescue 911," black plastic base, Siren Force .$8 – 10
12. black, "Pace Car Heuer," Siren Force ....$6 – 8
13. metallic gray, "Police 17," blue stripes, Light & Sound ....$5 – 6
14. ivory, "Emergency Doctor," "Rescue 911," black metal base, Siren Force ....$8 – 10

15. ivory, "Emergency Doctor," black metal base, Siren Force.................$6 – 8

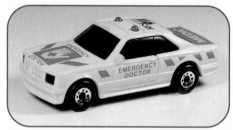

16. **ivory, "Emergency Doctor," black plastic base, Siren Force ...$6 – 8**
17. white, "500SEC" and silver stripes, brown interior, Saudi Arabia issue................................$20 – 25
18. white, "AMG," blue interior, Macau cast.....................................$4 – 5
19. white, "AMG," black interior.......$7 – 9
20. white, "1 Pig Racing Team," brown interior, Hong Kong issue.....$10 – 12
21. white, "7," red and blue design, black interior, gold chrome 8-dot wheels, Macau cast...........................$4 – 5
22. white, "7," red and blue design, black interior, silver chrome 8-dot wheels, Macau cast...........................$4 – 5
23. white, "7," red and blue design, black interior, new Superfast wheels, Macau cast ....$80 – 120
24. white with detailed trim, chrome windows, rubber tires on gray rims, World Class.....................................$7 – 9

25. **white, "Police," Rescue 911," red and blue stripes, Siren Force ....$8 – 10**
26. white, "Police," red and blue stripes, black metal base, Siren Force ..$8 – 10
27. white, "Police," red and blue stripes, black plastic base, Siren Force.$8 – 10
28. white, "Police 17," blue stripes, Light & Sound ....$5 – 6

Mercedes-Benz AMG C-Class, #35, 1996; #75, 1996, international

1. **metallic blue, "25 Camsport," 1996.................................$2 – 3**

2. metallic gold, 1997 75 Challenge series.................................$6 –
3. metallic gray, "25 Camsport," 199 Racing 5-pack.........................$2 –

4. **metallic gray, "Team Matchbox 1 rubber tires on chrome rims, P miere Collection #15 ....$4 –**

5. **yellow, "25 Camsport," black a red accents, 1997 ....$2 –**

Mercedes-Benz "Binz" Ambulance, 2⁷/ #3, 1968
1. black plastic wheels, ivory, with patient stretcher, rear hatch opens ....$15 – 2

2. **Superfast wheels, ivory, wi patient on stretcher, rear hat opens, 1970 ....$20 – 2**
3. Superfast wheels, ivory, rear hat doesn't open ....$8 – 1
4. Superfast wheels, olive, rear hat doesn't open, Two Pack ....$8 – 1

Mercedes-Benz CLK Convertible, #7 1999, Germany; #1, 2000, USA
1. **metallic green with tan interio 2000 Open Road series 1 .....$2 –**

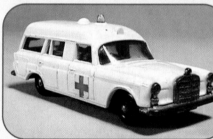

metallic green with black interior, 1999 Germany issue..........................$4 – 6

metallic green with tan interior, "Matchbox 2000" on windshield, 2000 Open Road series 1...........................$3 – 4

rcedes-Benz Coach, 2⅞", #68, 1965

turquoise ....$150 – 175

orange ....$12 – 15

rcedes-Benz Container Truck, 3", #42, 1977

red with beige container, "Sea/Land" labels ....$6 – 8

red with beige container, "N.Y.K." labels ....$6 – 8

red with beige container, "O.C.L." labels ....$12 – 16

red with beige container, "Confern" labels, Germany issue...........$40 – 50

red with white container, "Matchbox" labels ....$9 – 12

red with white container, "Mayflower" labels ....$9 – 12

red with white container, "Confern" applied over "Mayflower" ....$50 – 60

yellow with yellow container, "Deutsche Bundespost," Germany issue .$30 – 40

green with green container, "Confern" applied over "Mayflower" ...$120 – 160

green with green container, "Mayflower" labels ....$7 – 9

blue with blue container, "Karstadt," Germany issue.....................$40 – 50

rcedes-Benz E 430 Wagon, #34, 2001

metallic green, "Polizei," "K-9," 2001 ....$3 – 4

turquoise with red metal base, amber windows, mountain graphics, light blue interior, 2003 5-pack #10....................................$2 – 3

rcedes-Benz E Class 1997, #70, 1998; #65, 1999; #65, 1999, international

metallic pink, "Matchbox USA 20th Anniversary Convention," "Color Comp Inc. Conference," Color Comp promotional.................................$30 – 40

2. **metallic dark gray, "E Class," red pinstripe, red interior, 1998 Street Cruisers series ....$2 – 3**

3. metallic gray, "Intergalactic Research," 1999 Science Fiction series ......$2 – 3

4. cream, "Taxi 23000," Germany issue....................................$4 – 5

Mercedes-Benz G Wagon (see Mercedes-Benz 280 GE G-Wagon)

Mercedes-Benz GTC, #35, 1996

1. metallic cornflower blue with white and coral pink rally accents ....$2 – 3

Mercedes-Benz Lorry, 3", #1, 1968

1. **black plastic wheels, mint green with orange canopy ....$10 – 15**

2. black plastic wheels, mint green with yellow canopy ....$15 – 20

1. Superfast wheels, metallic gold with orange canopy.....................$20 – 30

2. Superfast wheels, metallic gold with yellow canopy.........................$15 – 20

3. Superfast wheels, red with yellow canopy, "Transcontinental Haulage, " Two Pack.............................$5 – 10

4. Superfast wheels, light olive with tan canopy, "USA48350," Two Pack.................................$10 – 15

5. Superfast wheels, dark olive with tan canopy, "USA48350," Two Pack.................................$75 – 90

6. Superfast wheels, light olive with tan canopy, "4TS 702K," Two Pack.................................$5 – 10

7. Superfast wheels, blue with orange yellow canopy, blue windows, "IMS,"Two Pack ....$15 – 25

8. Superfast wheels, blue with orange yellow canopy, purple windows, "IMS," Two Pack ....$45 – 60

Mercedes-Benz ML430, #77, 2000; #63, 1999, Germany; #57, 2000, international

1. **"The Osbournes," Kelly Osbourne, 2003..................................$6 – 8**

2. metallic maroon, "Matchbox," "Midwest Diecast Miniatures Customer Appreciation," custom promotional ....$16 – 24

3. metallic maroon, 5-spoke concave wheels, 1999 Germany issue.$5 – 6

4. metallic maroon, 10-spoke wheels, Target Eggmobiles 3-pack..........$16 – 20

5. dark green, no markings, 5-pack $2 – 3

6. **bright green, "Rugrats" and cartoon character illustrations, 2003 Nickelodeon 5-pack.....................$2 – 3**

7. dark blue, "If You Don't Collect Matchbox... Get Out Of The Way," custom promotional........................$16 – 24

8. dark blue, "Matchbox 2000," 2000 Snow Explorer series ....$3 – 4

9. **dark blue, 2000 Snow Explorer series ....$2 – 3**

10. **white, "Coca-Cola," "The Pause That Refreshes," illustration in circle, pale yellow lower half, rubber tires on chrome rims, Matchbox Collectibles Coca-Cola Collection ....$5 – 6**

Mercedes-Benz S500, #66, 1999, Germanyy; #32, 2000, international

Mercedes-Benz S500

1. yellow with blue stripe, 5-spoke concave wheels, 5-pack ....$3 – 4
2. yellow with blue stripe, 10-spoke wheels, 5-pack ....$2 – 3
3. black, 2000 Germany Classics series, international issue ....$3 – 4
4. metallic gray, 1999 Germany issue.......................................$4 – 5

Mercedes-Benz Sauber Group C Racer, 3," #46, 1985; #66, 1985

1. red, "BASF Cassettes," black airfoil, gold wheels, Macau cast ....$4 – 5
2. red, "BASF Cassettes," black airfoil, silver wheels, Macau cast ....$4 – 5
3. red, "Royal Mail Swiftair," red foil, Macau cast, UK issue...............$6 – 8
4. red and white, "Champion 51," maroon airfoil, China cast ....$2 – 3
5. red and white, "Champion 51," maroon airfoil, Thailand cast ....$2 – 3

6. **red and white, "Champion 51," red airfoil, China cast...................$2 – 3**
7. pale red with black, white and yellow accents, armaments, no airfoil, Roadblasters.....................................$6 – 8
8. fluorescent pink and blue, "Matchbox" and flames, blue airfoil, chrome and black windows, China cast, Lightning Wheels ....$4 – 5
9. fluorescent orange and yellow with lightning bolts, fluorescent yellow airfoil, blue chrome and black windows, China cast, Lightning Wheels ....$4 – 5
10. fluorescent yellow and orange, "Lightning," fluorescent yellow airfoil, blue chrome and black windows, China cast, Lightning Wheels ....$4 – 5
11. yellow and red, "Matchbox USA 11th Annual Convention & Toy Show 1992," red airfoil, China cast............$12 – 15
12. yellow with orange and blue accents, blue airfoil, Macau cast, new Superfast wheels....................................$4 – 5
13. yellow with orange and blue accents, blue airfoil, Macau cast, Laser Wheels ....$4 – 5
14. pale blue, "Grand Prix 46," black foil, Macau cast...............................$5 – 6
15. blue and fluorescent pink, "Lightning" and flames, blue foil, China cast, Lightning Wheels..............................$4 – 5
16. black, "Cargantua," black airfoil, Macau cast, new Superfast wheels...$16 – 24
17. white, "50," blue on sides only, pink on hood only, pink airfoil, silver wheels, China cast ....$2 – 3

18. white, "50," blue on sides only, pink on hood only, pink airfoil, silver wheels, Thailand cast...........................$2 – 3

17. **white, "50," red stripes, blue airfoil, silver wheels, China**

cast ....$2 – 3
18. **white, "50," blue and pink accents, pink airfoil, gold wheels, Thailand cast ....$2 – 3**
21. white, "50," blue and pink accents, pink airfoil, silver wheels, Thailand cast .$2 – 3
22. white, "Castrol Sauber 61," black airfoil, gold wheels, Macau cast...........$3 – 4
23. white, "Castrol Sauber 61," black airfoil, silver wheels, Macau cast ....$2 – 3
24. white, "Grand Prix 46," black airfoil, gold wheels, Thailand cast.........$2 – 3
25. white, "Grand Prix 46," black airfoil, silver wheels, China cast..............$2 – 3
26. white, "Grand Prix 46," black airfoil, 6-spoke spiral wheels, China cast...............$2 – 3
27. white, "Grand Prix 46," black airfoil, 6-spoke spiral wheels, Thailand cast ....$4 – 5
28. white, "Grand Prix 46," black airfoil, 8-dot silver wheels, Macau cast...........$2 – 3
29. white, "Grand Prix 46," black airfoil, 8-dot silver wheels, Thailand cast ....$2 – 3
30. white, "Jr. Matchbox Collector's Club," black airfoil, Macau cast, Australia issue...................................$9 – 12
31. white and orange, "Bisotherm," "Baustein," orange airfoil, Macau cast, Switzerland issue ....$10 – 12
32. white with blue and pink accents, pink airfoil......................................$2 – 3
33. white with white airfoil, gold wheels, no markings, Thailand cast, Graffic Traffic ....$8 – 10
34. chrome plated with black airfoil, no markings, Macau cast, custom promotional.................................$16 – 24

Mercedes-Benz Scaffold Truck, 2½", #11, 1969

1. metallic gray with yellow scaffolding, black plastic wheels................$9 – 12
2. metallic gray with yellow scaffolding, Superfast wheels ....$24 – 32

Mercedes-Benz Tourer (see Mercedes-Benz 350SL Convertible)

Mercedes-Benz TV News Truck, 3," #[...] 1989 – 1997; #62, 1999; #98, 20[...] #73, 1989 – 1997, international; 1998, international

1. red, "Intergalactic Research," bla[...] roof with metallic gray TV came[...] and antenna, 1999 Science Fict[...] series ....$2 – [...]

2. yellow, "Matchbox Cable TV," bla[...] roof with red TV camera and ante[...] na, 1997 City Streets 5-pack $2 – [...]
3. lime green, "Action Radar," "Xtre[...] Mission," metallic gray roof with met[...] gray TV camera and antenna, Ch[...] cast, 5-pack............................$2 – [...]

4. blue, "MBTV Mobile One," "7[...] News," metallic gray roof with lig[...] orange TV camera and antenna, Th[...] land cast ....$2 – [...]
5. blue, "MBTV Mobile One," "75 New[...] metallic gray roof with orange TV ca[...] era and antenna, Macau cast....$2 – [...]
6. blue, "MBTV Mobile One," "75 New[...] metallic gray roof with orange TV ca[...] era and antenna, Thailand cast ..$2 – [...]
7. blue, "TV 6," yellow roof with lime gre[...] TV camera and antenna, China cas[...] 1998 Around the Town internation[...] series ....$2 – [...]

blue and white with metallic gray roof, "Rock TV".............................$2 – 4

blue, "Super RTL Live!"; red roof with light gray TV camera and antenna, China cast, Germany issue ....$4 – 5

black, "Action TV," football graphics, yellow roof with yellow TV camera and antenna, China cast, 5-pack ......$2 – 3

black, "Action TV," soccer ball graphics, yellow roof with yellow TV camera and antenna, China cast, 5-pack ......$3 – 4

black, "Matchbox Channel 4," red roof, yellow TV camera and antenna, China cast, 1998 Around the Town 5-pack ....$2 – 3

black, "Mission Impossible, dark gray roof with dark gray TV camera and antenna, China cast, Star Cars...$5 – 6

metallic gray, "Weather, News at Noon, Sports," TV camera graphics, black roof with metallic gray TV camera and antenna, tinted windows, China cast, 2000 On the Road Again series ....$2 – 3

metallic gray, "Weather, News at Noon, Sports," TV camera graphics, "Matchbox 2000," black roof with metallic gray TV camera and antenna, tinted windows, China cast, 2000 On the Road Again series ....$3 – 4

metallic gray, "Weather, News at Noon, Sports," TV camera graphics, black roof with metallic gray TV camera and antenna, blue windows, China cast, 2000 On the Road Again series.................$20 – 30

white, "Action News 6," yellow roof with lime green TV camera and antenna, China cast, ASAP promotional ....$16 – 24

white, "American International Recovery," yellow roof with lime green TV camera and antenna, China cast, ASAP promotional......................$120 – 160

white, "Fox 8 WJW Cleveland," black roof with white TV camera and antenna, China cast, ASAP promotional ....$16 – 24

white, "Fox 8 WJW Cleveland," yellow roof with lime green TV camera and antenna, China cast, ASAP promotional ..$16 – 24

white, "Intercom City TV," blue roof with white TV camera and antenna, Thailand cast, Intercom City.................$8 – 10

white, "RCA," yellow roof with lime green TV camera and antenna, China cast, ASAP promotional ....$25 – 35

---

23. white, "Rock TV," multicolor diagonal lines, blue roof with white TV camera and antenna, Thailand cast ....$2 – 3

24. white, "Sky Satellite Television," dark blue roof with white TV camera and antenna, Thailand cast.............$2 – 3

25. white, "Sky Satellite TV," blue roof with white TV camera and antenna, China cast.............................$3 – 4

26. white, "World Cup Mobile Unit Television," blue roof with red TV camera and antenna, China cast, 5-pack ....$3 – 4

27. white, "World Cup Mobile Unit Television," blue roof with white TV camera and antenna, China cast, Action Pack.......................................$2 – 3

28. white with black roof, red TV camera and antenna, globe and satellite design, China casting ....$3 – 4

29. white with white roof, brown TV camera and antenna, no markings, Graffic Traffic ....$12 – 16

30. white with white roof, orange TV camera and antenna, no markings, Graffic Traffic ....$12 – 16

31. white with yellow roof, lime green TV camera and antenna, China cast, ASAP promotional blank................$30 – 40

Mercedes-Benz Trailer, 3½", #2, 1968
1. black plastic wheels, mint green with orange canopy....................$10 – 12
2. black plastic wheels, mint green with yellow canopy ....$16 – 18
1. Superfast wheels, metallic gold with orange canopy....................$20 – 25
2. Superfast wheels, metallic gold with yellow canopy...........................$15 – 20
3. Superfast wheels, red with yellow canopy, "Transcontinental Haulage" ....$5 – 7
4. Superfast wheels, light olive with tan canopy, "USA48350" ....$10 – 12
5. Superfast wheels, dark olive with tan canopy, "USA48350" ....$70 – 85
6. Superfast wheels, light olive with tan canopy, "4TS 702K"............$10 – 12
7. Superfast wheels, dark olive with tan canopy, "4TS 702K"............$70 – 85
8. Superfast wheels, blue with orange yellow canopy, "IMS"................$15 – 20
9. Superfast wheels, yellow with white canopy, "Alpine Rescue," Two Pack............$4 – 6
10. Superfast wheels, yellow with no canopy, no markings ....$3 – 5

---

11. Superfast wheels, red with white canopy, "Unfall Rettung," Two Pack...............................$4 – 6
12. Superfast wheels, white with orange canopy, "C & S" ....$4 – 6
13. Superfast wheels, red with white canopy, "Big Top Circus" ....$5 – 7

Mercedes-Benz Unimog, 2½", #49, 1967
1. tan with turquoise chassis, black tires on plastic hubs ....$9 – 12
2. blue with red chassis, black tires on plastic hubs..........................$7 – 10
3. blue with red chassis, Superfast wheels, 1970........................$20 – 30
4. metallic light blue with red chassis, Superfast wheels ....$20 – 30
5. army green with star label, Superfast wheels..............................$80 – 120
6. army green with "A" label, Superfast wheels..............................$9 – 12

Mercedes-Benz Unimog with snowplow, 3", #48, 1984
1. red, "UR83," white canopy, white stripes on red plow, Macau cast...........$3 – 4
2. yellow, "Rescue," white canopy, black stripes on white plow, England cast ....$9 – 12
3. yellow, "Rescue," white canopy, black stripes on yellow-orange plow, England cast...$4 – 5
4. yellow, "Rescue," white canopy, black plow, England cast ....$4 – 5
5. yellow, "Rescue," no canopy, black stripes on yellow-orange plow, England cast......................................$4 – 5
6. yellow, "Rescue," white canopy, black stripes on yellow plow, Macau cast ....$3 – 4
7. bright green, "The Lost World," metallic gray plow, includes metal dinosaur, Jurassic Park series.................$7 – 8
8. white, "C&S," black stripes on orange plow, Macau cast....................$3 – 4
9. white, "C&S," black stripes on orange plow, Thailand cast..................$3 – 4
10. white with gray and army green camouflage, army green plow and canopy, China cast ....$3 – 4
11. white with gray and army green camouflage, army green plow and canopy, Thailand cast....................$3 – 4
12. white with red and blue stripes, no canopy, plastic armament, Roadblasters, Macau cast.................$7 – 8
13. white with red and dark blue stripes, no canopy, plastic armament, packaged in Tomy box, Japan issue............$9 – 12

Mercury Capri (see Ford Capri, Hot Rocker, Maxi Taxi)

Mercury Commuter Police Station Wagon, 3", #55, 1971 (similar casting: Mercury Commuter Station Wagon)
1. white with red roof lights.......$16 – 24
2. white with amber roof lights.$90 – 120

Mercury Commuter Station Wagon,
3⅛", #73, 1968 (similar casting:
Mercury Commuter Police Station
Wagon)
1. metallic lime green, black plastic tires
   on chrome hubs, 1968 ....$16 – 20
2. metallic lime green, Superfast wheels,
   1970................................$20 – 30
3. red, Superfast wheels, cow head
   label..................................$80 – 120
4. red, Superfast wheels, cat head
   label....................................$20 – 30

Mercury Cougar, doors open, 3", #62,
1968 (similar casting: Mercury Cougar
Rat Rod)
1. pale yellow, black plastic wheels on
   chrome hubs, 1968........$750 – 800
2. metallic pale green, black plastic wheels
   on chrome hubs, 1968 ....$6 – 9
3. metallic pale green, Superfast wheels,
   1970................................$30 – 40
4. metallic green, Superfast wheels,
   1970................................$30 – 40

Mercury Cougar Rat Rod, doors don't
open, 3", #62, 1970
1. fluorescent lime green, "Rat
   Rod"................................$16 – 24
2. fluorescent lime green ,
   "Wildcat"..........................$25 – 30

Mercury Cougar Villager Station Wagon,
3," #74, 1978
1. metallic light green with green
   tailgate.................................$3 – 4
2. metallic dark green with green
   tailgate.................................$3 – 4
3. olive green with green tailgate, Brazil
   issue...............................$400 – 500
4. metallic dark blue with blue
   tailgate.................................$3 – 4

Mercury Park Lane Fire Chief, #59, 1971
(see Mercury Park Lane Police)

Mercury Park Lane Police, 3", #55,
1968, Superfast wheels unless noted
(similar casting: Mercury Park Lane Fire
Chief, #59, 1971)
1. red, "Fire" in shield label on doors, no
   hood label............................$40 – 50
2. red, "Fire Chief" hood label, "Fire" shield
   label on doors, #59.................$6 – 8
3. red, "Fire Chief" in square hood label,
   shield label on doors, clear windows,
   #59..................................$12 – 16
4. red, "Fire Chief" in square hood label,
   helmet and axes label on doors, clear
   windows, #59 ....$12 – 16
5. red, "Fire Chief" red and yellow hood
   label, helmet and axes label on doors,
   clear windows, #59.............$12 – 16
6. red, "Los Angeles Fire Dept.," Code
   Red.......................................$7 – 9
7. red, helmet and axes label on hood,
   shield label on doors, clear windows,
   #59..................................$12 – 16

8. red, helmet and axes label on hood and
   doors, clear windows, #59......$9 – 12
9. red, helmet and axes on hood, no label
   on doors, clear windows, #59 .$9 – 12
10. red, no hood label, "Fire" in shield label
    on doors, #59.......................$6 – 8
11. red, purple windows, #59 .....$30 – 40
12. metallic blue, bar lights, yellow, blue and
    red trim, plastic armaments, Road-
    blasters................................$6 – 8
13. black, Halley's Comet Commemorative
    Car, New Superfast wheels,
    1986...................................$8 – 10
14. white, "201" on hood, "Metro" on
    sides..................................$9 – 12
15. white, "Los Angeles Police," blue win-
    dows, Code Red......................$7 – 9
16. white, "Los Angeles Police," clear win-
    dows, Code Red......................$7 – 9
17. white, "Los Angeles Police" on hood, "Metro
    Police" on doors, blue windows ..$30 – 40
18. white, "Metro" on hood, shield on
    doors, blue windows...............$9 – 12
19. white, "Metro" on hood, shield on
    doors, clear windows..............$9 – 12
20. white, "Metro" on hood, shield on
    doors, tinted windows............$9 – 12
21. white, "Metro Police," blue
    windows...............................$9 – 12
22. white, "Metro Police," clear
    windows...............................$9 – 12
23. white, "Metro Police," tinted
    windows ....$9 – 12
24. white, "Police" with shield, clear win-
    dows...................................$9 – 12
25. white, "Police" labels, purple
    windows ....$35 – 45
26. white, "State Police," gray base, bar
    lights, blue windows, Laser
    Wheels ....$4 – 5
27. white, "State Police," gray base, bar
    lights, blue windows, New
    Superfast...............................$4 – 5
28. white, "State Police," black base, bar
    lights, blue windows, New
    Superfast..............................$9 – 12
29. white, "State Police" in orange and blue,
    black base, bar lights, blue windows, 8-
    dot wheels ....$80 – 120
30. white, no hood label, "Police" in
    shield label on doors, purple win-
    dows ....$40 – 50
31. white, no labels, blue windows .$9 – 12
32. white, no labels, clear windows $9 – 12

**33. white, Superfast wheels,
1970................................$16 – 24**
34. white with black fenders, "Metro," clear
    windows...............................$9 – 12
35. white with black fenders, "Police" in
    shield, blue windows..............$9 – 12

36. white with black fenders, "Police"
    shield, clear windows.............$9 –
37. white with black fenders, "Police"
    shield, purple windows..........$40 –

**38. white with blue dome light, black pl
tic wheels, #55, 1968.......$40 –**
39. white with red dome light, black plas
    wheels, #55, 1968.........$250 – 3

Mercury Sable Wagon, 3", #33, 198
#55, 1988
1. white with gray side stripe, metallic g
   base, white hatch, China cast....$3 –
2. white with gray side stripe, metallic g
   base, white hatch, Macau cast ..$3 –
3. white with gray side stripe, metallic g
   base, clear hatch, China cast, Ch
   issue................................$30 – 5
4. metallic pale green with woodgrain s
   panels, "The Brady Bunch," Star
   Cars ....$5 –

Merryweather Marquis Fire Engine, r
2¼", #9, 1959
1. tan ladder, gray plastic
   wheels..............................$30 –
2. gold ladder, gray plastic
   wheels..............................$30 –
3. gold ladder, black plastic
   wheels..............................$30 –
4. silver ladder, black plastic
   wheels..............................$20 – 2
5. tan ladder, black plastic
   wheels..............................$20 – 2

Merryweather Fire Engine, Superfast or
3," #35, 1969
1. metallic red with light gray base held
   by two clips........................$16 – 2
4. bright red with black base held on
   four rivets..........................$20 – 2
2. bright red with light gray base held
   by two clips........................$12 – 1
5. bright red with light gray base held
   by four rivets........................$6 – 1
3. bright red with tan base held on by tw
   clips.................................$20 – 2

Meteor Sports Boat and Trailer, ta
deck, blue hull, 2⅜", #48, 1958
1. metal wheels.....................$40 – 5
2. gray plastic wheels.............$60 – 8
3. silver plastic wheels...........$80 – 10

MG 1100, with driver and dog, 2⅝", #6
1966
1. light blue with Superfast
   wheels..............................$40 – 5
2. dark blue with Superfast
   wheels..............................$40 – 5

**green with black plastic
wheels** ....**$20 – 30**
green with Superfast
wheels............................$200 – 300

Midget Sports Car, 2," #19, 1956
with driver, made in England ..$50 – 75
Matchbox Originals commemorative
replica, green, 1993, made in
China ....$3 – 5

GA 1960, #502, 2001, Matchbox Collectibles Elvis Presley Collection with
Graceland diorama
maroon, detailed trim, rubber white wall
tires on chrome rims............$12 – 16

GA Sports Car, white, 2¼", #19, 1958
metal wheels, gold grille......$80 – 100
metal wheels, silver grille ......$60 – 80
gray plastic wheels.............$80 – 100
silver plastic wheels.........$125 – 150

GF 1.8L 1997, #66, 1998; #41, 1999,
international; #4, 2000, international;
#2, 2001?
red, 2000 Open Road international
series....................................$3 – 4
red, Target Eggmobiles 3-pack...$4 – 5
bright red, #2 ....$3 – 4

bright red, "Coca-Cola," 5-pack .$2 – 3

**yellow with orange band and "MG" logo,
1998 Street Cruiser series ......$2 – 3**
lime green, 5-pack ....$2 – 3
white, 1998 Street Cruiser international series ....$3 – 4
1999 Roadsters international
series....................................$2 – 3

Midnight Magic, 3", #51, 1982 (similar
casting: Tanzara)
1. black with silver sides, pearly silver
base, Macau cast ....$3 – 4
2. black with silver sides, pearly silver
base, Hong Kong cast ....$4 – 5
3. black with silver sides, pearly white
base, Macau cast ....$3 – 4
4. black with silver sides, unpainted base,
Hong Kong cast......................$3 – 4
5. white with red and blue graphics,
unpainted base, China cast, Premiere
Collection #13.........................$5 – 6

Military Jeep (see Jeep 4x4 Laredo)

Military Tank, 2⅞", #70, 1993 (similar
casting: Weasel)
1. tan (khaki) camouflage ....$2 – 3
2. army green (olive), 1996 ....$2 – 3

Mini Cooper, #75, 2003

1.   red, 2003 Car Shop series ....$3 – 4

Mini Ha Ha Mini Cooper, 2⅜", #14, 1975
1. red with blue windows...........$16 – 24

Mini Pickup 4x4 (see Toyota Mini-Pickup
4x4)

Missile Launcher, #82, 1999; #52, 2000

**1.   light green, "476 – Unit 61," 1999
Military Patrol series ....$2 – 3**

2. **tan with brown dirt, "United
States," "MLS 62," "314 6985,"
"10," 2000 Military series ....$2 – 3**

3. **"Man-At-Arms," He-Man & The Masters of the Universe 5-pack......$3 – 4**
4. tan with brown dirt, "United States,"
"MLS 62," "314 6985," "10," "Matchbox
2000," 2000 Military series........$3 – 4

Mission Chopper with retractable tail, 3,"
#46, 1985 – 1997; #49, 1998; #31,
1999; #66, 2000; #55, 2001; #57,
1985 – 1997, international
1. red with white base and skids, tail and blades,
"Rebels, Rescue, Air 1," Motor City...$2 – 3
2. red with white base and skids, tail and
blades, "Sheriff Air 1" ....$2 – 3
3. yellow with blue base and skids, white
tail and blades, "Canon," Nutmeg promotional issue ....$3 – 4
4. green with white base and skids, tail
and blades, "Polizei," Convoy ......$3 – 4
5. green with green base and skids, tail
and blades, brown and black camouflage, 1996 5-pack ....$2 – 3
6. army green with tan base and skids, tan
tail and blades, star and emblem, Skybusters SB – 12 1992 ....$2 – 3
7. army green with black base and skids,
black tail and blades, "AC15," Commando.................................$5 – 6

8. **army green with black base, skids,
and blades, army green tail, white
star, "AT-7521," 1996 ....$2 – 3**
9. fluorescent green with black base,
blades and skids, fluorescent blue tail,
"12 Air Patrol," 5-pack.............$2 – 3

10. **fluorescent green with blue base, skids
and tail, black blade, "12 Air Patrol,"
1997 Land Sea & Air 5-pack ....$2 – 3**

11. blue with white base and skids, blue tail, metallic gray blade, "Air Rescue," "Police," 1997 Police 5-pack ....$2 – 3

12. dark blue with metallic gray base and skids, white tail and blades, orange design ....$2 – 3

13. dark blue with metallic gray base and skids, metallic gray tail and blades, bull's-eye design, Macau cast.....$3 – 4

14. dark blue with metallic gray base and skids, white tail and blades, bull's-eye design, Thailand cast................$3 – 4

15. light purple with blue base and skids, yellow tail and blades, "Hanger 12," 2000 Air Travel series ....$2 – 3

16. light purple with blue base and skids, yellow tail and blades, "Hanger 12," "Matchbox 2000," 2000 Air Travel series ....$3 – 4

17. black with black base, skids, tail, and blades, "INGEN," "Lost World," gray armament attached, Jurassic Park series......................................$7 – 9

18. black with blue base, skids, tail, and blades, "SWAT Stand Clear 00256," 5-pack......................................$2 – 3

19. black with brown base, skids, tail, and blades, green and brown camouflage, 5-pack......................................$2 – 3

20. black with gray base, skids, tail, and blades, "AC99" Commando........$5 – 6

21. black with tan base, skids, and blades, black tail, tan and green camouflage, 5-pack ....$2 – 3

22. black with white base, skids, tail, and blades, "Police," Convoy cast......$3 – 4

23. black with white base, skids, tail, and blades, "Police Unit 2," gold star, 5-pack.......................................$2 – 3

24. light gray with black base, skids, tail, and blades, black camouflage, 5-pack.......................................$2 – 3

25. khaki with black base, skids, tail, and blades, "AT-7521," black star, 1998 Rough 'N Tough series..$2 – 3

26. khaki with black base, blades, and skids, khaki tail, brown camouflage, 1997 Desert Assault Force 5-pack................................$2 – 3

27. khaki with khaki base and skids, khaki tail and blades, green and brown camouflage, 1995 Military 5-pack ....$2 – 3

28. white with black base and skids, black tail and blades, "Unit 2," "Police," star crest, 1996 Police 5-pack ....$2 – 3

29. white with black base and skids, black tail and blades, "Unit 3," "Police," 5-pack.......................................$2 – 3

30. white with black base, skids, black tail and blades, black camouflage ....$2 – 3

31. white with black base, skids, white tail, and blades, "Police" ....$2 – 3

32. white with blue base, skids, tail, and blades, "Police Air Search" ....$2 – 3

33. white with blue base and skids, wh tail and blades, "Rescue" and gre crest, 5-pack..........................$4 –

34. white with blue base and skids, wh tail and blades, "Intercom City," "Polic Intercom City........................$9 –

35. white with fluorescent orange ba and skids, white tail and blades, "P tie 06-11," the Netherlands Conv issue...................................$4 –

36. white with fluorescent orange ba and skids, white tail and blade "Metro SWAT 7," 1993 Emergency pack.......................................$2 –

37. white with gray base and skid white tail and blades, gray and ar green camouflage, 5-pack ......$2 –

38. white with gray base and skids, wh tail and blades, gray camouflage, 199 Tundra Defense Force 5-pack ....$2 –

39. white with red base, skids, tail, a blades, "Sky," Nutmeg promotion issue...................................$3 –

40. white with red base, skids, and tail, wh blades, "Aces," Convoy issue.......$3 –

41. white with tan base, skids, tail, a blades, "Rescue" and green logo, pack...................................$4 –

42. white with white base, skids, ta and blades, "Storm Troope Reunion at the Mark 2000," ASA promotional ....$80 – 12

43. white with white base, skids, tail, a blades, ASAP promotional blank .$30 – 4

44. metallic gold with black base, skids, tail, a blades, 1997 75 Challenge series.$6 – 1

Mission Ford Van (see Ford Panel Van)

Mitsubishi Spyder, 1994, #28, 199 #22, 1995, international; #69, 199 #49, 1999

black with dark gray and black interior, detailed trim, rubber tires on chrome rims, Premiere Collection #1 ..:...$4 – 5
black with red interior, "Spyder" on sides, 1997 Convertibles 5-pack...........$2 – 3
black with red interior, "The Red Back" with spider and web design, Australia issue ....$4 – 5
blue with gray interior, "Spyder" on sides, 1998 Street Cruisers series........$2 – 3

dark green with tan interior, "Spyder," 1998 Street Cruisers series....$2 – 3
dark green with tan interior, "Fujihara Tuning Pros," ASAP promotional..$80 – 120
dark green with tan interior, "Yamaha Mufflers," ASAP promotional.$80 – 120
metallic blue with gray and black interior, detailed trim, rubber tires on chrome rims, Gold Coin Collection.......$16 – 24
metallic blue with pale green interior, light green splash design on sides and hood ....$2 – 3

0. **metallic blue with pale green interior, no markings** ....$3 – 4

1. **metallic blue with white interior, no markings**..........................$2 – 3
2. metallic gold with black interior, 1997 75 Challenge series ....$6 – 12

3. **metallic silver with red and black interior, detailed trim, rubber tires on chrome rims, J C Penney Premiere Collection**....................$4 – 5
4. red with dark gray interior, no markings ....$2 – 3
5. red with dark gray interior, skeleton and "Raptor," 5-pack ....$2 – 3

16. red with dark gray and black interior, detailed trim, rubber tires on chrome rims, Premiere Collection #1 .....$4 – 5

17. **yellow with gray interior, "Spyder" on sides, metallic gray interior, 1997**.................................$2 – 3
18. yellow with gray and black interior, detailed trim, rubber tires on chrome rims, Premiere Collection #12 ...$4 – 5
19. white with maroon and black interior, detailed trim, rubber tires on chrome rims, Premiere Collection #16 ...$4 – 5

Mitsubishi Galant Eterna (see Dodge Challenger/Mitsubishi Galant Eterna)

Mobile Canteen Refreshment Bar, 2⅝", #74, 1959
1. white with blue base and interior, gray wheels...........................$300 – 350
2. pink with light blue base and interior, gray wheels.....................$400 – 500
3. coral ivory with blue base and interior, gray wheels.....................$300 – 350
4. ivory with blue base and interior, gray wheels...........................$300 – 350
5. silver with gray wheels ....$30 – 40
6. silver with silver plastic wheels .$30 – 40
7. silver with black plastic wheels .$30 – 40

Mobile Crane (see Faun Mobile Crane)

Mobile Home, 3¼", #54, 1980 (similar castings: Airport Foam Pumper, Command Vehicle, NASA Tracking Vehicle)

1. **beige** ....$4 – 5
2. white....................................$4 – 5
3. white with stripes....................$5 – 6

Moby Quick (see Power Boat)

Mod Rod, 2⅞", #1, 1971
1. yellow with red wheels, wildcat label ....$25 – 45
2. yellow with black wheels, wildcat label..................................$15 – 20
3. yellow with black wheels, flower label..................................$15 – 20
4. yellow with black wheels, spotted cat label..................................$20 – 25

5. yellow with black wheels, scorpion label ....$30 – 45
6. silver plated with black wheels, stripes ....$60 – 80

Mod Tractor, 2⅛", #25, 1972
1. metallic bright lavender, black base, red seat.................................$40 – 50
2. metallic bright lavender, black base, yellow seat, headlights cast on fenders.$14 – 16
3. metallic bright lavender, black base, yellow seat, no headlights cast on fenders ....$12 – 14
4. metallic bright lavender, unpainted base, yellow seat ....$12 – 14
5. red with black base, yellow seat, Two Pack...............................$9 – 12

Model A Ford (see Ford Model A)

Model T Ford (see Ford Model T)

Modified Racer, 2 – 15/16", #12, 1989; #32, 1990
1. red, "2X," Nutmeg Collectibles ...$5 – 6
2. red, "37," Nutmeg Collectibles ...$5 – 6
3. red, "CraZ 8," Nutmeg Collectibles.............................$5 – 6
4. red, "Jamie Tomaino," "42," Nutmeg Collectibles.............................$5 – 6
5. red, "Jan Leaty," Nutmeg Collectibles.............................$5 – 6
6. red, "Jerry Cook," "38," Nutmeg Collectibles..............................$5 – 6
7. red, "Mike," "15," Nutmeg Collectibles.............................$5 – 6
8. red, "Parts Peddler," "69," Nutmeg Collectibles..............................$5 – 6
9. red, "Sherri Cup," "12," Nutmeg Collectibles..............................$5 – 6
10. red, "Spearpoint Auto," "21," Nutmeg Collectibles.............................$5 – 6
11. red, "Wayne Anderson," "15," Nutmeg Collectibles.............................$5 – 6
12. red with black interior, chrome exhaust pipes, "12" and stripes ....$4 – 5
13. red with orange-yellow interior, black exhaust pipes, "12" and stripes, Nutmeg Collectibles.......................$5 – 6
14. red with red interior, black exhaust pipes, "36," Nutmeg Collectibles..$5 – 6
15. orange, "73," Nutmeg Collectibles.$5 – 6
16. orange, "BR DeWitt," "61," Nutmeg Collectibles..................................$5 – 6
17. orange to red with black interior, black exhaust pipes, "12," Super Color Changers ....$4 – 5
18. orange to red with black interior, chrome exhaust pipes, "12," Super Color Changers.....................$4 – 5
19. orange with black interior, chrome exhaust pipes, "12," Macau cast .$2 – 3
20. orange with black exhaust pipes, "12," China cast ....$2 – 3
21. orange-yellow, "4 Bugs," Nutmeg Collectibles..................................$5 – 6
22. orange-yellow, "Satch Wirley," "4," Nutmeg Collectibles.......................$5 – 6

23. yellow, "Miller Brick Co.," "56," Nutmeg Collectibles..................$5 – 6
24. yellow, "Reggie 44," "Magnum Oils," Nutmeg Collectibles..................$5 – 6
25. powder blue, "5," Nutmeg Collectibles..................$5 – 6
26. blue, "Jimmy Spencer," "24," Nutmeg Collectibles..................$5 – 6
27. blue, "Mike McLaughlin," "3," Nutmeg Collectibles..................$5 – 6
28. blue and metallic gray, "Collector's Toys 95," "Gary's," metallic gray interior, chrome exhaust pipes, Parlor City Collectibles..................$7 – 8
29. dark blue, "Doug Heveron," "3," Nutmeg Collectibles..................$5 – 6
30. dark blue, "Hummels," "11," Nutmeg Collectibles..................$5 – 6
31. dark blue, "Ron Bouchard," "3," Nutmeg Collectibles..................$5 – 6
32. dark blue with black interior, chrome exhaust pipes, "12"..................$9 – 12
33. metallic blue, "JVB27 — Jan Leaty," Nutmeg Collectibles..................$5 – 6
34. dark purple with black interior, black exhaust pipes, "12," Action Pack..................$4 – 5
35. black, "Fyne Lyne," "39," Nutmeg Collectibles..................$5 – 6
36. black, "George Kent," "21," Nutmeg Collectibles..................$5 – 6
37. black, "NY," "7," Nutmeg Collectibles..................$5 – 6
38. black, "Rick Fuller," "44," Nutmeg Collectibles..................$5 – 6
39. black and gold, "O," Nutmeg Collectibles..................$5 – 6
40. black with white interior, chrome exhausts, "1," pink and white stripes, 5-pack..................$2 – 3
41. white, "1," Nutmeg Collectibles ..$5 – 6
42. white, "Maynard Troyer," Nutmeg Collectibles..................$5 – 6
43. white, "Phil's Chevrolet," "99," Nutmeg Collectibles..................$5 – 6
44. white, "Polar," "77," Nutmeg Collectibles..................$5 – 6
45. white, "Tony 1," "Universal Joint Sales," Nutmeg Collectibles..................$5 – 6
46. white, "U2 Jamie," Nutmeg Collectibles..................$5 – 6
47. white and blue, "ADAP 15," Nutmeg Collectibles..................$5 – 6
48. white and orange, "Perth Amboy Spring," "17," Nutmeg Collectibles..................$5 – 6
49. white and powder blue, "Tony Ferrante," "31," Nutmeg Collectibles..................$5 – 6
50. white with no markings, lavender interior, black exhaust pipes, Graffic Traffic..................$12 – 16
51. white with translucent blue interior, black exhaust pipes, "41" and stripes, Nutmeg Collectibles..................$5 – 6
52. chrome plated, with black interior, black exhaust pipes, custom..........$16 – 24

Monteverdi Hai, 2⅞", #3, 1973; BR 15 – 16, 1985 (similar casting: Rallye Royale)

1. orange with metallic gray base, ivory interior..................$16 – 24
2. orange with unpainted base, yellow interior, "3" labels..................$12 – 16
3. orange with unpainted base, yellow interior, no labels..................$12 – 16
4. orange with unpainted base, ivory interior..................$12 – 16
5. orange with unpainted base, ivory interior, "3" label..................$12 – 16
6. orange with unpainted base, ivory interior, "16" label..................$16 – 24
7. orange with black base, ivory interior, "3" label..................$12 – 16
8. orange with black base, ivory interior, "6" label..................$16 – 24
9. green with black windows, no, England cast, Super GTs BR 15 – 16, 1985..................$12 – 15
10. green with black windows, white and gold, England cast, Super GTs BR 15 – 16, 1985..................$5 – 8
11. black with translucent white windows, England cast, Super GTs BR 15 – 16, 1985..................$15 – 20
12. yellow, England cast, Super GTs BR 15 – 16, 1985..................$45 – 60
13. light tan, England cast, Super GTs BR 15 – 16, 1985..................$4 – 6
14. tan, England cast, Super GTs BR 15 – 16, 1985..................$6 – 8
15. gold, England cast, Super GTs BR 15 – 16, 1985..................$8 – 10
16. white, China cast, Super GTs BR 15 – 16, 1985..................$30 – 40
17. orange, China cast, Super GTs BR 15 – 16, 1985..................$3 – 5
18. green, China cast, Super GTs BR 15 – 16, 1985..................$8 – 10
19. blue, China cast, Super GTs BR 15 – 16, 1985..................$3 – 5
20. fluorescent pink, China cast, Neon Racer BR 15 – 16, 1985..........$4 – 6

Morris J2 "Builders Supply" Pickup, light blue, 2¼", #60, 1958
1. rear window, gray plastic wheels, red and black decals..................$30 – 40
2. rear window, silver plastic wheels, red and black decals..................$40 – 50
3. rear window, gray plastic wheels, red and white decals..................$30 – 40
4. rear window, silver plastic wheels, red and white decals..................$40 – 50
5. rear window, black plastic wheels, red and white decals..................$30 – 40
6. no rear window, black plastic wheels, red and white decals..........$30 – 40

Morris Minor 1000, 2," #46, 1958
1. light tan with metal wheels..................$700 – 900
2. dark green with metal wheels..................$50 – 60
3. dark green with gray plastic wheels..................$60 – 80
4. dark blue with gray plastic wheels..................$80 – 100

Motor Home [see Police Mobile Command Center, Truck Camper)

Motorcycle Trailer, #791, 1979
1. red with yellow motorcycles, England cast, Two Pack..................$3 –
2. yellow with black motorcycles, England cast, Two Pack..................$3 –
3. yellow with dark green motorcycles, England cast, Two Pack........$16 – 2
4. yellow with red motorcycles, England cast, Two Pack..................$3 –
5. yellow with red motorcycles, Macau cast, Two Pack..................$3 –
6. yellow with red motorcycles, no-origin cast, Two Pack..................$3 –
7. yellow with yellow motorcycles, England cast..................$8 – 1
8. blue with yellow motorcycles, England cast, Two Pack..................$3 –
9. black with dark red motorcycles, China cast, 5-pack..................$2 –
10. black with dark red motorcycles, no-origin cast, 5-pack..................$2 –
11. pearl gray with black motorcycles, no-origin cast, Two Pack..................$3 –
12. beige with black motorcycles, no-origin cast, Two Pack..................$3 –

Mountain Man [see 4x4 Mini Pickup]

Muir Hill Dumper [see Dumper, Muir Hill]

Mustang [see Ford Mustang]

Mustang, 1970 Boss [see Ford Mustang, 1970 Boss Mustang]

Mustang Cobra [see Ford Mustang Cobra]

Mustang GT350 [see Ford Mustang GT350]

Mustang Mach III [see Ford Mustang Mach III]

N

NASA Rocket Transporter [see Rocket Transporter; similar casting: Airplane Transporter]

NASA Tracking Vehicle, 3¼", #54, 1982, radar toward rear of roof (similar castings: Airport Foam Pumper, Command Vehicle, Mobile Home)

1. white, no side accents, clear windows, England cast..............$5 – 6

. white with side accents, clear windows, England cast ....$4 – 5

. white with side accents, clear windows, Macau cast..............................$3 – 4

. white with side accents, blue windows, Macau cast...........................$4 – 5

New Ford Transit (see Ford Transit Van)

Nissan 300ZX, no opening parts, 3", #61, 1990 – 1997; #37, 1991, international; #43, 1998

. metallic red with chrome windows, dark gray interior, rubber tires on gray rims, World Class ....$6 – 8

. metallic red, "Turbo Z," black and chrome windows, no interior, pink and red Lightning Wheels, on-package premium ....$6 – 8

. metallic red, "Turbo Z," black and chrome windows, no interior, silver and yellow Lightning Wheels, on-package premium...................................$6 – 8

. pearl pink, "Turbo Z," blue chrome and black windows, peach and silver Lightning Wheels ....$3 – 4

. orange-yellow, "D.A.R.E.," "Sanibel Police," D.A.R.E. series.............$4 – 5

. yellow, "300ZX" on doors, clear windows, white interior.................$2 – 3

. yellow, "300ZX" on doors, tinted windows, white interior.................$2 – 3

. yellow, "Turbo Z," black and chrome windows, Lightning Wheels........$3 – 4

. yellow, "Nationwide Auto Parts," "300ZX," clear windows, gray interior.....$30 – 40

10. yellow, **"North American Diecast Toy Collectors Association 1st Anniversary November 1994," custom..................$12 – 16**

11. yellow, detailed trim, black and gray interior, rubber tires on chrome rims, Premiere Collection #15 ....$4 – 5

12. bright orange, "300ZX," blue chrome and black windows, Lightning Wheels..$3 – 4

13. teal blue with yellow and pink streaks, clear windows, pink interior ....$2 – 3

14. metallic teal blue with yellow accents, hot pink interior, 1994 ....$2 – 4

15. metallic teal blue with hot pink, yellow and green accents, chrome and black windows ....$3 – 5

16. metallic blue, "300ZX," chrome and black windows, Lightning Wheels..........$3 – 4

17. metallic blue with silver and black riveted steel plate design on hood, pink interior, 1995......................................$2 – 3

18. black with orange and white lines on hood, white lines on sides, clear windows, fluorescent orange interior ....$4 – 5

19. black with orange-red and white graffiti, orange-red interior ....$2 – 3

20. black with white swirls, clear windows, pink interior ....$2 – 3

21. pearl white, detailed trim, chrome windows, dark gray interior, rubber tires on gray rims, World Class ....$6 – 8

22. pearl white, detailed trim, chrome windows, pink interior, rubber tires on gray rims, World Class ....$6 – 8

23. pearl white, detailed trim, chrome windows, white interior, rubber tires on gray rims, World Class ....$6 – 8

24. white, "ZX," orange and yellow design, 1998 Asian Cars series, international issue......................................$2 – 3

25. white with hot pink accents, blue chrome and black windows........$3 – 5

26. white, lime, and pink; "Z," "Turbo," black and chrome windows, Lightning Wheels.$3 – 4

27. white, orange, and black; "Z," "Turbo," black and chrome windows, Lightning Wheels ....$3 – 4

28. metallic gray and metallic blue, clear windows, fluorescent orange interior .$2 – 3

29. metallic silver with yellow and orange accents, "ZX" on doors, 1997...................................$2 – 3

30. metallic gold, 1997 75 Challenge series ....$12 – 16

31. chrome plated, Macau cast, custom...............................$16 – 24

32. chrome plated, Thailand cast, custom...............................$16 – 24

Nissan 300ZX Turbo, hood opens, 2⅞", #24, 1987

1. pearl gray with gold stripes, "Turbo"....................................$3 – 4

2. white, "Fujicolor" ....$3 – 4

3. red with red and orange stripes...$4 – 5

4. metallic red with red and orange stripes, Laser Wheels ....$4 – 5

5. white, "96," "BP Racing Team," the Netherlands issue ....$10 – 12

6. yellow, "4 Monkey Racing Team," Hong Kong issue..........................$10 – 12

Nissan Prairie, 2⅞", #31, US, 1991; #21, international, 1991; #45, 1998, international

1. dark green, gold "Nissan," 1998 Asian Cars series ....$2 – 3

2. metallic blue, silver sides...........$6 – 7

3. metallic silver, "Nissan".............$3 – 4

4. red, "Nissan".........................$9 – 12

5. white, no markings, Graffic Traffic ....$12 – 16

6. white, "Aqua" and diver design, 5-pack ....$2 – 3

7. white, "Paramedic PS" ....$3 – 4

8. yellow "City Wide Taxi Service," 1998 Around Town 5-pack................$2 – 3

Nissan Xterra, two kayaks on roof, #32, 2001; #65, 2001, international; #47, 2002; #39, 2003

1. metallic silver, "Matchbox" logo, "Xterra," gradient yellow to red kayaks, 2001 Sand Blasters series...............................$2 – 3

2. white with red, yellow, and black graphics; 2002 Weekend Cruisers series...$2 – 3

3. 2002 Matchbox Across America 50th Birthday series #16 Tennessee — Southern Collection, metallic dark gold, no kayaks....................$4 – 6

4. dark blue with red plastic base, "MHC Outfitters," 2003 Mom and Pop Shops ....$2 – 3
5. dark blue with red plastic base, "MHC Outfitters," 2003 Hero City 10-pack #2...$2 – 3
6. blue, "Kayaking Adventures" and wave design, yellow kayaks, 2001 international issue.............................$3 – 4

O

Oldsmobile Aerotech, 3," #62, 1989; #64, 1989
1. fluorescent orange, "Aerotech," Thailand cast ....$2 – 3

2. metallic purple and white, "Aerotech," purple flash, gold wheels, Thailand cast.....................................$2 – 3
3. metallic purple and white, "Aerotech," purple flash, silver wheels, China cast ....$2 – 3
5. metallic purple and white, "Aerotech," purple flash, silver wheels, Thailand cast ....$2 – 3
5. metallic purple and white, purple flash without "Aerotech," silver wheels, China cast.....................................$2 – 3

6. **metallic silver, "Quad 4," "Aerotech," "Oldsmobile," Macau cast ....$2 – 3**
7. metallic silver, "Quad 4," "Aerotech," "Oldsmobile," Thailand cast........$2 – 3

Opel Frogster, #74, 2003
1. metallic green, 2003 Car Shop series.....................................$2 – 3

Opel Calibra DTM, #66, 1997; #65, 1998

1. **orange with purple and white "33 Opel Racing," "Calibra" accents ....$2 – 3**

2. orange-yellow, "Sydney 2000," orange-yellow interior, 5-pack..............$2 – 3
3. orange-yellow, "Sydney 2000," orange-yellow interior, small wheels, 5-pack..$4 – 5
4. white, "Coca-Cola" and polar bear graphics, red interior, 5-pack.....$2 – 3

5. **white with blue and red "World Cup," "France 98" accents, red interior, yellow spoiler, 1998 World Cup 5-pack ....$2 – 3**
6. white with blue and red "World Cup," "France 98" accents, yellow interior, yellow spoiler, 1998 Motor Sports series ....$2 – 3
7. white with blue and red "World Cup," "France 98" accents, blue interior, yellow spoiler, Action Pack ....$2 – 3
8. metallic gold, no markings, 1997 75 Challenge series ....$6 – 12

Opel Diplomat, 2⅞", #36, 1966

1. **metallic gold with gray motor, black plastic wheels.....................$8 – 10**

2. **metallic gold with chrome motor, black plastic wheels ....$6 – 9**
3. sea green with gray motor, black plastic wheels............................$700 – 800
4. metallic gold, Superfast wheels, 1970 ....$30 – 40

Opel Frontera (see Isuzu Rodeo)

Opel Kadett (see Vauxhall Astra/Opel Kadett)

Opel Kadett Police (see Vauxhall Astra/Opel Kadett Police)

Opel Vectra/Chevrolet Cavalier GSi 2000, 3", #22, 1990; #41, 1991

1. **metallic red ....$3 – 5**
2. green, Germany gift set ....$10 – 1?

Opel Speedster, #6, 2003

1. **metallic silver with red interior 2003 Family Wheels series....$2 – ?**

Open Back Truck (see Mini Pickup 4x4)

Orange Peel Dodge Charger, 3," #74 1981 (similar casting: Dodge Dragster)
1. pink with snake illustration, China cast Premiere Collection #13 ....$4 – 5
2. purple with white, yellow and green flames, China cast, Adventure 2000..................................$2 – ?
3. white, "Orange Peel," Hong Kong cast.....................................$4 – 5
4. white, "Orange Peel," Macau cast.....................................$4 – 5

Over-Under Rescue Boats, #61, 2001 #38, 2002; #43, 2003

1. **white deck, metallic purple hull yellow-orange "Rescue" on sides bright orange interior, 2001 Scuba Dudes series ....$2 – 3**

2. **light blue deck, dark blue hull; yellow white, and blue lighthouse on sides fluorescent interior, 2002 Nite Glow series ....$2 – 3**

red deck, metallic blue hull, amber windows, metallic gray interior, 2003 Beach Patrol series ....$2 – 3
red deck, metallic blue hull, amber windows, metallic gray interior, 2003 Hero City 10-pack #1 ....$2 – 3

P

...nnier Tank Locomotive, 3", #47, 1979
dark green with black base ....$5 – 6
light green with black base ....$5 – 6
light green with brown base.....$8 – 10
light green with dark gray base ..$5 – 6
light green with unpainted base ..$5 – 6
light green with blue-gray base ...$5 – 6

...antera (see DeTomaso Pantera)

...assenger Coach (see Railway Passenger Coach)

...ersonnel Carrier (see M3 Army Halftrack Personnel Carrier, Army Saracen Personnel Carrier)

...ersonnel Carrier, 3", #54, 1976

. **army green with beige plastic figures seated in back** ....**$5 – 6**
. army green, no rear seats ....$5 – 6

...eterbilt Cement Truck, 3", #19, 1982; #8, 1998; #26, 1999; #93, 2000; #73, 2000, international

. **metallic red with white stripes, black barrel, metallic gray barrel base, 1998 Big Movers series** ....**$2 – 3**
. red, face and stripes, yellow wheels, lime green barrel, Live 'N Learn/Matchbox Preschool..........................$5 – 7
. red, black barrel, white barrel base, 1996.................................$2 – 3

4. red, black barrel, chrome barrel base, 1997 ....$2 – 3
5. red, orange barrel, Manaus cast, Brazil issue ....$35 – 40
6. red, white barrel, white stripes, packaged as #10 Peterbilt Quarry Truck, 1998 ....$24 – 32
7. dusty red, white barrel, 1999 Road Work series ....$2 – 3
8. light pink, "Readymix," white barrel, Australia issue ....$9 – 12
9. dirty pink, cream barrel with red stripes ....$2 – 3
10. orange-yellow, "Pace Construction," orange barrel ....$5 – 6
11. orange-yellow, "Pace Construction," red barrel ....$2 – 3
12. orange, black barrel ....$2 – 3
13. orange, cream barrel, translucent gray base, China cast.....................$4 – 6
14. fluorescent orange, no markings, black barrel, 5-pack ....$2 – 3
15. fluorescent orange, no markings, gray barrel, 5-pack ....$2 – 3
16. pumpkin orange, "Matchbox," gray barrel, 5-pack ....$2 – 3
17. yellow, "Dirty Dumper," orange barrel................................$45 – 60
18. yellow, "Pace Construction," gray barrel..................................$2 – 3
19. yellow, "Pace Construction," dark gray barrel, Motor City ....$3 – 4

20. yellow, "Pace Construction," red barrel ....**$2 – 4**

21. lemon yellow, "Highway Crew," green barrel, 1999 Highway Crew 5-pack ....**$2 – 3**

22. powder blue, black barrel, white stripes................................**$3 – 4**

23. blue, metallic silver barrel, orange barrel base, 2003 Hero City 5-pack................................**$2 – 3**
24. blue, "Kwik Set Cement," yellow barrel..................................$2 – 3
25. blue, "Kwik Set Cement," orange barrel..................................$9 – 12
26. metallic green, "Big Pete," orange barrel ....$3 – 5
27. bright green, "Matchbox," "MC05," white barrel, 5-pack ....$2 – 3
28. metallic gold, white barrel, 1997 75 Challenge series ....$6 – 12

29. white, "Cement Company," orange barrel, Manaus cast, Brazil issue.$35 – 40
30. white, no markings, gray barrel, ASAP promotional blank..................$30 – 40
31. white, "Hemler Bros.," gray barrel, ASAP promotional..............$80 – 120
32. white, "CAT Service Co.," gray barrel, ASAP promotional..............$80 – 120
33. white, "Redi-Way, Inc.," gray barrel, ASAP promotional..............$80 – 120
34. white, "Blue Ridge Construction," gray barrel, ASAP promotional....$80 – 120
35. dirty white, "Bilt," red barrel with white markings, pale gray base and grille, gray barrel base, 2000 Build It series...................................$2 – 3
36. dirty white, "Bilt," "Matchbox 2000," red barrel with white markings, pale gray base and grille, gray barrel base, 2000 Build It series ....$4 – 5

Peterbilt Conventional, 2³⁄₄", #43, 1982 (other variations exist as part of Convoy and White Rose Race Transporter series)
1. black with white and red design, amber windows, England (L) cast ....$5 – 6
2. black with white and red design, clear windows, England (L) cast ....$5 – 6
3. black with white and red "Ace" graphics, amber windows, England (L) cast .$5 – 6
4. black with white and red "Ace" graphics, amber windows, England (M) cast.................................$3 – 4

5. black with white and red "Ace" graphics, clear windows, England (L) cast..$5 – 6
6. black with white and red "Ace" graphics, clear windows, England (M) cast..$5 – 6
7. black with white and red "Z" graphics, amber windows, England (M) cast.......................................$4 – 5
8. black with white and red "Z" graphics, clear windows, Macau cast ......$3 – 4
9. black with white and red "Z" graphics, clear windows, England (M) cast .$4 – 5
10. black with white and brown "Ace" graphics, clear windows, England (L) cast...$5 – 6
11. black with white and black "Ace" graphics, clear windows, England (L) cast...$5 – 6
12. white with "NASA" and rocket graphics, clear windows, Macau cast ....$4 – 5

Peterbilt Dump Truck, with plow (also see Peterbilt Quarry Truck)
1. orange-yellow, "CAT," play set ....$4 – 5

Peterbilt Petrol Tanker (see Peterbilt Tanker)

Peterbilt Quarry Truck, 3", #30, 1982, US; #23, 1982, international; #19, 1997; #10, 1998
1. red with gray dumper, white stripes, 1998 Big Movers series ....$2 – 3
2. red with red dumper, "530SP," Manaus cast, Brazil issue ....$40 – 50

3. red with gray dumper, "530SP" and stripes, Manaus cast, Brazil issue ....$40 – 50
4. red with yellow dumper, "Joe Diesel," face and yellow design, play set..$5 – 6
5. orange with gray dumper, "Losinger," Macau cast, Switzerland issue.$10 – 12
6. fluorescent orange with black dumper, 5-pack......................................$2 – 3
7. pumpkin orange with gray dumper, "Matchbox," 5-pack ....$2 – 3
8. pumpkin orange with gray dumper, no markings, ASAP promotional blank ....$20 – 30
9. orange-yellow with red dumper, "Pace Construction" ....$3 – 4
10. orange-yellow with red dumper, no markings ....$2 – 3
11. yellow with gray dumper, "Dirty Dumper," England cast..........................$3 – 4
12. yellow with gray dumper, "Dirty Dumper," Macau cast ....$2 – 3
13. yellow with gray dumper, "Pace," Macau cast.....................................$2 – 3

14. yellow with gray dumper, "Pace," Thailand cast ....$2 – 3

15. yellow with yellow dumper, "CAT," Dirt Machines Dirt Movers set.......$2 – 3

16. yellow with red dumper, "Pace Construction" ....$2 – 3
17. yellow with red dumper, "Pace," Intercom City"..............................$12 – 16
18. white with gray dumper, "Cement Company," Manaus cast, Brazil issue ..$40 – 50
19. white with gray dumper, "Construction," Manaus cast, Brazil issue .....$40 – 50
20. white with gray dumper, no markings, ASAP promotional blank........$30 – 40
21. white with gray dumper, "Coast To Coast Hydraulics," ASAP promotional.$20 – 30
22. white with gray dumper, "CAT Service Co.," ASAP promotional ......$80 – 120
23. white with gray dumper, "Redi-Way Inc.," ASAP promotional......$80 – 120
24. white with gray dumper, "Blue Ridge Construction," ASAP promotional.$80 – 120
25. white with gray dumper, "Hemler Bros.," ASAP promotional ...$80 – 120
26. white with turquoise dumper, "Sagamore Insurance"...............$90 – 120
27. metallic gold with gray dumper, 1997 75 Challenge series ....$80 – 120

Peterbilt Tanker, 3", #56, 1982; #12, 1999; #5, 1982, international; #7, 1998, international; #12, 1999, international
1. red, "Amoco" on tank, "Getty" on door, chrome tank.......................$50 – 70
2. red, "Getty," chrome tank..........$3 – 4

3. fluorescent yellow, "Airways Caution Jet Fuel," chrome tank, 1999 Airport 5-pack ....$2 – 3

4. army green, "Gas," army green tan[k] Commando series ....$5 –
5. lime green, yellow tank, red wheel[s] Matchbox Preschool/Live 'N Lea[rn] series....................................$7 –

6. blue, "Fresh Milk," white tank, Far[m] gift set ....$20 – 3[0]
7. blue, "Milk" with red "Milk" on doo[r,] white tank...............................$5 –
8. blue, "Milk" with white "Milk" on doo[r,] white tank..............................$4 –
9. blue, "Milk" with no markings on doo[r,] white tank.............................$4 –

10. blue, "QTD-94712," maroon an[d] white stripes, chrome tank wit[h] printed gauges, flammable symb[ol] and pipes, 5-pack.................$2 –

11. blue, "Test Mission," gray tan[k,] 2000 Space Mission 5-pack...$2 – [3]
12. blue, white tank, no markings ....$6 –
13. black, "Amoco," black tank.........$4 –
14. black, "Amoco," chrome tank.$60 – 8[0]
15. black, "Amoco," white tank ....$40 – 6[0]
16. black, "Indy Racing Fuel," black tan[k,] Indy 500 series ....$12 – 1[6]
17. black, "Matchbox," "Getty," black tan[k,] Manaus cast, Brazil issue .....$40 – 5[0]
18. black, "Supergas," yellow tank ....$3 –
19. black, "Supergas," orange-yellow tank ....$3 –
20. black, "Supergas," chrome tank ....$60 – 7[0]
21. black, "Texaco," chrome tank, rubbe[r] tires on chrome rims, Premiere Colle[c]tion......................................$4 – 5

22. black and white, "Official Indy Fuel Truck," black tank..............$8 – 10

23. white, "100% Divine," chrome tank, ASAP promotional............$80 – 120
24. white, "American International Recovery," ASAP promotional.....$120 – 160
25. white, "Amoco," white tank.......$3 – 4
26. white, "Ampol," gray tank, Australia issue...................................$8 – 10
27. white, "Arco Lar 75," chrome tank, ASAP promotional.............$80 – 120
28. white, "Blue Ridge Construction," chrome tank, ASAP promotional.......$80 – 120
29. white, "BP," green tank, Australia issue $9 – 12
30. white, "BP Super," chrome tank, ASAP promotional......................$80 – 120
31. white, "CT Tank Removal," chrome tank, ASAP promotional.............$80 – 120
32. white, "Darry Brothers," chrome tank, ASAP promotional.............$80 – 120
33. white, "Dairy Line," cream tank, black cow spots, 1999 Highway Haulers series...................................$2 – 3
34. white, "Dairy Line" on cab only, cream tank, black cow spots, 1999 Highway Haulers international series.....$9 – 12
35. white, "Esso," cream tank, Manaus cast, Brazil issue.................$40 – 50
36. white, "Fullbright Oil Co.," chrome tank, ASAP promotional.............$80 – 120
37. white, "Giant Industries," chrome tank, ASAP promotional.............$80 – 120
38. white, "Hemler Bros.," chrome tank, ASAP promotional.............$80 – 120
39. white, "Maalcovich Pumping," chrome tank, ASAP promotional......$80 – 120
40. white, "Shell," gray tank.............$3 – 4

41. white, "Shell," chrome tank ...$2 – 3
42. white, "Shell" with "IC" on doors, chrome tank, Intercom City ...$12 – 16
43. white, "Supergas," yellow tank$30 – 40
44. white, "Systend Dairies," chrome tank, ASAP promotional.............$80 – 120
45. white, "Wisconsin," Matchbox Across America 50th Birthday series #30, Central Collection....................$5 – 6

46. white, "White's Guide Car of the Month #10 September 1999," chrome tank, ASAP promotional ....$10 – 15
47. white, cream tank, black cow spots, international issue.................$9 – 12
48. white, chrome tank, no markings, ASAP promotional blank..................$30 – 40
49. white, white tank, chrome pipes, no markings ....$40 – 60
50. white, white tank, gray pipes, no markings, Graffic Traffic..............$12 – 16
51. white and red, "Avia," white tank, Belgium issue ....$16 – 24

Peterbilt Wreck Truck, 3", #61, 1982
1. red, "Police," black booms, Manaus cast, Brazil issue ....$40 – 50
2. orange, "Eddie's Wrecker," black booms, amber windows ....$5 – 6
3. orange, "Eddie's Wrecker," black booms, clear windows ....$5 – 6
4. orange with black stripes, dark green booms, plastic armament, Roadblasters, Macau cast................$7 – 9
5. orange with black stripes, dark green booms, Tomy box, Japan issue, Thailand cast...................................$9 – 12
6. yellow, "Metro Recovery," blue booms, amber windows, 5-pack ....$2 – 3
7. yellow with car design, blue booms, amber windows, 5-pack ....$3 – 4
8. army green, "8," red and white stripes, black booms, Commando series.$5 – 6
9. blue, "C.P. City Police," black booms, Manaus cast, Brazil issue .....$40 – 50
10. blue with no markings, black booms, amber windows ....$160 – 240
11. white, "911," blue booms..........$3 – 4
12. white, "Police PD-22" and checkerboard pattern, orange booms, clear windows .$3 – 4
13. white, "Police M9," "Intercom City," orange booms, clear windows, Intercom City ....$8 – 10
14. white, "SFPD" and star, orange booms, clear windows.........................$2 – 3
15. white with black "9," black booms, Manaus cast, Brazil issue............$40 – 50
16. white with black "9," black booms, amber windows ....$3 – 4
17. white with black "9," black booms, clear windows ....$2 – 3
18. white with blue "9," black booms, amber windows ....$3 – 4
19. white with blue "9," blue booms, amber windows ....$2 – 3
20. white with blue "9," blue booms, clear windows ....$2 – 3

21. white with no markings, black booms, Macau cast............................$3 – 4

Petrol Tanker (see Bedford Petrol Tanker)

Peugeot 205 Turbo 16, 2¹¹⁄₁₆", #15, 1985; #25, 1991
1. white with red "205" and stripes, Macau cast...........................$3 – 5
2. white with black "205" and stripes, Macau cast...........................$3 – 5
3. white with purple "205" and stripes, Macau cast...........................$3 – 5
4. white with purple "205" and stripes, China cast ....$3 – 5
5. white with black "205," Manaus cast, Brazil issue ....$35 – 45
6. white with black "205," "Matchbox 11," Manaus cast, Brazil issue .....$35 – 45
7. orange-red with "Michelin," "Bilstein," "48"...................................$3 – 5
8. green with no markings, Germany gift set....................................$9 – 12
9. yellow with "Peugeot 205," "Bilstein," "48"...................................$3 – 5
10. dark gray with "Shell 37" and pink and yellow, Manaus cast, Brazil issue..$40 – 50

Peugeot Quasar, 2³⁄₄", #25, 1985, US; #49, 1987, international
1. maroon with yellow accents.......$2 – 3
2. orange, "Fanta," China issue.............................$160 – 180
3. yellow, "3," stripes and flames, Matchbox Preschool/Live 'N Learn series...................................$7 – 9
4. dark blue, "9" and pink stripes, new Superfast wheels ....$4 – 5
5. metallic blue, "9" and pink stripes, Laser wheels...........................$4 – 5
6. purple, "Quasar" ....$2 – 3
7. black with bright green and orange stripes, armaments, Roadblasters .$6 – 8
8. white, "Quasar"........................$3 – 4

Phantom Z (see Nissan Fairlady Z)

Pi-Eyed Piper, 2⁷⁄₈", #48, 1972 (similar castings: Big Banger, Cosmic Blues, Flame Out, Red Rider)
1. blue, "8" label on roof, amber windows ....$16 – 24
2. blue, "8" label on roof, blue windows ....$16 – 24
3. blue, "8" label on roof, "Red Rider" on base, Premiere Collection #13...$4 – 5

Pickfords Removers Van, 2⁵⁄₈", #46, 1960

1. **green, "Pickfords Removers & Storers," black wheels.............$20 – 25**
2. green, "Pickfords Removers & Storers," gray wheels.................$40 – 50
3. green, "Pickfords Removers & Storers," silver wheels ....$75 – 90
4. dark blue, "Pickfords Removers & Storers," gray wheels ....$60 – 75
5. dark blue, "Pickfords Removers & Storers," silver wheels ....$100 – 120
6. tan, "Beales Bealson," sunburst, black wheels............................$300 – 325

Pickup Camper 4x4, 3", #57, 1982; #35, 1986

Pickup (see Mini Pickup 4x4, Jeep Gladiator, etc.)

Pipe Truck (see Leyland Pipe Truck)

Piston Popper (see Ford Mustang Piston Popper)

Plane Transporter (see Airplane Transporter)

Planet Scout, 2³⁄₄", #59, 1971
1. red upper, beige lower, amber windows ....$12 – 16
2. metallic green upper, lime lower, amber windows ....$12 – 16
3. metallic green upper, apple green lower, amber windows ....$12 – 16
4. avocado upper, black lower, amber windows, Adventure 2000.........$30 – 40
5. avocado upper, black lower, purple windows, Adventure 2000.........$30 – 40
6. metallic blue upper, black lower, purple windows, Adventure 2000 ....$50 – 60

Plymouth Gran Fury Police, 3", #10, 1979
1. white with "Police" and shield, England cast.....................................$3 – 5
2. white with "Metro," blue windows, England cast ....$3 – 5
3. white with "Metro," dark gray windows, England cast ....$4 – 6
4. white with "Metro," blue windows, Macau cast.............................$4 – 6
5. white with blue "Police," blue windows, Macau cast........................$3 – 5
6. white with "Police SFPD," dark blue windows....................................$3 – 5
7. white with "Police SFPD," green windows..................................$80 – 100
8. white with "Sheriff SP-5," dark blue windows...................................$3 – 5
9. black and white, "Adam 12," "Police," Star Cars............................$5 – 7

Plymouth Prowler, with metal base, MLB97, 1997, White Rose Collectibles (compare to Plymouth Prowler, with plastic base)
1. "Anaheim Angels 1997," pearl white......................................$5 – 6

2. "Arizona Diamondbacks Inaugural Season 1998," metallic purple........$5 – 6
3. "Atlanta Braves 1997," metallic tan ....$5 – 6
4. "Baltimore Orioles 1997," black ....$5 – 6
5. "Boston Red Sox 1997," metallic red ....$5 – 6
6. "Chicago Cubs 1997," metallic blue ....$5 – 6
7. "Chicago White Sox 1997," black ....$5 – 6
8. "Cincinnati Reds 1997," metallic red ....$5 – 6
9. "Cleveland Indians 1997," metallic gray...$5 – 6
10. "Colorado Rockies 1997," metallic purple.......................................$5 – 6
11. "Detroit Tigers 1997," metallic orange ....$5 – 6
12. "Florida Marlins 1997," metallic gray ....$5 – 6
13. "Houston Astros 1997," pearl white ....$5 – 6
14. "Kansas City Royals 1997," metallic tan ....$5 – 6
15. "Milwaukee Brewers 1997," metallic green ....$5 – 6
16. "Los Angeles Dodgers 1997," metallic blue ....$5 – 6
17. "Minnesota Twins 1997," metallic blue ....$5 – 6
18. "Montreal Expos 1997," pearl white...$5 – 6
19. "New York Mets 1997," metallic orange ....$5 – 6
20. "New York Yankees 1997," metallic gray...$5 – 6
21. "Oakland A's 1997," metallic green...$5 – 6
22. "Philadelphia Phillies 1997," metallic red ....$5 – 6
23. "Pittsburgh Pirates 1997," black...$5 – 6
24. "San Diego Padres 1997," metallic gray...$5 – 6
25. "San Francisco Giants 1997," black...$5 – 6
26. "Seattle Mariners 1997," metallic tan ....$5 – 6
27. "St. Louis Cardinals 1997," metallic gray...$5 – 6
28. "Tampa Bay Devil Rays Inaugural Season 1998," metallic purple........$5 – 6
29. "Texas Rangers 1997," metallic red.$5 – 6
30. "Toronto Blue Jays 1997," metallic blue ....$5 – 6
31. "World Series 1997 Champions Marlins," turquoise.........................$5 – 6
32. "World Series 1997 Champions Marlins," turquoise, sealed in bat-shaped glass bottle ....$40 – 50

Plymouth Prowler, with plastic base, #34, 1995 – 1997; #18, 1998; #4, 2000; #58, 2001; #6, 1995, international (compare to Plymouth Prowler with metal base)

1. red with black interior, "Prowler"..$2 – 3
2. red with black interior, no markings ....$3 – 4

3. **red with black interior, detailed trim, rubber tires on chrome rims, Select Class #4..............................$4 – 5**

4. **red with gray and red interior, detailed trim, rubber tires on chrome rims, JC Penney Premiere Collection............................$4 – 5**
5. orange with gray interior, detailed trim, rubber tires on chrome rims, Premiere Collection #16.......................$4 – 5
6. metallic orange with gray interior, detailed trim, rubber tires on chrome rims, Premiere Collection ....$5 – 6
7. yellow, "Matchbox 1996 Line Preview," gray interior, rubber tires on chrome rims..............................$300 – 400
8. yellow with black interior, blue and red stripes, 5-pack ....$2 – 3
9. yellow with gray and black interior, detailed trim, rubber tires on chrome rims, Select Class #5 ....$4 – 5
10. yellow with black interior, no markings, Color Comp promotional blank .$30 – 40
11. yellow with black interior, "Convention 2000 Lion's Club — Honolulu Hawaii," Color Comp promotional........$30 – 40
12. yellow with black interior, "Tyler Elliot Memorial Model," "10," Color Comp promotional.......................$20 – 30

13. **blue with green interior, green and white design, 5-pack..............$2 – 3**
14. metallic dark blue with black interior, detailed trim, rubber tires on chrome rims, International Premiere Collection #1 ....$9 – 12
15. purple, "16th Annual Matchbox USA Convention 1997," custom....$12 – 16

16. purple, "Great Strides," "Cystic Fibrosis Foundation," Color Comp promotional ....$20 – 25
17. purple, "Mattel Wheels — Driving To Win, custom ....$300 – 500
18. purple, "Thank You For Buying From The Chris Getz Collection," Color Comp promotional ....$20 – 25
19. purple with black interior, no markings, Color Comp promotional blank .$30 – 40

20. **purple with gray interior, silver grille, 1995.........................$2 – 3**
21. purple with gray interior, plain grille, 1997.....................................$2 – 3
22. purple with gray interior, detailed trim, rubber tires on chrome rims, Premiere Collection #14.........................$4 – 5
23. purple with plain gray base, gray and purple interior, detailed trim, rubber tires on chrome rims, Premiere Collection World Class #1 ....$9 – 12
24. purple with detailed base, gray and purple interior, detailed trim, rubber tires on chrome rims, Premiere Collection World Class #1 ....$125 – 175
25. purple with white interior, detailed trim, rubber tires on chrome rims, Chrysler gift set ....$4 – 5
26. metallic gold with black interior, 6-spoke spiral wheels, 1997 75 Challenge series..................................$6 – 12
27. metallic gold with black interior, 5-spoke concave star wheels, 1997 75 Challenge series ....$20 – 30
28. metallic tan with black interior, 1998 Cool Concepts series ....$2 – 3
29. metallic tan with black interior, "White's Guide Movie #1," ASAP promotional.............................$60 – 80
30. black with plain grille, "Prowler" on sides, purple interior, 1998 5-pack ......$2 – 3
31. black with gray grille, "Prowler" on sides, purple interior, 1998 Cool Concepts series ....$2 – 3
32. black with orange interior, "Toy Fair 97," "Matchbox," US issue ..$80 – 120
33. black with yellow interior, "Toy Fair 97," "Matchbox," UK issue ....$20 – 25

34. **black with red interior, no markings, 2000 Open Road series........$2 – 3**
35. black with red interior, detailed trim, rubber tires on chrome rims, Gold Coin Collection............................$16 – 24
36. black with red interior, "Matchbox 2000," 2000 Open Road series.$3 – 4
37. gray with gray and purple interior, detailed trim, rubber tires on chrome rims, Select Class #1 ....$9 – 12
38. metallic gray with gray and purple interior, detailed trim, rubber tires on chrome rims, Premiere Collection #4 ....$4 – 5
39. white with blue interior, "Beep Beep The Clown," Color Comp promotional .$40 – 50
40. white with purple interior, "Prowler" on sides, plain grille, 5-pack ....$2 – 3

41. **white with purple interior, "Prowler" on sides, gray grille, 1998 Cool Concepts series ....$2 – 3**
42. white with blue interior, "Tyco Playtime Toy Fair 96".........................$40 – 50
43. white with blue interior, "Tyco Playtime Dallas 96"...........................$40 – 50
44. white with blue interior, "Tyco Playtime Hong Kong 96"...................$40 – 50
45. 2001 Wheeled Envy series........$2 – 3

Police Bus (see School Bus)

Police Car, #53, 2002; #27, 2003

1. **pearl white with blue, yellow, and gray design, 2002 Rescue Rookies series ....$2 – 3**
2. black with yellow door, "Highway Patrol," blue plastic base, red windows, 2003 Police Squad series ....$2 – 3

3. **blue with white, gold, and black, white plastic base, amber windows, 2003 Hero City 5-pack #7 .....$2 – 3**

Police Launch, 3", #52, 1976; #80, 1999

1. **red deck, white hull, "2416-134," blue sash design, yellow figures, 1998 Emergency Rescue 5-pack........$2 – 3**
2. yellow deck, black hull, "Rescue B-1," red and white stripes, cast horns, red figures, Real Talkin' series ....$4 – 5
3. yellow and black deck, white hull, "Base 2000," blue and black stripes, blue figures, Launcher 5-pack..............$2 – 3

4. **blue deck, white hull, "OD-593," light blue band, compass design, yellow figures, 2000 Ocean Dock 5-pack.$2 – 3**
5. metallic blue deck, dark blue hull, storm design, blue figures, Launcher 5-pack ....$2 – 3
6. white deck, blue hull, "Amity Police," "Jaws" labels, cast horns, light blue figures, Star Cars series ....$6 – 8
7. white deck, blue hull, "Police" labels, light blue figures, England cast...$5 – 6
8. white deck, blue hull, "Police" labels, cast horns, light blue figures, England cast..$6 – 8
9. white deck, blue hull, "Police" labels, cast horns, light blue figures, no-origin cast, Brazil issue ....$60 – 80
10. white deck, blue hull, "123," rope pattern, red figures, Matchbox Preschool/Live 'N Learn series..$7 – 9
11. white deck, dark blue hull, "Police," orange stripes, cast horns, China cast, Action Pack............................$3 – 4
12. white deck, red hull, "LA Fire," orange-yellow figures, England cast, Code Red series.................................$7 – 9
13. white deck, red hull, "LA Fire," light blue figures, England cast, Code Red series...............................$12 – 16

14. **white deck, red hull, white "UT-35-091M" and graphics, cast horns, China cast, 1999 Fire Rescue series...$2 – 3**

15. white deck, red hull, white "UT-35-091M" and graphics, no horns, China cast, Target Eggmobile series....$6 – 8
16. white deck, white hull, white figures, Graffic Traffic, China cast..........$6 – 8
17. black deck, dark gray hull, tan and gray camouflage, dark gray figures, Macau cast, Commando series ....$5 – 6

Police Mobile Command Center, #44, 2001; #15 Bloodmobile, 2003 (similar casting: Truck Camper)

1. **pearl white with blue door, blue and red, "Police," red roof lights, #44, 2001 Rescue Squad series ....$2 – 3**

2. **white with red door; red, black, and gray; "Metro Base 15," blue roof lights, #15 Bloodmobile, 2003 Hospital series...........$2 – 3**

Police Motorcycle, #35, 1999; 46,2001

1. **black with gray handlebars and saddlebags, "Police," 1999 Law & Order series ....$2 – 3**
2. blue with black handlebars and saddlebags, "Radio," 5-pack................$2 – 3
3. black with gray handlebars, black saddlebags, "MB1," 2001 Pull Over series..................$2 – 3

Police Motorcycle with Sidecar, #59, 2002; #28, 2003
1. yellow with yellow plastic fairing, blue seat, yellow base, 2003 Hero City 10-pack #1................................$2 – 3

2. **metallic blue with white plastic fairing, seat, and base, "No. 420 Police," 2002 Rescue Rookies series ....$2 – 3**
3. metallic blue with yellow plastic fairing, blue seat and base, 2003 Police Squad series..................................$2 – 3

4. **metallic blue with white plastic fairing, yellow seat and base, 2003 Rescue Heroes 5-pack ....$2 – 3**

Police Motorcyclist, Honda CB750 with rider, 2½", #33, 1977
1. black with "L.A.P.D." label ....$8 – 10
2. black with "Police" ....$3 – 4
3. ivory with "Polizei" label, wire wheels, Germany issue.....................$25 – 40
4. white with "Polizei" label, wire wheels, Germany issue.....................$25 – 40
5. white with "Polizei" label, mag wheels, Germany issue.....................$25 – 40
6. white with "Police" label, wire wheels, white seat..................$6 – 8
7. white with "Police" label, mag wheels, white seat..................$6 – 8
8. white with "Police" label, mag wheels, green seat.........................$16 – 24
9. white with "Police" label, mag wheels, black seat, black engine ....$3 – 4
10. white with "Police" label, mag wheels, black seat, chrome engine.........$6 – 8
11. white with "4" label, mag wheels, red seat, no rider ....$12 – 16
12. white with "Honda" and "Police" labels ....$3 – 4
13. white with Japan lettering ....$9 – 12

Police Patrol (see Range Rover Police Patrol)

Police SUV, #26, 2003

1. **metal flake gray with dark blue plastic base, blue windows; red, white, and two-tone blue; 2003 Police Squad series.............$2 – 3**

Police Trouble Tracker, 3", #52, 2001 (similar casting: Troop Carrier)
1. blue with khaki canopy, red tinted windows, "Police," 2001 Police series....................................$2 – 3

Pontiac 1970 GTO "The Judge," #70, 1996 – 1997; #38, 1998; #71, 1999
1. red with yellow and blue trim, 5-spoke concave wheels ....$3 – 4
2. red with yellow and blue trim, 5-spoke spiral wheels ....$120 – 160
3. orange with blue and red trim, rubber tires on chrome rims, Premiere Collection......................................$6 – 8
4. orange with yellow and blue trim, 5-spoke concave wheels.......$120 – 160

5. **orange with yellow and blue trim, 6-spoke spiral wheels, 1996 .....$2 – 3**
6. yellow with green and blue flames, rubber tires on chrome rims, Premiere Collection #11 ....$4 – 5

7. **yellow with red and blue trim, 1998 Classic Decades series ....$2 – 3**
8. dark green with orange and yellow trim, 6-spoke spiral wheels, China issue................................$80 – 120

9. **dark green with orange and yellow trim, rubber tires on chrome rims, Select Class #3** ....**$4 – 5**
10. metallic blue with red and white trim, rubber tires on chrome rims, Gold Coin Collection ....$16 – 24
11. dark blue with white, yellow, orange, and red trim, rubber tires on chrome rims, Premiere Collection #20 ...$4 – 5
12. dark purple with detailed trim, rubber tires on chrome rims, Matchbox Collectibles ....$16 – 24

13. **black with orange and white band, "GTO," 1999 Classics series** ..**$2 – 3**

14. **black with yellow and red trim, 1997 American Street Machines 5-pack** ....**$2 – 3**
15. dark gray with red and white trim, rubber tires on chrome rims, Premiere Collection #17 ....$4 – 5
16. white, "Coca-Cola Play Refreshed," rubber tires on chrome rims, Premiere Collection ....$4 – 5
17. white with blue and yellow trim, rubber tires on chrome rims, Premiere Collection #6 ....$6 – 8
18. metallic silver with blue and yellow trim, 6-spoke spiral wheels, China issue ....$80 – 120

19. **metallic silver with blue and yellow trim, rubber tires on chrome rims, Premiere Collection #3** ....**$6 – 8**
20. metallic gold with no trim, 1997 75 Challenge series ....$6 – 12

Pontiac Convertible, 2³/₄", #39, 1962
1. metallic lavender ....$80 – 100
2. yellow ....$30 – 40

Pontiac Fiero, 2¹³/₁₆", #2, 1985
1. white upper, blue lower, "Goodyear," silver wheels ....$3 – 5

2. white upper, blue lower, "Goodyear," gold wheels ....$5 – 10
3. white upper, red lower, "GT Fiero" ....$3 – 5
4. yellow upper, orange lower, "Protech," new Superfast wheels ....$5 – 7
5. yellow upper, orange lower, "Protech," 8-dot silver wheels ....$60 – 80
6. yellow upper, gold lower, "Protech," Laser wheels ....$4 – 6
7. black upper, red lower, "2 Dog Racing Team" ....$10 – 15
8. fluorescent orange upper, black lower, black flames, "Turbo" ....$5 – 7

Pontiac Firebird, 2⁷/₈", #4, 1975

1. **metallic blue with dual chrome hood scoops** ....**$6 – 8**

Pontiac Firebird Formula, #20, 1997; #72, 1998 (see Pontiac Firebird Ram Air 1997)

Pontiac Firebird Formula, #377, 1998, Taco Bell; Matchbox mold retooled by Strottman International Inc. through a licensing agreement with Mattel. Strottman manufactures toy premiums for Taco Bell. Base is marked "Made in China by S.I.I."
1. black with metallic silver windows, "Taco Bell," red and white flames, Taco Bell ....$4 – 5

Pontiac Firebird Racer S/E, #12, 1982; #51, 1984; #60, 1984; #12, 1986; #48, 1993 (see Pontiac Firebird S/E)

Pontiac Firebird Ram Air 1997, #20, 1997; #72, 1998

1. **yellow, 1997** ....**$2 – 3**

2. **black, 1998 Street Cruisers series, China cast** ....**$2 – 3**

3. metallic gold, 1997 75 Challenge series, Thailand cast ....$10 – 12
4. metallic gold, 1997 75 Challenge series, China cast ....$8 – 10
5. black, 1998 Street Cruisers series, Thailand cast ....$2 – 3
6. metallic gray, rubber tires on chrome hubs, Premiere Collection #14 ...$4 – 6
7. red, rubber tires on chrome hubs, Premiere Collection ....$6 – 9
8. yellow, "Coca-Cola Play Refreshed," Premiere Collection ....$4 – 6

Pontiac Firebird S/E, 3", #12, 1982; #51, 1984; #60, 1984; #12, 1986; #48, 1993
1. red, "Firebird," tan interior, clear windows ....$5 – 7
2. red, "Maaco" labels, red interior, clear windows ....$9 – 12
3. dark red, no markings, tan interior, clear windows ....$4 – 6
4. dark red, no markings, tan interior, amber windows ....$5 – 7
5. dark red, no markings, yellow interior, clear windows ....$4 – 6
6. dark red, no markings, yellow interior, amber windows ....$4 – 6
7. fluorescent pink with fluorescent yellow and white accents on sides and hood, 1994 ....$2 – 3
8. fluorescent pink with fluorescent yellow and white accents on sides, not on hood, 1996 ....$2 – 3

9. **fluorescent pink with yellow and white design, bright yellow plastic base, Thailand cast** ....**$2 – 3**

10. **yellow, "10," red and white, plastic base, new Superfast wheels** ....**$16 – 24**
11. yellow, "Pirelli 56" ....$5 – 6
12. yellow, "Son of a Gun 55" ....$5 – 6
13. pale green to dark brown, "Fast Eddie's 15," Super Color Changers ......$8 – 10
14. metallic turquoise with yellow and white hood and sides design, bright yellow plastic base, China cast ....$3 – 4
15. blue with white interior, blue windows, red, orange and yellow stripes, black metal base ....$9 – 12

16. blue with white interior, blue windows; red, orange, and yellow stripes; white metal base..............................$4 – 6
17. blue with white interior, blue windows; red, orange, and yellow stripes; white plastic base.............................$5 – 7
18. light blue, "10," blue and yellow, metal base, New Superfast Wheels.....$4 – 5
19. light blue, "10," blue and yellow, plastic base, New Superfast Wheels...$8 – 10
20. light blue with red interior, clear windows; green, yellow, and white stripes; Dinky.....................................$12 – 16
21. metallic blue, "10," blue and yellow, blue metal base, Laser Wheels........$4 – 5
22. metallic blue, "10," blue and yellow, blue plastic base, Laser Wheels .....$8 – 10
23. metallic blue with white interior, blue windows; red, orange, and yellow stripes; Laser Wheels ....$4 – 6
24. purple, "Firebird," red interior, clear windows, Super Color Changers......$4 – 5
25. purple with yellow and white design, bright yellow plastic base, Thailand cast.......................................$7 – 9
26. black, "Firebird," red interior, opaque windows ....$12 – 16
27. black, "Firebird," red interior, clear windows ....$3 – 5
28. black, "Firebird," tan interior, clear windows ....$4 – 6
29. black, "Go Pies! 1997," Australia issue ....$2 – 3
30. black, "Halley's Comet," gray interior, clear windows, 1986..............$9 – 12
31. black, "Knight Rider," tan interior, Star Cars series ....$9 – 12
32. black with red interior, clear windows, hot pink and bright blue accents ....$4 – 5
33. metallic gray with two-tone blue design, rubber tires on chrome rims, Premiere Collection #9..........................$4 – 5
34. white, "6 Horse Racing Team," Hong Kong issue..........................$9 – 12
35. white, "Fast Eddie's 15," blue metal base ....$3 – 4
36. white, "Fast Eddie's 15," blue plastic base, China cast....................$7 – 9
37. white, "Fast Eddie's 15," blue plastic base, Macau cast ....$4 – 5
38. white, "Fast Eddie's 15," blue plastic base, Thailand cast ....$3 – 4
39. dark brown to pale green, "Fast Eddie's 15," blue metal base, Super Color Changers...........................$8 – 10

Pontiac Firebird S/E Police, #456, 2000
1. red, "D.A.R.E.," "Police," D.A.R.E. series....................................$4 – 5
2. black and white, "D.A.R.E. To Resist Drugs & Violence," D.A.R.E. series....................................$4 – 5

Pontiac Firebird Trans Am, #16, 1979
1. metallic tan ....$6 – 9
2. metallic gold...........................$6 – 9
3. white......................................$5 – 7

4. dark blue, Manaus cast, Brazil issue..................................$60 – 80

Pontiac Firebird Trans Am T-Roof, #35, 1982; #16, 1983, international

1. **black, firebird design on hood, "Turbo," England cast ....$3 – 4**
2. black, firebird design on hood, "Trans Am," Macau cast....................$3 – 4
3. black, orange tiger stripes, Macau cast, UK on-package premium ....$12 – 16

4. **metallic silver, firebird design on hood, Macau cast ....$3 – 4**
5. red, "3 Rooster Racing Team," Macau cast, Hong Kong issue............$9 – 12
6. black, "Smokey & The Bandit," Star Cars series ....$6 – 7

Pontiac Grand Prix, 3", #22, 1964

1. **red with black plastic wheels ....$16 – 24**
2. red with Superfast wheels, 1970........................$2000 – 2500

3. **purple with Superfast wheels ....$55 – 65**

Pontiac Grand Prix, 1994, approximate`ly 1:43 scale, from White Rose Collectibles
1. yellow and black, red, and blue, "Black Flag 43," "French's 43".........$35 – 40
2. dark blue and white, "Cobra 24"....................................$12 – 16
3. light blue, "USA Bobsled Team 43"....................................$12 – 16

4. silver gray, metallic blue and pink, "Coors Light 42"..................$20 – 25

Pontiac Grand Prix 1996, WRP01, 1996, White Rose Collectibles
1. "MBNA America 72," black ....$5 – 6
2. "Skittles 36," "Starburst," red and blue..$5 – 6
3. "White Rose Collectibles," "December 25," dark green...................$60 – 80
4. "White Rose Collectibles," "Merry Christmas 1997," red ....$50 – 60

Pontiac Grand Prix Stock Car, #35, 1992; #22, 1993, international; #269, 1994, White Rose
1. "Black Flag 43," "French's 43"; yellow, black, red, and blue; Goodyear rubber tires on black rims, White Rose Collectibles..............................$40 – 50
2. "Black Flag 43," Goodyear rubber tires on black rims, White Rose Collectibles ....$4 – 5
3. "Cobra 24," dark blue and white, Goodyear rubber tires on black rims, White Rose Collectibles.........$12 – 16
4. "Coors Light 42," metallic blue and pink, Goodyear rubber tires on black rims, White Rose Collectibles, sealed in plexiglas box with metallic gray stand.....$20 – 30
5. "Coors Light 42," metallic blue and pink, Goodyear rubber tires on black rims, White Rose Collectibles, sealed in plexi-glas box with white stand ......$20 – 30
6. "Country Time 68," yellow, Goodyear slicks, White Rose Collectibles ...$4 – 5
7. "Evinrude 80," blue and white, Goodyear slicks, White Rose Collectibles ...$4 – 5
8. "French's 43," yellow, Goodyear rubber tires on black rims, White Rose Collectibles..............................$4 – 5
9. "Hulkster 43," red, Goodyear rubber tires on black rims, Team Convoy, White Rose Collectibles.............$7 – 9
10. "Kendall 40," black, Goodyear rubber tires on black rims, White Rose Collectibles..............................$4 – 5
11. "Medford Speed Shop," "Valtrol 48," white and yellow, Goodyear slicks, White Rose Collectibles.............$5 – 6
12. "Mello Yello 42," black and green, Goodyear slicks, White Rose Collectibles..............................$4 – 5
13. "Mello Yello 42," black and green, Goodyear rubber tires on black rims, White Rose Collectibles.............$5 – 6
14. "Nastrak 1," white and red, Goodyear slicks, White Rose Collectibles ...$4 – 5
15. "Nastrak 2," red, Goodyear slicks, White Rose Collectibles.............$4 – 5
16. "Nastrak 3," red and yellow, Goodyear slicks, White Rose Collectibles ...$4 – 5
17. "Nastrak 4," red and brown, Goodyear slicks, White Rose Collectibles ...$4 – 5
18. "Nastrak 5," red and yellow, Goodyear slicks, White Rose Collectibles ...$4 – 5
19. "Nastrak 6," blue and white, Goodyear slicks, White Rose Collectibles ...$4 – 5

20. "Outlaw Auto 7," black.........$3 – 4
21. "Pennzoil 30," yellow, Goodyear slicks, White Rose Collectibles.............$4 – 5
22. "Pennzoil 30," yellow, Goodyear rubber tires on black rims, White Rose Collectibles..............................$4 – 5
23. "Pennzoil 30," yellow, Goodyear rubber tires on gray rims, White Rose Collectibles..............................$5 – 6
24. "Pontiac Excitement 2," black, Goodyear slicks, White Rose Collectibles ...$4 – 5
25. "Pontiac Excitement 2," black, Goodyear rubber tires on black rims, White Rose Collectibles........................$5 – 6
26. "Pro Auto 10," yellow..............$2 – 3
27. "Richard Petty Pit Tour 43," blue, Goodyear rubber tires on black rims, White Rose Collectibles........$12 – 16
28. "Rumple 70," "Son's," blue, Goodyear rubber tires on black rims, White Rose Collectibles..............................$5 – 6
29. "STP 43," blue, Goodyear slicks, White Rose Collectibles.....................$4 – 5
30. "STP 43," blue, Goodyear rubber tires on blue rims, White Rose Collectibles..............................$5 – 6
31. "USA Bobsled Team 43," light blue, Goodyear rubber tires on black rims, White Rose Collectibles........$12 – 16
32. "White House Apple Juice 4," yellow, Goodyear slicks, White Rose Collectibles, on-package premium ...$5 – 6
33. "White Rose Collectibles 93," white and black, Goodyear slicks, White Rose Collectibles.............................$30 – 35

Pontiac GTO (see Pontiac 1970 GTO "The Judge")

Pontiac Stock Car, 3", #35, 1993
1. yellow, "Seaside 15," Goodyear slicks, 1993......................................$4 – 5
2. yellow, "Pro Auto 10," Goodyear slicks, 1994......................................$2 – 3
3. black, "Dirt Devil," Goodyear slicks, White Rose Collectibles.............$4 – 5
4. black, "Dirt Devil," rubber tires on black rims, White Rose Collectibles ....$4 – 5
5. black, "Duron 66," Goodyear slicks, White Rose Collectibles.........$9 – 12
6. orange, "Burn Foundation," "Motorsports 94," Goodyear slicks...$16 – 24
7. purple, "JP Graphics," Goodyear slicks ....$2 – 3

Pontiac Piranha, #73, 2002; #59, 2003
1. purple with silver doors, "Piranha" and illustration on sides, 2002 Kids' Cars of the Year series ....$2 – 3

2. yellow with fishbowl, cat, bird, and dog design, 2003 Kid's Shoppes series.................................$2 – 3

Pontiac T-Roof (see Pontiac Firebird Trans Am T-Roof)

Pontiac Trans Am (see Pontiac Firebird Trans Am)

Pontiac Vibe, #51, 2003
1. metallic silver, 2003 School Time series...................................$2 – 3

Pony Trailer, with two horses, 2⅝", #43, 1968
1. orange, Superfast wheels.........$5 – 6

2. yellow, black plastic wheels....$7 – 9
3. yellow, Superfast wheels ....$20 – 25
4. green, white roof, "Polizei," Superfast wheels...................................$4 – 5
5. beige, brown tailgate, Superfast wheels...................................$5 – 6
6. beige, lime green tailgate, Superfast wheels...................................$9 – 12
7. beige, white tailgate, Superfast wheels ....$3 – 4
8. white, blue-gray tailgate, "Polizei," Superfast wheels ....$2 – 3

9. white, lime green tailgate, Superfast wheels ....$2 – 3
10. white, red roof, white tailgate, Superfast wheels ....$2 – 3

Pop-Up Camper, #62, 2000; #42, 2000, international

1. red with white and black road design, white roof, tan interior, 2000 Great Outdoors series..$2 – 3
2. red with white and black road design, "Matchbox 2000," white roof, tan interior, 2000 Great Outdoors series ....$3 – 4

3. red-orange with forest, camper, and moon illustration, phosphorescent green roof, 2003 Camp Fun 3-pack with flashlight ....$2 – 3
4. metallic pale green with green and blue graphics, blue roof, 5-pack ....$2 – 3

5. white with red roof, footprints and turquoise graphics, aqua interior, teal base, 2003 5-pack #10 ..$2 – 3

Porsche 910, 2⅞", #68, 1970
1. red, "45" label on hood, amber windows ....$16 – 24
2. red, "45" label on hood, clear windows ....$16 – 24
3. red, "68" label on hood, amber windows ....$12 – 16
4. red, "68" label on hood, clear windows ....$12 – 16
5. red, "68" label on hood and sides, amber windows, gift set........$12 – 16
6. red, scorpion label on hood, amber windows..............................$180 – 240
7. metallic red........................$12 – 15
8. white, amber windows ....$40 – 50
9. fluorescent orange, China cast, Neon Racer BR 35 – 36, 1985 ....$4 – 6

10. lime green, China cast, Super GTs BR 35 – 36, 1985 ....$3 – 5
11. light blue, England cast, Super GTs BR 35 – 36, 1985 ....$4 – 6
12. light blue, "Drive," England cast, Super GTs BR 35 – 36, 1985 ....$8 – 10
13. light blue, China cast, Super GTs BR 35 – 36, 1985 ....$8 – 10
14. dark blue, England cast, Super GTs BR 35 – 36, 1985 ....$4 – 6
15. white, China cast, Super GTs BR 35 – 36, 1985 ....$8 – 10
16. silver, "49," England cast, Super GTs BR 35 – 36, 1985 ....$8 – 10
17. silver, "Drive," England cast, Super GTs BR 35 – 36, 1985 ....$4 – 6
18. silver, China cast, Super GTs BR 35 – 36, 1985 ....$8 – 10

Porsche 911 Carrera Cabriolet, #17, 1999, US; #72, 1999, Germany; #50, 2003, international
1. red with black interior, 5-spoke wheels, 1999 Germany issue ....$5 – 6
2. red with black interior, 10-spoke wheels, Target Eggmobile 3-pack ....$5 – 6
3. yellow with black interior, 1999 Germany issue ....$5 – 6

4. dark blue with tan interior, 2003 International issue ....$2 – 3

5. metallic graphite gray with light gray interior, black plastic base, 2001 Eurosports 5-pack ....$2 – 3
6. metallic silver with red interior, 2003 Auto Carrier Launcher 5-pack ....$2 – 3

Porsche 911 GT1, #68, 1998; #45, 2000; #58, 1998, international; #31, 1999, international; #35, 2000, international

1. metallic red, 2001 Eurosports 5-pack ....$2 – 3
2. yellow, "911GT1," 2000 Show Cars series.................................$2 – 3
3. yellow, "911GT1," "Matchbox 2000," 2000 Show Cars series............$3 – 4
4. metallic blue, "911GT1," Germany issue.....................................$4 – 5
5. metallic blue, "Matchbox," "GT1".$3 – 4
6. metallic gray, "Porsche" ....$3 – 4

7. white, "911 GT1," 1998 Street Cruisers series ....$2 – 3
8. white, "Citrix Vertigo," "CDN," ASAP promotional ....$80 – 120
9. white, "Citrix Vertigo," "Citrix.com," "CDN," ASAP promotional....$80 – 120
10. white with upside down "V" and radiating lines, ASAP promotional...$60 – 80

Porsche 911 Turbo, 3", #3, 1978
1. metallic brown, unpainted base, ivory interior, England cast............$40 – 55
2. metallic brown, black base, ivory interior, England cast.........................$8 – 12
3. metallic gray, black base, ivory interior, England cast ....$7 – 9
4. metallic gray, dark gray base, ivory interior, England cast...............$7 – 9
5. metallic gray, black base, red interior, England cast ....$4 – 6
6. metallic gray, brown base, red interior, England cast ....$8 – 12
7. metallic gray, dark gray base, red interior, England cast...............$4 – 6
8. metallic gray, brown base, tan interior, England cast ....$8 – 12
9. metallic gray, black base, tan interior, England cast ....$5 – 7
10. metallic gray, dark gray base, tan interior, England cast ....$6 – 9
11. gray, brown base, red interior, England cast ....$8 – 12
12. gray, dark gray base, red interior, England cast ....$8 – 12
13. metallic green, dark gray base, ivory interior, England cast..............$8 – 12
14. metallic green, dark gray base, red interior, England cast ....$8 – 12
15. metallic green, black base, red interior, England cast ....$8 – 12
16. metallic green, dark gray base, light orange interior, England cast.....$4 – 6
17. metallic green, black base, light orange interior, England cast...............$4 – 6
18. metallic green, blue-gray base, light orange interior, England cast.....$6 – 9
19. metallic green, unpainted base, light orange interior, England cast.....$6 – 9
20. red, black base, tan interior, "Porsche 90 Turbo," clear windows, England cast.$4 – 6

21. red, blue-gray base, tan interior, "Porsche 90 Turbo," clear windows, England cast ....$4 – 6
22. red, dark gray base, tan interior, "Porsche 90 Turbo," clear windows ....$4 – 6
23. red, dark gray base, white interior, "Porsche 90 Turbo," clear windows ....$4 – 6
24. red, black base, white interior, "Porsche 90 Turbo," clear windows..........$4 – 6

25. red, black base, tan interior, "Porsche 90 Turbo," opaque windows ....$12 – 16
26. red, black base, tan interior, no markings, clear windows, Macau cast.$4 – 6
27. red, black base, tan interior, clear windows, "Porsche" and "Porsche 911," Macau cast.............................$2 – 3
28. red, black base, brown interior, clear windows, "Porsche 90 Turbo," Macau cast.....................................$3 – 5
29. red, black base, blue interior, clear windows, "8 Dragon Racing Team," Macau cast, Hong Kong issue.............$9 – 12
30. orange-red, black base, white interior, "Porsche 90 Turbo," clear windows, England cast ....$6 – 9
31. white, black base, tan interior, clear windows, "Boss 14," Macau cast, Japan issue.................$9 – 12
32. white, black base, tan interior, clear windows, "Boss 14," Macau cast ....$4 – 6
33. white, black base, tan interior, clear windows, "Porsche," "3," Macau cast.....................................$9 – 12
34. white, black base, blue interior, clear windows, "Boss 14," Macau cast.....$4 – 6
35. metallic dark blue, black base, white interior, clear windows, "Wrangler 47," Macau cast, UK issue.............$9 – 12
36. black, black base, tan interior, amber windows, "Porsche 90 Turbo," Macau cast.....................................$3 – 5
37. black, black base, tan interior, clear windows, "Porsche," Macau cast...$9 – 12
38. black, black base, black interior, clear windows, "90 Porsche Turbo," "BP," Macau cast, the Netherlands issue ....$9 – 12
39. black, black base, tan interior, clear windows, "Porsche" and "Porsche 911," multipack, Macau cast..............$3 – 4
40. pale blue, black base, blue interior, clear windows, "Boss 14," multipack, Macau cast............................$4 – 6
41. dark blue, black base, tan interior, clear windows, "Porsche" and yellow stripes, Macau cast............................$3 – 4

154

42. red, black base, tan interior, clear windows, "Porsche" and "Porsche 911," Thailand cast............$2 – 3
43. dark blue, black base, tan interior, clear windows, "Porsche" and yellow stripes, Thailand cast............$2 – 3
44. yellow, black base, tan interior, clear windows, Porsche logo, Thailand cast, gift set.................$4 – 5
45. black, black base, tan interior, clear windows, "Porsche 90 Turbo," Manaus cast, Brazil issue.................$30 – 40
46. pale yellow, black base, black interior, clear windows, "Porsche" and spatter, Two Pack, Thailand cast...........$3 – 4
47. black, black base, tan interior, clear windows, "Porsche 90 Turbo," Manaus cast, Brazil issue.................$30 – 40
48. red, black base, tan interior, clear windows, "Porsche 90 Turbo," Manaus cast, Brazil issue.................$30 – 40
49. white, black base, red interior, clear windows, small Porsche logo, Thailand cast, Show Stoppers ....$3 – 4
50. white, black base, tan interior, clear windows, "Matchbox Fun Club," Thailand cast, UK issue.....................$9 – 12
51. black, black base, peach interior, clear windows, gold "Porsche," Thailand cast, Sports Pack ....$3 – 4
52. white, black base, blue interior, clear windows, "Boss 14," "14," Thailand cast, Sports Pack ....$3 – 4
53. blue, black base, blue interior, clear windows, "Porsche," Thailand cast, 5-pack.....................$2 – 3

Porsche 911 Turbo, #9, 2003
1. red with yellow and black on sides, 2003 Family Wheels series.......$2 – 3

Porsche 928, doors open except where noted, 3", #59, 1980
1. orange, "Lufthansa," red interior, clear windows, pearl silver base.........$5 – 6
2. yellow, "Porsche 928" and logo, red interior, clear windows, pearl silver base ....$12 – 16
3. metallic blue with brown interior, clear windows, black base.................$5 – 6
4. metallic blue with brown interior, clear windows, dark gray base..........$5 – 6
5. metallic blue with brown interior, clear windows, metallic gray base ......$5 – 6

6. **metallic blue with tan interior, clear windows, black base..............$5 – 6**
7. black, "Porsche" and stripe, brown interior, clear windows, metallic gray base.$9 – 12
8. black, "Porsche" and stripe, red interior, clear windows, metallic gray base.$4 – 5

9. black, "Porsche" and stripe, red interior, clear windows, unpainted base....$4 – 5
10. black, "Porsche" and stripe, red interior, clear windows, pearly silver base..$3 – 4
11. black, "Porsche" and stripe, red interior, light amber windows, pearly silver base ....$3 – 4
12. dark gray, chrome windows, detailed trim, rubber tires on gray rims, doors don't open, Macau cast, World Class....$6 – 8
13. dark gray, chrome windows, detailed trim, rubber tires on gray rims, doors don't open, Thailand cast, World Class..$6 – 8
14. metallic light gray with purple and blue design, red interior, clear windows.$4 – 5
15. metallic gray, "928S," detailed trim, purple and gray interior, clear windows, rubber tires on chrome rims, JC Penney Premiere Collection.............$4 – 5
16. pearl silver, "Martini Racing Porsche," red interior, clear windows, Japan issue.....................$8 – 10
17. white, "56 Porsche" with red stripes, red interior, clear windows, white base, doors don't open...................$12 – 16
18. white and metallic blue, "28" with "Cale Jenkins," red interior, clear windows, Laser Wheels...........................$4 – 5
19. white and metallic blue, "28" with "Cale Jenkins," red interior, clear windows, New Superfast wheels ....$4 – 5
20. white and metallic blue, "28" without "Cale Jenkins," red interior, clear windows, Laser Wheels.................$4 – 5
21. white and metallic blue, "28" without "Cale Jenkins," red interior, clear windows, New Superfast wheels .....$4 – 5
22. metallic tan with ivory interior, clear windows, black base ....$5 – 6
23. metallic tan with brown interior, amber windows, black base.................$5 – 6
24. metallic tan with brown interior, amber windows, brown base ....$8 – 10
25. metallic tan with brown interior, clear windows, black base.................$5 – 6
26. metallic tan with brown interior, orange windows, black base.................$5 – 6
27. metallic tan with light tan interior, clear windows, black base.................$5 – 6
28. metallic tan with tan interior, amber windows, black base.................$5 – 6
29. metallic tan with tan interior, amber windows, brown base ....$8 – 10

Porsche 935, 3", #55, 1983; #41, 1983
1. red, "41 Porsche," Macau cast..$2 – 3
2. red, "Autotech 35," New Superfast wheels...................................$4 – 5
3. red, "Porsche" logo, Thailand cast.$3 – 4
4. metallic red, "Autotech 35," Laser Wheels ....$4 – 5
5. light yellow with chrome windows, detailed trim, rubber tires on gray rims, World Class ....$6 – 8
6. yellow, "Porsche 10," Macau cast.....................................$3 – 4
7. yellow, "Porsche 10," Thailand cast.....................................$3 – 4

8. light blue, "Elf 71 Sachs," silver wheels.................$3 – 4
9. light blue, "Elf 71 Sachs," gold wheels.................$50 – 70
10. light blue, "Far Porsche 71 Sachs," Manaus cast, Brazil issue .....$40 – 60
11. black, "11 Ox Racing Team," Hong Kong issue.................$9 – 12
12. black, "935," chrome and black windows, Lightning Wheels ....$3 – 4
13. pearl ivory, detailed trim, chrome windows, rubber tires on gray rims, World Class.................$6 – 8
14. white, "935," fluorescent orange accents, blue chrome and black windows, Lightning Wheels ....$3 – 4
15. white, "Cadbury Buttons," UK issue.....................$9 – 12
16. white, "Elf," "Porsche," "Sachs," green wavy line and lavender stripes, Manaus cast, Brazil issue ....$40 – 60
17. white, "Porsche 10," gold wheels .$5 – 6
18. white, "Porsche 10," silver wheels.................$3 – 4

Porsche 944, 3", #71, 1988; #59, 1991
1. red, "944 Turbo," "Credit Charge," doors open, Macau cast, UK issue.....$9 – 12

2. **red, "944 Turbo," detailed trim, doors open, Thailand cast, International Premiere Collection #2 .$4 – 5**
3. red, "944 Turbo" and logo on sides, doors open, Macau cast ....$2 – 3
4. metallic red, detailed trim, doors open, Thailand cast, Gold Coin Collection....$16 – 24
5. yellow, doors open, Collectors Choice, White Rose Collectibles.............$4 – 5
6. metallic green, "944 Turbo," "American International Recovery," doors open, Thailand cast, ASAP promotional.$120 – 160
7. metallic green, "944 Turbo" and logo, doors open, Thailand cast ....$2 – 3
8. black, "944 Turbo" and logo, doors open, Macau cast ....$3 – 4
9. black, "944 Turbo" on sides, doors don't open, detailed trim, chrome windows, rubber tires on gray rims, Macau cast, World Class ....$7 – 9
10. black, "944 Turbo" on sides, doors don't open, detailed trim, chrome windows, rubber tires on gray rims, Thailand cast, World Class.............$7 – 9
11. white, "Duckhams," doors open, Macau cast, UK on-package premium..$16 – 24
12. white, "Duckhams," doors open, Thailand cast, UK on-package premium..$16 – 24
13. pearl white, "944 Turbo," detailed trim, doors open, Thailand cast, Premiere Collection #19.......................$4 – 5

Porsche 959, 2⁷⁄₈", #7, 1987; #51, 1994
1. metallic pearl gray with "Porsche" on doors ....$2 – 4
2. metallic pearl gray with "Porsche," chrome wheels, rubber tires, World Class..$6 – 9
2. white with "Porsche" on doors, white wheels.......................................$4 – 6
3. white with "Porsche" on doors, silver wheels.......................................$2 – 4
4. gray with "Porsche 959" ....$2 – 4
5. white with "Porsche 959"; red, yellow, and black stripes..................$8 – 10
6. pink with "Porsche 959"...........$3 – 5
7. purple with "Porsche 959" ....$4 – 5
8. white with "Redoxon" ....$25 – 35
9. white with "Pace Car," "Shell".....$4 – 5
10. white with "Pirelli Gripping Stuff 313"......................................$4 – 6
11. black with "Porsche" logo ....$5 – 6
12. chrome with no markings......$16 – 24
13. white with "Lloyds"...............$10 – 12
14. magenta with "Rage," black and yellow accents ....$2 – 3
15. hot pink with "Rage" on doors, accent on hood and roof ....$2 – 3

16. **metallic copper, 1999 Top Class ..$3 – 4**

17. **bright green, 1996 ....$3 – 4**

Porsche Boxster, #55, 1999; #5, 2000; #50, 1999, international
1. metallic red with gray and black interior, rubber tires on chrome rims, First Editions ....$6 – 8
2. light green, "Porsche Boxster," gold stripe, 5-pack ....$2 – 3
3. blue with rust interior, "Millennium Convention," Color Comp promotional................................$30 – 40
4. purple, "Millennium Toy Show," Color Comp promotional................$12 – 16

5. **metallic gray with rust interior, 1999 Beach series...............$2 – 3**

6. **metallic gray with black interior, 2000 Open Road series........$2 – 3**
7. metallic gray with black interior, "CFS Bowl 2000," ASAP promotional.......$60 – 80
8. metallic gray with black interior, "Matchbox 2000," 2000 Open Road series ....$3 – 4
9. metallic gray with rust interior, "Grand Opening Mattel-Die Cast Factory," "Matchbox," Color Comp promotional ....$250 – 300
10. metallic gray with rust interior, silver trim on windshield, 1999 Beach series...................................$4 – 5

11. **white with black interior, 2003 Hero City 5-pack #12....................$2 – 3**
12. unpainted with gray interior, rubber tires on chrome rims, First Editions ....$6 – 8

Porsche Turbo (see Porsche 911 Turbo)

Postal Service Delivery Truck, #97, 2000

1. **white, "United States Postal Service," 2000 On The Road Again series ....$2 – 3**
2. white, "United States Postal Service," "Matchbox 2000," 2000 On The Road Again series ....$3 – 4

3. white, "United States Postal Service," "Skillman, NJ 08558" decals, Color Comp promotional...............$20 – 30

Power Boat/Moby Quick, #21, 2001

1. **red deck, white hull, white "Unit 26," yellow "1462-PP12," 2001 Super Chasers series ....$2 – 3**

2. **white deck, black hull; yellow, white and blue "05 Police"; 2003 Hero City 5-pack #2.....................$2 – 3**

Pressure Refueler (see RAF 10-Ton Pressure Refueling Tanker)

Prime Mover Truck Tractor, 2¹⁄₈", #15, 1956
1. yellow with metal wheels ...$500 – 700
2. orange with metal wheels......$25 – 50
3. orange with plastic wheels.$175 – 200

Prime Mover Truck Tractor, Rotinoff Atlantic Super, orange, 2⁵⁄₈", #15, 1959
1. gray plastic wheels...........$350 – 425
2. black plastic wheels..............$30 – 45

Q

Quarry Truck (also see Articulated Dump Truck, Atlas Dump Truck, DAF Tipper Truck, Dodge Dump Truck, 8-Wheel Tipper, Euclid Quarry Truck, GMC Highway Maintenance Truck, GMC Tipper Truck, Leyland Articulated Truck, Mack Dump Truck, Peterbilt Quarry Truck, Quarry Truck)

Quarry Truck, Euclid (see Euclid Quarry Truck)

Quarry Truck, 2¹⁄₈", #6, 1955

metal wheels .... $40 – 55

gray plastic wheels .... $150 – 200

3. Matchbox Originals, 1993, blue with gray dumper, silver metal wheels, made in China .... $4 – 6

Quarry Truck, 2½", #6, 1957

1. yellow with gray plastic wheels .... $175 – 225

2. yellow with black plastic wheels .... $25 – 50

R

Racing Mini

1. **metallic orange .... $16 – 24**

2. **orange .... $12 – 16**

3. red .... $5 – 15

Racing Porsche (see Porsche 935)

Radar Plane, #41, 2001; #40, 2002; #34, 2003

1. blue with gray base, yellow wings and radar, 2001 Rescue Squad series .... $2 – 3

4. **black with black base, phosphorescent wings and radar, 2002 Nite Glow series .... $2 – 3**

5. orange-yellow with white base, orange wings and radar, 2003 Airport series .... $2 – 3

6. yellow with white base, orange-yellow wings and radar, 2003 Hero City 10-pack #2 .... $2 – 3

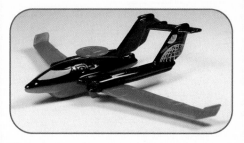

5. **black with red base, blue wings and radar, 2003 Hero City 5-pack #3 .... $2 – 3**

Radar Truck (see Weather Radar Truck)

RAF 10-Ton Pressure Refueling Tanker, 2⅝", #73, 1959

1. blue-gray with gray plastic wheels .... $5 – 10

Railway Passenger Coach, 3¹/₁₆", #44, 1978

1. red, "431 432" labels, beige roof, England cast .... $5 – 6

2. red, "431 432" labels, beige roof, Macau cast .... $3 – 4

3. red, "431 432" labels, beige roof, China cast .... $2 – 3

4. red, "431 432," "Kellogg's" labels, beige roof, Kellogg's on-package premium, China cast, the Netherlands issue .... $20 – 30

5. red, "5810-6102" labels, beige roof, England cast .... $9 – 12

6. red, "GWR" labels, beige roof, England cast .... $9 – 12

7. red, "NYK" labels, beige roof, no-origin cast, Brazil issue .... $120 – 160

8. green, "431 432" labels, beige roof, England cast .... $9 – 12

9. green, "5810-6102" labels, England cast .... $7 – 8

10. green, "British Railways," China cast .... $3 – 4

11. lime green, yellow, and red, Live 'N Learn/Matchbox Preschool series, Macau cast .... $7 – 8

12. lime green, yellow, and red, Live 'N Learn/Matchbox Preschool series, China cast .... $7 – 8

13. white, no markings, Graffic Traffic, China cast .... $12 – 16

Rallye Royale, 2⅞", #14, 1981 (similar casting: Monteverdi Hai, 1973)

1. **white upper, orange lower, "8," 1981 .... $9 – 12**

2. metallic silver upper, black lower body, "8" .... $9 – 12

3. metallic silver upper, black lower body, "14" .... $9 – 12

Range Rover Police Patrol (Rolamatic), 2⅞", #20, 1975

1. white, "Police" labels, frosted windows, orange dome, orange spinner .. $9 – 12

2. white, "Police" labels, frosted windows, blue dome, orange spinner .... $7 – 9

3. white, "Police" labels, frosted windows, yellow dome, blue spinner, large "Police" labels .... $7 – 9

4. white, "Police" labels, frosted windows, yellow dome, blue spinner, small "Police" labels .... $20 – 25

5. white, "Police" labels, frosted windows, yellow dome, orange spinner, large "Police" labels .... $7 – 9

6. white, "Police" labels, frosted windows, yellow dome, orange spinner, small "Police" labels .... $20 – 25

7. white, "Police" labels, frosted windows, blue dome, blue spinner, unpainted base .... $7 – 9

8. white, "Police" labels, frosted windows, blue dome, blue spinner, black base .... $9 – 12

9. white, "Police" labels, frosted windows, blue dome, orange spinner, unpainted base .... $20 – 25

10. white, "Police" labels, frosted windows, blue dome, orange spinner, black base .... $9 – 12

11. white, "Police" labels, amber frosted windows .... $9 – 12

12. white, "Police" labels, blue frosted windows .... $9 – 12

13. white, "Police" labels, yellow frosted windows .... $9 – 12

14. white, checkered "Police" labels .. $9 – 12

15. white, "Ambulance" labels, ... $20 – 25

16. white, "County Sheriff" .... $9 – 12

17. white, "Site Engineer" labels ... $20 – 25

18. white and black with Japan letters .. $9 – 12

19. beige, "Paris Dakar 83," "Lesney England" cast .... $7 – 9

20. beige, "Paris Dakar 83," "Matchbox International England" cast .... $7 – 9

21. blue, "Paris Dakar 81" .... $40 – 60

22. dark army green, "Ambulance" labels .... $70 – 90

23. dark army green, "Police" labels .... $70 – 90

24. light army green, "Ambulance" labels .... $7 – 9

25. light army green, red and yellow "Police" labels, black hubs .... $7 – 9

26. light army green, "Police" labels, chrome hubs .... $8 – 10

27. metallic tan, "Paris Dakar 83" .... $7 – 9

28. orange, "Site Engineer" labels .... $16 – 24

29. orange, "Police" labels .... $20 – 25

30. orange, "Ambulance" labels ... $20 – 25

Red Rider, 2⅞", #48, 1982 (similar castings: Big Banger, Cosmic Blues, Flame Out, Pi-Eyed Piper)

1. red, England cast.....................$5 – 6
2. red, Hong Kong cast ....$5 – 6
3. red, Macau cast.......................$2 – 3
4. red, China cast.........................$2 – 3

Refueler (see RAF 10-Ton Pressure Refueling Tanker)

Refuse Truck, 3", #36, 1980; #7, 1998; #3, 1999; #35, 2000; #19, 2001
1. red with yellow container and hatch, "Colectomatic" embossed on front of container, England cast.............$3 – 4
2. red with yellow container and hatch, no "Colectomatic" on container, England cast.....................................$20 – 25
3. red with yellow container and hatch, "Refuse Disposal," China cast...$9 – 12
4. red with metallic gray container and hatch, black recycling illustration, China cast...$2 – 3

5. **orange with dark blue container and hatch, "Metro DPW Unit 17".$2 – 3**
6. orange with gray container and hatch, "Refuse Disposal," China cast.....$2 – 3

7. **orange-red with light gray container, black recycle logos, 1996 ......$2 – 3**
8. orange with orange container and hatch, "Metro DPW Unit 17," recycle symbol, 1998 Big Movers series............$2 – 3
9. orange with white container and hatch, "Refuse Disposal," China cast.....$2 – 3

10. **bright orange with white container and hatch, "Disposal Unit 24," red recycling symbol, 1994 ....$3 – 4**

11. light orange with dark blue container and hatch, "Metro DPW" on doors, "Unit 17," white recycle symbol, 1998 Big Movers series ....$2 – 3
12. light orange with metallic gray container, "Ridge, NY Recycles," 1999 Matchbox USA series ....$2 – 3
13. fluorescent pale orange with white container, no markings ....$2 – 3
14. yellow with white container, "Disposal Unit" ....$2 – 3
15. green with metallic gray container, "Recycle," 1998 Around Town 5-pack ..$2 – 3
16. green with yellow container and hatch, "State City," China cast ....$2 – 3
17. green with yellow container and hatch, "Refuse Disposal," China cast.....$2 – 3
18. dark green with metallic gray container and hatch, "Recycle," China cast, 5-pack...$2 – 3
19. blue with orange container and hatch, "Metro" labels, England cast ......$3 – 4
20. blue with orange container, yellow hatch, "Metro labels, England cast........$6 – 7
21. blue with orange container and hatch, "Metro D.P.W. 66" labels, Macau cast.....................................$3 – 4

22. **blue with yellow container and hatch, "Metro D.P.W. 66" labels, England cast.......................$4 – 5**
23. blue with white container and hatch, "City of Cleveland Ohio," 2000 Matchbox USA series ....$2 – 3
24. blue with white container and hatch, "City of Cleveland Ohio," "Matchbox 2000," 2000 Matchbox USA series ....$3 – 4
25. bright blue with white container and hatch, "Fort Worth," metallic gray metal base, 2001 City Dudes series....$2 – 3
26. magenta with yellow container and hatch, England cast..................$3 – 4

27. **white with blue container and hatch, "Metro D.P.W. 66" labels, Macau cast ....$3 – 4**
28. white with blue container and hatch, "Metro D.P.W. 66" labels, China cast.......$3 – 4

29. white with blue container and hatch, "M Run" and flag, China cast, 5-pack ..$2 – 3
30. white with blue container and hatch globe, China cast, 5-pack ....$3 – 4
31. white with blue container and hatch, cartoo character, China cast, 5-pack ....$4 – 5
32. white with blue container and hatch Japan lettering, Macau cast, Japa issue.......................................$10 – 12
33. white with white container and hatch "Bulldog Castor Co.," ASAP promo tional ....$80 – 120
34. white with white container an hatch, "Renfro Cartage," ASAP pro motional ....$80 – 120
35. white with white container an hatch, "Waste Industries," ASA promotional ....$80 – 120
36. white with white container and hatch "Vince Coleen," heart design, ASAP pro motional ....$120 – 150
37. white with white container an hatch, maroon design, ASAP promo tional ....$80 – 120
38. white with white container and hatch ASAP promotional blank........$30 – 40
39. metallic gold with white containe and hatch, 1997 75 Challeng series ....$6 – 12

Renault 5TL LeCar, 2^{11}/$_{16}$", #21, 1978
1. blue with red interior, black base, clea windows, no markings ....$10 – 12
2. blue with red interior, dark gray base clear windows, no markings...$10 – 12
3. blue with tan interior, black base amber windows, no markings.....$5 – 6
4. blue with tan interior, black base, clea windows, no markings ....$5 – 6
5. blue with tan interior, dark gray base amber windows, no markings.....$5 – 6
6. blue with tan interior, dark gray base clear windows, no markings.......$5 – 6
7. blue with tan interior, metallic gray base amber windows, no markings .....$5 – 6
8. blue with tan interior, metallic gray base clear windows, no markings ....$5 – 6
9. pale blue with tan interior, black base clear windows, Manaus cast, Braz issue................................$80 – 120
10. metallic gray with black interior, blac base, clear windows, "Scrambler"..$5 – 6
11. metallic gray with red interior, blac base, amber windows, "LeCar"...$5 – 6
12. metallic gray with red interior, blac base, clear windows, "A5".....$16 – 24
13. metallic gray with red interior, blac base, clear windows, "LeCar".....$5 – 6
14. metallic gray with red interior, black base clear windows, no markings.....$20 – 25
15. metallic gray with red interior, blue-gra base, orange windows, "LeCar"..$5 – 6
16. metallic gray with red interior, dark gra base, amber windows, "LeCar"...$5 – 6
17. metallic gray with red interior, dark gra base, clear windows, "LeCar".....$5 – 6
18. metallic gray with red interior, gray-brow base, clear windows, "LeCar" ......$5 – 6

9. metallic gray with tan interior, metallic gray base, clear windows, "A5" ....$16 – 24
0. metallic gray with red interior, metallic gray base, clear windows, no markings ....$16 – 24
1. metallic gray with tan interior, metallic gray base, clear windows, no markings ....$20 – 25
2. red with orange interior, orange base, clear windows, "Turbo," Japan issue ..$16 – 24
3. red with tan interior, black base, clear windows, "Turbo" ....$20 – 25
4. white with dark yellow interior, black base, clear windows, "Renault"...$4 – 5
5. white with light yellow interior, dark gray base, clear windows, "Renault"...$4 – 5

6. **white with tan interior, black base, clear windows, "Renault" ....$4 – 5**
7. white with tan interior, black base, clear windows, "Roloil" ....$4 – 5
8. white with tan interior, black base, clear windows, "Roloil," Manaus cast, Brazil issue.................................$40 – 60
9. white with tan interior, cream base, clear windows, "Roloil," Manaus cast, Brazil issue ....$40 – 60
0. white with tan interior, dark gray base, clear windows, "Renault" ....$4 – 5
1. white with tan interior, orange base, clear windows, "Roloil" ....$16 – 24
2. white with white interior, black base, clear windows, "Renault" ....$5 – 6
3. white with white interior, black base, clear windows, "Roloil" ....$4 – 5
4. yellow with gray-yellow interior, dark gray base, clear windows, "LeCar"..................................$5 – 6
5. yellow with red interior, black base, clear windows, "LeCar" ....$10 – 12
6. yellow with red interior, black base, clear windows, "Le Toy Show," "Matchbox Road Museum," Color Comp promotional.............................$30 – 40
7. yellow with red interior, metallic gray base, clear windows, "LeCar" ..$10 – 12
8. yellow with tan interior, black base, amber windows, "LeCar" ....$5 – 6
9. yellow with tan interior, black base, clear windows, "LeCar" ....$5 – 6
0. yellow with tan interior, black base, amber windows, "Le Toy Show," "Matchbox Road Museum," Color Comp promotional.................................$30 – 40
1. yellow with tan interior, black base, clear windows, "Le Toy Show," "Matchbox Road Museum," Color Comp promotional.............................$30 – 40

42. yellow with tan interior, dark gray base, amber windows, "LeCar" ....$5 – 6
43. yellow with tan interior, dark gray base, clear windows, "LeCar" ....$5 – 6
44. yellow with tan interior, metallic gray base, amber windows, "LeCar"...$5 – 6
45. yellow with tan interior, metallic gray base, clear windows, "LeCar".....$5 – 6
46. yellow with tan interior, metallic gray base, clear windows, "Le Toy Show," "Matchbox Road Museum," Color Comp promotional........................$30 – 40

Renault 11 Turbo Alliance, 2¹⁵/₁₆", #33, 1987; #43, 1987
1. black.....................................$3 – 4
2. metallic blue, "Taxi Parisien" roof sign, James Bond........................$12 – 16

Renault 17TL, 3", #62, 1974
1. dark red, "9" label on hood......$8 – 10
2. orange-red, "6" label on hood...$8 – 10
3. orange-red, "9" label on hood...$8 – 10
4. orange-red, "Fire" label on hood ....$12 – 16

Renault Alliance (see Renault 11 Turbo Alliance)

Renault LeCar (see Renault 5TL LeCar)

Rescue Boat (see Over-Under Rescue Boats)

Rescue Chopper, #60, 1999; #7, 2000; #55, 1999, international

1. **blue, "Police"; white, silver, and red design; black base and tail, 2003 Hero City 5-pack #2 ....$2 – 3**
2. light blue, "Res-026," "067/299"; dark blue base, tail, and blades.........$2 – 3
3. bright blue, "Sydney 2000"; orange-yellow base, tail, and blades; 5-pack.......$2 – 3
4. white, "Alpine Rescue," blue base and tail, metallic gray blades, 1999 Wilderness Adventure series ....$2 – 3
5. white, "Alpine Rescue," "Matchbox," dark blue base and tail, metallic gray blades, Pleasant Books issue.....$4 – 5

6. **white, "Rescue Heroes," purple base, tail and blades, 2003 Rescue Heroes 5-pack ....$2 – 3**
7. white, "Med Air," yellow and dark blue stripes, red base and tail, black blades, 5-pack...................................$2 – 3

8. **white with bright orange and lime green design, blue base and tail, metallic gray blades, 2000 Ocean Explorer series.....................$2 – 3**
9. white with bright orange and lime green design, "Matchbox 2000," blue base and tail, metallic gray blades, 2000 Ocean Explorer series...............$3 – 4
10. white with red and yellow design, blue base and tail, metallic gray blades, 1999 Forest Run international series....$2 – 3

Rescue Crane, #72, 2001; #24, 2003

1. **red with orange crane, metallic gray boom, black plastic base, 2001 X-Treme Rescue series ....$2 – 3**

2. **white with red crane, yellow boom, black plastic base, 2003 Hero City 5-pack #9 ....$2 – 3**

3. **yellow with green crane, red boom, metallic gray plastic base, 2003 Bridge Crew series................$2 – 3**

Rescue Helicopter (see Hospital Helicopter)

Rescue Radar Plane (see Radar Plane)

Rhino Rod, #53, 1994 – 1997; #43, 1998; #24, 1994, international

1. **black with white eyes, 5-spoke concave wheels.........................$4 – 5**

2. **dark gray with red eyes, 6-spoke gold wheels ....$2 – 3**

3. **dark gray with orange eyes, 6-spoke silver wheels ....$2 – 3**
4. dark gray with black eyes, 6-spoke silver wheels.....................................$2 – 3
5. dark gray with white eyes, 6-spoke silver wheels.....................................$2 – 3
6. metallic dark gray with yellow eyes, 5-spoke concave wheels, 1998 Animals series.....................................$2 – 3
7. light gray with red eyes, 5-spoke concave wheels ....$2 – 3
8. metallic gold with black eyes, 5-spoke concave wheels, 1997 75 Challenge series..................................$6 – 12

Road Dragster, 2⅞", #19, 1970
1. red, "8" labels ....$16 – 24
2. red-orange, "8" labels ....$16 – 24
3. red-orange, no labels...........$16 – 24
4. red-orange, scorpion labels ...$40 – 60
5. light red, "Wynn's" labels...$100 – 150
6. purple, "8" labels ....$20 – 30
7. purple, scorpion labels..........$40 – 60
8. metallic red, "8" labels......$300 – 450

Road Roller, Diesel (see Aveling Barford Diesel Road Roller)

Road Roller, 2¼", #1, 1955
1. green with red metal wheels, dark tan driver ....$80 – 100
2. green with red metal wheels, light tan driver ....$80 – 100

Road Roller, 2 ⅜", #1, 1958
1. light green with red metal wheels............................$115 – 140
2. dark green with red metal wheels..............................$90 – 110

Road Roller, 2⅝", #1, 1962
1. green with red plastic rollers .$25 – 40

Road Roller, Bomag, #72, 1979; #40, 1991; #68, 1992; #68, 1991, international (see Bomag Road Roller)

Road Roller Paver, #36, 2001; #20, 2002; #23, 2003

1. **light orange with metallic gray interior, blue cage, 2001 Earth Crunchers series ....$2 – 3**

2. **red with metallic gray interior, black cage, 2002 Build It Right! series...............................$2 – 3**

3. **green with dark gray interior, yellow cage, 2003 Hero City 5-pack #9 ....$2 – 3**

4. **red with yellow interior, metal[l] gray cage, 2003 Bridge Cre[w] series ....$2 –**

Road Tanker, 1¾", #11, 1955
1. green with metal wheels ...$400 – 50[
2. dark yellow with metal wheels......................$75 – 10[
3. yellow with metal wheels ....$50 – 6[
4. red with metal wheels, "Esso" decal [on] rear ....$50 – 6[
5. red with metal wheels, "Esso" decal [on] sides..........................$125 – 15[

Road Tanker "Esso," red, 2½", #1[1,] 1958
1. gold trim, metal wheels.........$40 – 5[
2. silver trim, metal wheels ....$30 – 4[
3. gray plastic wheels...............$30 – 4[
4. silver plastic wheels.........$150 – 17[
5. black plastic wheels...........$80 – 10[

Robot Truck, #37

1. **black with white, yellow and blue cit[y] scene, phosphorescent chassis an[d] dish, 2002 Nite Glow series ...$2 –**

2. **black, "Jimmy Neutron," 2003 Nic[k]elodeon 5-pack.....................$2 –**

Rocket Transporter, 3", #60, 1990; #6[3,] 1999; #39, 2000; #40, 1985, inter[-] national; #58, 1999, internationa[l;] #24, 2000 – 2001, international (sim[i-] lar castings: Airplane Transporter)

red with yellow stripes, "Test Mission," yellow rockets, chrome hubs, 2000 Space Mission 5-pack...$2 – 3

lemon yellow with "Mission 1 Missiles," metallic gray rockets, 2000 Space Explorer series ....$2 – 3

lemon yellow with "Mission 1 Missiles," metallic gray rockets, "Matchbox 2000," 2000 Space Explorer series......$3 – 4

lime green with "Intergalactic Defence," black rockets, 1999 international Science Fiction series ....$2 – 3

lime green with "Intergalactic Defense," black rockets, 1999 Science Fiction series....................................$2 – 3

green with black and brown camouflage, green rockets, black hubs, Thailand cast, 5-pack ....$2 – 3

army green with "T7871-6" and star, army green rockets, black hubs, Thailand cast, 1996 .....$2 – 3

black with yellow and gray camouflage, dark gray rockets, black hubs, China cast, Commando series ....$30 – 40

black with green and brown camouflage, black rockets, black hubs, China cast, 5-pack ....$2 – 3

0. black with green and brown camouflage, black rockets, black hubs, Thailand cast, 5-pack ....$2 – 3

1. black with skull and crossbones, red rockets, black hubs, Thailand cast, Australia issue ....$4 – 5

2. white with "NASA" logo, U.S. flag, white rockets, chrome hubs, Macau cast....................................$2 – 3

13. white with "NASA" logo, U.S. flag, white rockets, chrome hubs, China cast ....$2 – 3

14. white with "NASA" logo and checkerboard design, white rockets, chrome hubs, China cast......................$2 – 3

15. white with "NASA" logo and checkerboard design, white rockets, chrome hubs, Thailand cast ....$2 – 3

16. white with gray and army green camouflage, army green rockets, black hubs, Thailand cast..........................$2 – 3

17. white with gray and army green camouflage, army green rockets, chrome hubs ....$9 – 12

18. white with gray and army green camouflage, gray rockets, black hubs, Thailand cast, 1997 Tundra Defense Force 5-pack ....$2 – 3

19. khaki with "T7871-6" and star, light brown rockets, Thailand cast, 5-pack.....................................$2 – 3

20. khaki with brown and olive green camouflage, khaki rockets, black hubs, 1995 Military 5-pack ...$2 – 3

21. beige with brown camouflage, beige rockets, black hubs, Thailand cast .....$2 – 3

22. beige with brown camouflage, black rockets, black hubs, Thailand cast, 1997 Desert Assault 5-pack..$2 – 3

Rod Roller, 2⅝", #21, 1973

1. yellow with green base, metallic red rear wheels ....$20 – 25

2. yellow with green base, red rear wheels................................$16 – 24

3. yellow with green base, black rear wheels ....$12 – 16

4. yellow with black base, black rear wheels................................$16 – 24

Rolls Royce Phantom V, 2⅞", #44, 1964

1. metallic tan, gray plastic wheels..............................$80 – 100

2. metallic tan, black plastic wheels ....$15 – 20

3. metallic gray, black plastic wheels................................$30 – 40

Rolls Royce Silver Cloud, metallic blue, 2⅝", #44, 1958

1. metal wheels.......................$30 – 40

2. gray plastic wheels ....$40 – 50

3. silver plastic wheels..............$40 – 50

Rolls Royce Silver Cloud, 3", #62, 1985, US; #31, 1987, international

1. **cream, England cast ....$2 – 3**
2. cream, Macau cast.................$2 – 3
3. cream, Thailand cast...............$2 – 3
4. purple, rubber tires on chrome rims, Gold Coin Collection.............$20 – 30
5. metallic gray, England cast, James Bond set...............................$9 – 12
6. metallic gold, chrome windows, rubber tires on gray rims, Macau cast, World Class............................$6 – 8
7. metallic gold, chrome windows, rubber tires on gray rims, Thailand cast, World Class.............................$6 – 8

Rolls Royce Silver Shadow, 3", #24, 1967

1. **metallic red, with black plastic tires on chrome hubs, 1967 ....$6 – 9**
2. metallic red with black base, Superfast wheels................................$12 – 16

3. **metallic red with gray base, Super-fast wheels ....$12 – 16**
4. metallic red with metallic green base, Superfast wheels ....$16 – 24
5. metallic red with pink base, Superfast wheels................................$16 – 24
6. metallic gold with black base, Superfast wheels, Japan issue ....$16 – 24
7. metallic gold with unpainted base, Superfast wheels, Japan issue.........$16 – 24

Rolls Royce Silver Shadow II, 3¹/₁₆", #39, 1979

1. metallic red, brown interior, clear windows, unpainted base, England cast.......................................$5 – 6
2. metallic red, ivory interior, clear windows, unpainted base, England cast ....$5 – 6
3. metallic red, light yellow interior, clear windows, unpainted base, England cast....................................$4 – 5
4. metallic maroon, white interior, clear windows, metallic silver base, Macau cast....................................$5 – 6
5. metallic purple, white interior, clear windows, black base, England cast ....$5 – 6
6. metallic purple, white interior, clear windows, metallic gray base, England cast....................................$5 – 6

7. metallic purple, white interior, clear windows, unpainted base, England cast....................................$5 – 6
8. metallic tan, white interior, amber windows, unpainted base, England cast....................................$4 – 5
9. metallic tan, white interior, amber windows, metallic gray base, England cast....................................$4 – 5
10. metallic tan, white interior, clear windows, unpainted base, England cast..........$3 – 4
11. metallic tan, white interior, clear windows, metallic gray base, England cast....................................$3 – 4
12. metallic tan, white interior, tinted windows, unpainted base, England cast....................................$3 – 4
13. metallic gray, red interior, clear windows, unpainted base, England cast....................................$5 – 6
14. gray, red interior, clear windows, unpainted base, England cast.....$5 – 6
15. black, gray interior, clear windows, black base, China cast, China issue ....$60 – 80

Rolls Royce Silver Shadow Convertible Coupe, Superfast wheels only, 3", #69, 1969

1. **metallic blue, orange-brown interior, tan tonneau, black base ....$20 – 30**
2. metallic blue, orange-brown interior, tan tonneau, dark yellow base .....$20 – 30
3. metallic blue, orange-brown interior, tan tonneau, light yellow base......$20 – 30
4. metallic gold, ivory interior, black tonneau, black base.................$20 – 30
5. metallic gold, ivory interior, black tonneau, silver base.................$20 – 30
6. metallic gold, orange-brown interior, black tonneau, black base .....$20 – 30
7. metallic gold, orange-brown interior, black tonneau, dark gray base ....$20 – 30
8. metallic gold, orange-brown interior, black tonneau, light yellow base ....$20 – 30
9. metallic gold, orange-brown interior, black tonneau, silver base .....$20 – 30
10. metallic gold, orange-brown interior, tan tonneau, black base ....$20 – 30
11. metallic gold, orange-brown interior, tan tonneau, dark yellow base .....$20 – 30
12. metallic gold, orange-brown interior, tan tonneau, light yellow base......$20 – 30
13. metallic gold, orange-brown interior, tan tonneau, silver base ....$20 – 30
14. metallic gold, orange-brown interior, tan tonneau, tan base................$20 – 30

Rolls Royce Silver Spirit, 3", #66, 1988; #55, 1990

1. **metallic red, tan interior, China cast ....$2 – 3**
2. metallic red, tan interior, Macau cast....................$2 –
3. metallic red, tan interior, Thailand cast...................$2 –
4. metallic red with crest, cream interio Thailand cast..........................$2 –
5. metallic green-gold, tan interior, Maca cast...................$4 –
6. metallic tan, tan interior, Macau cast...................$3 –

Rompin' Rabbit 4x4 (see Volkswage Rompin' Rabbit 4x4)

Rotinoff Atlantic Super Prime Move Truck Tractor (see Prime Mover Truc Tractor, Rotinoff Atlantic Super)

Rotovator, 1993 Farming Series

1. **blue with gray rotors ....$3 –**

Rotwheeler, lower jaw moves when rolle #73, 1995; #42, 1998; #47, 199 international

red with black collar, China cast,
1998 Animals series ....$2 – 3
red with black collar, Thailand cast,
1998 Animals series...............$2 – 3
black with red collar, Thailand
cast ....$2 – 3

brown with black collar, Thailand
cast ....$2 – 3
metallic gold, Thailand cast, 1997 75
Challenge series ....$6 – 12

over 3500, 3", #8, 1982, international
metallic bronze, tan interior.......$3 – 5
metallic bronze, white interior ....$4 – 6

over 3500 Police, 3", #8, 1982, international

white with "Police," England
cast ....$3 – 4
white with "Police," Macau cast..$3 – 4
white with "Police," China cast....$4 – 5
white with "Police," Manaus (Brazil)
cast.....................................$30 – 45
white with no markings, England cast,
Graffic Traffic ....$4 – 5

over Sterling, 2¹⁵/₁₆", #2, 1988; #31,
1988
metallic gray, "Rover Sterling" ....$3 – 4
metallic red with no markings ....$3 – 4
metallic pearl gray with red, white, and
blue stripes, Laser wheels.........$5 – 6
blue with yellow base, blue wheels, no
hood, Matchbox Preschool/Live 'N
Learn series.............................$7 – 9
yellow with no markings ....$9 – 12
white with no markings, Graffic
Traffic ....$12 – 16

uff Trek Holden Pickup (see Holden Ruff
Trek Pickup)

uff Rabbit (see Volkswagen Ruff Rabbit)

unway Hero (see also Airport Fire Pumper)

S

S.2 Jet, 2⅞", #2, 1981
1. black with yellow base, yellow wings,
England cast ....$4 – 6
2. light blue with white base, white wings,
England cast ....$3 – 5
3. light blue with white base, gray wings,
England cast ....$3 – 5

4. **dark blue with white base, white**
wings, Macau cast...............$3 – 5
5. dark blue with white base, white wings,
China cast ....$3 – 5
6. dark blue with white base, white wings,
Hong Kong cast...................$20 – 25
7. dark olive green, black base, dark
olive green wings, Commando
series ....$5 – 7

S&S Ambulance (see Cadillac S&S Ambulance)

S.P. Gun (see Self Propelled Gun)

Saab 9000, 2¹⁵/₁₆", #15, 1988; #22;
1989

1. **metallic red with brown**
interior ....$2 – 3
2. metallic blue with gray interior,
"Saab Turbo" and stripes, Laser
Wheels................................$8 – 10
3. white with brown interior, "Saab 22"
and stripes ....$3 – 4
4. metallic gray with brown interior, "Saab
22" and stripes ....$9 – 12
5. dark blue with brown interior, Germany
gift set ....$9 – 12

6. **dark ivory with yellow and brown**
interior, rubber tires on chrome
rims, Ultra Class ....$9 – 12

Saab Sonnet, 2¾", #65, 1973; BR 11 –
12, 1985
1. blue with yellow interior, unpainted
base ....$12 – 16
2. white with yellow interior, unpainted
base ....$300 – 400
3. orange with no interior, England cast,
Super GTs BR 11 – 12, 1985...$5 – 6
4. orange with no interior, China cast,
Super GTs BR 11 – 12, 1985.$8 – 10
5. green with no interior, China cast,
Super GTs BR 11 – 12, 1985...$4 – 5
6. blue with no interior, England cast,
Super GTs BR 11 – 12, 1985.$8 – 10
7. pale blue with no interior, China cast,
Super GTs BR 11 – 12, 1985...$4 – 5
8. tan with no interior, England cast,
Super GTs BR 11 – 12, 1985...$6 – 8
9. tan with no interior, China cast, Super
GTs BR 11 – 12, 1985..........$8 – 10

Safari Land Rover, 2⅜", #12, 1965
1. green with brown luggage on roof, black
plastic wheels........................$9 – 12

2. **blue with brown luggage on roof,**
black plastic wheels ....$9 – 12
3. blue with tan luggage, black plastic
wheels...................................$9 – 12
4. gold with tan luggage, black plastic
wheels................................$80 – 100
5. bright blue, Superfast wheels,
1970.....................$1,250 – 1,750
6. metallic gold, Superfast wheels,
1970................................$24 – 36

Saladin Armoured Car, 2½", #67,
1959

1. **olive green with black plastic**
wheels ....$30 – 40

Sambron Jack Lift/Fork Lift Truck, 3¹/₁₆",
#48, 1977; #28, 1991; #61, 1991,
international

1. orange-yellow with red stripes, 1994
gift set ....$3 – 4
2. yellow, no markings, black base, silver
hubs, 1977 ....$6 – 7
3. yellow, no markings, brown base, silver
hubs, 1977 ....$9 – 12
4. yellow, no markings, dark gray base, silver hubs, 1977 ....$6 – 7
5. yellow, no markings, dark gray base,
yellow hubs, 1977 ....$6 – 7
6. yellow, "Sambron," black base, silver
hubs, 1977 ....$400 – 500
7. lime green with red and white stripes,
1991 ....$2 – 3
8. bright green with red and white stripes,
1994 ....$2 – 3

9. **white with red stripes, 1993 Team
Convoy.................................$4 – 5**

Sand Digger Volkswagen Beetle, 2¹³/₁₆",
#49, 1983 (similar castings: Hi Ho Sil-
ver, Hot Chocolate, Volks Dragon, Dune
Man, Big Blue)

1. **metallic green......................$3 – 4**

Sand Racer, 2¹¹/₁₆", #72, 1984

1. **white, "Goodyear," "Union 211,"
Macau cast......................$20 – 30**

Sand Speeder (see Dune Buggy)

Saracen Personnel Carrier, army green,
2¹/₄", #54, 1958
1. black plastic wheels.............$20 – 35

Sauber Group C Racer (see Mercedes-
Benz Sauber Group C Racer)

Savannah RX7 (see Mazda RX7 Savannah)

Scaffold Truck (see Mercedes-Benz Scaffold Truck)

Scammell Breakdown Truck, olive green,
black plastic wheels, 2¹/₂", #64,
1959

1. **green metal hook ....$30 – 40**
2. silver metal hook..................$30 – 40
3. gray plastic hook..................$25 – 35

Scammell Mountaineer Snowplow, 3",
#16, 1964
1. gray plastic wheels..............$80 – 90
2. black plastic wheels.............$15 – 20

Scania T142, 3", #8, 1986; #71, 1986;
#72, 1986; other variations exist in
Convoy series
1. white with red, orange, and yellow
stripes ....$3 – 4
2. blue with red, orange, and yellow
stripes ....$3 – 4
3. white with red and black stripe...$3 – 4

School Bus, 3", #47, 1985; #12,
1998, #1, 1999; #31, 2000; #15,
2002
1. "1+2=3 abc," orange-yellow, green
wheels with blue hubs, Matchbox
Preschool/Live 'N Learn
series.............................$7 – 9
2. "1+2=3 abc," orange-yellow, green
wheels with green hubs, Matchbox
Preschool/Live 'N Learn
series.............................$5 – 7
3. "1+2=3 abc," orange-yellow, green
wheels with red hubs, Matchbox
Preschool/Live 'N Learn
series ....$7 – 9
4. "Atlantic Coast Surety," orange-yellow,
ASAP promotional.............$80 – 120
5. "Cap'n Crunch," "Quaker Oats,"
orange-yellow, ASAP
promotional ....$120 – 160
6. **"Carpenter High School," orange-yellow, China cast.....................$2 – 3**

7. "Downington Area School District," orang[e]
yellow, ASAP promotional ....$30 – 4[0]
8. "Durham," orange-yellow, ASAP prom[o]-
tional...................................$60 – 8[0]
9. "George Dapper, Inc. Iselin, NJ," orang[e]
yellow, ASAP promotional .....$80 – 12[0]
10. "Govt Property," army green ..$10 – 1[5]
11. "Govt Property," "Commando" hood log[o]
army green, China issue ....$30 – 4[0]
12. "Harvey World Travel," yellow, Austral[ia]
issue ....$9 – 1[2]
13. "Hofstra University," blue.........$9 – 1[2]
14. "Horlicks School Bus," yellow, Ho[ng]
Kong issue..........................$20 – 3[0]
15. "JMOA Engineering PC-K-12 Speci[al]-
ists," orange-yellow, ASAP prom[o]-
tional..............................$80 – 12[0]
16. "Martin Luther King Drug Free," orang[e]
yellow, ASAP promotional....$80 – 12[0]
17. "Matchbox Elementary," "Matchbo[x]"
orange-yellow, Pleasant Books ...$4 – [5]

18. **"Matchbox Elementary Schoo[l],"
orange-yellow ....$2 – [3]**
19. "Matchbox Elementary School," "Enj[oy]
Fanta," orange-yellow........$160 – 2[00]
20. "Montgomery High School," orange-y[el]-
low, promotional ....$16 – 2[0]

21. **"Mt. Laurel Preschool," bright pin[k],
1994 Collectors Choice from Whi[te]
Rose Collectibles...................$4 – [5]**
22. "ND Irish Mobile," orange-yellow, AS[AP]
promotional.........................$20 – 3[0]
23. **"Oaklyn Middle School PS33[0]"
"Go Team Go," orange-yello[w],
1997 ....$2 – [3]**

4. "Oaklyn Middle School PS33," "Go Team Go," yellow, 1998 Big Movers series .... $2 – 3
5. "Off To Northwestern," orange-yellow, ASAP promotional .... $30 – 40
6. "On My Way To Bowdoin," orange-yellow, ASAP promotional .... $16 – 24
7. "On My Way To Cal Poly," orange-yellow, ASAP promotional .... $16 – 24
8. "On My Way To Maryland," orange-yellow, ASAP promotional .... $30 – 40
9. "On My Way To RPI," orange-yellow, ASAP promotional .... $16 – 24
0. "On My Way To UCLA," orange-yellow, ASAP promotional .... $60 – 80
1. "On My Way To UGI," orange-yellow, ASAP promotional .... $30 – 40
2. "Penn State," "The Loop," white and dark blue, White Rose Collectibles...... $7 – 9
3. "Police 88," blue, Action Pack .... $4 – 5

4. **"Police Transport" with coiled barbed wire graphics, red with silver painted metal base, 2002 To The Rescue series** .... **$2 – 3**
5. "RCA," orange-yellow, ASAP promotional .... $20 – 30
6. "Ridge, NY Elementary," "Go Ridge Go," orange-yellow, 1999 Matchbox USA series .... $2 – 3
7. "Rutgers," orange-yellow, ASAP promotional .... $25 – 35
8. "Sage," orange-yellow, ASAP promotional .... $80 – 120
9. "School District 2," dark orange, China cast, gift set .... $9 – 12

0. **"School District 2," orange-yellow, China cast** .... **$2 – 3**
1. "School District 2," orange-yellow, Thailand cast .... $12 – 16
2. **"School District 2," yellow, China cast** .... **$2 – 3**

43. "School District 2," yellow, Macau cast .... $2 – 3
44. "School District 2," "Chef Boyardee," orange-yellow, on-package premium .... $10 – 12
45. "School District 2," "Chef Boyardee," yellow, on-package premium ...... $10 – 12
46. "St. Paul Public Schools," orange-yellow, China cast .... $40 – 50
47. "St. Thomas Elementary School, Rocky River, Ohio," 2000 Matchbox USA series .... $2 – 3

48. **"St. Thomas Elementary School, Rocky River, Ohio," "Matchbox 2000," 2000 Matchbox USA series** .... **$3 – 4**
49. "Storm Troopers Reunion at the Mark 2000," orange-yellow, ASAP promotional .... $80 – 120
50. "Van Lear," orange-yellow, ASAP promotional .... $80 – 120
51. "Vancom," orange-yellow ..... $80 – 120

52. **"White's Guide Car of the Month" in black lettering, orange-yellow, ASAP promotional** .... **$6 – 8**

53. **"White's Guide Car of the Month" in red lettering, orange-yellow, ASAP promotional** .... **$6 – 8**

54. "Wolfington," orange-yellow, ASAP promotional .... $60 – 80
55. orange-yellow, no markings, ASAP promotional blank .... $30 – 40
56. metallic gold, 1997 75 Challenge series............................... $12 – 16

School Bus, #16, 2001; #69, 2002; #52, 2003 (see Hummer School Bus)

Scissors Truck (see Ford Scissors Truck)

Sea Plane (see Seaplane)

Sea Rescue Boat, #43, 1999; #26, 2000; #38, 1999, international
1. red deck, white hull, dark blue railings, "489-4" and blue stripes, black wheels, 5-pack............................... $2 – 3
2. red deck, white hull, dark blue railings, "489-4" and blue stripes, white wheels, 5-pack............................... $4 – 5
3. blue deck, white hull, white railings, "Base 2000," 2000 Launcher 5-pack .... $2 – 3
4. dark blue deck, orange hull, red railings, lifesaver and storm logo, Launcher 5-pack............................... $2 – 3
5. white deck, black hull, metallic gray railings, red and silver stripes, 1999 Ocean series, international series .... $2 – 3
6. white deck, black hull, metallic gray railings, red and silver stripes, "World Ocean Explorer," 1999 Ocean series, US issue .... $2 – 3
7. white deck, metallic gold hull, black railings, red and black stripes, 2000 Fire Fighters series .... $2 – 3
8. white deck, metallic gold hull, black railings, red and black stripes, "Matchbox 2000," 2000 Fire Fighters series .... $4 – 5
9. white deck, white hull, white railings, "The Perfect Storm," ASAP promotional .... $80 – 120
10. white deck, white hull, white railings, ASAP promotional blank .... $30 – 40

Sea Rescue Helicopter, #41, 2003

1. **white with red base, propeller, and tail; red and blue swirl, 2003 Beach Patrol series** .... **$2 – 3**

Sea Speeder, #68, 2001; #44, 2003
1. red deck, white hull, metallic gray canopy and radar, "MHC Beach Patrol," 2003 Hero City 10-pack #2 .... $2 – 3

2. gray deck, blue hull, "911 Sea Police," 2003 Christmas 3-pack with gift box ....**$4 – 5**

3. red deck, white hull, metallic gray canopy and radar, "MHC Beach Patrol," 2003 Beach Patrol series ....$2 – 3

4. white deck, yellow hull, red canopy, blue radar, "NJBP" and graphics on sides, 2001 Storm Watch series........**$2 – 3**

Seafire Boat, 2¹⁵/₁₆", #5, 1975

1. white deck, fluorescent orange hull, no, blue plastic trailer ....**$2 – 3**

2. navy blue deck, green hull, blue plastic trailer ....**$2 – 3**

3. red deck, white hull, no markings, with trailer....................................$9 – 12
4. red deck, blue hull, no markings, with trailer.................................$30 – 40
5. white deck, brown hull, no markings, with or without trailer ....$90 – 120
6. red deck, yellow hull, no markings, with trailer.................................$40 – 50
7. black deck, yellow hull, no markings.$9 – 12
8. white deck, white hull, "Bacardi," white metal trailer ....$12 – 16

9. red deck, white hull, "Surf Rider," silver stripes, white plastic trailer ......$3 – 4
10. yellow deck, blue hull, "460," black plastic trailer ....$4 – 5
11. white deck, red hull, red and black, black plastic trailer ....$4 – 5
12. white deck, blue hull, no markings, with or without trailer.................$12 – 16

Seasprite Helicopter, small windows, 2³/₄", #75, 1977

1. white, "Rescue" labels, blue windows ....$5 – 6
2. white, "Rescue" labels, green windows ....$5 – 6

3. white, "Rescue" labels, purple windows..............................**$5 – 6**
4. white, "Rescue" labels, red windows ....$5 – 6
5. cream, "Rescue" labels, blue windows, Brazil issue ....$300 – 400
6. dark green, "Rescue" labels, blue windows, Brazil issue ....$300 – 400

Seaplane, #42, 1999; #67, 2000; #37, 1999, international; #47, 2000, international

1. red, red wings, white base, "EB32," red and black stripes, 2000 Air Traffic series..............................**$2 – 3**
2. red, red wings, white base, "EB32," red and black stripes, "Matchbox 2000," 2000 Air Traffic series ....$3 – 4

3. yellow, yellow wings, metallic gray base, blue stripes, Water Wings, 1999 Ocean series ....**$2 – 3**
4. dark blue, dark blue wings, white base, 5-pack....................................$2 – 3

5. white, blue wings, blue base, bl... stripes, 2000 Ocean Dock 5-pack ....**$2 –**
6. white, gray wings, red base, "Coca-Co... and reclining woman, Premiere Colle... tion.......................................$5 –
7. white, gray wings, red base, "Coc... Cola" and reclining woman, "www.coc... colastores.com," Color Con... promotional ....$60 – 8...
8. white, white wings, white base, no ma... ings, ASAP promotional blank..$30 – 4...
9. white, white wings, white base, "T... Perfect Storm," ASAP promotional ....$80 – 12...

10. white, red wings, red base, "Bea... Patrol," 2002 Sand Castle Resc... Team 5-pack with sand bucket..$2 –

Security Truck, #69, Matchbox 75 Serie... Superfast wheels

1. red with white roof, blue light, "Wel... Fargo" "732-2301" "Wells Farg... Armored Service Company" ...$3 –

Seeder, #712, 1993 Farming Series

1. green..........................$3 – 4

Self-Propelled Gun, Rolamatic, 2⁵⁄₈", #70, 1976

1. olive green, black treads........$3 – 4
2. olive green, tan treads.............$3 – 4

3. **olive green with tan and black camouflage, tan treads, China cast, Commando series.................$7 – 9**
4. olive green with tan and black camouflage, tan treads, Macau cast, Commando series ....$5 – 6
5. black with gray and yellow camouflage, tan treads, Commando series....$5 – 6

Setra Coach, 3", #12, 1970
1. metallic gold with tan roof, clear windows..................................$20 – 25
2. metallic gold with white roof, clear windows..................................$15 – 20
3. yellow with white roof, clear windows.............................$12 – 16
4. yellow with white roof, green windows ....$60 – 80
5. burgundy with white roof, clear windows ....$12 – 16
6. burgundy with white roof, green windows ....$12 – 16
7. purple with white roof, green windows ....$12 – 16

Sherman M4 A3 Tank, #85, 1999; #51, 2000

1. **light green with white "Power Striker," "476," "No. 33857," 1999 Military Patrol series ....$2 – 3**

2. light olive green with white "Power Striker," "476," "No. 33857," Premiere Collection.......................$4 – 5
3. olive green with tan camouflage, white star, 1999 Military Patrol series .$2 – 3
4. olive green with mud spatter, "Matchbox 2000," 2000 Military series ......$3 – 4
5. olive green with mud spatter, 2000 Military series............................$2 – 3

Sherman M4 Tank, 2001 Feature Cars, with opening features, designed to replace Premiere Collection
1. olive green with light blue camouflage, star ....$9 – 12

Shovel Nose Tractor Shovel (see Tractor Shovel)

Shunter (see Diesel Shunter Locomotive)

Side Tipper, #720, 1977, Two Pack
1. yellow with red tipper, England cast......................................$3 – 4
2. yellow with red tipper, China cast......................................$3 – 4
3. yellow with black tipper, England cast......................................$4 – 5
4. yellow with red tipper, Macau cast......................................$3 – 4
5. blue, "ABCD," yellow tipper, Macau cast, Live 'N Learn/Matchbox Preschool.$7 – 9

Silver Streak, Roman numeral I, 1978 (variation of #1 Mod Rod, 1971)
1. yellow with silver motor, Roman Numeral Limited Edition........$15 – 20
2. yellow with black motor, Roman Numeral Limited Edition.....................$20 – 25
3. silver plated with black motor, Roman Numeral Limited Edition ....$9 – 12

Site Dumper, 2⁵⁄₈", #26, 1976

1. **yellow with yellow dumper, black interior ....$5 – 6**

2. **yellow with red dumper, black interior ....$5 – 6**

3. orange-red with orange-red dumper, white interior.................$200 – 300
4. orange-red with metallic gray dumper, white interior..........................$5 – 6
5. orange-red with metallic gray dumper, white interior, yellow hubs.........$7 – 8
6. red with metallic gray dumper, white interior, yellow hubs ....$12 – 16

Site Hut Truck (see Leyland Site Office Truck)

Site Office Truck (see Leyland Site Office Truck)

Siva Spider, 3", #41, 1972; BR 7 – 8, 1985

1. **red with black trim ....$12 – 16**
2. red with silver trim ....$16 – 24
3. orange-yellow, England cast, Super GT BR 7 – 8, 1985 ....$8 – 10
4. yellow, England cast, Super GT BR 7 – 8, 1985...........................$8 – 10
5. dark blue with black trim ....$16 – 24
6. light blue with black trim........$16 – 24

Six-Wheel Quarry Truck (see Quarry Truck)

Six-Wheel Crane Truck (see Magirus-Deutz 6-Wheel Crane Truck)

Ski Boat (see Wave King)

Skip Truck (see Atlas Skip Truck, Ford Cargo Skip Truck)

Skoda 130LR Rally (European model), 2⁷⁄₈", #44, 1988

1. **white, "Skoda 44".................$4 – 5**

Sleet-N-Snow, Roman numeral II, 1978 (variation of U.S. Mail Jeep, #5, 1978)
1. blue, Roman Numeral Limited Edition..................................$9 – 12
2. olive, Roman Numeral Limited Edition..................................$15 – 20
3. yellow, Roman Numeral Limited Edition..................................$15 – 20

Slingshot Dragster, 3", #64, 1971
1. pink, "9" with flames label......$16 – 24

2. orange, "9" with flames label..............................$120 – 160
3. metallic blue, "3" with stripe label...............................$20 – 30

4. metallic blue, "9" with flames label ....$16 – 24
5. metallic blue, star with flames label...................................$60 – 80

Snack Truck, #96, 1998 (see Chevrolet Van 4x4)

Snorkel Fire Engine, with closed cab, 3", #13, 1977
1. red with blue windows, yellow boom and bucket, unpainted base.............$6 – 9

2. red with blue windows, yellow boom and bucket, metallic gray base$6 – 9
3. red with amber windows, yellow boom and bucket, unpainted base ...$12 – 16
4. dark red with blue windows, yellow boom and bucket, unpainted base........$6 – 9
5. dark red with blue windows, yellow boom and bucket, metallic gray base....$6 – 9
6. dark red with blue windows, white boom and bucket, unpainted base.......$6 – 9
7. dark red with blue windows, yellow boom, white bucket, gray base, UK issue..................................$60 – 80

Snorkel Fire Engine, with open cab, 2¹³/₁₆", #63, 1982; #26, 1998; #4, 1999; #27, 2000

1. "12th Rescue Squad," red with gold outline, metallic gray boom, China cast, 1995 ....$2 – 3
2. "12th Rescue Squad," red with white outline, metallic gray boom, China cast, 1995......................................$2 – 3
3. "FD No. 1 Fire Dept.," gold and black trim, red lower, white upper, metallic gray boom, China cast, 1996 5-pack.................................$2 – 3
4. "Fire Dept" and shield, red with white boom, China cast......................$2 – 3
5. "Fire Dept" and shield, fluorescent lime yellow with white boom, China cast, Action Pack.............................$4 – 5
6. "J.D.F.D. Fire Rescue 25," red with black boom, China cast, 2000 Fire Fighters series ....$2 – 3
7. "J.D.F.D. Fire Rescue 25," red with black boom, "Matchbox 2000," China cast, 2000 Fire Fighters series..................................$3 – 4
8. "Los Angeles," red with white boom, England cast, Code Red ....$7 – 9

9. "Matchbox Fire Dept.," red with white bands, metallic gray boom, China cast, 2000 Fire 5-pack .$2 – 3

10. "Matchbox Fire Dept.," dark purple with metallic gray boom, China cast ....$2 – 3

11. "Matchbox Fire Dept.," white with red bands, metallic gray boom, China cast, 1997 Fire 5-pack..........$2 – 3

12. "Matchbox Fire Dept.," red with metallic gray boom, China cast, 1998 To The Rescue series ....$2 – 3
13. "Matchbox Fire Dept.," maroon with white bands, 1997 ....$2 – 3
14. "Metro Alarm," "MA-ST1," red with gray boom, China cast, 5-pack..........$2 – 3
15. "Metro Fire," red with white boom, Macau cast.............................$2 – 3
16. "Metro Fire," red with white boom, China cast.............................$2 – 3
17. "Rescue Unit Fire 1," red with checkerboard design, white boom, China cast..........................$9 – 12
18. "Rescue Unit Fire 1," fluorescent orange with blue and white checkerboard design, white boom, "IC" logo, China cast, Intercom City ......$12 – 16

19. "Rescue Unit Fire 1," fluorescent orange with blue and white checkerboard design, white boom, China cast....................................$2 – 3
20. "Ridge, NY Fire & Rescue," red with white boom, 1999 Matchbox USA series.....................................$2 – 3
21. "Richfield Co.," red with black boom, rubber tires on chrome rims, China cast, Premiere Collection #7 .....$4 – 5
22. "Screamin' Red Fire Engines" in red print, white with white boom, China cast, ASAP promotional ....$12 – 16
23. "Screamin' Red Fire Engines" in purple print, white with white boom, China cast, ASAP promotional ....$12 – 16
24. "Seaside Fire Co.," "Snorkel Unit 2," metallic red with white boom, rubber tires on chrome rims, Premiere Collection #21 ....$4 – 5
25. red with Japanese lettering, white boom, China cast, Japan issue ....$10 – 12

26. turquoise with blue boom, separate labels included, McDonald's Happy Meal premium ....$4 – 5
27. white with gray boom, no markings, China cast, ASAP promotional blank...$30 – 40

3. white with white boom, no markings, China cast, Graffic Traffic (labels included in set)..................\$12 – 16

9. white with cityscape graphics, yellow boom, **2003 Hero City Fire Station**.............................**\$4 – 5**
0. metallic gold with black boom, no markings, China cast, 1997 75 Challenge series...................................\$6 – 12

Snow Doctor, halftrack vehicle, #6, 2001; #68, 2002

. **metallic blue with pearl white back section, 2001 Team Tundra ...\$2 – 3**

. **metallic rust with blue back section, 2002 Kids' Cars of the Year series**.....................................**\$2 – 3**

. **yellow with white back section, 2003 Hero City 5-pack #8** .....**\$2 – 3**

Snow Groomer, #57, 1999; #78, 2000; #52, 1999, international

1. orange, "FF-525," mountain scene, black plow and hatch, 1999 Forest Run international series...................\$3 – 4

2. **orange, "Hill Top Unit 3 Resort," white snow spatter, black plow and hatch, 1999 Wilderness Adventure series**.....................................**\$2 – 3**
3. blue, "42-06," metallic gray plow and hatch, cross and white design, 5-pack ....\$2 – 3

4. **metallic silver with blue plow and hatch, white and blue graphics, 2000 Snow Explorer series ...\$2 – 3**
5. metallic silver with blue plow and hatch, white and blue graphics, "Matchbox 2000," 2000 Snow Explorer series....................\$3 – 4

6. **gray with green plow and hatch; purple, white, and green graphics; 2003 Hero City 5-pack #8**..............**\$2 – 3**
7. white, "Test Centre," blue plow and hatch, polar bear graphics and hash marks, Launcher 5-pack ....\$2 – 3

8. **white with red band, yellow hash marks, black plow and hatch, 1998 Emergency Rescue 5-pack**.....**\$2 – 3**

Snowmobile/Turbo Ski, #94, 1999; #76, 2000; #8, 2001; #74, 1999, international; #56, 2000, international

1. **red with white design, black seat, yellow rider with black jacket, 1999 Mountain Cruisers series #19 ..\$2 – 3**
2. yellow with "8" and blue hash marks, black seat, dark gray rider, 5-pack........\$2 – 3
3. black with fluorescent yellow flash, red seat, dark blue rider with fluorescent green jacket, 2000 Snow Explorer series.................................\$2 – 3
4. black with fluorescent yellow flash, red seat, dark blue rider with fluorescent green jacket, "Matchbox 2000," 2000 Snow Explorer series ....\$3 – 4

5. **white upper with blue snowflake design, red lower with "+ Alarm" and graphics, black seat, red rider, 2003 Hero City 5-pack #8** .....**\$2 – 4**
6. white upper, orange lower, "TC-3," "Test Centre," hash marks, black seat, orange rider with blue jacket, Launcher 5-pack......................................\$2 – 3
7. "Colorado," Matchbox Across America 50th Birthday Series #38 — Western Collection...............................\$5 – 6

Snow Trac Tractor, 2³⁄₈", #35, 1964
1. white treads, "Snow Trac" decals.................................\$20 – 25
2. white treads, plain sides........\$20 – 25
3. white treads, "Snow Trac" cast into sides..................................\$20 – 25
4. gray treads, "Snow Trac" cast into sides..................................\$30 – 40

Soopa Coopa, 2⁷⁄₈", #37, 1972
1. blue ....\$16 – 24
2. pink with unpainted base, flower label...................................\$20 – 25
3. pink with red base, flower label...................................\$60 – 80
4. orange with "Jaffa Mobile" label, on-package premium ....\$120 – 160

Speedboat (see Sea Speeder)

Sports Boat and Trailer (see Meteor Sports Boat and Trailer)

Sports Boat and Trailer with outboard motor, 2⁵/₈", #48, 1961
1. gray wheels.........................$60 – 75
2. black wheels......................$30 – 40

Sprint Racer, 2¹⁵/₁₆", #34, 1990
1. red, "Allweld 14," Nutmeg Collectibles...........................$5 – 6
2. red, "Gambler 4," Nutmeg Collectibles...........................$5 – 6
3. red, "IW Lew," Nutmeg Collectibles...........................$5 – 6
4. red, "Joe Gaerte 7," Nutmeg Collectibles...........................$5 – 6
5. red, "Lucky 7"........................$2 – 3

6. red, "Rollin Thunder 2" ....$2 – 3
7. red, "Schoff 23S," Nutmeg Collectibles...........................$5 – 6
8. red, "Williams 5M" in blue letters, Nutmeg Collectibles......................$5 – 6
9. red, "Williams 5M" in white letters, Nutmeg Collectibles................$80 – 120
10. orange, "Williams Payless 5M," Nutmeg Collectibles...................$5 – 6
11. yellow, "Ben Cook & Sons 33X," Nutmeg Collectibles...................$5 – 6
12. yellow, "D. Blaney," "Vivarin 7C," Nutmeg Collectibles...................$5 – 6
13. yellow, "F&G Classics East 17," Nutmeg Collectibles...................$5 – 6
14. yellow, "Vivarin," "7c," "D. Blaney," purple background, Nutmeg Collectibles...........................$5 – 6
15. yellow, "Vivarin," blue background, Nutmeg Collectibles...................$8 – 10
16. light blue, "Schnee-D. Krietz 69," Nutmeg Collectibles...................$5 – 6
17. blue, "Ben Allen 1A," Nutmeg Collectibles...........................$5 – 6
18. metallic blue, "Rollin Thunder," "2".................................$9 – 12
19. metallic blue, "Lucky 7," Action Pack..................................$4 – 5
20. purple, "Hot Shot 34," 5-pack....$2 – 3
21. black, "Doug Wolfgang 49," Nutmeg Collectibles...................$5 – 6
22. black, "Gebhart's 4J," Nutmeg Collectibles...........................$5 – 6
23. black, "JW Hunt 69," Nutmeg Collectibles...........................$5 – 6

24. black, "TMC 1," Nutmeg Collectibles...........................$5 – 6
25. white, "Alvis O Rock 69," Nutmeg Collectibles...........................$5 – 6
26. white, "Maxim 11," Nutmeg Collectibles...........................$5 – 6
27. white, "Schnee 8D," Nutmeg Collectibles...........................$5 – 6
28. white, "Valvoline 11," Nutmeg Collectibles...........................$5 – 6
29. white, "Vanermark & Wahlie Im," Nutmeg Collectibles...................$5 – 6
30. white, "Weitkerk's Livestock 29," Nutmeg Collectibles...................$5 – 6
31. white, red, and dark blue; "Casey Luna 10," Nutmeg Collectibles..........$5 – 6

Stake Truck, maroon, 2³/₈", #20, 1956
1. gold grille and fuel tanks, metal wheels..............................$80 – 100
2. silver grille and fuel tanks, metal wheels................................$30 – 50
3. maroon grille and fuel tanks, metal wheels................................$30 – 50
4. silver grille and fuel tanks, gray plastic wheels...........................$100 – 125
5. dark red grille and fuel tanks, gray plastic wheels ....$90 – 120

Standard Jeep CJ5 (see Jeep CJ5 Standard)

Sterling (see Rover Sterling)

Stinger, helicopter-style fantasy vehicle, #68, 1995 – 1997; #41, 1998

1. orange and black, 1995, Thailand cast ....$2 – 3

2. yellow and black, 1996, Thailand cast ....$2 – 3
3. green and black, 1998 Animals series, China cast ....$2 – 3

4. green and black, 1998 Animal series, Thailand cast ....$2 – ?
5. metallic gold and black, 1997 75 Challenge series, Thailand cast ......$6 – 1?

Stingeroo, 3-wheel motorcycle, 3", #3? 1973
1. purple with chrome handlebars.....................$350 – 45?
2. purple with purple handlebars.........................$16 – 2?
3. purple with blue-gray handlebars.........................$20 – 2?

Stoat Armored Truck, 2⁵/₈", #28, 1974
1. metallic gold with chrome hubs ....$10 – 1?
2. army green with black hubs ....$7 – ?
3. army green with chrome hubs ..$8 – 1?
4. dark olive green with black hubs ....$70 – 9?

Street Cleaner, #96, 2000; #20, 2001 #3, 2002; #18, 2003
1. orange-yellow, "City Streets Department, dark blue bucket and brushes, black base, Pleasant Books issue ....$5 – ?
2. dark green, "City Service DO? 042076," fluorescent yellow bucket and brushes, black base, 7-spoke saw blade front wheels, 2001 City Dude series ....$2 – ?
3. dark green, "City Service DOT 042076, fluorescent yellow bucket and brushes black base, 8-spoke front wheels, 200? City Dudes series.....................$5 – ?

4. purple with bright green bucket and brushes, black base, 2002 Home town Heroes series ....$2 – ?
5. dark cream, "Metro Disposal," red bucket and brushes, metallic gray base, 2000 On The Road Again..................$2 – ?

dark cream, "Metro Disposal," red bucket and brushes, metallic gray base, "Matchbox 2000," 2000 On The Road Again ....$3 – 4

white with red dust bucket and brushes, orange base, 2003 Public Works series.......................$2 – 3

reet Streak concept car, #62, 1996 – 1997; #16, 1998

red upper, black lower, chrome windows, 1997 Cars of the Future 5-pack ....$2 – 3

metallic red upper, metallic gray lower, chrome windows, 1997.............$2 – 3
bright orange upper, black lower, black windows ....$2 – 3

blue upper, metallic gray lower, chrome windows, 1998 Cool Concepts series, China cast ....$2 – 3
blue upper, metallic gray lower, chrome windows, 1998 Cool Concepts series, Thailand cast..........................$2 – 3
purple upper, white lower, tinted windows.....................................$4 – 5

7. metallic gold, tinted windows, 1997 75 Challenge series ....$6 – 12

Street Sweeper (see Street Cleaner)

Stretcha Fetcha Ambulance, 2³/₄", #46, 1972
1. red, "Unfall Rettung" label, yellow interior, blue windows, red base, Germany issue ....$40 – 50
2. bright green, "Viper Van," ivory interior, amber windows, white base...$12 – 16
3. bright green, "Viper Van," yellow interior, amber windows, black base ...$12 – 16
4. bright green, "Viper Van," yellow interior, amber windows, unpainted base ....$12 – 16
5. bright green, "Viper Van," yellow interior, amber windows, white base ...$12 – 16
6. white, "Ambulance" labels, ivory interior, blue windows, red base.........$12 – 16
7. white, "Ambulance" labels, yellow interior, amber windows, red base......$16 – 24
8. white, "Ambulance" labels, yellow interior, blue windows, red base.........$12 – 16
9. white, no labels, yellow interior, blue windows, red base ....$12 – 16
10. white, red cross labels, yellow interior, amber windows, red base .....$16 – 24
11. white, red cross labels, yellow interior, blue windows, red base.........$12 – 16

Studebaker Lark Wagonaire, with hunter and 1 or 2 dogs, 3", #42, 1965
1. blue with white sliding roof.....$12 – 16

Submersible, #45, 1999; #6, 2000; #64, 2001; #40 Deep Diver, 1999, international
1. orange-yellow and blue, purple window, globe design, white and blue wave graphics, 1999 Oceanics series, international issue ....$2 – 3

2. orange-yellow and blue, purple window, globe design, "World Ocean Exploration," 1999 Ocean series, US issue ....$2 – 3

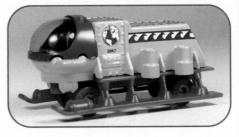

3. lime green and blue, amber window, globe design, white and blue wave graphics, 2000 Ocean Explorer series ....$2 – 3
4. lime green and blue, amber window, globe design, white and blue wave graphics, "Matchbox 2000," 2000 Ocean Explorer series ....$3 – 4
5. 2001 Scuba Dudes series........$2 – 3

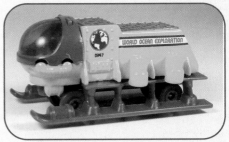

6. yellow and blue, amber window, "Base 2000," "BX-22775," Launcher 5-pack ....$2 – 3
7. metallic blue and yellow, blue window, globe design, yellow and red wave graphics, Pleasant Books issue ..$5 – 6
8. red and blue, amber window, "#042076" and storm graphics, Launcher 5-pack ....$2 – 3

Sugar Container Truck "Tate & Lyle," 2⁵/₈", #10, 1961
1. crown decal on back, gray wheels................................$65 – 80

2. **no crown decal, gray wheels.$30 – 40**
3. silver wheels ....$65 – 80
4. black wheels.......................$30 – 40

Sunburner (loosely based on Dodge Viper), 3", #15, 1992, USA; #41, 1992, international

1. **fluorescent yellow with sun and flames on hood, play set........$2 – 4**

2. white with sun and flames on hood ....$4 – 6

3. **metallic blue with white racing stripes, 1993.....................$2 – 4**

Sunberner Celica (see Toyota Celica XX)

Sunburner Maserati Bora, 3", #37, 1982
1. black with yellow and red flames, England cast ....$4 – 5
2. black with green and red flames, England cast ....$4 – 5
3. black with yellow and red flames, Macau cast ....$4 – 5
4. black with yellow and red flames, Hong Kong cast ....$4 – 5

Sunkist Mustang Piston Popper (see Ford Mustang Piston Popper)

Super Dozer, #37, 2001; #19, 2002; #67, 2003 (see Bulldozer Dirt Machine for photos)
1. red, "Matchbox 48," yellow plow, 2001 Earth Crunchers series ....$2 – 3
2. blue with yellow plow, 2002 Build It Right series ....$2 – 3
3. yellow with black plow, 2003 Heavy Movers series ....$2 – 3
4. yellow with red plow, 2003 Hero City 5-pack #9.................................$2 – 3

Super Porsche (see Porsche 935)

Swamp Rat Airboat, 3", #30, 1976
1. army green with tan hull, "Swamp Rat" labels ....$6 – 8
2. army green with tan hull, no labels ....$5 – 7
2. army green with tan hull, camouflage, tan driver, Commando series .....$5 – 6
3. army green with tan hull, camouflage, black driver, Commando series .$12 – 16

Swing Wing Jet, 3", #27, 1981
1. red with white base, white wings .$3 – 4
2. red with white base, gray wings...$5 – 6
3. black with gray base, gray wings, Commando series ....$5 – 6
4. gray with gray base, gray wings, "Top Gun," Star Car series ....$7 – 8

T

T-Bird Concept (see Ford Thunderbird Concept)

T-Bird Stock Car (see Ford Thunderbird Stock Car)

T-Bird Turbo Coupe (see Ford Thunderbird Turbo Coupe)

Tailgator, #27, 1994; #45, 1998

1. **bright green with gold-trimmed wheels, 1994 ....$2 – 3**
2. bright green with silver-trimmed wheels, 1994...................................$2 – 3

3. **dark green, 1996 ....$2 – 3**
4. metallic gold, silver-trimmed wheels, 1997 75 Challenge series ....$12 – 16
5. metallic gold with yellow base, gold-trimmed wheels, China issue ....$120 – 160

6. **purple, 1997......................$2 – 3**

7. **black, 1998 Animals series....$2 – 3**

Tanker Truck, #54, 2002; #48, 2003

1. **metallic red with translucent blue tank, 2002 Rescue Rookies series .....$2 – 3**

2. **red with white tank; red, maroo and silver; metallic gray plastic bas 2003 Hero City 5-pack #1.....$2 –**
3. white with translucent blue tank, 200 Forest Rescue series................$2 –
3. white with translucent blue tank, 200 Hero City 10-pack #1 ....$2 –

Tanzara, 3", #53, 1972 (similar castin Midnight Magic)
1. orange with chrome interior, amb windows ....$12 – 1
2. orange with chrome interior, blue-gree windows ....$12 – 1
3. white with chrome interior, amber wi dows.....................................$20 – 2
4. white with orange stripes, chrome int rior, amber windows............$12 – 1
5. white with red stripes, chrome interio amber windows ....$12 – 1
6. white with red stripes, chrome interio blue-green windows..............$16 – 2
7. white with red stripes, red interio amber windows ....$30 – 4

Taxi (see Austin FX4R London Taxi, Chevr let Impala Taxi, etc.)

Taxi Cab, #36, 2003
1. yellow, "Taxi," "36," wavy checkere stripe design, 2003 Mom and Po Shops series ....$2 –

Taxi FX4R (see Austin FX4R London Taxi)

Taylor Jumbo Crane, 3", #11, 1965
1. yellow weight box ....$15 – 2
2. red weight box....................$12 – 1

Team Matchbox Racer (see Hi-Tailer Tea Matchbox Racer)

Team Matchbox Formula 1 Racer, 2⁷/ #24, 1973
1. yellow with white driver, "8" label..............................$250 – 30
2. yellow with white driver, "4" label..............................$350 – 40
3. metallic blue with white driver, "1" label..............................$350 – 40
4. metallic blue with white driver, "5" label..............................$350 – 40
5. metallic green with white driver, "5 label..............................$50 – 6
6. red with white driver, "8" label ...$7 –
7. red with white driver, "8" label, label base, UK issue ....$60 – 7
8. red with white driver, "44" label ..$6 –

9. red with yellow driver, "44"
label..................................$20 – 25
10. orange with tan driver, "44"
label..................................$60 – 80
11. orange with yellow driver, "44"
label..................................$60 – 80

Thames Trader Compressor Truck, yellow, 2¾", #28, 1959
1. gray plastic wheels...........$160 – 180
2. black plastic wheels.............$30 – 40

The Buster, stylized pickup truck, #13, 1996; #20, 1998

1. **metallic blue with yellow, 1996 .$2 – 3**
2. metallic blue upper, bright yellow lower, hot pink, 1996 ....$4 – 6

3. **metallic gold, 1997 75**
Challenge ....$12 – 16
4. purple with yellow and white, 1997 ....$2 – 3

5. **metallic red with yellow and white,**
1998....................................$2 – 3
6. metallic green with yellow and white, 1998 ....$2 – 3

7. **metallic light green with yellow and**
white, 1998 ....$2 – 3

---

8. metallic blue with yellow, "American Iron Cruise 97" ....$16 – 24

The Londoner (see London Bus, The Londoner)

The Wall Eater (see Demolition Machine)

Tipper Truck (see Articulated Dump Truck, Atlas Dump Truck, DAF Tipper Truck, Dodge Dump Truck, 8-Wheel Tipper, Euclid Quarry Truck, GMC Highway Maintenance Truck, GMC Tipper Truck, Leyland Articulated Truck, Mack Dump Truck, Peterbilt Quarry Truck, Quarry Truck)

Tipping Trailer, 1993 Farming Series set

1. **red with black tailgate, black tires**
on gray rims.........................$3 – 4

Toe Joe Wreck Truck, 2¾", #74, 1972
1. red with green booms, black hooks, black base ....$175 – 225
2. red with red booms, black hooks, black base ....$175 – 225
3. red with red boom, red hooks, black base ....$175 – 225
4. yellow-orange with red booms, black hooks, unpainted base ....$4 – 5
5. yellow-orange with "Hitchhiker" label, unpainted base ....$150 – 200
6. yellow with green booms, black hooks, unpainted base ....$16 – 24
7. yellow with red booms, black hooks, black base ....$4 – 5
8. yellow with red booms, black hooks, unpainted base ....$4 – 5
9. lime green with green booms, red hooks, black base ....$5 – 6
10. lime green with green booms, red hooks, metallic gray base ....$5 – 6
11. lime green with green booms, red hooks, unpainted base ....$5 – 6
12. lime green with green booms, black hooks, unpainted base ....$5 – 6
13. dark lime green with white booms, black hooks, black base ....$150 – 200
14. dark lime green with green booms, red hooks, black base ....$5 – 6
15. dark lime green with red booms, black hooks, black base ....$16 – 24
16. dark lime green with red booms, black hooks, unpainted base ....$16 – 24

Tow Truck, #17, 2003 (see King Tow)

Toyman Dodge Challenger (see Dodge Challenger Hot Rod)

Toyota Celica GT, 2¹⁵⁄₁₆", #25, 1978
1. blue, "78," flat base, small rear wheels...................................$5 – 6
2. yellow, "Yellow Fever," raised base, small rear wheels.................$40 – 50
3. yellow, "Yellow Fever," raised base, large rear wheels.....................$5 – 6

Toyota Celica Supra, #30, 1995 (see Toyota Supra)

Toyota Celica XX, #77, 1981; #J-21, 1979, Japan
1. red, "Sunburner," US issued Sunburner Celica...................................$6 – 8
2. red, no markings, Hong Kong cast, Australia issue and US Speedsticks issue.......................................$4 – 5
3. red, Japan cast, Japan issue.......................................$16 – 24
4. ivory, Japan cast, Japan issue.......................................$16 – 24

Toyota Mini Pickup 4x4, issued with or without roof foil, roll bar, or tires in back, 2¾", #57, 1982; #13, 1983; #76, 1996 (also issued as Dunes Racer, Mountain Man, 4x4 Open Back Truck; similar casting: Toyota Mini Pickup Camper)
1. red with chrome windows, white and black splash design, yellow zigzag design, chrome plastic base, black roll bar, Super Trucks series...........$3 – 5
2. dark red with white, silver, and black stripes; no roof foil or roll bar ....$5 – 6
3. orange-red with white, silver, and black stripes; no roof foil or roll bar ....$5 – 6
4. orange with purple windows, "FWD," unpainted metal base, England cast.......................................$5 – 6
5. orange with orange windows, "FWD," unpainted metal base, England cast.......................................$5 – 6
6. orange with red windows, "FWD," unpainted metal base, England cast.......................................$5 – 6
7. yellow with red windows, "4X4," unpainted metal base, England cast ....$5 – 6
8. yellow with red windows, "4X4," metallic gray metal base, England cast ...$5 – 6
9. yellow with red windows, "4X4 Goodyear," pearly silver metal base, Macau cast...........................$4 – 5
10. yellow with red windows, "4X4 Goodrich," pearly silver metal base, Macau cast...........................$4 – 5
11. light blue, "Mountain Man" on roof, no roof foil or roll bar, black metal base ....$3 – 4
12. light blue, "Mountain Man" on roof, no roof foil or roll bar, black plastic base ....$2 – 3
13. metallic blue with red windows, pink, pink roll bar, black plastic base, Thailand cast ....$2 – 3

14. metallic purple with red windows, skeleton and triceratops, orange roll bar, 5-pack..............$2 – 3

15. white with red windows, "Bob Jane T-Mart," pearly silver metal base, Macau cast, Australia issue............$12 – 16

16. white with red windows, "63" and stripes, black metal base, Macau cast ....$2 – 3

17. white with red windows, "63" and stripes, black plastic base, Macau cast ....$2 – 3

18. white with red windows, "63" and stripes, black plastic base, Thailand cast.....................$2 – 3

19. white with chrome windows, blue and pink, pink roll bar, chrome plastic base, Thailand cast, Super Trucks series............$4 – 5

20. white with red windows, black ermine spots and dripping blood, red roll bar, black tires in back, red plastic base, Thailand cast..........$2 – 3

Toyota Mini Pickup Camper, 2³/₄", #22, 1982 (similar casting: Toyota Mini Pickup 4x4)

1. metallic silver with white stepped roof, yellow and black design, "Big Foot" ...$5 – 6

2. metallic silver with white stepped roof, yellow and black design, no side design, "Big Foot"..............$7 – 8

3. metallic silver with white flat roof, yellow and black design, "Big Foot," England cast ....$5 – 6

4. metallic silver with white flat roof, yellow and black design, "Big Foot," Hong Kong cast ....$7 – 8

5. metallic silver with white flat roof, yellow and black design, "Big Foot," Macau cast ....$5 – 6

6. metallic silver with black roll bar, yellow and black design, "Big Foot"...$40 – 50

7. red with white flat roof, "Aspen Ski Holidays," metal base.....................$4 – 5

8. red with white flat roof, "Aspen Ski Holidays," plastic base ....$3 – 4

9. white with white flat roof, "SLD Pump Service" ....$12 – 16

Toyota MR2, 2⁷/₈", #9, 1987; #74, 1987

1. white with "MR2 Pace Car".......$3 – 4

2. blue with "MR2" and pink stripes, new Superfast wheels ....$4 – 5

3. metallic blue with "MR2" and pink stripes, Laser Wheels ....$5 – 6

4. green with "7 Snake Racing Team" ....$9 – 12

Toyota Supra, 3", #39, 1982; #60, 1984, international

1. red, "Twin Cam 24," amber windows, black base, Japan issue ....$8 – 10

2. red, "Twin Cam 24," clear windows, black base, Japan issue ....$8 – 10

3. white, "41," red and black rally accents, amber windows, black base, 1982....................................$3 – 4

4. white, "41," red and black rally accents, amber windows, dark gray base, 1982.....................................$3 – 4

5. white, "41," red and black rally accents, clear windows, black base, 1982.$3 – 4

6. white, "Supra," pinstripes, amber windows, black base ....$3 – 4

7. white, "Supra," pinstripes, clear windows, black base ....$3 – 4

8. white with red, blue and yellow design, clear windows, black base, issued as a Dinky Toy, 1983 ....$9 – 12

Toyota Supra, #30, 1995; #44, 1998, international; #70, 2000, international

1. dark gray with red and black interior, clear windows, rubber tires on chrome rims, Premiere Collection #4 .....$4 – 5

2. black with black interior, tinted windows, red stripe, "Matchbox," 2000 Power international series ....$2 – 3

3. black with tan interior, clear windows, "Supra," 1998 Asian Cars international series.....................................$2 – 3

4. black with tan and black interior, clear windows, rubber tires on chrome rims, Gold Coin Collection ....$16 – 24

5. blue with black interior, green windows, ASAP promotional blank........$30 – 40

6. blue with black interior, green windows, "HEDIS Group," ASAP promotional ....$80 – 120

7. blue with black interior, green windows, "Mas 90 User Conference Lexington," ASAP promotional.............$80 – 120

8. blue with black interior, green windows, "Lucent Technologies," ASAP promotional.............................$80 – 120

9. blue with black interior, green windows, "Wenchey's Antiques...," ASAP promotional.............................$15 – 20

10. blue with white interior, clear windows; pink, orange, and white design, 5-pack...................................$2 – 3

11. chrome blue with white interior, clear windows; pink, orange, and white design, 5-pack.........................$2 – 3

12. chrome silver with purple interior, clear windows, lavender and pink design on sides and hood, 1997..............$2 – 3

13. fluorescent orange with red interior, clear windows, "Matchbox Get In The Fast Lane," "Toy Fair 1996," rubber tires on chrome rims............$20 – 30

14. metallic gold with black interior, clear windows, 1997 75 Challenge series...................................$6 – 12

15. red with yellow interior, tinted windows, white and orange design on sides .$3 – 4

16. red with metallic gray interior, tinted windows, black and white design on sides, 1997 Super Cars 5-pack.$2 – 3

17. **white with gray interior, red and yellow flames on sides and hood .$2 – 3**
18. white with red interior, red and yellow flames on sides and hood, 1996 ..$2 – 3
19. white with red interior, red and yellow flames on sides only ....$2 – 3
20. white with red and black interior, detailed trim, rubber tires on chrome rims, Premiere Collection #1 .....$4 – 5

21. **yellow with gray interior, rubber tires on chrome rims, Premiere Collection 8-car display set ....$4 – 5**

Tractor (see Ford Tractor)

Tractor Shovel, $2^7/_8$", #29, 1976; #13, 1998; #237, 1993; #29, 1997; #13, 1998; #28, 1999; #94, 2000; #39, 2001

1. red with black shovel, chrome hubs, black motor ....$2 – 3
2. red with metallic gray shovel, gray motor, 1997 ....$2 – 3
3. red with metallic gray shovel, black motor, 1998 Big Movers series .$2 – 3

4. **red with metallic gray shovel, chrome hubs, black motor, "Thomae Mucusolvan," Germany issue ......$30 – 40**

5. **red with red fork on metallic gray arms, black motor, 1993 Farming Series set ....$4 – 6**
6. orange with black shovel, chrome hubs, black motor, white roof, Germany issue ....$4 – 5

7. **orange with metallic gray shovel, chrome hubs, black motor, no markings ....$2 – 3**
8. orange with metallic gray shovel, chrome hubs, black motor, black stripes ....$2 – 3
9. light orange with black shovel, gray motor..........................$9 – 10
10. light orange with black shovel, chrome hubs, black motor, "Thomae Mucosolvan," Macau cast, Germany issue ....$25 – 35
11. light orange with red shovel, chrome hubs, black motor, red stripes, Action System/Action Pack.................$2 – 3
12. dark orange with black shovel, chrome hubs, gray motor ....$9 – 10
13. dark orange with red shovel, chrome hubs, gray motor ....$60 – 80
14. fluorescent orange with black shovel, chrome hubs, black motor, 5-pack .$2 – 3
15. fluorescent orange with metallic gray shovel, chrome hubs, black motor, 5-pack....................................$2 – 3
16. pumpkin orange with gray shovel, chrome hubs, black motor, 5-pack ....$2 – 3
17. pumpkin orange with gray shovel, chrome hubs, gray motor, "Hemler Bros.," ASAP promotional ...$80 – 120
18. pumpkin orange with gray shovel, chrome hubs, gray motor, "Redi-Way," ASAP promotional..............$80 – 120
19. pumpkin orange with gray shovel, chrome hubs, gray motor, "Blue Ridge Construction," ASAP promotional ....$80 – 120
20. pumpkin orange with gray shovel, chrome hubs, gray motor, "CAT Service Co.," ASAP promotional ......$80 – 120
21. yellow with black shovel, chrome hubs, black motor, "Thomae Mucosolvan," Germany issue....................$30 – 40
22. light yellow with red shovel, chrome hubs, chrome motor ....$9 – 12
23. light yellow with red shovel, black hubs, chrome motor ....$12 – 18
24. light yellow with black shovel, chrome hubs, black motor, "Thomae Mucosolvan," Germany issue ....$20 – 30
25. light yellow with black shovel, chrome hubs, black motor, "Thomae Mucosolvan," Germany issue ....$20 – 30
26. dark yellow with black shovel, chrome hubs, black motor, "Thomae Mucosolvan," Thailand cast, Germany issue...$30 – 40
27. dark yellow with black shovel, chrome hubs, black motor, "Thomae Mucosolvan," Macau cast, Germany issue ....$20 – 30

28. dark yellow with black shovel, chrome hubs, black motor, no markings ..$5 – 6
29. dark yellow with black shovel, chrome hubs, black motor, black stripes, "C" ....$3 – 4
30. dark yellow with black shovel, chrome hubs, black motor, black stripes, England cast ....$3 – 4
31. dark yellow with black shovel, chrome hubs, black motor, black stripes, Thailand cast ....$2 – 3
32. dark yellow with black shovel, chrome hubs, gray motor, black stripes ..$3 – 4
33. dark yellow with black shovel, chrome hubs, gray motor, no markings ..$3 – 4
34. dark yellow with maroon shovel, chrome hubs, black motor ....$5 – 6
35. dark yellow with maroon shovel, yellow hubs, black motor ....$7 – 8
36. dark yellow with red shovel, chrome hubs, chrome motor ....$7 – 8
37. dark yellow with red shovel, chrome hubs, black motor, no markings ..$5 – 6
38. dark yellow with red shovel, chrome hubs, black motor, red stripes ...$2 – 3
39. dark yellow with black shovel, chrome hubs, black motor, black stripes, Team Convoy ....$2 – 3
40. green with black shovel, chrome hubs, black motor, "Thomae Mucosolvan," Germany issue....................$40 – 50
41. green with dirt, gray shovel, chrome hubs, gray motor, metallic gray roof, 2000 Build It! series ....$2 – 3
42. green with dirt, gray shovel, chrome hubs, gray motor, metallic gray roof, "Matchbox 2000," 2000 Build It! series........$3 – 4
43. lime green with yellow shovel, chrome hubs, chrome motor, Germany issue....................$150 – 175
44. blue with red shovel, yellow wheels with orange hubs, red motor, Matchbox Preschool/Live 'N Learn series ..$7 – 8
45. blue with black shovel, chrome hubs, black motor, "Thomae Mucosolvan," Germany issue....................$30 – 40
46. blue with black shovel, chrome hubs, black motor, "Spasmo Mucosolvan," Germany issue....................$12 – 16

47. **blue with white shovel, chrome hubs, gray motor, 2001 Earth Crunchers series ....$2 – 3**
48. purple with black shovel, black motor, green and orange design, plastic armaments, Roadblasters ....$7 – 8

49. white with metallic gray shovel, chrome hubs, metallic gray motor, 1998 Big Movers series ....$2 – 3

50. beige with dirt, metallic gray shovel, chrome hubs, metallic gray motor, "3-MB34," 1999 Road Work series .$2 – 3
51. metallic gold with black shovel, chrome hubs, black motor, 1997 75 Challenge series................................$12 – 16
52. dull gold with black shovel, chrome hubs, black motor, Germany issue .$80 – 120

Tractor Shovel, 2000, Subway, "Mfd. by b. little" on base
1. pumpkin orange with black scoop and engine, black hubs ....$2 – 3

Trailer Caravan, 2⅞", #23, 1965

1. **yellow ....$12 – 16**

2. **pink................................$12 – 16**

Trailer Caravan (see Eccles Caravan)

Trans Am (see Pontiac Firebird Trans Am)

Trans Am T-Roof (see Pontiac Firebird Trans Am T-Roof)

Trash Truck, #57, 2002; #19, 2003

1. black with black dumper, metallic gray container and base, orange forks, 2002 Rescue Rookies series...................................$2 – 3

2. yellow with dark green dumper, black container and base, metallic gray forks, 2003 Public Works series ....$2 – 3

Travel Trailer (see Eccles Caravan Travel Trailer, Caravan Travel Trailer)

Travel Trailer (see Caravan Travel Trailer)

Travel Trailer (see Trailer Caravan)

Triumph Motorcycle and Sidecar, #4, 2⅛", 1960
1. metallic silver blue with black plastic tires................................$90 – 120

Trojan 1-Ton "Brooke Bond Tea" Van, red, 2¼", #47, 1958
1. metal wheels.......................$30 – 40
2. gray plastic wheels...............$40 – 50

Trolley Bus (see London Trolley Bus)

Troop Carrier, #36, 2002 (similar casting: Police Trouble Tracker)

1. white with black canopy, blue, turquoise and yellow "Metro Police," 2003 Hero City 5-pack #2 .....$2 – 3

Truck Camper, #58, 1999; #61, 2000; #53, 1999, international; #41, 2000, international (similar casting Police Mobile Command Center)
1. bright orange, 2002 Matchbox Across America 50th Birthday Series #44 Wyoming — Western Collection .$4 – 5
2. cream with blue and lavender design, blue windows, 5-pack................$2 – 3
3. light gray, "Candy Hill Campgrounds," red and yellow stripes, blue windows, Color Comp promotional........$20 – 30
4. light gray, "Matchbox 2000," red and yellow stripes, blue windows, 2000 Great Outdoors series ....$3 – 4

5. light gray with red and yellow stripes, blue windows, 2000 Great Outdoors series ....$2 – 3

6. white, "34 States and Still Going," black and yellow US map design, yellow windows, 1999 Wilderness Adventure series...................$2 – 3
7. white with blue and yellow design, yellow windows, 1999 Forest Run international series ....$2 – 3

8. white with red and black stripes, blue windows, 5-pack ....$2 – 3

Truck Camper Police (see Police Mobile Command Center)

[T]urbo Fury, 3", #69, 1973
red, "69" label, amber
windshield.............................$16 – 24
red, "69" label, clear
windshield.............................$16 – 24
red, "86" label, clear
windshield.............................$16 – 24
red, scorpion label, clear
windshield.............................$35 – 45

[T]urbo Ski (see Snowmobile)

[T]V News Truck (see Mercedes-Benz TV News Truck)

[T]V Service Van, with ladder, antenna, and three TV sets, 2½", #62, 1963
gray plastic wheels, "Rentaset"
decals..............................$125 – 150
gray plastic wheels, "Radio Rentals"
decals..............................$180 – 200
black plastic wheels, "Rentaset"
decals................................$30 – 35
black plastic wheels, "Radio Rentals"
decals................................$40 – 50

[T]yre Fryer, 3", #42, 1972
blue ....$12 – 16
orange "Jaffa Mobile," on-package premium, UK issue ....$90 – 120

[T]yrone Malone Bandit Bandit, 3", #65, 1982 (similar casting: Tyrone Malone Super Boss)
black with green and white stripes, "Tyrone" and four stripes on airfoil, England cast ....$4 – 5
black with green and white stripes, "Tyrone" and two stripes on airfoil, England cast ....$4 – 5

. **black with green and white stripes, no markings on airfoil, England cast..............................$4 – 5**

4. black with yellow and white stripes, no markings on airfoil, China cast ...$5 – 6
5. black with yellow and white stripes, "Tyrone" on airfoil, Macau cast...$2 – 3
6. black with yellow and white stripes, "Tyrone" and four stripes on airfoil, Macau cast..............................$2 – 3

Tyrone Malone Super Boss, 3", #66, 1982 (similar casting: Tyrone Malone Bandag Bandit)

1. **white, "Super Boss," "Detroit Diesel" on roof, decal, no stripes on spoiler, Macau cast..........................$2 – 3**
2. white, "Super Boss," "Detroit Diesel" on roof, tampo, no stripes on spoiler, Macau cast.............................$2 – 3
3. white, "Super Boss," "Detroit Diesel" on roof, four stripes on spoiler, Macau cast......................................$2 – 3
4. white, "Super Boss," "Detroit Diesel" on roof, no markings on spoiler, Macau cast......................................$2 – 3
5. white, "Super Boss," "Detroit Diesel" on roof, no markings on spoiler, green windows, England cast ....$3 – 4
6. white, "Super Boss," "Detroit Diesel" on roof, no markings on spoiler, red windows, England cast, Convoy.....$8 – 10
7. white, "Super Boss," four stripes on spoiler, green windows, England cast......................................$3 – 4
8. white, "Super Boss," four stripes on spoiler, Macau cast..................$2 – 3
9. white, "Super Boss," two stripes on spoiler, green windows, England cast......................................$3 – 4
10. white, "Super Boss," no markings on spoiler, green windows, England cast ....$3 – 4
11. white, "Super Boss," no markings on spoiler, China cast ....$3 – 4
12. white, no markings, China cast, Graffic Traffic ....$12 – 16
13. tan with orange, yellow and black stripes, metallic gray armament replaces spoiler, Macau cast, Roadblasters.................................$6 – 8

U

UFO, #61, 1999; #56, 1999, international
1. **lavender with blue-green windows, 1999 Science Fiction series ...$2 – 3**
2. **gold and silver, Real Talkin' series ....$5 – 8**

Ultralight (see Aero Junior)

Unimog (see Mercedes – Benz Unimog)

US Mail Jeep, "No.5 U.S. Mail Truck" on base, no gun, 2³⁄₈", #5, 1978 (similar casting: Army Jeep, with or without gun; #38, Sleet 'N Snow)
1. blue, white roof, "U. S. Mail" ......$6 – 8
3. pale blue, white roof, "U. S. Mail".$9 – 12

US Taxi (see Ford LTD US Taxi)

Utility Truck, #74, 1987; #33, 1989; #9, 1998; #15, 1999 (see Ford Utility Truck)

V

Vantastic, 2⁷⁄₈", #34, 1975; BR 23 – 24, 1986
1. orange with exposed engine, unpainted base, blue green windows, fish design label.................................$80 – 120
2. orange with exposed engine, white base, blue green windows, fish design labels ....$12 – 16
3. orange with exposed engine, white base, blue green windows, stripes labels ....$12 – 16
4. orange, no exposed engine, white base, blue green windows, "34" hood label ....$9 – 12
5. orange, no exposed engine, white base, sunburst hood label ....$16 – 24
6. orange, no exposed engine, white base, "Jaffamobile" label ....$400 – 450
7. orange, no exposed engine, white tab base, "34" label, UK issue .....$70 – 90
8. orange, no exposed engine, white tab base, "3" label, UK issue .....$80 – 120
9. beige, China cast, Super GTs BR 23 – 24, 1986 ....$4 – 5

10. blue, China cast, Super GT's BR 23 – 24, 1986 ....$4 – 5

Vauxhall Astra GTE/Opel Kadett, 2¾", #48, 1987, Europe

1. **red, "GTE" and stripes ....$3 – 4**
2. yellow, "Mobile Phone," "Telecom" .$4 – 5
3. yellow, no markings, Germany issue ....$10 – 12
4. black, "BP 52," "7," yellow stripe, the Netherlands issue ....$9 – 12
5. white, "AC Delco 48," silver wheels ....$2 – 3
6. white, "AC Delco 48," white wheels ....$3 – 4
7. white, "STP," "Sphere Drake" .....$2 – 3

Vauxhall Astra Police/Opel Kadett Police, 2⅞", #8, 1987; #24, 1999, international
1. white, "Police," red and blue stripes, white wheel hubs ....$5 – 6
2. white, "Police," red and blue stripes, silver wheel hubs ....$3 – 4
3. white and dark green, "Polizei" ...$5 – 6
4. white, "Police," orange and blue stripes and face on hood, yellow hubs, Live 'N Learn/Preschool series ....$4 – 5
5. white, "Police," yellow stripes, orange dot on roof ....$2 – 3
6. white, "Police," yellow stripes, no orange dot on roof ....$2 – 3
7. white, "Police," peach and yellow stripes ....$2 – 3
8. white, "59" in shield, yellow and black checks ....$2 – 3
9. white, "Police," "Hertfordshire" ...$2 – 3
10. black, "Police," commando emblem ....$16 – 24
11. white, "World Cup Security," "France 98" ....$2 – 3
12. metallic gray, "Police," red and blue stripes ....$2 – 3

Vauxhall Cresta sedan, 2½", #22, 1956
1. red with white or ivory roof, no windows ....$30 – 50

Vauxhall Cresta sedan, 2⅝", #22, 1958
1. ivory, no windows, metal wheels ....$40 – 50
2. ivory, no windows, gray plastic wheels ....$40 – 50
3. ivory, green windows, gray plastic wheels ....$45 – 55
4. ivory and turquoise, green windows, gray plastic wheels ....$350 – 400

5. gray and turquoise, green windows, gray plastic wheels ....$65 – 75
6. bronze and turquoise, green windows, gray plastic wheels ....$65 – 75
7. gray and pink, green windows, gray plastic wheels ....$50 – 60
8. gray and pink, green windows, silver plastic wheels ....$50 – 60
9. gold, green windows, gray plastic wheels ....$50 – 60
10. gold, green windows, silver plastic wheels ....$50 – 60
11. copper, green windows, gray plastic wheels ....$50 – 60
12. copper, green windows, silver plastic wheels ....$50 – 60
13. copper, green windows, black plastic wheels ....$35 – 45

Vauxhall Frontera (see Isuzu Rodeo)

Vauxhall Guildsman, Superfast wheels, 3", #40, 1971
1. pink, "40," green windows, unpainted base ....$16 – 24
2. pink with flames label, green windows, metallic gray base ....$12 – 16
3. pink with flames label, green windows, unpainted base ....$12 – 16
4. red, "40," amber windows, metallic gray base ....$12 – 16
5. red, "40," amber windows, unpainted base ....$12 – 16

6. **red, "40," green windows, unpainted base ....$12 – 16**
7. red with flames label, amber windows, unpainted base ....$12 – 16
8. red with flames label, green windows, unpainted base ....$12 – 16

Vauxhall Victor Estate Car, yellow, 2⅝", #38, 1963
1. green interior, gray plastic wheels ....$30 – 35
2. green interior, silver plastic wheels ....$35 – 40
3. green interior, black plastic wheels ....$25 – 30
4. red interior, silver plastic wheels ....$25 – 30
5. red interior, black plastic wheels ....$25 – 30

Vauxhall Victor Sedan, 2⅜", #45, 1958
1. red with no windows, metal wheels ....$900 – 1000
2. yellow with no windows, metal wheels ....$30 – 40
3. yellow with no windows, gray plastic wheels ....$30 – 40

4. yellow with green windows, gray plast wheels ....$30 – 4
5. yellow with clear windows, gray plast wheels ....$30 – 4
6. yellow with green windows, silver plast wheels ....$40 – 5
7. yellow with green windows, black plast wheels ....$20 – 3

Vectra Cavalier (see Opel Vectra/Chevrol Cavalier)

Volks Dragon Volkswagen Beetle, re 2½", #31, 1971 (similar castings: Ho Silver, Hot Chocolate, Sand Digge Dune Man, Big Blue)
1. red with unpainted base, purple wi dows, ivory interior, eyes sticker ....$12 – 1
2. red with unpainted base, purple wi dows, yellow interior, eyes sticker ....$12 – 1
3. red with unpainted base, clear window yellow interior, eyes sticker ....$12 – 1
4. red with metallic gray base, clear wi dows, yellow interior, eyes sticker ....$12 – 1
5. red with metallic gray base, purple wi dows, yellow interior, eyes sticker ....$12 – 1
6. red with unpainted base, purple wi dows, yellow interior, flower sticker ....$16 – 2
7. red with metallic gray base, purple wi dows, yellow interior, flower sticker ....$16 – 2
8. red with unpainted base, purple wi dows, yellow interior, no sticker ....$12 – 1
9. red with metallic gray base, purple wi dows, white interior, eyes sticker ....$12 – 1

Volkswagen 1200 Sedan, metallic ligh blue, 2½", #25, 1960
1. gray plastic wheels, clear windows ....$40 – 50
2. gray plastic wheels, green windows ....$40 – 50
3. silver plastic wheels, green windows ....$50 – 60
4. black plastic wheels, green windows ....$100 – 120

Volkswagen 1500 Saloon, 2⅞", #15 1968

1. **ivory with "137" on doors, black plastic wheels, 1969 ....$9 – 12**

ivory with "137" on doors, Superfast wheels, 1970.....................$20 – 25
metallic red with "137" on doors, Superfast wheels ....$24 – 36

olkswagen 1600TL, 2³/₄", #67, 1967

- **red with no roof rack, black plastic tires on chrome hubs ....$16 – 24**
  red with maroon roof rack, black plastic tires on chrome hubs ....$40 – 50
  metallic purple, no roof rack, black plastic tires on chrome hubs.............................$300 – 400
  red, Superfast wheels, 1970 ....$90 – 120
  metallic purple, Superfast wheels, 1970....................................$25 – 35
  pink, Superfast wheels ....$20 – 30

olkswagen Beetle 1962, #53, 1999; #12, 2000; #48, 1999, international
  red with black roof, "Coca-Cola," Avon 2-pack.......................................$6 – 8
  red with black roof, silver pinstripes, 5-pack.......................................$2 – 3

- **red with fishing graphics, 2003 5-pack #10 ....$2 – 3**
  red and white with black roof, "Things Go Better With Coke" rubber tires on chrome rims, Target multi-pack ....$5 – 6
  pumpkin orange, "Scooby Doo!" "Jinkies," "Velma," Warner Brothers series.....................................$6 – 8

- **metallic silver-blue, "Massachusetts," 2002 Matchbox Across America 50th Birthday Series — Northeastern Collection ....$4 – 5**

7. orange with black roof, "Xtreme Mission 33," 5-pack...................$2 – 3
8. metallic purple with black roof; black, blue, and lavender fish design, 5-pack.....................................$2 – 3
9. yellow with black roof, rubber tires on chrome rims, FAO Schwarz multipack................................$7 – 9
10. light blue with black roof, "Beetle," 5-pack......................................$2 – 3

11. **black with turquoise sides, black roof, "Matchbox," 1999 Beach series ....$2 – 3**
12. white with black roof, turquoise sides, "Northern New Jersey Toy Show," Color Comp promotional................$16 – 24

13. **white with turquoise sides, black roof, 2000 To The Beach series ....$2 – 3**
14. white with turquoise sides, black roof, "Matchbox 2000," 2000 To The Beach series...................................$3 – 4
15. white and red, "Coca-Cola," rubber tires on chrome rims, Premiere Collection...............................$5 – 6

Volkswagen Beetle 4x4, front opens, #31, 2001; #45, 2002

1. **yellow with blue plastic base, 2003 Hero City 5-pack #7 ....$2 – 3**
2. yellow with black base, "Desert Rescue," 2001 Sand Blasters series ....$2 – 3

2. yellow with red plastic base, 2002 Weekend Cruisers series ....$2 – 3
3. yellow with black plastic base, 2003 Beach Patrol series.................$2 – 3
4. yellow with black plastic base, 2003 Hero City 10-pack #1 ....$2 – 3

Volkswagen Beetle Big Blue (see Big Blue Volkswagen Beetle)

Volkswagen Beetle Dragon Wheels (see Dragon Wheels Volkswagen Beetle)

Volkswagen Beetle Dune Man (see Dune Man Volkswagen Beetle)

Volkswagen Beetle Flying Bug (see Flying Bug Volkswagen Beetle)

Volkswagen Beetle Hi Ho Silver! (see Hi Ho Silver! Volkswagen Beetle)

Volkswagen Beetle Hot Chocolate (see Hot Chocolate Volkswagen Beetle)

Volkswagen Beetle Sand Digger (see Sand Digger Volkswagen Beetle)

Volkswagen Beetle Volks Dragon (see Volks Dragon)

Volkswagen Beetle Taxi, #31, 2003
1. green with white roof, 2003 Airport series................................$3 – 4
2. green with white roof, 2003 Hero City 10-pack #2 ....$3 – 4

Volkswagen Camper, raised 6-windowed roof, 2⁵/₈", #34, 1967
1. metallic silver ....$35 – 50

Volkswagen Camper, low windowless roof, 2⁵/₈", #34, 1968
1. metallic silver ....$25 – 40

Volkswagen Camper/Dormobile, with opening roof, 2¹/₈", #23, 1970
1. blue with orange interior and roof ....$16 – 24
2. orange with orange interior and roof ....$150 – 200
3. orange with white interior, orange roof ....$12 – 16
4. olive with no interior, blue windows ....$7 – 9
5. white with no interior, "Pizza Van".......................................$10 – 15

Volkswagen Caravette Camper, light green, 2³/₄", #34, 1962
1. gray plastic wheels ....$40 – 50
2. black plastic wheels..............$40 – 50

Volkswagen Concept 1, #49, 1996 – 1997; #17, 1998; #18, 1999; #42, 2000; #60, 2001 (also see Volkswagen Concept 1 Convertible)

1. red, "17th Annual Matchbox USA Convention 1998," black roof, promotional..........................$15 – 20
2. red, "Coca-Cola," white wave, rubber tires on chrome rims, Premiere Collection.......................................$5 – 6
3. red, "Coca-Cola," "Always Coca-Cola," white roof, rubber tires on chrome rims, Premiere Collection..........$5 – 6
4. red, "Mark 1 V.W.S.," rubber tires on chrome rims ....$9 – 12
5. red, "Matchbox Collectors Club Deutschland," promotional.....$16 – 24
6. red, 2002 Matchbox Across America 50th Birthday Series #1 Delaware — Northeastern Collection ....$4 – 5
7. red with black fenders, opaque metallic silver windows, 1999 Taco Bell Matchbox Madness..........................$3 – 4

8. red with black roof, 1997......$4 – 5
9. red, "MICA Hershey 1999," Color Comp promotional..........................$20 – 30
10. dark red, "8th Toy Show Demo Model Hershey," Color Comp promotional..$16 – 24
11. dark red, "20th Annual MBUSA Demo Model," Color Comp promotional ....$16 – 24
12. dark red, "Matchbox," gold glitter, short card, "A Target Exclusive" on package ....$3 – 4
13. maroon, "Hope Spring Cancer Support Centre 1998," black roof, promotional ....$120 – 160
14. orange, "Bill Cairns Realtor," ASAP promotional ....$30 – 40
15. orange, "Hope Spring Cancer Support Centre 1998," black roof, promotional ....$20 – 30
16. orange, "Matchbox Convention Hershey PA 1999 Demo Model," Color Comp promotional..........................$30 – 40
17. orange, "MICA Hershey 1999," Color Comp promotional................$20 – 30
18. orange, "Matchbox World of Wheels," black roof, Color Comp promotional....................$120 – 160
19. orange, "RLI," black roof, ASAP promotional................................$80 – 120

20. orange with black roof, 1998 Cool Concepts series....................$2 – 3
21. orange, "www.sachs.com," ASAP promotional ....$120 – 160
22. pumpkin orange, "Hope Spring Cancer Support Centre 1998," black roof, promotional ....$120 – 160
23. yellow, "10 Jahre Mauerfall," "Berlin 1989 1999," promotional.....$30 – 40
24. yellow, "Happy New Millennium," "Y2K Bug," promotional ....$20 – 30
25. yellow with yellow roof, Germany issue.....................................$4 – 5
26. green, "17th Annual Matchbox USA Convention 1998," black roof, promotional................................$15 – 20

27. green with black roof, green base, 1997...................................$2 – 3
28. green with black roof, red base, 1997............................$120 – 160
29. light lime green, white flowers and globe design, rubber tires on chrome rims...................................$12 – 16
30. metallic lime green, white headlights....................................$4 – 5
31. metallic lime green, white headlights, "Matchbox," Pleasant Books issue.$4 – 5

32. metallic purple with black roof, 1997 Cars of the Future 5-pack ......$2 – 3

33. black with yellow stripes, 2000 Show Cars series.................$2 – 3
34. black with yellow stripes, "Matchbox 2000," 2000 Show Cars series.$3 – 4
35. brown, "Hope Spring Cancer Support Centre 1998," black roof, promotional............................$120 – 160
36. white, "Blue Angels," ASAP promotional............................$16 – 24

37. white, "Happy New Millennium," "Y2K Bug," promotional ....$20 – 3
38. white, "New Way Lunch," ASAP promotional.........................$60 – 8
39. white, "RCA," ASAP promotional.$20 – 3

**40. white with blue trim, 1999 To Class series ....$2 – **
41. metallic gold, 1997 75 Challeng series.................................$6 – 1
42. metallic silver, rubber tires on chrome rims, FAO Schwarz multipack.....$7 –

Volkswagen Concept 1, 1998, Taco Be Matchbox mold retooled by Strottma International Inc. through a licensin agreement with Mattel. Strottman ma ufactures toy premiums for Taco Be Base is marked "Made in China by S.I.I

1. red with black fenders, metallic silve windows, swirl design and lines, Tac Bell premium..........................$4 –
2. green with metallic silver windows, pl set......................................$9 – 1

Volkswagen Concept 1 Cabriolet (se Volkswagen Concept 1 Convertible)

Volkswagen Concept 1 Convertible, #8 2000; #1, 2001; #61, 2000, interna tional; #73, 1999, Germany

1. red with red trim on windshield, blac interior, rubber tires on chrome rims FAO Schwarz gift set ....$7 –
2. blue with no trim on windshield light tan interior, 1999 German issue...................................$9 – 1
3. blue with blue trim on windshield light tan interior, 1999 German issue ....$5 –
4. white, "Coca-Cola," 5-pack ....$2 –
5. white with white trim on windshield, ta interior, 2000 Worldwide Wheel series...................................$2 –
6. white with white trim on windshield, ta interior, "Matchbox 2000," 200 Worldwide Wheels series..........$3 –

7. metallic silver, "Coca-Cola" with bottle in red circle, red interior, Matchbox Collectibles Coca-Cola Collection ....$3 – 4

8. metallic silver with silver trim on windshield, "Beetle," 2001 Daddy's Dreams series.................................$2 – 3

Volkswagen Concept 1 Police, #465, 2000

1. "D.A.R.E.," yellow with black hood and doors, 5-pack ....$2 – 3

2. "D.A.R.E. Bellevue Police," white and black, D.A.R.E. series...............$4 – 5

Volkswagen Delivery Van, #72, 2000; #52, 2000, international (similar casting: Volkswagen Transporter)

1. green, "Georgia," Matchbox Across America 50th Birthday Series #4 — Southern Collection...............$4 – 5

2. blue, "Spongebob," cartoon illustrations, yellow base, 2003 Nickelodeon Spongebob Squarepants 5-pack ....$2 – 3

3. metallic light blue, "TNT Tours," motorcycle design, 2000 On Tour series.................................$2 – 3

4. metallic light blue, "TNT Tours," motorcycle design, "Matchbox 2000," 2000 On Tour series.......................$3 – 4

5. metallic blue with blue, yellow and black fish design, 5-pack ....$2 – 3

6. white, "All You Need To Know About Matchbox...," "Shabbir's Matchbox Website 5th Anniversary," Color Comp promotional..........................$25 – 35

7. white, "Coca-Cola Sign Of Good Taste," red roof, Avon Two Pack ....$6 – 8

8. white, "Farewell Vaarwell Wiedersehen 2000," "Welcom Welkom Willkommen 2001," "Matchbox Forum 2000 – 2001," Color Comp promotional ....$20 – 30

9. white, "Flashback Toys & Collectibles," Color Comp promotional........$35 – 45

10. white, "Iron City Beer," Color Comp promotional ....$35 – 45

11. white, "Manawatu Model Diecast Collectors New Zealand 2001," Color Comp promotional.........................$20 – 30

12. white, "MICA Goes To Hershey 2001," "Friday June 22 2001," Color Comp promotional.........................$20 – 30

13. white, "MICA Goes To Hershey 2001," "Saturday June 23 2001," Color Comp promotional.........................$20 – 30

14. white, "MICA Goes To Hershey 2001," "Sunday June 24 2001," Color Comp promotional.........................$20 – 30

15. white, "RCA," ASAP promotional.$25 – 35

16. white, "Scooby-Doo Christmas," Color Comp promotional..............$80 – 120

17. white, "Tyler James Elliot Memoriam Model 1," Monarch butterfly and sky design, Color Comp promotional...........$35 – 45

18. white, "We've Scored 20th Anniversary Matchbox USA Convention," Color Comp promotional.........................$16 – 24

19. white with chrome base, ASAP/Color Comp promotional blank........$35 – 45

Volkswagen Golf with rack and surfboards, 2⁷⁄₈", #7, 1976

1. metallic green with yellow interior ....$6 – 8

2. yellow with "ADAC" labels, roof light and antenna, no rack, Germanyy and Japan issue.................................$40 – 50

3. metallic green with red interior.$9 – 12

4. yellow with red interior..............$6 – 8

5. red with yellow interior..............$6 – 8

6. metallic silver with red interior ...$4 – 6

7. metallic silver with tan interior.$30 – 40

8. metallic silver with blue interior ....$300 – 400

9. black with red stripe , no rack....$6 – 8

10. black with red and orange stripe, "9," no rack, Dinky issue ....$9 – 12

Volkswagen Golf GTi, 2⁷⁄₈", #33, 1986; #56, 1986; #63, 1991

1. red, "Golf GTi".........................$3 – 4

2. white, "Federal Express"............$4 – 5

3. white, "Quantum," UK issue.......$6 – 8

4. dark gray, Two Pack.................$3 – 4

5. yellow, "PTT," Switzerland issue .$9 – 12

6. white, "Abstract" and graphics, UK issue....................................$4 – 5

7. white, "Lippische Landes-Zeitung," Germany issue.........................$16 – 24

Volkswagen Rabbit (see Volkswagen Golf)

Volkswagen Microbus, #72, 2002; #54, 2003

1. metallic two-tone light blue, no markings, 2002 Kids' Cars of the Year series.................................$2 – 3

2. metallic blue, "Bookmobile," 2003 School Time series...................$2 – 3

Volkswagen Panel Transporter (see Volkswagen Delivery Van)

Volkswagen Rompin' Rabbit 4x4, 2⁷⁄₈", #7, 1982

1. white with "Rompin' Rabbit" ....$6 – 8

Volkswagen Ruff Rabbit 4x4, 2⁷⁄₈", #7, 1983

1. yellow with "Ruff Rabbit" ....$4 – 5

Volkswagen Transporter/Ambulance Vanagon, 2⁷⁄₈", #20, 1986, international

1. white with ambulance markings and roof lights ....$3 – 5

2. black with green cross, "LS2081," Commando series ....$4 – 5

3. white with no markings, Graffic Traffic series................................$12 – 16

Volkswagen Transporter Microbus, #64, 1999; #57, 2000; #12, 2001; #59, 1999, international; #52, 2000, international (similar casting: Volkswagen Delivery Van)

1. lime green, "Scooby Doo," "Zoinks," "Shaggy," orange yellow interior, clear windows, Warner Bros. ....$6 – 8

2. light sea green and white with gray interior, clear windows, "Coca-Cola," rubber tires on chrome rims, Premiere Collection ....$5 – 6

3. light sea green and white with gray interior, clear windows, "Coca-Cola" and "www.cocacolastore.com," rubber tires on chrome rims, Color Comp promotional..................................$60 – 80

4. **red and white, "We Have Visitors," "They Are Here," 1999 Science Fiction US series.......................$2 – 3**
5. red and white with black and white illustrations, 1999 Science Fiction international series ....$3 – 4

6. **green, blue windows with curtains, 2002 Wilderness Tours 5-pack ....$2 – 3**

7. **metallic blue, "TNT," 2001 World Tour international series.......$3 – 4**
8. turquoise and white, detailed trim, rubber tires on chrome rims, FAO Schwarz multipack ....$5 – 6

9. **turquoise, dark blue and white with red, blue and white stripes, orange interior, "VW Transporter," 2001 Highway Heroes series ....$2 – 3**

10. **black, "Richie's Pizzeria," red interior, 2000 Speedy Delivery series····$2 – 3**
11. black, "Richie's Pizzeria," "Matchbox 2000," red interior, 2000 Speedy Delivery series ....$3 – 4
12. black, "Action Radar," "Xtreme Mission," gray interior, tinted windows, 5-pack.....................................$2 – 3

13. **white with red, yellow and teal bicycle and sun design, aqua interior, teal base, yellow windows, 2003 5-pack #10 ....$2 – 3**

Volkswagen Van, blue "Matchbox Express," 2¼", #34, 1957
1. metal wheels ....$45 – 55
2. gray plastic wheels ....$55 – 65
3. silver plastic wheels...........$80 – 100
4. black plastic wheels..........$125 – 150

Volvo 480ES (European model), 2⅞", #69, 1989
1. metallic pearl gray, "Volvo 480," green stripes, Laser Wheels ....$4 – 5
2. white, "480ES," gray metal base, Macau cast............................$3 – 4
3. white, "480ES," "Volvo," gray metal base, Macau cast ....$3 – 4
4. white, "480ES," "Volvo," gray plastic base, China cast......................$6 – 8
5. white, "480ES," "Volvo," gray plastic base, Macau cast ....$3 – 4
6. white, "Toys City" label on roof, gray metal base, Macau cast, Malaysia issue ....$80 – 120

Volvo 760 (European model), 3", #62, 1987
1. burgundy ....$8 – 10
2. purple, China cast ....$3 – 4
3. dark purple, China cast.............$3 – 4
4. metallic gray with detailed trim, rubber tires on chrome rims, Ultra Class.................................$9 – 12
5. metallic dark gray, China cast ....$3 – 4
6. metallic pearl gray, Macau cast .$3 – 4

7. white, China cast, Graffic Traffic ....$12 – 1

Volvo Aquarium Truck, with accessories #389, 1998
1. blue-green with dolphin and wave design ....$4 – 5

Volvo Cable Truck, with two metallic gray cable spools on back, 3", #26, 1984
1. orange with black base, blue windows ....$20 – 25
2. orange with dark gray base, blue windows...........................$20 – 25
3. orange with red base, blue windows ....$20 – 25
4. orange with red base, green windows ....$20 – 25
5. red with black base, blue windows ....$30 – 40
6. yellow with black base, blue windows ....$25 – 30

Volvo Container Truck, 3¹⁄₁₆", #20, 1986 #23, 1985; #62, 1990; #44, 1998 #1, 1998, international

1. **black with black container, "Cool Paint Co.," 1993 ....$2 – 3**

2. **black with yellow container, "Matchbox Auto Products," 1997.....$2 – 3**
3. blue with blue container, "Allders," UK issue.....................................$7 – 9
4. blue with blue container, "Comma Performance Motor Oils," UK on-package offer....................................$8 – 10
5. blue with blue container, "Crooke's Healthcare"............................$7 – 9
6. blue with red container, "Christiansen, Belgium issue ....$10 – 12
7. blue with white container, "Big Top Circus," gift set........................$10 – 12
8. blue with white container, "Coldfresh" labels ....$4 – 5

182

blue with white container, "MB1-75 #1 IN Volume Sales," UK issue ...$40 – 50

0. blue with white container, "Unic" ..$10 – 12

1. blue with white container, "Kellogg's," "Milch-Lait-Latte," Switzerland — Germany issue..........................$40 – 50

2. blue with yellow container, "Airways Air Cargo," 5-pack ....$2 – 3

3. metallic gold with black container, no labels, 1997 75 Challenge series ....$6 – 12

4. green with gray container, "Hikkoshi Semmon Center," Japan issue$12 – 16

5. green with white container, "M" and green stripes, Switzerland issue ..$10 – 12

6. gray with gray container, "Supersaver Drugstores" ....$9 – 12

7. orange with orange container, "Allied Van Lines," 1999 Speedy Delivery series....................................$2 – 3

8. orange with orange container, "Allied," "Pickfords" ....$2 – 3

9. orange with orange container, "Enjoy Fanta," China issue..........$160 – 240

0. orange with orange container, "Polar Power," White Rose gift set.......$4 – 5

1. orange with yellow container, black design and "Matchbox" logo on doors, "Get In The Fast Lane" ....$2 – 3

2. orange with yellow container, no design or logo on doors, "Get In The Fast Lane" ....$2 – 3

3. orange with yellow container, "N.A.D.T.C.A." label on doors, "North American Diecast Toy Collectors Association Second Anniversary November 1995" label on container, custom issue ..$9 – 10

24. orange with yellow container, "Matchbox Collector Edgar M. Strauss" label on container, custom issue ....$12 – 16

25. purple with purple container, "Continental Aero"............................$10 – 12

26. red with blue container, "Matchbox" with red arrow, International issue .....$2 – 3

27. red with brown container, "Merkur Kaffee" labels, Switzerland issue .$10 – 12

28. red with red container, "Coca-Cola" with polar bears, tinted windows ...$12 – 16

29. red with red container, "Coca-Cola" with polar bears, blue windows .....$30 – 45

30. red with red container, "Coca-Cola" with polar bears, amber windows ..$30 – 45

31. red with orange container, "Coca-Cola" with polar bears, tinted windows....$80 – 120

32. red with white container, "Big Top Circus" ....$2 – 3

33. red with white container, "Denner," Switzerland issue ....$10 – 12

34. red with yellow container, "Matchbox Animals" with dinosaur illustration, 1998 Animals series......$2 – 3

35. turquoise with black container, "Matchbox Auto Products," 5-pack ......$2 – 3

36. turquoise with black container, "Sagamore Insurance"...............$90 – 120

37. white and red with white container, "Auto Palace" ....$6 – 8

38. white with blue container, "The Matchbox Times," 1998 Around Town 5-pack ....$2 – 3

39. white with light blue container, "Co-Op People Who Care," UK issue .....$7 – 9

40. white with light blue container, "99 Tea," UK on-package offer ....$8 – 10

41. white with ivory container, "Federal Express" on container ....$3 – 4

42. white with white container, "Automotive Distributing Company," ASAP promotional...................................$60 – 80

43. white with white container, "Bill Cairns — Let Bill Move You," ASAP promotional ....$25 – 50

44. white with white container, "Bulldog Castor Co.," ASAP promotional....$30 – 40

45. white with white container, "Cendant Mobility," "We treat each move like it's our own," ASAP promotional..$60 – 80

46. white with white container, "Certainteed," "Synergy," ASAP promotional ..$50 – 75

47. white with white container, "Certainteed HVAC Insulation Products," ASAP promotional ....$80 – 120

48. white with white container, "CFU" in red on right side only, ASAP promotional ....$30 – 45

49. white with white container, "CFU" in blue on right side only, ASAP promotional ....$60 – 80

50. white with white container, "Cookman Accounting Services," ASAP promotional ....$24 – 32

51. white with white container, "Dupont Answers," ASAP promotional..$60 – 80

52. white with white container, "Dupont Floor Covering," ASAP promotional...$60 – 80

53. white with white container, "Dupont Floor Finishes," ASAP promotional.....$50 – 75

54. white with white container, "e=cycled.com," ASAP promotional ....$60 – 80

55. white with white container, "Family Trust," Canada issue ....$10 – 12

56. white with white container, "Federal Express" on container ....$4 – 5

57. white with white container, "Federal Express" on container, "XP Parcels" on doors ....$16 – 24

58. white with white container, "Federated Realty Group Inc.," ASAP promotional ....$45 – 65
59. white with white container, "Harty Press," ASAP promotional .$125 – 175
60. white with white container, "Hi-Speed," "Garvens," ASAP promotional.$40 – 50
61. white with white container, "Kellogg's," "Milch-Lai-Latte," Switzerland-Germany issue ....$40 – 50
62. white with white container, "Kit Kat," UK issue ....$30 – 40
63. white with white container, "Kuthasta Investment Supplies Group," ASAP promotional ....$30 – 40
64. white with white container, "Matchbox asi 33000," ASAP promotional...$80 – 120
65. white with white container, "Nestle," ASAP promotional...............$30 – 40
66. white with white container, "Office Depot," ASAP promotional.....$30 – 45
67. white with white container, "PC Van Go" on left side only, ASAP promotional...................$60 – 90
68. white with white container, "RCA," ASAP promotional...............$21 – 28
69. white with white container, "Scotch Corner" labels ....$9 – 12
70. white with white container, "TNT Ipec," Team Convoy series ....$4 – 6
71. white with white container, "Transply, Inc.," ASAP promotional........$60 – 80
72. white with white container, "Two Men and a Truck," ASAP promotional ....$12 – 16
73. white with white container, "UNIC"...................$8 – 10
74. white with white container, "XP Parcels"...................$5 – 7
75. white with white container, "Yorkie" ....$30 – 40
76. white with white container, no markings, ASAP promotional blank ....$16 – 24
77. yellow with yellow container, "Action System," on-package offer.........$10 – 12

Volvo Covered Tilt Truck, 3", #26, 1984, international; #49, 1990, US; #4, 1999, international
1. army green with tan canopy, "LS2020," Commando series ....$16 – 24
2. black with dark gray canopy, "LS1506," Commando series ....$16 – 24
3. blue with blue canopy, "Henniez," Switzerland issue ....$10 – 12
4. dark blue with yellow canopy, "Michelin"...................$2 – 3
5. metallic blue with yellow canopy, no markings, England cast.........$24 – 36
6. metallic blue with yellow canopy, "Fresh Fruit Co.," England cast.............$4 – 5
7. metallic blue with yellow canopy, "Fresh Fruit Co.," Macau cast..............$3 – 4
8. pumpkin orange with turquoise canopy, apple design, 1998 Farming international series ....$2 – 3
9. pumpkin orange with no canopy, "www.matchboxclub.de," Germany promotional ....$30 – 40

10. red with green canopy, yellow wheels, Live 'N Learn/Matchbox Preschool......$7 – 8
11. red with no canopy, "123" on doors, Live 'N Learn/Matchbox Preschool.....$7 – 8
12. red with white canopy, "Big Top Circus," Adventure 2000.....................$3 – 4
13. white with white canopy, "Federal Express" ....$3 – 4
14. white with white canopy, "Pirelli Gripping Stuff"...................$2 – 3
15. yellow with yellow canopy, "Ferrymasters Groupage" ....$3 – 4

Volvo Stake Truck, #315, 1997
1. blue, "MB Builders," wall frame payload, Action Pack...................$4 – 5
2. blue, no markings, straw bale payload, Action Pack...................$4 – 5

Volvo Tilt Truck (see Volvo Covered Tilt Truck)

Volvo Zoo Truck, 3", #35, 1982, international
1. red with blue cage, yellow lions..$20 – 25
2. red with gray cage, tan or brown lions ....$20 – 25
3. red with gray cage, white lions .$30 – 40
4. orange with gray cage, tan or yellow lions...................$20 – 25

VW (see Volkswagen)

W

Wall Eater (see Demolition Machine)

Watercraft with Trailer, #51, 1999; #46, 1999, international; #8, 2000

1. **teal blue hull, white deck, red seat and handlebars, yellow trailer, 2003 Hero City 5-pack #10 ....$2 – 3**
2. white hull with turquoise and purple design, turquoise deck, purple seat and handlebars, purple trailer, 1999 Beach series (US), 1999 Seaside series (international) ....$2 – 3

3. **white hull with orange and blue design, orange deck, blue seat and handlebars, blue trailer, 2000 Ocean Explorer series ....$2 – 3**
4. white hull with orange and blue design, orange deck, blue seat and handlebars, blue trailer, "Matchbox 2000," 2000 Ocean Explorer series...............$3 – 4

5. **white hull with yellow stripe, red deck, black seat and handlebars, black trailer, 2000 Ocean Dock 5-pack ....$2 – 3**
6. white hull with purple and blue octopus design, yellow deck, black seat and handlebars, gray trailer, 5-pack.......$2 – 3

Water Pumper (see Fire Water Pumper)

Wave King speedboat and skier, #41, 1999; #24, 2001; #36, 1999, international
1. yellow deck, white hull, two-tone blue design, blue driver and skier, 1999 Ocean series ....$2 – 3
2. blue-gray deck, black hull, maroon and white design, yellow driver, no skier, 5-pack.....................................$2 – 3

3. **turquoise deck, white hull, blue, purple and orange design, purple interior, 2001 Sun Chasers series .$2 – 3**

Weasel Armored Vehicle, 2⁷/₈", #73, 1974; #70, 1993 reissue; #77, 1996 error package (similar casting: Military Tank)
1. green with black and brown camouflage, Thailand cast, 5-pack ....$2 – 3
2. olive green, "M-3173," star, black hubs, Thailand cast, packaged as #73.$3 – 4
3. olive green, "M-3173," star, black hubs, Thailand cast, packaged as #77.$3 – 4
4. olive green, black hubs, England cast, Two Pack................................$7 – 9
5. olive green with tan and black camouflage, black hubs, Macau cast, Commando series ....$5 – 6
6. olive green, silver hubs, England cast, Two Pack................................$7 – 9
7. dark army green, black hubs, Two Pack................................$70 – 90
8. metallic green, England cast, silver hubs ....$5 – 6

9. black with yellow and gray camouflage, Macau cast, Commando series ..$5 – 6
10. beige with brown, black and white camouflage, black hubs, China cast ..$2 – 3
11. beige with brown, black, and white camouflage; black hubs, Thailand cast ....$2 – 3

12. khaki with brown and green camouflage, 1995 Military 5-pack ...$2 – 3

Weather Radar Truck, 3", #66, 2001; #43, 2002; #35, 2003
1. metallic dark red with blue tinted windows, metallic gray radar, 2001 Storm Watch series ....$2 – 3

2. metallic gray with smoke tinted windows, red radar, 2002 Airport Alarm series..........................$2 – 3

3. black with blue tinted windows, blue radar, 2003 Airport series ....$2 – 3
4. black with blue tinted windows, blue radar, 2003 Hero City 10-pack #2 ....$2 – 3
5. pale gray-green, "Satellite Radar," detailed graphics, 2003 Matchbox Heroes series.........................$3 – 4

Weatherhill (see Weatherill)

Weatherill Hydraulic Excavator, yellow, 2³/₈", #24, 1956

1. orange with metal wheels......$60 – 80
2. yellow with metal wheels .....$80 – 100

Weatherill Hydraulic Excavator, 2⁵/₈", #24, 1959
1. yellow with gray plastic wheels.$30 – 40
2. yellow with black plastic wheels.$20 – 30

Whitewater Raft Boat, #59, 1999; #65, 2001; #54, 1999, international; #37, 2000, international; #14, 2001, international

1. red deck, white hull, "Beach Patrol S.C.U.B.A." on yellow trailer, 2002 Sand Castle Rescue Team 5-pack ....$3 – 4
2. red deck, yellow hull, "Base 1," "A1697 – 935L," black trailer with "Base 1," 2001 Rescue series, UK issue ..$4 – 5
3. orange deck, orange hull, "RNLI Lifeboats," blue trailer with "Lifeboats," "RNLI," UK issue ....$4 – 5
4. yellow deck, turquoise hull, "Water Rescue," black trailer, 2000 Rescue series, international issue ....$4 – 5
5. yellow deck, metallic blue hull, "River Research," lime trailer, Pleasant Books issue..............................$6 – 8

6. blue deck, white hull, "Action Canyon," blue trailer, 1999 Wilderness Adventure series ....$2 – 3
7. white deck, yellow hull, "Louisiana," Matchbox Across America 50th Birthday Collection #18 — Southern Collection...$5 – 6

White Lightning, Roman numeral III, 1978 (variation of #48 Pi-Eyed Piper, 1972 and #48 Red Rider, 1982)
1. cream, Roman Numeral Limited Edition ....$9 – 12
2. white, Roman Numeral Limited Edition ....$9 – 12

Wildcat Dragster (see Ford Mustang Wildcat Dragster)

Wildlife Truck (see Ford Wildlife Truck)

Williams Honda F1 Grand Prix Racer, 3", #74, 1988; #14, 1989
1. white and light blue, "Goodyear," "Shell," "15"..........................$3 – 5
2. red, "Fiat," "27," metal base ...$2 – 4
3. red, "Fiat," "27," plastic base ...$8 – 10
4. red, "Scotch," "Target".............$3 – 5
5. yellow, "Pennzoil," "2".............$3 – 5
6. yellow, "Pennzoil," "4"................3 – 5
7. dark orange and white, "Indy," "4"...$3 – 5
8. chrome with no markings......$16 – 24
9. blue, "Panasonic," "7"............$3 – 5
10. white and blue, "Indy," "76"....$3 – 5
11. white and black, "Havoline," "Kmart," "6"...$3 – 5
12. orange, lavender, and white; "Indy".....................................$4 – 6
13. white and pink with blue spots, "7," 1994.....................................$1 – 3

Williams Renault Formula Racer, 3¹/₈", #28, 1982; #16, 1984; #74, 1996; #61, 1998; #246, 1994, Nigel Mansell issue
1. red, "Ferrari 27 Pioneer," black airfoil, F1 issue ....$4 – 5
2. red, "Fiat 3," black "Pirelli" on airfoil.................................$2 – 4
3. red, "Fiat 27," red airfoil, F1 issue....................................$4 – 5
4. metallic red, Manaus cast, Brazil issue..................................$40 – 50
5. orange, "MB Racing 1," dark blue airfoil....................................$2 – 3

6. yellow, "MB Racing 1," red airfoil, 1998 Motor Sports series ....$2 – 3
7. yellow, "Matchbox Racing Team," dark red "Goodyear" on airfoil............$2 – 4
8. dark green, Manaus cast, Brazil issue..................................$40 – 50
9. blue, "Renault Elf O" with red, white, and gold trim, F1 issue ....$4 – 5
10. blue, "Sasol 14," black airfoil, F1 issue..................................$4 – 5
11. blue, "Sasol 14," blue airfoil, F1 issue..................................$4 – 5
12. blue and white, "Cannon Williams O," white airfoil, F1 issue...............$4 – 5
13. blue and white, "Cannon Williams 5," white airfoil, Nigel Mansell issue .$5 – 6
14. blue and white, "Renault Elf O," white airfoil, F1 issue.......................$4 – 5
15. pale blue, Manaus cast, Brazil issue..................................$40 – 50
16. black, "Liqui Moly 30," black airfoil, F1 issue..................................$4 – 5
17. white, "Belterra," ASAP promotional issue................................$60 – 80

185

18. white, "Citrix CDN," ASAP promotional issue............................$60 – 80
19. white, "Comp USA," "SAP, $," ASAP promotional issue ....$30 – 40
20. white, "Footwork 9," white airfoil, F1 issue..............................$4 – 5
21. white, "Hewlett Packard," "HP2000C," "From Fast to 4X Faster," ASAP promotional issue........................$80 – 120
22. white, "IBM Infinity," ASAP promotional issue.............................$80 – 120
23. white, "IFS," ASAP promotional issue.............................$60 – 80
24. white, "Indy 98 Rotary," ASAP promotional issue...........................$60 – 80
25. white, "Loctite," "Hitachi 72," white airfoil, F1 issue ....$4 – 5
26. white, "MB Racing 1," dark blue airfoil....................................$2 – 3

27. white, "MB Racing 1," orange airfoil.................$2 – 3
28. white, "Matchbox," "Goodyear," blue "Shell" on airfoil.........................$3 – 5
29. white, "Mr. Juicy," "Sunkist," orange and green, yellow "Watson's" on airfoil...................................$20 – 25
30. white, "Network Associates," ASAP promotional issue ....$60 – 80
31. white, "Protective," ASAP promotional issue..............................$60 – 80
32. white, "RCA," ASAP promotional issue................................$25 – 35
33. white, "Site Smith," ASAP promotional issue...............................$25 – 35
34. white, "STB," ASAP promotional issue..............................$60 – 80
35. white, "Sun Microsystems," "Java," ASAP promotional issue......$80 – 120
36. white, "Uliveto," "Lee Cooper," "Ford 9, white airfoil, F1 issue...............$4 – 5
37. white, "UR #1," "Sealed Air," ASAP promotional issue ....$60 – 80

38. white, "White's Guide August 1999 Car of the Month #9" in black lettering, ASAP promotional issue .$12 – 16
39. white, "White's Guide August 1999 Car of the Month #9" in red lettering, ASAP promotional issue ......$12 – 16
40. white, four grasped hands logo, ASAP promotional issue................$60 – 80
41. white, no markings, ASAP promotional blank..................................$35 – 45
42. metallic tan, England cast.........$4 – 5
43. metallic tan, Macau cast..........$4 – 5
44. metallic tan, Manaus cast, Brazil issue.................................$40 – 50
45. metallic gold with black airfoil, 1997 75 Challenge series ....$6 – 12

Willys '33 Street Rod, 2¹⁵⁄₁₆", #69, 1982

1. blue with orange and white flames, "313" on roof, pearl silver metal base, Macau cast ....$2 – 3
2. blue with red and white flames, "313" on roof, light gray metal base, Hong Kong cast...............................$2 – 3
3. blue with red and white flames, "313" on roof, black plastic base, China cast .$2 – 3
4. blue with red and white flames, "313" on roof, black plastic base, Macau cast ....$2 – 3
5. blue with red and white flames, "313" on roof, pearl silver metal base, Macau cast......................................$2 – 3

6. metallic blue with pink and white design, 1996 Hot Rods 5-pack .$2 – 3
7. turquoise with pink, purple and white design, China cast....................$2 – 3

8. **turquoise with pink brush stroke on white band, 1997 American Street Machines 5-pack..................$2 – 3**
9. metallic turquoise with pink and white design, black plastic base, China cast ....$2 – 3
10. purple, "Bad To The Bone" and crossbones, black plastic base, China cast, Australia issue........................$4 – 5
11. black with pink and white design, black plastic base, China cast ....$6 – 8
12. black with red flames, "313" on roof, black plastic base, China cast, US on-package premium ....$8 – 10
13. white with orange flames, "313" on roof, metallic gray metal base, England cast..................................$4 – 5
14. white with orange flames, "313" on roof, unpainted metal base, England cast..................................$4 – 5
15. white with red flames, "313" on roof, unpainted metal base, England cast..................................$4 – 5
16. white with red flames, "313" on roof, metallic gray metal base, England cast..................................$4 – 5
17. pearl, "Grease" and silver flash, China cast, Star Cars........................$5 – 6
18. pearl with pink and yellow flames, "Pro Street," black plastic base, China cast, 1993.................................$2 – 3
19. pearl with pink and yellow flames, without "Pro Street," black plastic base, China cast ....$3 – 4

Wolseley 1500 sedan, 2⅛", #57, 1958
1. pale yellow-green with gold grille ....$60 – 80
2. pale yellow-green with silver grille.................................$40 – 50
3. pale green with silver grille ....$40 – 50
4. pale gray with silver grille ..$110 – 120

Woosh-N-Push, 2⅞", #58, 1972
1. metallic red with light yellow interior, "2" label...................................$16 – 24
2. magenta with light yellow interior, "2" label...................................$16 – 24
3. magenta with light yellow interior, "8" label...................................$16 – 24
4. yellow with red interior, flower label...................................$16 – 24
5. yellow with red interior, "2" label..$16 – 24

Wreck Truck, #11, 2001; #16, 2003 (see King Tow)

Wreck Truck, #13, 1955 (see Bedford Wreck Truck)

Wreck Truck, #13, 1958 (see Bedford Wreck Truck)

Wreck Truck, #13, 1961 (see Ford Thames Trader Wreck Truck)

Wreck Truck, #13, 1965 (see Dodge Wreck Truck)

2000 Chevrolet Suburban (see Chevrolet Suburban 2000)

4x4 Chevy Blazer Police (see Chevy Blazer Police 4x4)

4x4 Chevy Van (see Chevrolet Van 4x4)

4x4 Golden Eagle Off-Road Jeep (see Jeep Eagle)

4x4 Desert Dawg Jeep (see Desert Dawg 4x4 Jeep)

4x4 Dunes Racer (see 4x4 Mini Pickup)

4x4 Jeep (see Jeep 4x4, Jeep Off-Road 4x4)

4x4 Mini Pickup (see Mini Pickup 4x4)

4x4 Off-Road Jeep (see Jeep Off-Road 4x4)

4x4 Open Back Truck (see Mini Pickup 4x4)

4x4 Pickup Camper (see Pickup Camper 4x4)

4-Wheeler (see Four-Wheeler)

6-Wheel Quarry Truck (see Quarry Truck)

6-Wheel Crane Truck (see Magirus-Deutz 6-Wheel Crane Truck)

8-Wheel Crane Truck (see Eight-Wheel Crane Truck)

8-Wheel Tipper (see AEC Ergomatic Eight-Wheel Tipper)

MATCHBOX CHARACTER TOYS

In 1979, Lesney established an agreement with Universal of Hong Kong to produce a series of toys based on Disney characters. It is interesting to note that Universal purchased Matchbox from Lesney in 1982 and [purchased Dinky Toys shortly thereafter.

Disney Series 1979 – 1980
Donald Duck's Beach Buggy, WD-2, 1979
1.   Hong Kong casting ....$25 – 30
2.   Macau casting ....$65 – 80

Donald Duck's Ice Cream Truck, WD-11, 1980
1.   Hong Kong casting ....$35 – 45
2.   Macau casting ....$60 – 80

Donald Duck's Jeep, WD-6, 1979

1.   white with white base, Hong Kong casting ....$25 – 35
2.   white with black base, Macau casting ....$60 – 80

Goofy's Beetle, WD-3, 1979
1.   Hong Kong casting with ears not connected at shoulders ....$80 – 100
2.   Hong Kong casting with ears connected at shoulders ....$25 – 30
3.   Macau casting with ears connected at shoulders...........................$65 – 80

Goofy's Train, blue, WD-9, 1980
1.   Hong Kong casting ....$35 – 45
2.   Macau casting ....$60 – 80

Goofy's Train, red, WD-10, 1980
1.   Hong Kong casting ....$60 – 80
2.   Macau casting ....$70 – 90

Jiminy Cricket's Old Timer, WD-8, 1979
1.   Hong Kong casting ....$35 – 45
2.   Macau casting ....$60 – 80

Mickey Mouse's Corvette, WD-12, 1980
1.   Hong Kong casting ....$30 – 40
2.   Macau casting ....$60 – 80

Mickey Mouse's Fire Engine, WD-1, 1979
1.   Hong Kong casting, no casting to hold ladder ....$65 – 80
2.   Hong Kong casting with casting to hold ladder ....$25 – 30
3.   Macau casting with casting to hold ladder ....$65 – 80

Mickey Mouse's Jeep, WD-5, 1979
1.   "MM" on hood, Hong Kong casting ....$30 – 40
2.   "Mickey's Mail Jeep" on hood, Hong Kong casting ....$25 – 35
3.   "Mickey's Mail Jeep" on hood, Macau casting ....$60 – 80

Minnie Mouse's Lincoln, WD-4, 1979
1.   Hong Kong casting ....$25 – 30
2.   Macau casting ....$65 – 80

Pinnochio's Traveling Theater, WD-7, 1979
1.   Hong Kong casting ....$35 – 45
2.   Macau casting ....$60 – 80

Popeye Series, King Features 1981
With the modest success of the Disney series, a follow-up offering was produced in 1982 featuring *Popeye the Sailor Man* characters. Issues were designated CS, presumably for "Cartoon Series," implying that later additions were being considered.

Bluto's Road Roller, CS-14, 1981 ....$35 – 45

Olive Oyl's Sports Car, CS-15, 1981 ....$35 – 45

Popeye's Spinach Wagon, CS-13, 1981 ....$35 – 45

Looney Tunes Series
Most familiar of the character toy series from Matchbox is this offering from 1994, thanks to a limited licensing agreement obtained from Warner Brothers.

Bugs Bunny Mercedes Sauber Group C Racer, 1994 ....$4 – 5

Bugs Bunny Chevrolet Lumina Stock Car, 1994 ....$4 – 5

Daffy Duck 4x4 Pickup, 1994........$4 – 5

Road Runner Dodge Dragster, 1994 ....$4 – 5

Tasmanian Devil Sprint Racer, 1994..$4 – 5

Wile E. Coyote Chevrolet Lumina Stock Car, 1994 ....$4 – 5

Sesame Street 1998
Previously, Hasbro had the license to produce Sesame Street preschool toys.

In 1998, Mattel issued 12 die-cast-and-plastic models under the Tyco Preschool/Matchbox brand. Models are made in China, distributed by Mattel Australia Pty., Ltd., and sold (in the US) in sets of three for $5.99 or individually for $1.97 each.

1999 models were packaged under the Fisher-Price brand, but on the base is printed either "Matchbox" or "Tyco." Some 1998 models are no more than repackaged models from the previous year. Altogether, 19 different models resulted from several vehicles that used a variety of drivers and color schemes.

Baby Bear's Buggy, lime green with orange roll bar and base, blue wheels....$2 – 3

Bert's Tow Truck, lime green with blue boom, orange base, yellow wheels.........$2 – 3

Big Bird's Buggy, lime green with blue roll bar, orange base, yellow wheels ....$2 – 3

Big Bird's Fire Engine, red and white with yellow wheels........................$2 – 3

Big Bird's Mail Truck, red cab, white container, blue base and wheels......$2 – 3

Cookie Monster's Airplane, white with yellow trim and propeller, red base, blue wheels.................................$2 – 3

Cookie Monster's School Bus, yellow with blue base, red wheels..............$2 – 3

Elmo's Cement Mixer, blue and red with yellow base, silver barrel, red wheels. $2 – 3

Elmo's Dump Truck.......................$2 – 3

Elmo's Locomotive, blue with red smokestack and wheels, yellow trim.....$2 – 3

Elmo's Taxi, yellow with red base, blue wheels...$2 – 3

Ernie's Cement Mixer, yellow with red barrel and wheels.........................$2 – 3

Ernie's Dump Truck ....$2 – 3
Ernie's Police Car ....$2 – 3

Fozzie Bear's Dump Truck, blue with red dumper, yellow base, red wheels. $2 – 3

Fozzie Bear's Police Car, white with black doors, orange base, blue wheels. $2 – 3

Grover's Helicopter, red and yellow with blue skids, silver propeller and tailfin ...$2 – 3

Oscar The Grouch's Garbage Truck, silver with orange container, yellow base, lime green wheels...........................$2 – 3

Telly's Front Loader, yellow with lime green scoop and wheels ....$2 – 3

Zoe's Convertible, red with yellow base, blue wheels...........................$2 – 3

Accessory Packs

Occasionally, Matchbox offered items designated Accessory Packs that included service station accessories, roadsigns, buildings, a strange noisemaker, and one car transporter.

Brrroomstick (noisemaker), A3, 1971 (add 25% to value of model included in package)

Car Transporter, A2, 1957
1. blue cab and trailer, black-lettered decals, metal wheels...................$150 – 175
2. blue cab and trailer, orange-lettered decals, gray plastic wheels.............$150 – 175
3. blue cab and trailer, orange-lettered decals, black plastic wheels............$200 – 250
4. red cab, gray trailer, orange-lettered decals, black plastic wheels.$250 – 300

Garage, A3, 1957.....................$65 – 90

Home Store, A5, 1961..............$70 – 90

Pumps and Sign, Esso, A1, 1957.....................$80 – 100

Pumps and Sign, BP, A1, 1963..$60 – 80

Roadsigns, A4, 1960...............$60 – 80

Service Ramp, A1, 1970, ...$30 – 45

Matchbox by Manufacturer Number

Matchbox Forum member Christian Falkensteiner has made a comprehensive list with all manufacturing (MAN) numbers known so far. These numbers are found imprinted on the bases of most models issued since 1982, and in most cases are preceded by "MB." Numbers in parentheses represent the various model numbers as assigned on the package. These numbers are found imprinted on the bases of most models after 1980, and in most cases are preceded by "MB."

001 (01, 34) Dodge Challenger
002 (02) S2 Buccaneer Jet
003 (03) Porsche (930) Turbo
004 (04, 43) '57 Chevy
005 (05, 56) 4X4 Jeep/Jeep 4x4 with roll bar
006 (06) Mercedes 350 SL Convertible
007 (07) VW Golf
008 (08) Rover 3500 Police
009 (09) Ford Escort RS 2000
010 (10) Plymouth Grand Fury Police
011 (11) Bedford Car Transporter
012 (12) Citroen CX Break
013 (13) (GMC) Snorkel Fire Engine
014 (14) Leyland Articulated Tanker
015 (15) Lansing Bagnall Fork Lift Truck
016 (16) Pontiac Firebird
017 (17, 51, 28) London Bus/no name/ Leyland Titan
018 (18) Hondarora Motorcycle
019 (19) Peterbilt Cement Truck
020 (20) Range Rover Police Patrol
021 (021) Renault 5 TL
022 (22) Blaze Buster Fire Engine
023 (23) Atlas Dump Truck
024 (24) Diesel Shunter
025 (23, 25) Audi Quattro
026 (26) Volvo Cable Truck
027 (27) Swing Wing (F-14) Tomcat Jet
028 (28) Formula 5000
029 (29) Tractor Shovel

030 (30) Leyland Articulated Truck
031 (31) Caravan
032 (32, 06) Atlas Excavator
033 (33) Honda 750 Police Motorcycle
034 (34) Chevy Pro Stocker
035 (35) Volvo Zoo Truck
036 (36) Refuse Truck
037 (37) Talbot Matra Rancho
038 (38) Ford Model A Van
039 (39) Rolls Royce Silver Shadow II
040 (40) Bedford Horse Box
041 (25) Chevrolet Ambulance
042 (42) 1957 Ford Thunderbird
043 (43, 63) 0-4-0 Steam Loco
044 (44) Railway Passenger Coach
045 (45) Kenworth Cabover Aerodyne
046 (46) Ford Tractor
047 (47) SS 100 Jaguar
048 (28, 61) Sambron Fork Lift Truck
049 (49) Crane Truck
050 (50) Harley-Davidson Sportster
051 (12, 51) Pontiac Firebird SE
052 (52) BMW M1
053 (53, 55) Ford Flareside Pickup
054 (54) Nasa Tracking Vehicle/Command Vehicle
055 (55) Ford Cortina MK IV
056 (56) Mercedes 450 SEL
057 (57) Carmichael Commando
058 (58) Faun Dump Truck

059 (59) Porsche 928
060 (60) Holden Pickup
061 (61) Peterbilt Wreck Truck
062 (62) Chevrolet Corvette
063 (13, 63) Ford 4X4 Open-back Truck
064 (64, 09) Caterpillar D9 Tractor/Bulldozer
065 (65) Airport Coach
066 (66) Kenworth Super Boss
067 (67) Datsun 260 Z 2+2
068 (68) Chevy Van
069 (69) Armored Truck
070 (70) Ferrari 308 GTB/no name
071 (71, 12) Dodge Cattle Truck
072 (72) Dodge Commando Box Van
073 (73, 55, 25) Ford Model A
074 (09, 74) Fiat (131) Abarth
075 (75, 60, 30) Helicopter
076 (31) Mazda RX 7
077 (24) Datsun 280 ZX 2+2
078 (39, 60) Toyota SUPRA
079 (08) De Tomaso Pantera (Greased Lightning)
080 (14) Monteverdi Rallye Royale
081 (15) Volkswagen Hi Ho Silver
082 (26, 41) Cosmic Blues
083 (37) Maserati Sun Burner
084 (65) Kenworth Bandag Bandit
085 (46) Volkswagen Beetle Streaker (Big Blue)
086 (48) Red Rider

087 (51) Midnight Magic
088 (72) Ford Capri Maxi Taxi
089 (74) Dodge Charger Orange Peel
090 (63) Dodge Challenger
091 (31) Mazda RX 7
092 (25) Toyota Celica GT
093 (24) Datsun 280 ZX
094 (71, 32, 72) 1962 Chevrolet Corvette
095 (20, 14) 4X4 Jeep/Jeep 4X4 Canopy
096 (30, 23) Peterbilt Quarry Truck
097 (40, 62, 58) Chevrolet Corvette T-roof
098 (22, 35) Mini Pickup with Canopy
099 (07) Volkswagen Romping Rabbit
100 (56, 05) Peterbilt Tanker
101 (35, 16) Pontiac Firebird T-Roof
102 (44, 68, 26, 10) 4X4 Chevy Van
103 (41) Kenworth Aerodyne Conv. Cab
104 (60) Ford Mustang Piston Popper
105 (11) Ford Boss Mustang
106 (43) Peterbilt Conv. Sleeper Cab
107 (57) Mini Pickup with roll bar
108 (69) '33 Willys Street Rod
109 (SB-20) [CR/SB] Helicopter
110 (29) [CR] American LaFrance Fire Pumper
111 (63, 13) [CR] Snorkel
112 (59) [CR] Mercury
113 (52) [CR] Police Launch
114 (59) [CR] Mercury Fire Chief Car
115 (21) Chevrolet Corvette (Pace Car)

116 (06, 07) [IMSA] Mazda RX 7
117 (17, 09) AMX Protocker
118 (55, 41) Racing Porsche 935
119 (49) Volkswagen Sand Digger
120 (15, 55, 40) Ford Sierra XR4I
121 (58) Holden Ruff Trek
122 (11, 67) IMSA Ford Mustang
123 (14, 69) 1983/1984 Chevrolet Corvette
124 (44) Citroen 15 CV
125 (48) Mercedes Unimog with Plough
126 (67) Red Rider (Flame Out)
127 (28) 1984 Dodge Daytona Turbo Z
128 (68, 64) 1983/1984 Dodge Caravan
129 (50) 4X4 Chevy Blazer
130 (66, 46) Sauber Group C Racer
131 (37, 25) Jeep 4X4
132 (74) Ford Mustang
133 (72) Sand Racer
134 (18) Oshkosh Fire Engine
135 (43) Mercedes 500 SEC
136 (model not made)
137 (16, 06, 65) F1 Racer
138 (22) Jaguar XK 120
139 (26, 49) Volvo Tilt Truck
140 (42) Faun Mobile Crane
141 (41, 01) Jaguar XJ 6
142 (15, 25) Peugeot 205 Turbo 16
143 (54) Command Vehicle
144 (44) Datsun 280 ZX 2 + 2 Police
145 (40, 60) Transporter Vehicle with Rocket
146 (72, 65) Transporter Vehicle with Plane
147 (08, 71) Scania T 142 Cab
148 (20, 23, 62) Volvo Container Truck
149 (30) Mercedes-Benz 280 GE
150 (21, 53) Chevrolet Breakdown Van
151 (39, 28) BMW 323 I Cabriolet
152 (33, 56, 63) Volkswagen Golf GTI
153 (46, 57) Mission Helicopter
154 (67, 11) Lamborghini Countach LP 500 S
155 (60, 12, 48) Pontiac Firebird Racer
156 (17, 37) Ford Escort Cabriolet
157 (47) School Bus
158 (02) Pontiac Fiero
159 (23) Honda ATC 250 R Tricycle
160 (62, 31) Rolls Royce Silver Cloud
161 (33, 43) Renault 11
162 (48) Vauxhall Astra GTE/Opel Kadette GSI
163 (09, 74) Toyota MR 2
164 (51, 68) Chevrolet Camaro IROC-Z 28
165 (60, 57) Ford Transit
166 (06, 72) Ford Supervan II
167 (24) Nissan 300 ZX Turbo
168 (27, 51, 73) Jeep Cherokee
168 B (27, 51, 73) Jeep Cherokee with triangle roof light
169 (49, 72) Peugeot Quasar
170 (67) Ikarus Coach
171 (62) Volvo 760
172 (75) Ferrari Testarossa
173 (07, 51) Porsche 959
174 (04) Carbodies Taxi FX 4 R
175 (34) Ford RS 200
176 (44) Skoda 130 LR
177 (66, 55, 73) Rolls Royce Silver Spirit
178 (70, 45) Ford Cargo Skip Truck/no name
179 (08) Vauxhall Astra GTE/Opel Kadett GSI Police
180 (35, 16) Land Rover Ninety
181 (58) Mercedes-Benz 300 E
182 (20) Volkswagen Transporter Ambulance
183 (183) DAF 3300 Space Cab
184 (16, 51) Ford LTD Police
185 (10) Buick Le Sabre Stock Car
186 (17, 50) Dodge Dakota Pickup

187 (39, 35) Ford Bronco II
188 (21, 71) GMC Wrecker
189 (72, 65) Cadillac Allante
190 (15, 22) SAAB 9000 Turbo
191 (71, 59) Porsche 944 Turbo
192 (31, 02) Rover Sterling
193 (55, 33) Mercury Sable Wagon
194 (32, 12) Modified Racer
195 (69) Volvo 480 ES
196 (59, 61, 28) Ford T'Bird Turbo Coupe
197 (43, 24) Lincoln Town Car
198 (38) Ford Courier/Courrier Van
199 (38) Ford Courier/Courrier Combi
200 (02, 15) Chevrolet Corvette Grand Sport
201 (22, 41) Opel Vectra/Vauxhall Cavalier GSI 2000
202 (08, 39) Mack CH 600 Cab
203 (74, 14) Grand Prix Racing Car/no name
204 (14, 28) 1987 Chevrolet Corvette
205 (68, 73) Mercedes TV News Truck
206 (26, 31) BMW Series
207 (24, 70) Ferrari F 40
208 (34, 72) Sprint Racer
209 (09, 53) Faun Dump Truck
210 (62, 64) Oldsmobile Aerotech
211 (33, 74) Ford Utility Truck
212 (07, 39) Ford Thunderbird Stock Car
213 (44) 1921 Model T Ford Van
214 (214) Ford Aeromax Cab
215 (215) '39 Chevy Sedan Delivery
216 (35) Pontiac Grand Prix Stock Car
217 (217) Dirt Racer
218 (27, 73) Mercedes MBRAC 1600 Turbo
219 (61, 37) Nissan 300 ZX
220 (12, 33) Mercedes-Benz 500 SL
221 (54) Chevrolet Lumina Stock Car
222 (45, 69) Chevrolet Highway Maintenance Truck
223 (72) Dodge Commando Zoo Truck
224 (54) Chevrolet Lumina Stock Car
225 (06, 15) Alfa Romeo SZ
226 (31, 21) Nissan Prairie
227 (15, 41) Sunburner
228 (74, 14) [Indy] Grand Prix Racing Car/Indy 500 Racer
229 (57, 50) Mack Auxiliary Power Truck
230 (52) Isuzu Amigo
231 (01) Jaguar XJ 6 with roof light
232 (22, 49) Lamborghini Diablo
233 (08, 24) Airport Fire Truck
234 (38, 39) Mercedes-Benz 600 SEL
235 (53, 56) Ford LTD Taxi
236 (236) [FM] Ford Tractor with Shovel
237 (237) [FM] Tractor Shovel (new shovel)
238 (35, 22) Pontiac Grand Prix Stock Car
239 (31, 26) Jaguar XJ 220
240 (49, 02) BMW 850I
241 (model not made)
242 (model not made)
243 (model not made)
244 (41, 01) Jaguar XJ 6
245 (58) '39 Chevy Sedan Delivery
246 (74) Williams Renault FW 14 B/Formula 1
247 (74, 14) Indy Racer (no name)
248 (65) Ford F-150 (4 X 4) Pickup
249 (72) Chevy K-1500 (4 X 4) Pickup
250 (44) Ford Probe
251 (08, 54) Mazda RX-7
252 (52) Ford Escort RS Cosworth
253 (model not made)
254 A (43, 56) Chevrolet Camaro Z-28
254 B (59, 56) Chevrolet Camaro Z-28 with triangle roof light
255 (38) Chevrolet Corvette Stingray III
256 (03) Hummer
257 (15, 28) Ford Mustang Mach III

258 (53, 24) Rhino Rod
259 (27) Tailgator
260 (10, 12) Dodge Viper RT/10
261 (59, 63) Aston Martin DB 7
262 (262) 1993 Chrysler Voyager
263 (17, 41) Ferrari 456 GT
264 (model not made)
265 (model not made)
266 (55) [WR] Ford Flareside Pickup with load
267 (267) Chevrolet Lumina Stock Car
268 (268) Ford Thunderbird Stock Car
269 (269) Grand Prix Pontiac Stock Car
270 (22, 28) Mitsubishi 3000 GT Spyder
271 (30, 60) Toyota Supra Turbo
272 (40, 33) Ford Mondeo Ghia
273 (56, 59) Vauxhall Frontera/Isuzu Rodeo/Opel Frontera
274 (54, 61) Abrams Main Battle Tank
275 (47, 73) Rottwheeler
276 (01, 35) Dodge Viper GTS
277 (71, 43) Ford Mustang Cobra
278 (68) Stinger
279 (12, 31) Audi Avus Quattro
280 (34, 06) Plymouth Prowler Concept Vehicle
281 (15) Ford Transit
282 (40, 282) FJ Holden Panel Van
283 (283) Chevrolet Monte Carlo Stock Car
284 (284) Chevrolet Super Truck
285 (285) Zamboni Ice Maker
286 (13, 28) The Buster Pickup
287 (49, 58) Volkswagen Concept 1
288 (35, 75) AMG Mercedes Class (ITC)
289 (70, 64) '70 Pontiac GTO
290 (62, 72) Street Streak
291 (75, 21) Ferrari F 50
292 (63) Ford Falcon
293 (44) 1921 Ford Model T Van
294 (54) Holden Commodore
295 (04) 1997 Chevrolet Corvette
296 (03) Alfa Romeo 155 (ITC)
297 (25, 61) BMW Z3
298 (69, 20) '68 Ford Mustang Cobra Jet
299 (51, 17) Ford Ambulance
300 (48) '56 Ford Pickup
301 (66, 46) Opel Calibra (ITC)
302 (40) 1969 Chevrolet Camaro SS-396
303 (20, 66) Pontiac Firebird Ram Air
304 (54, 38) Ford Crown Victoria with Lopro roof light
305 (model not made)
306 (11, 34) Chrysler Atlantic
307 (43) [CCY] Peterbilt conventional Sleeper Cab
308 (214) [CCY] Ford Aeromax Cab
309 (45) [CCY] Kenworth Cabover Aerodyne
310 (41) [CCY] Kenworth Aerodyne Conventional Cab
311 (08, 39) [CCY] Mack CH 600 Cab
312 (29) [AS] Muir Hill Tractor Shovel (new shovel)
313 (18) [AS] Oshkosh Fire Engine (new ladder)
314 (42) [AS] Faun Mobile Crane (new boom)
315 (148) [AS] Volvo Truck with stakes
316 (21, 53) [JR/AS] Chevrolet Breakdown Van/ (no name)
317 (70, 45) [JR/AS] Ford Cargo Skip Truck with cage/no name
318 (318) [FE] Kenworth T 2000 Cab
319 (319) [JR] Mercedes M-Class with bucket (no name)
320 (36) 1957 Chevrolet Bel Air Convertible
321 (31) 1957 Chevrolet Bel Air Hardtop
322 (37) 1970 Ford Boss Mustang

323 (47) Bradley M 2 Fighting Vehicle
324 (46) 1997 Chevy Tahoe
325 (30) 1997 Chevy Tahoe with triang roof light
326 (50) 1997 Ford F-150 Pickup
327 (34) 1933 Ford Coupe Hot Rod
328 (32) 1970 Chevy El Camino
329 (03) [JR] Hummer with Armaments
330 (46, 57) [JR] Mission Helicopter w Armaments
331 (48) [JR] Mercedes Unimog Resc Truck
332 (71) Jaguar XK 8 Convertible
333 (66) MGF 1.8 I
334 (70) Mercedes-Benz E-Class
335 (68, 58) Porsche 911 GT1
336 (39) 1971 Chevrolet Camaro Z-28
337 (319) [JR] Mercedes-Benz M-Cla with roof load
338 (338) [COL] 1938 Dodge Airflow Va
339 (339) [COL] 1937 Mack Junior Van
340 (183) [CCY] DAF 3300 Space Cab
341 (08, 71) [CCY] Scania T 142 Cab
342 (72) Ford 1965 Mustang GT Fastbac
343 (343) [CAT] Caterpillar Front Shovel
344 (344) [CAT] Caterpillar Dump Truck
345 (345) [CAT] Caterpillar Bulldozer
346 (346) [CAT] Caterpillar Wheel Roade
347 (347) [CAT] Caterpillar Road Roller
348 (348) [CAT] Caterpillar Scraper
349 CAT Powered Peterbilt Dumper
350 (350) [CAT] Caterpillar Motor Grade
351 (351) [CAT] Caterpillar Challenge Tractor
352 (352) [CAT] Caterpillar Trailer
353 (353) [CAT] Caterpillar Backhoe/Loac
354 (354) [CAT] Caterpillar Soil Compact
355 (model not made)
356 (55, 50) Porsche Boxster
357 (40) Dodge Copperhead Concept C
358 (73) Chevrolet 1955 Chevy Bel A Hardtop
359 (46) Chevrolet 1955 Chevy Bel A Convertible
360 (67, 62) Ford Expedition
361 (75) Chevrolet 1957 Corvette Hardto
362 (362) Chevrolet 1957 Corvette Co vertible
363 (53, 48) Volkswagen 1962 VW Beet
364 (model not made)
365 (model not made)
366 (02) 1998 Chevrolet Camaro SS Co vertible
367 (08, 17, 68) 1999 Ford Mustan Coupe
368 (36, 12) 1999 Ford Mustang Convertib
369 (68, 63) 1998 Jeep Wrangler
370 (97) Postal Service Delivery Truck
371 (23) Ford Box Truck
372 (24) Chevrolet Chevy Transport Bus
373 (51, 46) Watercraft with Trailer
374 (374) [Taco Bell] 1962 Chevrolet Corve
375 (375) [Taco Bell] Humvee
376 (376) [Taco Bell/Car Wash] Volksw gen VW Concept 1
377 (377) [Taco Bell] Pontiac Firebird Formu
378 (61, 56) UFO
379 (76, 66) International Pumper
380 (56, 51) Mercedes-Benz A-Class
381 (381) [CAT] Caterpillar Material Handl
382 (382) [CAT] Caterpillar Tool Carrier
383 (383) [CAT] Caterpillar Tool Carrier Trac Shovel
384 (82) Missile Launcher
385 (385) Ice Cream Truck [Light and Soun
386 (386) Rescue Truck [Light and Soun
387 (387) Trash Truck [Light and Sound]

388 (388) [CAT] Caterpillar Peterbilt Dump Truck with blade

389 (389) [AS] Volvo Truck with Tank

390 (64, 59) Volkswagen (1967) VW Transporter

391 (50) [HD] Harley Davidson Chopper

392 (50) [HD] Harley Davidson Electra Glide

393 (393) [HD] Harley Davidson H FXSTS Springer Softtail

394 (394) [HD] Harley Davidson 1939 H Knucklehead

395 (model not made)

396 Fire Engine (Light and Sound)

397 (85) M4 Sherman Tank

398 (86) 1999 Chevrolet Silverado

399 (70, 65) 1999 Chevrolet Silverado 4X4

400 (71, 01) Mercedes Benz CLK Convertible

401 (07) Ford Cargo Scissors Truck

402 (68, 30) Dennis Sabre Fire Engine

403 (403) [CAT] Caterpillar Articulated Dump Truck

404 (404) [CAT] Caterpillar Skidder

405 (72, 52) Volkswagen 1967 VW Delivery Van

406 (66, 61) Land Rover Freelander

407 (43, 38) Sea Rescue Boat

408 (42, 37) Seaplane

409 (44, 39) Hydroplane

410 (45, 40) Submersible

411 (41, 36) Ski Boat

412 (35) Police Cycle

413 (55) Amphibious Personnel Carrier

414 (414) [PC] M 23 2.5 Ton Truck

415 (415) [PC] M 3 A 2 Half Track

416 (60, 55) Rescue Chopper

417 (58, 53) Truck Camper

418 (94, 74) Snowmobile

419 (57, 52) Snow Groomer

420 (34) Chevrolet Impala with V roof light

421 (91, 71) 4-Wheeler

422 (59, 54) White Water Raft Boat

423 (72, 50) Porsche 911 Carrera Cabriolet

424 (69, 19) BMW 328 I

425 (64) Mercedes Benz Actros 1857

426 (68) Mercedes Benz E 430 Wagon

427 (63, 57, 77) Mercedes Benz ML 430

428 (95, 75) Aero Junior

429 (92, 72) Dune Buggy

430 (93, 73) Dirt Bike

431 (21, 31, 50) Ford Transit with triangle roof light

432 (13) Kenworth T 2000 Cab without mirrors

433 (74, 44, 67) Audi TT Coupe

434 (66, 32) Mercedes Benz S 500

435 (model not made)

436 (80, 60) Chevrolet Suburban

437 (48) 1956 Ford Pickup (metal base)

438 (73, 61, 81) Volkswagen Concept 1 Beetle Convertible

439 (11) BMW 328I with square roof light

440 (69) Lotus Elise

441 (37, 04) Audi TT Roadster

442 (65, 45) Jeep Grand Cherokee (B: with raft)

443 (41, 14) Isuzu Flatbed Truck

444 (38, 23) Ford Panel Van

445 (48, 28) Isuzu Delivery Truck

446 (58) International Armored Car

447 (62, 42) Pop-Up Camper

448 (68, 48) Air Lift Helicopter

449 (75, 55) Golf Cart

450 (91, 71) Ford Dump Truck/Utility Truck/Ford F Series Truck

451 (83, 63) BMW 3 Series Coupe

452 (36, 21) X-33 RLV/X-33 Lockheed Martin

453 (41, 36) Ski Boat without skier

454 (model not made)

455 (455) [PC] Blimp

456 (456) [DARE] Pontiac Firebird SE with V roof light

457 (457) [DARE] Chevrolet Camaro Iroc-Z 28 with Lopro roof light

458 (59, 56) Chevrolet Camaro Z-28 with Lopro Roof Light

459 (54, 38) Ford Crown Victoria with V roof light

460 (460) [DARE] 1999 Ford Mustang Coupe with triangle roof light

461 (461) Caterpillar D11 Bulldozer

462 (462) Caterpillar Dump Truck (CD only)

463 (84, 64) Ford Focus

464 (464) [DARE] Chevrolet Corvette with V roof light

465 (465) [DARE] Volkswagen Concept 1 with Lopro roof light

466 (54, 38) [DARE] Ford Crown Victoria with triangle roof light

467 (model not made)

468 (90) Battering Ram Vehicle

469 (96, 03) Street Cleaner

470 (99) GMC Bucket Truck

471 (471) Jeep Grand Cherokee

472 (21, 31, 50) Ford Transit with V roof light

473 (473) [DARE] Chevrolet Corvette with Lopro roof light

474 (474) [DARE] Ford Panel Van with triangle roof light

475 (35) Holden Commodore with square roof light

476 (34) Mercedes Benz E 430 Wagon with square roof light

477 (477) Chevrolet Suburban with V roof light

478 (unknown) unknown

479 (unknown) unknown

480 (06) Artic Track Truck

481 (11) Wrecker Truck

482 (16) School Bus

483 (59, 56) [DARE] Chevrolet Camaro Z-28 with V roof light

484 (21) Tower Boat

485 (23) Ford Explorer Sport Trac

486 (25) '98 Jeep Wrangler Camper

487 (26) Airport Fire Pumper

488 (27) Ladder Truck

489 (50) Ford Expedition with triangle roof light

490 (32) Nissan Xterra with Kayaks

491 (31, 45) Volkswagen Beetle 4X4 (opening hood)

492 (36) Road Roller

493 (37) Bulldozer

494 (38) Demolition Machine

495 (40) Cement Mixer

496 (unknown) unknown

497 (41) Radar Plane

498 (42) Ambulance

499 (43) Ford F-Series Truck with Raft (with interior)

500 (500) [COL] 1955 Cadillac Fleetwood

501 (501) [COL] 1956 Cadillac Eldorado

502 (502) [COL] 1960 MGA

503 (44) Truck Camper with V roof light

504 (71) Jeep Liberty (Cherokee) 2002

505 (505) [COL] 1960 Jeep with Roof

506 (48, 33) Hummer Police

507 (507) 1955 Chevy Bel Air Hardtop with triangle roof light

508 (508) 1933 Ford Coupe Hot Rod with triangle roof light

509 (509) 1999 Ford Mustang Coupe with Lopro roof light

510 (47, 39) Armored Response Vehicle

511 (model not made)

512 (51, 37) Robot Truck

513 (51) Ford Falcon with triangle roof light

514 (52, 36) Troop Carrier

515 (57) 2000 Chevrolet Corvette Convertible

516 (59) Chrysler Panel Cruiser

517 (56) Dodge Viper GT SR

518 (61, 38) Rescue Boat

519 (62, 35) Hovercraft

520 (63) Airboat

521 (61) Ford Falcon (AU)

522 (69) Humvee

523 (66) Radar Truck

524 (67) Land Rover Discovery

525 (68) Speedboat

526 (73) Hummer H2 SUV Concept

527 (72) Rescue Crane

528 (53) Police Car

529 (54) Tanker Truck (with hose)

530 (65) Ice Cream Truck

531 (65) Ferrari 360 Spider

532 (09) BMW Z8

533 (533) [promo] BMW Z3 (opening doors)

534 (534) BMW 3 Series Cabrio

535 (535) [promo] BMW X5 (opening doors)

536 (55) Dump Truck

537 (66) Limousine

538 (74) BMW Z3 (shut doors)

539 (31) BMW X5 (shut doors)

540 (56) Bucket Fire Truck

541 (63) Rescue Helicopter

542 (57) Trash Truck

543 (74) Nissan Xterra

544 (69) Porsche 911 Turbo

545 (27) Ford Falcon (AU) with square roof light

546 (58) Chevrolet Avalanche

547 (59) Cycle with Sidecar

548 (60) Mobile Light Truck

549 (70) Volkswagen VW W12 Concept

550 (70) Chevrolet SSR

551 (61) Ice Breaker

552 (72) Volkswagen Microbus

553 (unknown) Ford Falcon (AU) with Lopro roof light

554 (21) Ford Transit with square roof light

555 (62) GMC Terradyne

556 (73) Pontiac Piranha

557 (557) [COL] 1965 Shelby Cobra 427 S/C (driver-only windscreen)

558 (558) [COL] 1961 Dodge Dart Phoenix

559 (559) [COL] 1957 Lincoln Premiere

560 (560) [COL] 1956 Ford Fairlane Sunliner

561 (73) Smart Cabrio

562 (64) Lift Truck

563 (75) Water Pumper

564 (67) Foam Fire Truck

565 (06) Opel Speedster

566 (01) Highway Rescue Fire Truck

567 (21) Cadillac Escalade

568 (26) Police SUV

569 (46) 4X4 Buggy

570 (unknown) [COL] 1960 Jeep with roll bar

571 (41) Sea Rescue Helicopter

572 (11) Emergency Rescue 4X4

573 (74) Opel Frogster

574 (27, 73, 51) Jeep Cherokee with triangle roof light

575 (71) Jeep Willys Concept

576 (16) Car Carrier

577 (36) Taxi Cab

578 (31) Volkswagen Beetle Taxi

579 (75) Mini Cooper S

580 (72) Chrysler PT Cruiser Convertible

581 (43) Ford F Series Truck with Raft (without interior)

582 (31, 45) Volkswagen Beetle 4X4 (shut hood)

583 (54) Tanker Truck (without hose)

584 (584) Troop Carrier without canopy

585 (51) Pontiac Vibe

586 (56) Billboard Truck

587 (unknown) [COL] 1965 Shelby Cobra 427 S/C (full-size windscreen)

588 (61) Dennis Sabre Ladder Fire Engine

589 (66) Dodge Ram SRT-10

590 (91, 71) Ford F Series Dump Truck/Utility Truck (without interior)

591 (unknown) Truck Camper with Lopro roof light

592 (66) City Police Car

593 (32) 4X4 Fire Truck

594 (31) Airport Fire Tanker

595 (unknown) TVR Tuscan S

596 (unknown) BMW X5 with square roof light

597 (model not made)

598 (unknown) Ambulance

599 (model not made)

600 (unknown) Checker Taxi

601 (unknown) unknown

602 Sky Fire (also 540 Bucket Truck)

603 (unknown) unknown

604 (unknown) unknown

605 (unknown) unknown

606 (unknown) unknown

607 (unknown) unknown

608 (unknown) unknown

609 (unknown) unknown

610 (unknown) unknown

611 (unknown) unknown

612 (unknown) unknown

613 (unknown) unknown

614 (unknown) unknown

615 (unknown) unknown

616 (unknown) unknown

617 (1) Whistle Wagon/whistle car, 2004

618 (2) Badge Blaster/badge car, 2004

619 (4) Fire Freezer/fire extinguisher, 2004

620 (unknown) unknown

621 (11) Buzz Helicopter/dragonfly helicopter, 2004

622 (unknown) unknown

623 (16) Y-Nossarus/dump truck, 2004

624 (17) Rumble Dozer/bulldozer, 2004

625 (26) Crime Capper/policeman's hat, 2004

626 (27) Squad Runnder/military helmet, 2004

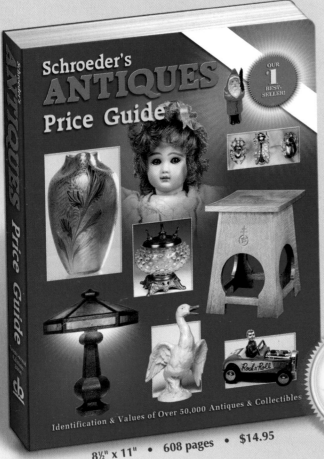